MODERN BRITISH HISTORY ★ A
Garland Series

Edited by
PETER STANSKY and
LESLIE HUME

THE CHURCH OF IRELAND
IN THE AGE OF CATHOLIC EMANCIPATION

Edward Brynn

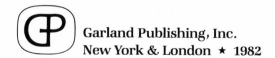

Garland Publishing, Inc.
New York & London ★ 1982

Library of Congress Cataloging in Publication Data

Brynn, Edward, 1942–
    The Church of Ireland in the age of Catholic
emancipation.

    (Modern British history ; 2)
    Originally presented as the author's thesis (doctoral
—Stanford University, 1968)
    Bibliography: p.
    Includes index.
    1. Church of Ireland—History—19th century.
2. Ireland—Church history—19th century.   I. Title.
II. Series.
BX5500.B79 1982   283'.3   81-48356
ISBN 0-8240-5151-3

All volumes in this series are printed on acid-free,
250-year-life paper.
Printed in the United States of America

TABLE OF CONTENTS

Challenged and then overshadowed by Roman Catholicism in the nineteenth century, criticized, reformed and disestablished by a largely Protestant Parliament at Westminster, the Church of Ireland was long consigned to the dustbin of history. Literate clerics penned some rambling elegant memoirs of their life on Ireland's ecclesiastical hustings, but the Establishment did nothing very extraordinary after precipitating the Oxford Movement in the 1830s. The thesis from which this book was prepared for Stanford University in 1967 and 1968, therefore, was designed to fill a gap in Anglo-Irish history, without at the same time pretending to supply a critical missing link in an understanding of modern Ireland.

Since 1968 interest in the Church of Ireland has revived remarkably. The centennial of disestablishment prompted some interest in what happened to the Anglican communion in Ireland after 1869. A new generation of Irish historians abandoned their fixation on the national trinity of O'Connell, Parnell and heroes of the Easter Rising. Professor R. B. McDowell at Trinity College demonstrated in a spate of books that analyses of administration could be at once instructive and interesting. J. C. Beckett restored a critical interpretative balance and recently scholars of genius such as F. S. L. Lyon have stimulated an enormous popular interest in Ireland's past. In short order my own thesis became only one of several studies on various aspects of the Church of Ireland in the nineteenth century.

Despite some inevitable overlapping, the several prominent studies on the Church address quite different questions and reach quite different conclusions. A. H. Akenson's two serious studies – one on Irish education and the other on institutional reform in the Church of Ireland in the nineteenth century – have served scholars well indeed. McDowell's much briefer but insightful look at the post-1869 era and Denis Bowen's inspection of Irish Protestantism's internal workings a century and more ago are also valuable. About a dozen articles linking Irish Church reform to British political developments suggest clearly what were the wider ramifications of the assault on the Establishment after 1800.

Although none of these studies did great violence to the arguments advanced in my Stanford dissertation, many of them offered instructive additions to my own research. To the extent permitted by an ambulatory life of a Foreign Service Officer in Asia and Africa, I have pursued my own investigations and published several smaller pieces shedding some additional light on the Church of Ireland. The opportunity presented to publish my dissertation also permitted me to incorporate recent research into this study.

I am grateful to many individuals and institutions for assistance in sustaining my interest in the Church of Ireland over the years: Richard W. Lyman, my advisor at Stanford; Robert B. McDowell of Trinity College, Dublin; the staffs of libraries at Stanford University, Trinity College, the British Museum, the Royal Irish Academy, the United States Air Force Academy, the Public Record Office of Northern Ireland, Armagh Public Library, and Colorado College. My mother, Mary Callahan

Brynn, typed several drafts of the manuscript. Christine Coulibaly resolved all problems stemming from preparation of the final type-script during my tour of duty in the Republic of Mali.

I am grateful above all to Jane Cooke Brynn, whose first year of marriage thirteen years ago was spent in Dublin while I pursued my research on the Established Church, and who has accepted with grace the subsequent transport of cartons of research materials to our posts on three continents.

Washington, D. C.
March 1, 1981

Chapter I: The Erastian Heritage   1535-1800

After 1800 the Protestant ascendancy, which had directed the
course of Irish history for more than two hundred years, began to
surrender its responsibilities to an expanded and invigorated administrative system and to a resurgent Catholicism.   The sinews which
bound together an alien landlord class and a minority ecclesiastical
establishment weakened under the pressure of a resurgence of Irish nationalism.   The landed class lost its monopoly of parliamentary power
and patronage, and the Church of Ireland was assaulted by reformers
demanding religious revitalization, by radicals promoting retrenchment,
and by Catholics seeking disestablishment.

The role of the landed class in nineteenth century Ireland and the
rise of nationalism have been the subject of several recent studies.   The
Church of Ireland's place in Irish politics, on the other hand, has
been less adequately studied.[1]   This book analyzes the impact of Irish
nationalism on the Church of Ireland from the Act of Union in 1801 to
disestablishment in 1869.   The emphasis here, then, is not on that revitalization which characterized much of the Church's spiritual life
during this period, but on the inexorable disintegration of the erastian system which had enabled the Established Church to play an important role in Irish politics, local government, education, and cultural development.   In this process the Church of Ireland became more
than merely an issue of Irish domestic interest.   The progress of reform and retrenchment brought into play the larger question of the role

of an established church in an increasingly secular political environment, the legitimacy of Parliament's assault on ecclesiastical privilege, and the wisdom of surrendering most of Ireland's inhabitants to
a religious system which had long been estranged from British political
traditions. Involved as well was the sanctity of private property,
on which the nation's landlord-tenant relationship was based. Even
the ability of a parliamentary system dominated by title and wealth
to accommodate the demands of an increasingly middle class, indus-
trialized society was questioned. Along with Catholic Emancipation
and the Great Reform Bill of 1832 the fate of the Established Church
reflected the breadth and intensity of a dramatic transformation in
Ireland, and stands today as a test of British institutional modern-
ization without revolution.

The legislative union of the British and Irish Parliaments in
1801 presaged the end of two centuries of an excessive preponderance
of aristocratic influence in Ireland. The union also revived within
the Anglican Establishment aspirations to become in fact what it had
sustained in theory since the Reformation: the Irish National Church.
The union represented a final effort to erase the barriers which centuries of separate traditions and divergent historical experiences
had raised between Ireland and Britain. In 1800 the Established
Churches of England and Ireland were merged, at least in theory, in
order that the Irish portion, precariously circumstanced by its minority status, by its endemic administrative abuses, and by its unhealthy
erastian character, might challenge the popular power of Roman Catholicism. The intent of the Act of Union was only partially realized.

A new level of probity was achieved after a series of reforms, not all of which were encouraged by the English connection. The calibre of the Irish clergy and the Church's administrative efficiency were heightened by the intervention of a Parliament free from the worst manifestations of venality encountered in the Dublin legislature of the eighteenth century. But exposure to a reforming temper in England made its greatest impact upon Irish erastianism itself, and disestablishment of the Church of Ireland in 1869 was belated admission that Ireland could no longer be controlled effectively by the ancient alliance of Protestant churchmen and Protestant landlords. Indeed, the very reforms which the Church of Ireland initiated or accepted contributed indirectly to its loss of official status. The Catholic majority remained unsatisfied, while those long-standing patronage and family connections which had induced Irish landlords to shield the Established Church from its enemies evaporated as administrative reforms increased. The legislative union, moreover, exposed Irish institutions, secular and ecclesiastical, to the emerging power of Benthamism, which stimulated the latent anti-clerical tendencies of the Whig party and the espoused hostility of bourgeois "radicals". Benthamism expressed itself in the conviction that the responsibilities traditionally assigned to the Irish Established Church, such as education, welfare, and certain aspects of local government, could be performed better by institutions free from religious trappings and commitments.

The last phase of the erastian experiment, therefore, was carried out in particularly distressing circumstances. The growing

sensitivity of Catholicism made proselytism difficult and perhaps inappropriate if the Church were to be accessible to all those seeking the
Church of Ireland's ministrations, especially where certain elements
among the ruling class in Ireland regarded Church reform as an assault
upon parochial property they had usurped or as unduly provocative to
their Catholic tenants. Attempts to refurbish its role as educator
focused attention on the Church's anomalies, its administrative abuses,
and its inefficient application of parliamentary grants and endowments.
The tithe problem increased in difficulty as population pressure on
limited land resources forced peasants subsisting at starvation levels
to choose between payment of rackrents or tithe obligations. Many
landlords acerbated this sensitive issue by encouraging tithe agitation in order to deflect attention from their increasing rapaciousness,
or by refusing to support the Church's legal claims. The astonishing
revival of Roman Catholicism after 1760 resulted from the relaxation
of penal codes and later from a growing intimacy between the Papacy
and Whitehall in opposition to Napoleonic France. When added to a revival of Catholic spiritual energy, this neutralized Protestant efforts
and made the Church of Ireland's adversary more formidable than ever.
Finally, growing concern within the Established Church itself that the
state connection tended to undermine its religious impact encouraged a
conviction in many quarters that erastianism was inherently unproduc-
tive.

In this study special attention must be given to those themes
which governed the relationship between the Church of Ireland and
various manifestations of British statecraft, and which influenced the

Church in its efforts to reform its administration, rekindle spiritual
fervor, and restore its influence in Irish affairs. This relationship
not only caused the Church to develop certain defensive characteristics which perhaps delayed the progress of substantive reforms, but
aroused in parliamentary circles an interest in reform which brought
legislative interference into hitherto untouched areas. Within the
context of the Church-state relationship, a wide range of factors
underlying Ireland's increasing economic malaise and growing nation-
alistic fervor were aired and discussed, and the Church of Ireland's
role in promoting Irish nationalism was perhaps exaggerated. For
ambitious reformers the Church became a symbol of all those policies,
mostly unenlightened, which had cast England's role in Ireland in such
unattractive terms. In reaction to this, the Church inclined towards
preoccupation with the question of its endangered temporalities as
the surest way to resist encroachment on its prerogatives. In time
such obsession with property rights further weakened its claim to be
the nation's spiritual counselor and prompted even more dramatic demands
by parliamentary radicals for ecclesiastical reform. Around such Benthamite catchwords as "utility" and the "greatest happiness for the
greatest number" gathered the Church's foes. In consequence the Irish
Establishment became the first great historical institution to be
measured by evidence of its usefulness to the nation. When this yard-
stick was applied, the Church of Ireland was found wanting.

Administrative reform, however necessary to any revival of the
Church of Ireland's place in national affairs and, more importantly,
to any increase in its spiritual efficiency, was only one dimension

of the nineteenth century dilemma. Equally important was the political context within which the drama of ecclesiastical reform took place.
The construction was erastian; the pace of events, therefore, was
determined as much by the sentiment of Parliament, successive ministries and political exigencies as by conditions within the Church of
Ireland itself. The ecclesiastical hierarchy, unfortunately, exerted
only a marginal control over ecclesiastical affairs; things spiritual
and temporal were opposed as often as allied within the Church's
structure; the personalities of politicans and political expediency
set the tone of reform, while bishops made futile gestures with pen
and in the pulpit. In a way peculiar to an erastian system the process of Irish ecclesiastical reform was essentially a political phenomenon, and cannot be understood in its true nature any other way.
This was obvious after 1830, when Whig measures recast the structure
of the Church in a radical way; it was also true before then, as politicians and prelates charted a course of action which skirted the
shoals of adverse public and parliamentary opinion. The reformation,
then, was in part ecclesiastical and in part political. One was impossible without the other, and it is the interaction between Church
and Parliament which forms the basis of this presentation.

For more than three centuries the Church of Ireland combined the
prerogatives of a national establishment with the limitations of a
minority membership. Crucial to an understanding of this anomalous
condition is an appreciation of the abortive nature of the Reformation in Ireland. To a disastrous degree, English political and ecclesiastical priorities were employed as a basis for the formulation of

Irish religious policy. Unlike England, Ireland had not witnessed development of an intimate Church-State relationship during the Middle Ages; the peculiar administrative dependence of the Celtic Church on monastic organization was ill-suited to civilian institutions of social control, which, in Ireland at any rate, were both transitory and exceptionally weak. The state did not, and indeed could not, defend the temporalities of the Church, and the Church was frustrated in its efforts to legitimatize the role of the state by disputes between Irish and English aspirants to power on one hand, and among the Irish chieftains on the other. For churchmen, the Pope was something of a distant father.

Nor, furthermore, was the Reformation in Ireland similar to that in England. In Ireland the Reformation occurred at a time when English power there was so circumscribed that the writs of Henry VIII ran unchallenged only in a small region near Dublin, and in several scattered seaport towns in the south and west. Irish leaders' occasional professions of allegiance to the English throne were largely symbolic, and nothing comparable to the English gentry existed in Ireland through which local government might put into effect the principal points of the Reformation program. Under Henry VIII, Edward VI, and Mary Tudor, the varying fortunes of the reformed Church in England made a light impression in the English pale and even less impact outside it. English rule in Ireland was centered in a group of families of Norman or English origin; they accepted the Reformation as another opportunity to express their desired alienation from the native Irish, but not as a heartfelt religious experience. Among royal officials and agents the fervor of acceptance reflected more their attachment to office than adherence to the new theology. There was no reformation of the heart; the restoration of the old religion under Mary Tudor found inhabitants of the pale and English coastal towns almost entirely sympathetic.[2] Outside the pale not even the facade of a reformation was yet evident. Papal appointments to most Irish sees were not effectively circumscribed; indeed, so little impact did the new royal prerogative make in Ireland that the English crown made no attempt to challenge nearly two-thirds of the pope's nominees, while at least one bishop believed as late as 1551 that Edward VI still forwarded candidates' names to Rome.[3] When Elizabeth was proclaimed queen in 1559, and a national church was again instituted in England and Ireland, the latter country still awaited its first reformation.

In Ireland Elizabeth's temporizing attitude towards Roman Catholicism, prompted by formidable obstacles, lost England the initiative. The Irish Catholic Church had never become deeply unpopular; it was not as wealthy as the English Church, and its somewhat tenuous association with Rome dampened resentment to foreign ecclesiastics. The mendicant orders were relatively popular, and the absence of an overblown diocesan structure made the reformed Church of England, when reproduced in Ireland, nothing very radical by comparison.[4] Dissolution of the monasteries released a flood of unpensioned, angry friars into the countryside, while the reformed Church's inability to supply parochial clergy left the field open for friars to vent their hostility towards the English-sponsored experiment.[5] Elizabeth could encourage the Reformation in Ireland only as fast as the extension of

English civil power would effect it. Meanwhile, the Counter-Reformation papacy was rapidly mending its fences and was by 1570 once more in a position to command sufficient resources for a religious offensive in Ireland. Not for another century, and then as a result of a Puritan and Presbyterian impulse, would Protestantism make a profound impact across the Irish sea.[6]

Herein can be seen the essentially defective nature of England's ecclesiastical policy in Ireland over the next three centuries and in part the difficulties experienced by the Church of Ireland even after 1800. The reformed Church remained largely an English import, and identification with Ireland was not enhanced by the Tudor injunction that ministers preach in English. The Church remained excessively dependent upon the civil administration for its very survival, and the state too often reciprocated by granting ecclesiastical dignities and property to supporters of the crown. Many livings remained in the control of Catholic nobles, who, while loyal to Elizabeth, rarely exerted themselves to see that the Anglican clergy were properly supported. By 1600 Roman Catholicism was again secure in the allegiance of the vast majority of the native Irish, and was demonstrating a remarkable capacity to absorb even English colonists who chose to farm the Irish countryside. In 1583, a quarter century after the accession of Elizabeth, and a full half century after Henry VIII had launched the Reformation, a report forwarded to London noted that not one Protestant church was standing between Dublin and the most distant parts of Munster, except in the ports.[7] Nor was much improvement in evidence in the next half century. While James I made a conscientious effort to raise the calibre of the bishops, the policy of plundering

the Church to satisfy political obligations continued. "Even in Dub-

lin," one observer noted,

> we find our parochial church converted to the Lord Deputy's
> stable; a second to a nobleman's dwelling house; the choir
> of a third to a tennis court, and the Vicar acts the keeper.[8]

The dispensation of ecclesiastical offices was scandalous. As one his-

torian has observed, "the idea that high Irish preferment involved

corresponding duties seemed to have been very imperfectly understood

at this time." One Mrs. Montgomery informed her relations that "the

King had bestowed on her husband three Irish bishoprics, the names of

them I cannot remember, they are so strange."[9] Charles I proved un-

able to reverse the trend. He was reluctant to press recusancy fines,

since his political position was decidedly precarious, and did little

to end practices of lay confiscation of Church property. As a result,

Catholics practiced their beliefs with impunity, while depredators

annexed whole parishes to the Establishment. In 1633 Charles I's

vigorous Lord Lieutenant Strafford summarized the condition of the

Irish Church in somber terms:

> The best entrance to the cure will be clearly to discover
> the state of the patient, which I find in many ways dis-
> tempered; an unlearned clergy, which have not so much as
> the outward form of churchmen to cover themselves with,
> nor their persons anyway reverenced or protected; the
> churches unbuilt; the parsonage and vicarage houses utterly
> ruined; the people untaught, through the non-residency of
> the clergy, occasioned by the unlimited shameful numbers
> of spiritual promotions with cure of souls which they hold
> by commendams; . . . the possessions of the Church, to a
> great proportion, in lay hands; the bishops alienating
> their very principal houses and demesnes to their children,
> to strangers; farming out their jurisdictions to mean and
> unworthy persons.[10]

Strafford instituted a number of reforms designed to enforce tighter discipline of the clergy within the Irish Church and to conform its liturgy to the High church tastes of William Laud, Archbishop of Canterbury. In Dublin churches were rebuilt and refurbished, and certain benefices were awarded to able ecclesiastical administrators. But Strafford soon returned to England to reinforce Charles' policies against Parliament, and was executed to appease anti-royalist zealots. Oliver Cromwell invaded Ireland, and the Anglican establishment was abolished. Some of the clergy fled abroad. A few adopted Roman Catholicism. Most retired to the countryside. Revenues were appropriated by the state, and later, the revolution's force dissipated, by Irish landlords.[11]

The triumphant restoration of the monarchy in 1660 was accompanied by a rapid revival of the Anglican establishment in England, where Presbyterianism and the more radical Protestant sects were widely identified as handmaidens of mayhem and revolution. In Ireland revival along the same lines was impossible. Powerful warlords openly proclaimed their allegiance to Rome, and the Church of Ireland's adherents were largely confined to Dublin and a few garrison towns. As in an earlier generation, Irish bishops spent little time in their bishoprics; they could not be compelled to do so when episcopal revenues were slight, congregations were scanty, and even accommodations were often non-existent.[12] Proposals were floated to abolish the diocesan system altogether, but the very thought raised the spectre of Puritanism and was vehemently rejected. A less dangerous idea, fusion of the Irish and English establishments, made much sense but little progress.

There was one important and enduring change; erastianism

was to remain a salient feature of the Irish scene until the Act of
Union. James II's Catholic sympathies and William's flirtations with
Irish Presbyterians meant that the Church of Ireland, when re-estab-
lished in 1689, was more dependent than ever on the state. The
Church proved strong enough to resist granting privileges to Presbyterians and to promote penal laws, but not strong enough to reform
itself. Indeed, ". . . the Church . . . surrendered the claim to
autonomy, allowed appointments to be governed by political and not
religious considerations, (and) became in fact a tool of the English
administration in Ireland; but in return insisted successfully that
the privileged position of the Establishment should be maintained."[13]
A stalemate necessarily followed: private reforms were obstructed in
court by hostile landlords; official reforms were shelved except
occasionally when it appeared the Established Church might collapse
completely; convocation, briefly revived, found many ecclesiastics
wanting in zeal and determination. By 1714, when the Hanoverians
came to the throne, it was as yet difficult to see that the joint
mission of Church and state to make Ireland Protestant and loyal had
succeeded on either account.

During the eighteenth century few of the Established Church's
problems were solved, but the Hanoverians gave it peace and security,
and the Protestant ascendancy strengthened. Proposals for substantial
administrative reform, such as William Petty's plan for division of
Ireland into uniform-sized precincts rather than parishes, abolition
of old endowments and a drastic reduction in the number of clergy,
were quietly put aside.[14] Jonathan Swift claimed, somewhat irrever-

ently, that while the government elevated "excellent and moral men"
for Irish bishoprics, "it unfortunately happened that, as these
worthy divines crossed Hounslow Heath on their way to Ireland,
they [were] regularly robbed and murdered by the highwaymen fre-
quenting that common, who seize[d] their robes and patents, [were]
over to Ireland, and [were] consecrated bishops in their stead.[15]
If this was aprocryphal, it was entirely true that under George I the
erastian character of the Church became more pronounced at the upper
levels where its archbishops played a major role in the civil government of the realm. Under Queen Anne convocation had been revived,
not so much to provide direction for the rudderless Church, but to
exercise more direct influetice on the Irish government. Failure to
call convocation after 1711 did not arrest this growing influence.
The lords lieutenant were largely non-resident, and during their long
absences the government was entrusted to two or three lords justice,
among whom one invariably was the primate or an archbishop.[16]

More important perhaps was the increasingly aristocratic origin of most Irish bishops during the eighteenth century, and the incentives fashioned to encourage them to play an overt role as politicians. In 1760 the increasing quantum of aristocrats was celebrated
by Dr. Thomas Newton, the future Bishop of Bristol and himself the
product of an unpretentious lineage:

> Though the apostles for wise reasons . . . were chosen from
> among men of low birth and parentage: yet time and circum-
> stances are so changed that persons of noble birth by com-
> ing into the Church, may add strength and ornament to it:
> especially as long as we can boast of some, who are honor-
> able in themselves as well as in their families; and whose
> personal merits and virtues, if they had not been nobly

descended, would have entitled them justly to the rank
and pre-eminence that they enjoy.[17]

Perhaps Newton was anxious to put the best possible face on the

inevitable. The percentage of bishops derived from plebian origins,

as measured by one modern observer, declined from one-fifth of the

episcopate in 1688 to one-tenth under George II and virtually to

zero by 1800. Bishops drawn from the aristocracy increased from

one-fifteenth under William II to one-fifth under George III.[18] These

trends were detectedin England and Ireland both. In Ireland the

tendency towards aristocracy was even more pronounced. By 1800 a

third of the Irish bench was aristocratic in class origin; almost

half of the men elevated to the Irish bench between 1791 and 1820

were sons or close relatives of peers.[19]

The rising tide of aristocratic influence within the Church

of Ireland reflected fundamental political conditions and considera-

tions. During the long period of Whig supremacy in the eighteenth

century Ireland served as a place to exile churchmen Whig in their

connections but unreliably radical in their theology. Some of these

Whig connections were useful and some indeed could not be ignored.

Under the Whigs, however, a good number still traced their pedigree

to the middle class. Thereafter, the return of the Tories intensi-

fied identification with the aristocracy. More important was the

growth of Irish nationalism after 1700. In Ireland even more than in

England episcopal appointments came to reflect purely political con-

siderations. Westminster's control over the Irish Parliament declined

when Poyning's Law was amended in 1782. Bishops became a reliable

if beleaguered interest in the Irish House of Lords; vacancies on

the Irish bench were dedicated with increasing regularity to the purchase of support of prominent Irish families. Political conditions
also called for accelerated translations to humor patrons with parliamentary influence.[20] These factors culminated in the patronage
exercise which attended the Act of Union. The preponderance of
ecclesiastical aristocrats on the Irish bench was not relieved until
the middle of the nineteenth century.[21]

Such an emphasis on politics inevitably undermined pretensions
to sanctity and even orthodoxy on the bench. Early on this distraction occasioned by such pronounced immersion in politics could be
seen in the career of one Irish primate, Richard Hoadly. His ambitions were so patently political that he did "not seem to have printed
anything, even the customary sermon or two." Archbishop Stone so
dominated the Irish government at midcentury that he built for himself an autonomous parliamentary interest which could oppose even the
government of the day.[22] Bishops were also deeply involved in affairs
distinctly unrelated to their ecclesiastical responsibilities, and
during their prolonged absences their dioceses deteriorated markedly.

The Church was sustained, where sustained at all, by ingenious
restraints on Catholics, gathered into a penal code, and by an impressive institutional structure of four archbishops, eighteen bishops and eight hundred clergy attached to some two thousand parishes.
The advent of a period of unprecedented tranquillity, however, dulled
rather than stimulated its energies. In 1715 Archbishop King of Dublin noted that the Church had fared better under William, who disliked it, than under Hanoverians who cossetted it; "the diligence,

piety, humility and prudent management of the clergy when they had

nothing else to trust proved much stronger motives to gain the

people than the favor of the government which put the clergy on

other methods and made them odious to the people."[23] As a result,

in several dioceses as late as 1750 a majority of the churches in-

herited from the medieval period or constructed subsequently were

in disrepair; the diocese of Clonfert had only ten beneficed clergy-

men, half of them non-resident, and Ferns had been divested of most

of its tithe income.[24] Laymen held the right of appointing the

clergy to many benefices; and retained most of the income for their

own purposes. Glebe lands attached to the churches, and intended to

support a residence for the clergy, had been seized by landlords and

sometimes by bishops. Income from tithes was often allocated hap-

hazardly, and sometimes directed outside the Church. Certainly

less than a third of the population adhered to the Established Church,

and perhaps less than a sixth. Even descendants of Cromwell's sol-

diers were now Catholic in areas where no Protestant clergy resided,

while others subscribed to the Church of Ireland only to avoid the

difficulties in landholding imposed by the penal code.[25]

There was no sharper critic of clerical behavior than Jonathan

Swift, as has already been seen. He focused his attention on the

bench of bishops, a place to which he aspired. Failing in his quest,

he painted the bench in satirical colors:

> The maintenance of the clergy, throughout the kingdom, is
> precarious and uncertain, collected from a most miserable
> race of beggarly farmers; . . . as soon as he is promoted
> to a bishopric, the scene is entirely and happily changed:
> his revenues are large, and as surely paid as those of the

> king: his whole business is once a year to receive the
> attendance, the submission, and proxymoney of all his
> clergy, in whatever part of the diocese he shall please
> to think most convenient for himself. Neither is his
> personal presence necessary . . . . The fatigue of or-
> dination, is just what the bishops please to make it,
> and as matters have been for some time, and may probably
> remain, the fewer ordinations the better. The rest of
> their visible office, consists in the honor of attending
> parliaments and councils, and bestowing preferments in
> their own gift. . . .[26]

The episcopal bench presented a spectacle of unhealthy subservience

to political interests. William Boulter, primate of Ireland from

1724 to 1742, was one of a series of churchmen who directed their en-

tire energies to the elevation of the English interest; though every

Archbishop of Armagh between 1702 and 1800 was English by birth, none

discouraged the Irish element with more zeal than he. Upon notifi-

cation of a vacancy at Cashel in 1727 Boulter noted that unless an

Englishmen were appointed, there would be thirteen Irish to nine Eng-

lish bishops out of twenty-two, "a dangerous situation."[27] His in-

sistence on Anglicanization soon aroused the angry genius of Dean

Swift, who was moved to write to the Lord Lieutenant in 1725 of

> the misfortune of having bishops perpetually from England,
> as it must needs quench the spirit of emulation among us to
> excel in learning and the study of divinity . . . . There
> is not another kingdom in Europe, where the natives, even
> those descended from the conquerors, have been treated as
> if they were almost unqualified for any employment either
> in Church or State.[28]

Englishmen used appointments to advance their fortunes and many

incumbents remained in England to pursue health cures or politics.

English-born prelates drew after them "colonies of sons, nephews,

cousins, or old college companions, to whom they bestow   their

best preferments in their gift."[29] Many of these were men of inferior ability and few scruples, and did considerably more mischief in Ireland than they ever had done in England. The native clergy were perforce relegated to the least remunerative, most frustrating assignments; it was not to be wondered that so little zeal was shown in improving either the spiritual or the temporal situation of the Church of Ireland.[30]

The subservience of the Irish Church to the English interest antagonized the resident gentry of Ireland. This hostility expressed itself in the first instance in opposition to the tithe, which was frequently collected by absentee incumbents' agents. It is a measure of its own dissatisfaction that the Irish Parliament, representing as it did only the Protestant minority in Ireland, should preceed with its opposition to the Church notwithstanding the dangers involved in splitting the Protestant ranks in the face of a sullen Catholic majority. The privy council was forced to intervene on several occasions between 1714 and 1730 to veto legislation hostile to the church. In 1735, in an extraordinary departure from the constitutional practice, the Irish House of Commons virtually halved the income of the beneficed clergy by removing pasture from the tithe jurisdication. At the same time it declared that those hereafter paying tithe on agistment were enemies of the nation. While the resolution did not have the force of law, the tithe on pasture was not collected for the remainder of the century.[31]

During the eighteenth century, as the danger of a Catholic restoration declined, relations between gentry and clergy, and within the clerical body itself, continued to worsen. As early as 1715 the

clergy were noted campaigning against the gentry in local elections;
their vociferous opposition in convocation had already moved the gentry to oppose any future meetings of that body.[32] The gentry antagonized the clergy by exploiting the benefices they held impropriate,
thus denying the clergy their salaries, and by resisting efforts of
conscientious bishops to build churches and buy glebe lands and houses
for resident incumbents. The gentry feared that a resident clergy
would press their tithe rights more effectively, and thus resisted
their attempts to reside; they did not hesitate, however, to condemn
absentees for evading their spiritual duties, especially when their
agents continued to collect the tithe.[33] The lower clergy, for their
part, directed some of their animus towards their ecclesiastical
superiors. They resented their almost complete exclusion from wealthier benefices and episcopal sees. Curates, most of whom were paid
miserable salaries by absentees to perform their duties for them,
were caught in a vicious cycle of poverty. "It is a miserable thing,"
complained Archbishop King to the somewhat less sensitive Bishop of
Cork

> to see men who have spent their strength and youth in
> serving the Church successfully, left destitute in their
> old age, and others, never served a cure, have benefices
> heaped upon them. But this is the way of the world; the
> more the pity. 'Tis a grief to me to consider, that I have
> above forty curates in my diocese, most of them worthy men,
> and some that have served near twenty years, and I not able
> to give or procure them a vicarage. . . .[34]

Irish clerics at all levels disliked the English, while the Irish gentry
found the English monopoly frustrating their efforts to secure positions
for their own sons. Finally, many bishops lived in a style which ex-

cited the jealousy of the greater landlords.[35]

Internal dissension of this magnitude would have destroyed the Church had not silent but potentially dangerous enemies, Dissent and Roman Catholicism, bound the Anglican interest together. Dissent, strong in Ulster, was forever threatening to secure by its quiet acceptance of the Hanoverian dynasty and its own indefatigable lobbying in London a measure of state recognition quite contrary to the wishes of the Established Church. In the settlement following the revolution of 1688 Dissent gained some measure of participation in public life, since a test act was not imposed in Ireland until 1704. Their remonstrances against the Established Church proved ineffective although renewed missionary activity drew more converts from Anglican than Roman sources. In 1714 the Church of Ireland, utilizing its considerable influence in Dublin and Tory strength in London, forced the termination of Dissent's privileges, including payment of the regium donum.[36] The Church insisted that its own minority position, coupled with the highly organized character of Ulster Presbyterianism, demanded that Dissent be proscribed. The chance that Presbyterians would identify with Catholics churchmen considered remote; any suggestion of Catholic resurgence would see Dissenters rallying to the Protestant cause.

These arguments did not appeal to the Whigs, who accompanied George I to the throne in 1714, only months after Dissent's role had been restricted. In 1719 they conceded Dissent a measure of limited toleration just sufficient to reduce the recipients' deeper discontent. After 1720 Dissent subsided into quiescence, preoccupied as it was with internal controversies. The fear within the ranks of the Estab-

lished Church that even limited toleration of dissident Protestants
must prefigure collapse of the erastian system reflected more
accurately its own insecurity than it did a sober analysis of the
danger posed by Ulster Presbyterians.[37]

Roman Catholicism could not be contained so easily. The government viewed it as a civil menace as well as an alien religious system,
and here the traditional ecclesiastical policy of erastianism was
expected to bear good fruit. By burdening Catholics with a code
designed to deprive them of their lands, the ministrations of their
clergy, and all public organization, the Irish government anticipated
the slow demise of the Roman Church. Since a Catholic had only to
foreswear his religion to be heir to all his father's property, un-
dutiful sons often conformed to the Establishment; the converts'
calibre, forged under such conditions, contributed little character to
the Church of Ireland, though the financial and political augmentation
was immense.[38] The Establishment also attempted to increase its
strength by proselytism and education. The assault on Catholicism was
not effective. Although outlawed, the Roman clergy continued to out-
number their Anglican counterparts three to one, and they labored
among their flock with a fervor which often contrasted sharply with
the widespread absenteeism of the Established clergy. Far from withering away, Catholicism seems to have improved its position in percentage
terms early in the century, and held its own thereafter. Indeed, instances of superficial conformity became so common that the Church of
Ireland demanded something more stringent; among lawyers in particular Catholicism continued to flourish, and even municipal officials

were known to have "popish wives and mass said in their houses."[39]

The Church of Ireland's dilemmas as a proselytizing institution were compounded by its erastian character, and not substantially relieved by ambitious efforts in the field of education. The government's insistence that all religious exercises be designed to disseminate the English language frustrated attempts to convert Catholics in rural areas, and strenuous efforts by conscientious clergymen to have Church publications printed in Irish were blocked in Dublin. In 1709 the lower house of convocation approved publication of an Irish bible, but the proposal was shelved by the bench of bishops; the identification of English and Protestant was so firmly imprinted in the minds of leading Church statesmen that no counter-arguments could prevail.[40] One alternative lay in an ambitious educational scheme, and in 1733 this found concrete expression in the founding of the Charter schools. Based on the principle that only by "abstracting" Irish children from their native environment could converts be made, these schools combined an education in handicrafts and scripture with room and board. As islands of the English interest in the Irish countryside they were perhaps "the best conceived educational institutions which existed in the world"; they were, however, ineptly administered despite lavish grants from the Irish exchequer, and were severely circumscribed by exclusion of the Irish language.[41] They managed to survive indifference and a long series of financial scandals only to be the occasion of considerable embarrassment to the Church of Ireland early in the nineteenth century.

By 1750 a state of equilibrium existed in which the Church of

Ireland, buttressed by the state, and Roman Catholicism, supported by the great majority of the population, had each secured defined positions in Irish national life. As a depository of an alien culture, distracted by administrative inefficiency, weakened by a largely absentee clergy bent on personal advancement, and opposed from time to time by its own gentry membership, the Church was unable to make the nation Protestant in religion or English in culture. Attempts to discipline the clergy proved ineffective. Bishops too often displayed a "haughty demeanor" and the clergy said only "consoling things" to their parishioners.[42] Despite a rising tide of prosperity, the Church's financial underpinnings remained weak. Deprivation of the tithe of pasture, which in effect exempted most great landlords from an obligation to support the Church, forced the clergy to exploit tithes on farm land more thoroughly than ever, exciting growing discontent among the great masses of impoverished tillage cultivators. At the same time, Roman Catholicism consolidated its hold over the peasantry and extended its activities as penal laws gradually eased.

But two generations of peace suggested to the Established Church that there was reason for expectation of eventual improvement. Whig hostility eased as the Hanoverian dynasty became more secure. The Church's strenuous support of the English interest prompted the government to ward off attempts by the Irish legislature to expropriate more of the Church's wealth. Catholicism, though not withering, was now protesting its loyalty to the crown. Priests discouraged displays of antagonism toward the Established Church, and some Protestant leaders joined in efforts to ameliorate and even abolish the penal codes.[43]

Presbyterianism, weakened by schism, was quiet. Ireland's tranquility during the Jacobite rebellion of 1745 was widely celebrated. If not a true national establishment, the Church of Ireland possessed the trappings of one, and by 1760 many observers believed that the erastian experiment would increase in stability and popularity as the years passed.

Between 1760 and 1800 the Church of Ireland's period of consolidation was disturbed by the appearance of new forces which underscored, sometimes dramatically, the inherent weaknesses of the Irish erastian system. The accession of George III, with his Tory convictions and strong religious tendencies, was greeted by the Church as the beginning of an era of ecclesiastical prosperity. Royal sympathy for the Church, however, proved slight compensation for the dangers posed by three powerful developments. One was the rise of Methodism. Another was the emergence of a distinct Irish nationalism within the very confines of the Protestant ascendancy. A third was the dramatic spread of tithe agitation and peasant unrest. Different in origin and orientation as each was, together they constituted an assault upon the Church of Ireland's religious prerogatives, its role as a link with England, and its property rights.

Irish Methodism, like its English counterpart, reflected some widely acknowledged defects of the Established Church as the representative of reformed Christianity. Little had been done to eliminate administrative abuses or to encourage clerical residence. Members of the Irish Parliament were quick to note the warping effects of excessive devotion to English patronage considerations. Non-residence was as prevalent after 1760 as before, and pluralism was practiced perhaps even more extensively than earlier. Lucius O'Brien, M. P. for Ennis, noted that in County Clare in 1764 there were seventy-six parishes but only fourteen churches. Of the latter, most were serviced by impoverished curates or not attended to at all.[44] Politicians distributed preferment to unqualified and sometimes rather unsuitable characters. In 1757 one bishop astonished the House of Lords by denying the existence of the Trinity and by recommending abolition of the Athanasian and Nicene creeds. The beneficed clergy followed the hunt with their landlord parishioners, and the clergy's identification with the gentry increased.[45]

Methodism developed in Ireland in response to abuses within the Establishment, as in England, but in Ireland it concentrated its efforts on onverting Catholics. Its zeal and forceful religious orientation, nonetheless, implicitly confirmed the gentry's increasing inclination to criticize not only the Church of Ireland's wealth, but its religious deficiencies.[46] Charles Wesley's message made a noticeable impact upon the lower clergy, but little on the bench of bishops and none on the administration. Methodism, however, was geared for missionary work; the Church of Ireland not only failed to convert large numbers of Catholics, but also aggravated divisions within Irish Protestantism and alienated many in its area of strongest concentration, Ulster. To the lower clergy Methodism implied an condemnation of patronage policies which had stymied any movement in the Establishment towards missionary activity, and they accepted readily the clarity, simplicity

and visceral characteristics of Methodism as an appropriate antidote
to fervent Roman Catholicism. To the extent, however, that Methodism
succeeded in raising the calibre of the lower clergy, so did it focus
on the upper clergy even more sharply. Unfortunately, by 1775 the
purging effects on the clergy's material instincts occasioned by
withdrawal of pasture from tithe jurisdiction had already been seriously blunted. An emphasis on tillage, necessitated by Ireland's rapid
population explosion, raised tithe income to unparalleled levels and
made the message of Methodism more relevant than ever.

As the danger of a Catholic restoration declined, Irish Protestants' dependence on the English connection, already made unpopular by
the exercise of English jobbery and by Ireland's parliamentary subor
nation, became increasingly unpalatable. After 1770 Britain's unhappy distractions in America gave the independence movement its
opportunity. Poyning's law, which since the reign of Elizabeth has
subjected Irish legislation to English parliamentary scrutiny, was
amended so as to give Ireland considerable autonomy in domestic affairs.
The Established Church was forced to accept a wider toleration of
Dissent, whose support was required to give the movement for independence wider appeal. Not only did this alarm Church leaders, who
doubted the established religion could long survive, but it aggravated
the difficulty of maintaining the English connection and increased the
odium of doing so as nationalism gained popularity among Irish Protestants.[47] The pattern of Church patronage which continued to relfect an
accommodation to the needs of ambitious Englishmen was attacked with
ever growing intensity after 1782. The dilemma was complete. To

abandon the English interest was to undermine the Church's role as the champion of English culture in Ireland, and therefore, perhaps, justification for being established. Yet to sustain the English interest was not only to aggravate the alienation of the native Irish but to endanger the Church's position in the eyes of the Protestant community as well. The Irish Parliament's approval of grants of wide toleration to both Presbyterians and Catholics in 1783 directly challenged the character and purpose of the traditional erastian system. That the Church of Ireland was extremely vulnerable to its enemies was made dramatically clear in the rise of tithe resistance after 1760 and the assault upon the Church of Ireland's prerogatives for more than two decades.

The lower classes had never completely reconciled themselves to tithes, but not until 1760 did they use the Protestant gentry's opposition to the Church's wealth to begin widespread resistance on their own part. The exemption of pasture from payment in 1735 threw the entire burden upon tillage, much of it only marginally productive, and almost all of it worked by tenants to whom even a light impost was a considerable burden. Since tithes constituted a percentage of the land's produce, increasing population pressures resulted in more intensive cultivation and also increased tithe revenues. Subdivision decreased the size of each tenant's plot year after year, raised rents by increasing competition for bids, and made subsistence difficult. By 1765 resistance to tithe payments was appearing in many parts of Ireland, and some pressure was exerted on beneficed clergymen to reside among their parishioners in order to reduce dissatisfaction.

Firm measures by landlords who saw in tithe resistance a conspiracy to restore a Catholic regime or who feared that the precedent might extend to rackrents, aided the clergy. Agitation subsided, but never ceased entirely, and it revived with unparalleled fury in 1786, when opposition assumed more concrete form. The Catholic peasantry objected to sustaining a Church whose principles they abhored and to supporting a clergy often nonresident. The clergy's agents, tithe farmers and proctors, increased their own income by zealous prosecution of tithe rights, and were particularly insensitive to tenants' needs when establishing schedules for assessment and collection.[48] All these elements and others contributed to a debate on tithes which convulsed the nation from 1786 to 1788. In Parliament Henry Grattan delivered some of his finest oratory in condemnation of the system. Whole villages joined the resistance to tithe. The established clergy were abused in pamphlet literature, and the abuse received oblique encouragement in the highest councils of the Protestant ascendency.[49]

Champions of the Church interest replied in pamphlet and pulpit. The most persuasive and most popular was Richard Woodward, Bishop of Cloyne, who identified the resistance with rebellion against the political order and with subversion of private property. He emphasized with considerable effect that the garrison character of Irish Protestantism made landlord tolerance of such defiance tantamount to destruction of the reformed religion. He predicted an end to the landholding system so painfully constructed during two centuries of British supremacy. When Irish officials obliged the Church by uncovering evidence of widespread conspiracy against tithes, the Protestant gen-

try once more felt obliged to assist their beleaguered Church;
by 1790 tithe agitation had subsided and tithes again managed to
survive in their ancient form.[50] Catholic priests, themselves upbraided for a certain efficiency in collecting dues for their services, counselled submission to the law. The outbreak of revolution
in France underscored Woodward's warnings, and the English interest
was restored to favor as the danger of an alliance between France
and Irish Catholics increased. William Pitt moved to strengthen
the Irish connection by reforming tithes but failed, and the Church
again emphasized the value of the traditional ecclesiastical policy.
Finally, rebellion in 1797 led to demands for a more durable English
connection. In 1801 the Act of Union, its passage secured by an
immense dispensation of honors, money, and promises, ended Ireland's
legislative independence and drew the British Isles together as never
before.

The Act of Union marked a decisive turning point in the erastian
experience. The submergence of the Irish Protestant ascendancy into
a larger, more stable British political, social and religious system
was expected to strengthen Ireland's minority ruling interest. The
Church hoped that less effort could be spent defending privileges and
prerogatives, and more attention devoted to proselytism. Insensitivity
to missionary work within the Church had been excused by the need to
promote a preponderant English interest in Ireland. Now it could be
undertaken. Administrative efficiency would increase the private
property rights be secured. A frequently hostile Irish Parliament
would no longer serve as a forum of grievances against the Establish-

ment, while the united legislature, with its heavily Tory sentiment, would refrain from intervention in ecclesiastical affairs. These were the sentiments of that large body of Irish Churchmen who saw in the Act of Union the seeds of a vast improvement. That the union was to lead to extensive legislative harassment and then to parliamentary reform of the Established Church, to Catholic emancipation, and finally to disestablishment in 1869, was hardly conceivable.

Chapter II: Politics, Patronage and Preferment

1. Repercussions of the Act of Union

Despite its limited membership and restricted spiritual responsibilities, the Church of Ireland at the beginning of the nineteenth century displayed an elaborate administrative system. With 4 archdioceses, 18 dioceses (some composed of more than one medieval jurisdiction), 33 cathedral chapters, and 2,400 parishes, the Irish Establishment was a considerable ecclesiastical structure.[1] The Irish primate, Archbishop of Armagh, outranked all but princes of the blood in Ireland. He constituted a factor of some weight in government circles at all times and a considerable influence when the office was filled by an energetic and able man as happened during the early nineteenth century. The primate's influence within the Church itself, however, was distinctly limited. His own jurisdiction contained six of the nation's wealthiest and, in numbers of Protestants, most populous dioceses, but entrenched landed interests and a vigorous Presbyterian community often frustrated

his programs. Alone among the archbishops the primate possessed
the right to grant faculties and dispensations in the other provinces.
This power was considerably circumscribed by the well-advertised
sensitivities of his colleagues on the episcopal bench, however.
Indeed, outside Armagh the influence of the Church as a whole was
quite inconsiderable. Dublin was an exception where members of the
Irish administration and leading Protestant barristers and merchants
constituted a vigorous community of adherents. Otherwise, most of
the island was overwhelmingly Roman Catholic. Most dioceses were
small, inefficiently administered, unevenly endowed, staffed by a
largely non-resident clergy, and filled with abandoned or unattended
parish churches. The middle ages cast a long shadow over the entire
administrative framework. Parish boundaries were oblivious to shifts
in population over the centuries. Large groups of parishes were
gathered into cumbersome unions to provide incumbents a large income.
Many diocesan offices were strictly sinecurial by tradition, others
treated so in practice. Many deaneries were handsomely endowed and
thirty of thirty-three lay in the gift of the crown, which exercised
its patronage rights with little concern for attendant responsibilities.
Many cathedral offices were also endowed far beyond attached duties.
In the course of the eighteenth century more and more of these offices
were placed at the disposal of sons and nephews of incumbent bishops.

Episcopal promotion set the patronage tone for the Church. The
erastian system by which Ireland was governed during the eighteenth
century relied heavily on the support of bishops, whose political
attitudes and family connections were given equal weight in the selec-

tion process. After 1800 the lords spiritual lost one function;
the Act of Union ended their declining influence in the Irish House
of Lords. Their importance in another area, however, increased:
elevations and translations appeased patrons, secured the acquiescence
of Irish families tempted towards fractiousness, and of course relieved the patronage backlog in England. In the context of pastoral
responsibilities contracted in the process of promotion, the candidates' credentials of good birth and good fortune were scarcely designed to promote the spiritual welfare of the Church's membership.
The translation process had in the course of the eighteenth century
appointed prelates to Irish sees with little regard for ecclesiastical requirements. As a result of the Act of Union translations became more frequent and therefore more disruptive to episcopal administration.[2]

Who secured Ireland's episcopal plums prior to 1800? A slight
majority went to Englishmen. "With the single proviso that clerics
resign their English livings before accepting Irish ones, there were
never any legal obstacles in the way of men being translated from
ecclesiastical positions in the one Church to those in the other."[3]
This policy of ecclesiastical free trade benefitted only Englishmen.
Between 1660 and 1790 about forty-five percent of all clerics named
to Irish bishoprics were born in England or Scotland. Swift observed
in the 1730s that two sorts of gentlemen gained Irish bishoprics:
English clergymen who succeeded "by the force of friends, industry,
solicitation or other means" unknown to Swift. The remainder were
Irishmen distinguished "by an implicit readiness to fall into any

measures that will make the government easy. . . ."[4]

A well worn path to the episcopacy passed through chaplaincies at Dublin castle, and it constituted an agreeable method for the introduction of Englishmen. The Lord Lieutenant enjoyed the customary prerogative of making his first chaplain a bishop. The Viceroy was always English; his protegés were invariably English as well. After 1800 this practice continued, even though at least one viceroy was Irish by birth; between 1801 and 1871 seventeen future bishops were chaplains to the Irish viceroy, and of this number twelve were English.[5] In truth Swift could complain how discouraging all of this was for native Irish aspirants.

Irishmen were more likely to advance through the cathedral offices. Both Irish and English candidates could hope for appointment to some of the poorer sees such as Cork and Ross, Killaloe and Kilfenora, or Clonfert; only Englishmen, however, could expect to reach the primacy or Dublin. This tendency towards one system of promotion for the Irish and another for the English produced friction and engendered a hothouse Irish nationalism among Irish incumbents which continued well into the nineteenth century.[6]

The pattern of parochial patronage was especially confusing. Towards the end of the eighteenth century the bench of bishops held the right of presentation in 1,339 of Ireland's 2,436 parishes. Laymen controlled 344 parishes, the Crown 282. Another 100 parishes were controlled by Trinity College (Dublin), cathedral chapters, and other institutions, and control of 349 was disputed or cannot be determined.[7] Incomplete returns published in 1824 reflect continued confusion, de-

spite a quarter-century's progress in eliminating the most notorious
patronage anomalies.[8] Episcopal appointment still represented only
one of several avenues to an Irish benefice. Except in Meath and
Ossory, the Bishop exercised the right of presentation to a majority
of the benefices, but these were often poorly endowed and were frequently granted to curates whose years and even decades of service
deserved recognition. Much of the tithe income in benefices where
the bench exercised right of presentation was controlled by laymen
and without episcopal support the livings would not have provided a
subsistence income; in Ferns, for instance, nearly one-half of the
parochial revenue went to sources outside the parish itself. The
crown exercised fewer rights of presentation, but the benefices involved were often lucrative and demanded the constant attention of
Dublin Castle. Lay presentations were even more disturbing, and turned on distinctly political considerations. In Down and Connor and in
Lismore more than one-third of the benefices were controlled by laymen, and in Ardfert and Aghadoe, Limerick and Ossory more than one-
fourth. After 1800 these rights, many of them the usurpations of
enterprising gentry families over two centuries, were subject to a
determined scrutiny by bishops' lawyers and were involved in lengthy
litigation. In other benefices the right of presentation was divided,
a fertile ground for dispute. Trinity College supported some of its
faculty by rights of presentation to several benefices in Ulster;
these incumbents were perforce rarely resident in their benefices.
Finally, patronage problems were complicated by control of tithe and
glebe incomes, with rectorial and vicarial tithes often in separate

hands.

Much of Ireland's impatience with the Established Church stemmed
from its observation of an overblown administration, with its inefficient allocation of revenues, unabashed manipulation of patronage,
widespread preoccupation with privilege and prerogative, and clerical
non-residence. After 1800 many looked to the united Parliament for
direction in ameliorating these abuses and in casting the administration of the Irish Church in more relevant terms. William Stuart, Archbishop of Armagh after 1800, was more aware than most that without substantial internal reform the larger task of weaning Ireland from Catholicism could never succeed. Shortly after his arrival in Ireland he confided to Charles Brodrick, Archbishop of Cashel and future partner in
promoting church reform, that

> the true state of the Church of Ireland, in great degree, con-
> sists of bishops without clergy, churches without clergymen,
> and clergymen without churches; parishes of considerable ex-
> tent without clergymen, Church or glebe, many parishes fre-
> quently consolidated into one, with a common Church too re-
> mote for parishioners to resort to. Can a Church so circum-
> scribed possess internal strength for its own defense against
> the mass of opposition exerted against it. . . ?[9]

In confronting this defective heritage, the Church of Ireland was required to deal with administrative problems on one hand, and with patronage on the other. A rational course might have seen the administration
revamped first; instead, the Act of Union with its attendant abuse of
ecclesiastical patronage, took precedence. The crisis, moreover, marked
a turning point in the development of Church-state relationships during
the nineteenth century.

Much has been written of the political chicanery which attended

Pitt's program of persuading the Irish Parliament to vote its own

abolition in 1801. The melancholy correspondence of the Earl of

Hardwicke, whoexecuted many patronage obligations connected with this

event, and recent studies which follow the union controversy through

its various stages, are vivid accounts of political machination at

its most cynical. Irish nationalist writers and British historians

of differing political convictions have been quick to note the crucial

importance of the Act of Union in nineteenth century Anglo-Irish re-

lations; the repeal movement in Ireland, the role of the Irish party

in British politics, and the final vindication of Irish nationalism

have all been traced to Pitt's decision to extinguish the Irish Parlia-

ment.[10]

The Act of Union was also an ecclesiastical settlement, designed

to fortify Protestantism and to stem the Catholic threat. Pitt had

promised Catholic prelates that in the wake of the legislative union

provision would be made for repeal of penal codes and reintegration

of the Irish Catholic majority into national life. At the same time

the Irish Established Church was to draw strength from its English

counterpart through administrative amalgamation and internal reform.

These praiseworthy objectives were obscured by the immediate need to

obtain the Irish Parliament's acquiescence in the union proposal, an

acquiescence which only lavish patronage commitments to its members

seemed likely to secure. The result was both unfortunate and inevit-

able. Negotiations regarding the Catholic Church were omitted complete-

ly. Those related to the Church of Ireland were superintended almost

entirely by Charles Agar, Archbishop of Cashel. His principal object was to obtain permanent parliamentary representation for the four

archbishops, and to exclude the remaining bishops entirely. In this

he failed. His second objective, a more important one, called for

explicit guarantees that the integration of the English and Irish

churches "be expressed as a fundamental part of the Union," and that

the position of the Church of Ireland be guaranteed irrevocably, as

was the Church of Scotland by the terms of the Act of Union of 1707.

This was duly inserted, although even the imperious Agar could not

make Parliament's pronouncement irrevocable.[11] The Churches of Eng-

land and Ireland were united in "doctrine, worship, discipline and

government;" the amalgamation was called "an essential and fundamental

part of the Union;" arrangements were outlined for the Church's re-

presentation in Parliament through two archbishops and two bishops.

But the legislation omitted all reference to Church reform, which

might alarm Ireland's hierarchy of vested interests, and committed

the government to an exercise in patronage destined to disorient pro-

motion patterns within the Church for a generation.

The critical importance of ecclesiastical patronage in obtaining

the consent of important Irish families to the union proposal has been

noted by G.C. Bolton in his study of "union engagements," a contemporary

euphemism which comprehended one of the most extensive and unabashed

exercises in jobbery in British history. Initially many churchmen

opposed the proposal, with the faculty at Trinity College leading the

resistance.[12] Some bishops were prepared to support the government for

a price. Of these, surely the most celebrated was Agar. His exertions

on behalf of British interests in Ireland were longstanding, though his

own Irish birth kept him from succeeding to Armagh in 1800. He recommended harsh and repressive measures during the Rebellion of
1798, acquired a large fortune through family control of Church lands,
and spent a good deal of time advising successive Irish viceroys.[13]
Lord Cornwallis, who superintended the negotiations which led up to
the extinction of the Irish legislature, described his interview
with Agar in this communication to the Duke of Portland:

> It was privately initiated to me that the sentiments of
> the Archbishop of Cashel were less friendly to the Union than
> they had been, on which I took an opportunity of conversing
> with his Grace on the subject, and after discussing some
> preliminary topics respecting the representation of the
> Spiritual Lords, and the probable vacancy of the see of
> Dublin, he declared his great unwillingness at all times
> to oppose the measures of the Government, and especially
> on a point in which his Majesty's feelings were so much
> interested, to whom he professed the highest sense of
> gratitude, and concluded by a cordial declaration of friend-
> ship.

Agar voted for the Union, received a Viscountcy the same year, and
became Archbishop of Dublin in 1801. He also received an earldom
shortly thereafter, an honor which enabled his son to enjoy the
benefits of a courtesy title on his European travels.[14] It is not
to be wondered that Agar enjoyed an unparalleled reputation for avar-
ice, and that his behavior on the occasion of the Act of Union should
move one observer to judge his "failings many and his virtues few."[15]

A few bishops opposed the union, and resisted the government's
promise of a "mark of favor."[16] Others, such as Thomas O'Beirne,
Bishop of Meath, vigorously supported the Union without first seeking
favors, though he was quick to find places for his relatives when
the opportunity presented itself.[17] Cornwallis blanched at the pros-

pect of trying to satisfy some powerful petitioners for ecclesiastical patronage, but he felt "obliged at this time to recommend" them.[18] Bishop Stock of Killalla published a barely anonymous pamphlet describing his treatment as a captive of the French force which made a brief landing in Mayo. A father and son distinguished for their work in ferreting out treasonable elements at Trinity College in 1798 asked for a deanery and benefice. One son's employment as a lieutenant in the artillery was not regarded as an insuperable obstacle to preferment, for he had attended some divinity lectures and was therefore prepared for ordination.[19] As a result of all these petitions, when Hardwicke reached Dublin he was confronted with some thirty pledges of ecclesiastical offices to bishops who had supported the bill in Parliament, to Irish peers seeking bishoprics and deaneries for relatives, and to English and Irish notables forced to surrender their Irish parliamentary franchises in the course of the legislative union.

But for the personal intervention of George III, Hardwicke might have confronted a Church completely bent to submission by the weight of its erastian responsibilities and privileges. Instead, the same scruples which had prompted the King to oppose Pitt's suggestion of Catholic emancipation led him on the eve of the passage of the Act of Union to intervene in direct opposition to the process of fulfilling union engagements. There was, of course, no dearth of willing candidates on the Irish bench and no flagging of aristocrats' pressure on behalf of favorites. And there was certainly no dearth of unsolicited, self-serving advice. Lord Clare, the dynamic and cordially hated Irish Lord Chancellor, looked for a "meek and firm

man" to fill the most important vacancy in Ireland, the primacy at
Armagh, which became vacant in timely fashion in 1800. Clare was
the son of an Irish merchant and the grandson of an Irish Catholic
peasant. To him the Established Church was a bastion against resurgent Catholicism, and having committed himself to the Protestant
cause, he was determined to see that Catholicism did not gain ground.
The eighteenth century Church had suffered from inept leadership and
lazy prelates; the new primate must be willing to "exert" himself
"with persevering moderation to correct the abuses which prevail in
our Church. . . .He ought not to be a political or a rapacious man"
for such vices would "induce him to acts of a very serious and extensive public mischief."[20]

In London, however, the favorite applicant was Euseby Cleaver,
protegé of the Grenvilles. Cleaver was Bishop of Ferns. His episcopal residence had been destroyed in the rebellion of 1798, and he
used this misfortune to advertise his suitability for the primacy.
Clare undermined the candidacy of this "most intemperate and over-
bearing priest" by circulating the story that in the management of
his see Cleaver had acted "solely upon the table of calculation which
he bought for half a crown."[21] Notwithstanding Clare's violent opposition Cornwallis in his last months as viceroy tried to press Cleaver's
case. Cleaver, Cornwallis asserted, was acceptable to Ireland because he was already on the Irish bench and he was acceptable to England and to the King because of his English birth.[22] Clare found
allies among those bishops who wanted the post for themselves. John
Porter, a bishop of only five years' tenure and already in command of

the lucrative see of Clogher, was favored   by the Whigs who had thrown

in their lot with Pitt at the beginning of the war with France.[23]

When Porter's candidacy raised hackles on the backs of Pitt's older

disciples, the Whigs advanced Thomas O'Beirne in his place. O'Beirne

had come to Ireland in 1782 as chaplain to Portland, the Whig vice-

roy. This former Catholic exercised considerable influence over

Portland, and only the Duke's brief tenure prevented O'Beirne from

becoming entrenched in Dublin castle. When Earl Fitzwilliam came to

Ireland as viceroy in 1790 O'Beirne served as his secretary.   In 1795

he became a bishop.[24]   Clare now kept him from becoming primate.

Cyril Jackson, Dean of Christ Church and a man of considerable

scholarly accomplishments, stood forth momentarily as a compromise,

but he, strange for the times, resisted the offer.[25]   Cornwallis was

eager to settle the question, but as the year 1800 advanced no candi-

date could be found who did not leave powerful interests bitterly

disappointed. Cornwallis warned London that if precedent was broken

and the place given to an Irishman, he dared not ignore Agar's claims.

If the primacy went to an Englishman, Cornwallis urged that a man al-

ready on the Irish bench be chosen. "It would have a very bad effect

at this time," Cornwallis complained to Portland, "to send a stranger

to supersede the whole bench of bishops, "and I should likewise be

much embarrassed by the stop that would be put to the succession

amongst the Irish clergy at this critical period, when I am beyond

measure pressed for ecclesiastical preferment."[26]

At length the King intervened, not only to preserve the ancient

practice of appointing an Englishman (or a Scot), but to thwart the claims and challenge the advice of his Irish advisors and govern-

ment.[27] The King, it transpired, was determined to consecrate the

new ecclesiastical amalgamation proclaimed in part five of the Act

of Union by translating an Englishmen to the Irish primacy. The

post was, however, despite its income and alleged prestige, a de-

cidedly unattractive one to English prelates of stature, and had

"gone literally a-begging"; the Bishops of Oxford and Norwich re-

sisted royal pleas that they cross over.[28] Among incumbents of the

poorer sees were few exceptional men. George III did, however,

finally satisfy his desire to strengthen the calibre of the Irish

bench by selecting William Stuart, Bishop of St. David's, for Armagh.

In doing so the King set in motion a reform impulse which neither he

nor his ministers could have anticipated.

The King's choice was remarkable in several ways: he defied

extremely strong pressure from the Irish administration to use the

primacy to satisfy pressing political engagements in Ireland; he

dared confront an almost universal hostility among Irish aristocrats

to English ecclesiastics; he settled on a man of heretofore unexcep-

tional achievements; and he expressed his support for reform in terms

which subsequently sustained Stuart in his confrontations with Irish

politicians. Stuart's previous advancement in the Church had de-

pended upon the persistent requests of the Countess of Bute, widow

of George III's favorite of forty years before. He became a canon

of ChristChurch, Oxford, in 1789, was offered and refused the Canonry

of Windsor in 1792, and became Bishop of St. David's in Wales shortly

after the death of his father the same year.[29] He preached before the

King the following year, having already gained a reputation in Church circles for his sober homilies. The King seems to have been favorably impressed.[30] The King's decision to press Armagh on Stuart seems to have followed another series of sermons delivered at court in the winter of 1799-1800. Writing to Stuart's wife's niece in July, he noted Stuart had been ill and the offer briefly delayed lest Stuart might advance his ill-health as justification for refusing Armagh. The see, the King added, was "in point of emolument. . .infinitely more lucrative than it is generally supposed; I know that will not actuate him, but at the same time with an increasing family it ought not to be disregarded."[31] Stuart proved genuinely reluctant, a point which he made much of in subsequent requests for royal support in Ireland. He cited his poor health, the great expense of taking possession of Armagh (which "would utterly ruin" his children if he died soon), the damp climate, and political problems. All these objections, even the climate, which the King praised, were at length overcome.[32]

Stuart's acceptance was greeted with considerable hostility by Irish politicians, who did not fail to see ominous implications in the King's confession to Pitt that the appointment was "essential to the quiet of the Irish Established Church, and to promoting religion and virtue in that island."[33] The King's obvious distrust of Irish ecclesiastics was resented and the traditional practice of reserving Armagh for an Englishman seemed even less reasonable now that the English and Irish Churches were joined legislatively.[34] The new primate kissed hands for the primacy October 21, 1801, and moved into

Irish politics shortly thereafter. "Shy and inaccessible," distressed initially at his exile, he appeared at first "to be disposed to
be as civil and accommodating to the Irish government as could
reasonably be expected after the manner of his appointment."[35]
Searching for clues as to Stuart's personality and possible reactions, Hardwicke referred to Johnson's "Dictionary" where he was described "with the advantages of high birth, learning, travel, and
elegant manners, an exemplary parish priest in every respect."
Hardwicke thought that his indicated "a common type of ecclesiastic,
and nothing more, and as to his individuality nothing further is
known than the dates of his promotions."[36]

The viceroy's assessment proved correct. Stuart was "a
high, proud, independent man, but with honorable principles and excellent understanding."[37] In matters political, however, he was
naïve, and this soon enough showed in his dealings with less than
scrupulous Irish politicians. But his impatience with and opposition
to traditional forms of ecclesiastical patronage manipulation by
Irish politicians was also made known.[38] The King had denied Armagh
to Irish interests; now Stuart was to become a focus of opposition to
the heritage of patronage abuse which had been so salient a feature
of the erastian system during the eighteenth century and which was so
flagrantly renewed in the wake of the Act of Union. Together with
Charles Brodrick,[39] Stuart was determined to protest against the
evils of indiscriminate distribution of patronage for political purposes and to implement a program of structural reform within the Irish
Church itself.

An examination of the "union engagements" controversy within the context of Stuart's protests, and with reference to the attitude of those bishops whose own advancement was delayed in order to accommodate supporters of the union, reveals distinctive aspects of Stuart's reformist views. It also underscores the utterly pragmatic and often shortsighted policy of the Irish government, and the naive and uninspiring attitude of many episcopal incumbents towards their own religious community. Eighteenth century Irish churchmen were, generally, an undistinguished lot, and even two luminaries, Swift and Berkeley, are rarely considered famous as ecclesiastics. The grandest bishops, such as Frederick Augustus Hervey, Earl of Bristol and Bishop of Derry, were wealthy magnates whose eccentricities often outshone their spiritual qualities, while the most obscure were often embittered relics of past political commitments which had advanced them to minor sees, where they had languished, completely forgotten.

That Stuart was a man of a distinctly different stamp was made painfully clear to the Irish government just as Hardwicke commenced fulfilling his "union engagements" in October 1801. The occasion was the seat vacated by Charles Brodrick at Kilmore, a diocese boasting a considerable Protestant population and a comfortable episcopal income. The aspirant was George de la Poer Beresford, son of John Beresford, a member of the last Irish House of Commons and, in popular parlance, "king of Ireland" by virtue of the boroughs he manipulated and the government patronage he controlled. The Beresfords represented within the Irish Church an extreme variant of that family influence which so seriously detracted from its zeal and probity. One archbishop and one bishop already testified to the importance of

the Beresford interest in the Established Church.

Stuart had wasted no time after his arrival in Ireland as-

certaining the number and condition of Church livings, government

plans for Church reform, and the extent of non-residence.[40] He

also inspected the qualifications of his bishops. His conviction

of the utter unworthiness of the latest nominee was not muted by

whatever appreciation he may have had of the family's immense in-

fluence:

> Mr. Beresford is reported to be one of the most profligate
> men in Europe. His language and his manners have given
> universal offense. Indeed, such is his character that
> were his Majesty's ministers to give him a living in my
> diocese to hold in commendam, I should be wanting in my
> duty if I did not refuse him institution.

To place him at Kilmore would be worse. "Perhaps it may be said,"

continued Stuart,

> that Mr. Beresford, being a bishop already it matters
> little whether he has two or four thousand per annum, or
> in what part of Ireland he is placed. This last circum-
> stance is, however, of the utmost importance. In the
> North, which is well known to be the Protestant part of
> Ireland, and where, therefore, if it be meant to preserve
> the Protestant interest, most care should be taken to place
> the government of the Church in proper hands, I have six
> bishops under me. Three are men of tolerable moral charac-
> ter, but are inactive and useless, and two are of acknow-
> ledged bad character. Fix Mr. Beresford at Kilmore and we
> shall then have three very inactive bishops, and what I
> trust the world has not yet seen, three bishops in one
> district reported to be the most profligate men in Europe.[41]

Hardwicke was shocked. If Addington was at first disposed to

interpret the Primate's fulminations as hot flashes of ill-temper, he

was disabused of this impression by Stuart's stubborn adherence to

principle. Hardwicke informed Stuart in a testily worded dispatch that the nomination should have been opposed at an earlier date.

Now the government's intentions had circulated to the point where

failure to appoint Beresford would constitute an insult to the en-

tire family.[42] He, Hardwicke, had not been aware of Beresford's

deficiencies and would seek Stuart's consent to all subsequent

appointments. Since Beresford was already a bishop, Hardwicke

added, a mere change of revenue could not be considered so serious

an innovation. Stuart did not agree. The Beresford nomination was

only part of the larger and much more serious question of the fate

of the Church. "You cannot be serious," he answered Hardwicke's

secretary,

> when you write that a translation from one see to another
> is simply a question of emolument. It is not so in any
> country, and in Ireland less than any other. . . .What
> will happen if the bishops of Ireland follow this example,
> and adopt this language--promote the most worthless clergy-
> man, because when a man holds a living a bad character is
> not to impede his preferment, as a removal from one parish
> to another is simply a question of emolument.[43]

To Hardwicke directly, he noted that

> by this measure, we are deprived of the advantage promised
> to us by the Union. In truth, the two Churches cannot be
> considered as united unless they are governed by the same
> principle. A bad moral character would in England be an
> insuperable obstacle to the promotion of a bishop--an
> obstacle which neither rank, nor wealth, nor parliamentary
> interest can enable a man to surmount.[44]

And to Addington, Pitt's successor as Prime Minister, he relayed his

most vigorous sentiments. He predicted that "the profession itself

would shortly cease to exist." He declared as well that there was

"no surer method of destroying the Church than by placing irreligious

and profligate men in those situations where the people have a right to expect examples of piety and virtue." Stuart would resign if the decision was not rescinded.[45]

The prospect of a resignation on the bench always created an embarrassing situation for an Irish administration. For the primate to do so was a serious constitutional crisis. Hardwicke complained to Addington of "this furious though honest zeal which disclaims everything short of theoretical perfection." He defended his own conduct in a long letter to the Prime Minister. The tone of his defense suggested more an attempt to settle his own conscience than to ease Addington's problems. He also decided to despatch Charles Lindsay, his brother-in-law and private secretary, to Armagh to show the irate ecclesiastic all the relevant correspondence.[46] Lindsay's mission was an utter failure. Stuart informed Hardwicke of his desire to resign the primacy, and wrote the King "in such a manner as will convince him that I most sincerely desire so to do."[47]

After sending his secretary to interview Stuart once more, Hardwicke was convinced that Stuart should be allowed to retire, "extraordinary and unprecedented as such a step would be."[48] Addington conceded that Stuart should have been apprised of the government's intention to translate Beresford, though in the past the primate's approbation was rarely asked for or even thought proper.[49] Addington asked Stuart to reconsider his request to resign the primacy. Stuart once again refused to change his mind. He told Addington that his decision "did not originate from pique, ill-humor, or party attachment," but from principle, and thus it was not subject to negotiation.[50] Resigning the primacy was not easy, but "if Dr.

Beresford be translated to Kilmore I should certainly have to struggle
with far greater evils, and should probably struggle in vain, for the
profession itself would shortly cease to exist."[51]

The violence of his language drew from Addington a remarkably
icy request, even a demand, for "some specification of the depravity"
which prompted Stuart's extreme language. And the next day Addington
informed Hardwicke that he considered Stuart's opinions to be unwarranted. Beresford's "gaity and irregularity at an early period of
his life" had been replaced by an "irreproachable" conduct on the
bench.[52]

Addington's distress at "the style and manner" of Stuart's
letters certainly prejudiced the primate's case. Beyond this, the
fact was that no one dared affront the Beresfords. The King was
disconcerted. He thought Stuart had been intemperate in drastically
condemning Beresford on the basis of what must have been some rumors
floated by Beresford's opponents. He urged Stuart to consider his
conscience relieved of its burden by this open and vigorous opposition to the Bishop. The King added that he could find no precedent
for surrendering the primacy, and that Stuart would harm the Church
by resigning.[53] Pressure on Stuart increased. He was upset by the
King's failure to support him. He was angered by reports that his
colleagues and government officials blamed him for not having averted
such a scandal by speaking out earlier. He protested that he had not
known of the planned translation, and that he would gladly have
surrendered his own private patronage to avert the scandal.[54]

At length Stuart succumbed to royal pressure that he remain at

Armagh. He decided to retain control of his province but to avoid

all participation in affairs of state until he had been vindicated

on the Beresford issue.[55] Addington invited Stuart to elaborate

on his accusations, but Stuart refused and declared that his word was

sufficient.[56] But Stuart's silence could not go on indefinitely.

Eventually his castigation of the government's patronage policies

produced some results. Lord Hawkesbury (later Earl of Liverpool)

promised Stuart in his capacity as Home Secretary that the government

would be more careful in the future. A prominent member of the Irish

administration, John Mitford, Baron Redesdale, the Lord Chancellor,

drew the appropriate lesson; "You may let a Lord or an Honourable

sleep in a Deanery without much mischief, and if he should chance

to prefer riot to sleep, the mischief he will do will be principally

the mischief of example, but such a man on the Bench may ruin Ireland,

or at least defeat the good effects of all the exertions of the rest

of the Bench."[57] It was a lesson not easily learned.

But it was far easier for Hawkesbury to placate Stuart than it

was to dampen the enthusiasm of preferment-seekers. Indeed, the pace

of patronage preferment quickened. The Beresford appetite remained

unsatiated and that of other clans was whetted at the sight of the

Beresfords' good fortune. A long hiatus in the mortality rate on

the episcopal bench between October 1800 and the death in 1802 of

Richard Marlay, one of two bishops who refused to support the union

legislation, increased pressure on Hardwicke to give even greater

priority to government promises. Marlay's death made possible the

elevation of Power le Poer Trench, son of Lord Kilconnel and brother

of Richard Trench, member for County Galway in the last Irish
House of Commons. Lord Pelham and Hardwicke exchanged letters on
Trench's candidacy in July 1802. In these letters Trench's qualifications for the bench were completely ignored and the requirements
of previous patronage commitments were discussed in elaborate and
even sarcastic fashion.[58] Trench's triumph was a source of deep
consternation to Irish episcopal incumbents, some of whom had
already long stood in line for a promotion.[59]

In 1803, the demise in Italy of that Whig grandee, Frederick
Augustus Hervey, opened the Bishopric of Derry, the most lucrative
in Ireland, to a deserving government supporter. William Knox,
scion of a powerful Ulster family, was nominated by Hardwicke. The
King thought him something of a pest but Hardwicke noted to Charles
Abbott, the Chief Secreatry, that a firm promise had been made to
him, and added a somewhat strained testimony to Knox's spiritual
zeal.[60] Lord Pelham, Home Secretary and an inveterate foe of the
Lord Lieutenant, tried to embarrass Hardwicke and complicate the
flow of union engagements by reviving one of the King's favorite
projects: an exchange of English and Irish bishoprics. So wealthy
a see as Derry was attractive even to some English ecclesiastics,
and Pelham suggested Euseby Cleaver of Ferns, who had been promised
promotion, might be sent to England. Derry then could be given to
an English nominee. Irish churchmen were enraged at the prospect
of an Englishman in Ireland's wealthiest see. Hardwicke was also
disturbed. The plan threatened to alienate the Knox family, with
their well-entrenched political interest in Ulster. For Cleaver,

"a very jobbing fellow," Hardwicke entertained no sympathy. For the policy of translating English and Irish bishops Hardwicke had nothing but scorn. And in regard to the prior commitment to Dr. Knox, Hardwicke recalled in sharp language that "every assurance, short of an absolute promise" had been made, and that a refusal now would excite hostility and perhaps would dishonor the government. Worst of all, Hardwicke's hopes to give Knox's present see (Killaloe) to his own brother-in-law Lindsay would be thwarted.[61]

At length Hardwicke prevailed and Pelham resigned. Lindsay obtained Killaloe. His new diocese was remote from Dublin, but he remained near Hardwicke and continued to act as the viceroy's financial advisor and private secretary It is not certain that he ever visited Killaloe. As compensation, however, he spent considerable time in London on viceregal business.[62]

When the Bishop of Raphoe, James Hawkins, showed signs of dying in May 1803 the union engagements controversy was renewed on a scale far greater in intensity than even that which was precipitated by the vacancy at Derry. Addington put forward the name of Charles Butson, Dean of Waterford. Butson was a school companion of Addington thirty years earlier, "the only friend" for whom the Prime Minister "felt extreme anxiety with a view to preferment in the Church of Ireland."[63] On behalf of the Beresford interest the Marquis of Waterford nominated Lord John George Beresford. Lord John held a lucrative preferment worth £4200 which he was willing to offer to the government. The Marquess of Ely and his relation Lord Loftus, member for Wexford and a Lord of the Treasury, also entered a claim.

Ely informed Addington that the Duke of Portland had promised Lord
Loftus a place on the bench for his younger brother Lord Robert
Tottenham Loftus as soon as possible after Tottenham reached the
age of thirty, the canonical minimum for a bishop.[64] Ely owned six
parliamentary boroughs at the time of the Act of Union and could be
counted on for eight votes. He supported the Union at an enormous
price: an Irish marquisate and an English baronatcy for himself,
the sinecure post of Postmaster-General in Ireland and a Treasury
post for his son, and of course ₤45,000 as "compensation" for the
extinguished boroughs. The bishopric was not included on the union
engagements list, but there was Portland's alleged promise.

The negotiations which followed suggest something of the intensity of the competition for ecclesiastical preferment, an intensity which even the unanticipated recovery of Bishop Hawkins did
nothing to abate. Addington was quite insistent that Butson be
elevated at the next vacancy. When the aging incumbent of Kildare
died in early 1804, Hardwicke found himself beseeched from all sides.
Butson was accused on the basis of deft research by his opponents
of having cultivated improper relationships with some Waterford wo-
men. Even his theology, lightly carried as theology was at that time,
seemed unorthodox.[65] Butsons's case, however, was not without its
merits. He held two lucrative preferments in commendam, and Hardwicke was sufficiently indiscreet to promise one of these to the
brother of Lord Enniskillen, a longstanding government supporter,
and another to a Dr. Lee, whose brother sat for Waterford.[66] Addington for his part determined to satisfy Butson unless Lord Ely could

produce satisfactory evidence that a prior promise had indeed been
made by Portland in favor of his son Robert Tottenham. Ely professed
that he could, but did not, and Butson was notified of his selection.

This was premature, for when Butson indiscreetly proclaimed his
victory in Waterford, the Beresfords and Ely both renewed their efforts.
Ely got Portland to admit that a promise had been made. Meanwhile the
Marquis of Waterford pressed the candidacy of Lord John Beresford in
a stream of letters directed to the viceroy, the Home Secretary, and
the Prime Minister. Addington was given a catalogue of Butson's
alleged indiscretions.[67] Addington refused to surrender Butson's
claims. Hardwicke dared not appease Ely when the Beresfords were unsatisfied.[68] Fortunately, the Bishop of Kildare died in April 1804.
Lindsay, who had yet to settle himself in Killaloe, was translated to
Kildare, and resigned his secretaryship at the same time. Dr. Nathaniel Alexander was translated from Clonfert to Killaloe.[69] Clonfert
was so poor that Hardwicke assumed neither Ely nor Waterford would
lay claim to it.[70] But Waterford showed interest and Ely wasted no
time in trying to pledge the Government to grant Clonfert to young
Lord Tottenham. Ely even closeted himself with Portland and Addington. Portland formally admitted that Ely had been pledged a bishopric as part of the union engagements and this forced Addington to
declare that this pledge must be redeemed without delay.[71] Addington was furious that Portland had made and then concealed so grave a
promise, although he thought Ely's representations ("which were not
deficient in earnestness, to say the least," he told Hardwicke), had
pressured the aging Portland to concede more than he wished.[72]

Hardwicke adopted a high tone of disinterest. He reminded
Addington that he "acted merely as a trustee of the late Government"
in dispensing ecclesiastical patronage. He had, at Addington's insistence, made a positive commitment to Butson and now he refused
to break it. Addington found himself out of office before the problem was resolved. Robert Stewart, Viscount Castlereagh, who made
many of the outstanding commitments in his capacity as Irish Chief
Secretary on the eve of the Act of Union, now urged Ely's case in
order to save him for the government, and Tottenham appeared at Dublin Castle to receive the episcopal commission. Hardwicke's fury
knew no limits. He condemned Ely for his rapaciousness, Addington
for giving way after pushing Butson's claims so energetically, and
London's officialdom for manipulating Irish patronage while ignoring
the viceroy's prerogatives. He told the young Tottenham that a binding commitment had been made to Butson, that "Addington's conduct
was not at all creditable," and that he, Hardwicke, "was not particularly fond of saying that what I called black one day was white
another." He informed Lord Hawkesbury that should Butson's elevation
be blocked he would resign.[73] Pitt agreed. Butson received Clonfert
and Ely retired from the ring when he secured first rights to the next
vacancy.[74]

The Beresford clan was also active during this period. The
Marquis of Waterford monitored the Butson-Ely negotiations closely.
He informed the Government that he would be willing to accept on his
brother's behalf the first "good bishopric" to come after Ely was
satisfied. He told candidate Lord John that nothing would distract

him from seeing him installed as a bishop.[75] In September 1804 Down

and Connor became vacant. Ely rushed to have this wealthy Ulster

see granted to Tottenham. Balked by Pitt on Clonfert, he was opposed

this time by the primate, who had been notified of the Government's

plan to satisfy Ely. The diocese, Stuart noted, contained many

Protestants. It was one of the most important ecclesiastical posts

in Ireland:

> Of Lord Robert Tottenham's moral character I have heard
> nothing, and, therefore, am willing to believe it not to
> be bad. But as I find it is universally said that he is
> utterly unacquainted with his profession, never having
> performed any clerical duties, I should conceive it would
> be improper to place him in a situation where even a slight
> imprudence might be extremely detrimental to the Church.

Stuart recommended instead Bishop Alexander, recently translated to

Killaloe.[76] Tottenham was accordingly despatched to Killaloe, where

his deficiencies, as Stuart saw them, might prove less severe. In

January 1805 the death of the Bishop of Cork and Ross provided an

appropriate occasion to meet the pledge given to the Beresfords. But

the Marquis of Waterford wanted Raphoe, whose incumbent was also

gravely ill. Raphoe's income was larger and Beresford lands lay with-

in its borders. Hardwicke had already implied that Cleaver could have

it. Fortunately the Beresfords proved less stubborn than Ely, and John

Beresford went to Cork and Ross. The Bishop of Raphoe recovered, and

Cleaver was once more frustrated in his efforts to escape Ferns.

The public could not fail to take note of this rapid and wide-

spread exchange of episcopal preferment. Hardwicke and English minis-

ters emerged exhausted and discouraged. Public opinion accused the

Beresfords and the Ely clan of treating certain Irish dioceses as spheres of influence. Castlereagh was moved to declare that if the

influence of these and other Irish families was not curbed the Church

would not survive another decade.[77] Hardwicke complained of the re-

ercussions of this scramble on the distribution of inferior eccles-

astical patronage.[78] Hawkesbury hoped that the government would

ee its way to avoiding promises for preferment to meet   political

bjectives. "The Church Establishment of Ireland deserves every

ttention that can possibly be paid to it."[79] Tottenham's elevation

as particularly disturbing. He told Stuart that

> Pitt entirely agrees with your opinion that the appointment
> of young men to the rank of bishops without any attention
> to their requirements and other qualifications must, on
> every account, be resisted in the future. The security of
> the Protestant religion and of order requires the utmost
> attention to be paid to the purity and respectability of
> the two benches. The union engagements have, in recent
> incidences, most materially counteracted these important
> objects, but it is to be hoped that they are now at an
> end, and that we may be enabled to revert to those princi-
> ples, and that practice, which can alone contribute to the
> tranquility and happiness in any country.[80]

One group in particular was quick to agree: those episcopal in-

umbents whose own services in support of union legislation had been

eglected in favor of the great magnates, and whose promised promotions

ere being frustrated by the influx of new personnel. Irish bishops

ere not a heroic lot; they expected promotion in the absence of evi-

ence of gross neglect of duty. The tenor of their requests to the

rish administration reflects this. Two episcopal petitioners stressed

heir right to promotion on the basis of the ordeals suffered during

he rebellion of 1798 and their decisions, cast in heroic terms, to

emain in their dioceses despite the turbulence. A half-dozen more pleaded their family connections as sufficient qualification. Others specifically noted their support in securing approval of the Act of Union. Two pleaded poverty. One declared that a wealthier bishopric was much more suitable for a man of his connections.[81]

The government was not insensitive to these claims, and in normal times they would have been satisfied as vacancies appeared. The special pressure of "union engagements," however, blocked the normal channels of promotion, and as Hardwicke noted, "until lay magnates find that the bench is not to be taken by storm" not much could be done.[82] Thus to the anger of a few prelates aroused to opposition by the low calibre of some appointees was added the dissatisfaction of the remainder at the Irish administration's insensitivity towards their personal complaints. Euseby Cleaver, for one, had suffered the indignity of having his episcopal palace burned down during the rebellion of 1798, and had been pressing for recognition of his tribulations in the wake of that event. Hardwicke, prematurely as it happened, promised him a promotion in 1804.[83] When Down and Connor became vacant in September 1804, Hardwicke was careful to consult Stuart about it, and the primate strongly disapproved of any further satisfaction of "union engagements" until the aspirations of those already on the bench had been recognized. The government's decision to satisfy the Beresfords instead prompted Cleaver to note that "partiality to my own claims induces one to think that Mr. Pitt did not weigh the disappointments of Lord John Beresford and my own in an equal balance."[84]

Cleaver had powerful friends and could not be ignored indefinitely. When he claimed he would take an English bishopric, "even

Bristol," so as to escape the discomforts attending future rebellion in Ireland, the government finally satisfied him by offering Dublin.[85] Others were less fortunate. While it is difficult to sympathize with the preposterous claims of some preposterous men, prospects for advancement had in the past encouraged devotion to duty. Incumbents' zeal and morale were not improved by elevating men with no tenure on the bench to positions higher than those of incumbents.

The evils of this decade of frenzied patronage exercises also permeated the lower levels of the Church, where the poorer relations of the great were given their places. Some awards represented efforts to restore the spirit of Trinity College after its alienation on the union issue.[86] Some obtained their positions by hearty exertions on behalf of the legislative union. Others impressed the Irish adminis-tration with their wit and suave manners: C. Mongan Warburton was a former Catholic and according to no less an authority than the King was the son of an Irish harper. During the rebellion of 1798 he not only remained at his post at Ardagh when most of the beneficed clergy fled that region, but he promoted his qualifications so effectively that he was recommended to the government "on account of his general good character." He managed to circumvent even royal opposition by marrying into wealth and respectability. He was ordained a bishop in 1806.[87]

For most, however, promotion within the Church during the period of "union engagements" was based upon personal connections. Some new members of the episcopal bench were situated in their sees only long enough to unpack their possessions before promoting the claims of sons,

brothers, and tutors. Stuart complained that patronage was distributed so arbitrarily that morale among those unable to claim the proper
connections was deteriorating rapidly.[88] There exists a voluminous
correspondence respecting the comparative value of deaneries, and how
they might be exchanged, augmented, and consolidated.[89] Viceroys pe-
titioned bishops to surrender patronage at their disposal, pleading
intense pressure from "friends at Westminster."[90]

Even the Lord Lieutenant indulged in the practice of finding
offices in the Church for his relatives. An interesting case can be
a poor relative, but not without high aspirations. He looked forward,
he confided to a friend in England, to an Irish bishopric, and while
episcopal incumbents were dying at a distressingly slow rate, he anticipated more activity in a year or so. The reverend chaplain, as it
turned out, moved no higher, but such was the buoyant spirit of those
involved in the Irish patronage gambit at the beginning of the nineteenth century that he could entertain such high expectations.[91] And
unusual enough at this time to merit comment was the inattention of
the Bishop of Raphoe to the clerical careers of his own sons, so that
as a result two of them with twenty years' service apiece had a combined income of only £450.

Behind the program of "union engagements" lay a problem of even
greater magnitude. The state Church was not master of its own house.
Whatever the propriety of a policy of awarding ecclesiastical benefices to those families whose connection guaranteed the establishment
of influence beyond what mere membership figures would otherwise have
allowed, the costs were exceedingly heavy. Rapid translations, to

which the Irish administration resorted with increasing frequency after 1800 in order to mollify as many claimants as possible upon the occasion of each vacancy, discouraged a strong identification of bishops with their dioceses. The easy distribution of patronage weakened the allegiance of those elements within the Church--ever more numerous after 1800--who expected some manifestation of evangelical zeal from prominent churchmen. At a time when the Established Church was forced to review its traditional relationship towards the state, cope with Catholic resurgence, face the possibility of the intervention of the united Parliament into its affairs, and meet widespread tithe resistance, patronage policies were promoting men of poor quality to important posts.

It says much for the dedication of a small number of reform-minded churchmen that in spite of this debilitating tendency, concerted protest against these patronage policies began to appear. This impulse was assisted by several developments. Stuart's refusal to allow "union engagements" to be satisfied by installation in his own province severely restricted the government's maneuverability. Hardwicke complained of Stuart's refusal to act as primate. His "supiness" acted to block the smooth functioning of those instrumentalities, such as the Board of First Fruits, which gave some coherence to the Irish Church.[92] But Stuart's stubborness slowly made its mark, and at length the Irish administration eventually saw the wisdom of conciliating the primate rather than leaving him "by his fireside in anger with all the world." Other bishops also demanded that they approve installation in their jurisdictions.[93] Hardwicke himself made a heroic effort to

mollify Stuart by referring decisions on episcopal promotions to the
primate when no single candidate had an unchallenged claim to the
vacancy.[94]

When Hardwicke left Ireland, however, much was required to be
done to effect a rapprochement between Church and State. The Whigs,
seemingly bent on a reform of Irish patronage policies and other
evils flourishing under indulgent Tory rule, fell afoul of the Irish
aristocracy and soon made their peace by shaping episcopal preferment
to mollify the great magnates.[95] When the Duke of Bedford surrendered his viceregal responsibilities to the Duke of Richmond and the
Tories in April 1807, Arthur Wellesley, the new Chief Secretary, noted
that promises had been made to Irish families on behalf of the Bishops of Cork, Waterford, Clonfert and Raphoe.[96] The petitioners'
constant reminders were made more vexatious by the fact that there
were no vacancies at the moment, a circumstance which induced Richmond, perhaps in self defense, to announce an "invariable rule. . .
not to promise Church preferment before it is actually vacant."[97]

Richmond's fine resolutions failed to compensate for his uneasy
relationship to the primate. Stuart steadfastly refused to go to
Dublin Castle, a resolution which in Richmond's mind was "attended with
some public inconvenience."[98] Richmond also complicated patronage
problems by compiling his own list of nominees upon his arrival in
Dublin. Among the most vexatious of these was a certain Charles Busby,
whose claims on Richmond's friendship were not likely to be satisfied
by elevation to one of the lesser Irish bishoprics. Busby's aspirations, and the resistance of officials in London, suggest something

of the intense jobbery which still attended Irish ecclesiastical preferment. Busby was offered Clonfert in 1807. He wanted this only if he could retain his stall at Westminster, an impossible demand. As an alternative Busby wanted another Englishman to take the Irish bishopric and surrender an English preferment suitable for Busby. Richmond was prepared to meet these extraordinary demands. Arthur Wellesley was not, and Hawkesbury was decidedly against it. When rumors of Busby's plan floated through London, Wellesley reported to Richmond that Irish Churchmen were angry: they did not want Irish preferment going to Englishmen and they most decidedly opposed the idea "that a bishopric should be given away . . . with a view to obtain a provision for another person." Busby's "repugnance to become an Irish bishop" was not relieved by Wellesley's disclosure that the King was now prepared to exchange Irish and English bishops on an extensive scale.[99]

These vexatious petitions and maneuverings were more than ever distracting to London. They tested a new commitment on the part of some English ministers, aided by Arthur Wellesley during his brief tenure as Irish Chief Secretary, to wrap up "union engagements" and establish new guidelines for the dispensation of ecclesiastical patronage. A primary consideration was the alienation of Irish bishops whose pretentions had long been ignored while commitments contracted in 1800 and 1801 were fulfilled. Bedford and Richmond were instructed on departing for Ireland not to ignore the claims of those on the bench, and some effort was made to reward the zealous and conscientious bishops by translation to more attractive sees. The translation of Cleaver to Dublin was one such instance, for it was opposed by power representatives of the "union engagements" residue.[100] A politically unimportant but professionally gratifying promotion in 1809 was that of Thomas Verschoyle, Provost of Trinity. The appointment demonstrated that appointments to the bench were "not always subordinated to political interests."[101] Other appointments were based squarely on ecclesiastical requirements. A few were successfully opposed because they might shock the reform element within the Church. When Elphin fell vacant in 1809, Liverpool pressed Richmond not to oblige either Lord Ely or the Beresfords but to translate "the most deserving bishop." He thought the claims of the Bishop of Killaloe best; "the latter not having applied is no objection; indeed, if his character is good, it is a recommendation."[102]

But good intentions were not enough. Richmond was particularly sensitive to the highly refined professionalism of Irish patronage seekers, and had great difficulty saying no, even when his Chief Secretary provided active support and inspiration.[103] Three other factors, however, aided the reform impulse : Parliament, in whose chambers discreditable nominees were now more likely to be exposed to public oppobrium; the new Prime Minister in 1809, Spencer Perceval, whose evangelicalism was enraged by traditional patronage practices; the King, whose last years of sanity were devoted to raising the tone of English public life, especially within the Established Churches. Under pressure Richmond declared his administration would no longer permit political considerations to determine episcopal appointments, and would resist both episcopal translations and exchanges of bene-

fices.[104] When Liverpool succeeded in convincing Richmond not to
grant Elphin to Ely's son Robert Tottenham, Ely complained that this
policy would vitiate the effect of the many thousands of pounds he
had expended to bring supporters for Perceval into Parliament.
The Marquis was chagrined to discover "that on this instance [Richmond]
seems to act up to his professions," and would regulate his conduct in
Parliament upon Perceval's reply.[105] Perceval sent a long letter to
Ely, outlining new principles upon which dispensation of Irish ecclesiastical patronage would henceforth be conducted. Ely's request,
Perceval asserted, was so phrased as to make it clear that Ely would
withdraw his parliamentary support were the claim denied. This tone
alone sufficed to deny Ely his request, whatever the worthiness of
Tottenham Loftus. Beyond this, the Church was in danger, according
to Perceval, and Richmond's new virtuousness on this score must be
encouraged. Indeed, Perceval concluded, he "would rather be driven
from [his] post tomorrow than purchase the continuance of it by break-
ing through so wide and proper a determination.[106]

Ironically, Perceval's good intentions coincided with a last
serious confrontation between the Church and the Irish administration.
That tempers were still agitated was confirmed in 1807 when the new
Tory ministry attempted to relieve pressures on the English Establishment's patronage. Richmond angered Irish Churchmen by repeating the
King's suggestion that Irish and English bishops occasionally exchange places.[107]

By 1810 the backlog of promises was unusually large. By now
deprived of Arthur Wellesley's tempering influence, Richmond deter-

mined to ease the pressure by a scheme of translations more elaborate and more comprehensive than anything since the Act of Union. Moreover, the very act of proclaiming a policy of patronage reform seemed to encourage Irish magnates to come forward to test it. The pathetic weakness of the Perceval ministry, aggravated by the Walcheren disaster, exposed the government to thinly-veiled blackmail. No one was more aware of the government's vulnerability than Ely, whose son's elevation to the bench in the first wave of union engagements was by now insufficient in terms of his continued services to the Tory cause.

Elphin, but recently filled, seemed about to be vacant again in the first days of January, 1801. On this occasion Richmond unwittingly put in motion a confrontation with Church reformers destined to cast a long shadow over the conduct, or misconduct, of Irish patronage affairs. The rumor of a possible vacancy at Elphin soon reached Ely, who demanded a lucrative preferment for Tottenham Loftus.[108] Richmond was at first inclined to favor the translation of Joseph Stock, Bishop of the remote diocese of Killala. In 1798 Stock had suffered the misfortune of seeing a French fleet under Admiral Humbert enter his town, occupy the episcopal palace, and detain the Bishop. Stock had never ceased to complain of his tribulations in connection with this abortive invasion, and thought no translation too weighty a compensation.[109] Richmond initially displayed considerable determination in advancing Stock's claims in the face of Ely's threats.[110] The pressure of parliamentary politics was intense, however, and Stock was placed at Waterford. Ely's opposition to the government on the impending Walcheren vote had to be averted, but to satisfy Ely while

leaving Ely's principal rival, the Beresfords, unrewarded, would invite political disaster.[111] Resolving this dilemma saw manipulation
of ecclesiastical patronage at its worst. Elphin was granted to Lord
John Beresford. Ely obtained a translation for Tottenham at the
first suitable vacancy; the minor offices attached to Elphin were
employed to secure friends for the Walcheren crisis.[112]

In September Clogher, the most valuable diocese after Derry,
became vacant. Far from relieving the government's embarrassment the
new vacancy increased it, for Clogher was worth substantially more
than Elphin and if given to Tottenham would raise the Beresfords' ire.
Richmond at first contemplated translating Bishop Bennett of Cloyne
to Clogher, his advancement having been temporarily delayed by a bout
of insanity. Tottenham would to to Cloyne, which "though inferior to
Clogher is very serviceable in having extensive patronage.[113] Ely was
not content with Cloyne. But Richmond had "many sufficient" reasons
to deny Clogher to Ely's son: Ely's bad manners; Loftus' retiring
nature (he was "so shy that he had hardly ever preached a sermon");
Beresford's jealousy and greater power; Ely's previous application for
Elphin which one might now remind him of while translating Beresford
to Clogher.[114] Richmond was on the point of giving Clogher to Beresford when Euseby Cleaver's condition deteriorated sharply and the prospect of a new vacancy threatened to derange the balance once more.
Cleaver recovered at year's end. As the government's fortunes revived
Richmond decided to give Clogher to Tottenham, leave Beresford at
Elphin, and promise the Beresfords further rewards at a later date.[115]

These machinations could not fail to ruffle the feathers of reform-minded Churchmen. Bishop Warburton, whose own career in the

Church included some dubious transactions in Church livings, wrote

to Stuart in the wake of the translations that

> I have no doubt the Duke of Richmond means well but much
> mischief is done by this system of clerical barter and so
> extensive a line of exchange; it sets every jobber at
> work; and draws down ridicule on the Church by exhibiting
> a set of clerical jockeys in the castle yard whenever a
> government preferment becomes vacant.[116]

Stuart, too, was incensed at Richmond's poor judgment. His clever

plans of moving bishops around like chess pieces discouraged those

elements within the Church which favored reform. Their letters re-

garding Richmond, Stuart told the Lord Lieutenant, were couched in

"language which I do not think proper to repeat but which is strongly

expressive of their feelings.[117] When visiting London Stuart was

shocked to discover how extensive was the Church of Ireland's notor-

iety: "indeed one scarcely meets a gentlemen in the street who has

correspondence in Ireland," he complained,

> who does not produce a letter giving an account of the ri-
> diculous stories circulated in Dublin at our expense . . .
> It is a very disagreeable duty to state to your Grace what
> I must shortly state to the public, that in my opinion,
> the Church Establishment cannot subsist under its present
> management. The nominations to the higher preferments have,
> indeed, been peculiarly unfortunate and have flung weight
> into the Roman Catholic scale, which is already too
> weighty.[118]

The manipulation of bishoprics undermined the good temper of re-

form-minded bishops. Subsequent revelations, related more particular-

ly to Bishop Stock, sparked an explosion. Richmond was surprised to

discover at the end of March that his proposal to translate Stock,

which he sincerely believed reflected his willingness to reward church-

men on a basis apart from family connections, was unpopular. "I never

heard anything against him till since his appointment has been known,"
Richmond complained. He added, however, as Addington had done in
1801, that what was done could not be rescinded.[119]

Richmond had seen only the tip of the iceberg. Stuart had
addressed himself to William Wellesley-Pole, the much harassed Irish
Chief Secretary, on the question of Stock's appointment. Stuart did
not mince words. Stock, he charged, had entered into fraudulent leases
when master of the school at Enniskillen. He had "made an agreement
with his successor of a most fraudulent nature, and that he had been
forced to surrender all the papers on the subject to avoid a prosecution which the late Lord Clare [the Lord Chancellor] planned to bring
against him." And finally, Stock was "a man of bad character who resided almost all of last year in England and had to be admonished on
the subject." These were serious charges. Stuart declared himself
ready to offer proof, although he did not want the scandal publicized.

As in 1801, the Primate succeeded in disorienting the ministry
of the day without insuring Stock's removal.[120] Perceval was apprised
of the charges, as was the bewildered Irish viceroy. Richmond pursued the Primate's allegations, and concluded they were overdrawn.
The leases had been granted "incorrectly" and Stock's family had
benefited, but "this system had been employed by others" and no legal
proceedings had ever been contemplated. Stock's inconstant residence
was due in part to the army's appropriation of his residence in Killala for a barracks. Richmond would, however, withdraw the nomination
if Perceval thought it proper.[121]

With the ministry in a weakened state and with the Whigs wait-

ing in the wings to assume power, Perceval was uncertain how to proceed. Evidence against Stock continued to pour in to Downing Street.
Members of Perceval's ministry confessed their opposition. "Ultras"
declared that the beleaguered bishop was pro-Catholic. But Perceval
conceded that it would be "extremely awkward" to rescind what was
so nearly completed; a public inquiry would have to follow. Perceval
therefore decided to proceed: "he cannot do much more mischief as
Bishop of Waterford than of Killala," Perceval reasoned fatalistically.[122]

Meanwhile, far from moderating his opposition to Stock, Stuart
received timely support from other Churchmen and determined to press
Richmond as much as possible.[123] The Bishop of Limerick reported
from western Ireland that "Bishop Stock's removal to Waterford did
certainly surprise everybody, nor can I imagine how the Lord Lieutenant came to think of him;"[124] Brodrick, a mild man and Stock's new
superior, doubted "how a worse appointment could be made."[125]

Stuart soon forecast the inevitable ruin of Stock's new see of
Waterford. "This case, a case in which perjury was combined with
fraud, is the strongest that can be imagined," he told Wellesley-Pole.
In Waterford, where Catholic priests were so powerful, Stock's nomination would prove fatal.[126] Wellesley-Pole and Perceval chose to remind
Stuart of the primate's disinclination to expose Stock to public scrutiny as the primary reason for their decision to proceed with the
translation.[127] Richmond was more than a little angered by Stuart's
censorious tone. "Had His Grace [Stuart] resided a little more in
Dublin," Richmond confided to the Chief Secretary, "I might have had

the opportunity of inquiring a little more into the character of the

bench, but in the three years I have been here I do not think he has

been ten days in Dublin . . . . With respect to exchanges [and trans-

lation] I am well aware they sometimes do harm but it is impossible

to attend to parliamentary interest without making them."[128] In a

long and elaborate review of his decisions concerning ecclesiastical

preferment, Richmond reminded Stuart of his dedication to the wel-

fare of the Establishment and of his immunity from political and per-

sonal opportunism.[129]

Stuart was enraged rather than soothed by Richmond's somewhat

specious self-defense. Stuart denied that Richmond could have been

unaware of Stock's "scandalous frauds, his shameful behavior, and

gross misconduct."

> Your Grace in promoting so many exchanges has been influ-
> enced, I have no manner of doubt, by great good motives, and
> the benevolent wish of rendering men happy and contented.
> But does it produce this effect? So far from it, that the
> appetite for exchange is increased by indulgence. The num-
> ber of applications is far more numerous than under any for-
> mer administration; a spirit of gambling has been excited;
> the unsuccessful, and those who have nothing to barter, are
> loud in their complaints against what they call the venality
> of government. All seem to consider exchange as the sole
> business of their profession, and never do I remember the[130]
> clergy so generally discontented as at this moment.

Stuart's admonitions, although couched in extreme language, reflected

an element of increasing sensitivity in the Church to the need for

reform; what had been allowed to pass in silence earlier was now

vociferously protested. A certain impatience was manifesting itself

and the Irish primate's warning was finding a wider response. In

part this continued to reflect the frustrations of those incumbents whose own aspirations had been ignored. But more than this was responsible. The steady growth of Catholic power in Ireland was not appreciated in English circles. A common enemy, Napoleon, made more attractive the proposition that all elements of Christianity must unite against Godlessness and while Catholics were busy protesting their loyalty to the crown, a small but growing element in Parliament was demanding that the Church of Ireland accept a program of comprehensive reform. The danger of an assault on the Church was making her friends more active. The period of "union engagements" closed; a new and more enlightened conduct of patronage began with the arrival in Ireland of a young chief secretary, Robert Peel.

2. Robert Peel and Irish Church Patronage 1812-1830

When Peel arrived in Ireland in 1812, he was under no illusions about the Irish Church. On his desk were petitions for benefices from all quarters. Even reformers such as Thomas O'Beirne, Bishop of Meath, could promote proposals for reform and places for his sons in a single paragraph. Peel himself was certainly not immune to political considerations, and in any case Richmond, with all his good intentions and careless promises, was still entrenched in Ireland. The Stock confrontation had dismayed the Perceval ministry and excited parliamentary criticism. Richmond found self-discipline painful and somewhat degrading, and on the eve of Peel's arrival he was the target of much criticism in and out of the ministry for his continuing indulgent attitude towards Irish Church patronage.[131] The viceroy was eager to share the blame with others. He complained that no one apprised him of

clergymen's deficiencies until they had been nominated. He alleged
that London made its selections on the basis of scholastic prowess
rather than practical ability. He even hazarded the guess that clergymen concealed the true value of their livings so as to gain the government's sympathy, and that there were too many idle clergymen in Ireland to avoid an occasional bad apple rising to the episcopal bench.[132]

Richmond was not alone culpable. Perceval's government, after
a brief period of recovery in early 1811, again drifted. This encouraged patronage seekers to show their hand and to take advantage
of its weakness.[133] Richmond was drawn into such foolish promises as
a peerage for the Archbishop of Tuam to silence the latest Beresford
offensive.[134] Peel's arrival in Ireland, however, gradually stiffened
Richmond's resistance. By 1813, with the veteran Irish viceroy looking
forward to surrendering his office, Peel was firmly in control.

Peel was not familiar with the intricacies of Irish patronage
upon his arrival, but Richmond's detailed if highly self-congratulatory
memorandum and a flood of correspondence from Irish peers and bishops
rapidly revealed the full extent of alleged and real promises of preferment. Peel concluded that Richmond had displayed poor judgment on
several occasions. He was particularly prone, Peel observed, to favor
the candidacy of members of the nobility. "It must be admitted," he
told Richmond in a rather forthright communication almost a year after
his first visit to Ireland,

> That the Bench in Ireland is rather overstocked with men of
> birth. There are the Bishops of Kildare, Kilmore, Derry,
> Killala, Raphoe, Cork, Ferns and Elphin who are all men of
> noble families, and three of the archbishops also. . . .It
> cannot be supposed for a moment that noble birth is a dis-

qualification for the bench but it is perhaps desirable to make it less a recommendation to preferment than in former periods. . . .[135]

Richmond agreed

> that we have a great many men of high family on the Irish
> bench and it would be good to reduce this so as to avoid the
> imputation of promoting for political motives. I don't,
> however, care about attacks made on me by newspapers as I
> feel no such motives have weighed with me and if people
> choose to examine the situation of those whom I have recom-
> mended it will appear clear that I could not. It is
> true that the brother of St. Laurence is an earl, but he
> has only ₺700 a year and no influence at elections. Joce-
> lyn's brother has political influence but the appointment
> was not politically motivated. Verschoyle has no relations
> higher than esquire. Hale the same. Leslie is distantly
> related to Wellesley and Ld. Harrowby, but I did not know
> that when appointing him. Fowler is brother-in-law to Lord
> Killarney, but Killarney has been locked up as a lunatic
> for years.[136]

Peel may or may not have been impressed by this and subsequent

protestations of innocence on the part of the Lord Lieutenant.[137] At

any rate, he found himself agreeing with Richmond when the death of

the controversial Bishop Stock of Waterford created a vacancy in 1813.

Stock's poor health stimulated petitions as early as April, four months

before his death. Richmond promised the position to the Bishop of

Cork, only to find that the new Prime Minister was determined to use

the occasion to grace the Irish bench with William Magee, Professor of

Divinity at Trinity and a considerable scholar.[138] Trinity scholars

had begun to make their mark on the bench, and more were to follow.

But Magee was a particularly controversial figure, a champion of

Catholic Emancipation, a political organizer among Trinity fellows,

and, with all this, a scholar of theology with a contemporary reputa-

tion equal to that of anyone in England. Liverpool was most eager to shore up the sagging scholarly credentials of the Irish bench. Stuart

hoped Magee's consignment to a bishopric some distance removed from

Dublin would end his political influence. Richmond viewed Liverpool's

extraordinary interest in Magee as a comment on his own patronage

practices, if not also a reflection of the prime minister's ignorance

of Irish conditions.[139] Peel held the balance, and in emerging as a

supporter of Richmond in this particular case he did much to elucidate

lines of conduct he hoped to pursue in the future:

> . . . A bishopric is not a mere mark of distinction; it
> has power and in fact political power attached to it. I do
> not think bishoprics should be made political appointments
> on any account, but I think if any clergyman took a very
> active though a very friendly part in politics it would. . .
> disqualify him for a bishopric. If he were qualified before,
> it would at least disqualify him in my opinion as much as if
> he took an active and hostile part.[140]

Peel's objections to Magee were sustained, much to Richmond's

satisfaction, but only by way of securing for him a deanery, which it-

self revived memories of Richmond's famous episcopal translations of

1810.[141] Liverpool was not about to surrender, however. He anticipat-

ed the early demise of Cleaver, who had finally become Arch-

bishop of Dublin. This would present a dramatic opportunity to raise

the tone of the Irish bench. "It is a lamentable circumstance," he com-

plained to Richmond, "to reflect how little learning and eminence there

is on the bench." Magee's political activity could be forgiven, for

it was inevitable in a college forum, and it would cease instantly were

he placed on the bench. In Liverpool's eyes the Irish Church had

suffered too long from an excess of "decent men" without any other

qualifications, and even these "decent men were often not to be depended on."[142]

If Peel and Liverpool disagreed on Magee, they were as one in opposing any return to the jobbery of previous years. Irish families soon discovered that the traditions of patronage preferment of the Richmond era were no longer in force. Peel shocked the Beresfords, whose ecclesiastical employments were by now a European scandal, by refusing their request for yet another bishopric in 1813. He gave as his reason a belief that the Irish bench had become a preserve of the nobility and must be curbed. He denied another request from the Bishop of Meath on grounds the candidate involved was patently not qualified for the Church. The Bishop of Derry was handled in similar fashion. The Bishop of Down and Conner, "that larder of lean earth," was violently upset when his son was peremptorily denied a deanery.[143] As Peel took pains to note, he was not in favor of overthrowing the patronage system as such, but only of raising the standards upon which the government determined its awards.

Peel's impact, therefore, was gradual. Modest reforms could not eliminate unsavory aspects of the traditional patronage system overnight. There were, for instance, the patronage requests of the regent, soon to become George IV, whose schemes for manipulating benefices infuriated Stuart and Brodrick. John Leslie, who presumed to know Peel intimately, apparently felt quite comfortable in requesting that Peel secure the translation of his brother from Dromore to Clogher, and justified it with some extraordinary observations. He told Peel that Clogher was

an object of the greatest importance from the circumstance

of two of my ancestors having been Bishops of Clogher. A great part of my property is held under that See and it would be the means of securing the representation of the County of Monoghan without a possibility of competition. Besides we should have it in our power to assist our connections and friends by an extensive patronage. Do then my dear Peel exert yourself on this occasion - it would not be a difficult matter.[144]

Leslie misjudged Peel, we may presume, although Peel was saved from the indelicacy of disappointing Leslie by the recovery of Archbishop Fowler of Dublin, whose place the Bishop of Clogher was rumored to take.[145] Lord Talbot meant no discredit on Peel in 1818 when he noted that, even after five years of reform, "the whole system of Church preferment as conducted, or rather as is wished it be conducted here, is disgraceful. . . I am determined to resist the jobbing (that is so disgusting even among laymen) in the pretensions to ecclesiastical preferment."[146] Not even Peel, working assiduously though he was, could root out the problem in five years.

Cynicism died slowly. Talbot in 1819 mourned the passing of Archbishop Trench of Tuam, but forced himself to "check the tear of sympathy" and address his attention to the clamor attending selection of the next incumbent. "I really fear as much from having another bishop to make, as I should do at the intelligence of a row."[147]

The death of the Archbishops of Armagh and Cashel in 1822 brought Peel once more into Irish patronage decisions. Now as Home Secretary he was obliged to concern his opinions with two other powerful and interested parties, the Marquess Wellesley as Irish viceroy, and Lord Liverpool. Stuart died from accidental poisoning, and because of this it was felt necessary to fill the primacy as quickly as possible.

The hostility of many Irish Churchmen towards the translation of Englishmen to Armagh had not dissuaded the ministry from advocating it.
The King made it clear that he was most anxious to see an Englishman
in one of the vacant archbishoprics.[148] Peel believed it was scarcely
possible to supply "a due proportion of men of learning and eminence
for the Church in Ireland" without having occasional recourse to the
universities of England, and had Oxford friends whom he thought deserved consideration.[149] Peel's Oxford mentor, Charles Lloyd, pointed
out to Peel the affront to Irish sensibilities involved in denying
the primacy to an Irishman, though of course none had filled the post
for more than a century. Wellesley suggested that Nathaniel Alexander,
Bishop of Down and Connor, an Irishman, and the holder of government
promise for promotion, be given Cashel, which Broderick had left vacant
upon his death. He urged that Lord John Beresford, who had been elevated to Dublin in 1820, be translated to Armagh. Beresford of course
was also Irish, but his English connections were politically powerful
and socially impeccable. The King would not have both vacancies go to
Irishmen, while neither Peel nor Liverpool thought much of Alexander.
At length Richard Laurence, a noted Egyptologist and Oriental scholar,
an Oxford academician and Englishman, was awarded Cashel, while Alexander, whose candidacy had been strengthened by rumor, was propitiated
by the promise of any future preferment.[150] The appointment was highly unpopular in Ireland, where wags made much of Laurence's eastern
tastes and western preferment.

Armagh was even more sensitive. Henry Goulburn, the Irish Chief
Secretary, noted that the weakness of the government at that time in

the Commons encouraged Irish gentlemen to believe they could force
acceptance of their nominees by threatening to withdraw political
support.[151] Wellesley, as noted, favored Beresford, despite his
recent installation at Dublin. Liverpool feared this would prompt
accusations of family pressure. He therefore suggested Thomas Elrington, Provost of Trinity, precisely because he was innocent of family
influence.[152] Wellesley prevailed, and Beresford became the first
Irish born primate in modern times. The vacancy at Dublin went to
William Magee, Peel's old foe, now considered properly conservative.[153]
For the first time since the eighteenth century the two primacy archbishoprics were staffed by Irishmen, a considerable compliment to the
rising tide of nationalist feeling even inside an ecclesiastical system which relied so heavily for support on the English connection.

A rash of vacancies on the bench followed the archepiscopal
appointments. Bubbling resentment over Laurence's elevation and his
close connections with Peel suggested to Churchmen that the Home
Secretary was primarily responsible for the translation of an Englishman. Pressure increased when Percy Jocelyn, Bishop of Clogher and an
Irishman, was deprived of his see in September 1822. Peel wondered
whether it might not be wise to exclude Englishmen as a rule. In the
case of Clogher he considered it imperative that an Irishman be selected; the appointment of an Englishman would "be considered a sort of
national reflection, as an intimation, that no Irishman could be found
to redeem the lost character of that benighted bishopric. Such an impression might be very unreasonable and unfounded, but still one very
much to be deprecated."[154] But Liverpool now echoed Peel's old posi-

tion: "If the Irish bench is to be made respectable, it can only be made so by an occasional infusion of English learning and respectability; . . . Trinity College Dublin cannot be expected of itself to feed adequately the Church of Ireland."[155] He did not insist on an Englishman at Clogher, however, and at any rate the government felt obliged to remember a promise made to Robert Tottenham, delayed by the King's intervention in favor of Jocelyn.[156] Tottenham as has been seen had caused Castlereagh and Hardwicke to differ in 1804, but Ely's importance in Irish politics was still immense. With the possible alienation of Lord Roden, Jocelyn's father, it was thought inadvisable to alienate another Irish magnate. Tottenham proved to be a capable administrator of this wealthy see.[157]

The decision to award Clogher to an Irishman buoyed hopes that Englishmen would not fill future vacancies. Between 1822 and 1826 episcopal patronage correspondence became increasingly vigorous. More vacancies appeared in 1822 than in any other year of the nineteenth century, and bishops scrambled for better situations. One of those favored with a translation soon discovered that it was not true that "everything suffered by translation except a bishop." He had become poorer, not richer, and requested assistance in making another move.[158] Bishop Alexander of Down and Connor blamed Peel for his failure to obtain Clogher, while Bishop Fowler of Kildare pleaded to be removed from "that horrible city of Kilkenny." St. Laurence noted that as the oldest member on the bench he deserved more consideration than he had received. Thomas Elrington, one of the Church's most prolific propagandists, wanted evacuation from "disturbed and miserable" Limerick.

Some claimants were not reluctant to force the hand of the government. "It was only with difficulty and at a cost of ₤500," Goulburn informed Wellesley on one occasion, that he was able to "prevent the publication, by the disgruntled Dean of Raphoe, of a manuscript describing accurately a disposal of Church patronage in Ireland for the past forty years, a history that reflects infinite discredit on the Church and much on the government."[159] Peel approved use of secret funds to stifle the publication. But he refused to support practices which might lend further credence to the Dean's assiduous researches. And while in each case Peel refrained from openly opposing the preferences of the incumbent Lord Lieutenant, his discreet suggestions were generally followed.

Peel's success in raising the tone of Irish patronage was due in part to the sympathetic hearing which he received from Lord Liverpool. Liverpool was a bastion of moderation and flexible conservatism as Prime Minister from 1812 to 1827. Liverpool demonstrated a keen awareness of the Church of Ireland's problems and absolutely refused to force the Church to receive Englishmen who could not be accommodated at home. He was also properly suspicious of the grasping tendency of Irish aristocrats; in 1819 he confided to Lord Talbot that

> the aristocracy of the nation will always expect to have some share in the patronage of the Church, and it is desirable even for the sake of the Church that this should be the case. . . .It is of great importance, however, that the proportion of men of rank raised to the bench should not be too large. In England there is no ground for complaint on this. I cannot quite say as much of the distribution of patronage heretofore in Ireland.[160]

Liverpool's principles were tested in 1826 upon the occasion of a vacancy at Cloyne. Wellesley wanted to appoint Dr. Kyle, Provost

of Trinity College, or his own brother Gerald, a beneficed clergyman

of indifferent accomplishments and tied to an English rural parish.[161]

Two points of controversy emerged. The proposed nomination of Kyle

was interpreted by John Jebb, the morose and mordant Bishop of Limer-

ick, as a rejection of his own claims to Cloyne and as proof of the

rumor that the government would no longer permit any translations on

the episcopal bench.[162] Goulburn persuaded Wellesley to abandon Kyle,

since "provosts made bad bishops" and because the vacancy at Trinity

would fall to the pro-Catholic Attorney General Plunkett's nominee.

But he suggested instead William Brinkely, who was not on the bench

either; Brinkley was an astronomer and a man of learning; although,

as Goulburn confessed, Brinkley was not what a bishop should be, he

was the best of an undistinguished lot.[163] Despite official denials

it seems quite clear that Goulburn, while denying Jebb's allegations,

did indeed want to avoid translating to Cloyne someone already on the

bench. He referred with some vehemence to Bishop Alexander's· com-

plaints that his new see was poorer not richer than his old one as an

example of the difficulties arising from such translations.[164]

Before Brinkely could get the post, however, Wellesley's claims

on behalf of his brother had to be disposed of, and the case was con-

siderably more serious. Gerald's very lack of success in his career

was something of an accomplishment in that of the five Wellesley bro-

thers three (Wellington, and Marquess Wellesley, and Wellesley-Pole)

had already received peerages and Henry, the fourth, was about to re-

ceive his. Gerald had made no such mark, but such were his connections

that under normal circumstances he might have expected a bishopric.
In 1807, while Arthur Wellesley was Irish Chief Secretary, an elaborate scheme was devised whereby Gerald might surrender his canonical
stall at Westminster for an English benefice, and then trade the
living for the bishopric of Cork. Liverpool opposed this, because of
the scandalous activities of Gerald's wife Emily Mary, daughter of
Earl Cadogan.[165] In partial compensation, Gerald became canon resi-
dentiary at St. Paul's in 1809. His wife continued to obstruct his
professional progress, but while they were separated in 1821 he refused to divorce her.

The initiative for a bishopric in 1826 proved more serious than
that of 1807. Wellesley gave Goulburn the impression that he wanted
to suggest Gerald but would not press for his elevation.[166] At the
same time, however, the Lord Lieutenant pressed Wellington to secure
Liverpool's assent. Wellesley added that he would interpret resistance
from Liverpool as an infringement upon the powers of the Irish executive.[167] Wellington took up the challenge and urged Gerald's candidacy in a strongly-worded letter addressed to the Prime Minister.[168]

Liverpool was not to be cowed by the Wellesley phalanx or by
charges of constitutional impropriety if he failed to oblige. He cited
Gerald's unwillingness to divorce his wife and his inability to live
with her as sufficient grounds for blocking Gerald's candidacy. He
quoted Saint Paul's first epistle to Timothy ("A bishop then must be
blameless, the husband of one wife, vigilant, sober, of good behavior,
given to hospitality, apt to teach. . . .One that rules well his own
house. . . ."). Wellington (who later on as Prime Minister might have

assisted his brother had he been so inclined) complained that Gerald

was the innocent party, but Liverpool stood firm:

> It is impossible to reflect on this subject without ad-
> verting to the peculiar situation of the Church of Ire-
> land. We live in an age of controversy as to religion
> and religious establishments. The Established Church of
> Ireland is from various circumstances exposed to severe
> criticism and obloquy beyond that of any other church
> in Europe. It is surely therefore the duty of those who
> have to distribute its patronage to be more than usually
> cautious as to the character and conduct of those who are
> to receive its honors and rewards. . . .[169]

Wellington murmured that many worse men than his brother had received

bishoprics.[170] Liverpool refused to reverse his stand and in with-

standing the pressure of perhaps the most important of all Irish

families the Prime Minister decisively influenced patronage trends

towards selection on the basis of merit.

After 1826 traditional themes in Irish ecclesiastical patronage

began to disappear. The growing influence of the liberal faction with-

in the Tory party restricted the power of Irish aristocrats, while the

onset of Catholic emancipation made reference to merit in choosing bishops

as well as other dignitaries more crucial than ever. Peel's influence

in the selection of bishops declined sharply, and he was distressed to

see so many "liberals" given episcopal preferment.[171] Goulburn noted

that such was the state of the times that public opinion was able to

dictate arrangements even on a parochial level.[172] As Catholic agita-

tion focused more and more unfavorable attention on the Irish Church

Peel was led to suggest that ways be found to transfer some episcopal

patronage to the Crown in order to reduce charges of nepotism. This

was difficult to achieve, for such transfers once detected would excite episcopal passions, while examination of the validity of government claims would be used by unscrupulous lawyers as an opportunity to place the patronage in lay hands.[173] Nevertheless, Peel dispatched a lawyer to Ireland to see what could be done.[174] Simultaneously, Archbishop Laurence of Cashel challenged the Primate's right to dispense patronage outside his province and accused Beresford of carving out a "petty tyranny" based on unabashed nepotism. Beresford's rights were upheld on legal grounds but popular and political sentiment favored Laurence.[175]

The triumph of the Whigs in 1830 saw an infusion of decidedly liberal Churchmen, of whom the economist-writer Richard Whately was certainly the most notable and most controversial. While the Whigs were anxious to change the complexion of the Irish bench, their own program of Church reform anticipated a sharp reduction in the number of bishops and the practical elimination of very lucrative preferments. This retrenchment significantly reduced the number of opportunities for exercises of patronage and encouraged close parliamentary scrutiny of the remainder.[176] When Peel returned to office at the head of a short-lived conservative ministry in 1834 he was prepared to select bishops almost entirely on the basis of their spiritual record and with very little reference to politics. He advised Lord Haddington, the Lord Lieutenant, how "absolutely necessary" it was "that every ecclesiastical appointment in Ireland, great and small, should be disposed of with reference to the single objective of strengthening the just--and by just I mean spiritual--influence of the Church of Ireland, and its hold upon public opinion."[177] The Whigs were not prepared to dispute the point.

Patronage did, of course, continue to influence the character

of the Irish bench in the last years of the Establishment, but the

factors which determined selection were now almost entirely related

to spiritual considerations. Of primary importance was the position

of the bench of bishops on the subject of national education. Although

started by the Whigs, Peel was determined to support it after his re-

turn to power in 1841. He refused to recommend candidates for the

bench who did not themselves support the system.[178] He discovered to

his consternation that the most prominent members of the Irish bench,

with the exception of Whately, would not cooperate in suggesting

nominees favoring national education. Ireland was still "a land of

jobbing" in which no one could be relied upon not to have "his own or

else some friend's interest to forward." He even contemplated appoint-

ing a Whig, but was dissuaded by the thought of a united "politico-

clerical" clamor.[179]

After 1830 as well the Church of Ireland saw an increasing num-

ber of suggestions for the elimination of the patronage system al-

together. Whately proposed a seminary for the Irish clergy and claim-

ed it was defeated by Irish conservatives whose sons would probably

have difficulty qualifying for admission.[180] Other sources called for

revival of convocation with full powers to establish qualifications

for the clergy, make the necessary appointments, and apply the required

discipline.[181] Part of this movement was stimulated by the growing

evangelical impulse, but part was also the result of real or imagined

encroachments on the Established Church's resources. A reduction of benefices and bishoprics in 1833 was not attended by a corresponding allocation of funds to Catholic priests. By 1845, however, even members of the government were seriously contemplating endowing the Catholic clergy, and in fact increased provisions were made for the seminary at Maynooth.[182] In 1854 a proposal to suspend another 395 benefices and to transfer the resources to the Catholics and Presbyterians was rejected, but it encouraged leaders of the Established Church to contemplate full termination of state patronage. This was accomplished in the disestablishment legislation of 1869.

Reform of the patronage system, unlike other aspects of the Church of Ireland's transformation between 1800 and 1869, was a completely informal process. Even the comprehensive Irish Church Temporalities Act of 1834 did not establish criteria for nominating candidates to Church offices on any level. The destructive character of "union engagements," which marked a nadir in the unpleasant patronage history of the Irish Church, did prompt a reaction which permeated elements of the Church leadership by 1810 and the civil administration within another decade. After 1820 the prospect of parliamentary intervention pushed even the unenthusiastic into acceptance of voluntary reform. Froude's effusive compliments on the calibre of Irish bishops and clergy in the 1840s reflect the immense transformation achieved in a generation. It is hard to avoid the conclusion that if this transformation had occurred fifty or one hundred years earlier the subsequent history of the Church of Ireland might well have been one of expansion rather than retrenchment. Patronage reform finally came, but came too late to stem the Catholic resurgence of the late eighteenth and early nineteenth century.

Chapter III: The Movement for Internal Reform 1800-1830

1. The Basis for Reform 1800-1810

The slow and uneven reconstruction of patronage priorities required the cooperation of both state and Church, but more responsibility necessarily lay with the state. In another area, administrative and clerical discipline, the initiative lay with the episcopacy. The tendency of many Irish historians to believe that the Established Church displayed little willingness to reform itself before Parliament intervened to do so after 1830 is based on a reading of reports of committees established after 1829 to look into the Irish Church question. Their descriptions of widespread administrative anomalies, of absentee clergy, of misdirected and inefficiently used financial resources, and of spiritual apathy do not make happy reading. Critical speeches by reform-minded politicians, Catholics, and Benthamites seem to substantiate their claims. Many of these charges were true. Often lacking, however, was a realization that conditions had been even worse thirty years earlier and that much had been done by reform-minded bishops with the limited legal powers and intangible moral suasion at their disposal. As a result, by 1830 there were some Irish dioceses which, in terms of efficiency and clerical zeal compared quite favorably with their English counterparts. These reforms were effected within the perimeters of a system which only Parliament could completely overhaul, but these changes did much to blunt the sharpest edges of the dislocation which attended parliamentary reform after 1830. Without them the Church of Ireland might well have found adjusting itself to Parliament's demands in the 1830s even more difficult than in fact it was.

As in the case of the partronage question, the initial impulse for internal reform came from a small number of the higher clergy, supported by an evangelical circle which was beginning to make its appearance in several Irish towns. And though internal reform did not demand a radical change in the government's policies, it was a good deal more complicated, and its constituent elements were highly interdependent. The central problem was clerical non-residence. Attached to this was the construction of churches and glebe houses, reform of parochial finances and recovery of lost revenues, increased episcopal control over the clergy, and development of a spiritual vitality long thought inconvenient and even improper by many clergymen and bishops as well. All of these facets demanded attention simultaneously. Residence could not be demanded if the clergy lacked quarters. Quarters were useless if the clergy refused to inhabit them. The clergy could not work effectively without churches. Churches were of little value if the clergy were non-resident. Facilities could not be constructed unless glebe lands could be procured nor the clergy paid if tithes remained uncollected. The need to assault the problem of internal reform on several fronts at once vitiated the effectiveness of the reform impulse, and led to considerable confusion. The legal instruments available to the reformers were rusty from long neglect and blunted by the resistance of vested interests.

Even public opinion was of little use, for Church leaders dared not

expose the full range of abuses to the world. For all of these

reasons internal reform was a particularly frustrating process, and

far from universally successful. It began, as did patronage reform,

in the wake of the Act of Union.

In 1800 the Church of Ireland was, in Stuart's opinion, the

most scandalous Christian denomination in Europe. Even the Church's

most dedicated apologists could not deny that the evils of non-resi-

dence, inefficient allocation of resources, spiritual indifference,

and frequent preoccupation with considerations of personal advance-

ment played a large part in the operation of the Irish Establishment.

A century and more of neglect during which time the Irish Church was

sustained by the ingenious application of penal laws, disrupted by

intermittent rebellion, and hampered by a dearth of dedicated per-

sonnel, was partly responsible. When unrest plagued the countryside,

those clergymen who had not already removed themselves to England or

to Dublin often fled their parishes, sometimes leaving their flock

in the hands of accommodating Catholic priests. Pastoral neglect was

compounded by the steady attrition of physical resources. Decayed

churches and abandoned glebes dotted the landscape. Lay patrons en-

joyed the revenues of scores of parishes, and discouraged Church

efforts to restore facilities.[1]

The reaction of some new appointees whose record of attentive-

ness to Church affairs was not a distinguished one suggests how diffi-

cult conditions were. Charles Lindsay, Hardwicke's secretary, informed

the Lord Lieutenant after a visit to Kildare that it was a case of
"scandalous men in scandalous livings."[2] Butson noted, "nothing can
be in greater disorder than this diocese and it is really surprising
that the reformed Church has subsisted in it at all. . . ." He could
not comprehend the extent of the disarray because no records had
been kept. Fifteen benefices encompassed fifty parishes and clerical
salaries were "scanty beyond all example in any establishement in
Europe." Only one glebe house remained.[3] Joseph Stock observed that
he could not build glebe houses and thus enforce clerical residence
because the glebe lands had been confiscated by the gentry over a
period of fifty years.[4] Alexander Knox, upon entering his wealthy see
of Derry, declared that he must have funds immediately in order to
repair his churches, many of which were actually collapsing and forcing their congregations to attend Methodist meeting houses. A similar
impression is obtained from the vantage point of the beneficed clergy.
The correspondence of Thomas Booke Clarke, absentee pastor of Innismacsaint, with his various ill-paid curates, is instructive. Clarke
discovered upon an examination of his new benefice that the glebe house
had collapsed and that tithes had not been collected for three years.[5]

At the heart of the problem was a woefully antiquated and inadequate diocesan administrative system. Variants and deviations from a
uniform pattern had become so profuse by 1800 that generalization is
difficult.[6] Each diocese except Meath possessed a cathedral consisting
of prebendaries and canons, entrusted with the government of the diocese in the absence of the Bishop. Because of the amalgamation but
not suppression of many Irish dioceses over the centuries, there re-

mained thirty-three deaneries. Their incumbents were in theory responsible for the care of cathedrals, a burden considerably eased by
decay of many cathedrals or their conversion to parish churches. The
deans, whether or not they in fact superintended a cathedral, advised
their bishops on the temporal and spiritual concerns of the diocese.
This responsibility was not often considered weighty until after 1810,
when "rural deans" were selected by reform-minded bishops as assistants
to their advisors. Almost all deaneries lay in the gift of the crown,
and deans were often selected by Lord Lieutenants to satisfy outstanding political obligations. Many of the preferments were lucrative;
even in the late eighteenth century Irish deaneries compared favorably
with their English counterparts.[7]

Most dioceses possessed archdeacons, episcopal vicars who substituted for an absent bishop. Their powers varied greatly from diocese
to diocese, and though much in demand during the heyday of eighteenth
century episcopal absenteeism, they too were often selected on political grounds and were themselves often permanently non-resident. In
England archdeacons translated episcopal directives into parochial
policies; in Ireland no such intermediary cemented superior-subordin-
ate relationships.[8] The chancellor was the secretary of the cathedral
chapter, and often served as treasurer as well. Irish dioceses might
also possess precentors, provosts, and other officers; there was
little uniformity in this portion of the cathedral chapter and few had
substantial duties. The diocesan administration itself as distinct
from the cathedral chapter was responsible for records, audits, and
correspondence; and by 1800 it was difficult to find more than a half

dozen dioceses in which these functions were being performed well.

The legal work of the Church of Ireland in defense of tithes or in efforts to recover lost properties was entrusted to a vicar general. Until 1800 this position, too, had been sinecurial, with surrogates entrusted with whatever work lay at hand. As late as 1815 one vicar general was surprised to learn that he had been appointed to the office more than a decade earlier; he had no idea whether a surrogate had been appointed or not.[9] Diocesan registers were often equally oblivious to their duties until Stuart pressed them after 1803 for information on the state of their dioceses. Together with the cathedral chapter, these diocesan officials constituted a corporation which in theory elected the bishops. Since these elections were subject to a binding suggestion from the crown, there was little to do here. The corporation was empowered to manage the diocese, to sue and be sued. After 1800 these latter responsibilities increased sharply.

Diocesan administration was as inconsistent in practice as it was archaic in form. Members of the chapters were usually prebendaries or persons holding rights to a revenue arising from the estates of a cathedral or collegiate church. There were usually more prebends than chapter offices. Saint Patrick's in Dublin contained nineteen, and in this way drew revenues from the land without supplying specific pastoral services. There were also canons, or persons possessing a revenue allotted for the performance of divine service. Since chapters' revenues were often derived from benefices attached to the various offices within the corporation, many incumbents were also cathedral

officers; if the benefice was far removed from the cathedral and if
the incumbent chose to situate himself at the cathedral, he could not
perform his parochial duties in person. Even after 1800 cathedral
duty was often sufficient defense against pressure for residence in
one's benefice, for to enforce cathedral officers to reside was to
dissolve the cathedral structure.

For other reasons as well the character of a cathedral chapter
varied from diocese to diocese. The right of presentation to these
offices was vested in a welter of laymen, high ecclesiastics, and the
crown, lending a certain air of jobbery and manipulation to many
appointments. Other factors complicated diocesan administration.
Meath possessed no cathedral, no chapter, and no dean; it employed a
synod composed of all the beneficed clergy and thus anticipated changes
of later years. Diocesan structures did not correspond in size to a
diocese's wealth or needs. Armagh was divided into "English" and
"Irish" parts, with the clergy of each area meeting in different
synods. Kilmore possessed neither cathedral nor chapter. Derry with
its very ample income supported only a dean, archdeacon, and three
prebendaries. Some western Ireland dioceses maintained a full range
of dignities, which appropriated the incomes of so many benefices that
non-residence remained a serious practical problem even after all
clergymen were theoretically busy at their work. The bishops themselves treasured their minor distinctions. The Bishop of Kildare normally resided in Dublin, outside his own jurisdiction, because he was
also dean of Christ Church. The Bishop of Down possessed no see city
at all. The Bishop of Dromore was addressed "by divine providence"

while most others managed with the less exalted "by divine permission." In Dromore as well there existed a petty court jurisdiction under the Lordship of Newry, with some pretension to issue writs normally controlled by ecclesiastical courts. Christ Church, Dublin, and the wardenship of Galway constituted collegiate churches, which possessed many attributes of cathedrals and which of course appropriated beneficed revenues for their support.

All of this directly affected the administration of the Church's resources. Since parish revenues were often appropriated to the use of diocesan or cathedral officers, many parishes went unattended, or were consigned to poorly paid curates. Many dioceses were inefficiently small and there were far too many of them. Some cathedral towns were merely villages which the tide of progress had long ago left behind. The village of Clogher, ecclesiastical headquarters of one of the wealthiest and most Protestant dioceses in Ireland, sat squarely on the episcopal estate. This rural orientation meant that revenues were often plentiful where people were scarce, while rapidly growing urban areas and whole stretches of southern and western Ireland rarely saw an Anglican clergyman at all.

Even administration of properties directly controlled by the episcopacy was fraught with abuse. Incomes were often drawn from rents on lands far removed from the see and indeed sometimes from properties outside the diocese altogether. This encouraged careless management. Since episcopal lands could not be leased for more than twenty one years, they were rarely improved and often poorly cultivated. Bishops were tempted not to renew leases so as to make them available to their own families on attractive terms. In 1780 Arthur Young estimated that the lands of Armagh, if let as a private estate, would have netted Ł100,000 rather than Ł8,000 per annum, Derry Ł50,000 rather than Ł7,000 and Cashel Ł30,000 rather than Ł4,000.[10] In Derry and Cashel the families of Bishop Hervey and Archbishop Agar accumulated such fortunes as to scandalize even normally insensitive observers. Agar bequeathed to his heirs an estate valued at Ł400,000. Apologists for the Church declared low rents showed compassion for the plight of rentiers; they were more correct when they noted its role in engendering enthusiasm among the Church's beneficiaries.[11]

The local structure of the Church was based on benefices, or livings, and on parishes. Three or more of them were often included in a single benefice. Benefices were variously defined as rectories, vicarages, perpetual curacies with care of souls, chapelries or districts annexed to various offices for administrative purposes, certain churches without territorial jurisdictions, and sinecures. Semantic vagaries provided endless opportunities for confusion, and Churchmen devoted much time explaining to politicians that pluralism in benefices did not always mean neglect of pastoral duties or lucrative incomes.

The parochial structure was equally archaic and even more inefficient. The number of parishes varied from 20 in Dromore to 180 in Meath. They were often ancient divisions of little contemporary relevance. The Bishop of Kildare discovered one in his diocese which consisted of two acres, on which was situated an illegal distillery. This, along with financial dislocations and the lack of Protestant communicants in large areas, lay at the basis of one of Ireland's most persistent administrative evils: unions. Because Irish parishes were unequal in size, common law allowed incumbents to treat several parishes as a single benefice, with the vexatious restriction that the inhabitants of one parish could not be assessed to build a church in a different parish of the same union. This effectively discouraged construction of new churches while accelerating disintegration of the old, as a single incumbent could not staff or maintain the small scattered parochial centers. Under Charles I the Lord Lieutenant and Council, with the consent of the metropolitan, bishop, patrons, and incumbents, were allowed to create new unions in which all parishes might be assessed evenly. Lay impropriators could not, however, be forced to relinquish their tithe revenue, and the system lapsed after twenty years. The experiment was re-instituted in 1715, and in 1723 was extended to permit benefices without care of souls to be appropriated to dignities and prebends having care of souls It also allowed bishops, dignitaries, and prebendiaries to exchange their appropriate rectories, vicarages and tithes for lands.

This effort to endow poor parishes and thus to avoid creation of more unions was not successful. Many parishes remained poor and even legislation once more permitting the several parishes of a union to be assessed for a single church found many parishes too poor to contribute. It seems likely, however, that rapid improvement of the country after 1715 would have allowed dissolution of a considerable number of unions had not the Irish House of Commons intervened in 1735 to remove tithe on agistment. Sharp reductions in tithe income led to another increase in unions, and subsequent legislation allowed bishops, with the consent of dean and chapter and other officials, to appropriate parishes to their see or to other parishes.[12]

By 1800 the process of consolidating Irish parishes had far exceeded sound administrative practices. The number of benefices had been halved, and pastoral neglect had forced Protestants in many rural areas to turn to Catholicism. Lay impropriators had success- fully avoided being forced to devote their revenues to church objec- tives. Unions created by consent of patrons could not be dissolved without their permission. Cathedral offices which had appropriated parochial income to their own purposes could not be forced to surren- der it without compensation. While unions were not a predominant fea- ture of the ecclesiastical landscape everywhere in Ireland, they were almost universal in the heavily Catholic sections of southern Ireland. In Munster 63 of 88 benefices were unions, and each union contained an average of 5 parishes. Some of these unions, stretching 40 miles across, afforded little opportunity for contact between pastor and flock, even when the incumbent constantly resided. In Ulster the 6 counties opened for Protestant settlement by the plantation charter of James I were constituted on a thoroughly reformed basis. In these areas tithes almost everywhere were used to support the active clergy.

Even here, however, there were some vexatious anomalies. In Down and Connor numerous occupiers of ancient monastic lands declared themselves extraparochial. Although they availed themselves of the services of nearby churches and clergy, they paid nothing for their support. Eliminating unnecessarily large unions, restoring sinecurial to incumbents performing duty, and making assessments more uniform was to engross the attention and tax the energies of a good many churchmen

in the nineteenth century. In the 1830s Parliament concluded that

better than restoring clergy to areas long without them would be aban-

doning the idea that the Church of Ireland should ever be truly nation-

al.[13] Failure to resolve the parochial administrative and jurisdic-

tional chaos was one of the most costly setbacks for the Church of

Ireland in the early nineteenth century.

The persistence of unwieldy unions reflected misallocation of

ecclesiastical revenues. This in turn was largely dependent upon the

tithe problem. The functional deficiencies of the tithe system must

be treated separately, but the allocation of revenues is of concern

here. With the dissolution of monasteries in the sixteenth century,

tithes belonging to religious houses "merely changed their masters and

their names." Instead of being attached to the parishes in which they

lay, most were bestowed on lay persons as temporal inheritances with

the new name of impropriations. Worse yet, many parish incumbents had

sought monastic protection in the unsettled conditions of pre-Reforma-

tion Ireland. Royal grants of monastic lands to impropriators provided

unanticipated opportunities for these great patentees to make "encroach-

ments on the parochial incumbents, under the pretense that the property

encroached upon was parcel of the ancient appropriations." Vicarial

as well as rectorial tithes were seized in some places, leaving nothing

to support the stipendiary curates.[14] The evil was so great by the

early seventeenth century, and so aggravated by voluntary alienations

and forced leases, that Charles I compelled patentees to restore usurp-

ed vicarages and impropriate rectories and tithes which the crown could claim, to return rectories to incumbents at the end of current leases, and to deny the right of clergymen to alienate any more ecclesiastical property. Other legislation encouraged return of Church property accepted in good faith from the crown. The Church pledged itself to apply the gifts to restoration of parochial revenues and if possible to dissolution of unwieldy unions. The crown also returned to the Establishment property forfeited by supporters of rebellion in 1641 and 1688.

These measures did not prove effective, and in 1800 perhaps one-third of all tithe revenue, plus many hundreds of glebes, remained in lay hands. Their parsimony, to curates and that of beneficed incumbents who enjoyed their incomes while living elsewhere, was notorious. Few curates were paid more than £75 per annum and many, especially in Munster and Connaught, survived on less than £50. Inadequate parochial income also contributed to the spread of pluralism where the crown could not be persuaded to approve the creation of more unions. Pluralism was particularly widespread in Connaught and the distance separating many incumbents' benefices meant especially unsatisfactory manifestations of pastoral care. In Connaught alone 131 beneficed clergymen were excused from constant residence in a benefice by virtue of obligations in another; the rest of Ireland contained an equal number of pluralists. In Cloyne nearly twice as many clergymen were absentees as resided. Some pluralists were fortunate enough to enjoy abutting benefices, but not many. Indeed, there was apparently little sensitivity to the problem of pluralism among many clergymen. Trading benefices in order to construct parochial empires was a common practice and one which Stuart and Brodrick, as will be seen worked

hard to control.

Two other by-products of financial dislocation and mismanage-

ment were the dearth of glebe houses and churches. Impropriation of

parochial revenues by laymen usually meant nothing could be obtained,

to maintain the glebe house. Absentee incumbents often evaded their

responsibilities as well. The eighteenth century saw considerable

use made of the quid pro quo in which incumbents maintained the house

for the curate if the bishop did not press the beneficed clergymen

to reside instead. In 1807 only Ulster had more benefices with glebe

houses than without. In Leinster almost one half possessed residences,

and in Munster and Connaught only one fourth. Rebellion and neglect

combined with normal deterioration to make the number of habitable

residences less each year as the eighteenth century came to a close.

Only 38 glebe houses were built in the decade prior to 1807, and per-

haps more than twice as many were abandoned during the same period.

In 2 dioceses in Munster there were only 3 residences for 33 bene-

fices. In Ferns and Leighlin, a prosperous and relatively accessible

united diocese in southeastern Ireland, there were only 9 glebe houses

in 1797; 16 were constructed in the next decade.

The dearth of churches was only slightly less lamentable. In

1807 bishops' returns indicated that 887 churches were in good, fair,

new, or "being repaired" condition, and 376 benefices had either none

or a church in "poor" condition. Since there were no guidelines es-

tablished for determining the categories, these figures were approxi-

mate, and if Stuart may be believed, the bishops tended to take a decidedly optimistic view. In Ulster and Munster relatively few bene-

fices lacked churches; in Connaught only one benefice in two boast-

ed a house of worship. The diocese of Limerick had only 35 churches

in "good" or "fair" condition for 95 parishes. Of these churches,

several were in the same benefice. The dearth of churches, while not

as serious from an administrative point of view as some of the Es-

tablishment's other problems, was deeply symbolic of the surrender of

the countryside to Catholicism during the eighteenth century. Without

glebe houses and without churches the Establishment's presence was a

tenuous one indeed.[15]

All of this led to the most serious problem of the Church of

Ireland; non-residence. In 1800 no defect was so incessantly be-

labored by its opponents, and so inadequately excused by its friends.

Decades of optimistic reports by bishops in all parts of Ireland had

neither stilled the criticism or resolved the problem, and the dislo-

cation occasioned by the rebellion of 1797 aggravated non-residence

even further. A more honest policy, encouraged by Stuart and at times

by the Irish administration, produced some exceptionally unattractive

substantiations of this most persistent and destructive of all church

problems. In 1798 the colorful and none too modest Dean Warburton of

Ardagh reported to Dublin that everything was peaceful in his area,

despite the rebellion, and that his parishioners had honored him with

a proclamation of their loyalty and support. But he was

> sorry to observe that it is the only instance of the kind
> that has yet taken place in the whole kingdom; and which,
> I have no scruple in telling your Lordship, is highly attri-
> butable to the shameful (and at this time) criminal neglect
> and non-residence of the clergy and gentry. Only look about

and observe the number of Irish bishops who are in England!
What can be expected from the inferior clergy when thus
deserted by their guides? The consequence is, what might
be expected, that the generality of the beneficed clergy
have betaken themselves to Dublin, to Bath, to London,
leaving their flocks to the certain seduction of revolutionary agents, who sleep not. And if a miserable curate
on the spot, as the representative of an absent rector, the
very station of this man is craftily turned by the republi-
cans into proof (convincing enough to the multitude) that
our whole Establishment is burdensome and unnecessary. . .
to counteract the evil effects of which (I do humbly think)
the government should (without delay) compel the residence
of every description of our clergy. There may naturally be
some delicacy felt in ordering the heads of our Church to
their duty, but surely this is not a time for ceremony.16

Brodrick, writing to the Bishop of Cloyne, whose diocese was a show-

place of administrative chaos, declared that non-residence was even

worse than the Church's enemies conceived it. There were "flagrant in-

stances of indiscretion" among the clergy, as well as "flagrant non-

residence," even among the curates. Hardwicke was informed that delay

in ending non-residence could not be tolerated.[17] The Duke of Bedford

upon his arrival in Ireland in 1806 confessed that he had not antici-

pated the extent of the evil, which "must inevitably tend to the decay

and probably terminate in the total ruin of the Established Church of

Ireland. . . ."[18]

Their sentiments were confirmed by episcopal surveys in 1807, even

after much warping of statistics to modify the extent of non-residence.

In two of the four provinces more clergy were absent than resident. In

Munster 57 to 83 clergy were permanently non-resident, half of them be-

cause of pluralism. Even in Ulster and Leinster over a third and near-

ly a half respectively were absent. In Kilmore, under the mismanagement

of Stuart's antagonist George de la Poer Beresford, 22 of 31 clergymen lived elsewhere. Only 8 dioceses claimed more resident clergy than absent. A small portion of the huge non-resident population lived in another benefice but did duty; lack of glebe houses prevented residence. Twenty pleaded infirmity. Only 41 offered as excuse the lack of a glebe house; to do so was interpreted as a commitment to build one if funds were made available. A small number pleaded no care of souls, and a handful were absent without permission. Most were attached to other benefices. It may be assumed that a goodly portion of these were in fact not resident on any of their benefices.

Within several months' incumbency at Armagh, Stuart was aware of the dimensions of the Church of Ireland's problems. He began a concerted effort to reverse the disintegration which had gone on uninterrupted during the previous century. The means at his disposal were not likely to engender much enthusiasm. His bishops were products of patronage excesses and he agreed with O'Beirne that unless their calibre was improved the clergy could not be expected to behave more satisfactorily. A couple were forced to dodge creditors; some were humiliated by family scandals.[19] Others responded with considerable hostility to critical comments on the state of their dioceses. The Bishop of Derry sold his episcopal house, despite Stuart's protests, and the Bishop of Cork, under pressure to rehabilitate his diocese, went insane.[20] Nor were many of the diocesan officials or members of the cathedral chapters cooperative. Most posts were looked upon as sinecurial and few bishops were anxious to assault their privileges.[21]

The prospect of a more energetic application of legislation governing clerical behavior was also discouraging. When the Bishop of

Cloyne moved against an absentee incumbent, the incumbent sent a certificate of ill health from his physician and departed for Europe. "Your Grace knows," the Bishop added,

> how difficult it. . . . is, with the present jealousy in all our great lawyers, to proceed to severities against the clergyman desiring absence on reasons, real or pretended, of ill health, supported by the oath of a physician, by high connections, and a good fortune.[22]

In many cases there was not much benefit in forcing a clergyman to reside if he remained sullen and uncooperative. One bishop complained that he "had more mad clergymen to contend with than any other bishop in the province." most of them gone insane because of their being forced to reside. The law protected the incumbent by treating the income from his benefice as a property right and therefore as almost unchallengeable. Bishops sometimes brought absentee clergymen to court but could rarely afford the exhaustive legal delays and usually surrendered without securing their point.[23] Indeed, without glebe houses the clergy could not be forced to reside, and many refused to apply for the grants necessary to build them.[24] These were the frustrations of resolving the Church of Ireland's problems through the channels of Church discipline and the law. Relations between reforming bishops and indifferent clergymen remained strained until the 1820s, when public opinion and more universal sensitivity among the clergy themselves left only isolated cases of opposition.

Two other major problems remained: application to Parliament for legislation which would tighten clerical discipline; and reform of financial resources available to the Church for construction of churches and glebe houses, which might in turn promote more frequent residence. Neither was without its dangers. Anti-clerical elements in Parliament professed to support reform efforts, but declared that clerical discipline should not be sought by granting bishops more power; the Church was already too much the beneficiary of prerogative. Many absentee clergy were identified with powerful vested interests who insisted that exemptions be included to cover a large number of specific situations. Legislative compulsion, in the absence of facilities for residence, seemed unfair. Finally, an increasingly vocal portion of Parliament was adopting the attitude that Ireland needed fewer, not more, beneficed clergymen, that rural Ireland should be surrendered to Catholicism in an attempt to reduce religious tensions.

Reform of financial arrangements was also difficult. In 1800 no one seemed sufficiently familiar with the Establishment's administrative structure to know what to suggest in the way of changes. Restrictions imposed by wills governing legacies, by an accumulation of legislation, by prescription, and by an absence of executive power made better application of resources somewhat difficult to plan. Without more effective control over clerical residence and without a transformation in the attitudes of many incumbents towards their spiritual duties it was unlikely that more efficient financial arrangements alone would reverse the Church's abdication of responsibilities in rural Ireland.

Between 1800 and 1810 Stuart and several of his bishops devoted their efforts to enlisting the support of the Irish administration and Parliament in combatting non-residence through legislative and administrative enforcement of clerical discipline. Brodrick, meanwhile, assumed control of the Board of First Fruits. This board supervised distribution of ecclesiastical revenues not committed to specified objectives. Brodrick worked with Stuart to seek legislation authorizing financial changes. Relations between the Church and the Irish administration were complicated by Stuart's protests over patronage policies, by the conflicting commitments of the government in Ireland, and by an element of distrust which permeated much of the correspondence between these two pillars of the ascendancy after 1800.

Prime Minister William Pitt's position was obscure. He went on record supporting parliamentary intervention to quicken the pace of church reform, but he refused to be specific.[25] Hardwicke was even more reluctant to take the initiative, especially in the wake of his difficulties with the primate. He was instructed to discourage formation of further unions, to encourage erection of glebe houses and churches, to enforce clerical residence, and to send lists of absentee bishops and "other dignitaries" to London from time to time.[26] Hardwicke seemed content not to "impede the salutary intention" of the reform-minded bishops. He did not exert a positive force; he read diocesan reports frequently but does not appear to have implemented their suggestions.[27]

The brief administration of the Duke of Bedford in 1806 and 1807 saw an intensification of reform activity at Dublin Castle. It would continue after the Tories returned to power, but it did not dispel Stuart's feeling of distrust. Upon reaching Dublin, Bedford wasted no time in making his own estimates of the effectiveness of the episcopal bench. Within a month he had written off the Archbishops of

Tuam and Dublin as "impracticable and indolent." He formed a highly

favorable impression of Brodrick and determined that Stuart should be

handled delicately.[28] Bedford promised Stuart that he would "pay the

most scrupulous regard to the character and dignity of the episcopal

bench in all recommendations" regarding ecclesiastical preferment and

other matters related to the Church. Stuart confided to Brodrick that

this "sounds well" and probably represented his real sentiments. "But

those who surround him," he added, "certainly entertain a different

opinion, and will use every method to adopt a conduct opposite to that

which it is his present wish to adopt." The primate forwarded a civil

but decidedly subdued reply. Bedford must have extracted every sugges-

tion of cooperation, for he waxed enthusiastic about his "cordial and

confidential intercourse" with Stuart and anticipated a marked improve-

ment in the Established Church under the influence of his administra-

tion.[29] Stuart's humor was not improved by Bedford's somewhat sim-

plistic proposals for sweeping reform. Nor was he unhappy when the

collapse of the Fox-Grenville ministry returned the care of the Church

to the Tories.[30]

Church-state relationships became considerably more complicated

after 1806. Stuart was no longer alone in pressing the government to

defend the Church. Some bishops' inopportune allegations of the

government's dereliction prompted intemperate responses from the Chief

Secretary and occasionally from the mild-mannered new Lord Lieutenant,

the Duke of Richmond. Some of the charges, such as failure to support

bishops' demands for franking privileges, were exceedingly petty.

Others, such as a widespread suspicion that Dublin Castle employed

manipulation of benefices to satisfy political requirements, were often
well supported by the evidence at hand.[31] Stuart was particularly
agitated at Richmond's propensity, his own declarations to the contrary, to permit exchanges of benefices so that both incumbents might
have an opportunity to negotiate increases in tithe rates. "To establish it as a system," he protested on one occasion, "that the
ecclesiastical favors of the crown are not to be given, but always
bartered, appears a most monstrous proceeding." Never had clerical
opportunism been so manifest, and never had the government been so
anxious to encourage this "spirit of gambling" for benefices.[32] Protestations of sympathy for the Church, vociferous though they were,
did not ring true when they were followed by strong directives from
Dublin Castle that bishops not disturb Irish tranquility by demanding
that their grievances be heard. As a result, mutual confidence diminsh-
ed rather than increased. The administration could not understand why
Stuart should be so unhappy; Stuart in turn noted that while the
government had been "profuse in their promises of supporting the
Church," he had "grown old," and found that confidence was "a plant of
slow growth in an aged bosom."[33] This lack of confidence, bred in the
first flush of "union engagements" and sustained through three successive Irish administrations, made even more difficult the highly sensitive task of negotiating with Parliament on questions of Church reform.

While it was necessary to proceed simultaneously with reform of
Church finances and clerical residence, Brodrick's assumption of the
control of the Board of First Fruits was a vital preliminary step.
Without some evidence of internal reform, Parliament could not be ex-

pected to react sympathetically to requests for financial assistance
or for disciplinary power over the wayward clergy. The Board of First
Fruits was the only centralized executive available to the Church of
Ireland through which internal reform could be stimulated. Unfortunately, in 1800 the Board reflected in microcosm most of the Establishment's administrative defects. The medieval Church had assessed each
incumbent his first year's income on entering a new benefice. One portion of these annates was forwarded to Rome. Another part constituted
a central fund out of which grants could be made for glebe house and
church construction. Two Reformation statutes (26 and 28 Henry VIII)
had appropriated first fruits to the Crown. Several succeeding statutes continued the annexation until 1710. The government seems to
have neglected almost entirely this source of revenue. By 1700 this
levy had been commuted to a fixed monetary sum. Despite periodic
attempts at revaluation, this sum increasingly represented a token fee
as inflation and intervals of prosperity enhanced the value of Irish
benefices. In 1704 the English Church abandoned collection of annates,
and agitation for a similar concession to Irish churchmen resulted in
creation of a Board designed to purchase lay impropriations, repair
and construct churches and glebe houses, and buy glebes. The pace of
improvement was far from startling. Revenues were small; solicitation of private contributions produced little income; and resistance
to reconstruction of church facilities was intense. By 1780 the track
record included lands purchased in 16 benefices, houses constructed in
45 locations, and impropriate tithes redeemed for 14 incumbents, all
at total investment of some £12,000.[34] In 1777 the Irish Parliament

began a long history of subsidies to the Board, and after 1785 settled

into a ₤5,000 annual advance.[35] Between 1791 and 1803 ₤44,000 was

expended for the construction of churches, ₤11,600 for glebe houses,

and additional sums for glebe lands. By 1800 the Board was relying

heavily on these annual grants to give ₤100 to promote the construction

of glebe houses for incumbents willing to match it with two years'

worth of their own income.

The system was peculiarly ineffective. Revenues at the disposal

of the board were manifestly inadequate for any program of reconstruc-

tion in Ireland after centuries of neglect. As a result, incumbents'

income increased steadily but the poverty of the Church's financial

administration increased as well. Since the burden of reimbursement

for grants made by the Board was spread over several successive incum-

bents, newly promoted curates were often confronted with a debt they

were unable to pay. Problems posed for small parishes were often

especially keen because no provision for repayment was included, and

because the Board limited its largess to benefices in which churches

had been abandoned for at least twenty years. Alas, the congregations

by this time were rarely more viable than the church ruins.[36] A para-

dox appeared: the Establishment's aggregate wealth became increasingly

obvious, but funds for improvement were so limited in amount and re-

stricted in use that the pace of physical decay quickened. By 1800

most grants for churches and glebe houses were devoted to repairing

deteriorating structures already in existence rather than to the con-

struction of new facilities.[37]

The contrast between the wealth of some higher dignitaries and

the poverty of many rural benefices did not escape the attention of
travellers, critics, and the government. A Church whose bishoprics
alone were capable of producing an annual revenue of some Ł223,000
after substantial discounting for leases, and many of whose cathedral
chapters commanded more than Ł3,000 a year, was relying on a parliamentary grant of Ł5,000 to sustain most of its construction program.[38]
Poorer benefices, of which there were several hundred, lacked sufficient funds to sustain an incumbent. This extreme inequity in allocation of church resources in Ireland prompted not only widespread criticism by outside observers, but made the Board of First Fruits a
forum for angry confrontations between rich and poor dioceses, between wealthy dignitaries and impoverished incumbents, and between careless administrators and unprincipled profiteers.

In 1800 Castlereagh suggested that proceeds from compensation
due the Church for destruction of ecclesiastical boroughs on occasion
of extinction of the Irish Parliament should be used to augment the
resources of the Board of First Fruits. Those bishops in whose jurisdiction the boroughs lay joined with the families who controlled them
in blocking the proposal.[39] The scramble for these funds which did
pass into the hands of the Board was so unedifying that at least one
bishop requested Hardwicke to intervene. So distracted and careless
was Agar's supervision of the Board that early in 1803 he was forced
to resign. As has been noted, the Board was placed under Brodrick's
jurisdiction.[40] Even Brodrick could not effect the needed improvements.
Stuart urged rapid expenditure of the surplus obtained by reversion of
ecclesiastical boroughs. Public opinion would not tolerate restrict-

ting the pace of construction to what could be obtained from the interest alone. Brodrick was entirely sympathetic, but most bishops preferred to discuss ambiguous and time-consuming long range plans. When
pressure was applied to act quickly, tempers flared and "warm and in-
decent altercation   usually resulted in rapid adjournement.[41]

Grants which were approved had a checkered history as well. Incumbents showed immense skill in frustrating efforts to force them
to accept funds for construction of glebe houses, and inefficient auditing meant the loss of many thousands of pounds of allocated funds.
Every session of the Board heard cases in which poor recipients attached the grant to their incomes, or built stables instead of a glebe
house, or who exchanged benefices with an incumbent in another diocese
and took the grant with them.[42] Recovery of grants was made almost
impossible by the bias of the law and the skill of lawyers. Compart-
mentalization of funds meant that grants could not be made where most
needed. A dearth of glebes prevented construction of residences, while
some of the gentry refused to sell land for glebe houses. Finally,
even successful efforts in reconstruction did not mean the clergy would
reside, and several years of neglect meant that the fruits of the grant
had been largely nullified.

Within months of Brodrick's accession to leadership of the Board
of First Fruits he was convinced that little could be done without
added funds and until legislation enforcing residence and restricting
church finances had been approved by Parliament. In 1801 a residence
enforcement bill attached to a proposed reform of the Board of First
Fruits had been submitted to the House of Commons and soon after with-

drawn. In 1802 the Bishop of Killaloe proposed application of funds derived from the government's purchase of ecclesiastical boroughs to build glebe houses in those parishes where glebe lands already existed. Hardwicke listened with interest and even suggested some changes, but urged that Irish churchmen rather than the government submit the bill to Parliament.[43] This was done but later the bill was withdrawn. The following year saw Stuart refer Brodrick once more to the matter of ecclesiastical boroughs extinguished by the Act of Union. If payments to lay magnates for their loss meant anything, the Church was also due generous compensation. Brodrick secured a generous ₤46,800 for three boroughs thus extinguished. After a tussle with bishops seeking exclusive control over funds derived from those boroughs which lay within their jurisdictions, he established a separate fund with proceeds from government debentures.[44]

This small triumph did not obscure the fact that not much substantive work could be done. Stuart was reluctant to expose the Church's anomalies to further parliamentary scrutiny. Brodrick, who was willing to brave a hostile audience, offered a bill in 1803 to facilitate interest-free loans to incumbents wishing to construct glebe houses.[45] The bill permitted trustees and commissioners of the Board of First Fruits to lend a sum not to exceed two years' income to the benefice, the sum to be repaid according to a fixed schedule and insured by a pledge binding on the signee and his successors. Default allowed the Bishop to sequester whatever parish funds were available. No construction was to be subsidized until building estimates had been audited by the Board. Within its distinctly limited realm of operation, this bill promised to regularize the role of the Board as a lending institution, and to grant the Church long requested authority to deal with defaulters.[46]

But while the bill encouraged those clergymen eager to reside if facilities could be constructed, it did not challenge habitual absentees' reluctance to solicit funds and therefore made little impression upon the problem of non-residence itself. Even this tentative and hesitant assault on non-residence did not find Parliament cooperative. The bill, unfortunately, was not introduced until late in the session. Despite Brodrick's summertime optimism that by this measure the Church would become more independent rather than less, the government decided instead to attach the bill to a direct parliamentary grant of ₤50,000, by which device Parliament would have a firmer measure of control over disbursal of funds for glebe house construction. The government's financial intiative delighted the Church, whose bishops convened in anticipation of parliamentary victory only to discover that the ministry was unwilling to press Parliament for early authorization of either the bill or the funds.[47] Growing impatience on the part of some bishops prompted Alexander Knox to introduce a separate bill permitting him to employ first fruits to repair his ruinous churches. The bill itself was innocuous, but Derry was a wealthy see. The prospect of Derry requesting additional funds promised to excite opponents of the Church to demand confiscation of episcopal revenues instead of a parliamentary subsidy.[48] Stuart's private suspicions that the ministry was prepared to use the Bishop of Derry's initiative as an excuse to force "hostile legislation" on the Church proved unwarranted. Brodrick's bill was approved, but the grant of ₤50,000 marked a new age of parliamentary scrutiny.[49]

Stuart's suspicions of the ministry's intentions were, in his own mind, soon confirmed. It became clear in the wake of Brodrick's inadequate assault on non-residence that Parliament was demanding, and the ministry prepared to support, a comprehensive investigation of the Irish Church. The grant of ₤50,000 itself was an invitation to parliamentary investigators. Stuart might have opposed this approach more vigorously had the Church been able to tap internal sources for glebe house funds instead. The provision which made application through the Lord Lieutenant a prerequisite for allocation of any portion of the grant to glebe house construction was secretly supported by some Irish bishops who believed their voice was rarely heard in the councils of the Board of First Fruits. But it greatly irritated Stuart, whose declared hostility to Hardwicke made it unlikely that the latter would miss any opportunity to embarrass the Church along the way.[50] The requirement that all expenditures be audited was both embarrassing and vexatious, for the Board of First Fruits was not in the habit of keeping accounts, and adjustment to new procedures came slowly.[51] "In truth," Stuart confided to Brodrick, "all we want is the money, and not parliamentary audits."[52]

Much worse was the suggestion of an even more thorough investigation. In his own province the returns would "be almost entirely free from those difficulties which are likely to occur in other parts of Ireland and which should excite in our mind very great alarm;" it would not be so elsewhere. By early summer, 1805, it was confirmed that Sir John Newport, Irish landlord and parliamentary gadfly, had

succeeded in forcing motions for a comprehensive inquiry of Irish

ecclesiastical finance and unions of parishes.[53] By October Stuart

seemed at a loss as to what to do:

> When I first read the motions which Sir John Newport pro-
> posed to make, I trembled for the consequences, and did my
> utmost to persuade the English ministers to reject them.
> They are, indeed, considerably altered, and some of the
> most obnoxious points have been deleted , but surely
> enough remains to do us great injury. Sir John Newport's
> real object is to subvert the Establishment, by making it
> appear, not only that the grossest abuses prevail, but
> that, in the greatest part of Ireland, the clergy are paid
> for doing nothing, while the Catholic priests, who alone
> perform the pastoral office, receive no emolument from the
> state. . . .I know not what to advise. The entering into
> a long detail to justify non-residence in particular in-
> stances, or to justify particular unions, will I fear pro-
> duce no good effect, for who will read it?. . .I once
> thought of writing a circular letter to the bishops, and
> recommending a general meeting in Dublin, but men meet so
> unwillingly, and such of my brethren as I had the oppor-
> tunity of consulting seem to be so little apprehensive of
> any ill-effects likely to result from these returns, that
> I dropped the design. At present, however, the matter is
> somewhat changed, and many of them begin to fear. . . .
> In truth, our situation is extremely perilous. In England
> the public opinion is decidedly against us. Our enemies
> are more active and industrious than ever: and our friends
> are either lukewarm or defend us with so many exceptions
> and reserves that their defence has all the appearance and
> all the effect of an attack.

Even the Irish Lord Chancellor, "whom the English suppose is well ac-

quainted with the ecclesiastical state of Ireland, and who is sup-

posed to be a biggoted admirer of our Establishment," had declared

that the Church was in a "most rotten state," that the Irish bishops

represented the state of their dioceses falsely, and that even good

men, such as Brodrick, were imposed upon by false friends.[54]

Newport's motions, relieved of their more hostile innuendos

against the Church of Ireland, were approved by the House of Commons
in October 1805. More than ever was Stuart reluctant to press for
legislation to support the reform movement within the Church. But
with the information to be placed at Parliament's disposal when returns were completed certain to excite displeasure and prompt calls
for disestablishment, the primate determined to press for a tighten-
ing of residency requirements. Besides the difficulties which attended the unwanted publicity engendered by legislative activity, there
were other dangers. Every law which distinguished the Irish Establishment from the English worked against those provisions of the Act of
Union which united the two Churches and which guaranteed the Irish
Church a measure of protection against its numerous opponents. Irish
bishops were increasingly sensitive to the difficulties which had resulted from their failure in 1800 to support a plan for recognizing
Canterbury's authority. In 1805 the House of Lords declared that the
union of the two Churches was only "nominal."[55] Parliamentary debates
also gave supporters of Catholic Emancipation further opportunity to
publicize their arguments and a chance to demonstrate how weak was the
organization and sentiment favoring the Church. When Whigs toppled
Pitt's ministry a strong undercurrent of hostility to the Established
Churches made it impossible for Stuart to persuade the new ministry to
give him power to enforce clerical residence. The subject of clerical
discipline was indeed a particularly sensitive one, prompting frenetic
efforts by vested interests to destroy the reform impulse and exciting
the barely latent anticlericalism of the Irish gentry.

On February 5, 1806 the government, under extreme pressure from

the Radicals, moved for a return on Irish clerical residence.[56] Two
weeks later Patrick Duigenan, member for Armagh and preeminent spokesman for the Irish Church in the House of Commons, presented a bill
giving bishops more power to enforce residence, partly to cure the
embarrassment itself, and partly to test the declarations of Newport
and Irish gentlemen that their only object in pressing for the returns
authorized earlier was increased clerical residence, not exposure of
the Church to criticism.[57] The bill gave bishops and archbishops the
right to command non-resident beneficed clergy to take up residence.
Those failing to do so might have their property sequestered and their
functions suspended until appeals were heard. Thereafter, following a
certain lapse of time, the benefice was to be considered vacant.[58]

The temper of the House was reflected in the remarks of leading
Irish members upon the bill's presentation. Henry Grattan declared it
stupid and absurd to enforce clerical residence in a region where there
was no Protestant population. Irish bishops, moreover, were political
persons, and they might force clergymen they disliked to live in remote
areas. The speaker of the House demonstrated his own adverse sentiments by ruling that a subsidiary bill designed to augment small livings out of private endowments was a private bill, subject to fees of
₤300.

Duigenen's defense of the bill was a study in legislative inepti-
tude. When confronted with the observation that the bill was vague,
ill-considered, and unenforceable, Duigenan claimed it was a reflection
of the wishes of the Board of First Fruits and the Irish bishops. This
was untrue. Incensed Irish Churchmen, many of whom opposed the idea of

legislative interference in the first place, urged Stuart to force

Duigenan to abandon his initiatives. Duigenan was not to be dissuaded

lightly, even though the first returns concerning non-residence pre-

sented on February 25, darkened the mood of the Commons. A second

series of fragmentary reports was presented on March 17.[59] Meanwhile,

Duigenan's bill was read a second time March 11, and was considered in

committee the following week. The bill was not itself thrown out.

But enthusiasm demonstrated in favor of another committee to deliber-

ate on the as yet fragmentary returns on non-residence made it quite

clear that the bill was being used as an occasion for castigating the

Irish ecclesiastical Establishment.[60]

By the time the bill was ready for its third reading the commit-

tee created to analyze non-residence was the center of attention, and

Stuart at length reluctantly intervened to have Duigenan's bill with-

drawn so as to deflect further attention from the Church.[61] Stuart

soon appeared to have regretted forcing abandonment of the bill. He

informed the government that as a result of recent court decisions

Irish bishops were "quite destitute of power to enforce residence, and

therefore ought not to be blamed or deemed responsible for the non-resi-

dence of the clergy." Canon law was now without effect. Procedures

in regular courts proved far too costly to be borne by most bishops.

It was "therefore now generally understood. . . that the clergy may

or may not reside as they think proper." After learning these senti-

ments and after examining some preliminary returns from the survey,

William Grenville as Prime Minister reluctantly agreed that the resi-

dence bill should not have been abandoned. So sensitive was the Church question, however, that the government dared not revive it.[62]

Of even greater concern to Stuart and Brodrick was the potential impact of the surveys on residence. By the spring of 1806 it was patently clear that the returns were inadequate, erroneous, and unintelligible.[63] Newport made clear his intention of moving for a new report on non-residence, with instructions shaped to preclude episcopal manipulation of the returns. To compete with Newport, Grenville suggested to Irish officials in April the possibility of a royal visitation, which might at once produce an accurate picture of the Church's condition and avoid heavy-handed parliamentary interference in the future. Duigenan's assertion that the returns were so complete as to make a visitation superfluous was roundly disputed by nearly everyone, including Stuart. The primate was forced to admit that they were "in truth not only unsatisfactory, but plainly evasive, and in every way unworthy of men of our station."[64] But Grenville also believed that even the visitation might be regarded as a hostile measure, and one which friends of the Church would see was effectively blocked. Stuart was particularly anxious to avoid it, so unlikely was it that the Whigs would appoint "unexceptional ministers."

The principal advocate of visitation was the Duke of Bedford. Stuart determined to cut through the crust of suspicion in order to impress upon him the wisdom of entrusting another survey to Stuart himself.[65] The primate excused the poor performance of the bishops by advancing the theory that the queries had been addressed to diocesan registers, who were incompetent to answer them, and that incomplete records frustrated the efforts of even the most cooperative bishops.

He believed a royal visitation would be regarded by most bishops and clergy with great suspicion. The proper device would be the ch-bishop, who exercised in Ireland

> a more extensive jurisdiction than is exercised by the arch-bishops in England. An English archbishop has little connec-tion with his suffragan and bishops, and no connection with the clergy under those bishops. But in Ireland an archbis-hop not only visits his own diocese every year, but each diocese in his province every three years, during which visit the power and functions of his suffragans are entire-ly suspended. He examines personally and publicly every clergyman, and puts what questions he thinks proper to the bishops who are obliged to answer them in the presence of all the clergy.[66]

The primate's letter proved persuasive. Bedford declared to Grenville his agreement with Stuart that a royal visitation would be hostile to the Church, and that "the benefits we look to. . . might be converted into the most serious mischiefs." The previous returns, to be sure, were extremely inadequate, and "not such as we ought to adopt as a basis of a salutary and effectual reform of the church." He attributed this in part to efforts by the bishops and the clergy to obscure their defective management of ecclesiastical resources. But Newport's motion was also considered

> an unnecessary exposure of the imperfections and defects of the Church, without a due allowance being granted for the local disadvantages under which it labours; and they, in consequence, set their faces against the parliamentary in-quisition (as they termed the measure) and withheld their assistance from those who were directed to carry the inquiry into effect. The information we desire to obtain must be sought with the entire concurrence and cooperation of the bench and higher orders of the clergy, or I fear our efforts will be of no avail.

Bedford's sympathetic response weakened the validity of Stuart's as-persions on the Irish administration which the Lord Lieutenant supervised. Bedford concluded his observations with a hope widely shared but perhaps less eloquently phrased elsewhere that a program of reform could be fashioned which might "tend not merely to prop the tottering fabric of the Established Church in this part of the United Kingdom, but to secure its strength and durability on a solid and lasting basis."[67]

Any lingering attachment in Grenville's mind to a royal visitation was apparently swept away by Bedford's forthright support of the primate; the prospect of a royal visitation was relegated to the status of "last resort" and Stuart was informed of the postponement.[68] Stuart was anxious not to be embarrassed by the obstreperousness of his bishops, and agreed with Bedford that the letters of instruction governing the new set of returns be backed by "the powerful motive of the King's sanction and authority."[69] Even this did not move the bench to concerted action. Stuart, however, managed to humor the ineffective and impractical Archbishops of Dublin and Tuam to join Brodrick and him in securing more credible returns.[70] On July 16 Bedford forwarded a series of questions to the archbishops, and these were immediately passed on to the bishops

The clergy and bishops proved to be only slightly more cooperative towards the Primate than they were to the government. By November Stuart was searching for devices which might make possible delaying submission of the new reports.[71] The search apparently proved fruitless, for the first bundle of returns, including Stuart's unaltered survey of his own province in 1806, the greatly amended submission of of Leinster, and the still incomplete returns of Munster and Connaught, were printed by the House of Commons the following July.[72] By far

the most extensive analysis in the history of the Irish Church, the

returns for the first time provided statistical evidence of the con-

dition of churches, glebe houses, and glebe lands, the pattern and

dimensions of residence and detailed reasons for absenteeism, the

number, duties, and remuneration of curates, and the number of bene-

fices, parishes and unions. For the first time Parliament and the

nation knew what Stuart had long suspected and discreetly noted: that

the disintegration of the Irish Church was far advanced, and could be

arrested only by heroic measures. These measures were certainly be-

yond the capacity of the Church alone, and perhaps beyond the ken of

Parliament itself.

The returns conveyed a new sense of urgency to demands for com-

pulsory residence. They prompted much recrimination against the Irish

ecclesiastical monstrosity and those who supervised it. Practices

once accepted almost fatalistically were now universally condemned.

The Irish administration upbraided the Church, and the Church criti-

cized the state.[73] On April 20, 1807, one week before the Grenville

ministry collapsed, the Irish Chief Secretary requested a select

committee to examine unions, churches, and glebe houses. Newport and

the "radicals" cheered the initiative; Duigenan for the Church inter-

est dared not oppose it.[74] Surprised perhaps at the extent of irregu-

larities within their own jurisdictions, Irish bishops managed to

overcome previous points of discretion and looked to Parliament, after

April 1807 once more controlled by the Tories. In August Newport de-

manded that clerical residence in Ireland be enforced immediately and without financial inducements. By summer's end, when compilations of Irish dioceses had been printed and circulated, the ministry and the Irish administration were in agreement that compulsory residence legislation was required.[75] Prosecution under canon law, as the new Irish Chief Secretary Arthur Wellesley observed, was so tedious and expensive that "neither the life nor the fortune of any bishop could be expected to hold out to its termination." He also believed that immediate moves to enforce residence would stimulate glebe house construction. If forced to live in Ireland, incumbents would quickly apply to the Board of First Fruits to build houses.[76]

Wellesley did not doubt that the Church was sufficiently rich to finance an extensive program of glebe house and church construction. But he appreciated difficulties and frustrations attendant upon trying to utilize this wealth, and moved to obtain supplementary funds from Parliament until clerical discipline was restored.[77] If uncooperative bishops hoped by their actions to delay consideration of deficiencies of the Irish Church, they were disappointed. Newport responded to the new yet inadequate returns with a proposal for a select committee to "take into consideration" the several acts relating to churches and glebe houses and to prepare the way for an audit of Ireland's Protestant population.[78] This was suppressed, but a bill designed to amend the 1803 Glebe House Act in favor of forcing clergymen to construct and reside in parochial residences reached the House of Lords in July, where it was hotly disputed and then allowed to die.[79] Despite considerable agreement between Stuart and the ministry as to what must be done, the government's bill was delayed until after supplementary returns were

obtained from Irish diocesan registrars in January of the next year.
This process was subsequently delayed by many bishops' evasive re-
plies.[80]

At the opening of a new session in Parliament in February 1808
Wellesley presented a new residence bill. Its main feature was to
extend to Ireland residence requirements enforced in England.[81] The
bill met with a hostile reception when presented to Parliament.
Arguments concentrated on the penalties to be applied for non-residence, which Radicals thought too lenient, and which many Irishmen
(especially those with Church connections) thought much too severe.
Stuart was soon unnerved. By March the clamor of those who opposed
the clerical residence bill as merely a means of shoring up the tottering ecclesiastical Establishment, and those who condemned it as
an assault upon the sanctity of freehold property, had thoroughly
disheartened the normally resolute Stuart, who urged the bill be
abandoned; it would, he observed be an "egregious folly," circumstanced
as the Church was, to continue, for "even if it were the best bill
ever brought into Parliament" it would not be worth the evils created
by any discussion of the Church's anomalies.[82]

The bill was not abandoned. Intense pressure on the Portland
ministry from the families of those clergymen who had most to
lose by compulsory residence requirements had its effect.[83] As
finally enacted, the bill empowered bishops to issue warnings to
any incumbent who lived in his benefice less than nine months of a
calendar year. If the incumbent failed to reside, the diocesan might
sequester the benefice and after three years declare it vacant and

appoint a new incumbent.[84] Sinecurists, bishops and archbishops were

exempt from the act, and as a sop to opponents of compulsory residence,

bishops were not obliged to implement the act at all.[85] Bishops here-

ofore determined to enforce residence, however, now had adequate

weapons to do so, and it was hoped that provision for a parliamentary

audit each year would encourage more indulgent bishops to invoke ex-

emptions only to protect those in poor health or exceedingly poor

livings.[86]

The new legislation represented at best a faltering step forward

in clerical discipline at the cost of considerable unfavorable publi-

city and much evidence of the government's lack of enthusiasm for de-

cisive reform measures. Bishops were not liable to provisions of the

new law, and the ease with which exemptions could be obtained by non-

resident clergymen blunted the impact of the new legislation. The

deficiencies of the Board of First Fruits came in for sharper criti-

cism by forcing funds for glebe house construction on recalcitrant

clergymen. Bishop Butson in a long and thoughtful letter drew Welles-

ley's attention to one evil when he described how unscrupulous archi-

tects charged the clergy enjoined to build houses high fees for inade-

quate advice, and how builders substituted poor materials for good.[87]

Wellesley thought it most important to tighten procedures surrounding

collection of first fruits, leaving problems in dispensing funds to

be addressed later.

Unfortunately, tales of the clergy's victimization, coupled with

Wellesley's call for more rigorous enforcement of first fruits collec-

tion, produced an unusual alliance of irate clergymen opposed to heavier taxation of their incomes, of Newport's friends demanding a new

valuation before collection was tightened, and even reformers in the

Irish Church who regarded Wellesley's injunction as a precedent which

could only result in a wider confiscation of church property at a

later date.[88] The government soon found itself urging slow implemen-

tation of the use of First Fruits Funds, citing the heavy expenses

which attended Irish dignitaries building residences suitable to their

style of living. This excited a mixture of mirth and anger and deeply

embarrassed the Irish Establishment, which was forced in the wake of

this discussion of its wealth to agree to substantial reduction in

the parliamentary appropriation for glebe house construction. Newport's

motion for heavier taxation and new valuations was narrowly defeated,

and the government dropped its much more modest plan to improve collec-

tion of existing levies.[89] O'Beirne saw fit to forward a long, poig-

nant letter to the government summing up the increased difficulties

facing the Church in the wake of the session's developments:

> Perhaps I was myself too sanguine in the expectations I had
> formed, from my knowledge of these friendly dispositions in
> the principal members of the administration, and I will not
> deny that I feel disappointment. I allow that it was a
> matter of great delicacy to bring the state of the Church
> in this part of the United Kingdom, into public discussion.
> But you had resolved to bring it before Parliament; you
> felt yourselves to be in suffecent strength to carry all the
> measures you might propose for our support and amelioration;
> and you well knew the hostile disposition of those who, on
> a change, would succeed to your power. I and others had,
> therefore, hoped that nothing would have been left undone
> by you which persons thoroughly acquainted with our wants
> and competent to advise on every necessary arrangement,
> might have suggested to you. . . . The British ministry
> seemed to be so nervous on all questions that affect us,
> that, with increasing difficulties, such as they have rea-
> son to apprehend, you will hardly find them disposed to set
> them afloat in another session. The consequence of all this

is that the disappointment of our friends is as marked as
the triumph of our enemies. It is not to be conceived how
dispirited all the thinking and respectable clergy whom I
have seen appear to be, or what fears the friends of the
Establishment begin to entertain. The events of this
session make them despair of that strong and vigorous support which our situation requires; and whether our ruin
shall be gradual, or accomplished at one blow, is the only
difference.[90]

Although Wellesley denied that the ministry planned to abandon

he Church to its own devices, and even produced for O'Beirne's bene-

it an unusually comprehensive plan for glebe house and church con-

truction,[91] it was more than ever apparent that the Church must now

ook to "internal devices" for further reform. Most of the abuses

which had prompted reformers to look to Parliament for amelioration

emained. Few progressives, however, and Stuart least of all, wanted

o resume the struggle the following year. The bad, on balance, had

utweighed the good. The passions of the Church's opponents had been

urther enflamed by each succeeding revelation of ecclesiastical ano-

alies in Ireland; the clergy who resided faithfully had grown ex-

eedingly sensitive to heavy-handed condemnations which appeared in

amphlet form and in parliamentary debates; those clergy who refused

o reside were provoked into further expressions of defiance by every

ttempt to force them to staff their benefices.[92] Church supporters

n Parliament had revealed themselves to be violent, ineffective,

eeply embarrassing to Establishment and vexatious to the Portland

inistry. The government thought the Church entirely insensitive to

he difficulties encountered in obtaining legislation in its behalf,

nd far too critical of its management of Irish patronage.

As a last effort to facilitate the process of internal ecclesiastical reform without returning to the quagmire of non-residence laws, the Church's friends obtained in 1809 from Parliament legislation further strengthening the administrative machinery of the Board of First Fruits and increasing its resources. The Board's diverse funds, including revenues from ecclesiastical boroughs, were consolidated. Restrictions on use of funds were removed, and the government's largess was considerably expanded. Apart from the Ŀ50,000 treasury advance in 1802 Parliament had, until 1808, seen fit to continue the traditional grant of Ŀ5,000. This was doubled in 1808 and 1809, and then raised to Ŀ60,000 for each year from 1810 to 1816.[93]

With the Board strengthened Brodrick immersed himself almost completely in the Board of First Fruits. In 1809 he drew up a plan for comprehensive reform of Church finances, in which 342 glebe houses would be constructed at a cost of Ŀ543,000, 341 glebes of twenty acres each purchased at a cost of Ŀ276,000, and 230 churches constructed at a cost of Ŀ230,000. Half of the total outlay would be obtained by floating debentures on the Board of First Fruits' anticipated revenues from more rigorous collection procedures, the remainder by bonding on state security. The memorandum never seems to have been circulated among the bishops, however, much less offered to the government.[94]

Indeed, the new largess could not relieve all of Brodrick's problems. Brodrick feared the government would decide not to continue its generous grants. Meddling ecclesiastics added to his bouts of indigestion. Euseby Cleaver, as Archbishop of Dublin, managed to alter the request for funds to include "repairs" to existing facilities as well as the construction of new churches and glebe houses. This, Stuart stormed, was "fatal": "once the vestries discover they can obtain funds from first fruits for repairs of churches, they will never again be induced to vote a penny for that purpose.[95] In 1812 and 1813 new fears circulated that government assistance would soon cease. Upon succeeding the unfortunate Spencer Perceval as Prime Minister Liverpool felt obliged to have Peel assure Stuart that the fate of the Church was still in friendly hands.[96] In 1815, just when Stuart and Brodrick again felt enough confidence in the government's favorable disposition towards the Irish Church to suggest public funds be appropriated for the augmentation of small livings, Liverpool announced that the grant would be reduced from ₤60,000 to ₤10,000 per year; the great age of physical reconstruction had closed.[97] In fact, the grant was only reduced to ₤30,000 until 1821. But even this less severe reduction meant that Board of First Fruit meetings became more acrimonious than ever, with Stuart supplying Brodrick with his distinctly uncomplimentary estimates of most of the bishops' requests and their sponsors. When Irish Chief Secretary Charles Grant informed the Board in June 1822 that no more government funds would be forthcoming, Brodrick and Stuart were not entirely unhappy.[98]

What had been achieved by this demonstration of Church and State cooperation? We can obtain a clear idea of the dimensions of the accomplishment between 1801 and 1815, when the subsidy was drastically reduced, by looking at two reports in the State Paper Office, Dublin.[99] During this period the revenues of the Board of First Fruits exceeded ₤636,000, of which ₤350,000 constituted direct grants by Parliament, ₤53,000 represented interest on Government securities, ₤61,000 obtained from the Borough Compensation Fund, ₺11,000 from repayment of loans,

₺36,000 from diverse governmental sources, and only ₺6,000 from first

fruits collections. Expenditures were as follows: gifts for churches,

₺97,370; gifts for the purchase of glebes, ₺27,646; gifts for the

construction of glebe houses ₺10,850; loans for glebe houses, ₺124,261;

increased gifts for glebe houses, as authorized under 48 George 3,

₺46,454, and loans for church construction under the same act, ₺111,359.

Another ₺198,658 was devoted to the purchase of debentures and govern-

ment stock; the income from this was expected to sustain construction

efforts after Parliament terminated its grants. About ₺9,300 was de-

voted to salaries, clerical needs, legal costs and lobbying. The di-

mensions of this program can be seen in the area of construction: 329

grants for churches, with 150 completed and 105 under construction at

the beginning of 1815; 390 grants for glebe houses, with 218 completed

and 85 under construction; 124 grants for glebes, with 86 purchased.

By 1822, when the program was terminated, the following record had been

established: ₺149,000 gifts in for church construction; ₺281,000 as

loans for the same; ₺211,000 as loans for glebe houses, and ₺110,000

as gifts; and ₺54,000 for the purchase of glebe lands. These disburse-

ments were flexible; no longer bound by legislative restrictions and

scarce funds, churches were rescued before they collapsed, often with

sizeable grants and loans. Even after 1822, with government funds un-

available, the Board received income from investments and repayment of

loans ranging as high as ₺16,000 per annum.[100] In 1829, at the end of

the era of internal reconstruction, nearly 700 churches had been re-

built or enlarged, 550 glebe houses constructed, and 193 glebe lands purchased.[101] The number of Anglican churches increased from 1001 to 1293, glebe houses from 354 to 829.[102]

The impact of legislation and internal reconstruction on cleri-cal residence was considerable. Between 1787 and 1832 the percentage of benefices with glebe houses increased from 31 to 59. Residence im-proved markedly. Between 1807 and 1819, under the influence of the exertions of the Board of First Fruits and residence legislation, re-sidence increased from 46% to 65%. The improvement was dramatic in Kilmore (28% to 69%), Ossory (29% to 59%), Cashel and Emly (34% to 67%), Killaloe and Kilfenora (44% to 80%), Waterford and Lismore (35% to 60%), and Tuam and Ardagh (39% to 63%). It was much less impressive in dioceses such as Clogher where so many benefices were controlled by cathedral chapters, Trinity College, or philanthropic institutions.[103]

In 1824 further legislation was enacted to remedy deficiencies of the Act of 1808. The new measure strengthened bishops' disciplinary powers on one hand and reduced the area of exemptions on the other. A graduated scale of fines was added for parochial incumbents' absentee-ism, which now could be prosecuted in civil courts. Cathedral digni-taries holding cure of souls were for the first time forced to reside at least eight months of the year in their benefices. Exemptions grant-ed in cases not explicitly defined in the act required archepiscopal approval, with the Lord Lieutenant exercising veto power.[104] As a re-sult, substantial further improvement of 10% could be discerned between 1819 and 1832. Improvement was especially marked in the province of Armagh, where by 1832 84% of the beneficed clergy were constantly resi-dent; in Derry alone residence jumped from 72% to 95%, in Dromore

from 61% to 76%, and in Kilmore from 70% to 85%. Because of the continuing widespread poverty of rural benefices and endemic unrest in
other provinces, improvement there was often less marked. In Cashel
and Emly and in Killaloe and Kilfenora non-residence actually increased, probably largely due to tithe agitation. The province of Cashel as
a whole, however, showed a small improvement.[105]

Attempts to restrict pluralism attended this assault on non-residence. Pluralism covered a multitude of sins and encompassed some
necessary and helpful administrative devices as well. About one-third
of all Irish parishes were parts of a union in 1819, but the incumbent
of a benefice composed of a union of parishes was not, in the technical
sense at least, a pluralist. On the other hand, small adjacent benefices, easily administered together and held by a single incumbent,
constituted pluralism. The 1819 returns suggested that the Church of
Ireland included about 160 pluralists. After 1820 pluralism, both legitimate and illegitimate, declined, slowly at first and then more
rapidly. Archbishop Beresford established effective restraints on
pluralism in his province, insisting that such faculties be granted
only when important duties, pressing financial considerations, and
administrative requirements were met. As a result, grants of faculties
to more than one benefice declined sharply.[106] Progress was substantially slower elsewhere, especially in Tuam, and pluralism was at length
eliminated more by redefining parochial jurisdictions than by refusing
multiple facilities.

By 1830, however, much had been accomplished. The Church of Ireland had enjoyed a decade of peace, its clergy were increasingly effec-

tive, and its position seemed relatively secure. Only two issues, tithes and education, stirred public opinion.

Chapter IV: The Irish Tithe Question 1800-1830

Of all the sad events which dominated Anglo-Irish relations before the twentieth century few present a tale more melancholy than tithes. A more vexatious impost for sustaining the Irish Church Establishment could not have been devised. Accident and determined adherence to the technical functions of the tithe created a system which did much to destroy Ireland's social and political cohesion, to disorient its economic life, to alienate the Church of Ireland from the nation, and to excite the passions of the great masses of the Irish people. Deficiencies in the tithe system itself were many times multiplied by the rackrents, by the absenteeism of much of the landlord and clerical class, by Ireland's excessive demographic burden upon limited agricultural resources, by the anomalies of prescription and legislative fiat, and by the volatile nature of the Irish people themselves. No problem seemed so little amendable to reform or extinction, for no system reflected the entanglement of so many vested interests over so long a period.

Tithes have been discussed often in books on Irish history, though not always without passion. They have not, however, been analyzed from the point of view of their relationship to the Church of Ireland, except in the most obvious instance: financial support. In fact the significance of the tithe was much more complex, for in an age thoroughly convinced of the sanctity of property rights and of the rights of prescription in general, the prospect of destruction of the tithe suggested uncomfortable parallels for the welfare of the Church as a whole. For these reasons, aggravated by deeper, almost visceral frustrations, the tithe was destined to obfuscate the internal transformation of the Establishment.

Even before 1800 the tithe problem touched upon almost all of the factors which were to sustain Irish disturbances from 1800 to the tithe's commutation in 1838. The medieval Church was organized on a monastic rather than a diocesan model, with monks living in communal conditions often paralleling the tribal organization of Irish life as a whole. Before the Norman invasion it was sustained by voluntary gifts or by the largess of the tribal leaders, whose own families often staffed the most important ecclesiastical offices. After the Norman invasion, the diocesan system preferred by Rome was made universal and uniform in Ireland. As a result of the decrees passed at the Synods of Cashel and Dublin in 1175 and 1186 respectively, ecclesiastical finances were based on a levy of one-tenth of the parishes' agricultural produce. Before the Reformation, however, tithing was practiced with consistency only within the narrow pale of English rule. In1541, in the context of the Henrician reformation, new legislation provided for the extension of the tithe system throughout the country. This law, too, was only haphazardly applied until systematic construction of the Elizabethan Church provided a basis for more rigid exaction of the tithe. During the period of colonization of Ulster under James I Presbyterians were also permitted to tithe; after 1660 Presbyterians were deprived of their tithes and the Church of Ireland's complete control was once more confirmed.

Agitation against tithes was not slow to emerge in the wake of the gradual extension of English rule. In 1612 one observer noted that peasants often resisted payment. Jonathan Swift a century later declared that the payment of tithes was "subject to so many frauds, wrangles and difficulties, not only from papists and dissenters, but even from those who profess themselves Protestants, that by the expense, trouble and vexation of collection or bargaining for them, they are of all other rents, the most precarious, uncertain and illpaid."[1] These "precarious" circumstances were in part due to unsettled conditions during the sixteenth and seventeenth centuries, which disoriented the tithe system in two ways. Many tithe rights fell into the hands of lay impropriators, who watched the decay of the Protestant Establishement without serious alarm and who easily forgot that recipients were supposed to provide, or see that others provided, religious services. Impropriators controlled the rectorial tithes in nearly one fourth of Ireland's parishes in the late eighteenth century, with the percentage ranging as high as 38% in Kildare and Waterford and Lismore, 46% in Killala and Achonry, and 61% in Elphin. One hundred eighteen parishes were totally impropriate.[2] As late as 1832 more than onesixth of all parochial income from tithes was still in lay hands.[3] Others were appropriated by bishops and cathedral offices, or by the Crown or Trinity, to sustain the higher clergy or diverse institutions of varying degrees of usefulness. In 1832 tithes appropriate amounted in value to Ł48,000, or about seven percent of the total.[4]

These handicaps notwithstanding, a generation of peace after
James II's abortive reign in Ireland in 1688 and 1689 saw growing agricultural prosperity and increased tillage provide the Church a level
of income far in excess of what Irish landlords and their clergy deserved.[5] The extent of ecclesiastical wealth focused attention on
their claims to tithe on pasturage, which increased as enclosure acts
became more common. In 1707 clerical tithe rights in Ireland were
confirmed by the Court of King's Bench; in 1722 landlord efforts to
relieve pasture from the tithe were again blocked by the courts.
Finally in 1735 a committee of the Irish House of Commons concluded
somewhat preemptorily that tithes need not be paid on cattle. Irish
churchmen were intimidated by threats of an open examination of the
Church. The tithe motion passed. It did not become law until 1800,
but was regarded as such from 1730.[6]

The legislative fiat by which the Irish House of Commons removing the tithe from pasture in 1735 discouraged tillage at a time when
the nation's population was increasing. It threw almost the entire
burden of supporting the Established Church on a Catholic peasant population.[7] By 1760 the masses of Irish tenants were, for several reasons, less disposed than previously to sustain the system without protest. Despite their unilateral and patently illegal suspension of
tithes on agistment or pasture, many Irish landlords, especially those
of modest incomes and constant residence, continued to criticize the
tithe and did little to discourage their tenants from resisting making
payments to the clergy. Rapidly advancing rackrents, facilitated by
ever more intensive cultivation of tillage plots, made tithes and rack-

rents an almost intolerable burden in some districts. When forced to choose between satisfying the landlords or clergymen, tenants in-variably favored the former. Irish Catholics' growing assertiveness and declining penal restrictions offered new opportunities for collec-tive opposition to the tithe. Finally, increasing use of proctors for evaluation and collection did much to alienate the beneficed clergy from their parishioners and to occasion semi-annual confrontations between these agents and tithe payers.

After 1760 tithe agitation began to take on a more menacing tone, although the existence of other factors complicates accurate analysis of Irish rural agitation. Throughout the century there had been spora-dic disturbances, especially in Munster. In 1761 agitation became more widespread and was sustained by semi-secret societies of peasant far-mers.[8] These disturbances were directed as much against enclosures as against the tithe, and Catholic priests found that they as well as the beneficed clergy were objects of peasant wrath.[9] Agitation diminished after several years and by 1770 even Munster, most sensitive to these periods of unrest, seems to have been quiet. After 1775 there was more trouble, and this time the tithe was the particular object of local dissatisfaction. By 1785 rural disturbance was sufficiently widespread to prompt a considerable pamphlet effort by the tithe's opponents and defenders alike, and the government sponsored bills for the protection of the clergy and more effective punishment for those engaged in con-spiratorial combinations.[10]

While many areas continued to remain quiet even in this period, the Irish legislature did see fit to launch the first of what would

prove dozens of investigations into the tithe question and to offer
suggestions for reform. The inquiry proved confusing: witnesses
followed one another with conflicting opinions as to the cause and
nature of the disturbance, the degree of conspiracy, the exactions
of the clergy, and the oppressiveness and vexatiousness of the impost
itself. Some clergymen directly accused landlords of fomenting agitation to deflect attention from the rackrents. Some landlords blamed
the problem entirely on clerical absenteeism and their proctors' greed
and insensitivity.[11] Countless tales of clerical murder and maiming
appeared in newspapers and debates, most of which proved to be the
product of agitated imaginations. A subsidiary debate tried without
success to determine whether tithe agitation represented dissatisfaction with the Protestant clergy themselves or with economic considerations. The Catholic clergy were accused on one hand of fomenting disturbance, and on the other charged with rapaciousness in their own
charges for ministrations.

As the tumult continued the tithe issue slowly became a source
of partisan controversy. The Irish government felt obliged to suggest
a plan. The Church would certainly oppose this initiative, Pitt informed the Irish viceroy, but if reform was dangerous, inaction was
worse.[12] The government sought the Church's advice and resolved to
defend the temporal prerogatives of the Irish Establishment. This
activity resulted in two tithe acts of limited effectiveness: 27
George III c. 15 addressed itself to illegal combinations and perpe-
trators of agrarian disturbance, to those who would destroy ecclesiastical property or defraud the clergy of their tithes, and to impedi-

ments to tithe evaluation;[13] a second act in the same year, 1787, compensated clergy for tithe losses, and permitted clergymen in specific areas to sue for tithes in secular rather than ecclesiastical courts. The first measure proved difficult to enforce; the second was renewed once and then suspended.[14] These palliatives were resisted by Henry Grattan and Irish Protestant nationalists, who opted for conversion of the tithe into a land tax. Grattan made a lasting impression on the Irish House of Commons but met with a series of legislative defeats by 1789.[15]

At length this agitation also subsided, but not without leaving indelible imprints upon Irish life. While the Irish Parliament might rail against tithe abuses, it was both unwilling and unable to recify or mitigate them because of complex vested interests and widespread fears that reform here would endanger the landlord' position.[16] On the other hand, forces friendly to the Church were beginning to mobilize their energies in an uncompromising support of the tithe. Richard Woodward, one time Dean of Clogher and now Bishop of Cloyne, responded to critics with a closely reasoned, strongly worded defense of the tithe in 1786; such was the popularity of the subject that his pamphlet went through six editions within four weeks.[17] The pamphlet's success heartened the Church and precipitated dozens more. Catholics and Presbyterians discovered, to their surprise, that they were allies against a common evil. Landlords realized rackrents were also threatened.

Most important was the formation of secret anti-tithe societies on a permanent basis. In Ulster Protestant groups began launching

daybreak house to house searches for peasants' arms and earned themselves the appelation Peep o'Day Boys. They supplemented their vigi-
lante work with attacks on Catholic houses and churches and destroyed
what they could. Catholics responded under the name "Defenders."
They soon moved beyond mere protection of their property and persons to
general agitation throughout Ireland, even in districts where Protestants were scarce. Both groups tended to degenerate into gangs of
thugs and robbers, insensitive to property rights in general, alive
to any pretext for agitation, and destined to undermine Ireland's
fragile peace during the next half century.[18]

The rebellion of 1798 set the stage for a full-scale confrontation between the Established Church and the Irish peasantry. The revolt itself was largely Presbyterian in origin and essentially political in nature, but disaffected Catholic peasants in Southern Ireland
soon translated it into a class war revolving around land. The Act of
Union was one response. The tithe question, meanwhile, was aired in
high circles. Pitt favored substantial reform, probably commutation
to land. His supporter Castlereagh may have suggested adding Presbyterian and Catholic clergymen to the list of beneficiaries of the
tithe.[19] Even the notorious absentee Bishop of Derry forwarded a
letter from Venice suggesting reform was necessary.[20] But the Church
was strongly opposed to any infringement on its rights, and only with
difficulty was it persuaded to support a bill to make permanent the
exemption of agistment from the tithe.[21] But Pitt dared not oppose
the bishops at a time when their patronage was desperately needed in
order to induce the Irish legislature to vote itself into extinction.

Plans for a more substantial tithe reform were therefore abandoned.

The lull which followed defeat of Wolf Tone and his comrades proved a short one. By 1806 a new wave of insurgency under the name "Thrashers" was convulsing Connaught and parts of Munster. So grave was the agitation that special commissions could not move through the country except under military escort. Summonses could not be delivered without dramatic displays of force. The rapidly deteriorating situation caught the attention of the new Whig administration which succeeded Hardwicke early in 1806, but it was not until the following winter, only three months removed from the collapse of the Whig experiment in Irish reform, that Grenville and Bedford came to grips with the problem.[22] Between 1800 and 1806 Castlereagh had continued to develop his own opinions. These came to Grenville's attention. They may have made some impression on the Whig ministry and are worth noting in detail. Castlereagh believed rents disruptive to good agricultural practices, attributed rural agitation to the collection process, blamed peasants for combinations against clergymen, and thought the tithe burden inequitably distributed. Castlereagh thereupon suggested conversion of tithes to a uniform money rate fixed by civil officials for twenty one years, with periodic revaluation. Adjustments would reflect grain prices. Proctors would be eliminated, and agistment again made liable to the levy. During the same period the fertile mind of the Marquis of Buckingham, Grenville's eldest brother, a Whig grandee, and onetime Irish Lord Lieutenant, was also active. Buckingham tended to complicate his proposals with burdensome amendments, but he too looked to a land tax pegged to grain prices.[23]

Grenville had apparently examined these suggestions in some detail prior to becoming Prime Minister. In March 1806 he devoted a long section in his dispatches to Bedford to suggestions for tithe reform, concentrating in the first instance on efforts to appease Irish Churchmen and only secondarily on substantive issues.[24] Grenville's approach, cautious as it was, seemed certain to invite the intrusion of Parliament into ecclesiastical affairs, and Bedford's declarations of confidence in Stuart's conciliatory tone did not remove his doubts.[25] Grenville referred to the Castlereagh-Buckingham land tax proposal with a pervasive air of resignation, and seemed no more enthusiastic about conversion of tithes to long leases or about the simple palliative of exempting indigent cottiers. Bedford for his part was eager, but also confused. At first he wrote from Dublin Castle arguing in favor of an institutionalized tithe evaluation program, with tithes being charged to owners, not tenants. Later he turned to commutation to land. He, as had Grenville, concluded that Parliament was unlikely to approve either solution and the ministry fell before he had time to develop new initiatives.[26] The tithe problem, once more, became part of the heritage passed on to the next administration.

The Tory restoration in 1807 saw the Duke of Richmond and Arthur Wellesley, on leave from the army, forced to confront the tithe issue directly. Their recognition of the gravity of the problem, prompted by massive expressions of popular discontent, coincided with a new surge of debate, the first since the Act of Union, on the question of tithe reform. Ireland now witnessed one of the most extensive pamphlet debates in its history. It is worthwhile to examine in detail those points of discussion and dispute which were destined to sustain tithe

agitation until the problem was finally resolved by Parliament in 1838.

We may divide this discussion into several parts; varying estimates of

revenue gained by the Church and by lay impropriators from the tithe;

the arguments employed by the Church to defend the tithe; the pattern

of tithe resistance; and proposals for reform.

Defining the tithe and estimating its value was long a principal

preoccupation of apologists and critics alike. In the eighteenth cen-

tury Sir William Blackstone defined the tithe as "the tenth part of

the increase, yearly arising and renewing from the profits of lands,

the stock upon lands, and the personal industry of the inhabitants."[27]

By 1800 economists and theologians distinguished three types: praedial,

which arose immediately from the ground, such as grain, hay, woods,

and fruit; mixed, which were based on objects deriving their value

from products of the earth, such as cattle; and personal, stemming

from the labor of man. Personal tithes were seldom paid in either

Britain or Ireland. Tithes were also divided into "great" and "small";

the former included corn, hay, and wood; the latter encompassed prae-

dial tithes of all other kinds and all mixed and personal tithes.

Tithes were not due from mines, a non-renewable item, or from turf or

gravel, because they were a part, not a product, of the soil. Barren

land converted to tillage was exempt from tithes for seven years, but

fertile lands, such as woods, if converted, must pay immediately.

Glebe lands were exempt if held by clergymen, but not if rented.. Ad-

judicating this welter of complicated formulas was the responsibility

of the ecclesiastical courts if the right was already established, and

of civil courts if the right itself was disputed.[28] The principal
inequity, it seemed, concerned the status of the potato. It was
generally exempt from taxation in the north but a mainstay of tithe
revenue in southern Ireland, where it also constituted the peasants'
principal foodstuff. Hay was often charged a flat fee, whatever the
size of the farm. On wheat the tithe might vary from 4/- per acre to
20/-. In one area even seafood was tithed.[29] As a result of these
uncertainties, estimates of the revenue accruing to the clergy ranged
over a wonderfully wide range from ₤200,000 to ₤3,250,000. Most
moderate estimates were near ₤600,000. The ecclesiastical commissioners estimate of ₤640,000 in 1832 probably marked a decline in tithe
rates of some thirty percent since 1815.[30]

Defense of the tithe rested on the twin foundations of property
rights and intrinsic advantage. Property rights were in turn extended
to comprehend allegations of a conspiracy to destroy the Established
Church altogether and identification of ecclesiastical prerogatives
with those of all other landed elements in the country. The tithe was
the basis of all order, for it sustained the Church which in turn
strove to convert the island to Protestantism, the only firm guarantee
of loyalty to the crown. The tithe for its part cemented the erastian
alliance by making the Church dependent on the state for its temporal
well-being and by intensifying the sanctity of private rights, the
basis of all order.[31] The tithe strengthened Britain's power in Ireland by appealing to the self-interest of lay impropriators, who could
see that the collapse of this species of property would endanger the
union itself.[32]

The Church placed particular emphasis on the interdependence of tithes and rents, an argument flexible enough to enlist the support of landlords and tenants alike. Landowners were constantly reminded that the habit of subversion reflected in tithe agitation must eventually undermine rents; Woodward made this a principal point of his exposition and it was so often repeated thereafter as to seem axiomatic. Lord Roden, a prominent Irish landlord noted that in Ireland landlords were not only reluctant to support the Church's property rights, but also actually encouraged tithe agitation as one way to deflect attention from rents, and indeed even took advantage of the situation to increase their own rents.

The obvious insensitivity of many landlords to this emphasis upon the similarity of tithes and rents induced churchmen themselves to present the other side of the coin to the tenants. As early as 1728 the Church developed the argument that disappearance of the tithe would result in increased rents: since landlords were more efficient than the clergy in the execution of their rights tenants would pay more than ever. This argument was put in a more sophisticated form by Adam Smith, who advanced the theory that "taxes upon the produce of the land are in reality taxes upon the rent, and, though they may be originally advanced by the farmer, are finally paid by the landlord. When a certain portion of the produce is to be paid away for a tax, the farmer computes. . . what the value of this portion is likely to amount to, and he makes a proportional abatement in the rent which he agrees to pay to the landlord."[33] This argument Archbishop Whately of Dublin thought a most effective opposition to the elimination of the tithes. Indeed others pressed on to declare that tithes actually encouraged industry since in each added increment of profit the proportion representing profit exceeded the ratio of profit to the previous base. The property argument was also employed to prove that tenants' complaints were completely unjustified, since the tithe rested in the land and was not paid by tenants at all. As a reserved rent inseparable from the land, the tithe was in fact paid by the owners, mostly Protestant, and not by Catholic rentiers. Catholics opposed to the tithe were free to forego taking leases; contracting to rent land signified a willingness to assume all the legal burdens attached.[34]

Landlords were unlikely to identify tithes with rent until agitation should endanger both rather than merely the former. Tenants were even less likely to be impressed by the idea of "reserved rent" while they were in fact forced to pay the impost. This did not vitiate property rights as an effective defense, for the Church could appeal with considerable force to current conceptions of property as an inviolable right, whatever the usefulness of the derived income and whatever the vexation encountered in sustaining it. Patrick Duigenan observed that no distinction could be made in the eyes of the British constitution between lay and ecclesiastical property. Both could be taxed, but neither confiscated. Both could be regulated, but neither diminished.[35] Many others, even some who were otherwise critical of the Establishment, felt obliged to agree. Even those who conceded that ecclesiastical property was held by the state in trust denied that the trustee's responsibilities went beyond defending it. Nor would the Church concede that tithes had ever belonged to the state; the

itle was medieval, preceding the state by centuries, and belonging
to the Church by virtue of its prerogatives as the Establishment.[36]
When clever antagonists then demanded the property be restored to the
Catholic Church, other researchers presented evidence that most property had been accrued by the Establishment's own devices after the
reformation.[37]

Whatever its defects, emphasizing that the tithe was indistinguishable from other property rights proved to be the most powerful
defense devised in long decades of verbal confrontation. The Church,
indeed, was often seen only in terms of its properties. Conservatives
"thought of nothing but of the Church in terms of defending that property. Radicals thought only of using that property for other purposes." The Church of course extended its arguments to include glebes
and episcopal holdings, but the main objective was the tithe, and such
close identification of the tithe with the larger question of the
efficacy of the Establishment suggested that the Church would rise or
fall on the property question alone.[38] The call to the barricades for
defense of property rights struck some others as absurd, but not the
beneficed clergy. The Church became enamoured of its own arguments and
tithe agitation was soon equated with subversion of the Irish and Eng-
list Establishments and Protestantism in general.[39] "Instead of seeing
the proud shield of the government and legislature extended over the
Church," these agitators expected "to find her discountenanced and un-
protected, and then they shall succeed in establishing an opinion that
popularity is to be purchased by mere plunder." Even senior members of
the bench believed this, and by 1830 so fixed was the notion that tithe

reform meant the end of Irish Protestantism that many bishops prepared
to tolerate substantial administrative reform and government intervention in redistribution of church revenues could not condone any
rearrangement of the vexatious tithe.[40]

Subsidiary points in defense of the tithe appeared as the occasion
warranted. Some optimists believed that increasing tithe agitation reflected Catholic efforts to destroy the rapidly reforming Establishment
before it would be challenged itself. Others denied that tithe agitation was more than a local problem. Tithes were held to encourage con-
sistent residence, for tithe collection was difficult if clergymen relied solely on proctors. The beneficed clergy, furthermore, were by
their residence demonstrating their ability to improve local agriculture, raise the level of education, and reduce social tensions. Indeed, the tithe was actually popular; for every instance of ill-feel-
ing caused by tithe process, there had been "a thousand instances
where the parishioners consider[ed] themselves well treated."[41] The
tithe was efficacious: England was better cultivated than Ireland and
yet paid a much stricter tithe; Scotland was poor because it did not
have the blessings of tithing. The tithe was flexible; it increased
in value during periods of prosperity, and dwindled in hard times.
It was collected with considerable compassion, so that no clergyman in
fact received a full tenth of the amount due him. Duigenan declared
that "the moderation of the established clergy was unparalleled."[42]
Indeed, such moderation encouraged condemnation of those clergymen who
pressed for their entire due. The tithe also deserved defense because
there had never been devised a way to support the clergy more appropri-

ite and more convenient to the nature of their calling. The clergy-

lan could not be expected to farm his own land. To add clerical

salaries to the county tax would aggravate already pronounced in-

equities and encourage widespread resistance to that impost. Commu-

ation would injure Protestantism by giving the large number of that

ody who wished to transfer residence from Ireland to England a chance

o sell their property. The tithe also kept the Church dependent on

he state and reduced the temptation to look to Rome or elsewhere for

upport.[43]

All of these subsidiary arguments were pressed with zeal and sup-

orted by ingenious if sometimes tortured reasoning. They were fash-

oned not so much to buttress arguments based on private property rights

ut to challenge the broad front of attack sustained by the tithe's

etractors. Opponents of the tithe refused to restrict debate to pro-

erty questions alone, where the Church's position seemed exceptionally

trong and at times impregnable. Instead, they spared no effort to

emonstrate that a tax so vexatious in its operation and so inefficient

n its purpose endangered the Irish government, the Established Church,

he national economy, and even the structure of society. The state,

herefore, could indeed exercise its prerogative in reforming or abol-

shing the tithe, for all discussion of property questions would be

cademic if the social system collapsed around the tithe. The beneficed

lergy were also severly criticized, much criticism attached to evi-

ence showing that the system defiled the clergy, rather than the

pposite, and that prospects for improvement and indeed the survival

f the Church demanded radical changes.

All opponents, whatever their reasons for reform, agreed that
the tithe was vexatious far beyond any redeeming features claimed by
its supporters and notwithstanding its alleged identification with
divine will and property rights. In 1788 Henry Grattan declared that
tithe owners, bent on enforcement of their rights, invariably converted
"authority into corruption, and law into peculation."[44] Others
contended that Catholics protested not the right, only the manner of
collection. Economists complained that the tithe forced good tillage
into pasture and discouraged improvements.[45] A generation later another commentator characterized the tithe as

> a tax more vexatious than oppressive, and more impolitic
> than either; vexatious, because paid directly and in kind,
> at unequal and fluctuating rates, impolitic, because it is
> vexatious - because a people, unanimous in this alone, de-
> claim against it - because it might be replaced by a more
> equal, certain, and satisfactory imposition.[46]

Much of this vexation reflected a hidebound allegiance to
antiquated methods of payment and evaluation which failed to accomodate
rapidly changing agricultural conditions in Ireland. In theory the
tithe could be paid in kind. In practice it was commuted to a money
payment supposedly somewhat lower than the market rate in order to encourage cash settlements. In Ireland payment in money was also necessitated by unions. No parson could be expected to gather in the produce
of a large, heavily cultivated region, and make arrangements for disposal before spoilage. During periods of resistance some areas reverted to payment in kind. This alarmed the clergy, who hastened to
court to enter charges of conspiracy. The courts agreed that payment
in kind was conspiratorial if the food could not be sold before spoil-

age, and looked with favor on any technical procedural fault a tithe payer might have committed in the process of declaring his intentions.[47] Payment in kind, where indulged, meant more assiduous effort at collection of the full tenth, which, as one observer noted, "would be attended with the ruin of the whole people."[48] Methods of evaluation were even more troublesome. Tenants complained that harvest estimates were often made in mid-summer, before early frosts or heavy rains destroyed portions of the crop. Appeals against evaluations were generally useless, since they were heard in ecclesiastical courts with their inescapable prejudices, exhorbitant costs, lack of publicity and summary judgments.[49] Constant subdivision of plots complicated the work of tithe surveyors, and proved to time-consuming that few clergymen were inclined to superintend it themselves. Responsibility for the execution of the clergy's rights, as a result, gravitated to tithe proctors, whose peculiar characteristics must be reserved for separate scrutiny.

Legal devices intended to enforce payment and punish the recalcitrant were often worse than the disease. Irish tithe enforcement legislation, while more rigorous than that in England, was not adequate. In theory tithe "was recoverable by a cumbrous process in ecclesiastical courts, in the Exchequer by a bill of equity, when a number of defendants could be proceeded against at a time, by summary proceedings before two magistrates for sum up to ₺10 or by distress, when an individual's goods could be seized and sold."[50] These seemingly formidable agencies were in fact defective in terms of most tithe payment problems, associated as they were with Ireland's minute tenant holdings. One tenant, with tithe obligations of only a shilling found his cattle impounded several times a year; he pleaded as an excuse the sheer impossibility of keeping up with his vestry and grand jury cesses and crown rents along with the tithe, "all this upon a plot of ground not exceeding an acre."[51] All these functions of the tithe alienated many who supported the tithe in principle; there were many who "would . . . pay cheerfully for the maintenance of the clergy provided it was levied in another manner than everlastingly struggling to wrench from he payee] the tenth of his hard earnings."[52]

A second and insuperable objection to tithes in the minds of opponents was the invidious mold in which the operation of the system cast the Established clergy. It was a sufficient objection that the tithe was paid by largely Catholic tenantry to a Protestant clergy; it was worse yet that many of the recipients resided in their parishes infrequently or not at all.[53] Those clergy most conscientious about their pastoral duties were often the most vociferous in their opposition to the tithe system as it stood. There was a "positive inconsistency" between the aspect of the clergy as gentle shepherds and their role as tithe collectors. If gentle, parishioners refused to pay their tithes, and if harsh, they violated the character appropriate to the religious calling.

This sense of alienation was most forcefully reflected in the Established Church's dismal proselytism record. Tithes were "the original sin" attached to Irish land. Tithes so enflamed the laity that they would "purchase [the clergy's] absence" if they could.[54] "The virulence indeed with which men speak of the clergy universally, in respect to the drawing of tithes," commented one dispassionate ob-

erver, "can leave no doubt that this bias of mind has taken deep root
and will be difficult to eradicate."[55] Whatever the legal question,
the tithe was "inconsistent with Christianity" and could not be sustained. Instances in which clergymen hoisted themselves over fences,
seized cattle, forced the gates, and thus avenged a defaulting tithe
payer, or summoned a military contingent to force payment, were pro-
ably less frequent than generally alleged. They were sufficiently
commonplace, however, to lend credence to popular stories and newspaper
accounts.[56]

A most unfortunate side effect was the opportunity afforded a
minority of unprincipled clergymen to advance their revenues by assiduous cultivation of the legal complexities which surrounded the tithe.
As early as 1785 Grattan remarked of the Established clergy that "when
their God, their Redeemer, and their Country" were in question, they
were silent; "but when a twelve-penny point on their tithe" was
brought forward, they were "vivacious." There were more subtle methods
of improving one's lot. Tithes were customarily renegotiated upon the
installation of a new incumbent, with attendant opportunities for early
expressions of bad will between pastor and parishioners.[57] Those
dissatisfied with the contract might follow a pattern similar to this
manifestly biased and unsympathetic account:

> Suppose, the contract was concluded for the incumbency of the
> parson, and, he, forgotten man! had been doomed to remain
> longer in his parish than his virtues or his expectancy de-
> served; he becomes sad, and merely to divert his sorrow, he
> wishes to advance his tithes. Perhaps, the neighboring par-
> son has just made a more advantageous bargain with his people.
> He laments his situation; his brothers cannot refrain from
> sympathizing with so interesting a sufferer so peculiarly
> afflicted. A conference is called; the contract is reviewed,

> and if found technically defective is annulled. If it be
> valid, alas! . . . All make common cause. Fortunately
> for the whole clerical corporation, another parson finds
> himself aggrieved, in a similar manner. The sufferers meet,
> and . . . they agree to exchange; the difference in value
> of the livings is arranged. . . and the superintending
> authorities ratify the sacred work. By this means the
> leases of both their parishioners are voided, and each is
> let loose on the other parish, to exact with improved vigi-
> lance.[58]

This was hardly a commonplace event, but it did happen, and it was,

understandably, hotly resented. It was not the only type of fiscal

manipulation known to this small minority of the clergy, most of whom

were products of unsalubrious patronage practices and almost always

non-resident. Some clergymen were careful to grant preferential treat-

ment to large landlords, and thus to make it appear their tithe de-

mands were universally mild. Instances of forcing acceptance of a

revised agreement which illiterate peasants did not understand or of

manipulation of parochial groups against each other also occurred.[59]

These practices were not common, but many, perhaps most, Irishmen chose

to believe otherwise, and the reputation of the clergy suffered griev-

ously as a result.

Because unsavory connotations were frequently attached to evalua-

tion and collection of the tithe, many clergymen preferred to entrust

their rights to agents, or proctors. These agents have commanded a

place in Irish history almost unique in terms of disopprobrium and

universal bitterness. Most were engaged by the clergy to set the tithe

at harvest time and to receive payments the following spring. Some

were hired by the vestry to supervise composition agreements. Many of

them also worked for landlords as rent agents, and tenants would not be xpected to differentiate too carefully between the proctors' work as

erald of rackrents and as collector of tithes. Tenants were not alone

n their fulminations against the proctors; many incumbents were

hemselves victims of their proverbial greed and complained that they

ere defrauded of their tithe more frequently than tenants were driven

o excessive payments. In defense of the proctor, it must be noted

hat the role of middleman finds few champions in any society. Tithe

valuation and collection was an immensely complex task. As the party

ost immediately concerned with the operation of the system the proctor

as certain to be the recipient of a goodly part of peasant wrath and

lerical suspicion. This allowance, however, does not remedy what re-

ains one of the saddest chapters in modern Irish history.

The institution of the tithe proctor reflected the vexatious na-

ure of the tithe itself. The clergy defended their employment by re-

erring to the cumbersome nature of collection, with its time-consuming

djustments and tendency to encourage acrimonious confrontations.[60]

ithe collection also required a financial ken quite foreign to most

lergymen, and resistance to payment forced many incumbents otherwise

nclined to supervise the tithe personally to enlist proctors' assist-

nce. It is clear that many clergymen believed themselves, not the

easantry, the most frequent object of proctors' manipulation.[61] It is

lso true that many proctors aggravated their relations with other par-

ies by resorting to unwholesome practices in collecting imposts. They

tuffed ecclesiastical courts with petty claims and warped the law to

it their requirements. They forced entry into private quarters with-

ut warrant and appropriated property without authorization. They encouraged peasant indebtedness and increased their incomes by charging

exhorbitant interest rates. Few clergymen received a full tenth.

They regarded tenants' protests that they paid much more than a tenth

as groundless. Proctors even staffed bars and saloons within which

lightheaded clients ratified tithe increases.[62] Many of the clergy

were ignorant of these malpractices, though ignorance, where founded

on constant non-residence, merits little sympathy.[63] Others felt obliged

to   tolerate these disreputable devices of their agents because of

the recalcitrance of tithe payers. A few were convinced that resis-

tance merited whatever procedures proctors felt inclined to employ.

The proctor, then, was a symptom of Ireland's, and the Church's, prob-

lems. As long as the land remained subject to unwieldy and unpopular

imposts it was unlikely to expect proctors would either disappear or

alter their tactics. And as long as clerical absenteeism remained wide-

spread it was extremely difficult to control these agents and circum-

scribe their abuses. The proctor flourished with rackrents and the

tithe, and died out only with their abolition.[64]

Tithe resistance reflected widespread peasant dissatisfaction

stemming from intrinsic difficulties with the tithe itself. But a

further source of opposition reflected landlords' attitudes, over which

the Church had almost no control and whose grievances were not always

associated with the tithe system at all. Early in the eighteenth cen-

tury Archbishop Boulter complained that landlords were obstructing tithe

collections by ignoring the verdicts of ecclesiastical courts.[65] Land-

lords avoided their magisterial duties of enforcing tithes by refusing

to lease out land on which tithes were paid so as to be able to declare

a conflict of interest. At other times they undertook to help the
clergy only if promised a portion of the revenues. By 1780 clergymen
were complaining that some members of the Protestant gentry were encouraging acts of terrorism.[66] In 1797 a group of West Ireland landlords signed a proclamation opposing tithes. Arthur Wellesley as Irish
Chief Secretary felt obliged to express his astonishment "that any set
of gentlemen having landed property should ever have thought of passing
resolutions the effect of which must be to shake the title of all landed property," destroy the Established Church, and undermine British
control.

Wellesley's strictures seem to have made little impression; his
successors continued to hear allegations of a gentry conspiracy.[67] In
1825 a select committee of the House of Commons was informed that
tithes were opposed as much by Protestant landholders as by Catholic
tenants; indeed, there was "a remarkable coincidence in the language
of the two classes upon the subject."[68] The persistence of this estrangement of the largely Protestant landlord class from the tithe system was explained by the Church as a reflection of greed for its property, by landlords themselves by reference to the tithe-engendered
turmoil, and by nonaligned observers as a gentry effort to deflect
popular clamor from evils of rackrent. Boulter in 1728 thought that
landlords resented the clergy's participation in Ireland's increasing
prosperity, and wanted everything produced by tenants beyond their own
subsistence requirements to accrue to the gentry. He repeated these
sentiments to Walpole nine years later.[69] Woodward again referred to
hem in 1786 when he went so far as to lay the blame for the renewal of

tithe agitation squarely on the shoulders of the middling gentry.
Woodward's remarks were regarded as inflammatory, but after 1800
there was considerable evidence that landlord dissatisfaction was a
hearty exercise among the less affluent gentry. Their own constant
residence made them sensitive to rural dislocation and their resentment of greater landlords' monopoly of Church preferment vented itself on attacks on the ecclesiastical Establishment.[70] After 1830,
with the renewal of widespread tithe agitation, the middle gentry
proved less willing to countenance resistance, for at last Wellesley's reference to the destruction of all property rights seemed about
to come true. The gentry's conversion, such as it was, came too late
to salvage the tithe, and perhaps to save rackrents as well.[71]

The obvious religious connotation of the tithe led some clergymen to conclude that tithe resistance was primarily a vehicle for
Catholic opposition to Protestant theology and proselytism. Statistics
offered ready proof that tithe resistance was most widespread in the
most Catholic areas of Ireland. Tithe resistors were Catholic in a
percentage even greater than the Catholic proportion to the population,
and since the intensity of opposition rested among those paying the
smallest tithes, religious factors must be looked to as a primary cause.
Against this extraordinary reasoning one could note that most tillage
farmers were Catholics; largely Protestant graziers escaped the tithe.[72]
Catholics represented the poorest sector of the population and suffered
from the tax far more than others, and had less to lose by recourse to
resistance in periods of intense distress.

While many clergymen had long claimed to see a relationship beween Catholicism and tithe resistance, no effort was made to cast

he connection in statistical terms until 1825, when a select commit-

ee addressed itself to the problem. Most of the testimony given be-

ore the committee proved inconclusive; Catholics did indeed oppose

he tithe, but not, it seemed, to an appreciably greater degree than

rotestant and Presbyterian tenants.[73] Daniel Murray, the Catholic

rchbishop of Dublin, argued with some force that the clergy found

rotestant resistance, though more subtle, also more effective, for

rotestants could avail themselves of court delays and outspend the

lergy. Others believed that Catholic peasants' resistance to the

emands made by their own clergy suggested that their opposition to

he tithe was not primarily religious. Lord Melbourne, Irish Chief

ecretary briefly in 1827 and 1828, thought he saw a similar pattern

n his observations when larger farmers, again mostly Protestant, pre-

erred to turn to grazing rather than be subject to the tithe.[74] After

830 resistance gradually became almost entirely Catholic as Protes-

ant alarm at the Catholic resurgence encouraged more assiduous defense

f the Establishment.

In the sixty years encompassing large scale and concerted tithe

esistance suggestions for reform were understandably numerous and com-

lex. Three very broad categories of questions presented themselves:

ould the tithe be reformed or abolished?; should the tithe be retained

nd its revenues directed to new objectives?; could the tithe in its

resent form be abolished without a clear violation of vested property

ights? The first question in turn suggested two areas of concern:

ere tithes divine or human in their origin?; what powers did the state have in supervision of ecclesiastical wealth? Debate over the

tithe's divinity inevitably shed more heat than light. Church scholars

rushed into print with detailed and closely documented scriptural

exegesis and long before 1800 were satisfied that the tithe was divine

in inspiration and therefore unalterable. After 1800 Churchmen in high

places proved reluctant to base their defense on the rock of scripture.

One Dean of Ferns cast a popular sentiment in concise terms when he

questioned the opinions of those who denied the tithe could ever be

extinguished. "The law of moral and political necessity superseding

all tithes places but little regard to the fanciful intangibility of

any distinct species of property, however insulated by prejudice, or

sanctioned by time." There came a time wherein all property must bow

to public necessity. This view was gradually accepted by others.[75]

The right of the state to deprive the Church of its tithes, how-

ever, was not so readily conceded. Private property was an issue of

immense sensitivity, and tithe opponents were perforce reluctant to

confront the question directly. A few commentators adopted the pre-

mise that tithes, like slavery, were unchristian and thus could be

extinguished. Most observers however emphasized the right of the

state to alter the method by which the erastian structure was sustained.

The Reformation was an instance of state intervention in ecclesiastical

affairs, and when Churchmen dared to complain that this was itself

illegal, others demanded that the property revert to Catholics. In-

exorably the idea of the Church as a public corporation gained ground;

its property had been set apart for a specific purpose, and if subverted

the state could restore this property to its original function.[76]

Opposition to this view, however, subsided only very slowly, and as late as the 1830s a very considerable portion of public opinion was not yet prepared to countenance the idea of alienation of ecclesiastical property to secular uses. Determining what did and did not constitute a legitimate degree of intervention remained one of the most sensitive points of contention throughout the entire period of legislative reform.

For those satisfied that reform was necessary, and state intervention permissible, the logical next step was the nature of the proposed changes. Those points related themselves to changing the species of the property itself may be postponed until a discussion of parliamentary attempts to reform the tithe after 1800. A smaller number subscribed to imaginative formulas by which the taxation mechanism would remain but the revenues themselves would be redirected. Of these by far the most significant concerned revitalization of Ireland's rudimentary and archaic welfare system and concurrent establishment of the three principal Christian denominations. The possibility of using tithe revenue to alleviate Irish poverty exercised a peculiar fascination over some social reformers, whose enthusiasm at the prospect of channeling an already established comprehensive taxation system towards indigency obscured in their minds the vexatious, cumbersome and uneven character of the tax itself. In their effort to protect their rights the Established clergy found themselves opposing a worthy project. Their discomfort increased when diligent researchers uncovered precedents in scripture and in medieval Irish practice for devotion of one-fourth of the tithe to paupers. Nor did the clergy improve their image when they claimed that the portion intended for the poor had been confiscated by lay impropriators instead.[77]

Proposals for concurrent establishment, on the other hand, were less embarrassing to the beneficed clergy but far more dangerous in their larger implications. Some observers proclaimed their readiness to accept the Church's belief that tithes were divine, inviolable, and ecclesiastical in nature; they disputed, however, whether the Church of Ireland was a proper recipient. Others contended that a sharing of tithe revenue among all clergymen would nullify popular objections without raising the conundrum of property rights.[78] Far from undermining the Establishment, these optimists maintained, the new system would grant all groups a stake in society and opposition to the Establishment would disappear. Finally, Benthamites added that more efficient management of ecclesiastical property in general would provide considerable revenues of Presbyterians and Catholics without reducing that allocated to the Establishment.[79]

Proposals for redirection of revenue from the tithe floundered in almost insuperable objections. Most Protestants preferred complete extinction of the tithe to the application of even a small portion to the rival Catholic colossus. The implications of concurrent endowment, even in a limited area, were so dangerous that Church champions could scarcely contain their distress when alluding to the proposal. Even from a purely secular standpoint, alienation of property from the corporation whose prescriptive rights had not been challenged for two centuries was a dangerous course, and many middle class elements who thought the Irish Church otherwise indefensible could not bring themselves to support so radical a suggestion. But above all, the intrinsic difficulties of the impost itself militated against reforms which affected modes of distribution and not collection of revenue. The nub was in the operation of the impost as much as in its purpose, and here only an assault on the mode of collection could be expected to have satisfactory results.

The two principal proposals for reform of the tithe were composition to a land tax and commutation to land, with revenues from either designed to approximate a sum gained from the tithe at the time of conversion, and, with periodic adjustments, to equal anticipated revenues in the future. In that both proposals were closely involved in periodic legislative assaults on the tithe problem after 1800, the refinements of both may safely be considered in the context of their legislative appearance. Proposals for a tax raised several larger questions: 1) upon what species of property should the tax fall?; 2) who should be held responsible for collection of the tax?; 3) what form of taxation would most likely approximate tithe income at the time of conversion, and prove sufficiently flexible to correspond to what might have been the tithe income at a future date?; 4) should composition to a tax be considered a final settlement, or an intermediate step on the way to commutation? In this context, the tithe proved peculiarly difficult to convert, for it was not a burden on all the land, only tillage, and was not a uniform burden on tillage. It was not generally collected in its entirety. Its beneficiaries often held concurrent jurisdictions, and received a fraction of the tithe, not the whole. It encompassed potatoes and even seafood in some portions of Ireland, but not others. For all these reasons proposals for composition were exceedingly complex. Some suggested a tax on cattle and corn, some wanted pasture included, some affixed it to rent; some wanted landlords to collect it, others demanded special commissioners. Some wanted a permanent unalterable settlement; others suggested flexible and graduated scales.[80] For all these reasons, composition was destined to have a long and singularly unhappy parliamentary history in the nineteenth century.

The challenges of commutation to land were equally formidable. The clergy, and most bishops, displayed a solid opposition to commutation. Their determination was eroded neither by diminished revenues in periods of tithe agitation nor by arguments in favor of tithe commutation. Many believed it less permanent than the tithe, an attitude not easy to explain when the tithe resistance increased. Many were irreconcilably suspicious that commutation would be attended by massive efforts to defraud the Church of its property rights. Some forcast that the Establishment would be forced to deal with recalcitrant tenants in much the same fashion as it now was involved in tithe resistance. Some opponents of the Church also opposed commutation; the Establishment was already a considerable landowner in Ireland.[81]

There were, nonetheless, attractive, indeed almost irresistable, features. Commutation promised to end tempestuous clergy-laity altercations over tithes, to ameliorate the uncertainty of payment, and avoid recourse to cumbersome, expensive and largely ineffective ecclesiastical courts.[82] In the long run it could be expected that rents would appreciate even more rapidly than tithes, thereby avoiding the unhappy prospect of periodic revaluation. It was unlikely that renting the land would require more financial expertise than managing composition arrangements, and it promised less difficulty than tithe collection.[83]

Despite some clear English precedents for commutation, the conversion process did not promise to be smooth. During the eighteenth century enclosure movements in England had encouraged tithe commutation at a rate uniformly generous to the parson.[84] In Ireland enclosure was impossible as long as the rural population could not find urban employment. Landlords, moreover, were not likely to negotiate with the clergy in a spirit of good will. Land could not be purchased in a short period without raising land prices dramatically and thus disorienting commutation. Creation of a lucrative central fund during the transition period might tempt Parliament to direct ecclesiastical resources to other objectives. Gradual transition might encourage large scale peasant resistance and destroy the Church's temporal position entirely. For all of these reasons and others, commutation, although convenient in theory, was a particularly sensitive proposal and one which remained impossible to implement until the very end of tithe controversy in 1838.

While the nation disputed the tithe question in the public forum, the new Tory administration found itself in 1807 forced to contemplate reforms to confront intense agitation in the west of Ireland. Wellesley broached the subject in a long, thoughtful letter to Liverpool in October 1807. Wellesley noted that assemblies were adopting resolutions by unanimous vote protesting tithes. While the Irish government might intervene to prevent some of this protest in the future, it could not extirpate such feeling unless the Church presented a persuasive case in favor of the existing system or put forth proposals for reform. Wellesley considered reform both impossible and unpalatable. The present system, he urged, demanded a spirited and articulate defense. But even defending tithes demanded that Irish bishops supply accurate information on the tithe system as it operated within their jurisdictions. Such a request would alarm Churchmen who feared that their rights would be destroyed in the future, or that opponents' expectations would increase, or that it would raise hopes for a permanent settlement. "It was impossible to do anything," Wellesley concluded.

Stuart informed Wellesley that he was equally pessimistic. Whatever the utility of a tithe inquiry, he observed, many bishops and most clergymen would refuse to cooperate. Even a "private and confidential communication" through the archbishops was difficult. Brodrick and Stuart would cooperate, but of the other two archbishops one was indifferent and the other, Agar, was "wild upon the subject" of reform of any kind.[85]

Having raised the problem with Liverpool, Wellesley directed his energies towards opponents of the tithe, some of whom he hoped to convince that opposition to tithes meant opposition to the Established Church. To Lord Clarina, who had urged Wellesley to overturn the system completely, Wellesley expressed horror that Irish landlords would express such sentiments. "The same arrangements which lead to the conclusion that tithes ought to be <u>abolished</u>," he lectured Clarina, "would apply to a resolution that no rent ought to be paid." Not only will rents be undermined, but the Church, the state, and the British connection would all dissolve in their turn.[86]

Wellesley recognized that lecturing wayward Irish aristocrats was not enough. He communicated instructions to County lieutenants for mustering the militia and urged reinforcement of the army in Kerry.[87] These measures, he was satisfied, would prevent some of the meetings and had already "softened the violence" of resolutions in meetings which could not be prevented.[88] His appeals to London, meanwhile, were somewhat confusing. Adamant in his conviction that reform was impossible, he nevertheless thought it necessary to urge that the ministry develop a tithe reform proposal sufficient to parry criticism in Parliament. Lord Redesdale, the government's chief legal officer in Ireland, advanced a plan for compulsory composition based on an arbiter's estimate of clergymen's average receipts over the previous five years. Wellesley objected to Redesdale that this plan would violate private property tenets, and believed that exhaustive surveys, immense expenditures, and the imposition on the clergy involved in Redesdale's plan would accomplish nothing. Wellesley fashioned some suggestions of his own: a voluntary short-term composition coupled with strict enforcement of clerical residence. This he hoped would raise the tone of the relationship between the clergy and the people without undermining the private property concept involved in tithes.[89] But because Wellesley did not believe in the efficacy of reform, his own suggestions seemed insincere.

While Wellesley devoted his time to deprecating expressions of
tithe agitation in Munster and to dispelling the fears of Irish Churchmen, Liverpool attempted to frame suitable legislation in his capacity
as Home Secretary.[90] Stuart in his disconcerting but characteristic
way declared that if reform was indeed contemplated, it should be radical reform. His solution called for dismissing long leases and exempting cottier's holdings as mere palliatives. He called instead for a
system of regular, comprehensive tithe evaluations by the government,
and held out the prospect of eventual conversion of the tithe into
annuities and perhaps even into land.[91] While the primate would be
vindicated in 1838, he angered such Churchmen who were apprised of the
proposals and drove the Irish government into temporary though ill-
concealed confusion. Wellesley and Richmond were unable to contemplate so drastic an assault on property rights. The Chief Secretary
was strongly opposed to compulsory composition unless it reflected a
full tenth due the clergy, since rates reflecting the average revenue
of previous years would serve to perpetuate the earliest settlement.
He believed upon reflection that financing a rate-setting scheme would
be enormously expensive. He also suspected that tithe resistance really
reflected unhappiness with rents and clerical non-residence, both of
which must be reformed first. Spencer Perceval, who with Portland and
Liverpool led the Tory Administration, was not particularly impressed
by Wellesley's observations, but for different reasons; Perceval favored composition and Liverpool wanted commutation.[92] Perceval prevailed,
and the heads of proposals for a system of voluntary composition were
forwarded to Dublin for Wellesley's consideration prior to Christmas.

Prospects for legislation were soon dimmed by the Irish Church. Wellesley had already anticipated difficulties and although he saw no chance for reform he wanted this demonstrated by others and not by himself. In an interesting memorandum forwarded to Liverpool he outlined an elaborate method of enlisting the support of Irish bishops, starting first with the primate and Brodrick, then proceeding to a half-dozen bishops with liberal inclinations. Agar and O'Beirne were to be circumvented altogether, the first because he opposed all reform, the second because the plan might "not suit his peculiar view of the affairs of the Church."[93] Wellesley's pessimism was soon supported by the reaction of the Churchmen. Many clergymen refused to submit information on their tithes as requested by the government through Stuart and Brodrick, and rushed into print with pamphlets and broadsides proclaiming the Church was in danger. The Portland ministry actually reached the point of contemplating a twenty-one year leasing bill. The Richmond papers contain an elaborate undated memorandum with seven questions apparently addressed by the Irish government to some Churchmen. Included are some responses. Despite this effort, the government at length decided to abandon the proposals for reform and hoped that improving agricultural conditions in Ireland would blunt the sharpest edges of rural agitation.

For a while the question was carried forward by a small but vocal band of parliamentary radicals. Sir Henry Parnell, M.P. for Queen's County, the site of endemic unrest, moved for a return of public papers relating to Irish tithes in 1808.[94] He conferred with Perceval, who became Prime Minister in 1809, discovered that the ministry was afraid

to forward its own proposals, and introduced the leasing plan as a
prelude to more thoroughgoing reforms. The bill was easily defeated.[95]
Parnell pressed on. He contributed some intelligent speeches on the
subject which distinguished Irish from English tithe regulations, and
was finally discouraged by Parliament's disinterest and improving
agricultural conditions.[96] To the immense relief of the Church and
Perceval ministry alike, resistance subsided after 1808 and remained
limited for almost a decade.[97]

While British involvement in the Napoleonic wars continued, Irish
agriculture enjoyed a brief but heady prosperity, translated by Irish
landlords into rapidly expanded tillage, more intensive exploitation
of the land, increased subdivision, and higher rents. Expanded tillage
accommodated a growing peasant population, and tithes doubled in a
space of ten years. The clergy renewed their confidence in the traditional tithe system, and proctors made their appearance in ever greater
numbers in order to administer an increasingly lucrative but also increasingly complex system. Parliament responded to reports of clerical
manipulation with short spurts of uninspired rhetoric and tabled occasional proposals for tithe reform. In Ireland the question continued to
receive widespread popular attention. Richmond thought it sufficiently
important to grace the final year of his viceroyalty with a nine page
exposition on the need for modest procedural reforms to strengthen the
principle of property rights.[98]

When the European peace settlement of 1815 was translated into an
abrupt decline in Irish agricultural prices, however, rents and tithes
once more became an object of popular contention.[99] Insurrection acts

were applied to repress the most serious manifestations of dissatisfaction. In 1816, legislative deliberation on tithe reform resumed.[100]
Some of the clergy again reacted with vigorous proclamations of "no
surrender," whatever the element of justice and compassion involved
in tenants' distress, and whatever the immediate inconvenience involved,
most clergymen thought better to "submit to continued loss and inconvenience, than purchase the quiet possession of a good increase at any
risk to the permanent interests of the order."[101]

In 1816 the Earl of Kingston, a South Ireland landlord, circulated petitions against the tithe and in Parliament demanded the repeal
of a law of 1800 forbidding simultaneous payment of tithes in kind.[102]
Brodrick was able to shelve Kingston's proposal by focusing Parliament's
attention on the evils of rackrent. But new evidence of Parliament's
impatience with the Irish Church indicated that further difficulties
were on the way.[103] In 1817 a tithe bill passed the House of Commons
but died in the Lords. The bill was a modest one and does not seem to
have alarmed Irish Churchmen. In 1820 Henry Parnell introduced a
stronger tithe composition bill. Newport spoke in favor of it, and
the government remained neutral.[104] In 1821 an agricultural depression
was aggravated by a widespread potato failure. General starvation and
rebellion was averted only by parliamentary grants, a visit to Dublin
by George IV, and by appointment of a "Catholic", the Marquess Wellesley, as Lord Lieutenant. The Irish landlords and clergy were quick to
suggest that peasant tribulations be eased by reduction of tithes and
rents respectively, and by early 1822 it was painfully obvious that the
government must make a more concerted effort to reform tithes than had

been attempted in the past or face widespread rural rebellion.

The intervention of the Liverpool ministry came at an inauspi-
cious time. Verbal battles between the two Archbishops of Dublin and
evidence of growing peasant cohesiveness under the direction of Daniel
O'Connell were raising religious tensions and prompting acrimonious
exchanges on the parochial level.[105] There was, however, little alternative. Tithe resistance breasted now not only on a wave of hostility to imposts on the land, but on a rapid, even catastropic decline of agricultural prices, which led Irish gentlemen to join peasants in reform agitation. Furthermore, a catalyst had appeared--
the Marquess Wellesley--who was determined to reverse the tide of
frustration which had marked his political career since his return
from India and to make of his Irish viceroyalty a watershed in Irish
history. His arrival in Dublin in December 1822 marked the emergence
of a new initiative in the search for a solution to the tithe problem. This initiative was one which Peel as Home Secretary felt obliged to cultivate rather than discourage, and one which the newly-install-
ed Chief Secretary, Henry Goulburn, sustained through his dogged if
reluctant assaults on Parliament's inertia.

The new assault on tithe problems may be dated from January 1822.
The optimistic and energetic Marquess began soliciting reports from
articulate Irish observers, demanded statistical information from Irish
bishops, and forwarded lengthy commentaries to London. Wellesley's
observations were highly tentative, and he refused at that early stage
to commit himself to any particular proposition. His initiative, however, was timely. Indeed, Goulburn as Irish Chief Secretary wrote

Wellesley at the opening of Parliament in February reporting rumors
that radicals contemplated an investigatory commission on tithes.[106]

Wellesley was far from prepared to put forward a comprehensive
solution. Distracted by an insurrection in Ulster and a famine in
parts of Galway, Clare and Mayo, he disassociated himself from the
tithe issue until the following autumn.[107] Peel and Goulburn therefore opted for a strategy of delay and modest concession. Joseph
Hume, spearheading the radicals' initiative, was informed that Wellesley was at the moment engaged in a massive study of the problem, and
that in time the government would come forward with a comprehensive
solution. Hume was not easily appeased; he informed Goulburn that
his motion proposed to examine all aspects of the Irish Church.
Goulburn informed Peel that Hume's larger ambitions would normally
alienate a large portion of the membership of the Commons, but so unpopular was the tithe that the motion might well succeed. Goulburn
persuaded Hume to delay his motion from February 22 to early March,
complained to Wellesley that tithes constituted the most intractable
dilemma he had ever encountered, and embarked upon proposals for
immediate piecemeal reforms.[108]

Goulburn had more to do than appease Hume. Irish bishops in-
timated they would oppose any concessions to that unpalatable gadfly,
much as they had resisted Newport's initiatives in 1807. Liverpool
conferred with Irish bishops in London and informed the primate that
the government saw no need to interfere with the existing system where
it was operating smoothly or to obstruct locally popular changes, but
that it must compel some sort of settlement where agitation was in-

tense.[109] Goulburn, meanwhile, made it quite clear that the government's obstructionist tactics of 1807 would not suffice now.[110] On
March 14 the Duke of Devonshire upstaged Hume by introducing a motion
on tithes in the Lords. Goulburn and Peel, after consulting Liverpool and Irish officials, agreed that only immediate tangible concessions, and a public commitment to comprehensive legislation within
a year, would avert a parliamentary catastrophe.[111] The list of immediate concessions reflected considerable panic and little forethought:
a short bill ending exemption on agistment, which was certain to enrage
further the Church's opponents; an exemption on potatoes, which would
lower clerical and lay impropriator incomes in Munster.[112] Within one
week Goulburn perceived the error of his strategy. Specific groups
had been alienated, and advocates of tithe reform had not been con-
ciliated. A simpler plan permitting agreements for composition of
tithes for twenty-one years with collection by landowners, was offered
instead.[113] Wellesley agreed with Goulburn, desperate for support on
this item, that "the state of the collection of the tithes is certainly
a primary and most vexatious cause of misery to the lower order of the
people in Ireland," but offered no further support.[114]

Hume proceeded with his own promise to pursue the question.
This sparked vigorous debates on the subject in May and June. Hume
inevitably alienated some possible support by extending his list of
grievances against the Irish Church. Nevertheless, when Newport asked
the House of Commons to pledge itself to entertain a tithe bill during
the subsequent session his motion was defeated by only seven votes.[115]
Wellesley, indeed, believed that the government had allowed itself to

be outflanked by pledging its honor to piecemeal legislation and per-

haps limiting its maneuverability on the larger question.[116]

On June 13 Goulburn interrupted Hume's attacks to submit his

leasing bill to the House of Commons. He reminded the M.P.s of the

sanctity of private property and he detailed the evils of the tithe

system. He proposed in his bill to enable (but not to force) "eccle-

siastical and other persons in Ireland to grant leases of tithes so

as to bind their successors."[117] Radicals believed that the bill was

only a device to avert the need for stronger legislation. Conserva-

tives forcast a revolutionary expropriation of private property.

After a rough parliamentary passage the bill became law, but only

after the government declared that the bill incorporated "no great

plan" and was in fact "only an interim measure."[118]

While Goulburn was piloting his tithe palliative through Par-

liament, Wellesley was slowly gathering material for a decidedly

more comprehensive scheme. In the first instance Wellesley turned,

appropriately enough, to his two brothers, Wellington and Maryborough,

who had served in Ireland as chief secretaries. Wellington replied

that he had gone to Ireland in 1807 with "great hopes" of resolving

the question. At that time he was convinced that the difficulty was

essentially procedural, and confident that adoption of long leases

was the apporpriate answer. Upon closer examination he had deter-

mined that the clergy did not in fact obtain more than two-thirds of

the amount due. He had therefore concluded that long leases, which

he believed must in the context of property rights be based on a

full tenth, would meet universal resistance by tithe payers. Maryborough agreed with him that there was no solution.[119] Bishops and

clergymen submitted reports which contained scarcely-concealed allegations of the government's perfidy in raising the question at all.

They were almost universally opposed to any reform.[120] Beresford

informed Liverpool and Wellesley that no proposal should isolate

the Irish from the English portion of the united Church. He observed

"that the property of both [was] interwoven with the stability of the

kingdom."[121] Even the government, burdened with pledges of reform,

thought nothing was possible. Liverpool declared in the House of

Lords that he agreed with the Duke of Bedford's assertion in 1807

that he "had given the subject every possible degree of consideration

[and] was, at last, obliged to confess himself unable to fix on any

plan for removing the causes of complaint."[122]

These heady discouragements were adequately balanced by the

unpalatable possible repercussions of letting the issue pass into the

hands of the opposition. In June a large gathering of M.P.s at the

Thatched House Tavern in London declared their opposition to tithe payments in any form. They threatened to amend Goulburn's palliative

tithe bill to reflect these sentiments. All this confirmed ecclesiastics in their views that the Establishment would soon be destroyed.[123]

Wellesley refused to despair of a solution and determined to

allow his thoughts to mature slowly and solidly. By October, fortified by massive statistical returns from Ireland's dioceses, prodded

by Goulburn, Peel, and Liverpool, and deluged with memoranda from

Irish observers, he was prepared to commit his proposals to paper.

In doing so he put into motion the quest for a comprehensive tithe solution which would continue for fifteen years.[124]

What Wellesley submitted to Liverpool in November was a tithe plan designed to provide a permanent, comprehensive, and uniform composition to a money payment payable by landowners rather than tenants. The composition was to be made for twenty-one years, subject to revision every seven years at the average amount and value of produce for the preceding seven years. In each parish a select vestry of landowners would establish the amount needed to cover parochial expenses and clerical incomes, with compulsory government arbitration applied when required. Assessments on individual landowners would be determined by the vestry. Landowners could appeal assessments to Quarter Sessions. All Irish parishes would be required to effect composition.[125]

Wellesley's plan was a dramatic assault on traditional conceptions of property rights. It was designed in the first instance to remove tenants from the process, and, by compelling periodic reassessments, to insure the clergy's rights to share in the increasing productivity of the land. Landlords would attach tithes to rents. This would eliminate proctors and seasonal evaluations of crops, and terminate the exclusion of pasture proclaimed in 1735. The proposal was remarkably similar to Stuart's suggestion of 1807, and, as it developed, akin in principle to the legislation of 1838. To Wellesley's distress, the plan was greeted with expressions of intense dismay in London. Goulburn had already concluded that compulsion was impracticable, for landowners would press to see that composition settlements would be so structured as to defraud the Church of its property.[126] Peel was slightly less pessimistic. He agreed with Wellesley that only a "fully comprehensive plan" would do, but was convinced that compulsion would alienate many M.P.s otherwise holding moderate views. Liverpool agreed with the essential aspects of the Wellesley plan, and laid it before the cabinet on December 9. Two objections appeared, one relatively small and the other, concerning compulsion, more serious. Wellesley's suggestion that landlords be permitted to raise their rents so as to accommodate parochial assessments under the composition rate was opposed by some ministers who were conscious of the growing problem of arrears in rents and afraid further rent increases would stimulate resistance to payments. Liverpool argued that tenant income freed from tithe payments constituted a reserve applicable to rents. Wellesley's provision stood, with modifications.

The compulsion clause was modified at Liverpool's own initiative. Under his plan, if present parochial arrangements were congenial, no changes need be made. If the composition agreement was opposed by either the clergy or the vestry, the project would be suspended temporarily. Compulsory arbitration would be made available at the request of either party after a suitable pause.[127] Wellesley's reliance on compulsion was thereby made an ultimate rather than an immediate weapon. Finally, Wellesley's "select vestry" (i.e. Protestant), was replaced by a vestry of all who paid tithes, regardless of religion.

The amended bill was returned to Wellesley, who forwarded it to Goulburn.[128] Goulburn devoted most of December 1822 and January 1823 to drafting suitable legislation based on the proposal. He was prepared to lay it before Parliament in February. Neither Goulburn nor

Liverpool was confident of success. The stopgap legislation of 1822 had made little impact upon Irish problems. Any tithe payer's opposition to voluntary agreement was sufficient to obstruct the leasing system in a parish. Expectations of more comprehensive legislation had dissuaded others from entering into twenty-one year leases. Rural distress had made rent collection difficult, and landlords did not want to assume the burden of collecting tithes as well.[129]

The opposition of Irish Churchmen to the new bill proved far more serious than even Goulburn in his most pessimistic moments had contemplated, and underscored the drawbacks of Wellesley's rather cavalier treatment of Irish bishops. Beresford was not sent the heads of the bill until February 14. He complained bitterly of being among the last to be informed, and of being discouraged from suggesting amendments. His list of objections was long, and he expressed his displeasure forcefully. The bill was "destructive to the Church, inappropriate to Ireland." Liverpool had ignored the Church, undermined clerical confidence in the state, and moved to dissolve the erastian connection. The previous year's tithe bill, Beresford complained, had been satisfactory in principle but inoperative in practice because the ministry had seen fit to ignore Beresford's advice. Reliance on compulsion was shortsighted; it would not arrest agitation, and it would flail the clergy. It would eventually destroy the Church by "betraying it to popular clamor," destroying "the landmarks of all property," and facilitating full expropriation of ecclesiastical wealth."[130]

Goulburn, at least, was properly impressed with this demonstration of episcopal wrath. Liverpool assumed the burden of attempting to mitigate it.[131] In his answer to Beresford Liverpool argued with

spirit that to have refused to produce a bill would have been tanta-

mount to throwing the Church into hostile hands. The House of Commons,

he observed, would on its own initiative have appointed a committee on

which "the predominant power . . must have been the landowners of Ire-

land who would all from self-interest and some from faction have en-

deavored to impose upon the clergy the most disadvantageous terms."

He asserted that the bill did recognize that conditions in Ireland

differed from those in England. This was shown in the fact that com-

pulsion was an "ultimate" and not an "immediate" remedy. Composition

had been accepted in principle on certain articles in the past. The

vestry system would not become an agency to defraud the Church because

the clergy would resist unequal settlements and could rely on the gov-

ernment's sympathetic support.[132]

Liverpool failed to mollify Beresford, who had the satisfaction

of seeing two archbishops and fourteen bishops join in a formal pro-

test against the "destruction" of the Irish Church.[133] The clergy dis-

played similar misgivings. One observer noted that the clergy were con-

vinced the legislation would expose them to abuse and fraud. Revalua-

tion at the end of the first term would be accompanied by wholesale

manipulation of rents by which tithes were to be reset. Uncertainties

in the law would lead to illimitable litigation.[134] Goulburn was not

insensitive to the clergy's complaints. Those lower clergy at the edge

of starvation because of tithe resistance, he noted, however, were

much less critical than those clergymen with large, well-secured in-

comes.[135] The danger of fraud bothered Goulburn, but to incorporate

urther safeguards for the clergy in negotiating the parochial com-
osition would almost certainly alienate those Irish gentlemen whose
upport he required in Parliament. Looking ahead to eventual commuta-
ion of the tax to land, Goulburn conceded that inflated land prices
esulting from Ireland's superabundant population would make it diffi-
ult for the clergy to attain sufficient land to provide an income
qual to their property rights under the tithe system. But that, at
ny rate, was a problem for the future. At the moment he dared not
tter the word commutation aloud.[136]

Irish landlords had already expressed their sentiments. The
rinciple of composition to a tax had been opposed in the heady pro-
lamation at the Thatched House Tavern that "nothing short of a gener-
l commutation of tithes [to land] would satisfy [them] or could re-
ieve Ireland."[137] Newport was especially bitter, complaining that
omposition was insufficient to bring peace to Ireland, but drastic
nough to discourage other remedies.[138] Even Lord Palmerston, a
ember of the Liverpool ministry, noted that David Ricardo had proven
o the satisfaction of most landlords that a tax on land in lieu of
ithes would fall directly on landlords and could not be transferred
y them to their tenants in the form of higher rents. Palmerston
eared that the Wellesley-Goulburn plan might alienate Irish land-
ords and jeopardize Britain' already tenuous control in Ireland.
inally, Hume's contention that the Irish clergy would in fact be
iven a pension financed by the landlords reflected quite accurately
ie hostility of the Irish gentry.[139]

Goulburn introduced the legislation on March 6, 1823, in the form of two bills. This provided opponents an opportunity to combine their efforts, whatever the differences in their motives. One bill was relatively non-controversial, but died of disinterest before Parliament turned to it. This bill proposed creation of a board of "Commissioners for the Commutation of Tithes in Ireland," to consist of several ranking ecclesiastics and civil officials. Incumbents or lay impropriators agreeing to composition might request the board to secure land of equal value in return, with the government empowered to lay a parochial tax to reimburse itself for the lands thus purchased. The bill was designed to give incumbents freedom to choose lands or a composition tax. Its premises depended upon legislative approval of compulsory composition and thus generated little immediate enthusiasm.[140]

The second and more important bill called for temporary composition. The plan was voluntary in that composition would not proceed unless approved in a parish vestry limited to large tithe payers (to avoid "tumult and confusion"). It was compulsory, however, in that it either the vestry or the clerical incumbent could not reach an agreement through their respective commissioners, or could not agree on binding arbitration, the Lord Lieutenant could select an umpire empowered to set the composition rate. As his reference he would use the amount in tithes which the clergy could claim under the law (ten percent).[141]

The first reading of this bill produced only isolated protests, including a vigorous personal attack on Goulburn by the Archbishop of Tuam. Goulburn was incensed and employed his Latin to good effect.[142]

Before the second reading, however, criticism of the compulsion provision intensified, and Goulburn was sorely tempted to substitute a scheme for voluntary settlement instead.[143] Wellesley's disapprobation sufficed to hold the line for the moment. Clauses fixing uniform rates of assessment were also subject to controversy. David Spring Rice, an Irish M.P., claimed that settlements should be based on what the clergy were accustomed to receiving, not on their theoretical rights under the law.[144] This was agreed to, with the approvision - narrowly approved - that commissioners might raise composition rates one-third above existing levels where tithe agitation had depressed receipts substantially.[145] The government defeated a motion to set valuations on the receipts of the previous three years rather than the previous seven years. The shorter period would have depressed clerical incomes in disturbed districts. The government also resisted Hume's move to forbid all payments to non-resident clergymen.[146]

The tithe bill barely survived the committee stage in the House of Commons, and passed over strenuous objections by many clergymen and opponents of the clergy. In the Lords proponents of compulsion now that the bill was weighted against the clergy) pressed Liverpool. e agreed that compulsion might be introduced later; this was "not a ermanent measure, or ⋯ one which might not require modification."[147] ut Liverpool opposed compulsion in composition settlements at this oint. To insert it would entail returning the bill to the House of ommons, where radicals who still believed that the bill was too faorable to the Church would try again to defeat it. The Prime Minis-

ter closed his case by admitting that "it was only by the operation
of the present bill that the real difficulties of the bill could be
understood."[148]   On that note of uncertainty the tithe reform act of
1823 passed.

Liverpool was entirely correct. The new legislation was weak
and extraordinarily complicated. Applications could be made by the
incumbent or by five owners or occupiers of land paying at least £20
per annum. These applications would call for composition of tithes
for twenty-one years, reset every seven years. Cottier tenants could
not initiate requests for composition against the wishes of major
landowners or major tenants. Upon receiving an application, the
viceroy would summon a special vestry. If the vestry opposed composition the process ceased. The vestry would inform the Irish Chief
Secretary that negotiations were concluded. If negotiations were
approved in principle, the incumbent on his own behalf and the vestry on behalf of the parish were each empowered to nominate one
commissioner. The incumbent must notify his bishop within seven days,
and also notify churchwardens, the Chief Secretary and any lay impropriators with tithe rights in his parish that negotiations were to begin. Bishops were permitted to veto any of the commissioners nominated;
this was designed to protect clergymen from local landlords' pressure
on the clergy.

If the clergy and the vestry agreed on a settlement the commissioners' responsibilites were limited to insuring that the amount
agreed upon was not less than the average annual receipts for seven
years preceding 1821. This, and the required approval of bishop and

patron, further shielded the clergy from an imposed settlement and was, in Goulburn's mind, intended to avoid long negotiations by commissioners, with the heavy attendant expense. In the absence of direct negotiations, commissioners were empowered to negotiate terms subject to approval by all parties concerned. If no settlement was made, proceedings were suspended and the Chief Secretary was notified. If negotiations were successful commissioners were empowered to make a new applotment. If they failed to do so the incumbent could demand a copy of the last applotment from each collector of parish cess, and the composition would be levied on the basis of this applotment.[149]

This legislation, remarkable for its cumbersome provisions and complicated procedures, was no sooner launched than subject to proposals for reform. Goulburn complained he was forced to spend "much time preparing summaries of the act "for those who will not read it, or upon reading it do not understand it." The clergy, he noted, initiated most requests for negotiations. This was a heartening sign, except that the higher classes in each parish frequently moved to block any agreement which would force them to pay higher taxes. Wellesley was advised initially to grant permission for summoning the select vestry only where success seemed likely. Later Goulburn urged granting permission except when failure seemed inevitable in order to give the act as wide an application as possible.[150] By mid-September Goulburn's initial enthusiasm had cooled to the point where he began to contemplate seriously the formulation of amending legislation for Parliament's consideration early in 1824. The obstructionism of graziers tended to drive tillage farmers and the clergy into alliance, while Catholic priests identified themselves with graziers in order,

in Goulburn's view, to promote hostility to incumbents. This ironic

if temporary alliance meant that by mid-October of 600 applications made

to the Lord Lieutenant, only 71 agreed to proceed to negotiations, and

only 51 of these actually negotiated.[151] Goulburn proposed to resolve

this by substituting tithe payers, who were largely Catholic tillage

farmers, for vestry cess payers, who were for the most part graziers

and, even more germaine, mostly Protestants. A second defect, the

complicated procedures, was vexatious and not easily rectified.[152] A

third was the widespread hardship occasioned by adjustments in payment

schedules. The new annual payments meant that during the transition

period either the clergy were six months late in obtaining their in-

come, or tithe payers were assessed six months earlier than heretofore.

The law, Goulburn admitted, would not be generally successful. It

would, he hoped, be successful enough so that by amendment it could

be extended elsewhere.[153]

The next twelve months saw a gradual extension of the 1823 tithe

act. Parliament accepted some relatively minor changes. Opposition by

the episcopal bench declined. By January 1824 applications from 966

parishes had resulted in 467 parishes voting on the issue. From this

there were 216 votes in favor of negotiations, and this led to 31 com-

position agreements.[154] By October applications had risen to 1188 and

434 parishes had reached the point of appointing commissioners to treat.

Composition agreements rose to 121. No agreements were reached in

Armagh, Down, Connor, Derry, Raphoe, Ilmore and Dromor. These were

all Ulster dioceses, where existing arrangements were generally satisactory. In Emly, Ross, Kilmacduagh, Killalla and Achonry the fail-

re was more serious, because tithe agitation was widespread there.

rdagh, Kildare, Ardfert and Confert boasted the best percentages,

ith Ardfert coming up with 19 composition agreements in 67 parishes.[155]

oulburn interpreted these figures in the best possible light. He

oted that without the act at least several dozen parishes where

greements had been reached would be potential areas of agitation.[156]

Painful progress was recorded in Ireland. At Westminster events

oved very slowly. Wellesley once more applied himself to the tithe

roblem. He concluded, almost inevitably, that without the threat of

ompulsion little could be done to reduce the tithe problem in the

ost agitated areas.[157] In March Goulburn offered several modifications

f the 1823 measure to the House of Commons. He noted that the 1823

ct had received a moderately warm reception (507 applications from

hurchmen, and 523 from laymen), but that several difficulties had

ppeared in the process of negotiations in the vestries. To remedy

hese he suggested a system of enforced arbitration which would insure

doption of composition after it had been accepted in principle by the

estries. Voting qualifications should also be changed so as to re-

uce the influence of agistment owners; their obstinacy had derailed

any negotiations. Goulburn also recommended that the basis for de-

ermining composition rates be extended. Tithe payments were to be

iven priority over rents, and the clergy's property rights were to

e strengthened by a more precise description of composition equiva-

ents.[158] Most importantly, Goulburn recommended that compulsion be

eintroduced. Debate on this particular issue had clearly indicated

that Churchmen, who had strongly opposed compulsion a year earlier,
were now so alarmed at the continuing spread of resistance to the
tithe and were so delighted at the terms they had secured under the
1823 act that they were now predisposed to accept force in settlements.
Against them were the Radicals, who saw a consolidation of ecclesiastical property rights as the inevitable result. The great Irish
landlords also opposed compulsion; they continued to dislike
thoroughly the idea of paying tithe on agistment after nearly one
hundred years' exemption.[159]

Goulburn's recommendations were accepted by the government and
amending legislation was presented to Parliament. Compulsion was
again resisted, although procedures for securing tithe composition
after the vestry had accepted it in principle were successfully inserted into the amended act. But these amendments did little to
accelerate the spread of composition agreements. On the other hand,
settlements began to appear in areas of greatest unrest.[160] By 1829
nearly one thousand parishes had accepted composition agreements,
and Wellesley departed Ireland confident that considerable headway had
been made in removing this particular problem from the Irish scene.[161]

An examination of tithe applotment books for Clogher between
1824 and 1832 underscores some great difficulties encountered by the
negotiating parties even in a diocese rather lightly afflicted by the
agitation. Many parishes contained more than 700 tithable plots. In
only one case did the landlord group them together and collect the
tithe himself. In at least two instances the clergy nominated Protestant extremists who might be trusted to make the most grudging con-

essions. Tithe rates varied according to the quality of the land,
which more active cultivation was changing, and according to custom,
which defied rationalization. Many laymen were engaged in negotiations in several parishes, sometimes simultaneously. Frequently
tithes were owed to several ecclesiastical persons and to lay impropriators as well.[162] Amassing the material incorporated in the applotment books was an elaborate and expensive exercise; one wonders that
any agreements were reached at all. By 1829, nevertheless, half of
Ireland's parishes had effected composition. Tithe composition tabu-
lations in 1832 revealed 1,500 parishes settled, covering some £42,000
of £704,000 due.[163] Areas of traditional disturbance, while rarely included in the new composition agreements, were also quiet, finding
respite in temporary expedients. For a few short years it appeared
that the tithe problem was no longer a major source of discontent on
the Irish countryside.

After 1825 the true significance of the Wellesley-Goulburn legislation became more apparent. The acts reduced the distinction between
rents and tithes and "ensured that opposition to rents and to tithes
would be concurrent and simultaneous."[164] Voting regulations heavily
favored the larger landowners. They of course often worked to defeat
composition, which would suspend their 1735 exemption. The occupying
tenants still paid the tithe. Tenants were allowed, under subsequently
negotiated leases, to deduct tithes from rents, but landlords merely
added the new composition to the rent. As a result, the Established
clergy were further implicated in the landlord-tenant relationship.
Grain prices, used as the basis for new rents, were comparatively high

between 1814 and 1821 and included several years of extremely high prices. Compositions based on these figures were not popular among tithe payers.[165]

The fragility of these tithe reforms was shown in the resumption of tithe agitation in Kilkenny in 1830. Popular preoccupation with the meteoric rise of O'Connell, with Catholic emancipation, and with a gradual extension of tithe composition agreements to rural Ireland obscured for several years following enactment of Goulburn's legislation the continued widespread hostility to the tithe itself. Whiteboy agitation had never ceased entirely in the most Catholic counties. Failure of the potato in 1822 had emphasized the inequity of a system which taxed the potato outside Ulster but not in Presbyterian areas. A continuing decline in grain prices, amounting to almost twenty-five percent between 1820 and 1830, and more severe declines in beef prices, gradually made even tithe rates fixed by composition agreements difficult to sustain.[166] Increasing evidence of Protestant proselytism, marching under the banner of "The New Reformation," alarmed Catholic peasants and induced their bishops to encourage, as discreetly as possible, resistance to tithes.[167] Finally, a new consciousness of their influence when highly organized, a lesson learned during the drive for Catholic emancipation, prompted peasants to renew tithe agitation on a larger scale than ever before. Thus when cattle distrained for tithe in the Parish of Graig in Kilkenny were put up for sale in December 1830, authorities were astounded to discover that while a large crowd attended, none bid for the stock. There had emerged a highly effective system by which no tithe owner could gain com-

pensation for his losses, for none in the crowd dared purchase his
property. Soon, penny taxes were being collected in parishes to cover
peasants' prosecutions and court expenses.[168] The tithe issue had
been joined, once more, this time not to be abandoned until permanently resolved.

The course of tithe agitation during the 1830s has already
attracted considerable popular and scholarly comment. Homicides,
which had been infrequent before 1830, now became common. Law and
order in southern Ireland threatened to disappear completely. In
early 1833 Earl Grey informed the House of Lords that

> between the 1st of January and the end of December 1832, the
> number of homicides were 242; of robberies, 1,179; of
> burglaries, 401; of burnings, 568; of houghing cattle, 290;
> of serious assaults, 161; of riots, 203; of illegal reviews,
> 353; of illegal notices, 2,094; of illegal meetings, 427;
> of injuries to property, 796; of attacks on houses, 723;
> of firing with intent to kill, 328; of robbery of arms, 117;
> of administering unlawful oaths, 163; of resistance to legal
> process, 8; of turning up land, 20; of resistance to tithes,
> 50; taking forcible possession, 2.[169]

Proclamations of resistance circulated under the noses of authorities
who dared not prosecute too vigorously. By 1833 the beneficed clergy
were loud in their complaints to London that they faced starvation, and
tithe agitation so disoriented the functioning of local government that
vestry meetings were adjourned _sine die_. As it became increasingly
apparent that tithes would not be collected, composition agreements
were suspended as well. After 1830 Ireland once more looked to Parliament for a comprehensive solution.

Chapter V: The Established Church and Irish Education

Interesting analogies can be made between tithes and education
and the relationship of both to the Church of Ireland in the first
half of the nineteenth century.   In both cases certain developments
over which the ecclesiastical establishment had little control worked
to undermine vested interests.   The Church was forced to confront an
assault on its prerogatives at a time when its own options seemed
severely restricted, and when Catholic identification with the forces
of change prompted arguments which often shed more heat than light.
The Church reacted by making a vigorous assertion of its prescriptive
rights.   This approach gained immediate support but sacrificed the
opportunity of a wise adjustment to inevitable changes.

By 1800 the Anglican Church of Ireland had, perhaps unwittingly,
squandered its best chance to convert Ireland through control of primary and secondary education.   Judging from the frequency of royal decrees and legislation in the field of Irish education since the Reformation, one might well have concluded that the Established Church
supervised a system which incorporated intelligent fiscal principles
and a comprehensive, practical curriculum suited to peculiar Irish
conditions.   In 1537 the Irish Parliament, on Henry VIII's advice,
directed that a system of parochial schools be established to promote
the Protestant religion and the English language.   Responsibility for
the schools was assigned to the beneficed clergy.   The statute was
renewed in 1695.   In 1722 it was complemented by another enabling the

clergy to grant land in each parish for support of a resident Protestant schoolmaster.[1] Further legislation facilitating endowments was passed early in the reign of George III.

Unfortunately, practice fell far short of theory. In 1800 there were parochial schools in only one-fifth of Ireland's parishes, and the condition of facilities, the qualifications of the faculty, and the rigor of the curriculum left much to be desired. Their deficiencies, moreover, represented only a part of the gap between law and fact. Starting with Elizabeth, grants were made for diocesan schools and other foundations, whose care was entrusted to the presiding bishop or some commissions.[2] The Stuarts contributed their own remedy, royal schools, which were concentrated in Ulster. They seem to have shown a bit more vitality than either parochial or diocesan schools during the seventeenth and eighteenth centuries. Finally, as in England, charity schools, supported by private subscriptions, dedicated to universal education, and intent upon inculcation of basic Protestant principles, appeared in Ireland after 1700. Under Archbishop Boulter these were gathered together into a corporation in 1733. When even this proved insufficient to sustain them, the crown was induced to make annual grants. In 1747 Parliament also began to contribute to these schools. This practice continued until 1831.[3]

By 1800, then, there existed on paper an ambitious and complicated structure of primary and secondary schools. In reality, Irish education was more inadequate than ever. Catholics had rebounded from the restrictions imposed by the penal code early in the century to develop a vigorous albeit haphazard collection of hedge schools. These schools reflected an inextinguishable passion for learning on one hand, and

a determination to avoid Protestant control on the other. The Estab-

lishment's effort remained almost universally dismal. The financial

scandals which attended the management of the Charter schools in par-

ticular excited both mirth and amazement. In 1791 a report solicited

by the reinvigorated Irish Parliament declared that parochial schools

should be removed from the control of the Protestant clergy, whose

record of attention and interest was notorious, and entrusted to a

body controlled by laymen. Even more significantly, the commission

recommended admission of Catholics to the controlling body, attempted

to reduce proselytism by inviting clergymen of the various denomina-

tions to instruct members of their flock enrolled in the schools, and

proposed establishment of a central board to supervise most of Ire-

land's educational facilities. Whatever the evidence of bold and

advanced thinking incorporated in the commission's proposals, the re-

port was ignored. It was revived a decade and more later by the next

group of commissioners. An abortive legislative effort to implement

the report in 1799 rounded out a dismal century of educational mis-

management.[4]

Beset by confrontations over patronage, the status of the Church

under the Act of Union, tithe resistance, and clerical non-residence,

the Establishment continued for the most part to ignore the question

of education until 1806. In 1802, to be sure, there was a flurry of

activity when Stuart attempted to block a proposed grant for a new

library at Trinity from a charitable fund specifically directed at

education of the Irish poor. In the same year O'Beirne, a trusty bellwether of approaching storms, pleaded with the government to make each bishop account for the decayed condition of schools in his juris- diction.[5] In 1805 an outburst of pamphlet literature emphasized the plight of the Charter schools. The government hinted to Stuart that they should be abolished. Stuart wondered whether this solution thus might not result in "many evils," admitting in the same breath that the schools were "ill managed, . . not productive of the good intended, and extremely expensive."[6]

In 1806, however, at the request of John Newport and the Whig ministry, and with the acquiescence of Stuart, a statutory commission of inquiry into Irish education was initiated.[7] The membership, com- pletely Protestant and dominated by Stuart himself, implied that nothing very radical could be expected. At first it apparently was intended that as the Board issued periodic reports the Irish government would take whatever remedial measures seemed appropriate. Upon publication of the first report in 1807 (regarding schools of Royal and Private Foundation) Arthur Wellesley proposed the creation of a commission with some power to reform the most neglected institutions in that cate- gory.[8] Nothing was done at the time.

Six years and fourteen reports later, however, the commission concluded its lengthy labors by making some dramatic recommendations. The first thirteen reports, based on the grudging submissions of em- barrassed clergymen, confirmed what was already widely suspected: ex- isting educational foundations were not only in an advanced stage of administrative torpor and decay, but were a poor basis for any revita- lization of Irish education.[9] The Charter schools, which Wellesley and even Stuart at first believed could be revived and refurbished, were determined on further investigation to be in the worst possible condition.[10] Royal schools, diocesan institutions, and various other private and public foundations were condemned for their overblown administrative systems, dearth of pupils, incompetent teachers, frequent peculation of funds, and inadequate teaching materials. The rector of Monaghan, for example, in response to the commission's request for information on the state of the diocesan school entrusted to his care, reported no schoolhouse, no free students, no day scholars, and one boarder. To the instructor went ₤30, and another ₤77 was missing.[11]

The Fourteenth Report concluded that only central supervision would make possible rehabilitation of these schools. But the report went further; the new board should not only be permanent and have authority to inspect and to discipline, but should also be allowed to create new schools where needed, and to place them under their direct control. These "supplemental" schools were not to "influence or disturb the peculiar religious tenets of any sect or description of Christians." Texts would avoid denominational bias. Literary and moral instruction, then, was to be kept separate. This proved to be "a germ of the principle that was to be the heart of the national system."[12]

The appearance of the Fourteenth Report in 1812 followed closely upon the establishment of a new genre of schools in Ireland destined to play a crucial role in nineteenth century Ireland. The private society idea, first tried a century earlier and destroyed by public

apathy, was revived at the end of the eighteenth century in connection with isolated manifestations of evangelicalism within the English
and Irish Establishments. The first of these new societies was the
Association for Discountenancing Vice and Promoting the Knowledge and
Practice of Christian Religion. It was founded by Anglican clergymen
in 1792, and, after an uncertain period, was incorporated in 1800.
Soon after its incorporation the government began providing annual
grants in successively larger amounts. Although controlled completely
by the Established clergy, t!.e society refrained from active proselytism and controversial teaching methods until the early 1820s, when a
large-scale Catholic exodus soon had the effect of reducing the schools
to impotency.[13] Thus died a promising method whereby the Establishment might control Irish education without the disadvantages of government intervention.[14]

A second experiment, the London Hibernian Society, made no attempt
to obscure its proselytizing tendencies. "Built on the anticipated
reduction of popery," the society's statistical claims were usually
overblown, and Catholic suspicions began to develop shortly after its
schools first appeared in 1806. In their zeal to penetrate Catholic
bastions they often situated their schools in remote areas, where "too
little regard" was paid "to cleanliness, order and regularity."[15] After
1820 these schools were the object of violent Catholic hostility, and
the Society's protests to the contrary, the schools declined rapidly
in numbers and effectiveness.[16] Indirect grants from the public treasury were also quietly suspended. Of the three smaller societies also
engaged in the work of Irish education, least active was the Baptist

Society for Promoting the Gospel in Ireland, founded in Ireland in
1814 along lines similar to the London Hibernian Society and claim-
ing nearly one hundred day schools in 1825.[17]

The most interesting experiment was conducted by the Irish
Society for Promoting the Education of the Native Irish through the
Medium of their own Language, established in 1818 not to preserve the
Irish language but to use it as an effective means of education and
proselytism. The Irish Society had to fight both "extreme prejudice"
against use of Irish in the Protestant churches as well as Catholic
suspicions. It claimed forty day schools in 1822, and seventy-one
in 1827. Its budget was slim, and the schools relied on substantial
outside assistance.[18] The last, The Sunday School Society, coordinat-
ed the efforts of various local bodies in the attempt to convert
Catholics and distributed scriptural material. It claimed to be non-
sectarian and to instruct more than 150,000 scholars by 1822.[19]

Another of an entirely different character was the Society for
Promoting the Education of the Poor in Ireland, generally called, from
its Dublin situation, Kildare Place. One salient recommendation of the
Fourteenth Report of the commissioners of education was the creation of
a national system of education for the poor. Only one year earlier
there had been founded a society dedicated to scriptural readings without note or comment and to exploitation of advanced educational techniques, later subsumed into the national system.[20] It sought, and in
its early years obtained, the approval of many Catholic clergymen.
Indeed Lord Fingall, a Roman Catholic nobleman, became a vice-president.
Parliament soon recognized its work in implementing the commissioners'

suggestion for education of the poor by an initial grant of ₤6,000 in
1816, increased to ₤30,000 per annum in 1831. Eventually Kildare
Place taught 137,000 children in more than 1,600 schools, a considerable achievement.[21] Its textbooks and training schools suggested
a commitment to national education far beyond even what endowed schools
had achieved in the past. By 1819 it appeared that the recommendations
of the 1806-1812 committee were being implemented on a large scale,
if not by Parliament directly, at least through generous appropriations to Kildare Place.

All this was effectively compromised after 1820 by a swell of
Protestant religious pressure and a Catholic counterattack. In 1820
Kildare Place authorized grants to Protestant proselytizing societies
and permitted proselytism by the Established clergy in their own
schools. Catholics responded with their own society and with demands
for state aid. Catholic pressure and Benthamite criticism pushed
Kildare Place into even closer ties with the proselytizing agencies
despite the society's fervent protests of complete impartiality.[22]
Once again promising developments in Irish education had been destroyed
by sectarian considerations.

The Fourteenth Report, meanwhile, had been transformed by Parliament and by the opposition of the Established clergy into something
quite different from what its authors had intended. The report had
recommended creation of a board of education supervising lower class
elementary education leaving the motley array of endowed schools to
flounder in their own seemingly insuperable difficulties. So black a
picture of these schools had the earlier reports painted, however,

that Parliament rushed instead to shore them up by putting them under the board. Prospects for a truly comprehensive board were thus increased, only to be dealt a severe blow when plans to place both new elementary schools for the poor and existing parish schools under the authority of the commissioners met the decided disapproval of the Anglican clergy. Proponents of the national system struggled against the clergy and against public apathy for three years. At length, all sides were exhausted by tortuous argumentation and the proposal was shelved. Because the defeat destroyed the Established clergy's last opportunity to supervise a national system in the spirit of Henrician legislation, it is worthwhile to examine what motives prompted the Church of Ireland in its opposition.

The lively activities of the private societies and even livelier criticism of the endowed schools after 1800 focused attention upon the plight of the moribund parochial schools, on the statutory responsibilities of the Established clergy, and on the abysmal record of neglect and malfeasance which had attended the actions of these state-appointed guardians of Irish primary education towards schools in their benefices. By law, the clergy were obliged to sustain and supervise parochial schools open to children of all faiths free of charge. In fact, the clergy usually discharged their obligations and eased their consciences by a miniscule grant of two pounds a year. They made occasional and lackadaisical efforts to secure a schoolmaster and contributed generous doses of theology which, along with tuition requirements, effectively deterred most Catholic children where the schools functioned at all. In some parishes the vestry provided assistance.

In others funds were raised by private subscription; in still others
private societies contributed funds on the condition that their particular education formulae be reflected in the curriculum. In many
parishes the idea of comprehensive elementary education was ignored
altogether.

Before 1825 no concerted effort was made to secure accurate information on the condition of the parish schools. The returns of the
clergy in 1807 were notorious for their glaring, intentional inaccur-
acies while the reports of the commissioners were sharply critical but
statistically vague. Mason's survey in 1812, itself largely composed
of interviews of the Established clergy, reveals something of the
problems involved without attempting to provide a serious analysis of
the schools' defects. Mason reported that in Rathcline, County Long-
ford, there was "no desire for education." The only school was "run
by a Catholic who bought his books from wandering peddlars." In
Tathconrath, County Westmeath, education was "rather limited," there
being no schools. Many clergymen admitted that Catholics displayed
a great deal more desire for schooling than their own flock. Most
parishes had hedge schools, and some as many as twelve. Most reported
that schools were conducted only when the children could not gain employment; a prosperous year agriculturally meant a decline in liter-
acy. To the extent that the peasantry was securing education, it was
agreed, the hedge schools, not parochial schools, deserved the credit.[23]

The commissioners' report determined that in 1810 there existed
549 parish schools educating 23,000 children. Four dioceses had no
parish schoolhouses whatever, an interesting deficiency in this approach

to "national education." It concluded that the schools were no longer necessary in their present form for diffusion of English and were highly ineffective as a proselytizing device. The clergy, it observed, should be relieved of the Henrician oath which bound them to support a parish school, since most ignored it except when called upon to support some more onerous plan. Instead, parish schools should along with new schools as needed, be nondenominational, national, uniform, and financed by parliamentary grants distributed through the new National Board.[24]

These logical and relatively innocent proposals soon prompted a controversy as complex and acrimonious as the parish schools were defective. Upon receipt of the recommendations in 1813 Robert Peel set out to formulate proposals acceptable to Protestants and Catholics alike. His first move was to bring in a bill creating a new board for the endowed schools, much as Arthur Wellesley had suggested in his memorandum of December 1807. Next, he agreed with the Commission that no system of public education could survive without Catholic cooperation, but he opposed surrendering existing parochial schools – those superintended by the Established clergy – to a system where denominational instruction must necessarily be weakened. He proposed to the cabinet at the end of March 1813 that there be two sets of commissioners: one for the regulation of existing parochial schools and the other for the supervision of such public schools as might proceed from recommendations of the Fourteenth Report. The existing schools would continue to serve Anglican children. They would be supported and managed by the beneficed clergy, with control as needed from a central commission composed exclusively of salaried Protestant laymen. The new schools would be entrusted to a board of Catholics and Protestants. The Established clergy would not be obliged to support them, and the role of religion in the curriculum would be determined by the Board itself.

The proposal was a thoughtful one. Parochial schools in the eyes of the law were "strictly establishments of the Church, supported by the revenues of the Church, and solely under the control of its members." Because of these factors, Catholics were not likely to attend these schools in great numbers, even if the schools were resuscitated.[25] But any new system of education could not exclude the Catholic majority, and for this reason a new system completely divorced from the old seemed to Peel most appropriate.[26]

The prospect of being required to support parish schools in a meaningful way horrified many of the beneficed clergy. To demand such support for schools in which there would be not certain opportunity for proselytism on behalf of the Anglican Establishment was doubly unpalatable. As a result, Peel proved unable to gain the cabinet's support. And because Grattan's motion for Catholic relief threatened to destroy the Liverpool ministry in May and June 1813 the more comprehensive system was quickly and quietly shelved. Parliament evaded the central issue by establishing a board of commissioners to manage only the endowed schools.

Early in 1814 another attempt was made to implement the suggestions of the Fourteenth Report concerning parochial schools. By early March of that year Peel had been convinced by Thomas Elrington, Provost of Trinity College, and by James Verschoyle, Bishop of Killalla,

that he must continue to support plans to abolish the old Henrician

oath. The clergy, they noted, had long ignored it. Attempts to in-

corporate it into the legislation of 1813 had only generated wide-

spread clercial hostility. But Peel was equally convinced that the

legislature would not permit the Established clergy to escape responsi-

bility for parish schools. Brodrick, fresh from a meeting with Peel,

wrote to Stuart that "no substitute could be thought of by us, which

would not in a degree and in fact tax the clergy separately from the

laity. In a choice of difficulties it remained then only for us to

take that which was subject to the fewest exceptions." They chose to

insist that upon presentation to their benefices the clergy take an

oath to support the school, or to enter into a written obligation to

appoint and support a schoolmaster. If at the end of three months no

schoolmaster could be procured, the bishop would then exercise the

right to appoint a schoolmaster or not, according to circumstances,

and to apply two percent of the incumbent's income to his support.

In this way Peel hoped to avoid implementation of the Fourteenth Re-

port's call for a national board of education, with its danger of

eventual Catholic predominance, its difficulties in choosing textbooks,

and its thinly disguised secular tendencies. Instead, parochial

schools, free from proselytism but controlled and sustained by the

Established Church, would gradually fill Ireland's educational vacuum

while keeping Catholicism at bay.[27]

Peel's solution did not prove a happy one. Stuart for his part

was incensed that undue tenderness towards clerical sensibilities and fear of the secular tendencies of the national scheme prepared under

his supervision were to be used to destroy the salient features of the

Fourteenth Report. He noted that the clergy had always been exclusive-

ly taxed. Indeed, he observed, "it would be difficult to point out

the time when they were not, in some degree, burdened with the educa-

tion of the people." Their negligence over the centuries should not

have the force of prescription against their responsibilities in the

future, and the new plan, with its easily evaded promises and its de-

pendence on the weak reed of bishops' attentiveness, was hardly likely

to succeed where the oath had failed.[28]

Stuart's discomfort, however, was light in comparison to the un-

happiness of the clergy at the prospect of being taxed to support

schools they could not control. A denominationally neutral system of

elementary education, in which the clergy must defray the expense of

a school and schoolmaster was combined with the invidious possibilities

for extension of their burden as the system expanded. Such conditions

not only earmarked a particular social class for financial ruin, but

destroyed the erastian principle of unfettered clerical control over

education. John Jebb, eventually to become a member of the Irish bench

himself, decried selective taxation. He preferred that the clergy

surrender the principle of being exclusive educators in Ireland than

"get strapped with the burden of educating everyone."[29] "National

education," declared O'Beirne in a rather trite play on words, "is not

the responsibility of the parochial clergy;" the nation should pay if

it wants non-denominational schools.[30]

The hostility of Stuart against any undermining of national education on one hand, and the beneficed clergy's unhappiness at revival of parish schools on the other, led to considerable confusion within the government. Liverpool and Peel dared not appear to abandon the idea of educational reform lest the opposition, led by Newport, bring forth a proposal of its own. Thomas Elrington in desperation suggested that the commissioners should reverse their stand, oppose any financial imposition on the clergy, and even declare their opposition to supplemental schools and national education entirely. This would eliminate the need for any implementation of the report at this time. Elrington hoped, somewhat optimistically, that the clergy would be stimulated by the threat of future legislative intervention to revive their support for parochial schools. This would preclude the need for future legislative intervention.[31] Stuart in opposing exempting the clergy from this burden was in the minority.

By a massive and dextrous display of inactivity, the 1814 legislative effort eventually died, and the opposition proved unable to revive it. Parliament eased its conscience by inaugurating its plan of support to private societies. Emphasis was directed to Kildare Place, whose plan most accurately reflected what the Fourteenth Report thought should be done in Irish education. Meanwhile, the new board of education authorized in 1813 proceeded to enjoy a "long and undistinguished history" because its jurisdiction, the endowed schools, were shielded from close scrutiny by other legislation. This left only a few "odds and ends." The board managed to treat these with a certain indifference by a narrow interpretation of its own powers of inspection.[32] The Established clergy, for the most part, attempted to

improve parish schools in their jurisdictions but made them more
Protestant than ever. In overwhelmingly Catholic areas no effort
was made to improve elementary education on the premise that Roman
Catholics would refuse to attend schools supervised by Anglican
clergy.[33] The erastian ideal of national education controlled by the
state Church was quietly surrendered in order to avoid responsibilities
for support. In schools which remained, Protestant children were
given preference in admission. The religious division in Ireland
was more pronounced than ever.

Vigorous efforts by private societies satisfied Parliament until
1821. Inflated statistics and energetic propagation of the benefits
of the various programs set a tone of progress and accomplishment which
no one could effectively challenge. In 1822, however, the movement for
national education revived. Endowed schools continued to show evidence
of neglect and malfeasance. Diocesan schools had long since surrendered
their efforts to teach the poor. By charging high fees they had long
been transformed into schools of classical training with a "decidedly"
Protestant character.[34] Even new schools soon succumbed to mismanagement. A consolidated fund established in 1819 empowered the Lord Lieutenant to make grants to schools established by voluntary subscriptions.
This fund was soon restricted to Protestant applicants and catered to
scholars of independent means.[35]

More alarming was the impact of increasing Catholic militancy on
Irish education. A harbinger of this trend was O'Connell's attack on
Kildare Place, the largest and least denominational of the private ed-
ucation. This destroyed prospects for an evolutionary approach to

comprehensive education for the poor. Increasing religious tensions began to undermine the work of other private societies in overwhelmingly Catholic areas.

New surveys of parish schools revealed that much less than hoped for had been accomplished in this quarter.[36] Clergymen continued to fulfill their Henrician oath with a contribution of forty shillings a year, hardly a worthy sacrifice. Unbeneficed clergymen sought to improve their inadequate salaries by teaching, a distraction which often weakened their effectiveness both as ministers and as teachers.[37] Records were kept haphazardly or not at all, and vestry allocations were often misappropriated. Contributions from private societies led to considerable confusion, with parish schools attempting to meet demands put down by all societies. Many parochial schools closed, and thereby transferred their burden to the private society schools.[38] All this led to a somewhat precipitate attempt in 1821 to remove all parish schools from clerical control, and to forbid all books objected to in any way by Catholics. Stuart sent an alarming letter to Brodrick opposing this. The two of them impressed upon the Liverpool ministry the inevitability of the Church's collapse if the government did not oppose the bill. The prelates were successful and the motion was rejected.[39]

A Catholic initiative in 1824 led to the founding of a new committee on Irish education. Complaints of proselytism had increased in frequency and intensity, and rumors of financial scandals circulated in London and Dublin.[40] To the annoyance of the bench of bishops, the first Catholic in modern times to be appointed to any commission of

inquiry was included in the panel. After three years and nine reports, the commission obtained Catholic concurrence for schools with
Protestant and Catholic instructors supervising literary instruction
in common, and with special days set aside for religious classes.[41]
It asked that aid to private societies be limited and eventually extinguished, and outlined a proposal for a new government board to
manage schools of general instruction. As a sop to the Established
Church, it recommended termination of the Henrician oath; the Established clergy should be responsible only for education of the Protestants. The experiment soon collapsed; attempts to have texts compiled by cooperative ventures of the Anglican and Catholic bishops
failed miserably.[42]

In 1828 another commission was launched under the aegis of Thomas
Spring Rice. The report, issued in record time, was a model of con-
ciseness and clarity. It contemplated the creation of a new board to
found and manage all schools, to oppose religious orientation, to
receive applications for assistance and dispense aid to schools of
general instruction. Texts would be approved by both Catholic and
Protestant bishops. No schools would be built without local cooperation.[43] But the new era of religious confrontation had already sharpened Protestant zeal. Now, unlike 1814, the prospect of loss of control over elementary education far outweighed the question of financial support in the eyes of the Anglican clergy. Whereas in 1814
the Established clergy refused to assume direction over parochial
schools if forced to subsidize them, now they demanded unfettered control of all schools and were willing to make allotments from their in-

comes. With Catholicism increasing in power, the prospect of loss of all control now apppeared especially invidious.

The reports of 1825 through 1828 were greeted with dismay by the Church of Ireland. Demands for detailed returns on parochial schools met with widespread hostility.[44] One principal policy oracle of the Church denounced this "sinister" attempt to concede Ireland to Catholicism. It opposed separation of literary from religious instruction, and demanded that the Church be confirmed in its prerogatives.[45] Wellesley reported that the "Protestant part of the community uniformly contend against government intervention in Irish education. The clergy complained that limitation of religious instruction to week-end periods would be insufficient to correct Catholic-inspired errors accumulated during the week. Wellesley added that even Protestants who were inclined to accept the substance of the reports believed that only Catholic recommendations had been implemented.[46] Kildare Place and its more vigorous proselytizing counterparts, angry at the prospect of implementing the recommendations of the Spring Rice commission, also opposed the idea of central supervision of all schools.[47] Kildare Place claimed that it was unable to understand how the committees could champion their own principles on one hand but contemplate terminating grants to the society on the other.[48]

As in 1814, the government was unable to fashion a policy favorable to all parties. Again, it dared not ignore the question, for "expectations had been excited by the commission" and deficiencies of the existing system generally "admitted and confirmed." It would be, Wellesley added, more difficult to make a case against the reports, than to "justify passing it over altogether." On the other hand, no member of the Liverpool ministry was prepared to adopt the proposal wholeheartedly. Goulburn opposed abandoning grants to the private societies until and unless proof existed another system of elementary education would work in its place. Burdened with these reservations and deeply suspicious of Catholic intentions, the ministry resolved to do nothing dramatic. Indeed, as it happened, it did nothing at all.[49]

Unlike 1814, the matter was not destined to rest again for a decade. Tempers had flared and expectations raised and Catholics were prepared to take the offensive in securing for themselves the benefits of well publicized parliamentary largesse to Irish education. It was far better, the Irish primate observed, to withdraw all grants from all the private societies than to give money to the Catholic bishops for parochial schools.[50] Ironically, this was also the conclusion of the new Irish secretary, Edward Stanley, appointed when the Whigs gained power at the end of 1830. Stanley noted Kildare Place was spending sums granted to it with furious alacrity in an effort to demonstrate its central role in Irish education. This in turn induced Catholics to forward demands for a share of the grant. Stanley reached the conclusion that the only recourse was a comprehensive system along the lines of Spring Rice's proposal of 1828.[51]

Years of legislative intervention in Irish education, coupled with Catholic approval of national education, the attack on the private societies, and the liberal turn in political developments after Catholic emancipation all played their part in the formation of a new system. The most salient feature was the creation of a new education board

equipped with full powers to regulate Irish parochial and endowed
schools. The board could dictate textbook requirements, select
teachers, and finance support. The breathless pace with which the
new system came into operation caught everyone by surprise. Despite
a stream of petitions from Irish and English Protestants, despite
protests from Kildare Place at the prospect of being deprived of
government funds, and despite angry confrontations between Liberals and Conservatives in Parliament, Stanley proceeded to create a
board by the end of 1831.[52] The dominant personality on the new
board was Richard Whately, the Whig appointed Archbishop of Dublin.
Whately was a confirmed Liberal and a noted economist. His economic
theories inclined him to recommend some severe measures for treatment
of Ireland's unemployed paupers. He subscribed to the wage fund
theory, which held among other things that productivity rather than
any redistribution of income was the only way to relieve the lot of
the poor.[53] He was not, however, insensitive to the real deprivations
which Ireland's poor faced, and he gave generously in a most discrete
way.[54] As part of his package of solutions, moreover, he advocated
an impressive program of public works.[55]

In all these respects Whately was separated almost completely
from the remainder of the Irish bench. Brushing off totally unfounded but widely circulated allegations that he had received Dublin after
agreeing to support national education,[56] Whately proceeded to direct
his associates on the board (which included three Protestants, two
Catholics, and two Presbyterians) to the construction of a general
system of elementary education. He managed to prevent the system at

the same time from being destroyed by theological divisions.[57] The

achievement was immense: 3,500 schools attended by 400,000 children,

equipped with inexpensive, orderly, informative texts. There were

also several model schools and workable operational guidelines. Be-

cause of Whately's dynamism even Peel dared not challenge the system

during his brief ministry in 1835, much to the consternation of

Churchmen and political conservatives alike.[58] Upon their return to

power in 1835 the Whigs raised parliamentary grants and accelerated

expansion of the system. By 1840 the national schools were a perman-

ent feature of the Irish scene.[59]

The dilemma of the Established Church was acute. In the House

of Lords the Irish bishops led a vigorous assault on Stanley's system.

A few months after the scheme was made public, Beresford and sixteen

other members of the Irish bench complained in a petition that the pro-

posed national schools deprived the Established Clergy of their right

to superintend national education. It transferred to Catholic priests

that "preference and predominating influence, which has hitherto been

assigned to the purity and authority of religious truth than to the

numerical supremacy of the members of any communion in a single part

of the united empire."[60] He repeated his plea in February 1832.

In March he reaffirmed that the "clergy could not subscribe to any

system of national religious education in which right of reading the

scriptures should be either avowedly or impliedly denied, or even held

in doubt."[61]

Beresford's tireless petition campaign had no effect on the Whigs,

and even Peel proved peculiarly insensitive to his ringing denunciations of popery. In March 1836 a move for a new commission on Irish education was denied by Melbourne, the Whig Prime Minister.[62] Outside Parliament a wave of pamphlet literature fortified the determination of most Anglican clergymen not to attach their schools to the system. The Christian Examiner painted the national system as the tool of Rome, forced on Ireland by the papacy as part of a large and ingenious international plot to eradicate Protestantism in Europe. The magazine, and by implication many Anglicans, refused to accept the principle that priests should be allowed "to make use of the schoolroom for the purpose of teaching the peculiar dogmas, the superstitious rites, the intolerant sentiments, the blasphemous fables, the dangerous deceits, and, in a word, all the errors of popery."[63]

The pronounced opposition of Beresford and most of the bench eventually expressed itself in a heroic effort to construct by private subscription a national system which would conform to the principles of the Established Church. By 1835 it was clear that parliamentary opposition to national education and heavyhanded tactics by Anglican landlords to suppress local support for national schools was ineffective. Attempts to attract students by conducting classes in the Irish language resulted in only temporary successes for the Established Clergy. At length many landlords sought local peace by ending their opposition to the national schools and by contributing land for their construction.[64] Presbyterians negotiated with the board for concessions which allowed them to participate in the national education scheme without surrendering their religious scruples. But the Church of Ireland raised the banner of "no surrender". It eschewed all attempts at ompromise with the system, and moved ahead with its own denomina-

ional program under the auspices of the Church Education Society.

ounded in 1839, the society was directed by the primate and eleven

ishops, an array of lay nobles and gentry, and a host of deans and

rchdeacons. A flood of endowments and expressions of geniune en-

husiasm gave the experiment an early momentum, with grants,

f some Ł10,000 increasing to more than Ł50,000 by 1847. Schools expan-

ed from 825 in the society's first year, with 43,000 pupils, to

ore than 1,800 schools and 100,000 students at its peak in 1844.[65]

he clerical apathy of 1814 and 1824 had been turned to energy and

o a devoted attention to education. The response of the laity

uggested an unparalleled level of religious enthusiasm. Goaded

y Whigs and Catholics to action, it appeared by 1845 that the Estab-

ised Church had conquered its own internal weaknesses and had

uccessfully defied the government as well.

The experiment, however, could not be sustained forever. There

as, in the first instance, considerable division of opinion within

he Church itself as to the merits of a policy of defiant indepen-

ence. Beresford's celebrated petitions of 1832 had not obtained

he signatures of all the bishops. Many clergy defied their superiors

d organized local groups to apply for grants from the national educa-

ion board. In Whately the proponents of national schools had an elo-

ent and able spokesman. He reasoned that the Established Church

uld not educate the entire nation. Neither the will not the re-

urces were present. The national education system was, on the other

nd, "more likely to be successful than any other." "There were objections, undoubtedly, against the education of Roman Catholics and Protestants together; there were objections, and stronger, to their education being conducted separately; there were also objections – the strongest – to not educating them at all."[66] The government was not trying to provide a complete educational program for the poor, but only a rudimentary grid, to which should be added the work of the Churches.[67]

Whately convinced a few who were not already inclined to accept the march of events. After 1838 he threatened to quit the board unless the Church changed its attitude.[68] Other voices were also raised in opposition to the Church Education Society. Gladstone suggested to Whately and others that a distinction be made between "vested" schools in which the national board retained full control, and "non-vested" schools, in which local patrons would receive some assistance from the board but still have considerable autonomy in determining curricula. These fertile thoughts found little response within the Church of Ireland.[69] Only one initiative in favor of national education emanated from a Church body. The clergy of Raphoe and Derry, upon amalgamation of their dioceses in 1834, called for a modification of the system so that Roman Catholic children need not attend scripture classes but could not leave the school during these hours to obtain religious instruction from their priests. Under this proposal the schools under control of the Established Church would be allowed to teach religion. Whatever chance this most modest concession from Church attitudes towards elementary education might have had was destroyed by the protests of the Irish clergy themselves, who held fast to a "no compromise" tance. This made it impossible that through negotiation the Church

ght obtain the required funds and still be able to impress its

eligious values upon the children.

After 1840 opposition to the national schools began to decline,

r rather was made futile by the rush of events. The very success

f the Church Education Society drew Anglican children from national

chools, which reinforced Catholic control. After Peel's return to

ower in 1841 the Church again pressed for dissolution of the national

ystem and for grants to denominational groups. Peel wavered, then

efused the request, fearing denominational emphasis would only bring

nrest in its wake.[70] Beresford refused to surrender without a final

ppeal. He interpreted Peel's refusal of separate assistance in

842 as reflecting fears of "rendering the National Board exclusively

Roman Catholic one." Subsequently Peel supported a grant for the

atholic seminary at Maynooth, which he had earlier opposed. "Apparent-

y," observed the primate, "he does not think much of this argument

nymore,"[71] and felt that Peel would eventually approve grants to

hurch Society schools.

Beresford was only deceiving himself. In 1845 he presented Peel

petition, signed by most of the bishops, 1,700 of the clergy, 1,600

f the nobility and gentry, and 60,000 people. The petition made a

onsiderable stir. But Peel again declared that denominational edu-

ation would make Ireland hard to govern and refused to support separ-

te grants to the Church Education Society.[72] Only a minor concession,

hat which deleted the provision that children of another faith must

e excluded during proselytizing exercises, was obtained. This was nothing more than what had in practice been conceded to Presbyterians before 1840 in order to gain their support. Even this latest rebuff at the hands of the ministry did not prompt an early surrender. At mid-century nearly three-fourths of the clergy, and half of the hierarchy, including Beresford, continued to oppose all suggestions for association with the national schools.

Financial considerations, however, had to be faced. Petitions to Parliament increased in number after 1850, when the central society's income levelled off and then began to decline. Finally, in February 1860 Beresford conceded in an address to the Clogher Diocesan branch of the Church Education Society that schools in trouble must conform to the national system. The alternatives were a generation of ignorant Protestant children or complete usurpation of national education by Catholics.[73] This flag of surrender did not quiet the troops. Indeed, Beresford was called a Judas Iscariot and perhaps two-thirds of the clergy continued to oppose surrender. Further negotiations between government officials and diehards proved both pointless and fruitless. Spokesmen for the no-surrender party proclaimed their willingness to respect the prohibition of "religious instruction" as followed in the national schools, if by "religious instruction" it was not intended to include readings from the Bible. The board refused; it dared not condone a principle which was in fact already being widely practiced by Presbyterians and Catholics informally, and it realized that with Beresford now committed to national education it need not negotiate with the die-hards. Finally in 1866 large numbers of the clergy determined to surrender, proclaiming their preference for united education over a denominational system.[74] Meanwhile,

annual receipts of the Church Education Society continued to decline,

and scholars decreased from nearly 70,000 in 1863 to 52,000 in 1870.

By the advent of disestablishment the Church Education Society was

but a skeleton of its former self.

The moral of the story involving the Church of Ireland and edu-

cation in the first two-thirds of the nineteenth century was not a

happy one. Everyone was preoccupied with religious considerations,

and these considerations led all parties to fight the battle for in-

fluence and control on the elementary school level. The role of the

Establishment here was encumbered by narrow thinking and a strange

inactivity at crucial times. In retrospect, the presentation of the

Fourteenth Report in 1812 offered the Church of Ireland a golden

opportunity to revive parochial schools and play a part in the task

of educating Ireland's poor. It is impossible not to wonder what the

wholehearted development of these parochial schools under the super-

vision of the national board might have meant for the vitality and

growth of the Church in the nineteenth century. Failure to use the

respite which followed Parliament's abortive work in 1813 and 1814 to

good advantage, by restoring to effectiveness the endowed and parochial

schools entrusted the Church, also represented a lost opportunity of

immense proportions. The impact of the "New Reformation" during the

1820s, and its contribution to proselytizing efforts in the schools

of the private societies, led to destruction of one system congenial

to the Church and the almost inevitable emergence of another far less

palatable. Finally and most important was the stubborn refusal to

recognize the dangers involved in ignoring national schools after
1831. This refusal was sustained in a heroic proportion within the
Church Education Society, but it allowed the new system to gravitate
by default to the Roman Catholic Church. Unwillingness to compromise
with the system was both shortsighted and unnecessary. It was shortsighted because it gave impetus to parochial tendencies within the
national education scheme. It was unnecessary because Presbyterians
had already proven by 1840 that small concessions and perspicacious
application of pressure could bend the schools to fit the Church's
priorities. Again one can only speculate what might have been the
long term results of a fusion of clerical zeal for education, so manifest after 1830, with access to the government educational cornucopia.

The implications of the educational drama extended far beyond
the classroom. Disputes over the question led to a serious alienation of Church and government from each other in a period when the
Church was most in need of assistance and protection. In 1845 Beresford confided to the Archbishop of Canterbury that the Establishment
had been ill-treated even by its erstwhile firmest supporter, Robert
Peel. Beresford accused the conservative ministry of bestowing preferments and dignities on the supporters of the national schools. He
alleged that previously uncongenial clergymen had been bribed to
announce their support for national education in exchange for a high
office.[75]

The education controversy also led to a sharp division of opinion
within the Church itself. Whately and Beresford, the only archbishops
remaining to the Church after provisions of the Act of 1833 came into

lay, were constantly at loggerheads, and the beneficed clergy moved
into opposing camps. It also prevented an easing of tensions with
the Catholic Church which might otherwise have followed final settlement of the tithe question in 1838. Whately resigned from the educa-
ional board in 1853 after a petty dispute over textbooks. This not
nly reflected continuing religious tensions, but destroyed the possi-
ility that Irish education might be an avenue to national unity. With
hately gone, Catholics became more aggressive than ever in their de-
ands for control over education and other questions. In losing the
attle for the children the Church contributed, albeit unconsciously,
o a deepening of divisions in Ireland. Many of them remain.

Chapter VI: Irish Church and Parliament in the

Age of Church Reform 1822-1833

1. Introduction: Church and State on the Eve of Catholic

Emancipation

Reviving interest in and increased appreciation of Whig reform
rograms between 1830 and 1838 have encouraged new studies on the re-
ationship of the Established Churches to critical nineteenth century
ebates on the nature of private property, the emergence of a secular
ociety, and the state's responsibilities in the spread of education.
s a major vested interest with extensive resources and privileges,
he Church of England was vulnerable to Radicals' demands for retrench-
ent. It weathered the crisis posed by the Whig ministries by accele-

rating internal reform and by identifying its interests with Peel and moderate conservatism.[1] The Church of Ireland, meanwhile, exhibited a series of deficiencies far more extensive than those of the English Establishment. Indeed, its problems called into question the efficacy of Establishment itself. The crucial importance of the Irish Church in prompting the collapse on the question of property rights of both the Grey-Melbourne ministry in 1834 and Peel's brief ministry in 1835 has recently been noted. The aristocratic character of the Whig interest was sacrificed to a more dynamic, middle-class liberalism. No-popery was fashioned by Conservatives as a campaigning instrument.[2] The Oxford Movement received a powerful stimulus by the accession of those opposed to traditional erastian practices. The entire system of vested rights which had sustained the Protestant ascendancy in Ireland was brought into question.[3] Parliamentary reform itself excited no more intensive and sustained debate concerning the prerogatives of government and the direction of British politics.

Increasing appreciation of the importance of the Irish Church issue in accelerating the pace of reform has done little to illuminate the Church's relationship to Parliament during this period, or to suggest to what extent the Church was more than a mere pawn of larger political forces. It has been implied, indeed, that the Irish Establishment played little or no role in determining the direction of reform.[4] These observers hold that the Church was unable to vindicate its position on any substantive issue, and that Church reform itself was limited to a short period in the 1830s when parliamentary pressure was intense and direct.

The process of reform, as has already been suggested, was in
fact more comprehensive than the tithe and "appropriation" debates
might indicate. The Church leadership engaged in an active and not
entirely futile exercise in modifying the direction of reform itself.
Prominent politicians, moreover, did not conceive of the Irish Establishment as merely a convenient abstraction for the elaboration of
reform principles. They found themselves moved by private considerations to modify their abstract principles to meet specific conditions.
Finally, since the reform impulse in the Church not only preceded the
collapse of the Wellington ministry in 1830 but had found expression
in Parliament as early as 1824 in terms of tithe legislation, the
events of the 1830s were not entirely the product of new forces and
new conditions.[5]

Until 1830 full appreciation of the Irish Church's exposed position escaped the notice of most political observers. Lord Liverpool's
reluctance to press the issue reflected several factors. Liverpool
himself was ambivalent as to the merits of Catholic Emancipation. He had
a healthy appreciation for the iconoclastic power of any "no-popery"
crusade. Finally, his exposure to the Church's reactions to the tithe
legislation of 1822, 1823 and 1824 suggested how difficult any reform
might prove to be.[6] In the course of Goulburn's work Beresford made
it emphatically clear that the Church regarded its property rights as
absolute, and its ecclesiastical status as indistinguishable from the
Church of England; there was no room for negotiation.[7] Nothing, including the Marquess Wellesley's admonition of Irish landlords for
their public denunciation of tithes, found Beresford appreciative. In

Beresford's eyes every move to negotiate implied that the Church's position would be modified.[8] Beresford informed Wellesley in an "accusatory tone" that tithe legislation set "at naught the rights and interests of the clergy." He hoped that the ministry, which had made a noble stand for thirty years against Jacobinical principles," would "not soon give way to the torrent which would destroy the landmarks of all property" and bring on "revolutionary confiscation."[9] In the wake of all this, Liverpool and Peel were understandably reluctant to agitate Beresford again.

There were, of course, rumblings of dissatisfaction in quarters much less sympathetic to the Church than was the government. In 1819 Newport submitted a motion for inquiry into the Irish Establishment. It was approved by the House of Commons after substantial reduction of the scope of the investigation.[10] The formation of the Catholic Association in 1822, and the increasing prominence of Catholic Emancipation as a parliamentary question thereafter was seen by most "Protestants" as an oblique assault on the Church Establishment.[11] In 1823 the Church Establishment was the subject of a motion by Joseph Hume. Hume moved to declare that the property now controlled by bishops, deans and chapters was public and therefore available for redistribution among all religious denominations. He asked that the Establishment be reduced and tithes be commuted. He assaulted the Church's property rights rather too vigorously. It alarmed champions of property in general and impressed upon Irish bishops in London the need for more vigorous attention to their ecclesiastical and parliamentary duties.[12] Hume repeated his motions in 1824 and 1825. In these debates Hume produced figures suggesting that Irish bishops obtained huge sums as renewal fines, while tenants lost all benefit from their capital improvements. So serious was episcopal mismanagement of its property and so rich was the Church, according to Hume, that Ireland's economic and social difficulties could not be alleviated until Church property was confiscated.

Hume's motions were easily defeated in a lightly attended House. But the strength of Hume's support in 1824, totalling some 79 votes, indicated that sentiment against the Church was increasing.[13] More alarming was a debate on proposals submitted to Parliament, also in 1823 and 1824, to reform "first fruits." Hume requested that this ancient levy be revived, so that the first year's income of every clergyman in a new benefice could be used to replace public assistance to the Church and to subsidize public welfare projects. The government declared that the clergy was fulfilling all its legal obligations and Goulburn accused Hume of impugning the clergy's integrity. The motion was negatived on a very close vote, 39 to 29, in 1823, and was again narrowly defeated, 87 to 71, in 1824.[14]

Even more attention was drawn to the ill-conceived request made by the Bishop of Derry that an appropriation be granted to Derry to repair the cathedral. This innocuous proposal invited Radicals' inquiries as to why the cathedral had been allowed to decay. They embarrassed the Church by producing evidence that a fund once established for cathedral maintenance had been squandered.[15] The government launched some halfhearted initiatives of its own, partly to steal thunder from the Whigs, partly to impress upon the Church the need for further exer-

tions. Goulburn brought in a mild residence bill in February 1824.
He was not a little vexed at the failure of many bishops to supply
returns as ordered by the House of Commons for every year after
1809.[16] Goulburn's magnificently innocuous proposal offered to tighten
the 1808 requirements by further limiting bishops' discretion to excuse the clergy from residence. Newport asked that pluralism be outlawed if one benefice was worth £400 or more. Goulburn parried this
but in turn withdrew his own bill.[17] Newport thought well enough of
his own proposal to introduce it again in 1825. This time he barred
all pluralities and urged repeal of statutes permitting creation of
episcopal unions. Leave was granted to bring in the bill, but it
was defeated.[18] Hume then offered a motion declaring Irish Church
property to be part of the public domain. He requested that a select
committee be established and instructed to determine how this property
should be disposed. George Canning in opposing this motion referred
to the Act of Union's commitment to the Church, and Hume's motion
was easily defeated 126 to 37.[19]

In March 1826 the Earl of Kingston moved that large unions be
divided. Neither this nor Newport's renewed call for a select committee to examine inequities in the collection of first fruits gained
much attention.[20] Isolated opposition continued thereafter, but not
until 1829 did developments take a more serious turn. In April of
that year Edward Stanley, a respected and talented Whig politician,
proposed a reform of episcopal leases. He charged that Church reform
was not only attractive to the Radical fringe but to the main body of
respectable and moderate reformers in Parliament. Lord Leveson Gower,

the Irish Chief Secretary at the time, joined with Peel in urging the
ministry not to attempt to defeat the motion.[21] The session also saw
Cobbett offer a motion in favor of disestablishment. Proponents of
the motion were left in a small minority, but Cobbett's initiative
marked the boldest challenge to date on the subject of the Irish
Church.[22]

In this context, Wellington's decision to support Catholic emancipation, while only indirectly related to the Establishment, meant
an inevitable resurgence of alarm within the Church and prompted
Beresford's vigorous opposition. In this case Beresford could not
complain of an assault on the Church's prerogatives or property rights.
He did forward a series of demands for Protestant guarantees which
would if accepted by the government have insured Catholic rejection
of emancipation.[23] He also wanted compensation in the form of parliamentary grants for churches and glebe houses. When Wellington rejected
these demands Beresford consulted with the "ultras" and mustered sixteen episcopal Irish bishops to declaim against the bill.[24] All this
activity established in hostile minds a picture of the Irish "church
militant" contesting every inch of ground and fighting "in some broken
pot-works, from which she is driven with confusion."[25]

When the Whigs took power, the Irish Establishment was already
clearly on the defensive. The Catholic political revolution had already undermined the traditional erastian system in Ireland. The
government could no longer afford to abuse the Established Church by
pernicious uses of its patronage. The Church could no longer expect
protection from its enemies within and without Parliament. The Es-

tablishment was seemingly involved, in one way or another, with virtually every Irish grievance: the tithe; the cess; its immense properties improperly managed. While some clergymen conceded in private that the Church's anomalies could not be tolerated longer, most did not. The majority also resented the somewhat simplistic implication that all of Ireland's problems would be resolved were the Establishment destroyed. Indeed, the shortsightedness of the Church not only vexed liberals, but conservatives as well. It might be true that it was "the strongest bulwark for securing the union" of England and Ireland, but under present conditions the price paid in Irish agitation and parliamentary unhappiness was a costly one.[26]

In part the painfulness of the prospect of legislative intervention stemmed from a recognition that the considerable progress of the period 1810-1830 was not enough. And yet much had been done. Under Parliament's ever closer scrutiny glebe houses, churches, and glebe lands had been acquired and improved, so that by the 1820s the physical reconstruction of the Irish Church was much advanced.[27] Nonresidence had been reduced everywhere in Ireland, and most strikingly so in the South and West. But anomalies remained, many of which could not adequately be eliminated without recourse to Parliament. And the Established Church, whatever the magnitude of internal improvement and perhaps because of it, was a source of discontent. Therefore the inevitable move towards Church reform by Parliament got underway in 1830.

2. Stanley, Beresford and the Beginnings of Church Reform

The first move to prepare the ground for legislation in the area of Church reform preceded the collapse of Wellington's ministry in 1830. A year before this the government contemplated including Ireland in a royal commission on ecclesiastical law.[28] This was rejected. Early in 1830 Beresford himself proposed that Parliament investigate opposition to tithe payment. His advisors noted any such investigation would almost inevitably be extended to include non-residence and other anomalies, and this in turn was withdrawn.[29] The third initiative, this by Sir John Newport, was not to be parried so easily. On March 4, 1830 Newport proposed a comprehensive investigation of parochial unions: their value and their possible dissolution; curates' salaries and the exercise of pluralities. During this investigation the Crown was not to exercise its rights in parochial preferment. The government was unable to stomach so comprehensive an initiative, but after taking the pulse of Parliament it agreed to all investigation suggestions. Patronage functions were not suspended, but an accounting of all dispensations to permit pluralities during the previous ten years was undertaken. Peel in supporting these concessions launched a scathing attack on ultra-conservatives for abusing the aging Newport.[30]

While still digesting concessions made in response to Newport's motion on parochial unions, on May 18 the government faced a second Newport initiative. This time the first fruits issue was revived again. As noted earlier, the Papal impost of a first year's income from each new incumbent's benefice had been transferred to the state during the reign of Henry VIII. The law had been studiously neglected for most of the next two centuries, and first fruits were restored to the Church in 1710. Faced with the choice of reviving this ancient tax or obtaining funds from Parliament, the Irish Church had chosen to appeal to Parliament, fearing that the clergy would refuse steadfastly to surrender a portion of their income. A vigorous program of church and glebe house construction had been carried out under the aegis of Archbishops Stuart and Brodrick. There remained, however, the legal obligation of the clergy to pay first fruits. When pressed to resume these payments, Irish clergymen either denied that the tax was still valid, or remitted the amount paid in the Reformation era, which amounted to only a pittance. As a result, very small sums trickled into Church coffers. During the ten year period preceding January 1821 only £3752 was collected. During the decade preceding January 1830 only £5142 was received. The latter decade had seen fifteen bishoprics and four archbishoprics become vacant and therefore liable to first fruits. Since 1800 out of nearly 1000 benefices granted to new incumbents 467 had never been assessed anything, and in another 366 benefices the incumbents had chosen to ignore the assessment. The remaining 250 benefices contributed a total of £2000. Sir John Newport estimated (and his estimate was not challenged) that had first fruits been collected rigorously from 1800 to 1830 it would have exceeded that £686,000 granted to the Church by Parliament between 1800 and 1822. Indeed, Newport's estimate was conservative. Derry, with an annual revenue of nearly £20,000, paid only £250 as first fruits. Cashel contributed £93, Cloyne £10, Killaloe £20, Clogher £350, and Cork and Ross £50. One

English diocese, Winchester, paid more than all Irish dioceses combined.

After 1800 several efforts had been made to restore first fruits
as a principal source of revenue for the Church, in every case by requesting a new valuation of annual incomes and by initiating more vigorous efforts at collecting amounts due. Newport had sponsored a
motion to this effect in 1808, when it was rejected by only 17 votes
in a lightly-attended House. Another motion in 1824 was defeated by
only 12 votes. Between these two parliamentary initiatives Shaw Mason,
the first Receiver of First Fruits after revival of the Central Board
under Brodrick, was empowered "to collect, levy and receive, and to
examine and search for the just and true value of all and singular
archbishoprics, bishoprics, and all other ecclesiastical dignities
and benefices whatever in Ireland." To the consternation of many
clergymen, Mason at once demanded payment of first fruits from those
who had never done so. Mason also demanded that new valuations be
made. The Attorney General and the Solicitor General declared this
illegal. In 1822 Shaw appealed to the ministry for redress. Goulburn
at that time ordered Shaw to desist. Shaw reluctantly complied.[31]

Newport's third motion, offered May 18, 1830, brought a prompt
denial from Levenson Gower that the Henrician statutes cited by Newport permitted, much less demanded, a new valuation. He labelled
Newport's proposal simply "a question of taxing the Irish clergy for
the support of the Irish Church." If this principle was admitted,
Leveson Gower continued, it would also be valid to say that "the Church
of Ireland was established for the benefit of the clergy and not for

that of the country."[32] Another Whig, Thomas Spring Rice, supported
Newport with a sharp and sarcastic assault on the doctrine of ecclesiastical immunity from care of the Church. Irish bishops, he ventured,
would not "be looked on with less reverence if the churches were built
and kept in a state fit for worship, as in olden times they were, out
of the wealth of the Church itself rather than by taxes wrung from the
people." Newport's motion was defeated, but the message was clear.
In the wake of this debate Wellington's ministry moved to appease
liberal elements within and without the government by fashioning an
Ecclesiastical Commission of its own. It was given wide powers to
examine unions, non-residence, and payment of curates' salaries.[33]

The prospect of an ecclesiastical commission and the inevitability
of Church reform in its wake did not excite general alarm among supporters of the Irish Church. The likelihood of Wellington's government remaining in power seemed excellent in the spring of 1830, and suggestions for reform would therefore be moderate. The commission itself,
"if properly dealt with," might save the Church from a full exposure
of its anomalies.[34] Beresford's belligerent opposition began to moderate, and he himself admitted that "some legislative interposition
[was] absolutely necessary to enforce our very defective discipline."[35]

Beresford had further reason to be satisfied when the government
moved to select members for the Commission. Francis Leveson Gower
suggested that Beresford preside. He accepted most of the primate's
recommendations as to membership on the Commission, and even proposed
additional nominees likely to defend the Church.[36] As constituted,
the Board included three bishops, two laymen strongly sympathetic to

the Establishment, two moderates, and John Erck as Secretary. Erck's two decades of work on various ecclesiastical commissions seemed likely to insure that the Board's transactions would not take a radical turn.[37]

The Commission fulfilled the Church's most sanguine expectations. Its first report, issued a year later, was a model of decorous language and dull exposition. The report dealt only with the province of Armagh (where the Church was efficiently conducted) and aroused little excitement. The recommendations were also modest: creation of a legal instrument to dissolve unions where this was practicable; an end to the appropriation of parochial incomes to Church dignities and ecclesiastical bodies; fusion of vicarial and rectorial tithes; conversion of perpetual cures into rectories or vicarages; and adjustment of parochial boundaries.

Other inquiries, however, were also being proposed. Even as the Commission of Ecclesiastical Inquiry was being organized Parliament entertained recommendations that the Church vestry, its powers already restricted, be abolished.[38] The tithe question was also revived. Indeed, in terms of property questions alone, the Establishment was vulnerable not only to Catholics, but to Protestant landlords who expected to profit from confiscation of some of its resources. More than ecclesiastical considerations were at stake in Irish Church reform.[39]

The Whigs' initiatives gradually waxed more vigorous and more comprehensive. In August 1832 a Royal Commission was created to examine ecclesiastical patronage and revenue in Ireland. The Commission

was formidable in size. It included in addition to two archbishops
and five bishops four Irish noblemen, four government officials,
Newport, Parnell and eight others, whose views were certain to upset
many Churchmen. This commission did not begin to issue its reports
until legislative reform was well underway. Its comments on patronage
anomalies and on administrative inefficiency, however, sustained the
demand for reform after 1834.

The work of the 1832 commission, which in effect supplanted the
1830 Commission of Ecclesiastical Inquiry, extended over most of the
remainder of the decade. To discuss the board here anticipates the
chronology of reform but since its impact on day-to-day political
developments was slight, a word may be appropriate. Four reports, the
first appearing in March 1833 and the last in July 1837, covered almost every aspect of ecclesiastical revenue and patronage. The first,
and most controversial, dealt with the revenue of bishops and archbishops and, appearing in isolation, seemed to vindicate a highly popular impression of unbounded ecclesiastical munificence. The ₤17,000
income and 100,000 acre landholdings of the primate excited the envy
of some of Britain's most prominent peers. A second report, on cathedral chapters and dignitaries, highlighted pockets of inefficiency.
The third and fourth, dealing with patronage and income questions on
the parochial level, helped to discount overblown reports of ecclesiastical wealth, but not in time to save the Church from its confrontation with high priests of Benthamite reform.[40]

The decade, finally, was graced with a series of reports on other
aspects of the Church of Ireland, all of which underscored the new

emphasis on administrative efficiency and expanding governmental responsibility in national life. A religious census in 1834 was directed towards the number of resident clergymen, benefices with churches
and glebe houses, and the religious configuration of the Irish population. It revealed that only 11 per cent of the nation was Anglican,
only 8 per cent Presbyterian, and 81 per cent Roman Catholic.[41] In
July 1835 parishes with fewer than 50 adherents were enumerated,
and later a count of benefices without vestigatory commission involved
ecclesiastical courts and the relationship between civil and canon
law.[42]

The advantage of immediate administrative reorganization, whatever the verdict of all the commissions, was dimmed by the end of
1830 by several developments. The accession of the Whigs brought
forward the question of parliamentary reform, temporarily obscuring
the plight of the Irish Church. Irish bishops were decidedly less
enthusiastic at the prospect of Church reform under Whig direction.
In a lengthy private memorandum Lord Wellesley, viceroy in Ireland
for the second time in 1833 and 1834, reviewed ecclesiastics' opposition to reform. He admitted that he admired the adroitness of Churchmen in preventing the commission from asking embarrassing questions,
in delaying the submission of required questionnaires, and indeed in
isolating opponents from any voice in the commission's proceedings.[43]
Indeed, the bishops did little to expedite the work of the ecclesiastical commissioners, and after the Whigs took office the eruption of
tithe agitation distracted attention from administrative anomalies.
Legislators turned their energies to larger questions involving the

Church.

3. Tithe Agitation and Legislation

Resurgence of tithe agitation in 1830 began with a collision between the incumbent and tithe payers in Graignuenamanagh, County Kilkenny in November and December 1831.[44] In this, an area of high cultivation and resultantly lucrative tithes, the price of grain had
fallen by one quarter since 1820. Reduction in the tithe was the
principal object of the local agitators.[45] A particularly pusillani-
mous curate, prominent in the "New Reformation" movement, aggravated
tensions by his refusal to negotiate with tithe payers.[46] By intimi-
dating prospective buyers of goods distrained for tithe Catholics not
only effectively nullified tithe collections, but found immediate
response in other parts of Ireland.[47] Attempts to suppress agitation
by forceful application of the law at Graig were thwarted. This demonstration of legal impotence became an open invitation to resist
tithe payments elsewhere.[48] Sporadic resistance was reported in the
spring of 1831, but large scale opposition awaited the autumn applotment.[49] By then John Doyle, the Catholic Bishop of Kildare, had justified resistance to tithes and blood had been shed in two clashes in
May and June.[50]

Parliament was also forced to confront the Irish tithe problem
once more. In December 1830, even as the Whigs assumed office, a broad
based attack on tithes was mounted by Irish landlords of all economic
backgrounds, and petitions began to swell in number.[51] Protests against
English   tithes were also numerous, following a government promise

to submit a tithe reform bill along the lines of the Irish bill of

1824.[52] In February a combination of English and Irish radicals

brought in a bill to exempt the potato. Edward Stanley for the Whigs

and Goulburn for the Tories declared that this would be an illegal

appropriation of church property.[53] Each new report of tithe resis-

tance prompted reciprocal accusations. The Irish clergy blamed priests

and radicals and O'Connell chastised the absentee clergy.[54] Prominent

Liberals blamed the Tory bill of 1824. Spring Rice accused Goulburn

of having destroyed hopes for an effective compulsory tithe composi-

tion system by his public ridicule of the plan of 1823, a year before

he was forced to adopt it.[55] By late autumn, Irish clergymen were

petitioning the government to counter growing tithe resistance by

using force. The Whigs realized the question could be delayed no

longer.[56]

A promise of tithe legislation was made from the throne in

December. The task fell to Stanley, whose disinclination to confront

the problem was already well known in Parliament.[57] He was under no

illusions as to the potential disaster represented by tithe resistance.

He was energetic, imaginative, decisive, and a supporter of the Irish

Establishment. As his biographer has noted:

> Of the complicated questions with which Stanley had to deal
> the one most intimately associated with him was that of the
> Irish Church. Involved were two of Stanley's most strongly
> held ideals--Protestantism and private property, for he felt
> the fate of the Church of England, control of Ireland, and
> the rents and properties of landlords were united closely
> with the Irish Church.[58]

Stanley was quick to realize the significance of the Kilkenny agita-

tion. In November 1830, even before Irish agitation had begun to spread, Stanley noted to Blomfield, the Bishop of London that

> the payment of tithes will in a very few years cease, on
> account of combinations keeping within the law, which all
> the powers of the government are insufficient to resist
> and which are spreading and will spread from the success
> that is attending them, until without any struggle or
> breach of the law the Protestant Establishment will cease
> to exist.

He did not dispute the Church's legal right to full enjoyment of its

tithes. He doubted, however, that this right could be sustained.

Concessions were necessary, and the clergy must make them. Until

the tithe was forcibly cast as a money payment, and then commuted to

land, agitation would continue and erosion of the Irish Church would

follow in its wake.[59]

Stanley's solution to the tithe problem was restricted by per-

sonal scruples and political necessity. He had been tapped for the

Irish Chief Secretaryship in an attempt to appease rival factions on

the Irish Church issue. By his zealous defense of the Establishment

in the 1820s it was hoped Church supporters would be comforted;

"Catholics" would remember his support of the Emancipation bill.[60]

The government was unclear in its general program for the Irish Church.

Lord John Russell believed the Grey ministry had been founded on the

principle of reform but "ultras" pushed out of the Tory party by

Catholic emancipation were obviously unable to accept this view.[61]

Again Stanley was seen as a symbol of compromise. He could not, how-

ever, take full advantage of the support which he enjoyed in the new

ministry. He would not challenge ecclesiastical property, which he

believed lay beyond the reach of Parliament.[62] The tithe, as private

property, could not be abolished, as O'Connell demanded, without

irreparable harm to all rights of ownership.[63] Stanley was also
determined to force payment of arrears as an act of justice to the
Church. His room for maneuvering was limited. He might invite the
Church to "come forward with a liberal proposition which would give
its friends a firm basis for giving it zealous support" but he could
not force it to do so.[64] He might offer what to him seemed a radical
reform of the tithe and still not satisfy liberal Whigs, whose ministerial influence was increasing.[65] He felt obliged to enforce tithe
rights in Ireland but feared this would increase resistance. He
recognized the need for legislative reform but concluded correctly
that rumors of reform would strengthen the resolve to resist the
tithe.[66] He was committed to composition, despite its tendency to
invite invidious comparisons, reduce flexibility in payment, and tax
previously exempt graziers. He anticipated eventual commutation,
despite widespread suspicion among Irish landlords that the lands
held by the Irish Church were already far too extensive.[67]

The Irish Establishment too, was deeply suspicious of Stanley's
methods and motives. Despite threats and terrorism, the clergy was
not prepared in 1830 and 1831 to surrender their legal rights.[68]
Beresford himself noted that the Church's importance was not appreciated by the government and that "even the friends of the Church" were

> but too willing to listen to every scheme of spoliation
> which may hold out a precarious hope of tranquility. In
> such a temper of the public mind was the emancipation bill
> carried and in the same temper are various schemes for re-
> modeling and disposing of Church property discussed in the
> present day. Everyone feels the conviction that the former
> remedies so much relied on have done nothing for our cures
> and as in all desperate cases everyone is willing to try
> the first new remedy that is offered. I am aware of the

embarrassment created to the government by our unhappy
divisions. It cannot at all times do what it would desire.
The very physical danger against the Church both here and
in England is not to be disregarded by them and I am free
to admit that no sacrifices of individual interest, however
great, nothing short of a surrender of religious principles,
would be too costly. in order to make of us a united and a
contented people. [64]

He could not, however, support commutation. There was in most cases

no land available for purchase in lieu of the tithe, and the result

would necessarily be the accumulation of large sums in the hands of

tithe commissioners. The temptation for expropriation thus posed would

not easily be resisted by anti-clerical elements in Parliament. The

1824 decision had not worked, he believed, because of the opposition

of graziers, whose influence would also destroy Stanley's more ambi-

tious scheme. But the violent course of events could not be sustained.

The Church was forced to choose between commutation and resistance

"to every proposal of innovation, as tending to the ultimate surrender

of the Church's property."[70] The temper of Parliament supported vio-

lent assaults on its property. The clergy's generous concessions in

composition agreements concluded under the 1824 act had been forgotten.

The clergy's openhanded allocation of tithe revenues to charitable

purposes had gone unrecognized.[71]

The ministry's decision to press for immediate reform of the Irish

tithe system came in 1831, and Stanley was commissioned to fashion legis-

lation which might somehow conciliate the welter of conflicting inter-

ests. Beresford resigned himself to the inevitability of commutation.

Within the cabinet itself, however, there was considerable disagreement

as to the proper scope of reform. Stanley proposed to limit the tithe bill to the immediate problem of non-payment, and to leave other serious matters, such as the extent of Church lands and revenues, the question of state support for the Catholic clergy, and the vexatious vestry cess, to another time.[72] The Marquess of Anglesey as Lord Lieutenant wanted to introduce a scheme incorporating reduction and sale of bishops' lands and payment of the Catholic clergy.[73] Stanley, however, had the decisive advantage of knowing Anglesey's proposals before their appearance before the cabinet. He fashioned his objections accordingly, and succeeded in having Anglesey's ideas rejected.[74] Stanley in turn proposed that a committee of both Houses be established to investigate the tithe. This was approved. Catholics were excluded, to the immense relief of the Irish Church, and the committee was placed under Stanley's direct control.[75]

The committee was not, however, very popular with any section of Parliament. Peel had earlier condemned it as the best way to sustain agitation in Ireland. Stanley said this was avoided by a wintertime deliberation, when no tithes were due.[76] O'Connell was angry that Catholics had been barred from the committee. To this objection Stanley replied that since it was "a subject which bore immediate reference to the Protestant Established Church," the alterations "should not appear to be forced [on it] by those who did not belong to it."[77] The Lords suspected Stanley intended to cloak a general spoliation of the Church under the guise of a committee. Wellington in particular accused Stanley of deliberately and systematically destroying the Church.[78]

In January 1832, with the committee still deliberating, Stanley circulated his own observations within the ministry. The Composition

Act, he believed, should be made permanent and compulsory and the bur-

den eventually transferred to the owner in fee. The clergy would be

removed from a direct confrontation with tenants by commutation to

land. Liberal terms should be offered landlords by which device the

tithe could be redeemed by a fixed payment or by voluntary appropria-

tion of land to the clergy. The clergy would pay a premium of 15 per-

cent to encourage landlords to purchase the tithe. Funds derived from

the redeemed tithe would be invested in land for the clergy.[79] To meet

immediate problems, the Lord Lieutenant was to be empowered to relieve

the clergy's distress by grants from the Consolidated Fund. These

grants were later limited to £60,000, payable on a sliding scale, with

smaller proportional amounts to those with larger incomes. Stanley's

complaisant committee incorporated these suggestions into its own re-

port, released in March 1832. Again perhaps on Stanley's intiative,

the committee recommended establishment of an ecclesiastical corpora-

tion, composed of bishops and beneficed clergy, which would manage

Church finances in their respective dioceses.[80]

It was not sufficient, however, to propose a tithe commutation

formula. Without a bill authorizing the Irish government to intervene

to collect the tithe, Catholic Ireland might proceed to contemplate

destruction of the tithe by sheer agitation. It did not appear diffi-

cult to secure simultaneous passage of the arrears and reform bills in

the House of Commons. It was unlikely, however, that the Lords would

accept the reform bill. A suspicious House of Commons could not be

expected to accept the arrears bill, favorable to the Church, until it was assured of the Lords' favorable disposition regarding the package.[81]

On March 8 resolutions incorporating the tithe reform, collection, and arrears provisions were introduced in both Houses of Parliament. There was little difficulty in gaining approval for them in the House of Lords, although the phrase "complete extinction" ruffled some feathers.[82] Stanley had a much rougher time in the Commons. Here even defenders of the Establishment sought to disorient Stanley and delay considerations of provisions. One by one the resolutions were approved. By the end of March Parliament had assented in principle to radical tithe reform.[83] The government moved immediately to translate these resolutions into legislation. The arrears bill passed by the House of Commons on April 16 without serious difficulty, although the Radicals' language was so extreme that Stanley was visibly upset.[84] As passed, it ratified the £60,000 limit on withdrawals from the Consolidated Fund. It authorized clergymen to obtain relief equal to no more than two-thirds of the tithes due them for 1831, but never more than £500. Upon accepting the grant the incumbent surrendered his tithe rights, which in theory the government could exploit.[85] In the Lords passage was assured, and Stanley felt no need to concede even minor points to the Tories.[86] Even Beresford proclaimed the expedient as "seasonable, necessary, and just."

The primate's blessings proved small consolation for those burdened with the responsibility for putting the Arrears Act into effect.[87] The legislation was a palliative, and not a completely satisfactory one at that, for it made the government "the virtual tithe-holder general for a large portion of the Irish clergy."[88] The consequences

of all this would become more apparent in the autumn tithe evaluation
season.

Within the cabinet itself, Anglesey remained unreconciled, calling the system by which the Established Church was maintained in Ireland "odious, oppressive, and postively obnoxious."[89] With little
pretense to discretion Anglesey continued to criticize Stanley's
tithe reform bill, the next part of the legislative package, even as
it was introduced in the House of Commons in July 1832.[90] He was not
alone. Between March and July the report of the committee had been
subjected to sharp discussion, punctuated by more petitions against
tithes, and enlivened by O'Connell's proposed amendments.[91] Peel was
particularly adamant in his opposition to commutation. "If a prescription of 300 years can plead nothing in favor of the present settlement of the property of the Church," he argued, "how unlikely it is
that a prescription of 150 years can plead in favor of the settlement
of lay property." The question, he believed, was not reform but enforcement of the law; for protection of property people created society and government, pay taxes, and "submit to a thousand restraints."
Commutation was none of these; it was illegal appropriation of private property.[92]

But when Stanley introduced the bill in July, Peel had reason to
adopt a more moderate tone, for it was apparent that Stanley had backed away from "total extinction" and was thinking instead in terms of
an extension of the Goulburn—Wellesley formula of 1822—24. Stanley's
sensitivities in the area of alienating Church property were apparent.
Moderate Tories, such as Peel, supported the bill as the best of an

inevitably uncomfortable series of options available to the Church.
Ultra Tories joined other "ultras" driven into the Whig camp during
Catholic Emancipation in raising the cry of Catholic conspiracy and
no-popery. Peel also objected to the lengthy interim period between
composition and commutation, during which time the Church would remain
vulnerable to harrassment. He regretted that the compulsory discounting of the tithe in order to excite landlord enthusiasm would one day
be used to destroy all private property. He also opposed treating the
Irish Church as distinct from the Church of England.[93] Churchmen for
their part opposed the inflexibility of composition procedures, which
would see re-evaluation of the tithe, barring commutation, only once
every seven years.[94]

Attacks from the right represented a spirited defense of private
property, but those from the left were far more dangerous in terms of
ministerial unity. Stanley's surrender of "extinction" (Stanley was
destined to be plagued by loaded terminology in all aspects of his
church reform work) was made all the more galling to Radicals because
t was apparent that the ministry, deeply divided over the larger
question of property rights, had salved their consciences by mouthing
the term "extinction" while at the same time leaving control of the
bill squarely in Stanley's hands.[95] The term itself suggested aboli-
ion, not composition or commutation, and the disappointment of Radi-
als on receiving Stanley's bill was immense.[96] Relations between
Stanley and O'Connell were already disturbed.[97] O'Connell had been
arrested in 1831 for inciting disturbance, and, he firmly believed,
: Stanley's instigation. O'Connell pressed Stanley to confirm the

suggestion of appropriation, or at least to affirm that Church property could be expropriated. Stanley refused to do so.[98] Radicals, as a result, loosed all restraints in their fulminations against that "monstrous pile" of a Church.[99]

Harried by the right and left, Stanley moved ahead with the bill throughout July. The proposition was presented as three distinct bills: permanent and compulsory composition; investiture of Church revenue obtained from sale of tithe rights in a board of ecclesiastical commissioners; redemption of tithes by a land tax.[100] His poise under pressure from the conservatives for a pledge against confiscation, and from Radicals demanding confiscation, was remarkable. "The question as to the future application of revenues of the Church" was to be "left perfectly open," he declared; the important thing at the moment was to get the tithe bill through.[101] Two radical attempts to destroy the bill were defeated by wide margins.[102] Peel agreed to support the measure and although Russell moved towards a declaration that Church property could be diverted to secular uses, Stanley managed to keep him in line.[103] The bill reached the Lords August 6, where a string of petitions against tithes made little impression. The House of Commons agreed to minor amendments on August 15. A new tithe law was now in force.

As placed on the books, Stanley's tithe legislation extended the Goulburn composition scheme by empowering the Lord Lieutenant to enforce a settlement whatever the disposition of the local parties. Compositions were made perpetual. Revaluations could be made every seventh year, and, like the initial settlements under the new act, were

he responsibility of specially-appointed commissioners. Landowners
ould pay the tithes where tenants' leases were three years duration
r less. This was significant; more than any other portion of the
ill it was a harbinger of future developments in tithe legislation.
ther clauses enabled landlords to purchase the tithe from the clergy,
or whom land would be purchased instead.[104]

The weaknesses of Stanley's bills covering arrears and tithe
eform had been obscured by his masterly handling in every stage of
egislative discussion; now, however, these became painfully obvious.
he diocesan corporations of bishops and clergy soon discovered that
andlords did not find a discount of fifteen per cent sufficient in-
ucement to buy tithe rights at the specified rate of sixteen years'
alue. In turn, the corporations were unable to purchase land for
he clergy. The new and extremely complicated regulations afforded
riests every opportunity to thwart the tithe act without violating
he law.[105] By encouraging tenants to pay the tithe on the approach
f the police or magistrate, but at no other time, the priests insured
hat a demonstration of force in one locality was no help elsewhere.[106]
he arrears bill proved almost completely ineffective. Arrears no-
ices were posted on the doors of Catholic chapels in defaulting areas,
 here they were burned or ignored.[107] O'Connell estimated that it
ost the government Ł15,000 to collect Ł14,000 in the first year of
peration.[108] Stanley professed to have confidence in the eventual
uccess of the measure, but in private noted that he was not san-
uine.[109] The Tithe Act of 1832 did not provide that peaceful forum
o much desired for the next and more radical round of Church reform.

4. The Church Reform Bill of 1833:   Church-State Negotiations

The Irish Church Temporalities Act of 1833 has served historians

for more than forty years as a convenient litmus test of liberal and

conservative principles. Of late it has assumed a fashionably pivotal

role in sorting out the political confusion which followed Liverpool's

demise in 1827. In all this the role of the Irish Church itself in

the political transformation of the 1830s has been almost universally

ignored.[110] This distinction between the politicians' plans for

Church reform and Churchmen's attitudes have suggested that the Estab-

lishment proved unable to influence even the details of the proposed

legislation or to summon the latent power of the no-popery element to

defend its prerogatives. Neither is correct. On one hand Stanley

succeeded in involving Beresford in the formation of legislation to

such a degree that the Archbishop was effectively compromised as a

critic of the bill; on the other Peel emerged as the architect of

moderate ecclesiastical reform in the wake of the pleas of Irish Church-

men and did much to protect the idea of Establishment itself.[111] The

relationship between Stanley and the cabinet and Beresford must be ex-

amined in some detail; from these interlocking relationships emerged

the Whig measure for Church reform.

Stanley was pledged to the preservation of the Irish Church. He

refused to undertake the preparation of a reform bill without being

assured by his Whig colleagues that reform would not exceed certain

concrete limitations. Anglesey's efforts to identify reform with tithe

legislation in 1831 had prompted Stanley to express alarm at the Lord

Lieutenant's disregard for ecclesiastical property and to seek Angle-

y's transfer to India.[112] Grey doubted whether the ministry would
rvive office-changing. Stanley acquiesced in the prevailing arrange-
nts after extracting from the cabinet the principle "that the proper-
 of the Church was not to be diverted to other than Protestant
urch purposes.[113] Having established this condition, Stanley was
:epared to propose a program of Church reform encompassing abolition
f the church cess, reduction in the number of bishoprics and sinecure
ignities, formation of a commission to investigate church revenues
d patronage, and dissolution of parochial unions.

The moderate tone of Stanley's initiative was both congenial to
nd a reflection of well-established Whig principles on the erastian
onnection. Whigs believed in the idea of an Established Church. But
hey insisted that it conform to sentiments of the country, and not
o the niceties of theology. "They had no special attachment to the
hurch of England to make them view the Presbyterian Church of Scotland
ess favorably, and not all of them were so attached to Protestantism
hat they could not bear the thought of a Roman Catholic Establishment
n Ireland.[114] Stanley's plan was designed to engender support among
hose Whigs who were willing to give the Church of Ireland one final
hance. It was already apparent, however, that this benign approach
ight not be sufficent to curb more enthusiastic reformers.

In Stanley's short tenure as Irish Secretary the question of
hurch reform had already engaged the attention of several prominent
arliamentary spokesmen. In November 1830 O'Connell introduced a mo-
ion for comprehensive Church reform, declaring that only the support
iven the Irish Establishment by the Act of Union had sustained it so

long.[118] Stanley responded with a bill designed to meet O'Connell's
objections in the area of vestry rights. This was later withdrawn.[116]
In July of the next year Lord King, an Irish landlord with strong
anti-Church sympathies, demanded legislative intervention to abolish
Irish pluralities since Church leaders had failed to effect the reform
on their own.[117] A proposal to build chapels of ease in areas with an
expanding Protestant population was blocked.[118] Even the vestry act
of 1826 was hotly disputed.[119] In September 1831 O'Connell called on
the nation to resume control of the temporal possessions of the Irish
Church. This proposal finally bestirred some Irish landlords to a
spirited defense of private property.[120]

The most celebrated initiation into Irish ecclesiastical reform
was occasioned by the vacancy at Derry. With a revenue estimated by
some to be in excess of ₤30,000 per year and landholdings of 96,000
acres, Derry was a celebrated instance of concentrated ecclesiastical
wealth. In July 1831 Hume referred to the precedent of a partial disendowment of the bishopric of Malta as justification for a similar
treatment for Derry.[121] He withdrew a motion to that effect in September when Lord Althorp promised to put Hume's proposal under consideration.[122] Reducing Derry's temporalities was easily accomplished;
the vacancy went to Richard Ponsonby, Earl Grey's brother-in-law, on
condition that Ponsonby would abide by any decision to reduce the
bishopric's value.[123] Although this was regarded by radicals as defective implementation of its promise to Hume, the commitment to the
principle of Church reform seemed to have been confirmed.

Rumbles from Parliament went far to force the Whigs into pro-

sing ecclesiastical reforms. The history of the ecclesiastical
mmission of 1830 provided disconcerting proof that reform by
mmittee was impracticable. In two years of fitful labor the 1830
mmission managed to report only on unions of parishes in the province
Armagh. Even this unimpressive forward movement was slowed in
gust 1832 when most of the members of the 1830 commission were also
pointed to a new commission on Church revenues. This new challenge
s a considerable one, and in six months the new commission produced
set of returns so fragmentary and imperfect that further delays
re inevitable. As a result, the new legislative initiative of
tumn 1832 was destined to proceed on grossly insufficient data, a
rcumstance which committed Whig ministers to furious and sometimes
intelligible controversies on the nature and direction of Church
form.[124]

Stanley's plan for ecclesiastical reform, first presented to the
abinet in October 1832, reflected the work of an astute politician
opeful of conciliating Whigs and Conservatives by obscuration of
rinciple, circumvention of sensitive points of controversy, and
imitless pragmatism and improvisation. The first point provided for
he abolition of the church cess. This was a source of constant vexa-
ion among Irish Catholics, who resented their exclusion from the ves-
ry for purposes of determining the tax, but not for purposes of tax-
tion itself. They resented maintaining the facilities of the Protest-
nt parish, and were deeply suspicious of the clergy who presided over
he vestry and over allocation of funds entrusted to their care. Abo-
ition of the cess, however, meant that new sources of revenue were

needed to build and maintain Protestant churches and glebe houses.

In England this object had been met by first fruits, which were

technically paid to the crown but in fact allocated to smaller livings.

In Ireland this charge of a year's revenue upon each new incumbent, as

has been seen, had long been frozen at a nominal payment.[125] Rather

than restore it to full vigor, a burden which the Irish Church might

be unable to sustain, Stanley proposed to exchange the cess for an

annual tax on benefices throughout the entire period of incumbency.

The tax was to apply to all benefices valued at over Ł200 per year

after deductions, such as the 15 per cent charge to landlords for

collection of tithes. The value of benefices would be determined from

compulsory tithe evaluations as stipulated in the legislation of 1832.

The tax itself would represent 5 to 15 per cent of the value of the

benefice, established on a sliding scale. Livings worth Ł200 to Ł500

would be subject to a 5 per cent tax; those between Ł500 and Ł800 at

7 per cent; those between Ł800 and Ł1000 at 10 per cent; those above

Ł1200 at 15 per cent.[126] Lower rates would apply to the present in-

cumbents; pluralities would be taxed as a single benefice. Stanley

estimated that the tax would average no more than 6 per cent of all

the tithe income of the Established clergy.[127] Revenues engendered

by the tax would be paid to an ecclesiastical board, which would then

allocate the funds among the respective parishes and submit periodic

returns to Parliament.[128]

Stanley doubted whether revamping first fruits would meet en-

tirely the financial deficiencies caused by abolition of the cess.

He was therefore prompted to propose the further financial expedient f reduction of the number of bishoprics. That 800,000 Irish Church-

en were more than adequately served by 18 bishops and 4 archbishops

as admitted by all but the bishops themselves, who referred to their

esponsibilities as resident gentlemen and "pastors once removed" in

1arge of the millions of Irish Catholics. Stanley proposed that six

rish sees, in his happy phrase, be "incorporated with those adjoining

o them" and their revenues placed in a general fund for Church pur-

oses administered by the Board.[129] To this revenue was to be added

avings derived from the abolition of dignities where neither resi-

ence nor spiritual duties were required and from taxation of bene-

ices on a sliding scale.[130] These revenues were to be employed to

ugment poorer livings. The board, then, would operate within cer-

ain defined limits in allocation of its resources, compensating for

oss of the cess, augmenting smaller livings, constructing new churches,

nd pursuing "such other purposes, not particularly specified, as

nall appear to the Commissioners to be connected with the support of

he Established Church, and shall have been previously sanctioned by

arliament."[131]

Stanley's direction in these suggestions was clear. By com-

elling the Church to maintain its property by taxing its benefices

nd from savings produced by administrative rationalization, Stanley

as able to lay to rest the Radical contention that tithes be allocat-

d to this purpose.[132] He acknowledged the justice of those, whether

nfluenced by Benthamite ideas or not, who held that substantially the

ame level of ecclesiastical activity could be sustained in Ireland at

smaller cost.[133] He ended the cess, an impost by which ₤50,000 was

gained at the cost of immense public disturbance. He went far to
satisfy the grievances of many Irish evangelicals concerning the
inexcusable poverty of many hardworking curates and equally intolerable wealth of some virtual sinecurists.

Another financial proposal, however, proved considerably more
controversial A principal grievance of efficiency-minded critics of
the Irish Church was the method of renting bishops' lands. The
Commons' committee on the tithe had noted that

> the bishop being almost compelled to renew, under the
> penalty of forfeiting the annual fine, which constitutes
> the greater part of his income, the tenant has, in fact,
> a permanent interest in the land, but under conditions
> which may tend to discourage any improvements, as an in-
> creased fine may at any time be demanded by the bishop.[134]

This inconvenience was, in fact, less disruptive than might have been
thought, but because of reasons hardly likely to discourage Church
critics from intervening. Most leases were held by Irish aristocrats,
and indeed by members of the bishop's family who enjoyed use of some of
Ireland's finest lands at nominal rents and fines. As a result, the
Church was in fact subsidizing the aristocracy to sustain the influence of the Church itself. Stanley was eager to reform the system.
Ostensibly Stanley wanted to rectify the alleged difficulties confronted by tenants, in fact he hoped to destroy this pernicious and pervasive exercise in self interest which made competition among Irish
magnates for bishoprics an unseemly and dangerous affair. Stanley
suggested that tenants might contract a permanent interest if they
were permitted to purchase perpetual leases. The longer leases would
raise the value of the lease, running at twelve and one-half purchase
price under the old system, to twenty years'. Tenants would be able

secure permanent interest by tendering six years' purchase.
he sum, never having been the property of the Church, would be
vailable, after satisfying Church needs, for such use as Parlia-
ent might desire.[135]

This single departure from Stanley's firm commitment to "non-
lienation" was a remarkable exercise in semantic compromise.[136]
ontemporaries did not fail to see in it some evidence of Stanley's
trained efforts to avoid an occasion for secular employment of
cclesiastical property in principle. At the same time it provided
iberals with something which they could regard as a direct assault
n the sanctity of the temporalities of the Irish Church.[137] Lord
olland noted to Sir Denis Le Marchant, Brougham's secretary, that
with Stanley's views on the nature of Church property, we are
bliged to resort to fallacies to obtain his consent to liberal
easures."[138] It was certainly not designed to conciliate either
he Church or conservatives and was probably an uncomfortable exer-
ise for Stanley when forced to defend it. It represented, never-
heless, a concession to intense pressure within Grey's cabinet for
more pronounced assault on the Irish Church's vaunted prerogatives.

The proposal, in all, was an extensive one. Even Anglesey's
lan, so dreaded by Stanley, had not suggested that the episcopacy
e reduced, a proposal bound to inflame the passions of some Church-
en. Yet the Stanley plan was not likely to satisfy all members of
he cabinet. Stanley had not provided for the elimination of parishes
vithout cure of souls, and he had refrained from broaching the subject
f subsidizing the Catholic clergy. The elimination of non-cure

parishes threatened to open the larger question of the Church of

Ireland's right to national Establishment. The question of support-

ing the Catholic clergy was even more dangerous. Anglesey had attempt-

ed to insist on it, Grey had supported it, and even the King was not

hostile.[139] Stanley himself could extend the reform bill further only

at the cost of violating his own principles. He determined to resign

his office if either extensive widening of reforms already incorporated

in the bill or new principles were introduced.[140]

In presenting his bill to the cabinet Stanley was forced to con-

sider on one hand the disposition of Whig elements hostile to the pre-

tensions of the Irish Church, and those Whigs, and the great body of

Tories, who publicly supported the Establishment on the other. Ad-

herence of the former depended upon Stanley's success in demonstrating

that his reform was both substantial and adequate. Retaining the alle-

giance of the second required evidence that fundamental erastian prin-

ciples remained inviolate and that the Irish Church itself was not

opposed to reform. Within the Cabinet Stanley could rely, in the first

instance, on Lord Grey, who despite his readiness to place relatives

in its most lucrative preferments, believed the Establishment was ad-

ministratively unsound and opulent beyond its needs. But Grey also

considered the Church a bastion of stability that the House of Lords

would not let be destroyed by radical propositions.[141] Grey was sen-

sitive to the limits placed on reform by conservative tolerance. He

noted Irish tranquility must not be delayed while more radical propo-

sitions sought public support: one could not govern Ireland with "the

sword in one hand and a ukase in the other;"[142] reform was necessary, out on "a conservative principle."[143]

Stanley could also rely on Melbourne, who as Home Secretary was responsible for Ireland. Stanley held that the Church was an artificial grievance, but one requiring resolutions before tithe resistance undermined other species of property.[144] Melbourne, indeed, believed coercion more than conciliation was required in Ireland, and held that the Protestant interest should be cultivated more carefully.[145] Without Stanley, moreoever, Whig reforms of the Irish Establishment could hardly expect to receive sympathetic attention among conservatives.[146] Finally, Stanley could rely for support in the cabinet on Sir James Graham, the First Lord of the Admiralty, and the Duke of Richmond, both firm Churchmen and admirers of Stanley's political expertise. Neither was prepared to advance farther along the road to reform than Stanley had done already.[147]

Cabinet dissidents, however, were equally numerous and strongly convinced that Stanley had treated the Irish Church too gently. Anglesey, the Irish viceroy, though neither in London nor in the cabinet, provided considerable support for the anti-Stanley faction by declaring that it was impossible to keep peace in Ireland while Stanley's Church prejudices were being sustained.[148] In the cabinet itself Lord Althorp, leader of the House of Commons, offered the most formidable opposition. He was ably supported by Lord John Russell, Lord Durham, and, somewhat inconsistently, by the erratic Lord Brougham. Althorp was sensitive to the Stanley-Anglesey rift, which if not silenced must in time disrupt the cabinet. He devoted the weeks prior to Stanley's submission of the Church bill to cabinet scrutiny to efforts to shuffle the cabinet so as to remove Stanley from his Irish post.[149]

Durham and Russell reacted to intimations of what Stanley intended

to present in his reform bill by threatening to resign. Stanley

therefore faced a badly divided cabinet when he presented his bill

for the first time on the evening of October 19, 1832.

By this date Stanley had taken the initiative on another front

in an effort to gain wider support. He sought to enlist the services

of the Irish primate. By doing so Stanley wanted to gain not only the

support of Irish churchmen and their friends in Parliament, but to

fashion a case for feasible reform which might silence critics with-

in the Whig cabinet itself. The Whigs, Stanley was eager to show,

had never opposed the concept of the Established Church. They were

dedicated to making it a popular one.[150] Stanley interpreted this to

mean that Ireland should not be considered alone when justifying the

Protestant Establishment. As part of the United Kingdom, Irish

Protestantism was the majority confession. To convey his support for

the Irish Church and to gain Beresford's confidence in return, Stanley

approached the primate through an intermediary in the middle of Septem-

ber, one month prior to submission of the Church reform proposal to the

cabinet. The intermediary painted a somber picture of hostility to

the Church and suggested in cogent terms the advisability to Beresford

cooperating:

> . . . Unless Mr. Stanley can take the confidence of the pri-
> mate, and the heads of the Irish Church, our cause is lost.
> He is most anxious to save the Irish Establishment, and has
> made great personal sacrifices to do it. His present union
> with an ultra-Whig administration increases his difficulty,
> as it necessarily creates a suspicion in the minds of others
> of the soundness of his own principles. . . . Mr. Stanley

wishes for the primate's confidence and he is worthy of it.
The Church would have been actually given up but for him.
Unless he is met with reciprocal confidence and kindness he
will be moved from his present position, to occupy one more
disadvantageous than even the one he now holds.

Beresford was advised that J.C. Hobhouse, a man of more decided liberal

principles, would replace Stanley immediately if Beresford refused to

discuss the reform proposals with him.[151] Stanley was prepared to

assure Beresford that he did not regard the Church's wealth as too

large, or amenable to application to secular purposes. But he felt a

redistribution of its property among its members was inevitable. If

the Irish primate withheld his confidence, he could not guarantee a

more radical distribution and even expropriation would not result.[152]

Beresford consented to treat. This encouraged the Chief Secretary

to inform Beresford that the cabinet contemplated a reduction in the

number of bishops, and asked Beresford to suggest what formula might

be applied to eliminate six bishoprics with least discomfort to the

Church. Beresford in turn declared no reductions were necessary un-

less funds were to be appropriated to secular purposes:

> In such matters I deprecate all innovation of which the
> necessity is not urgent, and even from a secular point of
> view the bishops with their connections and dependents form
> a valuable class of resident clergy, diffusing throughout
> a wide circle the influence of superior information and good
> example and the benefit of liberal expenditure.[153]

If reductions were inevitable, he recommended Clonfert, Dromore, Raphoe,

Cloyne and Kildare be attached to neighboring dioceses, along with the

archdiocese of Cashel. Tuam should be reduced to a bishopric.[154]

Beresford also volunteered comments on reform of Church property, the

principal points of which Stanley had outlined in his letter. Beresford believed that the prevailing system of renewal was not unpopular,

based on the high value this type of property bore in the market.

He hoped Stanley would "pause" before being "induced by any theore-

tical plan" to proceed against episcopal property. He thought es-

tablishment of a common corporation to manage this property and in-

come from other sources a dangerous invitation to future parliament-

ary demands for expropriation. Finally, he hoped efforts to eradi-

cate the tithe were ended. Since composition was now compulsory and

permanent, there could be no plausible objection to rigorous enforce-

ment of the clergy's rights.[155]

Stanley chose to place an optimistic construction on this first

round of correspondence with Beresford. Grey reciprocated by noting

that Beresford "surprised some ministers with what appeared to be a

greater disposition towards reason than they were willing to concede to

a clergyman of Irish Establishment."[156] Stanley informed the primate

that his response afforded

> the hope that we may be enabled to do something effectual for
> the security of the Protestant Establishment not by conciliat-
> ing the leaders of the Catholics, for of that, with you, I
> entirely despair, but by gaining the power of making a suc-
> cessful resistance to them, supported by all the reasonable
> Protestants of both countries, and unopposed, if not assisted,
> by a considerable portion of the Catholics themselves who are
> desirous of preserving the union of both countries. . .[157]

This somewhat artificial euphoria constituted an introduction to Stanley's

next series of requests for concessions from Beresford. After outlining

his plan for a graduated tax on all benefices in lieu of first fruits,

without specifying the percentage to be demanded, and after hinting

that landlord reluctance to assist compulsory composition by assuming management of tithes meant commutation could not be delayed, Stanley hoped Beresford would not object to "one additional proposal." Noting that appropriation of sinecures by certain Irish families constituted "one of the glaring blots of which the opponents of the Church avail themselves and which give the erroneous idea of the general wealth and absence of duties in the Church," Stanley advised Beresford to agree to block the filling of sinecure vacancies.[158]

Beresford's reply was lengthy and impassioned. The Irish Church was the "firmest rock of support" for the English connection; alienation of additional revenue from bishops' lands

> would not answer the end of any wise government. It would revolt the Church's friends, without conciliating her enemies. It would be a precedent of evil omen to the security of all vested property. . . Such a measure I should consider as the first breaking up of the mounds opposed to radical cupidity.

Taxation of benefices likewise constituted a dangerous innovation. First fruits was always a "fraudulent state intervention" in its taxation of ecclesiastical fees and should be eliminated outright. Taxation restricted to those benefices requiring glebe houses might be acceptable; a general levy would not. Regarding abolition of pluralities, the evils Stanley complained of could be removed by placing strong diciplinary power in the hands of the bishops. Beresford again emphasized the danger of a consolidated Church fund, especially when enlarged by Stanley's insistence that the compulsory composition of tithes must be transformed into land. Finally, the primate noted that the plan to allow the crown to suspend the living to a benefice having no Church, for the purpose of augmenting still further the general fund, was susceptible to obvious abuses by any hostile ministry. Instead of eliminating parishes possess-

ing absent pastors, non-residence itself should be eliminated by
placing further disciplinary power in bishops' hands.[159]

Stanley chose not to pursue the Beresford correspondence further until the cabinet's reaction was clear. He could not afford to
make further commitments to the Primate when evidence was increasing
that substantial modification might result from Stanley's confrontation with Althorp, Durham, and Russell. The exchange of letters revealed Beresford's unhappiness with most of Stanley's proposals.
But Stanley was correct in interpreting Beresford's willingness to
continue the correspondence as significant for the success of the
Church reform bill. By admitting that if some moderate concession
would preserve the Irish Establishment it should not be opposed,
Beresford was unwittingly appearing to give his consent to Stanley's
plan. This interpretation, indeed, has persisted in modern accounts
of this period.[160] Beresford's correspondence with Stanley later
caused him endless embarrassment. It was not, at this stage, so much
a question of determining Beresford's ultimate position on Church reform as it was to present him to the cabinet, then to Parliament, as
a reasonable man. Stanley succeeded in doing this, notwithstanding
Beresford's growing discomfort. To this extent Beresford was the vic-
tim of a carefully laid plan, a plan which Beresford could later expose
only at the risk of making himself appear something of a dupe.

On the evening of October 19 Stanley faced the cabinet on the
Church reform issue for the first time. He moved immediately for a
pledge from all members of the cabinet that they would resist any
attempts in the Commons to extend the reform measure by amendment.

Durham objected to the government's pledging itself, with Althorp and Russell expressing less pronounced disapproval.[161] The meeting adjourned. The three opponents failed to concert their actions. Russell, who held that the index of a clergy's effectiveness ought to be religious ministrations, wanted abolition of benefices in those portions of Ireland containing few Protestants. This plan, if enacted, would have seen a large-scale withdrawal of the Church of Ireland from the countryside, and Stanley refused to support it. Russell therefore offered to resign at the convenience of Grey.[162] Althorp shared Russell's sentiments. He believed that the minority Establishment had no right to its superfluous revenues, which should be devoted to general purposes instead.[163] He was reluctant to resign, but hinted to Grey he would do so if some concessions were not forthcoming.[164] He confided his feelings to Russell, who realized that his own resignation would mean the collapse of Grey's ministry. At length he allowed himself to be persuaded by Althorp, Grey and Lord Holland to remain in the government.[165]

Althorp's reluctance to resign was more than matched by Durham's readiness to provoke a crisis, and by Anglesey's renewed enthusiasm for his own plan of extensive reform.[166] Durham had alienated virtually everyone in the government during the brief history of Grey's ministry. He was unable to solicit the cooperation of Russell and Althorp. Anglesey, writing from Dublin, demanded immediate abandonment of Stanley's "Church prejudices" and the imposition of radical measures upon Parliament and the crown. Without radical reform there could be no salvation for "this wretched country and its Church."[167]

Prospects for saving the bill depended equally on Grey and
Stanley, the former through his preservation of the cabinet's unity,
the latter through his willingness to make further concessions. Grey
was painfully aware that continued bickering would lead to an early
collapse of the ministry. He hoped to encourage a compromise by refusing to identify himself with either party. He prevailed upon Althorp not to resign by threatening to resign himself if Althorp departed, and by showing him the evil repercussion a more extensive
measure of reform would have on the attitude of the Church of England.[168]
Althorp was secured. Grey turned to Russell with similar arguments.
The bill was not inconsistent with Russell's principles, as Lord
Holland noted on Grey's behalf, and the Lords would not swallow a
stronger measure.[169] Anglesey was also reconciled if not mollified,
by Grey's and Holland's strenuous efforts.[170] By dextrous efforts,
Grey thereby managed to hold the Whig ministry together. The separation of matters of principle from matters of practicality allowed
Russell and Anglesey to believe that they had not surrendered the former but conceded only the latter. Finally, by casting moderation in
terms of expediency Grey was able to curb radical tendencies which
perhaps violated his own increasingly conservative attitude towards
change.[171]

Grey's success in sustaining Stanley's plan did not relieve the
Irish Chief Secretary from all his problems. There remained, above all,
the potentially dangerous Durham. His disinclination to resign on the
Irish Church issue was matched by his connections with radicals in and
out of Parliament.[172] Durham was not satisfied that Stanley's bill had

incorporated a substantial reforming principle; it merely "stuffed the saddle more equally—but did not take off the weight."[173] He was chagrined to see Russell and Althorp, so recently prepared to confirm his views, now reacting to Stanley's bill with conciliatory silence.[174] Having lost his support within the cabinet, Durham felt no reluctance to divulge portions of the Church reform bill to radical elements in Parliament in the hope of disrupting the plan and undermining Stanley's powerful hold upon Grey.[175]

To accommodate Durham's pressure, Stanley was forced to seek further concessions from Beresford, even at the risk of alienating the Irish primate and destroying the good relations engendered by the September round of correspondence. On October 30 Stanley informed Beresford that he had told the cabinet of Beresford's willingness to support certain reforms within the Irish Church. Although impressed by Beresford's conciliatory tone, the cabinet decided that it was necessary to recommend a further reduction of bishoprics, leaving 12 of the present 20 bishoprics and 2 of the 4 archbishoprics.[176] Beresford, clearly displeased, asked to be allowed to consult Irish Church leaders on so momentous a retrenchment;[177] Stanley refused.[178]

Apparently on his own initiative Beresford decided to employ tactics similar in procedure but opposite in objective to those already adopted by Durham. On November 10 the primate directed a long letter to Howley, Archbishop of Canterbury, and to the Bishops of Down and Connor and Cloyne. Beresford dared not venture further unilaterally. Indeed, he neglected to mention the question to bishop's leases and implied that reduction of bishops was only a possibility, not, as

it was, an integral part of Stanley's program. The letter marked
the beginning, however feeble, of the Irish Church's counter-offen-
sive and deserves thorough scrutiny. After outlining Stanley's proposals Beresford professed himself prepared to accept abolition of
Church assessments, substitution of a graduated income tax in lieu
of first fruits, restriction of pluralities and enforcement of residence, and institution of a central fund for construction of glebe
houses and churches: "If equitably carried into execution, and without the covert purpose of ulterior innovation, I can confess I see
no insuperable objection."[179] Abolition of Church assessments could
be justified by the Irish Church's minority position and the "unavoid-
able collision" with Catholics which had recently attended enforcement
of this "invidious" charge. Pluralities were "in fact already abolished,
not a single faculty having been granted during the last four years."
Sinecure dignities were few, but "not perhaps in the most proper hands."
All these concessions, however, did not make a proposed reduction of
bishoprics palatable. The Church had exhausted its store of concessions:

> I believe it will be admitted that a consolidation of seven
> or eight of the Irish sees might be made without inconvenience
> in the administration of Church affairs, were that alone to
> be taken into consideration. But as to any benefit to be
> derived from this reduction, independently of the aid given
> to the proposed fund by the contribution of their income, I
> can see the expectation to be quite illusory. Even in a
> secular point of view, these ecclesiastical establishments
> are eminently useful in Ireland, where resident gentry of
> superior information, and of approved principles, with their[180]
> connections and dependents, are so much wanted. . .

Beresford was not yet prepared to revolt against Stanley's program, which he believed would be adopted anyway. But the Irish Church
could no longer escape the necessity of constructing its own policy

towards imending developments.

The response of the primate's correspondents betrayed shock,

surprise, and rapid recovery. Richard Mant, the Bishop of Down and

Connor, in his reply called for a strategy of selective cooperation.

The abolition of Church assessments was

> an avowal that the Protestant Episcopal Church is no longer,
> to a certain extent at least, to be regarded as the Establish-
> ed National Church of Ireland. I should pause before con-
> sidering voluntarily taking upon myself a portion of the
> responsibility of recommending or bringing forward such a
> measure. . . . It is the government, to which by the way we
> are in no small degree indebted for the necessity, which
> should attract the credit or discredit of effecting the de-
> gradation.[181]

He believed, unlike Beresford, that the remaining parts of the reform

program could be digested with minor difficulty. An exception to this

was taxation of benefices, which was "iniquitous and oppressive," and

it continued what had always been an unjust tax levied by the state.

Reduction of bishoprics was not in his mind a matter of extreme sensi-

tivity. On the whole, he recommended cooperation with Stanley on the

"precise condition" that no funds will be alienated from the Church.

Canterbury's reaction was mild, even fatalistic, though not in

agreement with Beresford's strategy to this time. Voluntary accession

to reform measures, Howley ventured, was ill-advised in that it des-

troyed the chances of negotiating concessions once the government plan

was proposed. It also suggested unhealthy precedents for future reform

in the English Church, where the results would be catastrophic. He

strongly opposed abolition of the Church cess, for such a move consti-

tuted as "gratuituous concession to dissenters. . ." to be "followed

by extensive desertions of our communion and delapidation of our churches." His advice to Beresford was none too clear-cut: "opposition to government might hazard the subversion of the Establishment." It was also possible that "by binding ourselves to their measures we may eventually appear to have committed suicide." Howley could describe the horns of the dilemma for Beresford, but not ease the discomfort.[182]

Beresford's "unauthorized" quest for advice provided little inspiration, while Stanley's request for further concessions from Beresford failed to remove Durham's objections. On November 3 Stanley renewed his demand that the cabinet pledge itself not to accept appropriation of Church revenues to secular purposes at some future date.[183] Althorp suggested that Stanley be offered a Secretaryship of State as one way to detach him from the Irish problem and yet honor him for his talents.[184] Grey demurred. He feared that any shifting of personnel would destroy the cabinet and was determined to sustain Stanley in his Church reform program.[185] Stanley rescinded his demand for a pledge, and prepared "to plod on in the everlasting round of abuse and faction inseparable from everything Irish."[186] Durham, however, immediately revived discord by circulating a paper in the cabinet condemning Stanley's plan.[187] A semantic battle ensued. Stanley supported his position from Dublin. Durham declared that non-alienation of Church property in this bill implied permanent inalienability. Stanley replied by stating that he was not binding the government's hands in the future.[188] When Durham persisted, Stanley determined to revive demands for a pledge; Durham must "yield or go."[189]

Grey saw the imminent collapse of the cabinet if either Stanley or Durham resigned. He persuaded Stanley once more to modify his stand on the pledge, appealing to the imminent death of Durham's child as a reason for political charity.[190] Russell with a certain insensitivity took the occasion to remind Stanley that he too supported Durham. Brougham proposed to Grey that Stanley be removed from Ireland altogether.[191] Stanley wisely ignored these sallies, and Grey directed his badly split party through a successful general election.[192]

As before, quiet in the cabinet was quickly followed by further problems with the Irish Church itself. After his soul-baring letter to Howley in early November, and Howley's gracious but indecisive reply, Beresford had determined to divorce himself from the government connection. In December, however, Howley initiated a direct overture to Grey after having determined from his clergy that the proposed abolition of Church rates, circulating as rumor, portended in their minds "the absolute ruin" of the English Church. Howley wanted an explicit promise from Grey that the Irish precedent would not be extended to England.[193] Beresford in return decided to publicize the discomfort of the Irish clergy stemming from continued non-payment of tithes. Howley, on the heels of his own overtures to Grey on Church cess, found it difficult to discourage Beresford from permitting petitions to be forwarded to London on the tithe question.[194]

Howley's burgeoning concern that Irish Church reform might destroy the prerogatives of the Church of England, Beresford's new determination to expose clerical grievances stemming from tithe resistance, and Stanley's unresolved confrontation with Durham and Russell isolated

Beresford not only from Stanley but from many English and Irish Church-

men as well. Blomfield, Bishop of London, suggested that the Irish

Church increase its charity and decrease its petitioning. Beresford

charged that the English clergy were slow to support the Irish Church

on the tithe issue for fear of focusing attention on their own wealth.[195]

Beresford demanded from Stanley substantial aid for the distressed

Irish clergy; "never perhaps in any civilized country was an entire

order of men visited with ruin so sudden, so universal, and so unpro-

voked as that which has fallen upon the Irish clergy."[196] The govern-

ment, Beresford added in another letter, must repress tithe agitation:

"another year of forebearance like the past and the government will

have lost the firmest supporter of English connection."[197] Stanley in

reply declared he "dare not make such a proposal in the House of

Commons," and busied himself instead with last minute negotiations on

the reform bill itself.[198]

In this confusion of tithe agitation, panic among English Church-

men for their own fate, and Beresford's acrimonious correspondence with

Churchmen and politicians alike, Stanley felt obliged to demand of

Beresford even more concessions before the Reform bill reached the floor

of Parliament in early February. Pressed by Durham and Russell, whose

strategic disclosures to radicals increased popular demands for a more

vigorous assault than Stanley would permit, Stanley informed Beresford

on January 16 that it "might be necessary" to abolish 10 rather than 8

bishoprics, plus 2 archbishoprics.[199] Beresford in reply denied the

wisdom of this suggestion, and declared that the "public will not fail

to discern a precedent of spoliation."[200] With Durham on his flank,

Stanley could not afford to tolerate Beresford's ill humor. On February

9, Stanley sent his last letter:

> There are indications in the House [of Commons] that nothing
> but very extensive measures of reform will obtain for us the
> cordial support of the vast majority of the House of Commons--
> more especially reform in the Church and most of all in the
> Church of Ireland. It is most important for us to be able to
> draw at once a broad line of distinction between the Government
> and the Destructives, and that the first trial of strength
> should set them not merely in a minority, but in a very con-
> siderable minority. . . . Upon the issue of that measure
> depends not merely the existence of the Church and of the ad-
> ministration, but I conscientiously believe, the existence
> of any government. . . .

This introduced the last concession Beresford was asked to ac-

knowledge: a suspension of appointments of parochial incumbents in

those benefices where divine service had not been performed during

the previous three years. The power to suspend appointments would re-

main with the commissioners. Stanley thought this arrangement more

acceptable than suspension in parishes containing few Protestants be-

cause "in point of fact" he believed there would not be many parishes

to which the three year rule could apply.[201] Beresford's reply, which

did not reach Stanley until after the bill had been introduced, was

extremely critical. Beresford pointed out that henceforth in "entire

districts. . . the Roman Catholic Church will be described as exclu-

sively recognized." Instead, he thought, these unattended districts

should be amalgamated to existing Protestant congregations, in order to

preserve the form of national presence and to sustain the hope for ex-

pansion later.[202] Stanley took note of the suggestion and promised to

draw up an amendment to the effect.[203] With this final, minor sop to

the Irish primate the Irish Church Temporalities Bill entered Parliament.

Chapter VII: The Irish Church and Parliament in the Age of Church

Reformation: 1833-1838

1. The Church Reform Bill in Parliament

With the Irish Church reform bill before Parliament, the complexion of the Church-state relationship changed dramatically.   No
longer could Stanley and Beresford fashion a reform program between
them.   No longer was the nature of the reform hidden from the Church's
clerical and lay supporters, whose conservative tendencies and traditions showed themselves in strong disapprobation of any negotiations
with the Whigs.   The Conservatives, under Peel's guidance, and the
ultra-Tories vigorously but haphazardly led by peers of an uncompromising stripe, could now expect to re-establish close connections
with the Irish bench.   Grey's ministry itself offered a new face to
Church reform, for Stanley succeeded in exchanging the Irish Secretaryship for the Home Office just as the bill was presented to the House
of Commons.   Finally, continued inflammation of tithe problems meant
that any efforts in the direction of Church reform must be accompanied
by disciplinary legislation for the Irish countryside.

Lord Althorp, assuming Stanley's office, introduced the reform
bill in the House of Commons on the evening of February 12, 1833.
Althorp's presentation was consciously, almost painfully restrained.
The bill, he declared, incorporated no "abstract principle"; it was
"not necessary now to decide whether Parliament has or has not a right
to interfere with Church property."   The Church had first rights to

the fruits of the reformed system; at a later date Parliament could decide "the manner in which the surplus ought to be applied."[1] So modest a measure, thought the Whigs, would gain broad support and insure passage.[2] Despite Althorp's efforts, the terms of the bill caused an immediate sensation. O'Connell declared it "wise" and thought that it contained "the seeds of future amelioration." Other radicals were loud in their approval;[3] their joy, Peel confided to an Irish Churchman, "made him sad." Stanley was elated. He believed, prematurely as it developed, that O'Connell would now support tithe collection and discourage rural agitation against the Established Church.[4]

Peel spoke on behalf of the moderate Tories. He condemned the graduated income tax as destructive of property rights. He also questioned the appropriateness of reforming bishops' leases, and concluded with the hope that the bill could be revamped rather than destroyed. Henry Goulburn, Peel's lieutenant and member for Armagh, informed Beresford that the Conservatives dared not react harshly and demand a vote which might, "by an early demonstration of weakness, have given encouragement to further pillage."[5]

The most vociferous response, decidedly negative, came from ultra-Tories and Churchmen in England and Ireland. Inglis declared that it would force the King to violate his oath to support it, contravene the Act of Union, attack the Church when it had already reformed itself, and offer a dangerous precedent for further reform.[6] To his considerable consternation, Beresford found himself condemned by his erstwhile friends as a conspirer with the Church's enemies.[7] Howley declared that the bill had caused a "great sensation" among the English clergy.[8]

The ultra-conservative Duke of Cumberland admonished Beresford for his association with Stanley, and others declared Beresford had obviously been badly compromised.[9] Nor was Beresford's position strengthened when Stanley declared he had Beresford's support. Indeed, he wanted the primate to attest to it publicly.[10]

Beresford's defense reflected the embarrassment of a Churchman unaccustomed to the vagaries of politics and uncertain of the wisdom of his association with Stanley. Beresford found himself defending his actions on several fronts at once. The English clergy seized upon taxation of benefices and elimination of sinecures as "portending a destruction of their deans and chapters, the income of the Irish chapters being so small so as not to warrant a legislative interference, except as a precedent for the richer possessions of this country." Irish bishops feared their exclusion form Parliament. They viewed the Establishment of a new commission to administer the central fund as a stigma upon their character.[11] Beresford unburdened himself to Howley:

> I am quite aware of the unpopularity to which I shall be
> exposed both in England and Ireland on account of the part
> I have taken. I would ask the most zealous friends of the
> Church, whether they are prepared, or whether they are satis-
> fied that they possess means to maintain the points which I
> thought myself constrained to give in upon the hope, I con-
> fess a very doubtful one, of securing what was essential to
> the permanence of the Establishment. . . . My opposition or
> concurrence can be of little avail as to the final carrying
> of the measure, but it would relieve my mind from much
> anxiety to learn that my views have not been widely different[12]
> from those of some at least of the Church's best supporters.

It was better to concede graciously what would be wrestled away in any case.[13] He believed that certain members of the ministry were eager to exaggerate Beresford's influence in preparation of the bill, and asked Goulburn to explain his position among the generally hostile Conservatives.[14]

Increasing appreciation of Beresford's peculiar position and his gradual turn to condemnation of the bill transformed the hostility of Church supporters to a pity-tinged sympathy. Howley confided that under the circumstances he "would probably have taken the same part." "The government," he added, "in fairness to you should have stated the whole of their plan to you at once, and not asked your consent to a part, intending to go farther."[15] Beresford in turn admitted that the bill was defective in many respects. While he could not sympathize with those who thought reduction in bishoprics catastrophic and perhaps profane, he did fear that non-appointment of incumbents in certain benefices was "most dangerous."[16] He refused to bar the circulation of a clerical protest to the bill, but decided not to sign the petition himself.[17] By the time the bill reached the Lords Beresford had moved into the ranks of opposition.[18]

Beresford's anxious defense of his connection with Stanley, the excited petitioning of Churchmen against the bill, and the loud but ill-conceived protests of "ultras", obscured momentarily the fact that the fate of the bill and its eventual form depended upon a contest of wits between the ministry and Robert Peel. Peel's sensitivity towards the Church has been the subject of several analyses in connection with a dissection of his political and personal principles.[19] As has been seen, his special interest in this area was a longstanding one, dating from his Irish service as Chief Secretary between 1812 and 1818.[20] His concern for property rights and the Protestant constitution had moderated after 1825, but his essential commitment had not changed. His success in sustaining and finally reviving the Conservative party in the wake of Catholic emancipation, which split it, and parliamentary reform, which reduced its power, had already given him immense personal influence over other Conservatives. His party was, however, particularly difficult to define, with ultras jostling moderates and Canningites whose talents had not found a place in the Whig party. His dexterity in shaping and sustaining a moderate measure of Church reform during the spring of 1833 remains one of the most dramatic displays of his command of the techniques of early nineteenth century parliamentary politics.

The introduction of the Church reform bill into Parliament immediately focused attention on Peel. His own position was not easily determined, for he heartily disliked certain portions of Stanley's bill and yet doubted a measure more favorable to the Church would appear in the future. Politicians and Churchmen of all shades of conservatism expected his support, and sublimated their conflicting views in order to construct a common front against the more radical elements in Parliament.[21] Peel's own inclination led him to oppose the graduated tax on benefices and the famous 147th clause, with its appropriation of unearned income from reform of bishops' leases to secular purposes. He doubted that twenty-two bishops were too many, and was deeply disturbed by Stanley's failure to make a statement of general principles regarding the future course of Church reform.[22] On the other hand, he could not countenance the more extreme suggestions of the ltras, including advice to the King that he use the coronation oath

o block the bill. "If it be meant that all rights and all privileges

f every description then [1689] pertaining to all classes of the

lergy must be exactly preserved," he noted, "some very inconvenient

onsequences will follow. Few kings, I fear, have rigidly observed

heir oath."[23] If the bill were to be defeated, it should be done by

arliament, which meant the House of Lords. And the Lords should not

osition themselves in direct opposition to the bill until every oppor-

unity for moderating the measure was exhausted.

Peel devoted a considerable portion of his energies in the spring

f 1833 to amelioration of Stanley's bill. Althorp presented Church

eform on the night of February 12 as a "redistribution" rather than an

appropriation" bill in order to avoid the abstract question of appro-

riation and perhaps to mitigate the opposition of conservative peers.[24]

rmed with a preliminary report of the Commissioners on ecclesiastical

evenue and patronage, Althorp produced figures which suggested that

fter conversion of bishops' leases and satisfaction of the Church's

eeds, which admittedly came first, a substantial surplus would reamin

or secular employment.[25] Peel adopted the strategy of attempting to

rove that no surplus would exist, and that as a result the controver-

ial 147th clause was abstract and unnecessary. There would be no sur-

lus if he could procure amendments in other areas reducing the central

und available for church and glebe house construction and increasing

he endowment of the poorer benefices.

After securing Stanley's admission that Church needs did indeed

ave priority over all other uses of the leases increment, he demanded several modifications of the reform program.[26] On the very night of

Althorp's presentation, therefore, Goulburn moved for a return of all

benefices in which divine service had not been performed for the last

three years, carefully avoiding the term parishes, many of which in

all parts of Ireland must not have seen divine service, while the

unions of parishes had.[27] O'Connell's attempt to alter "benefices"

to "parishes" was defeated, an early but important victory for friends

of the Church.[28] Six weeks later Peel pressed hard against the pro-

posal to substitute a tax on clerical incomes for the cess, declaring

that this implied that the clergy themselves had a special interest and

obligation in keeping churches in repair.[29] He obtained no satisfaction

here, but he did gain the ministry's consent to exemption of incumbents

who had paid first fruits.[30]

On May 6 the Church reform bill was read for the second time.

By this date Peel had made major inroads into the Whig program. Amend-

ments had considerably reduced the amount of money available for re-

distribution, and Peel again asked whether there was any surplus at

all.[31] Althorp answered that by his estimates there still remained a

considerable surplus.[32] But Peel's question manifestly disturbed the

radicals, who now came to believe, contrary to their earlier impression,

that the bill was meant to maintain and strenghten, rather than reform

and diminish the Church of Ireland.[33] Peel had further ammunition.

He could not comprehend how those who agreed that the character of

ecclesiastical property differed in no way from other species of pro-

perty could at the same time maintain that Parliament might apply the

improved value it gave to any property to state purposes. What could e done to Church property, then, could be done to any property, an

nference which Benthamites and most radicals could not admit.[34]

inally, he moved a step further in neatly destroying the theory that

he state had added any value by noting that an act of Parliament which

ad limited the power of bishops was now to be repealed. Restraints

ere removed but no value created.

While Peel pursued his moderately tempered and practical opposi-

ion, more extreme elements from both left and right attempted to ob-

cure issues or win minor, meaningless victories. Deep-dyed conserva-

ives were particularly concerned about the proposed reduction of

ishoprics. Theological questions aside, the reduction was alleged

o insure the destruction of whole towns dependent on bishops' incomes,

hile transfer of administrative powers to the commissioners reflected

dversely upon episcopal competence.[35] From the left came a series of

mendments, some which attached minor provisions to the bill, others

hich demanded abolition of the Church altogether.[36]

The bill survived the second reading by a handsome margin but

he Whigs were now deeply divided. Stanley and Althorp could no longer

aintain that the appropriation of funds under Clause 147 did not con-

titute a spoliation of Church property. The cabinet sought ways to

ave the measure, and, by implication, the government. The King agreed

o lecture the Archbishop of Canterbury on the danger of short-lived

overnments and to create five or six peers as a demonstration of sup-

ort for the Whigs.[37] He would not go further. Stanley, meanwhile,

pened a correspondence with Peel with an eye to modification of the

ppropriations clause. Peel agreed with Stanley that concert was pre-

ferable to disunity among the Church's friends.[38] Peel dared not
take the initiative, however, for his own party's mind was unclear.
'It seems," he confided to Goulburn, "as if I was asking people to
make a concession of their own opinions to mine, when I am merely
laboring to bring about a general agreement as to the practical course
to take."

While the appropriation clause was the most sensitive point
within the Tory and Whig parties alike, the Conservatives were far
from reconciled on other points as well. Goulburn doubted that the
measure tended to make the Church more efficient, and exclaimed that
reduction in bishoprics "would condemn many parts of Ireland to the
misfortune of never seeing a Protestant bishop."[39] Ultras were far
from reconciled by Peel's success in ameliorating the bill. Since the
coercion bill intended as a sop to conservative peers had already
passed, they were not inclined to negotiations on the reform bill.
Churchmen continued to proclaim in a loud voice against the perfidy
of the Whigs and to elaborate on the distress of Irish clergymen re-
sulting from the anti-Church tone cultivated by the government. Per-
iodicals favorable to the Church raised a storm of protest on almost
every aspect of the bill. From wholesale violations of oaths to
clerical impoverishment, they declared, the bill was a veritable
"sevenfold division of iniquity."[40]

Peel determined to pin his hopes on elimination of the appropriation clause. Stanley's sensitivity towards the claims of the Church's
supporters reflected his estrangement from the Whigs. The cabinet was
not disposed to allow him to negotiate away the principal parts of the

bill itself. Instead, Peel's friends urged him to consider changing
the objectives of any surplus under the terms of the 147th clause from
unspecified to "religious" or "ecclesiastical." Peel refused, noting
both would permit allocations to the Catholic Church.[41] Perhaps pressured by Stanley, perhaps, as Peel believed, by "a positive order from
the King," the cabinet gave way and abandoned the clause, to the intense
consternation of Irish radicals and some members of the cabinet itself.[42]

The concession produced new problems. The radicals now determined
to throw out the bill on the third reading. O'Connell accused Stanley
of reneging on his promise to confirm the appropriation principle.
Stanley hotly denied he had made any such commitment.[43] "With the exception of the vestry-cess," O'Connell complained, "the bill does not
propose to reduce the burdens of the people of Ireland by a single
shilling."[44] After the defeat of the appropriation clause by a vote
of 280 to 149 O'Connell moved to abolish the vestry cess altogether
rather than permit it to be used for non-Church purposes, as proposed
in the reform bill. The Whigs and Peel concerted their efforts to retain it. To them vestry appropriations constituted a substitution,
however inadequate, for a poor law system and should not be destroyed
in a fit of anger.[45] O'Connell was badly defeated on this amendment.
Another one suspending appointments where no service had been held for
three years was accepted however.[46] At the end of debate O'Connell
concluded that he was "almost at a loss to know whether to vote in
favor or against" the bill. He decided to oppose it.[47]

If conservatives were still unsatisfied, they could make common cause with the radicals. This course of action Peel instinctively opposed. Peel doubted that "in the present temper of the House of Commons, looking particularly at the influence now possessed under the reform bill by the dissenters," a better bill could be passed in the future. Alienation was popular with the cabinet, and it might be dangerous to speculate about the chance for a better bill.[48] But if Peel was able to convince others of the legitimacy of his call for approval, he could not so easily convince himself. On the third and final reading Peel joined such unlikely bedfellows as O'Connell, Shields, Lefroy, and Gladstone in opposing it.[49] The bill moved to the upper house and the Irish Church awaited its fate there.

The conservative cast of the House of Lords threatened to destroy the Whig bill. In this bastion of traditional values bishops' fears were treated with respect. The large "Irish interest" was predominantly Tory.[50] Here too, the recent passage of the Great Reform Bill, coming after threats to pack the House with liberal peers, made further concessions difficult. Peel had gained important modifications of Stanley's original bill by convincing Grey that the Lords' approval of the original bill was out of the question.[51] Now Wellington, confronted by the well-organized ultras, was unable to insure passage of the modified measure.[52] He confessed to Peel that

> the majority of the House of Lords are decidedly against the bill. It is very difficult to restrain them, and they are very much displeased.

He thought it better to "displease them than to increase and aggravate the confusion of the times," but it was "not so easy to make men feel that they are of no consequence in the country, who had heretofore had o much weight, and still preserve their properties, and their stations in society, and their seats in the House of Lords."[53]

The bench of bishops was confused. They brought forth a petiion against the bill, but there were some conspicuous absences in he episcopal list, and the effect was mixed.[54] Beresford was by ow disillusioned with his own identification with Stanley. He had o cope with the bitter reproaches of Church zealots, and with the .eform Bill itself. He resolved to oppose the measure. Archbishop Whately of Dublin, on the other hand supported. While "God forbid e should ever sacrifice principle to expediency, in a question of his kind," he declared, "the principle and the expediency must go ogether." He was supported by Bishop Blomfield of London, who saw n it no tampering with the Church's spiritual autonomy,[55] and feared hat the Church would be in "extreme danger. . . if this bill was reected."[56] Those who opted to follow Beresford into the opposition counters were agreed in a determination not to be mollified by mere modifications of the existing bill, but they were unable to coordinate their arguments.[57] The Archbishop of Canterbury, meanwhile, belabored the question of property rights, which did nothing to improve the ministry's temper.[58]

Wellington was thus faced with a confused and frustrated chamber. Grey informed the King that if the bill failed the government would resign forthwith.[59] It was exceedingly unlikely that the conservatives could form a government themselves, he observed. Instead, another ministry founded on perhaps more radical principles would press Church reform upon the Lords in an attempt to break their power.[60] On its second reading the ultras dragged in the question of the coronation oath. On July 11 Wellington spoke so violently against the bill that Grey was barely able to restrain the cabinet from resigning on the spot; Althorp talked of the "dead majority against us."[61] Grey was encouraged by King William, who was induced by Anglesey to advise Grey that he would not accept the Prime Minister's resignation unless a new government could survive.[62] Grey was thus resolved to see the bill through.

Wellington, too, showed a change of heart. Peel was now strongly opposed to the bill's defeat; radicals were prepared to use the occasion to demand expulsion of the bishops.[63] On July 15 Wellington admitted to a collection of peers that he would not oppose the bill and indeed might support it.[64] Bishops split 14 to 11 against the bill, which favored the bill more than earlier expected. The ultras applied sufficient pressure to keep Wellington neutral on the vote on the second reading. The government, nevertheless, carried the vote after strenuous lobbying by a margin of 59.[65]

Wellington's resolve not to oppose the bill was based on his espoused conviction that the Church required reform and that amendments could be made in committee. In private, however, he feared the consequences of the collapse of the present ministry and the Conservatives' dim prospects in any election that followed.[66] In committee, Wellington attempted to conciliate the increasingly uncontrollable ultras by suggesting that if the Irish bishoprics could be amalgamated by exercise of royal prerogative, they could be separated by the same device later.[67] Grey refused to accept this and Wellington's friends narrowly escaped seeing the bill destroyed by a decision of diehards to press for a division.[68] The Tories then resolved to save face by amending the clause suspending appointments to benefices in which no service had been held for three years. Their amendment allowed funds derived from such suspension to accumulate with the intent of building churches and glebe houses at a later date. The amendment passed by a margin of only two votes, with ultra-conservatives and Whigs opposing a united block of bishops and moderates.[69]

On the heels of this amendment members of the cabinet again pressed for resignation. Grey thought the amendment of little significance, which it was, considering the small number of benefices in which there had been no cure of souls during the previous three years. Grey warned the Tories that any further exercises in amending would result in the government's resignation.[70] The full bill passed the House of Lords July 30, by a vote of 135 to 81.[71] It then returned to the Commons. O'Connell did "not think the Lords had made the bill much worse than it was before they received it. It was a delusion to suppose that the people of Ireland would be satisfied with the bill."[72] An exhausted house accepted the amendments with equanimity, and Church reform was law.

What did the law entail? The most obvious transformation took place on the diocesan level with the amalgamation of four provinces into two, and eighteen already partially united dioceses into ten. The most significant of these were related to the new central agency, the Ecclesiastical Commissioners for Ireland, and to various devices for its funding. The reduction in revenues of Derry, which the incumbent Richard Ponsonby had agreed to accept in principle upon his appointment in 1831, and a similar reduction at Armagh, to occur upon the next vacancy, established important precedents. The graduated tax upon livings reinforced the principle of transferring property. Complex provisions for administration of episcopal lands meant in effect that bishops became salaried servants and were no longer landed magnates. Their tenants gained considerably. Heretofore many had been bishops' relatives or powerful aristocrats who enjoyed the lands at low rents. Now tenants gained complete control in return for a purchase price and a small annual fine. The Commissioners also gained power to suspend patronage in all jurisdictions not in lay control where divine service had not been celebrated for three years prior to vacancy. This was without much immediate impact, but the potential for long range reform was immense. From all these sources the Commissioners anticipated and in fact obtained, a revenue which by 1861 approximated ₤3,000,000, a substantial sum indeed. The financial resources, when mobilized in areas of jurisdiction confirmed to the Ecclesiastical Commission by the Act, vindicated Benthamite precepts of institutional efficiency. The commissioners took over the Board of First Fruits' work in sustaining and expanding the Church's physical establishment. They assumed responsibilities once carried by the parochial cess, determined whether large benefices and parishes might be divided, and in general acted as a central executive much as any other department of state was managed.

What did the new law forbid and destroy? It ended much of the pressure for patronage competition by limiting the opportunities for lucrative self-aggrandizement among those families receiving prefer-ent. It discouraged large-scale episcopal translations by making

iocesan jurisdictions more equitable in terms of both pastoral

esponsibilities and income. It destroyed the erastian character

f the parish, a development of considerable yet often neglected

mportance. It ended financial decentralization, which for genera-

ions underlay much of the Establishment's inefficiency. It ended

he chaos in the area of "middle management" so long a curse of the

hurch. By expanding the responsibilities of rural deans, dignitaries

f cathedral chapters, and archdeacons in liaison and disciplinary

unctions between the top and bottom levels of the ecclesiastical

ierarchy it bridged the gap between bishops and the parochial clergy.

entralization also meant increased uniformity as to norms of disci-

line, pastoral work, clerical character, and administrative procedures.

he eighteenth century Church had been destroyed but in retrospect more

ad been gained than had been lost.[73]

Passage of the Irish Church Temporalities Act was both more and

ess than what Parliament had bargained for. The reforms inaugurated

n era of administrative retrenchment within the Irish Church. Tithe

gitation still raged, and because of it retrenchment, haphazard and

ll-designed, would have come anyway. A reduction in the number of

ishoprics precipitated a shortlived effort in Ireland to consecrate

hem underground. This was a romantic and ill-conceived device which

ven most "ultras" could not accept. In England, however, the contro-

ersy expressed itself in Newman's declaration of "national apostasy."

rom this sprang the Oxford Movement, one of the transcendent religious

evelopments of the century.[74] Internal reform had been forced upon the Irish Establishment. It was also an indication to the Church of

England that its own condition must be attended to. Only a large

measure of internal reform to forestall heavy-handed parliamentary

intervention would permit the wealthiest Establishment of all to

weather the approaching storm.[75]

The shadow cast by the reform bill extended beyond the Establish-

ed Churches. Peel in retrospect thought the Irish Church bill offered

conclusive evidence that the lower house now exercised supreme power

and that the Lords were in decline.[76] The sanctity of private property

had been challenged; assaults on other vested interests would soon

follow in the form of the Municipal and Factory Acts. Finally, the

great issue of appropriation, refined and then rejected in debates

during the spring of 1833, was to become the basis of a far more

dangerous assault upon the Irish Church than anything heretofore

attempted. Before it was settled, Grey's ministry would be replaced

by Peel's, and Peel's by Melbourne's. Melbourne was to lead the

first liberal government, much as Grey, for all his forward thinking,

had presided over the last Whig system.

2. The Tithe Question Resumed

The progress of the tithe legislation of 1832 had disappointed

its supporters, alarmed the Irish administration, and emboldened the

clergy to complain louder than ever. Statistically the forward move-

ment looked impressive enough; about £644,000 of £700,000 in tithe

values were reputedly operating under composition agreements by 1834.

Only £200,000 of this amount, however, had been added since 1832.

Moreover, a broad consensus, shared by radicals, moderates, conservatives and Churchmen, held that the Church Temporalities Act was not a sufficent response to the tithe question, which Stanley's act of 1832 had done little to resolve. O'Connell had attempted to referee events in Ireland so as to relieve the Whig government from embarrassment, but elimination of the appropriation clause in July removed his incentives here. The Whigs, by their concessions on the Church bill, especially the abandonment of the provision suspending appointments for non-cure benefices, did much to cool radicals' ardor towards the ministry. Conservatives read into the Whigs' reluctance to proceed with enforcement of tithe collection in the autumn of 1833 an intent to destroy the Irish ministry, indirectly but nevertheless effectively. The Whigs' position was confused. Stanley's Act remained in force, though tithe collection had practically ceased. During the spring several plans for extinction of the tithe circulated in Whig cabinet meetings. Lord Duncannon wanted commutation of the tithe to an acreable tax paid by the tenant to the state as a quit rent. He planned to reduce its burden by implementing the plan only in parishes which had cure of souls after the Church reform bill had passed. Elimination of provisions for abolishing non-cure parishes destroyed, in his mind, much of the effectivenss of his plan.[77] The confusion was heightened by Althorp's declaration that the coercion bill, then struggling through the Commons, would not be employed to sustain tithe collection.[78] This, however, was not communicated to Anglesey in Ireland, who resumed enforced tithe collection following spring elections. In this confusion there remained the Whig commitment to propose a tithe

commutation bill to carry Stanley's Compulsory Tithe Composition Act
of 1832 one step further.[79] Edward Littleton, a Whig intimate of
the second rank became Irish Chief Secretary in July 1833. He maintained that frequent changes in the tithe system had occasioned a
"singular state of uncertitude as to what ought now to be considered
the law."[80] Littleton, indeed, complicated the problem further by
expressing bewilderment at his lack of expertise in this area. He
protested that he was merely filling in until someone else could be
induced to assume the position of Irish Secretary, "incomparably the
most arduous under government."[81]

Until the Lords saw fit to act on the Church reform bill in July
the Grey ministry moved slowly on the tithe question. Were the reform
measure defeated, the government would fall and any advance preparation
on the tithe bill would be nullified.[82] Until July 10 Littleton contented himself with the church cess problem. Parish vestries had voted
the cess in liberal amounts during the previous spring, anticipating
that they would not have to pay it. Now that the Church bill had been
amended in the Commons to delay application of the tax upon present
incumbents, the funds were needed and the liberal grants must be collected.[83] Littleton also made some move to encourage completion of
composition valuations according to Stanley's act after he learned, indirectly, that the ministry would indeed proceed with a new bill to
substitute a land tax for the tithe.[84]

In early July the tithe question was broached in the cabinet.
Prevailing sentiment favored merely a commutation of tithe arrears,
arguing that under the anticipated progress of the 1832 Tithe Composi-

tion Act the occupying tenant would no longer be responsible for tithe by the time a comprehensive tithe reform was promulgated.[85] This specious thinking was characterized as a none too subtle evasion of the real problem. The cabinet then looked at the possibility of converting the tithe to a land tax fixed on proprietors, rather than tenants, in the form of a quit rent due the crown. Littleton, under Althorp's influence, initially approved this. He later abandoned the plan when Irish landlords complained it would saddle them with huge annual taxes.[86]

The problem defied solution. Tenants by law were responsible for the tithe or an equivalent, but their resistance made collection impossible. Landlords, who recognized the plight of the Church, doubted they should pay the impost when it seemed unlikely they could obtain sufficient compensation in the form of higher rents. To abolish the tithe without compensation would be to undermine property rights, a precedent which landlords were not about to establish. Beresford for his part noted "I feel myself called on to declare that the passing of the bill in its present shape would be more injurious to the Church" than none at all, with its reduction of clerical rights and revenues.[87] And William Plunket, the Irish Lord Chancellor, summarized the dilemma in declaring that tithe reform would involve either robbery or bloodshed.[88]

The ministry, faced with these alternatives, concluded it wiser to concern itself only with arrears, itself a touchy problem. In June Grey had disclosed what frustrations attended efforts to collect arrears by force; of £104,000 due the clergy for the tithes of 1832 alone, only

£12,000 had been collected, and this at an expense greater than the
amount received. Many claims were for less than one pound.[89] Littleton confirmed these figures in August. He introduced the government's
bill to compensate tithe owners for arrears of 1830-31, less 25 per cent
to balance expenses which tithe owners would confront in attempt to
collect them personally, and less a 15 per cent deduction for arrears
of the past year.[90] The grant, nearly one million pounds, was greeted
by pro-Church ultras as a concession to tithe resistance and, in terms
of the deductions, something of a punishment to be inflicted on the
clergy. Radicals condemned further grants to a "useless" establishment
and demanded that the grant be made from the ecclesiastical funds.
O'Connell, however, identified himself with those who thought the prospect of peace worth the purchase price.[91] The party liable for composition in each parish under Stanley's Act of 1832 would be responsible for repayment, after having 25 per cent of it discounted for
their trouble. This did not encourage landlords' enthusiasm, despite
glowing predictions of peace by members of the government. The bill
passed in late August, with a considerable body in the Lords denying
it would do any good.[92]

The bill proved in no sense a solution to the tithe problem. It
was extraordinarily complicated. Indeed, its passage may have been
facilitated by the fact that so few people understood what it included.[93] It did not affect future tithe collections. Another year of
resistance would restore the problem to its original form. It had not
eased the government's embarrassments, for the Church complained of
irresolution in prosecution of its tithe rights, while radicals re-

garded the million pound grant to the clergy as a massive sell-out.
It had not healed divisions within Ireland or in the cabinet. The
Protestant party was increasingly alienated by what seemed a cavalier
attitude towards property in general and Church property in particular.[94] Wellington concluded that the act, when bound to recent reforms, not only established a blueprint for the destruction of the
Irish Establishment, but the English as well, and even of the gentry,
of which the clergy were the most important parts.[95] The fact that
the clergy chose to be reimbursed by the tithe act rather than demand
payment from tenants encouraged a period of tranquillity in Ireland
in the fall and winter 1833-34, but nothing permanent was achieved.[96]
The clergy's real temper was shown in their concerted demand for compensation for the loss of the church cess; again the ministry decided
it should appropriate the sum rather than force a confrontation.[97]
The Coercion Act, moreover, remained necessary as long as the tithe
problem existed, and coercion itself so enflamed O'Connell that tithes
were further removed than ever from permanent solution.[98]

A feeling of desperation in ministerial circles fostered ever
more radical solutions. This radical cast in turn was sufficient to
insure their defeat. One expedient was a land tax to be shared by
Catholics, Protestants and Dissenters alike, thus avoiding the past
problem of taking the tithe off the shoulders of one party and putting
it on another without changing the beneficiary. The Cabinet, distracted by other issues, suffered Littleton to hammer out another plan so
complicated that few professed to understand it. Littleton now pro-
prosed to make tithe a crown rent redeemable in land, money or perpe-

tual rents. After five years the crown rent not redeemed by commutation to land or money would become a charge on the estate of the owner.
He in turn might indemnify himself by charging the interest on the
under tenants.

This plan had one virtue and several vices. It gave the clergy
an opportunity to purchase lands over a longer period of time, thus
avoiding the prospect of inflated land prices during a single seige of
commutation of tithes or tithe composition revenues to land. It also
permitted clergy and landlords to avoid commutation if composition
worked satisfactorily in the five year period. It made the crown, not
the clergy, the recipient of the land rent. This would deprive tithes
of some unpopularity among Catholics, and made the clergy pensioners
of the state. Unfortunately, Littleton's plan raised the question of
the price to be set for purchase of land, a matter which the Irish
Secretary must determine county by county.[99] Where commuted to land,
the residual rent needed to pay for it remained an extra charge on
rents. Landlords remained unconvinced it could be collected. Commutation raised the problem of land purchase arrangements. Most thought
in terms of individual glebes. Whately thought large estates rather
than glebes should be acquired; "keep the land in a lump" and it
would give the Church a patrimony which she could employ as needs arose
rather than being strapped to parochial boundaries.[100] Beresford
thought this much too radical, and the prospects for a bill which
Littleton devised on this basis were further dimmed.

3. The "Appropriations" Controversy Resumed

Littleton need not have worried about his tithe bill's unpopular features. There remained in the first instance the unresolved problem of "appropriation" which Stanley had opposed and which he had expunged from his Church reform bill earlier in 1833. Until settled the larger question of tithes could make little progress. The appropriations controversy had been divorced from Church reform by Stanley on the grounds that the interdependence was artificial. A majority of both Houses had agreed with him. The tithe question, however, offered no such easy separation. The Millions Act, as it was popularly called, had thrust the state into the role of tithe payer. English taxpayers could not be expected to defray for an indefinite period the debt due to the Irish clergy, just because the responsible party, the Irish peasants, refused to pay the impost. The refusal of the Lords to approve provisions in the Church reform bill regarding elimination of non-cure parishes also suggested to many that a Church wealthy enough to sustain these luxuries was indeed too wealthy for Ireland.[101] While Littleton did not suggest appropriation in his tithe proposals, his radical tone brought to the surface the latent enthusiasm for it among the more liberal Whigs.[102] Duncannon referred to the need for it in December while demanding a new survey of the Irish Church to ascertain how it could be reduced further.[103] This was rejected as premature, but Althorp concluded, however, that the appropriations issue could not long remain hidden and that the government must soon collapse.[104] Most important was Russell's canvassing in early February 1834 for support to amend Littleton's tithe bill to include the appropriation clause.

The speech from the throne on 4 February heralded the next attempt to fix the tithe question "as may extinguish all causes of complaint, without injury to the rights. . . or to any institution in Church and State."[105] Littleton followed with his new tithe bill two weeks later. He reviewed the sad history of the tithe and noted that Stanley's 1832 measure had reduced the number of tithe payers but had not facilitated collection. "The nature of the tax, and not the extrinsic impulse of agitation," he concluded, "raised the outcry against" tithes.[106] The new bill, already described, established as financial inducements for conversion a 60 per cent level of tithe value as the price landlords would be asked to pay to assume the burden. This was a bargain. The clergy, however, would receive 80 per cent of the tithes' value, the missing 20 per cent to be otained from revenues arising from the sale of leases under the Temporalities Act (lay impropriators would be compensated out of the Consolidated Fund).[107] Littleton's two-tiered conversion table was ingenious; landlords could buy low and tithe owners could sell high simultaneously. The twenty per cent difference, paid from Church funds to clergymen, seemed to avoid appropriation. Along with provisions for gradual delay already outlined, the conversion scheme reflected much credit on Littleton's attempt to deal with a most difficult problem.[108]

All went for naught. As in 1832, there was condemnation from all quarters. The radicals noted that redemption precluded further re-duction of the tithe. O'Connell argued it was a mere subterfuge by which the name changed but the tithe remained the same. It was "the idlest thing ever yet proposed--of all the delusions ever attempted, this was the greatest of all;" the people of Ireland would not be fooled.[109] O'Connell offered a substitute measure so drastic that its reliance on appropriation seemed in conservatives' eyes the least objectionable part of the measure.[110] Henry Grattan, son of the Irish hero of fifty years before, offered a motion recognizing the right of the Established clergy to state support but declaring they were in practice overpaid. This was rejected 190 to 66.[111] Conservatives noted that a portion of the Church perpetuity fund, which Peel had successfully shown to be Church property in May 1833, was now to go to the Irish landlord, who was in some quarters suspected of supporting tithe agitation.[112] Beresford had already made known his opposition to employing landlords rather than rate collectors appointed by the government to collect the tithe, and also denounced discounting the clergy's income.[113] Finally, to complete Littleton's embarrassment, Russell let it be known in the cabinet that he decidedly favored appropriation; he was soothed only by Brougham's philippic on the need for unity.[114] Littleton found that his ingenuity had brought him the worst of both worlds. Conservatives interpreted the 20 per cent grant to clergymen as "appropriation" because it robbed the Church as an institution of funds in order to resolve a question of property rights for which it had no direct responsibility. Radicals saw the movement of funds from the Church to the clergy as merely a financial sleight of hand, and believed appropriation excluded.

But Littleton's bill survived the first reading. Prior to a second reading, therefore, a motion to appropriate surplus Church re-

venues to general education was introduced by a dissatisfied radical.
After a flurry of discussion with Althorp and others, Littleton was
relieved to find that the member had decided to postpone his attempt
until the second reading.[115] Then Littleton decided to move off the
fence and appease conservatives by amending the land redemption method
to be more favorable to the clergy.[116] To test the strength of the
opposition Robert Sheil on O'Connell's behalf called for a postponement of the tithe bill. He demanded that rumors of division within
the cabinet be confirmed or denied by each minister's testifying on
appropriation.[117] Stanley replied that since the bill did not en-
compass appropriation Sheil's request was not relevant.[118] Shiel's
motion for postponement was easily defeated, and the ministry's
precarious unity seemed sufficent to guide the bill through the second
and third readings.

The course of debate on May 6, when the second reading took
place, not only destroyed the illusion of Whig unity but raised the
Irish Church issue to high drama. There were to be serious long-range
consequences for Whigs as well as for the Church Establishment.
O'Connell opened the debate with a complicated proposal of his own,
adding that he would be willing to retire from Parliament if Ireland's
grievances were satisfied.[119] Stanley in response again skirted the
question of appropriation.[120] Russell followed. He noted that the
debate concerned two primary questions: the amount to be paid; and
appropriation. The bill at hand, he noted, dealt with the first of
these questions. Once Parliament had vindicated its property in
tithes, he continued, then he would assert his opinion on appropriation

even at the risk of divorcing himself from the Whig party. In his

opinion "the revenues of the Church of Ireland were larger than

necessary" for the religious and moral instruction of its member-

ship, "and for the stability of the Church itself." Indeed, "if

there were ever a just ground of complaint on the part of any people

against any grievance, it was the complaint of the people of Ireland

against the present appropriation of tithes."

He must abide, in the face of all opposition, by his own princi-

ples.[121] Stanley at once complained to Graham that Russell had "up-

set the coach;" he would now be forced to vote against that part of

the tithe bill which made it acceptable to defenders of the Church.[122]

Russell's motives in making an issue out of his well-known sympathies

remains a matter of dispute,[123] but it drove Stanley and other friends

of the Church to resign at once.[124] Russell attempted to justify his

position by denying he intended hostility towards the Irish Establish-

ment. Radicals forced consideration of the appropriations question

despite continued protests from Russell that the bill before the House

of Commons did not involve the appropriation issue. It seemed that the

Grey ministry must collapse.[125] Althorp fended off the radicals' ini-

tiatives by promising a new commission on the Irish Church to ascertain

by an enumeration of Church membership whether a surplus of revenue

existed.[126] Meanwhile those clauses of the tithe bill which provided

for redemption in land would be omitted. If a surplus was found to

exist, the revenues gained from sale of tithes to landlords could be

directed to secular uses. Stanley was not placated; an Established

Church by its essence was designed to offer its services throughout the land, whether the number of adherents was great or small.[127]

But the device did, by a vote of 396 to 120, allow the Whig remnant to survive, since Peel refused to unite with the radicals to force its resignation.[128]

The radicalization of the Whig ministry by virtue of the resignation of four of its most conservative members, led by Stanley, suggested that the Church of Ireland was now more than ever exposed to wholesale legislative destruction. In fact, however, conservative forces were beginning to mobilize their energies in support of the beleaguered Establishment. For one, the King agreed to the commission but refused to be bound by its verdict.[129] He encouraged the government to continue only because there was no alternative, and because he hoped Grey's conservative instincts would restrain the liberals.[130] The King even addressed himself to the Irish bishops. He pledged his support, a task quite different from his admonition to the Archbishop of Canterbury the previous year. Stanley, now adrift between liberals and conservatives, resolved to oppose appropriation as an independent. In the House of Lords, Grey offered a tactless defense of a commission to examine the Irish Church. The circumstances were "so anomalous" he observed, "that nothing like them was ever known before in the history of the world." This excited the displeasure of an ever wider circle of peers.[131]

Once more primary attention was focused on Peel.[132] He refused to unite with radicals in bringing down the Whigs. This refusal was based on the premise that it "would probably . . . alienate from the support of the Church many lukewarm supporters and might make the con-

dition of the Irish Church even worse than it is at present." Only
if the Whigs collapsed because of internal disunity would Conservatives have a basis for an appeal to the country.[133] By avoiding
"cunning schemes" there was hope for a broad turn towards support for
the Establishment.[134] He opposed the commission, agreeing with Stanley
that it implied acceptance of appropriation. He refused to be drawn
into political maneuvers which might make formation of any other
government possible now, but in the longer run of events dangerously
ineffective.

There was still no tithe legislation, and the Irish Church faced
the autumn of 1834 harvest with alarm and resignation. Ward's motion
was defeated, but it had done its work. Even the Whig rump could not
discover unity. Liberals were disappointed that the appropriation
question had again been skirted by the device of a commission. Althorp
and others were angered by Russell's heedless espousal of appropriation
at such an inopportune time.[135] Loss of conservative support forced
the ministry to negotiate with O'Connell, however distasteful this
might be. Changes in the tithe bill reflected this turn.[136] The
amended version, scarcely recognizable in its new form, was confined
to a land tax payable by the same parties liable to the composition
under Stanley's measure of 1832. After five years four-fifths of the
tax would be converted to a rent charge on the first estate of inheri-
tance. This charge would be payable to the Church commissioners who
would transfer it to the tithe owner, minus a small percentage for
collection expenses. There would be no commutation to land. This
reflected liberals' fear of increasing the Church's political influ-

ence and honored the pledge to keep the question of allocation of revenues open. The landlords in effect were to become tenants of the Church.[137]

Since appropriation was not included in the bill, it was thought necessary to negotiate with O'Connell for his support. The government's principal lever was an offer to suspend the coercion law. Unfortunately, negotiations were begun, and O'Connell's support gained, without Grey's knowledge.[138] When the government proceeded with its original coercion bill O'Connell disclosed his agreement with the Marquess Wellesley and Littleton. Grey resigned, followed by Littleton and others.[139]

It appeared the Whigs must relinquish power, but the King was anxious that Melbourne form a new ministry, including Peel, Stanley and all moderates if possible.[140] Melbourne demanded freedom to proceed with the new commission on the Irish Church and "such measures for the reform of the hierarchy in England and Ireland as may appear to be advisable.[141] Peel was opposed to this commission and to the tithe bill, and Stanley resolved to avoid a coalition.[142] The King relented in his project. A new Whig ministry was formed, and in July Althorp announced the government would persevere with the tithe bill. The five year delay before commutation to a land tax was now amended to allow landlords to assume immediately and voluntarily the burden of the rent charge. An incentive was to be provided by a lien on the proceeds of the Perpetuities Purchase Fund established by the Church Reform Act a year earlier.[143] O'Connell proposed that the rent charge be made compulsory at once, to the disgust of the Irish Church and Irish

landlords alike.[144] This was accepted by the government and the
tithe bill passed the House of Commons on August 5, with especially
fulsome praise from O'Connell himself.[145]

By this time Conservatives' opposition to the tithe bill had
solidified. Peel declared that men were justified in raising the
cry of the "Church in danger" when Dissenters championed its divorce
from the state and when Whigs promised appropriation.[146] He added
that use of ecclesiastical funds for settlement of the tithe problem,
"could not but tend to shake all confidence in the decision of the
government, and of the legislature." The Whigs did not want to help
the Church, even if the tithe problem could be resolved at the same
time.[147] It was, he concluded, "one of the most complicated and
mischievous measures" ever to pass the House of Commons, and a violation of the commitments made by clergymen in all preceding composition measures.[148] Stanley widened the gap between himself and his
former colleagues by declaring the amended bill resembled the skill
of those who, "by dexterous shifting of a pea, [place] it first under
one thimble, then under another, and call on the bystanders to bet
which thimble it was under;" it changed names but failed to resolve
the problem.[149]

Many peers and most Churchmen needed little encouragement to
reject the bill. The Duke of Wellington had been waxing more conservative since the previous winter and his election as Chancellor of
Oxford fortified the Church connection.[150] The ultras now pressed
Wellington to oppose the tithe bill. Wellington declared, to their
satisfaction, that his vote would be guided by the bishops. The

bishops hurriedly convened at Lambeth and pronounced their opposition; even the liberal-minded Blomfield, Bishop of London, called it an act of spoliation.[151] Beresford mobilized sentiment against the measure, though his pressure on wayward prelates may not have been as intense as Whigs believed.[152] The main objections of the Church, beyond the principle of appropriation, rested on a conviction that deficiencies in the Perpetuity Fund would not permit it to be employed as part of the tithe computation machinery for twenty-five years or more. Meanwhile the clergy would have to be paid out of the consolidated fund, that was to say, out of the taxpayers' pockets. To this they would never consent.[153]

The lay peers added arguments of their own. Wellington agreed that the Irish clergy under this measure would become stipendiaries of the British government. This would abrogate the independence of the Church of Ireland, since, again, the Perpetuities Purchase Fund could not meet the charge itself.[154] The Earl of Ripon noted that when, if ever, the Perpetuities Fund did become sufficient to reimburse Irish landlords for their troubles, the sums advanced would in fact be coming from the pockets of Irish clergymen.[155]

The prospect of an early defeat of the tithe bill induced Melbourne to declare that if the bill failed the clergy would be obliged to repay the debts owed the government for borrowing under the Tithe Arrears Act of the previous session. The present bill planned to cancel these debts. Melbourne said that the government would not propose another grant for the relief of the Irish clergy. The clergy would be liable to past debts without the possibility of collecting obligations. Therefore they would be confronted with immediate ruin.[156]

This, far from cowing Beresford, enflamed him and the Irish bishops,

who moved among the peers with pleas for early defeat.[157] The Lords

obliged on the second reading by a vote of 189 to 122, disregarding

a late appeal from Stanley that the bill be pruned of its offensive

features and returned to the Commons.[158]

The Tory victory did not negate the gist of Stanley's warning.

No legislature would "furnish to the clergy, acting independently,

the means of recovering their composition." Attempts in November by

the clergy to collect their own imposts inevitably brought violence.

As it stood, the Tories had rejected the bill and upon them lay the

onus of future trouble.[159] English tithes would now be infected, and

a remedy must be devised quickly.[160] Beresford was not slow to seek

identification in England with the Church of Ireland's woes, to the

signal discomfort of many English Churchmen. The clergy, he confided

to Howley, "must lie still and be killed or do something in their own

defense."[161] The English Church must shake off its apathy and help

Irish Protestantism.[162] The response, however, was less than enthus-

iastic. Beresford complained to Wellington in November that more

resolutions must be passed by the universities and by political groups

to emphasize the plight of the Irish clergy.[163] To the Duke of North-

umberland he outlined his plans for the Clerical Society and complained

of landlords' apathy in Ireland itself.[164] Finally, he urged, there

must be a conservative ministry to reverse the radical tendencies of

the times and restore the country to sanity.

How to bring the Tories to power and thus rescue the Church in

the absence of strong evidence of national support was the conundrum.
It was well known that King William was sympathetic towards the Irish
Church. He had so proclaimed it to the bishops and they had published
his remarks. Wellington noted that there was "nothing that people care
so much about as the Church, excepting always their own properties."[165]
There was a general if poorly defined feeling that the Whigs and radicals had over-reached themselves on the Irish Church issue, that "no
popery" was gaining currency in the land, and that the Whig ministry
must soon collapse. In November Lord Spencer, Althorp's father, died,
and Althorp moved to the Lords. Melbourne was forced to find a new
leader for the Commons. The King saw his chance to dispense with Melbourne's services. He complained that he could not tolerate further encroachments upon the Irish Church, which Duncannon and Russell seemed
to be prepared to do with the results of the Commission of Inquiry.[166]

What, indeed, the Whigs had intended to do concerning the Church
remains a matter of conjecture. In September Russell had proposed to
Melbourne that Parliament be reconvened to consider a new tithe bill.
It would have had all advances made by the treasury repaid out of
ecclesiastical property, with a suspension of all Irish livings where
less than one-tenth of the population belonged to the Established
Church.[167] Melbourne refused to be drawn into a confrontation with
the "High Protestants" in Ireland and nothing was done.[168] Moderate
Whigs, such as Thomas Spring Rice, held a more ambivalent position:

> I will never overthrow or diminish the efficiency of the
> Protestant Church of Ireland. . . . But sure I am that
> wealth nearly double to that which is possessed by our
> British incumbents is a source of danger. . . to the Irish
> Church. With respect to surplus the just appropriation is

to provide for the Christian education of our people. We can teach them in our schools if we cannot teach them in our Churches. The one is the road to the other.[169]

The position of other ministers was sufficiently vague to leave the disturbed King convinced that further encroachments upon Church pro-perty in Ireland would soon follow.[170] William would not tolerate a "revolution once a year" and dismissed the Whigs on the Church issue.[171]

The King's action was arbitrary and perhaps unconstitutional, but as a device for stalling further encroachment on the Irish Church it had, in perspective, considerable success. Grey and Melbourne had between them sustained a reform program in Parliament and other matters which cast a long and generally wholesome influence over nineteenth century affairs. The Irish Church problem, however, had defied solu-tion. In efforts to grapple with this problem the Whig party had lost some of its leading men without being able to deliver more than the moderate bill of 1833. In part the character of the Irish Church, despite its anomalies, had offered protection. Its right to property was based upon the same principles as that of many of the great Whig magnates themselves, and this blunted the sharp edge of the assault upon Church property. Moreover, the Act of Union, no matter how much ignored in practice, suggested a connection between the Irish and Eng-lish Establishments which could not be forgotten; in response, the Tory cry of the Church in danger was both relevant and politically attractive. All these factors, while contributing to an understanding of the Whig dilemma, did nothing to solve the Irish Church question. It remained to be seen whether the Tories could do better. The price of failure was the slow disintegration of the Church of Ireland under

pressure of continued tithe agitation and perhaps a full-fledged
agrarian revolt.

4. The Tories in Power

The call to power in November 1834 found Peel in Italy. Wellington held all offices of state until he could be returned. Peel was not
entirely happy at the prospect of forming a government on the Irish
Church issue. He had refrained from blind obstructionism, and took
advantage of the election in December 1834 to issue in his Tamworth
Manifesto a pledge of support for Church reform in Ireland, but opposing at the same time lay appropriation.[172] If he entertained any
illusions concerning the weakness of his party in the country, the
election results disabused him of this. He was forced to face Parliament in February with only a minority of the House of Commons in his
favor. He tried to broaden his support by an appeal to Stanley to join
with him in sustaining the Irish Church. Stanley replied that agreement on the Church itself could not be the basis of a party with other
items still unsettled.[173] Peel had to content himself with this.[174]

The Whigs had been "kicked out" of office. They had not been
destroyed. Even as Peel grappled with the Irish Church problem in
January 1835 Russell was taking the lead in preparing a new Whig government based squarely on the appropriation principle.[175] Peel was painfully aware of this, and felt obliged to propose to Parliament an
immediate practical solution of the tithe question, even if it proved
a rather severe jolt to the Irish Church itself.[176] The core of his
"equitable and final adjustment" was to amend Littleton's bill of the

previous summer in favor of the landlords. They would now be able to buy up tithes for 75 per cent of their value, rather than 80 per cent.[177] The clergy would pay for this inducement by a corresponding decline in their payments to 75 per cent. The ecclesiastical fund would remain untouched.[178] He justified this last decision not by an appeal to property rights alone, but by a computation that the abolition of Church rates by the Act of 1833 had transferred to the Perpetuity Purchase Fund an annual bill of ₤70,000, while revenues accruing to this fund derived from suppressed bishoprics and taxation of benefices amounted to only ₤40,000. Appropriation, as he had ventured to note a year earlier, was academic when the revenues of the Perpetuity Purchase Fund were less than expenses.[179]

Finally, there remained the question of arrears. Three alternatives existed: the military could be used to collect arrears; the clergy could be left to their own devices; the residue of the million fund, amounting to ₤360,000, could be employed to sustain the clergy for another year. The first would precipitate further agitation in Ireland, where a fray at Rathcomac had already brought O'Connell to his feet in great exercises of oratory. The second would mean virtual impoverishment, since the clergy could not collect the tithe unaided. The third was best, although the amount in the fund was insufficient to compensate for lost tithes.[180] Peel dared not even broach the question of having the clergy repay the million pound loan, lest the clergy react by making a more concerted effort to collect their tithes.[181]

The bill disappointed Irish Churchmen, who expected to be assured full compensation for loss of the tithe, rather than less than the Whigs had promised. Beresford's advisors had already protested various as-

pects of the Whig bills in great detail, and had even regarded the

million pound loan for arrears as vexatious.[182] The clergy complained

in loud terms of the collapse of authority in Ireland, and the appear-

ance of a sympathetic government encouraged more rather than less

lamenting.[183] It was obvious, however, that if Peel's solutions were

harsh, those of the opposition would be more severe yet. Beresford

was urged not only to accept the tithe bill, but to undertake substantial

internal reform of clerical salaries or have it done by Parliament in-

stead.[184] Peel enlarged on this in a direct appeal to Beresford on

February 14:

> Of all public matters that were ever presented to my consi-
> deration, this is (mainly on account of the acts and pro-
> ceedings of the late Government) in the most embarrassing
> and difficult state. . . . We feel impressed with the abso-
> lute necessity of proposing to Parliament some immediate
> practical solution of those difficulties, with the utmost
> earnestness. . . Our only hope is that something may be
> devised, through the consultations of a government friendly
> to the Church, with spiritual authorities, sensible, like
> your Grace, to the extreme difficulties of the question, of
> the danger to the Church of further delay, of the necessity
> of considerable sacrifices for the sake of increased security,
> which may conciliate the good will of the great mass of Pro-
> testant proprietors, and induce them to lend that crucial
> aid and assistance to the law, without which mere legislative
> enactments will continue, I fear, to prove as they have[185]
> hitherto proved, delusiory and powerless.

The second reading of the tithe bill on March 20 did not convince

the Whigs that much had changed. Russell wondered what real difference

could be discerned in paying the clergy out of one fund or another.

Reducing clerical income was a form of secularization, at which Peel

had feigned to recoil in horror.[186] Hume called Peel's measure "dis-

honorable," so close was it to Whig proposals in the past. O'Connell was equally critical, but from the opposite point of view: "If they gave not Ireland the principle of appropriation, they would give them nothing."[187]

All this, however, was only postponing the main point, for the Whigs had already decided to challenge Peel's minority position in the Commons. The thought of proposing an amendment to Peel's bill was broached in Whig circles by Spencer and Russell even before Peel had introduced the bill into Parliament.[188] Melbourne assented after discovering that this reflected widespread Whig sentiment.[189] It was a question which promised to topple Peel, especially if the amendment were vaguely and judiciously worded so as to gain approval from radicals and moderates alike.[190] And it was better it be raised by the Whigs than by the radicals, for "this great question of principle" should not be left to a minor group when it could be used to wean Stanley's followers away from him and to re-establish the Whigs in power.[191]

Even without the assent of Stanley himself, which the Whigs made a last effort to obtain,[192] Peel was under no illusions as to the durability of his ministry. Russell's motion, originally scheduled for March 23, was postponed a week, but final strategy was fixed.[193] On March 25 Peel circulated a paper within his cabinet asking "shall we continue responsible for the government of Ireland, and shall we proceed with measures relating to the Church of Ireland founded on an opposite principle?"[194] Wellington favored continuing the ministry. On the 29th the King was informed that there was no ground for believing that Peel's perservering in office would help the Church.[195] At the

same time Peel circulated another memorandum asking his colleagues "of
what avail would it be, if the Lords amended or rejected a popular
tithe bill passed by the House of Commons? Can you settle the tithe
question? Can you collect the tithe, if a majority of the House of
Commons is ranged on the same side with the vast majority of tithe
payers in Ireland?"[196]

The inevitability of the ministry's collapse did not detract
from the drama of Russell's amendment. In moving his amendment to
the tithe bill on March 30, Russell declared that the Irish Church had
forfeited its pretentions to special consideration. It was time to
ask whether the large sums (he estimated the total sum at ₤300,000)[197]
entrusted to it had been

> applied to the religious instruction of the people, or to
> whose benefit it has been applied? - whether, while during
> the last century there has been this enormous increase in
> the revenues of the Church there has been a corresponding
> increase in the number of conversions to the Protestant
> religion? - whether the activity and zeal of the clergy has
> been such, and whether such has been their success, that
> the greater portion of the inhabitants of Ireland have be-
> come attached to the Protestant Church, and whether this
> beneficial change has been owing to the instruction of its
> ministers? I am sorry to say, the result has been too much
> the reverse.

Russell then proposed his resolutions:

> That this house resolve itself into a committee of the whole
> house to consider the temporalities of the Church of Ireland.

> That it is the opinion of this committee that any surplus
> which may remain after fully providing for the spiritual
> instruction of the members of the Established Church of Ire-
> land, ought to be applied locally to the general education[198]
> of all classes of Christians.

There followed eight days of vigorous debate, during which time
Russell established himself as a leader of the Whig party and completely

estroyed Stanley's chance of returning.[199] This event can be seen

s the watershed between an aristocratic and a popular tendency in

he Whig party. Russell captured the attention of the House of

ommons.[200] Peel fought doggedly, and even managed to gain some allies.

ames Graham, who had resigned in May 1834 with Stanley, now threw in

is lot with Peel and prophesied the "loss of all principle" if Russell

as not contained.[201] Hardinge, the Irish Chief Secretary, produced

igures proving to the satisfaction of his own party that 51 years

ust elapse before the Board of Ecclesiastical Commissioners was out

f debt.[202] Peel defended every inch of his tithe bill in extraordin-

rily lengthy debates, but finally succumbed when Russell's appropria-

ion motion was approved on April 7 by a vote of 285 to 258.[203] On

pril 9 his government resigned. Peel declared that the appropriation

ote, "implying as it did, the necessity of a total change of system

n Ireland, so far as the Church revenues were concerned, it would im-

ose such difficulties in the practical administration of Government

n Ireland, by parties opposed to the principle of the vote, that they

ere fairly entitled to decline the responsibility which others were

ound to incur.[204]

Peel's effort to resolve the tithe problem had failed, but his

fforts on behalf of the Church of Ireland had not been totally barren.

y his steady and skilled handling on the Irish Church issue he raised

is reputation and had, he believed, created a party strong enough to

bstruct any violent measures by the Whigs. He predicted that the

higs' inconsistency would ruin them, and that the Church issue was

'not a popular one in the country [England], where nothing like favor

to the Catholics of Ireland or their religion is agreeable to the
masses.[205] He had been able to impress upon leaders of the Irish
Church the necessity of a major sacrifice in income to maintain the
principle of the inviolability of their property. He was not unhappy
to have the more extreme measures authored by Russell given a chance
to impress upon Beresford how perilous was the situation of the Irish
Establishment. Peel had done much to detach those Whigs whose sensitivity for the Irish Church made cooperation with Russell impossible,
and he looked forward to closer cooperation with Edward Stanley in its
future defense. In all, the brief conservative experiment was not
without some elements of success.

5. The Return of the Whigs

But the immediate problem was Russell. The new government immediately ratified the principle of appropriation of Church property to
secular uses. During these debates Peel responded to the observation
that length of time had sanctioned the abuse of tithes by asking
whether there was no right which prescription was given laymen to their
property, which was not at least in equal degree given to the Church.[206]
A tithe bill incorporating the appropriation clause was not introduced
until June 26. It imposed on the landlords for every ₤100 of tithe a
rent charge of ₤70, from which would be deducted a 5 per cent charge
for collection, giving tithe owners 67.5 per cent. Arrears prior to 1834
were to be extinguished: for 1834 tithe owners would report amounts
owed to the Attorney General, who would proceed against landlords.
Some composition settlements would be readjusted. Benefices with

ewer than 50 Protestants were to be extinguished and duties assigned
o a neighboring parish or a curate at a cost of less than ₤100 per
ear. The income from the suppressed parishes, estimated at ₤85,000,
ould be placed in a reserve fund along with the unspent residue of
he million pound loan. After paying the clergy and readjusting com-
osition, the remainder would be given over to the consolidated fund
or the "moral and religious instruction of all classes of Ireland."

When the bill reached the committee stage Peel moved to divide
he appropriation clauses from the remainder of the bill. Stanley and
raham supported Peel, but the ministry was pledged to the controversial
rinciple and could not countenance its deletion.[207] Two weeks
ater, on July 21, Peel charged that the question of appropriation
as still academic, for there would not be a surplus in the perpetuity
und for forty years.[208] Peel's parliamentary efforts were accompanied,
ut not complemented, by efforts in other quarters to defend the Church.
he fall of Peel's ministry had galvanized the Irish bishops, and eight
f them promised to assist the primate in London during the summer
ebates.[209] When English and Irish bishops gathered, the traditional
recedence of the English at table was overturned, and the bishops
ixed together as a manifestation of solidarity and as a salve to inured Irish feelings.[210] A petition was drawn up in deliberately
rovocative language, calling Ireland a "land where disaffection to
he British name, contempt of legal authority, and blind obedience to
he Papal See appear in their undisguised forms."[211] Melbourne scolded
he bishops for deliberately alienating Catholics and for delivering
sweeping condemnations of the Whigs.[212] The King responded sympathe-

tically, but his blustering references to the impeachment of Russell
and his studied impoliteness to the new government alarmed Peel as
well as the Whigs.[213] The Whigs recorded every rumor of the King's
alleged intention "to play Melbourne another trick" but it persevered
nonetheless.[214] The King's brother, the Duke of Cumberland, spread
rumors of a change in government and painted his opposition to the
tithe bill in violent terms.

The tithe bill did not receive its third reading in the Commons
until late July. An alternative bill, which removed, in Graham's
phrase, "every well-founded objection to the present establishment,"
was offered by the Conservatives in June, and its rejection by only
39 votes suggested that the Whigs were already in great difficulty.[215]
A later test saw the difference reduced to 27 votes.[216] Rumors that
the appropriation clause would be dropped proved premature, and the
bill reached the House of Lords on July 25. It was clear that the
Lords would reject the bill if the clause were not removed. But the
Whigs could not discard the appropriation principle easily, for both
Russell's reputation and an understanding with O'Connell depended on
it. The Lords removed the controversial clause. The amended bill
passed, over Melbourne's objections, and on August 2 the bill returned
to the House of Commons. Russell urged rejection in a vigorous speech
and was sustained by a narrow margin of 29 votes.[217]

Another tithe bill was thus rejected, but the tithe problem in
Ireland remained, and there could be no peace until it was settled.
Upon collapse of the tithe bill another was introduced to relieve the
Irish clergy of repayment of the million pound loan: it passed both

houses.[218] The next eighteen months were spent consolidating political positions. The Whig administration which took office in 1835 was
more popular in Irish Catholic and liberal circles than any administration since the Union. Earl Mulgrave, the Lord Lieutenant, was energetic and flamboyant; but even he was overshadowed by Thomas Drummond,
who reduced the profile of the Irish constabulary and ruled over an
increasingly peaceful countryside. The tithe question became a preoccupation of Conservative strategy. Stanley noted to Lord Ripon, a
member of Russell's ministry, that the difficulties were "almost insuperable," and that Russell's adamant stand on alienation precluded
settlement. He saw a glimmer of hope in the very gradual spread of the
operation of his tithe legislation of 1832, which the Whigs could not
repeal.[219]

Peel for his part underlined his identification with the principle
of Church Establishments by accepting the rectorship of Glasgow University. On that occasion he declared that he would "support the national establishment which connects Protestantism with the state in
the three countries."[220] Russell was unwilling and perhaps unable to
desert the alienation principle. Melbourne, however, thought the principle absurd and was eager for a compromise.[221] Ripon hoped that the
ecclesiastical commissioners would report there was no surplus; this
would remove the subject from the realm of practical politics.[222] Lord
Morpeth noted that he still favored "appropriation", but not to secular
purposes. This was a considerable change of heart.[223]

The new moderation appeared again in the putative Church reform
bill of 1836. Appropriation remained, but the revenues were not to be

obtained, as in the 1835 proposal, by a mass elimination of all parishes with fewer than 50 adherents. Instead, Morpeth suggested that
clerical salaries be paced to match the limited pastoral responsibilities of these jurisdictions. The new tithe provisions were also
more favorable to the clergy. Morpeth proposed discount of 25 per
cent rather than 30 per cent. The bill, inevitably, was bled to death
by amputations in the House of Lords.[224] In 1837 yet another attempt
led to similar results. The appropriation sections were made even
more gentle but the principle retained. Ecclesiastical Commissioners,
under the supervision of the Privy Council, were to obtain funds to
sustain the appropriation fund by a tax upon all benefices, dignitaries
and bishoprics becoming vacant after the bill's passage. No parishes
or benefices would be eliminated. The bill was rejected.[225]

Beresford, meanwhile, was alternately emboldened by increasing
evidence of support of the Irish Church, and subdued by reminders that
only a compromise would relieve its present distress. Thus in Parliament in August 1836, on the occasion of the introduction of yet another
tithe bill, Beresford accused the government of trying to confiscate
Church property. He charged that the government intended to convert
incumbents into "mere stipendiaries of the government, with an allowance scarcely equal to ordinary wants, fully disproportionate to the
station of the men." The suppression of bishoprics by unilateral
action on the part of the state left only the "semblance of an Established Church." This guaranteed the ascendancy of Rome. Was Britain
prepared "to surrender the Church Establishment to the clamor and
menaces of the agitating party?"[226] The Irish Church could not on the

other hand subsist forever without its revenues. The rapid development of clerical aid societies was not a permanent solution. Impoverished curates demanded more than the incumbents could pay. Although
the laity responded with generous advances, this pace could not be
continued forever.[227] "Years of austerity," one Church supporter
noted in Parliament, "had forced the Established clergy to take up
the Roman practices of fasting and celibacy."[228]

Whately, who as the Whig-appointed Archbishop of Dublin was not
on friendly terms with Beresford, confided to Melbourne in 1835 that
the Church could tolerate reduction in revenues without difficulty if
incomes were consolidated and the Church administered on a congrega-
tional system. This would also alleviate the need of abolishing parishes. The Church by these devices would lose a "few ounces of blood
instead. . . of a limb, mortified and the mortification likely to
spread." Beresford, he noted, had opposed this pooling of incumbents'
resources just as he had opposed a central fund for management of other
Church revenues. But to Whately consolidation of tithes would allow
the clergy to be stationed where needed most, and would end the
Church's dependence on Catholic clergy.[229] Whately's flexibility was
one indication of a new willingness to compromise. If concessions
could be obtained from Russell, the tithe problem might be settled.

By the end of 1837 Russell's adamancy had softened; he even
talked of the Irish Church in "complementary terms."[230] There were
many reasons for this, some more important than others. Russell himself was less interested in tithes than before. He had exploited the
issue in order to oust Stanley, his chief rival for the party leader-

ship, and to cement an alliance between Whigs and Radicals.[231] Stanley

was now gone. Many Whigs had become disillusioned with O'Connell's

demands for Irish reform, demands which seemed to grow more inflated

with each government concession. When asked why the ministry did not

come to an agreement with Rome to "establish" the Catholic Church in

Ireland, Melbourne replied candidly that this was simply not necessary.

He quoted the pope as saying that "for a long time past . . . no piece

of preferment of any value ever fell vacant in Ireland that the Bri-

tish government did not nominate a candidate for it."[232]

Melbourne also displayed a new spirit of accommodation towards

Peel. He informed Peel through Lord Wharncliffe that "I can't help

thinking that things are soothing down . . . and as to the appropria-

tion clause I can't [say] so publicly yet, but we should give that up

without much difficulty."[233] Mulgrave in Ireland reported that the

appropriation question could safely be postponed without undermining

the Irish administration. He promised that O'Connell would not oppose

the abandonment.[234] Mulgrave added that appropriation was little more

than "a badge of attachment to the Party at present in power." No one

expected to profit from its enactment, and Irish M.P.s would have to

determine on an individual basis how closely tied to it they were.[235]

The old opposition to the Established Church was beginning to

decline in other quarters. Graham echoed the sentiments of many:

> It is quite clear that the Roman Catholics have basedly
> cheated all those Protestants who trusted them, when the
> grant of equal civil rights was conceded, and they are
> pleased even to mock us with insults, and to laugh at our
> credulity, when we gave credit to their oaths and written
> declarations, and believed that they would rest satisfied
> with civil equality, while the ascendancy of the Protestant

Church in Ireland is maintained.[236]

Even Dissenters, whose radical complexion in Parliament had sustained
Whig ministries in the past, now feared the growing power of Catholicism.[237] Anglicans feared for their own Establishment and emphasized
their historical mission in Ireland.[238] The critical attitude of the
radical Edinburgh Review towards the clergy in the 1820s had become
something much more savage by 1835. Anglicans noted that no distinction
was made in radical circles between Churches in England and Ireland.[239]
Indeed, a few Dissenters were now no longer satisfied with a modification of the Church Establishment, but demanded its elimination. The
Whigs, much less English conservatives, were not disposed to be agents
facilitating this process.[240]

"No-Popery" again became an important political weapon, and in
the election of 1837 those who were salient supporters of the assault
on the Church of Ireland found their numbers weakened.[241] At the
same time, Peel's continuing disinclination "to get the government out
on the Protestant point" was coming under fire.[242] The Whig-Dissent
alliance, constructed by Russell after Grey's retirement in 1834, now
became a source of embarrassment, "a millstone around their necks."[243]
As the Whig commentator Grenville noted, the issue

> was not unlikely to produce the dissolution of the government.
> Strange that this Irish Church in one way or another [was]
> the insuperable obstacle to peace and tranquility in Ireland,
> and to the stability of any administration here; and yet it
> [was] fought for as if the prosperity or salvation of the
> state depended on it.[244]

As Melbourne noted, the Irish Church itself was moving ahead with substantial reforms, and in time these reforms must make the more radical

demands of the Whigs both foolish and unnecessary.[245]

By 1837 the Ecclesiastical Commission was able to report substantial improvement in administration and morale.[246] The prospect of
"clearing the ground of so many Protestant clergymen" in Ireland would
perhaps provide sufficient funds to make alienation possible but at
the cost of leaving "free scope for the growth of popery.[247] Voices
of moderation within the Church began to be heard over the earlier
ill-tempered clamor of frightened bishops and distraught clergy. Of
these, the voice of Whately was the most articulate and the most heeded,
for his credentials, even in radicals' eyes, were creditable. Whately
noted that statistics alone should not constitue a sufficient reason
for a reduction in Church temporalities. In the first place, the
radicals' idea of equal work for equal pay was inappropriate. Inequity
in livings promoted ambition and service, with younger clergymen in
poorer livings working towards a more lucrative preferment. Secondly,
equalization of pay discouraged men of high ability from entering the
Church at all. Finally, the Established Church must be expected to
devote a proportionately larger share of its resources in rural areas
than efficiency would warrant or it would forfeit large parts of Ireland. Parliament's preoccupation with property rights was not only
unfortunate, Whately added, but it obscured the fact that temporalities
would not be superfluous if the scope of the Church's spirituality was
increased. Rather than reducing ecclesiastical resources to meet its
limited spiritual responsibilities, Parliament should encourage litur-
gical and administrative reforms which would induce Catholics and
Dissenters to convert.[248] Finally, it was quite clear that without

some resolution of the Irish Church question other legislation concerning Ireland would never be approved.[249]   Around the tithe problem
revolved the larger question of the British presence in Ireland.

Early in 1838 the Whigs determined to make a new effort in the
direction of the tithe problem and enhanced the possibility of success
by abandoning, in a somewhat complicated manner, the appropriation
question. Melbourne was eager to keep the government in power. Even
O'Connell, at long last, could not sustain his objections to a tithe
settlement free from the appropriation clause.

> I wish with all my heart that the ministry were decently
> freed from that dilemma. If there were a proper deduction
> from the tithe, there would for the present be no surplus,
> and it is really too bad to risk on such a point a ministry
> who are for the first time in history conquering the anti-
> Saxon spirit of Ireland and adding 8,000,000 to the King's
> subjects.[250]

After O'Connell's surrender Russell was in no position to resist the
Crown's strong wishes and those of Melbourne.[251]   Russell himself at
length admitted that "the efforts of the clergy to persuade the country
that the measure of the present ministry respecting the Church of Ireland . . . would shake and ultimately destroy Church property have had
a considerable effect on the public mind."[252]   It remained for the political process to dispose of the problem with as little embarrassement
as possible to all parties concerned.

Russell's change of heart was made explicit in April in a series
of resolutions presented to the House of Commons. Several principles
might be noted: existing compositions should be commuted into a rent
charge at 70 per cent of the tithe's value, which in time would be purchased by the state at sixteen years' rent. The money thus advanced by

the state would be invested by the Ecclesiastical Commissioners as
they saw fit, and the proceeds would be given to the clergy. The
state might collect the tax as it wished, and would devote the proceeds to education and local expenses heretofore defrayed by the
Treasury. Better distribution of Irish ecclesiastical revenues would
be outlined by supplemental legislation.[253]

The plan was a generous one, but in the first instance the
generosity was interpreted by Conservatives as evidence of weakness.
They moved to strike down the provision concerning application of
the land tax to educational purposes. These ultras believed "appropriation" was thriving in a new costume. The government would profit from pegging the conversion rate at 70 per cent, and the profits
would accrue in the considerable revenue which would be derived by the
state from a tax so cheaply purchased. On May 13, 1838, therefore,
an opposition member moved that the conversion clause be stricken from
the bill. This heavy-handed attempt to force the government into
surrender, however, was not likely to promote an amicable settlement.[254]
There were elements within the Church who believed Stanley's 1832
bill was now making sufficient progress to raise hopes that the tithe
matter could be settled without recourse to new legislation, which
would at best dig deeply into the clergy's share of tithe revenues.[255]
Conservatives' opposition to the new bill strengthened the resolve of
these Churchmen not to sacrifice even a portion of their tithe income.
The center of the resistance now proved to be Beresford himself. He
was abetted by Irish conservatives led by Frederick Shaw, who contemplated amendments which would increase the composition rate and deny

radicals all suggestions of vindication. When the matter was first

broached by Russell on March 17 in private conversations with Shaw,

Shaw recalled Beresford's intimacy with Stanley in 1832. He advised

the primate not to enter into any direct negotiations with Russell,

and above all to make no premature concessions:

> The Church cannot be assured what the final course of the
> government might be or that they would not use the assent of
> the Church to draw the Church into further concessions, or
> indeed to say that if the Church objected to these further
> concessions it would be to blame for the ruin of the bill.[256]

There was little danger that Beresford would collaborate with the

Whigs. Although Peel's tithe bill of early 1835 had included provi-

sions for a substantial discounting of tithe revenue in order to obtain

landlord participation in the commutation process, similar provisions

now raised Beresford's anger. He reported to Goulburn that the pro-

posals had been laid before a body of the clergy and that they pro-

nounced them "utterly destructive to their interests and the stability

of the Church." As it was, he complained, landlords already paid more

than half of tithe composition as directed by Stanley's act. To pro-

vide further incentive to them to do what they were already doing as re-

quired by law was absurd. Furthermore, eventual commutation to land

would no longer require landlord intervention even in those areas where

they have not already assumed the tithe, and yet they were to be paid

handsomely for alleged expenses which might arise. Again he objected

to the lapse of time before the land was purchased for the clergy. He

accused Russell of sinister motives, of wanting to make a large profit

from the sale of rent charges, and of wanting to use the consolidated

for secular purposes. Beresford refused to agree on any higher discounting than 25 per cent. Finally, he wanted the rent charge to be given directly to the clergy, as the tithe was before 1832 and composition sums were after 1832, even though it must have been clear that the tax as such would inevitably foment agitation on the part of the Catholic peasantry.[257]

Beresford, then, was still adamant on two points. He believed that composition of the tithe into a tax upon the land was perhaps inevitable. But he wanted the proceeds from the new form of collection to go directly to the clergy, not to a central fund, which would constitute a standing invitation for government appropriation. Secondly, he still opposed commutation to land, which yielded an income difficult to increase and susceptible to charges of Church wealth. He could not believe that Russell was in fact eager to settle the tithe question. Even without affirmation of the appropriations clause the scheme was "contrived for keeping ministers in and for gaining for them in five years the support of all the priests and Roman Catholics of Ireland."[258]

This time, however, almost no one would listen to Beresford. On June 2 Peel and Russell made speeches committing themselves to compromise, an exercise in congeniality which ruffled the right-wing Tories.[259] An attempt by Irish members to revive the appropriation clause was rejected 270 to 46, a crushing defeat.[260] Opposition to the compromise proved weak in the Lords and a permanent settlement was finally reached.

The Tithe Act of 1838 was much less dramatic than its role as a legislative culmination to years, decades, and even centuries of tithe agitation might have suggested. Composition was replaced by a rent charge of 75 per cent of the old composition and paid semi-annually by head

landlords. These landlords were entitled to a handsome bonus, not

exceeding 25 per cent, for their work. They were entitled to append

the tithe charge to the rents of their immediate subtenants. The ex-

emption of tenants-at-will or year-tenants, established in Stanley's

act of 1832, was confirmed. Rack rents (full rents, without fines or

deductions of any kind) were reduced by a quarter of the tithe compo-

sition, the difference between the old composition and the new rent

charge, and these rents were based on a standard of grain prices com-

puted for the seven years previous. All arrears between 1834 and 1837

were written off. Provision was made for the collection of future

arrears by the government; arrears continued to appear and in fact

the government rarely exerted itself to collect them.[261]

The tithe problem had effectively paralyzed the Anglo-Irish

Church for more than a decade. It had bred every conceivable suspi-

cion between the two pillars of the erastian system. It had served

to divorce the Irish Church from the bulk of the people for a century

and more. It had done more to focus unfavorable attention on the

Church than had any other aspect of its institutional structure. It

had involved the question of property rights and had in this sense

alarmed the champions of mammon as well as the ministers of the Lord.

It had, finally, led to a full-scale governmental assault on the prero-

gatives of the Irish Church and had indirectly countenanced the belief

that it could never really serve Ireland as the national religious

establishment.

Church reform, coming in the middle of the tithe controversy,

was the object of deep suspicion as well, and the unfortunate contest
did much to force Churchmen into finding something of value in arrangements and conditions which could not in conscience be justified. Beresford devoted perhaps too much of his energy to focusing attention on
rights of prescription and not enough on the religious problems which
engendered so much of the Church's unpopularity in Ireland. Bishops
and lower clergy too often cut ridiculous if sincere figures with
their voluminous petitions, their protestations of poverty, and their
aspersions on Ireland's peasantry.

But much of lasting value emerged, though scarcely appreciated
by observers at the time. Two tremendous accomplishments should not
be ignored: permanent settlement of the tithe problem; and substantive Church reform. These did not, it is true, save it from confrontation with the forces of disestablishment. Both, one indirectly and
one directly, did facilitate adaptation of the Irish Church to a new
and more hostile environment, and indeed to survival after disestablishment in 1869.

The larger implications of the Irish Church question from 1828
to 1838 have sometimes escaped modern historians. Legislation affecting the Church marked the beginning of an era in Irish administrative
reform. The appropriations clause acted as midwife in translating
Whiggery into Liberalism. The larger question of the efficacy of erastianism was debated, and the Oxford Movement was given its impetus.
The essentially secular tone of modern politics was established in
these debates. The Tory party, under the leadership of Robert Peel,
abandoned its fundamental commitment to conservatism in favor of grad-

ual change. The Church of Ireland had made its imprint upon British politics no less than politics had determined developments within the Church.

6. The Politics of the Status Quo: 1838-1869

The thirty year span bracketed by the definitive tithe legislation of 1838 and disestablishment in 1869 witnessed little of the political tumult which the Irish Church issue had heretofore brought to British politics. The tranquility convinced careless observers that a watershed had been crossed, that internal reform would in time produce a vigorous and fruitful proselytism among Catholics, and that politicians and troublemakers would direct their indignation elsewhere. This tranquility, however, was not only deceptive, it was contrived. Wise and wearied students of ecclesiastical statecraft labored to keep the Church of Ireland out of the public eye, foreswearing those heady traditional prerogatives, or what remained of them, and seeking in turn the safe harbor of obscurity. For some twenty years events favored their objects. The Maynooth controversy of 1845 gave clear focus to anti-popery, long active in popular politics and especially so since Catholic Emancipation and Church reform. Reaction to the Oxford Movement reached something of a crescendo in 1850 in the wake of Cardinal Wiseman's breathless oration "outside the Flaminian Gate" and distracted many who might otherwise have supported disestablishment and disendowment in Ireland. The convulsions which attended the great famine, the emergence of Irish demands for repeal of the Act of Union, and the first suggestions of the collapse of the traditional landlord-tenant system allowed the Church of Ireland to avoid the public eye. The road to disestablishment, as a result, was poorly posted with signs of impending danger and suggested little of the abrupt confrontation to come after 1860.

More than ever the Church of Ireland's perception of the nature of the erastian connection was a contradictory one. Until 1850 the Church looked to Robert Peel for understanding and assistance, and received little of either. As has already been seen, Peel refused to destroy the national education system constructed by the Whigs, and indeed exercised his patronage prerogatives to reward men whose own views on this score were agreeable to his friends and the Whigs alike. Peel stoutly maintained his adherence to the principle of establishment in Ireland, without however fully satisfying Irish Churchmen.[262] While the Church of England recovered its self-confidence and even its popularity after the difficulties of the 1830s and resumed an active if discreet role in the politics of the nation, the Irish branch found no reservoir of support. When in 1847 Whately briefly abandoned the Church's policy of avoiding parliamentary attention and submitted legislation enabling the Lord Lieutenant to restore bishoprics suppressed in 1833, Parliament yawned and the bill was withdrawn without benefit of a second reading.[263] Gladstone, whose resignation from Peel's ministry on the occasion of the Maynooth Grant of 1845 marked him as a potential champion of the Irish Church, was already confiding to Manning that he was in doubt whether the Irish Establishment should be continued.[264] Lord John Russell flayed the Vatican for appropriating ecclesiastical titles attached to Eng-

lish sees and thereby gratified a large anti-papal interest, but he
also wanted state funding of Catholic priests in Ireland and indeed
supported concurrent endowment of all churches.[265]

Among politicians of all persuasions the erastian connection
came to be considered purely in terms of political convenience and
administrative efficiency.[266] The Church was an instrument of government – the composition of the Ecclesiastical Commission certainly confirmed this – and whenever it became an obstacle to rather than a
useful instrument of good government in Ireland it need be retained
no longer. Thus Parliament in 1854 reduced and in 1857 eliminated
"ministers' money," an urban income dating from Charles II and an increasingly unpopular impost source. In the same frame of mind the
government intervened in ecclesiastical affairs on two or three
occasions to address some aspect of administrative efficiency. For
the rest the Church was left to its own devices; little was required
of it (the Town Improvement Act of 1849 removed the last vestry responsibilities and in 1856 the Archbishop of Dublin surrendered his
ancient prerogatives in the Liberty of St. Sephlcher) and, apart from
the Privy Council's vestigial superintendence over burial grounds and
the configuration of parishes and unions, little attention was devoted
to it.

During the final years of the Establishment one movement was
patently sympathetic to the Church: the Protestant Association, established in 1835 to comprehend the Orange lodges (themselves revived
a decade earlier when Catholic Emancipation became imminent), evangelicals (reacting in part to the Tractarians), devout aristocrats and

a new generation of English nationalist politicians.[267] The new movement boasted an impressive constituency; British workers alarmed at
an intrusion of poorly paid Irish Catholic labor; the principal elements of Dissent as well as orthodox Anglicans; the Anglican and
Presbyterian interests in Ireland; Tory politicos looking for a
popular basis upon which to reconstruct a Conservative hegemony; and
imperial enthusiasts fearful of a Catholic (ie. French) challenge to
British power overseas. The Maynooth controversy of 1845 revealed
that the Protestant Association, through an efficient executive and
endless publications, could exert considerable influence. By treating
the Irish question as a religious one the Protestant Association reinforced the popular identification between Protestantism and nationalism, labelling Whig liberalism as seditious and even Peel's support of
the Maynooth grant as perfidious.

The Church of Ireland derived sympathy and political support from
this neo-no-popery movement. In turn it contributed its own perfervid
evangelical wing, and hoped that the sharp reaction against the Whig
assault on the English and Irish Establishments would assure indefinite
protection against Catholicism. Even within the Protestant community,
however, dangerous and disruptive tendencies were showing. One, the
Oxford Movement, was of course begun originally as a reaction to state-
sponsored Church reform. The peculiar biases of its adherents, with
their highly articulate but rarified views and labyrinthine pronounce-
ments, tended to turn the Oxford Movement against the Irish Church.
Loud in denunciations of state interference, Puseyites advocated disestablishment lest the Church be defiled by utilitarian manipulations;

steadfast in its opposition to low-Church tendencies, the group lent
credence to the ancient suspicion that the Established Church was
seditiously Roman; upset by suppression of Irish bishoprics and
ancient ecclesiastical practices, the movement obscured the more pressing problems of the Irish Church. By the time disestablishment agitation became a public question the Oxford Movement had diverted part
of its energy and personnel to Catholicism and the remainder to theological disputation. Its impact in Ireland in the 1850s and 1860s
was therefore limited. But in its first decade of activity Pusey,
Newman and others articulated a case for disestablishment which appealed to many high Churchmen and which those who favored disestablishment
from other motives appropriated to their own advantage.[268]

Prior to 1860 the unabashed support of the Church of Ireland
from the Protestant Association and the somewhat disorienting advice
from Oxford publicists was matched by those Protestants who opposed
the principle of establishment in general and Irish Catholicism, which
opposed the Church of Ireland in particular. Though both interjected
the Irish Church issue into politics from time to time, neither cast
its arguments in terms specifically related to disestablishment. That
the Church of Ireland's position escaped a frontal assault was due in
large measure to the Maynooth issue. Peel's bid to increase state
support of the celebrated seminary was sure to prevent a Dissent-Catho-
lic alliance on the disestablishment question. If the Protestant Association opposed the Maynooth grant on the grounds that it undercut Protestantism, it could hardly question the principle of state support for
religious institutions. It remained to the "Voluntaries," those Whigs,

radicals and Dissenters who advocated free trade in religion, to sustain the position that "establishing" the Catholic Church (via Maynooth) was as pernicious as maintaining the incumbent establishment. Indeed, so pervasive were laissez-faire principles that early in the 1840s Edward Miall, architect of agitation against Maynooth, tried to enlist the proponents of disestablishment, Corn Law repeal, and universal suffrage under the same banner.[269] The arrangement proved exclusive rather than comprehensive, and Miall was far more successful when he directed his efforts against the Maynooth grant alone. In this cause "regular" Protestants and Voluntaries could cooperate. The former feared that Catholicism would overwhelm the Established Church. The latter feared that the principle of concurrent establishment would protect the Church of Ireland from pressure for disestablishment.[270]

During the Maynooth controversy, then, it was almost impossible for spokesmen for the Established Church in Ireland to find a more congenial political atmosphere. Churchmen could afford to be discreet: were Maynooth defeated, Irish Protestantism would stand vindicated and the Establishment's position indirectly ratified; were Maynooth approved, Protestant opinion would sustain the Church of Ireland and indeed the state would be dedicated more than ever to the principle of public support for ecclesiastical institutions. Indeed, "establishing" the Catholic Church was not necessarily dangerous. Edward Ellice, monitoring the pulse of English ecclesiastical opinion, noted that many Churchmen "would rather - if we are to admit the Catholics to terms of equality - see a sister establishment in an efficient state to assist them against the inroads of the Voluntaries, than have the Catholics added to the latter force."[271] The Irish Protestant Establishment might have subsisted indefinitely under such conditions. Had not a radical re-orientation of Catholic priorities brought that communion into agreement with the Voluntaries twenty years later, it is difficult to see what danger could have arisen. The long Indian summer of tranquility would finally end, but not before new forces had surfaced within the ancient communion, forces geared to preservation of the Church when the erastian system was dismantled.

Chapter VIII: The Life of the Church 1800-1869

1. The Church as a Society

The Church of Ireland was a product of, and a contributor to, the landed classes which governed the island, shaped its economic development, and established its cultural and moral tone. The bishops regarded themselves and were accepted by others as aristocrats whose station for the most part reflected the proper family connections, adequate incomes, and the required breeding. They displayed a sense of heady independence in their correspondence with the government, much as secular peers conducted their own affairs.[1] Below them, the beneficed clergy sought identification with the gentry. This identification eluded some of them because of economic difficulties and landlord hostility. Curates also strove for the status of gentlemen, but their poverty, hard work and ingrained hostility towards a system which offered so little hope of advancement made them uncomfortable auxiliaries of the landlord class. As a society apart from the larger Protestant interest, the Church depended for its strength upon a system of discipline loosely defined and haphazardly enforced. Its vitality depended upon the solidity of the landlord interest, but its effectiveness as a religious body was connected to the pace of internal reform. During the eighteenth century the stresses of this large and important organization were carefully sublimated. After 1800 this was no longer possible. Within the ancient shell there occurred a considerable transformation, so that the Church of Ireland at disestablishment differed far more from the Establishment of the year 1800 than the latter differed from the Henrician Church.

The bench of bishops in the last era of the Establishment was still, to a considerable degree, the preserve of aristocratic families, though by 1869 priorities had shifted considerably. Whatever their pedigrees, the bishops were men of an individualistic stamp and were not always disposed to cultivate each other's friendship. Stuart was hard pressed to find much good in any of them, except Brodrick, for whom he never seems to have had an unkind word. It took more than just attention to duty to elicit a favorable reaction from Stuart on any issue, "as he of all men never expressed kindness merely as a compliment," and we must on this account discount some of the acerbity of his comments. He was, however, an acute observer of the Irish scene.[2] As has been seen, he concluded that in his own province six of the seven incumbents were unworthy or listless in 1801. The only exception was Thomas O'Beirne, whose tenure at Meath lasted until 1823. During this time O'Beirne labored indefatigably to discipline both his clergy and the ministry of the day, to their common and considerable annoyance. His predecessor at Meath, Bishop Henry Maxwell, had also been the scourge of politicians, and O'Beirne's letters to Wellesley and Peel continued a tradition of frankness which his colleagues tried hard to avoid. O'Beirne was not, however, a shrew; he sustained public works for the poor, praying morning and evening with reverence, not, however, devoting so much time to prayer "as to interfere with business or pleasure."[3]

As for the remaining bishops, it is hard not to agree with Stuart's low opinions. Not one of them made a mark on events in the Church and not one was subsequently translated. The most famous of this group was undoubtedly Frederick Augustus Hervey. He was a wealthy politico who found the richest diocese in Ireland, Derry, too confining. His support for relaxation of penal codes and British control conformed to the Whig tradition. His successor, Alexander Knox, lived in Londonderry only four months of the year, and quartered in London most of the remainder. His munificence was both ample and unrestricted; every worthy project obtained his support. He used the immense political influence at his disposal to increase his family's fortune, and often angered the ministry of the day by offering parliamentary seats for sale at inflated prices. His summer parties at Londonderry marked a new chapter in Derry propriety; no cards were permitted and gates closed promptly at eleven.[4] Knox's successor, Richard Ponsonby, reigned more than twenty years at Derry, scrupulously avoided antagonizing Catholics, pursued the liberal policies of Lord Grey in a gentle way, and died a popular man.[5]

A succession of bishops at Clogher brought both good and bad.
John Porter, whom Stuart had included among his indifferent bishops,
left behind a diary which shows the gradually civilizing life style
of a late eighteenth century gentleman. He was succeeded by Lord
John George Beresford, the future primate, in 1819. Beresford remained at Clogher only a year before moving to Dublin, and only two
years in Dublin before obtaining the primacy.

His successor was the unfortunate Percy Jocelyn. Jocelyn's
career in the Church had been promoted by Lord Roden, spokesman for
the ultra-Tory interest in Parliament. Jocelyn combined all the worst
characteristics of those ecclesiastical leaders whose claims were
based solely on political influence. He became a bishop while still
young. His transparent unfitness for this office did not bar him
from the important diocese of Clogher, which he reached in 1822.
Clogher was one of the wealthiest dioceses of the country, and the
mentally unbalanced bishop was soon reported to have sold the very
furnishings of his palace. In the same year he was apprehended on
a morals charge in London. His partner in the crime was a "common
sailor," and critics of the Church did not fail to notice that Jocelyn
was granted bail while the sailor was consigned to a miserable life in
prison.[6]

Jocelyn's case soon became the subject of a lively correspondence
involving the Viceroy, Lord Wellesley, the Chief Secretary Goulburn,
the Prime Minister and the new primate Beresford.[7] They finally decided that the Church would suffer less if Jocelyn was deprived of
office quickly and quietly in return for a commitment by Lord Roden to

keep him out of sight. But Jocelyn jumped bail and fled overseas.
Peel and Goulburn made no attempt to secure his return, and vowed
only that he would be prosecuted severely if he did so.[8] Jocelyn did
return, but so discreetly that few were aware that he spent the remainder of his life as a servant in his own brother's house. King George
IV drew from this melancholy episode the lesson that Irishmen made
bad bishops.[9]

Jocelyn's successor was Lord Robert Ponsonby Totenham Loftus,
Lord Ely's young son of yesteryear. His supervision of this wealthy
and heavily Protestant diocese during the age of parliamentary reform did him immense credit and would have surprised Stuart. George
de la Poer Beresford, whose translation to Kilmore had precipitated
Stuart's intervention in union engagements, remained at Kilmore in
discreet anonymity for an entire generation; his work too was better
than Stuart acknowledged.

The primate from 1822 until almost the end of our period, Lord
John George Beresford, combined the attributes of an eighteenth century grandee and the concern of a nineteenth century Church administrator. Stuart had given the primacy real moral power, and Beresford
was determined to sustain it. His rise to power, however, conjured up
shades of the past. After taking orders he moved at once to the
deanery of Clogher, no minor post, and seven years later to the bishopric of Cork. In 1807, only a year later, he moved to Raphoe, and ten
years later to Clogher. In 1820 he was translated to Dublin, and
thence to Armagh in 1822, where he remained more than forty years.
During his sixty-four years of clerical service he received from the

Church an estimated ₤887,900, and his family benefited to the sum of three or four million pounds. His generosity, however, mitigated the worst evils of such acquisitiveness. Armagh and Trinity College still bear witness to his largesse, some of which was directed towards projects more pleasing to the eye than useful to the community.[10]

The province of Dublin traditionally attracted men who entertained strong political ambitions, especially in the see of Dublin itself. Charles Agar, Earl of Normanton and Archbishop of Dublin as a result of the Act of Union, had pursued his interests in statecraft with a distinctively secular enthusiasm as Archbishop of Cashel. He would have continued to do so at Dublin but for reasons of health and because of a diminished enthusiasm for his services among leaders of the Irish administration. His successor, Euseby Cleaver, was regarded in 1790, before all his plaintive requests for removal from Ferns and Leighlin, "as perfect a character as human nature can produce."[11] He was, however, a man of stubborn conservative views, which Stuart and Brodrick circumvented on some occasions and ignored on others.

Cleaver's conservatism was tested early, and perhaps his refusal to be just another pliant bishop is worthy of further notice. Even before the end of the eighteenth century he dared to defy none other than the powerful Irish Lord Chancellor, the Earl of Clare. The issue was financial. Cleaver had laid an exhorbitant fine on the governors of Swift's Hospital in Dublin, the lands of this institution being leased from the good bishop. Clare appealed to Cleaver to be generous. Cleaver refused "in terms of very brutish violence and indignation," to quote Lord Clare.[12] Fortunately his rise in the Irish Church was due to the patronage of the Duke of Buckingham, and Cleaver was therefore doubly fortunate that Archbishop Agar chose to pass away when the Whigs were briefly in power in 1806 and 1807. Euseby's brother William was a prelate in the English Church, and held a series of bishoprics without residing in any of them.[13] Euseby resided faithfully in Ireland, and indeed had earned the sympathy of the government by virtue of the destruction of his residence during 1798. He was completely ineffectual as Archbishop of Dublin from 1807 until his death in 1812.

The most difficult high ecclesiastic to analyze was William Magee. He was installed as Archbishop of Dublin in 1822. As Professor of Divinity at Trinity College he gained one reputation as a noted theologian, perhaps the finest theologian of his age, and another as a political liberal. His success in mobilizing fellows of the College to support parliamentary efforts to secure Catholic relief in 1812 and 1813 distressed the Irish government and delayed his bishopric. He became Dean of Cork instead, and after a period of good behavior was raised to the bishopric of Raphoe. Thereafter his liberalism began to wane. His birthplace was County Fermanagh, a land of longstanding religious tensions. They surfaced in Magee's case in a deep dislike of Catholicism. When he became Archbishop of Dublin in 1822 Magee was convinced that Protestantism was on the threshold of a resurgence in Ireland.[14] The vestiges of liberalism, which probably helped him to get favorable consideration from the Marquess of Wellesley in 1822, gave way to a contentious, narrow-minded conservatism.[15] He became

involved in a raging dispute with Dublin Catholics over the question
of access to churchyards after funerals. His inelegant though pithy
aphorisms describing political and ecclesiastical opponents pleased
very few. He incurred Beresford's wrath by defending one of Trinity's
fellows against the leaders of the College. He fared better, however,
on the issue of Catholic Emancipation, where he worked strongly against
it. The King confessed to Magee that there were no politicians he
could lean on to prevent the Catholic triumph. But Magee returned to
Ireland and to his bed. He died in 1831.[16]

Magee's successor, Richard Whately, was perhaps the most unusual
man to staff the Irish bench in the entire period. London born and
widely educated, he served as Principal of St. Alban's Hall, Oxford,
from 1825. He succeeded Nassau Senior as professor of political
economy in 1829. Whately's appointment engendered considerable controversy. His rise was dramatic in that he circumvented the usual steps
of dean and bishop; he moved directly from his academic situation at
Oxford to Dublin. Bishop Philpotts of Exeter charged Whately held
dangerous theological opinions, including a denial of the sacredness of
the Sabbath. Others thought him too brusque, too impatient, and too
much impressed with his own mental superiority.[17] His training in
political economy made him "hard, logical, unimaginative, and to some
extent intolerant," and his readiness to dominate the proceedings of
the Irish Privy Council gained him few friends.[18] His elevation was
widely though erroneously attributed to Whig plans for a scheme of
national education in Ireland, though in fact Grey could not recall
having any opinion of Whately before inviting him to take Dublin in

eptember 1831.[19] More likely the appointment reflected a complete

earth of sympathetic bishops on either the Irish or English benches,

circumstance which drove the Whigs to offer the see to Henry Bath-

rst, Bishop of Norwich and at 87 in no position to execute his own

esponsibilities.[20]

Whately hotly opposed the growing influence of evangelicals.

hen the Rev. R.J. Nolan, a Catholic priest and instructor of Maynooth,

urned Protestant, Whately not only gave him no encouragement but

uestioned his credentials as a scholar. Archdeacon Thomas Magee, son

f Whately's predecessor, gave Nolan a pulpit in opposition to the

rchbishop's express commands.[21] He condemned use of charity to gain

onversions in a charge "On the Right Use of National Afflictions" and

ocialized with Lord Wellesley, twice Lord Lieutenant and married to a

atholic.[22] Whately's disdain for convention was magnificently ex-

ressed in other ways. He viewed his jurisdiction as an experiment

hich had failed, and believed he would be the last Archbishop of Dub-

in. He wanted his salary reduced, offered to help support Catholic

riests out of the revenue of the Established Church and tried to

irect Church revenues to religious purposes.[23] His enthusiasm for

ational education disturbed most of the Church and Beresford seems to

ave been afraid of him.[24] Like Beresford, he too remained a leading

orce in the Irish Church almost to disestablishment, and did much to

eform the lax discipline of his diocese.[25]

Most bishops of the province of Dublin were men of distinctly

nferior stamp. Charles Lindsay, Hardwicke's secretary, seems to have

een a man of petty instincts and suspicious feelings. Peel detested him and Stuart thought him "not only troublesome but extremely absurd."[26]

Risingstandards of episcopal character arrested his advance, despite his own pleas, and he spent much time disagreeing with and then apologizing to his conversants.[27] His diocese seems to have demanded and received little attention, and upon Lindsay's death it was united with Dublin. Of the remaining dioceses, in Ossory and Ferns and Leighlin the one notable personality was Thomas Elrington, one-time provost of Trinity and Bishop of the latter united diocese from 1822 to 1835. An able Church propagandist, he played an important role in the Irish education inquiry under Perceval and Liverpool and defended the Church with conviction and considerable agility. In Cashel the dominant figure was Charles Brodrick, translated from Kilmore in 1801, architect of ecclesiastical fiscal policies for more than twenty years. Brodrick was a man of many interests, corresponding with Hannah More on social problems, making observations on the weather, dabbling in fiscal projects for Church and state, and incurring the wrath of fundamentalists for his moderation.[28] His successor, Richard Laurence, was an intimate of Peel, Regius Professor of Hebrew at Oxford, an indefatigable scholar and man of liberal sympathies even to the point of voting for Catholic emancipation. Upon his death Cashel ceased to be an archbishopric and became subject to Dublin.

Within the province of Cashel were gentlemen of decidedly precarious social pretentions. One of these was C. Morgan Warburton. Warburton's consientious work as bishop helped to ease suspicions that he had never received orders and his marriage to a wealthy lady after the death of his first wife removed him from the shadow of poverty.

e was suave and debonair, friend and confidant to a generation of

rish politicians.[29] He maintained a profitable friendship with

he Price of Wales, later George IV. Warburton never permitted his

chievements to pass unnoticed, and he forwarded frequent and un-

olicited advice on how the Crown should manage the Irish Church.[30]

is political acumen was vindicated elsewhere, too. He was among

he first Churchmen to measure accurately the threat O'Connell posed

o existing order, and he used his episcopal visitations to combat

hat man's "mischievous" initiatives.[31]

Another colorful gentleman was Power Trench, Bishop of Water-

ord and Lismore (1802-1810) and Elphin (1810-1819). "He had known

ome ups and downs in life. . . having begun life as a land-agent, he

. . finished it as an Archbishop." His was popular, but belonged to

he Church militant. While at Elphin he put himself at the head of a

etachment of the Third Light Dragoons, and rode off to put down local

isturbances. His letters to Peel are among the most prescient anal-

ses of Irish rural problems in the early nineteenth century.[32]

tuart thought him irresponsible.[33] Trench established a chair for

he study of the Irish language at Trinity, but his use of grants from

he Board of First Fruits, while not wasted on himself, seems to have

een largely misdirected.[34] He made himself popular, however, by re-

using to punish defaulting tenants and by assisting those who were

arrassed by insensitive landlords.

Two other bishops of the province of Cashel were prominent, though

or different reasons. One, John Jebb, was a considerable scholar

ho felt deeply the privations of Irish rural life. He was also an inveterate correspondent, an able pamphleteerist, and perhaps Brod-

rick's closest friend. Jebb combined a wealth of learning with

considerable strength of feeling on controversial and often unrelated

questions. He pursued his arguments with undistracted zeal for a while,

and then lapsed into periods of boredom and frustration.[35] He did not

obtain a bishopric until 1822, and then apparently as a reward for

having kept his parish quiet during tithe agitation in his area. Under

his influence standards of examination of candidates for orders were

raised sharply. In this he anticipated further improvements made by

Archbishop Whately after 1830. The excellence of his speechmaking in

Parliament contrasted sharply with that of most of his fellow bishops.

His reasoned explanation of opposition to the tithe commutation bill on

July 10, 1824 was described by the aging Wilberforce as "one of the

most able ever delivered in Parliament."[36] He suffered a stroke in

1827, retired to England, and, as John Henry Newman later noted,

strongly influenced the beginnings of the Oxford Movement.

The other, William Bennett, arrived in Ireland in the 1780s as

chaplain to the Earl of Westmoreland, moved to Cork in 1790, and to

Cloyne in 1794, where he rested until death in 1820. Age overtook him

and his diocese became a hotbed of non-residence at a time when others

were showing substantial improvement. Bennett excused his negligence,

noting that

> I have no longer the activity with which I was once able to
> counter all the difficulties of the Episcopal Church; that
> I am the oldest bishop on the bench, distressed more than
> any, by those severe domestic misfortunes, of which we have
> all a share, and . . . pressed by a distemper, which by in-
> capacitating me from taking exercise, must soon break up my
> constitution.[37]

At the end of the second decade of Stuart's tenure there were
still many bishops in Ireland who, though less infirm than Bennett,
were equally inactive. "I have indeed had occasion to observe,"
Stuart wrote to Brodrick towards the end of his life,

> what little reliance can be placed upon the assertions of
> bishops [respecting] the state of their dioceses. Some are
> extremely indolent, and endeavor to conceal the effects of
> the indolence, by very bold assertions. Others from vanity
> exaggerate most extremely the benefits of their exertions
> and therefore give a false account of the buildings under
> their care.[38]

In 1825 Archbishop Magee informed a parliamentary committee that clerical behavior had improved substantially, largely due to the higher
calibre of the bench. In 1829 the clerical propagandist Newland in
one of his apologies declared that the "duties of a bishop in Ireland
engross his whole time"; indeed, he could state "with perfect truth"
that he knew of one dignitary "who undeviatingly devoted from seven to
eight hours daily" to his work.[39] This was hardly heroic labor, and
the next generation of bishops was to do much more as the evangelical
impulse grew within the Church.

After 1840 evangelicalism gained its first fully committed champions on the Irish bench with the elevation of Robert Daley and James
T. O'Brien. O'Brien, as Bishop of Ossory and Ferns and Leighlin after
1842, was representative of a new breed: a prolific writer on justification by faith and constant opponent of the Oxford Movement and
disestablishment. He spoke out forcefully even on controversial issues
and demonstrated tremendous dedication to the movement for reform.[40]

Another, John Gregg, was the last of a long series of distinguished preachers in the Irish Church in the early nineteenth century. In

1862 he became Bishop of Cork, Cloyne and Ross.[41] Perhaps his popularity as preacher is explained by his shorthand guide for the preparation of sermons: "thirty five minutes, explain text, reason on it, urge it home strongly, exhort warmly, conclude prayfully and close simply."[42]

The character of the beneficed clergy at the beginning of the nineteenth century was not always exemplary. Surviving documents by their nature tend perhaps to convey the worst rather than the best instances of clerical conduct. In some cases the clergy's weaknesses reflected a defective vocation; one clergyman asked Brodrick in 1815 to decide promptly whether he might have a certain benefice as to "enable him without further loss of time to endeavor to make out for himself some other employment or line of life" were the post unavailable.[43] Powerful families managed to have relatives with little general education and less exposure to theology and spiritual training installed in livings. O'Beirne noted in 1803 that "residence is among the most especial objects we ought to have at heart; but it is equally essential that we should labor to render that residence effectual to its purposes, and that can only be done by endeavoring to restore the spirit of their profession, as well as the knowledge of learning of it among the clergy."[44]

This problem eased considerably by 1830. By midcentury clerical academic credentials were impressive. Religious training, however, remained somewhat haphazard despite Whately's attempts to organize a seminary.[45] And notwithstanding O'Beirne's pertinent remarks, non-residence remained a serious problem. It was not only invidious in

itself, but hurt the Church most noticeably in overwhelmingly Catholic
areas, where the clergy were least likely to reside. Even Protestants
accused these clergymen of thinking of their parishioners as only
"tenants at will, as they do themselves lords in transit."[46] Absentees,
of course, were often the most ambitious for promotion to a more lucrative preferment. It lent credence to a popular advice in jingle form
to

> . . . let it be your ambition
> [to] be an intriguing, shrewd, Church politician.
> Politicians in Church, aye, as well as in state
> for nothing but interest succeeds there of late.
> The news advertisements, moreover, attest
> That livings are given to those that bid best.[47]

Such abuses must not be belabored, even at the beginning of the
nineteenth century. Many commendable men also staffed Ireland's
parishes. But the high incidence of absenteeism meant that the impetus
for religious activity moved by default out of the regular Church and
into the hands of Methodists and evangelicals. Their work was limited
in scope before 1815, but even this threatened to undermine the casual
attitudes of the less zealous beneficed clergy, and did eventually, as
will be seen, lead to a marked improvement in the character of the Irish
clergy as a professional body.

Our picture of the curates is even less happy, though their defects were to a considerable extent part of the system and not personal.
In 1800 Irish clerical absenteeism was in part rectified, or rather excused, by the employment of curates at salaries rarely in excess of Ł40
a year. Their indigence in a Church otherwise well circumstanced was
a public scandal. One outspoken incumbent reacted in response to a
proposal to raise curates' salaries by predicting that if salaries were

increased to ₺75, "the curates . . . will become head landlords, and incumbents their tenants."[48] Later on, Stuart tried, over vehement protests of incumbents, to force salary increases. He noted that rapidly increasing tithe revenues had done nothing to raise curates' salaries above those of "menial servants".[49] These attempts proved only partially effective, for curates' salaries rose very slowly indeed until 1830.

Curates' poverty had both commendable and unfortunate ramifications. It tended to identify their plight with the peasantry, who responded with evidence of affection rarely reserved for incumbents.[50] Their education was generally rudimentary, and their level of sophistication low.[51] They were receptive to evangelical tendencies.[52] They sought preferments for themselves, although their letters reflected little confidence that their requests would be granted.[53] To meet the demands made on their small salaries by growing families they often became estate agents, tithe proctors and farmers, and even tenant farmers. This involved curates in heated disputes with parishioners and incumbents alike. The former resented tithes and rents; the latter were suspicious that the curate-proctor was cheating them. When bishops arrived on their annual visitations, curates were disposed to criticize their absentee clerical supervisors, sometimes with considerable effect. They, like some beneficed clergymen, also tried to accumulate curacies, and as a result non-residence was not unknown even among curates. In the absence of the beneficed clergy they also exerted their authority, sometimes so heavyhandedly that parishioners demanded their removal. One cannot, however, help sympathizing with their poverty and difficulties involved in representing on a local level a religious establishment often insensitive to pastoral responsibilities.[54]

2. Discipline within the Church

The Established Church in Ireland, like its counterpart in England and in the Catholic tradition, was hierarchical in structure. The primate exercised authority over the bishops, and the bishops disciplined beneficed clergymen and their curates. By 1800 discipline within the Church was practiced somewhat more in the exception than in the rule. Inattention by those in positions of authority had elevated clerical autonomy to a prescriptive right, one not to be surrendered without difficulty. The gentry tastes and pretentions of the clergy induced them to strive for recognition as landlords' equals – and to resent episcopal strictures – while bishops' aspirations were reinforced by family connection and private wealth. The insensitivity of the bench to Stuart's demands, even when reinforced by parliamentary mandate, has already been noted. Indeed, the primate had little legal influence in his own province, and almost none outside it. The primate dared not forward chastisements directly to absentee bishops, but depended upon the government to nominate a higher calibre of personnel in the future. For their part the bishops responded to requests for information with uneven enthusiasm until 1820. After 1820 criticism from evangelical elements and the prospect of substantive reform, combined with a distinctly higher episcopal specimen, raised the level of episcopal exertions dramatically.

Bishops who ignored directives from Stuart and from Parliament ex-

pected, and received, little obedience from the beneficed clergy. Even
before 1820, however, a considerable minority of the bishops were refur-
bishing their disciplinary weapons and restoring their powers of moral
suasion inside their jurisdictions. The instruments available in this
task of insuring discipline were, as has been noted, highly defective.
Bishops were obliged to visit each benefice once each year to interview
incumbents and to inspect parochial facilities. Many bishops discharged
their responsibilities by dispatching obliging surrogates, whose in-
spections were often cursory and observations innocuous. Not until the
1820s do we see a majority of bishops keeping detailed records on the
condition of churches and glebe houses, the aptitude of curates, parishioners complaints, tithe values, and frequency of service and communion. As late as 1823 no Protestant bishop had seen fit to visit Conne-
marra in the west of Ireland. Those bishops prepared to confront wayward incumbents were often obliged to enter into an extended correspondence and protracted court suits, an effective discouragement for
all but the most zealous.

Between 1800 and 1830, by which time most salient problems had
been substantially modified, active bishops directed their disciplinary
energies in six directions: enforcement of residence; prevention of
pluralities and exchanges of benefices; encouragement of church and
glebe house construction; satisfaction of patronage requests without
injury to the Church's pastoral responsibilities; assignment of curates to assist incumbents in large benefices; and resolution of parochial disputes. Non-residence was the most persistent theme of reform-
minded bishops' correspondence during the first three decades of the

nineteenth century. O'Beirne set the tone for more rigorous enforce-

ment in his charge of 1800:

> I owe it to our general interests, to the credit of our
> Church, to the cause of religion and morality, that I should
> labor to cut off this subject of reproach at once, and to
> joy to our adversaries, and regret and mortification to our
> friends; my determinations are therefore fixed. In no in-
> stance will I excuse the residence either of the incumbent
> or his curate, where there is a Church, and in what so many
> are pleased to call and to make, non-cures, I will be deter-
> mined by circumstances, whether I shall enforce the residence
> of either, or not.[56]

O'Beirne implemented this resolution with a vigorous hounding of his

"rotten sheep." He advertized his determination through pamphlets,

and even established a surveillance system wherein parishioners were

encouraged to report instances of their incumbents' lax behaviour.[57]

Other bishops were equally determined, and Stuart tried to get

the government to use its patronage rights to strengthen these bishops'

hands.[58] But progress was slow. Once confirmed in their benefices,

incumbents proved to be an intractable lot. Publicity often aggravated

matters, for Parliament, which assumed that the bishops should be

able to give orders and have them obeyed, often accused the bench of a

defective zeal. The clergy felt no hesitation in applying to their lay

patrons for support against the bishop. They fashioned highly ingen-

ious reasons for their absence; one incumbent explained his failure to

attend the episcopal visitation by saying he had failed to see the no-

tice in the London newspapers![59] Sometimes, as Stuart noted, the clergy

took leave of their jurisdictions "without even the formality of a letter."[60]

Perhaps the clearest and most depressing evidence of a harrassed bi-

shop's frustrations came to Brodrick from William Bennett, the aging and

heretofore none-too-zealous Bishop of Cloyne, in 1819. It deserves quoting in some detail:

> . . . The vicar general informs me, that he was directed by your Grace to say that you expected me to prevent Mr. Blackwood's winter journeys to England. I wrote to him on the subject, but received an answer that he was directed by his physicians to go to the waters of Rathbone, enclosing a certificate on the oath of one of them to this effect. He sent me afterwards as an excuse for not going that season the state of Europe at the time, but actually went since, and talks of the benefit received and the necessity of going again. Your Grace knows from Bishop Cleaver's case, how difficult it is in the present time, and with the present jealousy in all our great lawyers against episcopal exertion of this sort, to proceed to severities against the clergyman desiring absence on reasons, real, or pretended, of ill-health, supported by the oath of a physician, by high connections, and a good fortune. In short, this gentleman, half-deranged as he is, is much above my single hand, and all I wish is that your Grace interpose with your superior authority at the next triennial [visitation], and I will engage under that authority to execute what you direct. I confess I was in hopes from his brother's leading interest in the county of Down, that Lord Castlereagh would have taken him off my hands before this time and planted him in one of the northern deaneries. He is much the most troublesome man we have to manage, and yet my opinion is he will submit rather than endanger his preferment. . . .

Lister is another of the unmanageable set. He is certainly in very bad health, asthmatic and dropsical as his appearance shows, and has been of late very generally absent at Bath, answering my inquiries and orders by volumes rather than letters, and certificates of his illness, of the truth of which I have no reason to doubt. He has no house and neither money or credit to build one, nor do I think that if the Board [of First Fruits] advanced money, there would be any chance of its being properly expended. I am afraid his death is the only benefit he will ever confer upon his parish.

. . . Your Grace order[ed] . . . that Rev. King of Kilblane . . . should reside, which he obeyed, and has resided ever since at the cabin, not much I fear to the advantage of his parishioners. This man, like Blackwood, is undoubtedly deranged, and it is very hard upon me to have more mad clergymen to contend with than any other bishop in the province. . . He [is] everyway so incompetent to the care of a parish, that it [is] best to leave him his non-cure, . . . and put some active curate into the cure. . . . I stated my intention to King himself, and nothing can more clearly satisfy your Grace of his state of derangement, than his thinking himself very

ill-used and persevering to harrass me with letters to give
him a better living, . . . that he may redeem his injured
character.[61]

Preventing manipulation of benefices was equally frustrating,

although in time bishops' powers to reduce the evil bore considerable

results. The practice of exchanging benefices in order to augment

revenues was widely developed before 1800, and strongly negative re-

actions by reform-minded bishops after the Act of Union forced aspir-

ing exchangees to devise subtler excuses. One applicant noted rough

handling in the late rebellion. Others went to considerable length

to prove that the two clergy involved were equal in income and age.[62]

Until 1805 even Stuart and Brodrick were somewhat indulgent; after-

wards, exchanges were rarely approved.[63] Sometimes, however, the

preferments lay entirely in the gift of the crown, which led to more

flagrant exercises of the aspiring clergyman's art. As Stuart noted

to Richmond on one occasion:

> Only consider the case of Dr. Steward, whom your Grace would
> certainly not have suffered to exchange, had you been
> acquanted with his real motive. You gave him two livings,
> with the value of which I am well acquainted, for the single
> living which he then held; happy and contented he was,
> but this contentment did not last a single month – he then
> applied to exchange one of these large livings with Mr.
> Ponsonby . . . . He is again discontented and will think
> himself ill-treated if he has not the deanery of Clogher,
> which he imagines will be vacated in this disgraceful
> scramble.[64]

The exchanges could be complicated; the following, described in

the Brodrick correspondence, reveals the finely honed system which

decades of indulgent bishops had allowed to develop:

> Mr. Symes [holding a benefice in Ferns] has devised a scheme
> of eluding the residence laws. Mr. Radcliff, rector of
> Enniscorthy in the diocese of Ferns, is also rector of Porta-

> ferry in the Diocese of Down . . . Mr. Radcliff has agreed
> with Mr. Symes to this exchange, and Mr. Radcliff has just
> sent a petition to the primate for a faculty, enabling him
> to hold Enniscorthy and Castle Ellis. Sir Thomas Forster,
> who has the benefice of Castle McAdam in the diocese of
> Dublin, is to exchange Castle McAdam for Portaferry, and
> Mr. Symes by such means to have Castle McAdam.

Unfortunately for the aspirants, Stuart refused to grant the faculty.
If the Bishop of Down and Connor, however, allowed Forster into Porta-
ferry, Symes could move to Castle McAdam, residing there rather than
in Ferns, and pleading, quite legally, that he may live on either of
his benefices. Brodrick, then administering Dublin as a trust during
the final illness of Cleaver, refused to accept Forster's letter of
resignation. Symes pleaded with Brodrick to reconsider; after all,
Forster had not been resident in Dublin, nor he in Ferns. By the exchange both would reside, because they found the new areas congenial.
He concluded by noting that with his "character and conduct I trust being
unexceptionable I am at a loss to know on what grounds I am refused a
request so reasonable." Brodrick was not swayed by such guile, and the
transaction collapsed. Such initiatives became fewer thereafter.[65]

Encouraging glebe house and church construction represented in
the minds of recalcitrant clergymen an assault on their property rights.
Even Parliament's contribution of legislation assisting bishops in
forcing the clergy to apply for loans was not entirely successful.
Bishops were understandably reluctant to approve allocations of funds
in those instances where the clergy were determined not to reside.
Sequestration was somewhat unwieldy. If the incumbent was a pluralist,
and the revenue small, and he finally exhausted all legal procedures,
it was often convenient just to abandon the benefice to the bishop.

The more stringent sequestration provisions of the 1807 legislation,
were, however, used with considerable effectiveness in some dioceses
whose bishops possessed and the clergy knew they possessed sufficient
resources to withstand long court cases.[66] Sometimes incumbents resisted grants because they entailed employment of a curate, or an
additional curate, in their farflung benefices.[67] Sometimes as well
the local gentry resisted the bishop, lest a resident clergyman be
more attentive to his tithes.

Bishops were under considerable pressure from neighboring gentry
and more distantly situated members of the peerage to accommodate minor
relatives who, even in Ireland, could not aspire to begin life in the
Church with a deanery. When bishops felt obliged to comply, they often
soothed their own injured pride by delivering notification of the
largesse in unmistakably sarcastic terms.[68] Later bishops felt a bit
more secure, as when one told a peer that he refused to admit a clergyman with care of souls "who leaves another in consequence of inability
of attending to his duty."[69] Pressure was also exerted from Dublin
Castle, especially in the case of deaneries, where the crown held the
right of preferment but wanted the acquiescence, if not the enthusiastic
agreement, of the presiding bishop.[70] Finally, of course, beneficed
clergy and curates made their own direct representations. They pleaded
prior promises, recent service to the Church or state, affliction,
large family, poverty, or poor accommodations.[71] Some efforts must
have melted even those episcopal hearts inured to the tribulations
of the rural clergy. Others were equally renowned for their audacity
and presumptuous language; all were attempts to move up the preferment

ladder when the proper connections could not be brought into play.

Bishops' attempts to increase the effectiveness of local parochial activity often took the form of recourse to curates. In large
benefices they made unwieldy jurisdictions manageable and restored the
Protestant presence in those areas abandoned during the eighteenth
century. Some of the most vociferous protests to reach the episcopal
palace were triggered by plans to force incumbents to sustain additional
curates. Many pleaded financial inability. Others took a higher line
and interpreted the move as a reflection on their own effectiveness as
ministers. One clergyman in a long missive noted that while almost
sixty he was still in good health, if only because he dreaded the
suggestion that a curate be appointed to assist him. "With respect
to a curate," he pleaded "do not think of it."

> I am . . . able and willing and accustomed to duty; but
> this I could by no means afford; no one knows better than
> your Lordship the circumstances of this poor parish . . .
> [after paying Ł200 to a local family holding rectorial
> tithes] what remains, between paying my proctor, and being
> robbed and cheated to the right and left, is really little
> more than that sum; nor is my own patrimony equal to aid
> me. I have a wife and seven children. . . .[72]

A more sophisticated device was a perpetual curacy. This was a
favorite way of restoring the Protestant presence and having some
assurance that it would remain so. Perpetual curacies were endowed
sub-parochial jurisdictions ideally suited to large benefices. Citizens
of a remote part of the union sometimes lobbied for a permanent Church
and curate in their area, offering to create a small endowment. The
incumbent was asked either to promise an annual sum, or to surrender
tithe revenues in the area encompassed by the new jurisdiction.
Neither invitation much suited the clergy, but upon each vacancy some

progress was made in establishing more perpetual curacies.[73] Bishops

were also involved in rearranging parochial boundaries to meet modern

commitments. This was extremely difficult. It required approval of

the bishop, the Lord Lieutenant, the agency holding right of presen-

tation, and the Privy Council and called for an act of Parliament.

Only the most notorious parochial jurisdictions were amended.

In part this deficiency was remedied by extension of "rural

deans." The idea of subdividing dioceses was an old one, and one which

survived the Reformation in England better than in Ireland. Rural deans

had been employed in Ireland on occasion in the seventeenth century,

once or twice in the early eighteenth, and more commonly near the close

of the century.[74] By 1820 rural deans were to be found in 16 or 22

dioceses, usually several in each diocese. Some were members of

cathedral chapters but reformist bishops tended to rely on popular

clergymen to effect the necessary liaison work. Rural deans had the

power to inspect and report. As such, they were seen by lethargic

clerical elements as spy agents, a prejudice which died as the pace of

local renewal quickened.[75] Such was the progress made in this area

that Whately after 1830 was able, and willing, to wage war upon re-

fractory curates or incumbents for acts which partook of the nature

of breaches of etiquette rather than offenses against "faith or

morals."[76] An earlier generation of reformers would never have bothered

with these things.

The relationship between curates and beneficed clergy was not at

all similar to that of the clergy and the bishops. The clergy, it is

true, exercised one form of control over curates which bishops could

not use: financial. Other factors were far more important. Where
the incumbent resided, the curate might be little more than an em-
ployee, occasionally a colleague. Where the beneficed clergyman was
an absentee, or where the union was so large that several curates and
a resident pastor could all work within the same jurisdiction and yet
have little day to day contact, the curate was often a man of substantial influence in the community. This was especially true when
he was able to combine the prerogatives of his superior with the
relatively greater popularity enjoyed by curates in the countryside.
Many taught in the parish school, and had few responsibilities beyond
that. They sometimes drifted away, or emigrated; rarely were they
dismissed, so difficult was it to find others prepared to work for a
pittance. Two forces eventually altered their condition dramatically:
Parliament's intervention in Church affairs brought a sharp rise in
their salaries by 1850; the Church's retreat from the countryside
meant fewer curates were needed.

3. The Church and Irish Society

The importance of the Church of Ireland to the nation during the
early nineteenth century was a subject of considerable, even, constant,
dicussion. This interest encouraged wide dissemination of unsubstantiated
statistics and manipulation of numbers to partisan advantage. The question, moreover, addressed intangible relationships between bishops and
clergy and landlords and tenants, the somewhat confusing impact of the
Church in urban areas, and its considerable economic influence. Determining even the number of adherents was a provocative exercise. Poli-

tical economists observing the Irish scene during this period concluded

that the ratio of Catholics to Protestants had increased from 2 to 1

in 1731 to 4 to 1 in 1805; Newenham included Dissenters in the Pro-

testant population.[77] Mason, basing his estimates on parochial re-

turns from the Established clergy and including all Protestants, be-

lieved that the ratio in 1814 was 2.75 to 1.[78] Defenders of the Church

took a decidedly more optimistic view. One observer concluded that

"Protestants in Ireland are at least equal to the Catholics;" Newland,

more moderately, thought the ratio was 2.60 to 1 in favor of Catholics,

but tending towards Protestants.[79] The religious census of 1834, car-

ried out in connection with Church reform, produced the first detailed

figures:

Established Church (including Methodists)	852,064
Roman Catholics	6,427,712
Presbyterians	642,356
Other Protestant Dissenters	21,808

The ratio was more than 4 to 1 in Catholics' favor. It was immediately

seized upon by Protestants as inaccurate, the product of "hostile"

commissioners.[80] One was forced to conclude that either Protestant

estimates, and those of neutral observers, had been decidedly conser-

vative, or that Ireland was moving into the Catholic camp at an ex-

ceedingly rapid pace. In 1861, according to a census which did much

to precipitate agitation for disestablishment, the membership of the

Irish Church stood at 693,357 out of a total population of 5,798,977.

This represented a drop in proportion of the total population from 13

to 11 per cent. These latter figures, following four decades of

evangelical activity and internal renewal, and coming in the aftermath of a widespread Catholic exodus during the famine, suggested that the Established Church was indeed becoming, demographically, a constantly smaller force on the Irish scene.

Distribution of membership did much to concentrate Anglican influence in northeastern counties and in urban areas. Armagh and Clogher, the latter with 26 per cent of the population belonging to the Established Church and thus the most Protestant diocese in Ireland, contained nearly one-fourth of the entire membership in 1861. Dublin and Kildare contained more than one-seventh. Killalla and Achonry, Tuam, Clonfert, Kilfenora and Kilmacdaugh, Killaloe, Ardfert and Aghdoe, Limerick, Cashel and Emly, Lismore and Waterford and Meath, 10 of the 22 dioceses before the reform bill, contained only 77,000 members in 1861; indeed, all Connaught and Munster had only slightly more than 100,000. The minority position of the Church was buffered slightly by the Presbyterians. But they were concentrated in the northeast to an even greater degree than the Establishment and therefore Anglicans in southern and western Ireland were isolated indeed.

This concentration in urban areas and in Ulster was only slightly suggested in the structure of episcopal and parochial preferments. The medieval Church had contained 2,400 parishes and about 3,000 clergymen. The number of parishes remained constant but were subsumed into unions after the Reformation. In 1803 there were 1,120 benefices. This increased to 1,200 in 1824, to 1,396 in 1829, to 1,402 in 1838 and to almost 1,500 in 1861. Many incorporated two or more parishes; sometimes ten or more were thus united. This was especially true in Meath, with its exceedingly large number of minute medieval jurisdictions, and in western Ireland, where Protestants were scarce. Clonfert possessed 60 parishes but only 17 benefices, Killaloe 138 and 50, Elphin 75 and 29, and Tuam 89 and 23, in 1803.

These ratios were subsequently slightly reduced, but the Established Church continued to support many benefices with few members. In 1835, 41 benefices contained no members ar all, 90 contained fewer than 20, 120 more than 20 but fewer than 50, 160 more than 50 but fewer than 100, 221 more than 100 but fewer than 200, 286 more than 200 but fewer than 500, 139 more than 1,000 but fewer than 2,000, 91 more than 2,000 but fewer than 5,000, and 12 contained more than 5,000. Thus more than one-third of Irish benefices were home to fewer than 100 members of the Established Church. On the eve of disestablishment, after extensive administrative reorganization and consolidation, 487 benefices contained fewer than 100 members, 76 more than thirty years earlier. The burden of rationalization took place in the division of those with large memberships into smaller units; the Church was still trying to maintain its national scope.[81]

In the decade before disestablishment the parochial clergy numbered some 2,000, including 500 curates. The clergy were distributed across Ireland by virtue of factors clearly outdated and uneconomical. Armagh possessed nearly one-half of the beneficed clergy: Armagh and Dublin between them possessed two-thirds. In fact, however, the clergy should have been even more concentrated. An incumbent in the diocese of Down and Connor and Dromore superintended 1000 parishioners; in the united diocese of Cashel, Emly, Waterford and Lismore the number was only 135. Curates did a little, but not much, to equalize the workload. The vast distances of sparsely populated western parishes of course required more clergy, but underemployment was a substantial problem in the South and West.

Clerical incomes varied greatly and reflected no particular relationship to the work. On the eve of disestablishment, after forty years of considerable effort to rationalize incomes, 109 incumbents enjoyed net incomes in excess of ₤1000 per annum, while 40 per cent (720) had incomes of under ₤200 per annum. Three hundred incumbents were paid less than ₤100 per annum. Curates' salaries were generally very low.[82]

The national aspirations of the Church were sustained by economic resources far in excess of limited membership. This prompted observations that even despite its limited membership, Anglicanism did indeed play an important role in Irish society. There were, in the first instance, fees received by the bishoprics for rental of land. These lands were normally rented at low rates and renewed at fines well below market value to Irish families upon whom the Church depended for its support. In Armagh some 100,000 acres were leased at less than 4 shillings per acre to Protestant peers and gentry. This rate was only one-third of the market evaluation. In the remainder of Ireland the abuse was less extensive only because lands were less improved. Even at these reduced rates, however, episcopal revenues on the eve of the reform bill were sufficient to make many bishops among the wealthiest men of the land. A total of some ₤150,000 in annual income was unevenly divided among the 22 bishops, so that Armagh, with ₤17,000, Derry with ₤14,000, and Clogher with ₤10,000 were very substantial preferments indeed. To these incomes was often added revenue from incumbents' family estates. Many bishoprics, especially those in Munster, were much less lucrative, but in the context of the rural poverty surrounding them their emoluments seemed attractive enough.[83] In addition, there was some ₤500,000 in tithe revenue distributed among 1,400 benefices, or ₤245 per capita. The average was relatively innocuous. Unfortunately, more than 230 benefices received less than ₤100 per year, while over 550 received more than ₤500 per annum. The larger amount represented an income upon which a comfortable gentry life-style could easily be sustained.

The concentration of ecclesiastical wealth in a few bishoprics and in the higher preferments encouraged a considerable exaggeration of the Establishment's financial resources. Hume computed the total rental of Ireland at 14 millions, and since the Church owned over one-fifth of the land, he computed the rental of Church lands, if properly let out, at 2.5 million. The addition of parochial tithes brought total estimated annual revenue to 3.2 million. A much more sober estimate of ₤800,000, low rentals discounted, was advanced by radicals in 1835.[84] Parliament concluded that if tithes were fully collected and lands rented at current competitive rates the Church's income would approximate 1.2 million.

The crisis of the 1830s found the Church at her wealthiest. Thereafter this wealth was gradually reduced by discounts encountered in the composition process, diversion of income previously obtained from vestry cess, state liens upon bishops' lands, and other factors. By 1868 no bishop received more than ₤10,000. Armagh and Clogher

as a united diocese received one-third of the income the two dioceses
had enjoyed in 1835. The total of episcopal revenue was about ₤50,000,
again one-third of the amount received thirty years earlier. Incomes
of the beneficed clergy also declined sharply. Especially disturbed
were the lucrative preferments, which suffered reductions of 50 per
cent and more. The Church of Ireland's financial stake in the nation
was thus sharply reduced at the time of disestablishment. Until 1835,
however, its revenues were such as to make it a powerful voice, whatever its minority status, in Irish society.[85]

Equipped with these interesting credentials, a minority membership and a powerful economic stake in Ireland, the Established Church
was exposed to the thrusts of its critics, and not always defended
successfully by its friends. The Church aspired to be regarded as
a pillar of the Protestant interest, as a stabilizing force in society,
as an agency of social control. Critics agreed that by this measure-
ment the Irish Church was a decided failure. "Never did opulence and
knowledge make so few friends or do so little good," observed one of
them. It is inimical to the cause of religion, which it affects to
support; and not the less detrimental to the national morality which
it is instituted to protect . . . It would be difficult to state the
national benefits gained by the mass of the people. . . ."[86] Bishops usually identified themselves with the great Irish landlords, and the
beneficed clergy with Ireland's vigorous gentry. After 1800 the Church
faced an increasingly hostile environment. This trend was not reversed
until after 1835. Then its decreasing influence and rising Protestant
alarm at the continued growth of Catholic power, combined with clear

evidence of reform within the Church, stilled most critics.[87] Until

then criticism was more common than were compliments. As a social

force, the Church was often represented as wealthy and impotent, a

preserve of vested interests cloaked in theological garb.[88] As a

pillar of the ascendancy it was seen as a puppet of English peers

and a hitching post for their worthless sons.[89] The beneficed clergy

were resented for their tithe-engendered incomes, for their preoccupa-

tion with signs of social acceptance, for their emphasis upon unpro-

ductive scholarship as a means to rise higher than perhaps their for-

tunes would have otherwise permitted, and in their fawning dependence

on family connections.[90] Dissenters declaimed against their unenthu-

siastic sermons, their confusion of Godliness with social respectabil-

ity, their hierarchial proclivities, and their aversion to proselytism.[91]

In 1822, as part of a surge of animosity against the Establish-

ment, John Doyle, Catholic Bishop of Kildare, issued a pamphlet whose

immediate popularity was in part due to the following observation:

> What state of the Protestant Church and of its revenues in
> Ireland would present itself to the view of an . . . unpre-
> judiced judge? He would find, . . . that an overwhelming
> majority of the population were of a different religion, and
> in a miserable state of poverty, supporting, however, their
> own clergy in decent but unassuming station: he would find
> the minority in numbers, and deists in religion, with clerical
> pastors, the highest orders of whom possess enormous revenues,
> much greater, in proportion to the circumstances of the two
> countries, then the same class in England, and having com-
> paratively little or nothing to do but to collect and enjoy
> them, many of them having not perhaps seen some of the
> parishes from which, through tithe farmers, they derive their
> incomes, or a portion of them, a dozen times in their lives,
> and engage some curate, at fifty or sixty pounds a year, to
> attend once in each Sunday to read prayers (often, perhaps,
> to the parish clerk alone), the rector himself, for twenty
> years together, not having been seen in his reading task
> or pulpit, except perhaps to attend his bishop. In other

parishes he would find (whether the fault rests with the
proctors or the clergy, the clergy themselves, the gentry,
or odious nature of the impost) acrimonious conflicts between individuals of the upper classes of the Protestant
laity and their own clergy, exhibited to the view of their
Catholic neighbors, and no infrequent, and distressing contrast, recording that acrimony, would be seen in the evident
reluctance with which the squire of a parish prevails on himself to accept the bread and wine from the hands of his parish minister while the Catholic priest is observed on the
terms of most hospitable cordiality with the same class of
his flock. He would find many of the men who actually perform the clerical duties, presenting to his commiseration
grey hairs and large families, with salaries scarcely sufficient to keep them from mendicancy, poor compared with their
neighbors, the Catholic priests, whom their own peasant flock
from their scanty earnings, preserve from such penury. . . .[92]

The innuendo of criticism was marked in 1822 by an immense pamph-

let activity. In part it was engendered by Catholics, but in part by

evangelical elements who concentrated on the defects of a clergy as

pastors and missionaries. Certain prelates, Magee in particular, were

the subject of abusive language. A book proporting to be a biography

of the Archbishop of Dublin was denounced by his friends as a "papist

plot."[93] O'Beirne noted that the clergy were "daily traduced. . .

and held up to popular odium as rapacious and unfeeling oppressors of

the industrious and the poor."[94] In 1822 both O'Beirne and Magee agreed

that disrespect to the clergy had never been so great, nor the Church

more unpopular.[95] Clerical appeals to Parliament were denounced as

"barbarous jargon." Parliamentary critics painted the state of the

Church in terms more heinous than ever before.[96] This hostility was

directed not so much against Protestantism, as against the Protestant

Establishment, and not so much against the Church as a religious organi-

zation, as against its social activities. During the eighteenth cen-

tury religious vitality had rarely interfered with the Church's civic connections. Now spiritual renewal proved a complicating factor, by putting in sharper focus the deficiencies of those corners of the Establishment not yet reformed.

4.   The Landlord Interest

In looking at the role of the Established Church in Irish society between the Act of Union and disestablishment it is convenient to divide our observations into three larger categories: relations with the landlord interest, overwhelmingly Protestant at the beginning of our period and still largely so at the end;   the place of the Church in the urban environment, where most Protestants and an increasing number of Catholics lived;   and shared attitudes and antagonisms with the lower classes, mostly Catholic, but in part Presbyterian and Methodist.   Unfortunately, documentation does not always correspond in amount to points of importance. Our knowledge, for instance, of the role of the Established clergy in rural localities is drawn largely from their own descriptions or from occasional outside observers.   The former were naturally anxious to defend their work.   The latter emphasized the extraordinary and often the atypical defect.   We also know a great deal more about relations between landlords and the clergy than between Catholic priests and peasants and the clergy, and yet we must presume that the second category was of at least equal importance.   And with certain exceptions, such as the Outrage papers and occasional parliamentary commissions, we have little chance to measure any of these relationships in statistical terms. Assiduous researchers have reconstructed early nineteenth century Ireland in much greater detail than thought possible even two decades ago, but there are large gaps where inference and scholarly judgment must complement available documentation.

Most of what is known of the Church-landlord connection is not particularly pleasant. During the eighteenth century resident Irish landlords resisted expansion of tithe income. They impropriated tithes and glebe lands, encouraged tithe resistance, and forestalled efforts to make more of the clergy resident. Several factors contributed to this hostility. There was a resentment against the Church's English orientation in values and personnel; strong anticlercial themes were appearing at this time almost everywhere in Western Europe. Landlords' financial interests were sometimes challenged by the Establishment. Finally, there was a fear, sometimes justified, that an active Protestant presence would disturb relations with Catholic tenants.

After 1800 these conditions were slowly modified. The clergy were forced to reside more frequently, whatever the landlords' attitudes. The rapid growth of Catholic power made many farsighted landowners fearful for the continued vitality of the Protestant ascendancy. Rising levels of income and education among the clergy made them proper companions for the gentry. Indeed landlords resident in remote areas began to see in the clergy a symbol of civilized life which they were more and more disposed to emulate. Certain strains persisted, however, and new ones appeared as the reform movement gained momentum. The success of the clergy in advancing their tithes became a source of sharp controversy as landlord's tenant policies increased the number and reduced the standard of living of Catholic peasants. More crops were being produced than ever before by this intensive cultivation, but there were many more mouths to feed and less money available for rents and tithes. The clergy retaliated against evidence of landowners' encouragement of tithe resistance by charging that land policies had driven Protestants from rural Ireland, had reduced Catholics to starvation, and had, in times of tithe resistance, even reduced the Established clergy to want.[97] During tithe convulsions in the 1820s and 1830s, and during agitation for Catholic Emancipation, many clergymen made pointed remarks about landlord dereliction in the task of social control, their provocative friendliness towards Catholic priests, and their resistance to clergymen zealous in exercising their pastoral responsibilities.[98] Often landlords were afraid of growing Catholic power, and even those most disposed to assist the Established clergy dared not provoke Catholic sensitivities. The Protestant press gave considerable publicity to landlords who helped the clergy during the tithe agitation of the 1830s. The publicity itself suggests that assistance was not universal. Even well-established social functions such as King William's birthday were increasingly shunned by the landlords. When at length tithe agitation was permanently settled in 1838 the clergy followed this example.[99] As land leagues appeared near mid-century we find more landlords sympathetic towards clerical complaints. Ironically, by 1860 landlords and not the clergy were the principal object of peasant agitation.

The process of Church reform, which many landlords wanted ardently, also brought strains. Aggressive bishops began to press landlords to restore impropriated tithes and even challenged their rights of presentation to vacant benefices. A celebrated struggle over right of

presentation to the deanery between the Bishop of Clogher and the
Dacre interest in Clones, County Monaghan, lasted almost ten years.
Prominent landlords supported Dacre and condemned the bishop's usurpation. The struggle, conducted semi-publicly while the incumbent
hung on to life, ended in a face-saving settlement for Dacre, and a
victory for the Church.[100] The same bishop challenged the powerful
Ely interest in another instance. The Marquess of Ely reacted swiftly.
He rushed his nominee to Ireland to confirm his title, since "possesion,"
as he told his candidate, was "many points of the law." Bishops'
efforts to enforce residence also met sporadic landlord resistance,
and episcopal pressure on vestries to help construct churches or on
impropriate titheholders to allocate funds led to altercations. The
leading gentry found it convenient to boycott vestry sessions called
to discuss construction plans, and then complained they had not been
consulted. Since vestries rarely dared defy the leading local landed
interest, and the clergy refused to endanger their good standing,
nothing was done. In several cases the bishop took the case to court,
and even to Parliament.[101]

A fruitful area for dispute was the tenant relationship assumed
by leading Irish families on Church lands. Before 1800 these lands
were almost always granted, as has been seen, to family interests at
low rates. After 1800 a larger number were granted to prominent local
landlords in order to cement the Protestant interest in an increasingly
hostile environment. Under the whip of criticism engendered by low
rentals, some bishops tried to bring rates up to competitive levels.
The bishops did not on the whole seem to have been very successful.

Finally, bishops were sometimes called in to adjudicate parochial disputes between different classes of the Protestants themselves. Landlords often ran vestry affairs in a high-handed way, allocating welfare funds as they saw fit, distributing pew rights to their advantage, and forcing the clergy to ignore popular demands for increased vestry rates for community projects. Petitions from the lower class element, directed to the bishop, put them in the uncomfortable position of appearing to discourage popular measures if they defended the landlords, and of favoring the masses if they refused. Bishops, naturally enough, tended to procrastinate, not always successfully. The congregation became bolder in its charge against landlords and accusations against the bishop himself, while landlords made it sufficiently clear what they thought the bishop must do.[102]

Differences of opinion and policy, no matter how severe, could not delay the clergy's tendency to seek identification with the gentry class. Despite many recorded instances of exchanges of benefices to secure better incomes or to avoid the wrath of reforming a bishop, the beneficed clergy changed their venue rather infrequently, and especially after 1825. Once appointed to the benefice, the average length of their tenure approximated the life-span of a landed gentleman after inheriting his estates. The average tenure in a benefice exceeded sixteen years in Clogher, where special conditions perhaps added several years to the national average. If those tenures terminated during the first three years are removed, the duration rises to twenty-one years. Those clergy residing in one benefice more than six years could expect to remain twenty-four years more.[103] These conditions gave those constantly resident considerable local authority and expertise.

Their pastimes reflected their gentry aspirations. They displayed interest in agricultural improvement, if only because it improved their tithe revenues as a result. Many clergymen were themselves the younger sons of landed families, and their interests were therefore deeply ingrained. If clerical incomes were somewhat less than those of the well-situated gentry, their level of education was higher. They often followed the hunt. After 1800, however, they seem to have turned more to literary pursuits, both because their educational accomplishments made this a satisfying pastime, partly because criticism of their participation in such sports as hunting and racing was gathering force under the influence of evangelicalism. Many, indeed, were authors of more than a mere local reputation. Ireland, Britain, and the whole empire were later to see a large number of writers, civil servants, and professional men begin their day as children of this generation of Irish clerical families.[104]

The clergy made inroads into the families of Irish peers through judicious marriages. Early in the century the great landlords regarded the beneficed clergy in large part as distinctly inferior in social rank. By 1815, however, rising tithe revenues were making many clergymen suitable prospects for super-abundant daughters of noble families, and younger sons of other leading families made the best of tightened residence requirements by obtaining benefices in the area of their family's power. Again in Clogher, for which statistical evidence is available, of the 128 beneficed clergy holding preferment between 1800 and 1841, 76 came from gentry families or married into them, while

another 14 were attached to the peerage. The connections also tended
to become local; at least 29 of the 129 were related to the half dozen
most prominent local families, and another 33 to the gentry of the
country. The number related to some Protestant family within the
diocese was probably just over 100. For the clergy this trend was
highly beneficial, and in immediate and practical terms did much to
mitigate their sufferings during the long period of tithe resistance
after 1830.[105]

Dr. R.B. McDowell has recently produced a convenient analysis of
the social origins of the Church of Ireland clergy on the eve of disestablishment. The upper class connection remained strong. Of 1300
beneficed clergymen out of a total of 1500 in 1868 whose family circumstances are known, 15 per cent were sons of members of the peerage.
Twenty-seven per cent came from decidedly prominent families. More
than one-half were sons of professional men, lawyers and clergymen.
Twenty clergymen were sons of bishops. Only 11 per cent were sons of
businessmen and only 4 per cent were sons of farmers. Most were graduates of Trinity College; indeed, in the year before disestablishment
a third of all Trinity graduates took orders. Trinity, the upper and
upper middle classes and the Church corporation continued to form a
very close-knit society.[106]

Trinity, indeed, was the true center of the Church of Ireland.
The school was not only strongly Protestant, with compulsory chapel
and catechetical lectures for the 80 per cent of its students who were
members of the Established Church, but it was also prominent in the
evangelical movement. The staff of the Divinity school were often men

of weight, and they did much to raise the caliber of the clergy who
passed through Trinity's portals after 1820.

Whether the Church profited otherwise from this gentry-orien-
tation is more doubtful. The prospect of a resident beneficed
clergyman supplying the deficiencies of a callous and absent gentry
was applauded by some observers, but it led to the clergyman possessing "in the eyes even of his own proper flock nothing more than the
characteristics of a well-bred and perhaps humane and charitable
country gentleman.[107] The movement was not only resented by many of
the gentry themselves, but viewed with alarm by more zealous bishops.
In 1822 Magee warned his clergy of the danger involved in the "parish
priest becom[ing] lost in the country gentleman, and the spiritual
guide superseded by a sociable companion."[108]

5. The Middle Class

The role of the Established Church among the middle classes was
more closely identified with spiritual ministrations. This class,
which for purposes of analysis will be extended to include small freehold farmers and Protestant town tradesmen as well as the administrative
and banking classes of Dublin, tended to judge the clergy on the basis
of their religious obligations more than on their social connections,
and on occasion to find them wanting. They resented the espoused ambition of many clergy to elevate themselves into the gentry class.
They saw this as reinforcing the clergy's landowners at the cost of
alienating the hard-working, generally egalitarian middle class, often
of Scots ancestry.[109] Many instances were cited in which the poorer

Protestant, deserted by his socially ambitious pastor, turned to

Catholicism or to the dissenting sects, or where the parson, intent

upon raising his social stature by increasing his income, alienated

himself from the Protestant tenant class and assumed in their minds

the guise of a crafty businessman.[110]

Because the middle classes were constantly resident in Ireland,

they tended to take a more active role in ecclesiastical affairs than

did their social superiors. And since their religion was an important

factor in securing for them a higher social position than Catholics

in a similar economic stratum, they were quick to rebuke the Church

for its deficiencies and to attempt to correct them.[111] If landlords

tended to lack respect for the clergy as a class, they nevertheless

liked many of them as individuals. The middle class, however tended

to respect the profession more than some of those who constituted a

part of it. One devout bourgeois traveler was shocked to find how

unworthy many clergymen appeared to be regarded by the middle class,

"and still more afterwards when I perceived how justly the majority

deserve it."[112] The middle class figured prominently in vestry efforts

to maintain local peace, partly because the incomes of many, especially

those of the middlemen, were extremely vulnerable to tenant unrest.

They supported the clergy's tithe rights, which they identified with

the security of their Church on one hand and perhaps with their own

land rents on the other. They staffed the Orange lodges during Catho-

lic emancipation, and together with town-dwellers formed a large part

of private militias. They sponsored bible societies and formed the

lay corps of the evangelical movement. Despite their vigorous activity, however, they could not arrest the growing gentry bias of the clergy. Thus the Church as a whole continued to share the values of the landed classes, and not those of the Protestant middle orders.

Dissent also flavored the relations between the Established clergy and the middle classes. The Presbyterian interest was inclined to minimize distinctions between the Anglican and Catholic Churches. By 1800 much of its higher gentry had passed into the Church of Ireland. The Church in consequence was composed mainly of townsmen and freehold farmers in Ulster. Among these farmers considerable opposition to tithes encouraged local cooperation with Catholic agitators until 1830. Thereafter this resistance became so closely identified with the general Catholic assault of the Protestant ascendancy that cooperation was no longer possible. Dissenters were suspicious of attempts by the Established clergy to convert them, but they gravitated to the Church of Ireland when Presbyterian congregations were not convenient. In Ulster they were especially sensitive to the burden of the parish cess. They disliked the tax itself and resented their inability to determine the application of funds.

Although the Established clergy often reported Presbyterian membership to be declining, Dissent was more vigorous in its efforts to convert Catholics. Indeed, its lack of moderation in championing the Protestant interest was often condemned by the beneficed clergy. Rather more bitterness was evident in pamphlet literature between these two Protestant denominations than between the Establishment and Catholicism. Archbishop Magee's celebrated aspersions on both sects in 1822 ("We are hemmed in by two opposite descriptions of professing

Christians - the one, possessing a Church without what we can call a religion, and the other, a religion without what we can call a Church") was deeply resented by Presbyterians. It triggered a new wave of Dissenting criticism of the pretensions of the beneficed clergy and the Establishment's wealth. This criticism was to endure until the eve of ecclesiastical reform and disestablishment.[113]

6. The Catholic Church

While Catholicism and the lower classes in the early nineteenth century were not synonymous in economic terms, the strength of religion as a demarcator of the social structure was sufficiently well developed to make the identification a valid one. Catholics were almost every-where the majority, and outside Ulster often an overwhelming majority. They occupied 90 per cent of Irish tenancies, including almost all of the smallest. The peasant character of the Catholic Church was but slightly modified by a growing Catholic body of merchants, barristers, and clerks in Dublin. Confronted by this alienated majority, the Es-tablished clergy were forced to cultivate a pattern of connections with Catholics more intricate than would otherwise have been necessary.

This large task saw many clergymen choose to sublimate their de-nominational instincts in order to pursue the goal of amicability with Catholics. There is evidence of considerable local cooperation be-tween the Churches prior to Catholic emancipation. It diminished thereafter. Cooperation was especially marked in three areas: Protes-tant support for the construction of Catholic chapels and indirect assistance in the maintenance of the priests; Catholic priests' efforts

to encourage law-abiding instincts among the lower and often economic-
ally desperate classes; relationships forged between the Established
clergy and priests in the distribution of relief supplies and promotion
of local civic projects.

By 1800 most beneficed clergymen had convinced themselves, or
had been prompted by the desire to avoid trouble, that proselytism
among Catholics was shortsighted and generally useless.[114] More feasible
was the attempt to gain a measure of local influence by offering the
Catholic peasant the prospect of assistance in ameliorating some grievances identified with the traditional system of Protestant rule. The
task was not an easy one. Memories of the penal code, which had cost
Catholic families their lands and often their self-respect, were still
young. The tithe system constituted a standing grievance. Clerical
absenteeism meant that many Catholics had never met the Established
clergy, and knew of them only through the priests. Centuries of Catholic emphasis on Protestantism's wayward theology and "diabolical" per-
secution of Catholics was translated into a deep-seated suspicion not
easily erased.

With increasing residence, the clergy assigned to overwhelmingly
Catholic areas found two types of overtures immediately beneficial;
support in the construction of Catholic chapels; and remittance of
tithe obligations for the Catholic clergy. Between 1820 and 1840,
Protestant aid in chapel construction played a large and often incon-
gruous role in Irish life. In many cases the funds were obtained
through the vestry cess. Local clergymen enlisted the aid of landlords
to insure the vestry impost was over-subscribed. John Jebb was so

successful in his work of conciliating Catholics in Abingdon in central Ireland that he entered his bishopric with a reputation as liberal.
Evangelicals fulminated at his willingness to be seen inside Catholic
chapels, the cost of which had been largely borne by his own exertions.
The clergy also often exempted priests from tithes. In the poorest
parts of Ireland priests often rented plots themselves and in other
areas their churches and residences were constructed on tithed ground.
In these areas, where the beneficed clergy could operate with some
effectiveness, the results were often impressive, and widely applauded.[115]

These overtures often encouraged priests to exercise their own
influence to facilitate collection of the tithe. They condemned
harrassment of Protestants during Sunday services, and encouraged
peasants to seek redress within rather than outside the law. This
seems to have worked most effectively between 1820 and 1829. The
atmosphere was explosive with charges and countercharges as Daniel
O'Connell's Catholic Association confronted Orange lodge activity, and
the priests had reached a high point in prestige. With O'Connell behind their efforts to avoid violence, the parochial priests were
usually able to exercise considerable control within their jurisdictions. With the likelihood of early success in the emancipation
movement, Catholic leaders were prompt in expressions of respect for
the Church of Ireland and loyalty to the crown. After 1829 the resumption of tithe agitation, O'Connell's own disinclination to preach
submission to the law, and Orangeism's growth reduced priests' willingness to labor to keep the peace.[116]

The Established clergy were not slow to see the increasing prestige of the priests, not only among their own flock, but with the gentry as well. "The state of Catholic society and of the Catholic
Church of Ireland is considerably altered," noted one pamphleteer:

> The humility or the obscurity of former times has entirely
> disappeared and is forgotten. The country priests now hunts
> with the country squire, keeps sporting dogs, controls elec-
> tions, presides at political clubs, and sits "cheek by jowl"
> at public dinners, and public assemblies, with peers of the
> land and members of Parliament.[117]

This was overdrawn, but the tendency was unmistakable. John Doyle as
early as 1819 reprimanded some priests for attending the horse races.
Some priests later reached a level "not far removed from that of the
petty gentry." They circulated constantly, ate out twice a week, and
were both popular and feared.[118]

The Established clergy reacted in different ways to the rising
power and prestige of the priests. Instances of intimate friendship
are not wanting, though generally the relationship was better described
as "cordial." Mason's survey of Irish parishes in 1812 revealed a
fairly highly developed exchange of information between clergymen of
the two Churches, although there was little evidence of social intercourse.[119] In times of local crisis, however, the relationship often
became very close. Shortsighted rackrent policies discouraged peasants
from trying to save any money, and one bad harvest often meant famine.
The 1823 potato famine saw considerable cooperation between the Established clergy and priests. In Cork, a Catholic priest wrote after the
event, the incumbent took on "the most troublesome share" of family relief, including distribution of supplies, daily inspection and the

auditing of accounts in the   parish.   "His indefatigable exertions to

procure the means, and his very judicious management of them" would

long be remembered.[120]   In Derry a charitable loan society was founded

in 1809, sustained by annual sermons in Churches of all denominations,

and managed by a board on which all religious leaders sat.[121]

Friendship and cooperation between the beneficed clergy and

Catholics were not, unfortunately,   the only themes which governed their

relationship in the nineteenth century.   The years 1822 and 1823 stand

out rather sharply as the beginning of a period of unparalleled tension

and hostility destined to last twenty years.   From that period dates a

self-imposed isolation   of the Established clergy destined to endure un-

til disestablishment.   The blame can be distributed rather evenly.   On

the side of the Established Church the growing influence of evangeli-

calism prompted the bishops and clergymen to cast their opposition to

Catholicism in sharper terms.   O'Connell's work bred a sense of fear

and frustration which the clergy vented in inflammatory speeches and

pamphlets.   Catholics for their part became decidedly more aggressive,

encouraged by the growth of the   Canningite interest in Parliament to

expect early resolution of the emancipation crisis.   Peasants were more

militant, their tenancies reduced by population pressure and their

attachment to existing institutions undermined by their   poverty.   The

Catholic clergy, as already noted,   were now more powerful, better edu-

cated, and better motivated than ever before.   The tinder was dry, and

the spark was struck in 1822.

Magee's ill-considered criticism of both Presbyterianism and

Catholicism in 1822, whatever the Archbishop's subsequent attempts to

modify the remarks, loosed a torrent of printed invective unparalleled
in Irish history. In July the Catholic-oriented New Irish Magazine
and Monthly National Advocate began publication. In response the Irish
Protestant and Faithful Examiner appeared in November. Neither spared
abuse and purple rhetoric; both were widely applauded and extensively
quoted.[122] The Examiner raised its circulation by some multiples with
a list of the latest immoralities of Catholics (which included "swind-
ling" or being caught naked after being stripped of clothing, including
"inexpressibles," while drunk). The Advocate published its own list.[123]
Bishop Doyle refuted Magee's now famous aphorism. Magee was in turn
supported by the Rev. Harcourt Lees, a fiery evangelical writer capable
of much heat and little light. While the debate continued through
several exchanges over four years, the confrontation took on a more
physical case elsewhere. In Ardee a calf's head was placed on the alter
of a Catholic chapel, and Curtis, the Roman Catholic primate, jumped
to the conclusion that Magee's speech had been the inspiration for the
desecration.[124]

Much more serious was the confrontation over burial rights. Most
Irish churchyards abutted the Anglican churches. While Catholics had
refused to enter the churches since their conversion to Protestant use
in the sixteenth century, they had continued to bury their dead in
consecrated ground. The custom was confirmed by statute in 1822, but
graveside prayers and ceremonies by Catholic priests were expressly
forbidden. Protestant clergymen for their part often overlooked their
canonical obligations to superintend all burials within the churchyard.
But in September 1823 at St. Kevin's Church in Dublin politically ac-

:ive Catholics determined to challenge custom and 1822 statute. They enlisted the aid of several militant priests in conducting a grave-side service. The parish sexton on his own initiative interrupted the service and was beaten and chased. Protestants responded by demanding government intervention to sustain the law. Catholics throughout Ireland moved to repeat the St. Kevin's confrontation, and Magee was abused in handbills posted on Dublin street corners.

The confrontation found the ailing Archbishop of Dublin taking the waters at Leamington Spa in England. Dublin Castle proved unable to defuse the agitation. Magee demanded that the law be enforced now that Catholics had precipitated the confrontation. At the same time he denied that, as the Catholic press charged, he wanted Catholics and their priests excluded from churchyards altogether.[125] Goulburn rushed to confer with Plunkett, the Irish Attorney General. His pro-Catholic political inclinations found him reluctant to support Magee. Other elements in Dublin Castle strongly supported Magee, and paralysis resulted. The Archdeacon of Dublin, in whose jurisdiction St. Kevin's belonged, determined to move against the trespassers but found it impossible to enlist lawyers willing to brave the wrath of enflamed Catholic opinion.[126] Magee complained of the "new state of things" in which "the heads of the Established Church immediately under the eye of the Government of the Country [were] held up to public contempt and execration by a set of popish priests. . . ."[127] Goulburn moved to obtain the Law Officers' confirmation of the Established Church's prerogatives. Wellesley was so reluctant to forbid Catholic prayers and services, however, that the practice entended itself almost interrupted while Protestant clergymen waited in vain for instructions from Dublin.[128]

Early in 1824 the burial question moved into Parliament. First it took the shape of a motion by Sir John Newport to permit unfettered Catholic activities in the disputed churchyards. Later it appeared as a bill proposed by the government conceding some of Newport's demands.[129] The government's strategy combined confused objectives and furious activity. The confusion reflected differences of opinion between Goulburn and Wellesley, while the pace of activity reflected fears of increased agitation in Ireland. Goulburn first thought to persuade Catholics to bury their dead elsewhere. He hoped by repeal of Williamite legislation compelling burial under Protestant auspices to remove the occasion of friction.[130] Wellesley realized Catholics would not consent to exclusion from sacred ground.[131] Goulburn and Irish bishops agreed to concede the Church's right to superintend all burials and to permit Catholic priests to say private prayers if in turn all vestments, formal services, and images were excluded.[132] After two weeks of intense activity in the Cabinet the bill was presented to Parliament. It was "hurried forward" despite protestations from those hostile to the Church's prerogatives and was enacted into law a month later.[133]

The temper of the times, unfortunately, did not permit the new law to eliminate all confrontations in churchyards. Priests gradually increased their use of vestments, elaborated the ceremonial and disregarded prohibited hours for entering the burial area. This excited Protestant antipathy and led to sporadic local clashes. Gradually the Established Church resigned itself to sharing control of the area with Catholics.[134]

The pattern of physical violence continued until the end of the tithe wars. It reflected little credit on either the Establishment or on Catholics. The beneficed clergy much more than the priests were vulnerable to outrages against their persons and although assaults were fewer than one might have anticipated under the circumstances, each received wide attention, and where possible Orange lodge membership was mobilized for a campaign of retribution.[135] Occasionally the Established clergy took the lead in confronting Catholic agitators. More often they sought the protection of the landlords and by 1840 had sharply restricted their attempts to play the role of "social mediators." This, to an increasing degree, fell to the Catholic clergy.[136]

7. The Church and the Community

The erastian system expressed itself most forcefully at opposite ends of its structure. At the top bishops contributed their advice to the Irish administration. At the local level the clergy played a pivotal role in government and politics until the Irish Church Temporalities Act and subsequent poor law and municipal reforms legislation transferred responsibilities to secular agencies, or surrendered it to the Catholic clergy. The deteriorating intimacy of Church and state in the early nineteenth century is discussed elsewhere (Chapter IX). By the 1820s episcopal alarmism, the predictions of an "approaching explosion," the "defiance of all established authority," and the prospect of "all the horrors of a religious war" were taxing the patience of the nation's political leaders.

After 1830, moreover, the Irish bench was increasingly ignored.[137] The bishops were, however, more than mere adjuncts to the
Irish administration in terms of their community responsibilities.
They, were, in the first instance, the government's most articulate
source of information on conditions in rural Ireland, a role which
increased in importance as bishops' residence improved.[138] Their
charities set a standard for gentry generosity, and their appeals
for relief supplies in periods of distress were usually highly effective.[139] Bishop Trench of Elphin carried his responsibilities a bit
farther. He led the Enniskillen Dragoons "at so rapid a rate across
the country with which they were little acquainted, that they, being
worse mounted than he, actually tumbled after him." Elphin's esca-
pades continued to color Irish correspondence for a decade.[140]

Bishops were considerable agriculturalists. George de la Poer
Beresford found a safe refuge from Stuart's aspersions in raising his
Devon sheep in Kilmore, and producing a specimen unsurpassed in the
British Isles. O'Beirne, it appears, was "a great tillage farmer, as
well as an extensive breeder of the long-horned cattle."[141] More constant residence also expressed itself in restoration of episcopal
palaces in the palladium style, a process which enhanced the episcopacy's credentials as important men of the countryside.

The role of the clergy in the community was more complex, and
the contradictions inherent in their position taxed their finesse and
goodwill. As "social mediators" they were expected to avoid excessive
proselytism. As representatives of the ruling interest they were expected to eschew violent retaliation when injured in person or proper-

ty. As recipients of funds from England in times of distress, they

were expected to supervise relief operations without always knowing

the pattern of poverty. As the "national" clergy they were discouraged

from identifying too closely with distinctive Protestant associations.

The role of the Established clergy as social mediators was much

discussed in pamphlets devoted to proving the Church of Ireland was

national, even if not popular. The character and life-style of the

beneficed clergy was offered as an example of what a national clergy

must be, and, implicitly, as proof that Catholic priests and perhaps

Dissenting clergymen could never fulfill the role. As one observer

noted:

> . . . Nor does that order consist of men removed from the
> charities of social life, and cut off by celibacy from those
> connections which bind the citizen to his country; but
> combined the sacred character of a minister of religion with
> all the relations which knit together the bands of society.
> The clergy of the Established Church are involved in the
> same common interest with all other classes of citizens;
> they contribute equally to the support of the state: they
> are subject to the same laws: their property is employed,
> as much as that of any other men, in the encouragement of
> the manufactures and of the industry of Ireland; their
> expenditure is more equally diffused over the whole country,
> and more immediately beneficial to those from whom it is
> derived than that of any other class of society.[142]

The responsibilities associated with "social mediation" were never

clearly defined, but a generation of pamphleteerists and preachers left

no doubt that this held the key to the Establishment's survival and

prosperity in Catholic Ireland. As early as 1800 O'Beirne tried to

suggest some themes appropriate to social mediation in a charge to his

clergy: they must avoid "that fastidiousness, haughty and supercilious

distance" with which the lower order had so long been kept in their place; they must "live among the lower and middling orders of other communions in the discharge of all the varied charities of a friend and neighbor. . . , mediate for them in their various connections with the upper classes of his own communion, . . . visit them under their roofs, . . . offer them his advice and assistance."[143] In addition to providing a means of communication among the classes, the clergy embodied a civilizing influence, and by "spreading . . . to the remotest corners of the land" sustained the English connection.[144] Their "ingenious and enlarged education" was "calculated to impress the peasants with a sense of superior intelligence."[145] To the clergy were also entrusted duties of social control, combined with religious teaching if possible. This would tend to prevent "suicide, mania, despair, anguish, dissentions in families, contempt of domestic charities, estrangement of kindred, disturbance of neighborhoods, civil wars [and], overthrow of states." This was not, it appears, an inconsiderable burden.[146] Beyond this, they supplied the deficiencies of the gentry when that class was absent or insensitive to local responsibilities. They championed the law. They refrained from proselytism efforts which might destroy their good relations with all classes.[147] For the most part it was hoped, to quote the florid language of the day, that the clergy would "connect the high and low, . . . be the mediators between the rich and the poor, . . . soften the selfishness of wealth . . . and assuage the envy of want."[148]

While implementation of some of these objectives might have dismayed Solomon himself, the concept was more than a figment of publicists' fertile imaginations. Indeed, the law demanded of the Established clergy cooperation in supervising the operation of the parochial vestry, responding to parliamentary inquiries, performing marriage ceremonies, and maintaining local records. Their assistance was invited as magistrates, as members of borough corporation councils, and as dispensers of relief supplies. Their contributions were welcomed in agricultural improvement, and in local civic societies. Their exemplary conduct befitted a person of weight and responsibility in the community.

The role of the Established clergy in the vestry system was an important though not always clearly defined one. The vestry disintegrated rapidly as a form of local government after 1815. This process was complicated by the role of the Church cess in stimulating agitation in Ireland. The vestry became a matter of parliamentary concern and makes a discussion of its operation in the context of the decay of erastianism more appropriate than here. It is perhaps sufficient to note in this context that the clergy's participation in the vestry both widened their opportunities for community involvement and subjected the clergy to frequent, almost incessant criticism in an area detached from religious responsibilities. Thus they were "so occupied in enforcing their rights that they [had] no time or mind for performing their duties. It was alleged that they ruled their vestries like oriental despots and held the whole population in utter contempt and that they exuded a "spirit of jobbery."[149] Their achievements in the vestry were widely ignored. They confronted an increasingly restive population who blamed the resident clergyman for their grievances against British rule, and who failed to distinguish between the man

and the system. Their attempts to satisfy Parliament's demand for
information and records were also deemed unsatisfactory. O'Beirne
noted to Stuart at one point the deficiencies of the clergy in record
keeping: "there is not a family in Ireland that can produce legal
certificates either of the birth, or the marriages, or the deaths in
any of its branches." Even claims for peerages, O'Beirne hazarded,
were often based on hearsay. This judgment was supported by an examination of returns and parochial record books. But it failed to consider the vastness of some rural jurisdictions, the reticence and
hostility of peasants confronted by complicated queries, and the unwillingness of Catholics to register births, baptisms and deaths with
the clergy in an alien Church.[150] Most clergymen were not inclined
to business by training or inclination, and found these tasks of
auditing accounts, completing returns, maintaining records, and ferreting out the necessary information laborious and sometimes even unintelligible. After 1820, however, as the calibre of the resident
clergy increased, attentiveness to these details also improved. Vestry records became more elaborate and parochial registries more
accurate. On the eve of disestablishment Ireland was compiling a
remarkable accurate statistical self-portrait, with the Anglican clergy
playing an important role. These responsibilities reverted to secular authorities in 1870.

Outside the confines of the vestry and the record room lay a
larger forum for clerical activity as magistrates, members of borough
councils (where applicable), and dispensers of largesse to the poor.
As magistrates incumbents attracted both applause and opportunism. The

burden of enforcing law and order was not, on the face of it, fully
congruent with the clerical profession. But a case could be made, and
frequently was, that absence of a resident gentry, combined with the
clergy's undenied attachment to the law and a less universally acknowledged sense of compassion, made them effective magistrates. Ireland,
it was alleged, was like a ship in a storm abandoned by her officers:
"in this case all hands must work;" the clergy's qualifications were
irrelevant if no one else could be found to serve.[151]

Many disagreed, some vociferously. Magisterial duties resulted
in explicit or implicit conflicts of interest, such as in tithe resistance, where an incumbent might use military force to collect his own
tithe arrears. No less destructive of their effectiveness as magistrates was non-residence, compounded by a tendency to seek refuge
elsewhere when agitation appeared in their locality. In both cases
the clergy's behavior improved markedly after 1800, but the wholesale
desertion of the countryside in the rebellion of 1798 was not quickly
forgotten.[152] In larger terms, "to see the rector or curate of the
country parish head a party of the police and sally forth to apprehend
a felon excited no particular veneration."[153] For many, the martial
role of the clergy prompted bitter descriptions whose exaggerations
and misrepresentations did not always rob them of a certain credibility
in peasants' eyes. As one writer noted sarcastically:

> Being appointed officers in the Church militant, they are
> frequently found at the head of armed detachments; and
> from a love of justice, and hatred of hearing the name of
> the Lord profaned, it is almost impossible to find a bench
> of magistrates not studded with them: indeed, it is at
> petty sessions they often discharge the more weighty duties
> of their profession, in issuing decrees for the recovery

of tithes. . . .[154]

Whatever the incongruities involved, clergymen continued to serve as magistrates until 1833, when the Whigs excluded them from lists of commissioners of the peace. Thereafter they served only if invited by popular petition.[155]

Much brighter was the story of the clergy's role in relief activities. While there is occasional evidence of callousness in the face of hardship, the clergy were a compassionate lot. They were eager to appeal to philanthropic groups in England in time of need, and usually were prepared to distribute supplies without reference to religious distinctions. In 1822 and 1823, during widespread potato famine, clerical participation in relief work was widely noted not only in the popular press, but in letters of appreciation from the Catholic clergy. Their efforts were hampered by a lack of familiarity with the gravity of the problem, the pattern of distress, and a knowledge of Irish, especially in rural Ireland. After 1830, moreover, widespread tithe resistance often left incumbents financially unable and tempermentally unwilling to offer much assistance. The bitterness engendered during this long period of chaos was not easily dispelled. In 1834 relief work was often tinged with bias, at least Catholics so alleged, and the spirit of improvisation seemed lacking.

The great famine which began in 1845 prompted charges of "souperism." The term meant that the Church of Ireland, which served as the government's principal agency in the distribution of relief in Ireland, was allegedly using its status to encourage conversions as the basis for eligibility for charity. A detailed study on the subject suggests that these grave allegations were not based upon fact, other than in isolated instances.[156]

In the vestry a less cooperative tone did appear. Charges of religious discrimination often resulted in cessation of welfare appropriations shortly after 1830.[157] Debates in Parliament over the wisdom of introducing a poor law system into Ireland sometimes included proposals for entrusting the system to the beneficed clergy. This was less heard of after 1830; Irish society had been polarized too far to make the suggestion practicable.[158] The role of the Established clergy in other areas also declined. Participation in non-denominational mendicity societies, in road commissions, and in borough corporations declined either because of informal pressures, or as in the case of boroughs, because of abolition of the old corporations under terms of the Irish Municipal Reform law in 1840.[159] During tithe agitation more effort was directed to denominational societies, such as the Association for the Relief of Distressed Protestants, founded in October 1836, or the School for Sons of the Irish Clergy.[160]

Partisanship in philanthropy was not an isolated tendency. Catholic, Presbyterian and Anglican clergymen also marked the 1820s with a growing involvement in partisan politics. The role of Catholic priests in organizing peasants holding tenancies on Irish estates to vote for the more liberal candidates was well established before 1800, though penal code restrictions reduced the effectiveness of this exercise by barring Catholics from sitting. After 1823, however, political organization quickly disoriented the Irish political system by placing Catholics in seats they could not hold. The salient role of the priests in O'Connell's agitation did not escape the notice of

the Established clergy. Until the 1820s most Irish incumbents had

abstained from political involvement. They had called on occasion

for military assistance to quell disturbances associated with reli-

gious meetings, and had discouraged flagrant displays of the symbols

of King William and the Orange lodges. But the rise of the Catholic

association marked a loss of confidence in the ability of the priests

to contain violence. Skirmishes between Catholics and Protestants in-

creased in frequency.

After 1827 few priests dared defy the Catholic Association, and

Anglican clergymen were driven to attachment to Protestant organiza-

tions as violence reached the doorsteps of episcopal palaces and

churches.[161] Two organizations were especially prominent; Orange

lodges, a fixture of varying power on the Irish scene for three de-

cades; and Brunswick Clubs, founded during the high point of Catholic

emancipation agitation to combat the "popish conspiracy." Before 1820

respectable Protestants were generally careful to dissociate them-

selves from the Orange lodges, which, in their estimation, catered to

distinctly lower class elements, both Anglican and Presbyterian. In

1822, however, the Irish Protestant and Faithful Examiner came out in

support of them, and slowly more moderate bodies agreed.[162] In 1828

most Protestants joined the Brunswick Clubs. The clergy were actively

involved in soliciting members, and in holding services commemorating

Guy Fawkes and other decidedly Protestant holidays.[163] This movement

declined shortly after Emancipation arrived, but the Orange lodges had

a decade of vitality left to them, during which time the clergy often played a prominent part. As in the case of philanthropic trends, the decline of the Orange lodges after 1835 saw many local Protestant groups spring up to take their place, in which the clergy were included. In a very real sense this clerical allegiance marks the end of the clerical role in the community as social mediators, and the development of a more intensive commitment to the minority Protestant interest.

8. The Church Spiritual

The most striking feature of the spiritual life of the Established Church between 1800 and disestablishment in 1869 was internal reform and renewal. Historians observing the intensity of parliamentary criticism of the Church during the 1830s, and noting continuing deficiencies in residence and distribution of ecclesiastical resources, have been perhaps too anxious to conclude that the widespread spiritual torpor of the eighteenth century Church had not been much altered after the Act of Union. Whatever the anomalies of the Church in 1869, they had been considerably greater in 1835, and whatever the reasons for criticism in 1835, they had been much stronger in 1800. It can be shown, moreoever, that a great deal of the reform impulse had already manifested itself before Parliament intervened in the 1830s. Indeed, by 1830 the Church had gone about as far in rearranging priorities in the direction of greater efficiency as was possible without legislation to recast the basic administrative structure. Reform was also apparent in the tone of spiritual life. This was intangible and difficult to measure statistically, but it was expressed rather forcefully in the spread of evangelical tendencies, in the

rising calibre of the preaching clergy, and in clerical behavior and
zeal. Exposed to almost incessant criticism from without, and directed by motivated leadership from within, the Irish Church responded to
clear signs of danger with a reforming zest too often underestimated
by modern observers.

Part of the process of renewal is reflected in statistics: the
decline in non-residence; the construction of churches; the procure-
ment of glebes and construction of glebe houses. In the area of non-
residence, the greatest strides towards elimination of this evil may
have taken place between 1800 and 1819. In 1807, 561 beneficed clergy
were non-resident, and 560 resident. In 1819, 826 resided constantly,
and 307 were classed as non-resident. It is worth noting that the
greatest improvement took place in the provinces of Ulster and Munster,
presided over by Archbishops Stuart and Brodrick respectively. In
Ulster the number of beneficed clergymen increased by 97, and in
Munster by 106, compared to 33 for Leinster and 30 for Connaught. In
Connaught the percentage change was dramatic, with more than twice as
many beneficed clergy resident in 1819 as in 1807, although a full
third of the clergy at the latter date were still non-resident.[164]
The improvement between 1819 and 1835 was much less impressive. The
number of resident beneficed clergymen increased by only 19, and non-
resident clergymen actually increasing by 40, for a net loss of 21.

Several factors account for the lack of improvement. Tithe
agitation drove some normally resident incumbents to safer havens.
Stricter reporting procedures were introduced, which defined residence
in terms tighter than those employed in 1807 and 1819. Most important-

ly, difficulties within the Church administration impeded increased residence without structural change. This last consideration is extremely important. Of the 347 incumbents still non-resident according to the returns of the 1835 Commission of Inquiry, 160 were exempt from residence because of permanent assignment in other benefices, or work as chaplains, officers in ecclesiastical courts, diocesan administrators, teachers at Trinity and other employment. Another 83 were technically non-resident, but lived close enough to their jursidictions to do duty. In these cases the parochial jurisdiction was often inconveniently shaped, so that residence at a point outside the jurisdiction was more convenient to all parts of the benefice than any location inside. In other cases absence was enforced by want of adequate accommodation. Only 187 clergy, therefore, were absent without license. Until offices comprehended in cathedral chapters and other dignities could be dissolved or made wholly sinecurial, only moderate improvement could be expected by the bench of bishops.

Church construction after 1800 offers a startling contrast to the record of the eighteenth century. During the eighteenth century only 134 churches were erected, raising the average number per diocese from 18 to 31. Even this achievement must be discounted, for coincidental neglect meant that one of every three churches in 1800 was in poor condition. Many in fact were unsafe for divine service. In 1807, after several years of concerted effort to build new churches and repair the old, 109 more churches were available for public worship. By 1819 another 245 had been built or restored, bringing the total to 1,112. By 1829, when the program virtually ceased, the total was 1,320.

In thirty years more than 600 churches were either repaired or constructed, equalling the effort of the Church during the previous 270
years.[165]

Glebe house improvement shows a similar dramatic change. In
1807 there were 418 glebe houses. Only 163 of these had been constructed during the eighteenth century, and many of the remainder were
understandably in a state of advanced disrepair. Between 1800 and
1819 the number of glebe houses increased by 347 to 765. During the
next decade only 12 more were built, reflecting Parliament's decision
in 1817 not to proceed further with generous grants to the Board of
First Fruits. Again, the most dramatic improvement came in Munster,
where the number of glebe houses in new or good condition almost
doubled.

In all Ireland, the frenzy of glebe house construction was also
reflected in a precipitous decline in the number of non-resident clergymen justifying the absence on the basis of inadequate accommodations.
In 1807, 728 of 1,197 benefices lacked glebe houses ; in 1819, 533 of
1,267, or a decline from 61 per cent to 42 per cent. Again, eliminating the remainder was difficult. Many benefices were small and could
be served by a clergyman domiciled nearby. Some produced an inadequate
revenue. Others were controlled by hostile laymen who refused to facilitate construction of glebe houses. Still others had no Protestants.
If anything, the zeal for construction was perhaps excessive, for Catholics were disturbed by demands made upon the vestries, and Parliament's
rationalization of the Irish Establishment after 1830 saw abandonment
of some benefices in which church and glebe house had recently been

erected.

An examination of the episcopal visitation records compiled during the period not only suggests something of the intensity of the reform effort, but also shows the wide range of obstacles confronting the improving bishop. Before 1815 they offered elaborate, interesting insights into the pattern of reform. O'Beirne in 1804 concluded that the most outstanding factor he had observed was "the continuing decline of the ardour of the masses, and the rise of a toleration not founded on charity, but on indifference."[166] In 1818, however, he could report considerable activity: church and glebe house construction; new schoolhouses; parishioners active in criticizing wayward pastors. He himself exposed a perpetual curacy being embezzled by its incumbent, arbitrated a conflict over the location of a proposed church, berated a congregation for its refusal to lay a cess for a new church, congratulated others on a total of 23 churches and 27 glebe houses recently constructed or being built in the diocese, and disciplined several inattentive incumbents. He was able to report 25 glebes procured, 66 glebe houses constructed or acquired, and 62 churches built since his own incumbency.[167]

The impact made by a conscientious bishop can be noted in the contrasting visitation reports of 1818 and 1821, the first compiled by Percy Jocelyn, later deprived of the see of Clogher, and Robert Loftus, his successor as Bishop of Ferns. Jocelyn reviewed his diocese and contained all the anomalies he noted to a couple of pages; Loftus interviewed his clergy personally and entered elaborate reports. He asked one curate residing three miles from his Church why he did not move in closer. He determined that another had never attempted to obtain a glebe, the deficiency of which he had used as a reason for no residence. He demanded of a third why he had made no return as requested. To complaints that impropriators were refusing to repair churches in their control he issued opinions that impropriators thereby forfeited their rights. He denied another clergyman's request that eventide lectures be given in a house since only four people attended them. His questions regarding Leighlin were equally probing.[168]

The resident bishops were not alone in asking questions. Parliament demanded thorough returns in 1807, 1819, 1824 and frequently thereafter. In each case the number of questions increased and the details demanded became more elaborate. By 1826 archbishops in the course of making triennial visitations to each diocese in their province were not only exerting themselves to make the inquiry less formal and more meaningful, but were employing rural deans to provide supplementary information. In 1826 Beresford demanded of his bishops and their clergy an estimate of the number of Catholics, Protestants and Dissenters in each diocese, and whether each group was increasing or decreasing in size. The value of this exercise might be disputed (almost all reported Protestants increasing, Catholics only holding steady, and Presbyterians decreasing). But the motive was obvious, disturbingly so to some incumbents who attributed whatever lack of success they conceded to emigration of their own flock and to early marriage among the others.[169]

After 1830, the burden of inquiry in the Church of Ireland was taken over by the Commission of Ecclesiastical Inquiry established in

the final days of the Wellington ministry. The nation was offered a
wealth of statistics on the Irish Church. One wonders, however, whether
these comprehensive but perhaps less sensitive probes proved as chasten-
ing to defective clergymen as the rigorous visitations which came into
vogue during the 1820s and which distinguished the internal effort for
reform for another generation.

That the improving tendency within the Irish Church confirmed by
compilations of statistics, by inquiries, and by returns made a considerable impression on the defenders of the Church is unquestioned. For
the most part, however, public opinion continued to be shaped by im-
pressions obtained from newspapers and pamphlets, from conversation
and rumor. Bad news, as always, travelled faster and farther than the
good. This in part accounted for continued publicized instances of
the Church's defective spiritual condition. Criticism, however, probably intensified between 1800 and 1830, and did so for several additional reasons. Increasing exposure of ecclesiastical anomalies impressed upon the Irish reading public for the first time the full extent of the Church's difficulties. Higher criteria as to what should
be expected of the clergy meant that practices once viewed with indul-
gence were now severely chastized. This was manifested in other denominations besides the Established Church, but the latter was perhaps
the most vulnerable. Declining confidence in the ability or desire of
government to sustain the Establishment was underscored by a sense of
urgency at the prospect of parliamentary reform. This encouraged elements within the Church of Ireland to demand of their clergy, and of
themselves, a greater display of spiritual zeal.

The most important area of comment on the beneficed clergy continued to touch on non-residence. In 1816 O'Beirne declared that it was "no longer possible for the people to reproach the clergy of gross non-residence." This observation reflected more wishful thinking than considered judgment.[170] Indeed, parishioners observed that their censures of wayward clergymen would be heeded by bishops. After 1820 several dozen vestry meetings became, in spite of or at the instigation of the curate, a forum for publicizing the non-residence of their incumbent. At least one series of remonstrances appeared in pamphlet form and was widely circulated; whether distorted by the intensely public nature of the crusade or not, the confrontation deserves examination as an example of parishioners' grievances. Lord Blayney addressed a series of letters to Beresford regarding parishioners' efforts to remove both an absentee rector and his incongenial curate. The Bishop of Clogher visited the parish but delivered nothing more than a "severe verbal censure." As a consequence, "the greater part of the respectable parishioners," Blayney reported, withdrew "themselves from the Established Church," some gravitated to Sectarians and others emigrated to America. Some attended a new Methodist meeting chapel. "Thus we have," concluded his lordship in somewhat convoluted prose,

> in this instance among a multiplicity of others in confirmation of the opinion that in proportion as the Church is largely provided for in Ireland, in the same proportion, far too many of the clergy of that Establishment irritate the feeling of the people, and neglect those duties, which they are alike bound to perform by the precepts of the gospel, and the law of the land.

Lest Blayney be thought to hold a personal grudge, several dozen residents added their own comments, noting that 1,000 Protestants, because f the non-residence of their pastor, received "no spiritual comfort,

o paternal admonition. . . in the difficulties of life." As a result,

roselytism was making "alarming strides," while "wealthy and respect-

ble Protestants who cannot continue in danger of losing a proper in-

lination for the rights of the Church" were leaving the area.[171]

Non-residence also continued to intrude into parliamentary de-

ates. In 1819 the parish of Galoon in north central Ireland based its

efusal to pay tithes on the constant absenteeism of the incumbant.

The only visit the parishioners ever received from anyone connected

ith the Church," read the brief submitted to Parliament, "was an

ccasional one from the tithe proctor, and the only reason they had to

now that their pastor lived was from seeing his name four times a year

t the head of a civil bill for the recovery of tithes."[172] In 1835

n M.P. from County Monaghan reported in Parliament that in the barony

f Farney, which comprised a considerable portion of his constituency,

here was not one resident beneficed clergyman, despite the fact that

he value of two benefices exceeded ₤750, and of another two exceeded

1000.[173]

More constant residence among the Irish clergy did not in itself

liminate criticism. Some parishes were shocked to discover that in-

umbents disgruntled at being forced to reside could display some un-

ttractive characteristics. When proclaiming in 1817 that clerical

on-residence was no longer a problem, O'Beirne had hastened to add

hat they must now bear good fruits in their pastoral work, or be

harged with laziness. Indolence appeared most frequently in any

ist of clerical deficiencies. One reputedly unbiased traveler in

Ireland noted that he had "seen many pious and well intentioned men;
but few active men, . . . whose listlessness rendered their calling
ineffectual for any good purpose. . . ."[174] Another declared that
while a "friend to religion, I am an enemy to salaried idleness. To
twenty-five hundred parishes I would have twenty-five hundred parsons;
no curates at fifty, no absentees at two thousand pounds a year; no
starving zeal, no lazy affluence."[175] We can accept the aspersions
cast upon the Established clergy by Bishop Doyle with a grain of salt,
but their behavior before the 1824 committee on the state of Ireland
was not entirely felicitous. Even Whately, upon his arrival in Ireland, was distressed with the character of many of his clergy, and
confirmed the verdict of a current pamphlet that they were, in spite
of their relatively advanced education level, often doctrinaire and
occasionally simply stupid.[176]

So strong was this impression in Whately's mind that the Established clergy were not properly trained for their profession that in
the autumn of 1833 he outlined a proposal for the education of the
clergy. His proposal called for a School of Divinity, separated from
Trinity but sharing in part the same faculty. This would provide
clergymen with "vocational" training in scripture and composition,
both of which Trinity treated inadequately for the clergy's needs.[177]
Whately's school met with instantaneous opposition. The alarm intensified when the Irish government through Lord Wellesley promised a
building. Trinity fellows believed the school would destroy the
College's Protestant character by drawing religion out of its curriculum and permitting an influx of Catholics. Beresford believed the

lergy resented the idea of professional training which would set

hem apart from the Protestant gentry.[178] A sharp exchange between

hately and Beresford followed, with several bishops supporting

hately. Trinity, however, was almost unanimous in its opposition.

hately felt the opposition was largely a reflection of his liberal

rinciples. No conservatives, he observed, shied away from asking

or patronage at his disposal.[179] But in fact the idea of a seminary

macked of connotations foreign to the clergy's training as gentlemen,

ot theologians. None of Whately's concessions could allay these

ears.[180] Legislation to establish the School of Divinity was aban-

oned by the Gray ministry and Whately's efforts to establish it on

private basis and to restrict it to his own diocese collapsed.

The litmus test of the clergy's qualifications and limitations

as their work as spiritual advisors and ministers of religion in

rish parishes. The clergy were understandably sensitive to charges

hat they were only lightly employed, a charge made no easier to bear

hen constant residence was demanded of them. Descriptions of Sabbath

ervices attended by a small handful of the Protestant faithful con-

rasted sharply with the overflow in Catholic Churches. In 1813 Curwen

n the course of his travels noted that in one village Presbyterian,

atholic and Anglican services coincided; "the bells of the Establish-

d Church were rung, apparently in vain — for not a single individual

id we see enter the doors."[181] In another instance one of Thomas

reevey's Irish correspondents painted an even more graphic picture:

> Now I have seen a real Irish Protestant church. When I
> entered it, two parsons were sitting in a row at a reading
> desk - the rector and archdeacon of Ossory — the other his

curate. We were fifteen from the house and four from the
chief justices. Dungannon and Lady Dungannon, man and
maid were there, and so help me God! not a soul else. The
parish is a large and populous one, but without a single
Protestant in it except these two families - nay, not even
amongst their servants.[182]

This was, of course, not the picture everywhere. But in rural

Ireland the newly refurbished or constructed churches were often dis-

turbingly empty, especially in the three decades which preceded Catho-

lic emancipation. The ineffectiveness of the clergy was a frequently

discussed topic, and Churchmen searching for instances of zeal and

growth often by the very intensity of their efforts suggested that

they were well aware of the substance of some of these charges.[183]

The optimistic censuses of Protestants submitted by the clergy to

their bishops in 1829 were almost 50 per cent higher than those re-

corded by the ecclesiastical commissioners in 1834. One suspects that

the discrepancy was due in part more to an earlier exaggeration than

to a precipitous decline in membership.

By 1825 the coincidence of improved discipline in clerical re-

sidence, expansion of parochial facilities, and the growing power of

Catholicism had served to encourage the emergence of the most important

expression of spiritual vitality in the Church of Ireland during the

nineteenth century: evangelicalism. The growth of this force after

the Napoleonic wars was an expression of a reform impulse quite un-

like anything experienced on a general scale in the history of the

Church of Ireland. In part evangelicalism reflected the Methodist

impulse in England - Wesley visited Ireland twenty-one times. Often,

however, it was closely associated with the Irish upper class, as was revealed in the work of the countess of Huntingdon after 1770. Under her influence spirited English preachers invaded Dublin and other towns and shocked and often converted local social leaders. Government protection was promised so long as Methodist efforts were directed against Catholics alone.[184] When the Church as a body refused to accept the evangelical challenge, evangelicals established their congregations on the periphery of the towns.

But the impulse was far from abortive. Evangelicalism was forced to challenge the traditional description of organized religion as an agency "to regulate the dispositions and to improve the characters of men."[185] In assaulting this view evangelicalism triggered changes which after 1800 produced an influential group of reformers within the Church itself. The movement remained one of personalities more than principles, however, even after 1820 when it provided Irish Protestantism with a vigorous counter to the rising tide of Catholicism.

By 1820 the evangelical movement was expressing itself through three channels. One which perforce anticipated emergence of the others was the growth of evangelical tendencies within the Established clergy themselves. In this context, perhaps the most famous early evangelical was the Rev. Peter Roe of Kilkenny. His situation in what was popularly called the "Versailles of Ireland" tempted him to assert the spirit of moral and religious reform with a disconcerting vigor and directness. Under his guidance groups of clergymen initiated a series of weekly and then monthly meetings among themselves to plot a program of spiritual education. These meetings, which began about 1800, found a sympathetic bishop in O'Beirne. As Bishop of Ossory before 1802 O'Beirne actually had sponsored a clerical association to encourage bible reading and discussion among his clergy. These meetings were, however, often strongly opposed by O'Beirne's successors and other bishops. They thought the side-effects of antagonism and agitation to be dangerous, and they resented the implied reproach of their own less zealous pattern of life. Roe's work, however, gradually spread, and when Roe assaulted the theatre in Kilkenny and was silenced by a former Trinity Provost, Bishop John Kearney, he directed his energies to an even wider area and was gradually vindicated.[186]

The new clerical zeal soon found satisfactory employment in the development of the Bible Society. Founded in 1814, the society soon precipitated a vigorous open debate between those who feared preoccupation with scriptural education would alienate Catholics and push the Establishment towards fundamentalist Protestantism, and those who saw in reliance on the Bible and on a rekindling of spiritual enthusiasm the only road to revival of the Established Church as a whole. The controversy began in earnest in 1816 with the publication of numerous pamphlets on the benefits and deficiencies of the society's program for the Church. Daniel O'Callaghan, a persuasive enthusiast of the traditional stripe, condemned the Bible Society as a motley collection of "bishops, socinians, deans, deists, deacons, quakers, ministers of state, jumpers, whigs, tradesmen, tories, methodists, lords, gospel ministers, ranters, magistrates and antipedital baptists." He abhorred the idea of putting the Bible into the hands of ignorant peasants without instructing them, and saw the society as an "engine or [the Church's] destruction."[187]

O'Callaghan apparently touched sensitive nerve-endings, for the
esponse of the society's defenders was prolific and pointed. O'Beirne
ed the defense, and was supported by beneficed clergymen, curates,
ethodists and several interested laymen. O'Callaghan thereupon ex-
anded his charges against the society to call it "Jacobinical and
estructive of the fabric of the state and an aid to sectarians and
atitudinarians."[188] O'Beirne lamented that the controversy had re-
uced itself to maligned aspersions on personalities, and regretted
hat so many of the clergy refused to support it.[189] The society did,
owever, gain considerable support among lay and clerical evangelicals,
who by 1822 were loud in its praise.[190] O'Callaghan, however, was
etermined to continue the controversy, and in 1827 offered Ireland
n unforgettable if boldly drawn caricature of the new spirit of
ealous proselytism manifested by the Bible Society:

> When they [Bible Societies] issue their marching orders to
> a regiment of Bibles, to reinforce the garrison of a parti-
> cular town, the march is preceded and followed by a numerous
> rabble of irregulars, composed of handbills, – newspaper
> squibs – speeches revised and reported – pious tracts –
> evangelical essay – serious reviews, and more serious
> magazines, in all which popery and its priesthood are
> described as the most abominable of all possible abomina-
> tions, and clothed with the choicest attributes of hell and
> Satan, while the members of the holy alliance of prosely-
> tising fanatics, are held out as ministering angels,
> descending from heaven, on errands of mercy. These are
> dropped on the roads, scattered in the fields, given to
> good children, read in stagecoaches, forgotten at public
> houses. . . .[191]

O'Callaghan's fulminations contained at least one germ of truth.
The Established Church could not support unlimited private judgment
without conceding ground to Dissent, nor sustain vigorous proselytism

without endangering relations with the Catholic Church. This was the
attitude of most bishops.[192] They were supported by many clergymen,
who began to complain that in their areas Catholics and Protestants
were drawing apart. It could not on the other hand merely watch the
accession of Catholic strength without attempting to meet the challenge.
Something broader than small clusters of evangelical clergymen defying
their bishops by their efforts at personal purification through prayer
sessions, and Bible societies with their vigorous scriptural message,
was needed to make revitalization universal. The third avenue was the
"new reformation" and a national proselytizing effort directly supported
by the Church.

The nature and direction of the "new reformation" reflected in
general Protestant fears in the wake of concessions to Catholics and
in particular the work of Rev. Sir Harcourt Lees, English baronet,
Irish clergyman, and political pamphleteer. The proper course of action,
it struck many Protestants, was not reliance upon the Bible Society and
its narrowly Christian viewpoint, but a program which stressed high
Church principles against evangelical tendencies, and prescriptive
rights against Catholic usurpation. Not unlike Newman's work in England a decade later, but more virulent and popular, the "new reformation" challenged the growing secularism of the age and decried the pernicious influence of its primary political agent, the Whig party.
Evangelicalism represented an intensely personal solution to the Establishment's problems. It avoided the tendency towards institutionali-
zation wherever possible. But the "new reformation" attempted to begin where structural reform left off: to emphasize the essential

egitimacy of the erastian principle, and to attribute most defects
within it to a pervasive papal-Whig conspiracy. Catholic clergymen
were invited, or sometimes goaded into, public debate upon sensitive
religious differences. The results of these were shaped by polemni-
ists into victories for their side and distributed throughout Ireland, causing much bad feeling. Local debates were often staffed by
eloquent if unlettered peasants after priests were forbidden to
accept invitations.

The most famous of these debates took place in the Rotunda of
the old Parliament building in April 1827. The debate lasted six
days and debated such things as whether a mouse could run off with a
consecrated host. A bellicose layman named Maguire captained the
Catholic contingent. He was a coarse but witty spokesman, and at a
later date O'Connell would be called upon to defend him against a
charge of seducing an innkeeper's daughter. For the moment, however,
Catholics were incensed that Protestants would try to convert Maguire
by bribery.[193] Everyone became involved. Harcourt Lees added more
fuel to the religious conflagration with such intriguingly and elabor-
ately titled publications as Theological extracts selected from a late
letter written by a popish prelate to his Grace the Archbishop of
Dublin, with observations on the same, and a well-merited and equally
well-applied literary flagellation of the titular shoulders of this
mild and humble minister of the gospel; with a complete exposure of
his friend the Pope and the entire body of holy impostors.[194] Titles
told the story.

Harcourt Lees' own influence waned after 1830. His audience was exhausted by his forecasts of eminent papal coups at Whitehall, of assassination attempts on members of the royal family, and his own hyperboles.[195] The "new reformation" impulse continued, but was translated into more durable institutional forms. When the effort to defeat Catholic emancipation proved ineffective, the "new reformation" gradually merged with still-expanding evangelical tendencies. This accelerated the pace of self-purification on one hand, and launched new proselytizing efforts towards Catholics on the other. By 1835, indeed, evangelicalism no longer was required to prove its durability or popularity. Non-resident clergymen were rapidly being frightened or shamed into constant attendance. The quality of preaching and pastoral care improved. The probity of most clergymen stood in startling contrast to the unevenness noticed by friends and critics only a decade earlier. New churches were founded in Dublin on the initiative of evangelical laymen willing to make substantial contributions in order to hear Protestant theology in an evangelical accent.[196]

Relations with Dissent, so acrimonious in 1822, became friendlier. As early as 1835 Presbyterian clergymen proclaimed that it was the duty of "all Protestant clergymen to support the Establishment's privileges," and the Church responded by supporting their chapels as "helpmeets in the great cause of Christianity."[197] Indeed, so pervasive did evangelicalism seem that those bishops not entirely sympathetic with its levelling tendencies wondered whether the Church of Ireland was doing enough to stress its own unique heritage.[198]

The proselytizing effort towards Catholicism between Church reform and disestablishment was enthusiastic, if somewhat disjointed and not always entirely effective. Before 1830 several societies designed

to disseminate Protestant literature and to support the Church's role

in Irish education had arrived on the Irish scene. After 1830 the

organizational impulse turned first to clerical self-help societies to

relieve distress occasioned in the tithe war, and then moved on to more

ambitious projects. Two of these, the Irish Protestant Association

and the Society for the Relief of Distressed Protestants, were both

founded in 1836. They evolved into the more important of a prolifera-

tion of Protestant mutual aid societies. Small annual dues were soli-

cited from members. In turn these funds were used to finance the cir-

culation of religious literature among poor Protestants, registration

of sympathetic voters for crucial elections, assistance to those suffer-

ing at the hands of Catholics, and most importantly, loans to Protes-

tants to establish themselves in business or agriculture.[199] Other

groups were more ambitious. The publication of the Irish religious

census in 1835 revealed for the first time how tenuous was the role of

the Established Church in national life. With only 11 per cent of the

population, Anglicanism was the religion of a small minority. In the

province of Tuam, only 4 per cent was Anglican, in Cashel 5 per cent.

Clearly, there was much to be done, and a missionary psychology

was not inappropriate. Thus the Church Missionary Society, founded in

1836, attracted the support of the lower clergy, although it was re-

sisted by most of the bishops, who naturally reflected a continuing

faith in the state connection long after the lower clergy were skepti-

cal of its value.[200] New efforts were made to reach the Irish in their

native language, a strategy which aroused considerable agitation among

Catholics.[201] The most ambitious, and ultimately perhaps the least successful, project involved a settlement scheme on Achill Island off the western coast. Here the Protestant Association under the direction of the Rev. Edmund Nagle procured a large tract of reclaimable mountain in 1838. On this land houses were built for missionaries, school teachers, scripture readers and a steward, along with a church and a schoolhouse. The society admitted to its cottages those "expressing a desire to be sheltered from the tyranny of the Roman Catholic priests and their police, and to receive spiritual instruction for themselves and their children." Local Catholics effectively ostracized the settlers. Large subsidies were required from England, and at length only 92 of the 6,000 persons on Achill were converted by the mission.[202]

After 1840 the missionary effort was restricted more and more to education. This device offered the greatest hope for the ultimate conversion of the Irish peasantry. It also promised, at least until the eve of disestablishment, to be more effective than the work of the missionary societies among a suspicious and zealous Catholic population. The great famine prompted new allegations of ulterior motives in the Church's philanthropic efforts. Whether the crisis was in fact an occasion for proselytism may be doubted, but some Catholics were not reluctant to accept that point of view. It is probably safe to say that on balance the efforts of the missionary societies "so far from Protestantising Ireland, . . . made it more intensely Catholic than ever." Even concentration on education was distracted after 1840 by renewed tension between high Church and low, a topic of intense concern in the English Church and one which did not fail to divide the

Irish clergy as well.[203]

Parliamentary reform of Church temporalities, evangelicalism, and even administrative retrenchment did not squelch all plans for further change within the Church. Two questions loomed large as disestablishment approached: internal autonomy; and the efficacy of the state relationship. As early as the beginning of the 1830s Whately pressed Lord Grey to appoint commissioners to "devise, digest, and submit to Parliament some form of government. . ." for the Church. Whately apparently wanted the establishment of a mixed assembly of clergy and laity modelled after the Kirk of Scotland "to legislate on ecclesiastical matters, or at least to declare that changes were or were not needed."[204] Whately feared that were this not done the government would do it for the Church. This was at least partially confirmed in the reduction of bishoprics, dignities, revenues and prerogatives in 1833. His suspicions were vindicated more directly in the establishment of the Irish Ecclesiastical Commissioners, who were empowered to allocate revenues from the suppressed sees and suspended dignities, and from taxation on clerical incomes. These, with vestigial rights of the Privy Council over unions of parishes, parochial revenues, management of glebe lands and churchyards, meant the Church was, after 1834, as little the master of its own house as it had been before 1800.

The obvious solution, at least to Churchmen, was revival of convocation. Encouraging trends across the water, such as revival of convocation at Canterbury in 1853 and York in 1861, quickened the hearts of Irish high Churchmen. In 1860 the Irish bench lodged a pro-

test against the implementation of any changes in the doctrine or
discipline of the "united Church of England and Ireland" without the
participation of the Irish branch. As Bishop Fitzgerald of Cork noted,
the Act of Union had affirmed the unity of the Church. The prospect
of Canterbury and York legislating on their own was dangerous. Unfortunately, this logic made little impression on the incumbent Whig
ministry. It refused to summon a "general synod of the United Church"
and showed no interest in permitting convocation in the Irish branch
of the communion.[205] The Whigs were fearful of doing anything which
would stress the erastian character of the Church of Ireland.

Faced with an insensitive ministry, a group of active clergymen
urged the Irish archbishops to summon provincial synods at Dublin and
Tuam. The law officers responded to this initiative by holding that
a Henrician statute forbidding such meetings without the Crown's permission applied to Ireland as well as to England. Somewhat impolitely
these officials also held that such meetings were illegal under the
Irish convention act of 1793![206] As a result, the Church of Ireland
was forced to look on helplessly while Canterbury and York proceeded
to amend their canons and ceremonies. All this emphasized the fragility of the connection incorporated into the Act of Union. Eventually
Gladstone would grapple with the problem with heroic dispatch.[207]

The government's insensitivity on this score almost inevitably
prompted discussion inside the Church as to the efficacy of the state
connection. Such discussion was not new.[208] Now, however, developments added intensity, since any government determined to forbid to
the Church so fundamental a prerogative as convocation might well be

regarded as less an ally than a master, less a friend than an antagon-

ist. Maziere Brady, beneficed clergyman of decidedly unorthodox (and

among his associates, unpopular) views, believed that "in proportion

as the Church Established seeks more earnestly to live as a Church, so

will her position as an Establishment become less tolerable.[209] What

Brady's friends within the Irish Church perhaps did not entirely rea-

lize was that the decline of the erastian connection was in fact quite

far advanced. The threads binding state and Church together had already

been frayed in several crucial respects.

Chapter IX: The Road to Disestablishment 1822-1869

Of themselves, neither administrative reform, whether internal or

imposed from without, commutation of tithes to land, nor even a growing

spirit of alienation from the state's priorities constituted a direct

assault on the principle of erastianism in Ireland. Indeed, both Tories

and Whigs made much of their promise that Church reform, whatever the

momentary pain involved, would lead to a more fruitful Church-state re-

lationship. A few Irish ecclesiastics, such as Whately, believed this

to be true. The remainder, whatever their reasons and prejudices, were

understandably skeptical. A casual observer could not fail to note the

growing influence of Catholics in government councils, or remain in-

sensitive to the implications of Benthamite reform for the ancient sys-

tem. The surrender of rural Ireland was implied in the abolition of

benefices with few Protestants. This left only Ulster and urban centers

as a forum for the influence of the Established Church. The pace of
the decline, however, could not be observed by most Churchmen, for it
was best reflected in minor legislative changes, in the declining role
of the clergy in national administration, and in a loss of confidence
and intimacy between leaders of Church and state. In this sense the
process of disestablishment was much more than the belated recognition
of the Church of Ireland's weakness after 1860 or of William Gladstone's
sudden determination to appease Catholic Ireland.

In retrospect, the last decade of Stuart's primacy, extending
from 1812 to 1822, must be regarded as the final phase of a fully functioning pattern of Church-state cooperation. During this decade, as
has been seen, Robert Peel's service as Irish Chief Secretary brought
to bear on the erastian connection a sensitivity for the Church's
problems far greater than that of his predecessors and even his
successors. A conservative reaction to twenty years of revolution
on the continent buttressed the claims of all venerable institutions.
The advantages of established religion and regulated piety were more
widely recognized than at any time in more than a century. The excesses of union engagements had passed. The tone of patronage distribution had risen. A determination to avoid undermining the Church's
dignity in this fashion was frequently proclaimed to be a part of
official policy. Stuart was widely respected for his rugged probity, and Brodrick for his realism and moderation. At the beginning of
the third decade of the nineteenth century the fortunes of the Establishment seemed more promising than ever before.

The problems which disturbed this new sense of confidence were

largely outside the control of the Church. The sincere but inex-
perienced Lord John George Beresford would assume the primacy in
1822 after Stuart's death from accidental poisoning. This translation coincided with tithe agitation, O'Connell's political activism,
educational reform, new assaults on the Church's civil prerogatives,
and heightened religious tensions. Brodrick also died in 1822.
Thomas O'Beirne, who played a considerable if somewhat confusing
role in the reform movement as Bishop of Meath for most of the period,
died the next year. The new hierarchy was committed to reform as
never before, but it was hard pressed to cope with so many problems
simultaneously. After 1830, moreover, the ministry of the day would
often be Whig, with its heritage of anticlericalism and hostility to
ecclesiastical claims. And after 1841, with the Tory recovery, Peel
no longer felt his allegiance to the Irish Church could take precedence over Catholic claims. Peel might be understanding, but he could
not afford to be indulgent. More and more the Irish Establishment
saw its opinions ignored in the formulation of policy. Politics drew
apart from the life of the Establishment and when at last the government momentarily overcame its indifference, it did so to effect
disestablishment.

Several major themes dominated the Church-state relationship
after the death of William Stuart and Charles Brodrick. One dealt
with the vestry system and its related local institutions. The vestry symbolized the erastian connection on a parochial level and
afforded the resident clergy a convenient instrument for influencing
and even dictating local government. Collapse of the vestry system

marked an end to one large area of ecclesiastical responsibility in Ireland. Another theme reflected the growing agitation for Catholic emancipation, an issue of vital consequence to the Establishment, and one in which the Church's opinion was vociferously expressed and rather openly ignored. A third, which derived its momentum from concessions to Catholics, was the debate over the efficacy of the Establishment itself. The discussion was not only intrinsically important but underscored the Church's diminishing hold on the loyalty of the Irish people. Finally, and perhaps most important, was the growing isolation of ecclesiastical leaders from the government of the day. This changing relationship marked by increasing bitterness, distrust and frustration on one hand, and indifference, insensitivity, and secretiveness on the other.

Through the operation of the parish vestry the Irish erastian system most nearly approximated the principles of a theocracy. Theoretically, the vestry was composed of all members of the parish. On Easter Monday and occasionally other times of the year, the membership gathered under the direction of the pastor to elect parish officials, lay a cess on property for civic and religious functions, pass regulations for local tranquillity, fulfill whatever responsibilities might have been laid on the vestry by Parliament during the previous session, and offer resolutions on important questions of the day. In Ireland, however, the system had experienced a considerable metamorphosis in the wake of religious and political turmoil, landlord influence, clerical absentism, indifference to the law, and ignorance. The first major step was the denial of voting rights to

Catholics after 1720. This exclusion was justified by the vestry's role in regulating the affairs of the local Church, and by the penal system's deprivation of Catholic lands and thus Catholics' liability to the vestry cess. The second was the expansion of vestry activities in civil affairs to compensate for the weakness of the national administration and in reaction to frequent rural lawlessness. By 1800 the vestry, then, was often an oligarchical body wielding considerable power in local life. The restrictions imposed on it by vague and outmoded legislation were often evaded. Its effectiveness and influence varied from one parish to another.

The vestry's officers gave life to the system. Of these, the most important were the incumbent clergymen. They presided over the vestry itself and by skillful manipulation of its membership often exercised considerable power in the community. They were of course, not elective. Parish clerks were in theory responsible for the proper conduct of church services. They also maintained civil and ecclesiastical records and managed the parish in the absence of other officials. By 1800 the clerks' responsibilities had atrophied, and their capabilities had suffered a decline. They kept records in a cursory and haphazard way, and displayed contempt for Parliament's inquiries. Often they regarded their positions as perfectly sinecurial, which allowed them to act as tithe agents and tax collectors.[1] Sextons assisted the clergy in Sunday services; many parishes got on very well without sextons.

Most important were Churchwardens, "officers instituted to protect the edifice of the Church, to superintend the ceremonies of public worship, to promote the observance of religious duties, to form and

execute parochial regulations, and to become, as occasion may require,

the legal representatives of the body of the parish."[2] These ambitious

parochial empire-builders were generally chosen by negotiation be-

tween members of the vestry and the minister. In many areas the

attendant difficulties had been resolved by binding custom, subject

only to the common law courts' approval of the validity of local

arrangements. Exemptions from office were granted to peers, clergy-

men, and members of Parliament, the militia, Catholics, dissenters

and surgeons. No person living outside the parish was eligible. The

Churchwardens could sue or be sued on behalf of the Church. They

seated parishioners on Sunday, managed all profits of benefice, glebes,

and tithes during the absence of the incumbent, procured curates,

assembled parishioners to lay the cess or laid it themselves if the

vestry failed to convene, provided for illegitimate children, con-

sented to burials, collected fines for spoiled cheese and butter

and supplied the Church with provisions. They also posted the ten

commandments on church doors, expelled rowdy elements during the ser-

vice, tended the graveyard, levied penalties for profanity and drunk-

enness, licensed peddlers, fined truants on Sunday, controlled alms,

schoolhouses and legacies designated for pious purposes, oversaw the

welfare of the poor, and directed the parish clerk to record all

burials, births, christenings and marriages. Their activities as

champions of law and order constitute some of the most intriguing

material for Irish local histories. They closed stores on the Sabbath,

and stopped all traffic during divine service. They ferreted out

illegal distilleries and were put in charge of armed groups patrol-
ling the countryside. They applotted the cess, a delicate and sometimes dangerous task if it taxed powerful landlords too heavily.[3]

The scope of vestry responsibilities gave the Established
Church a role in local life far beyond what its small membership
and landlord hostility might otherwise have permitted it. Since the
cess was generally relatively small, often less than Ł50 per annum,
few Protestants took the time to audit the records with care. They
usually entrusted the clergyman to disburse funds for charitable
purposes according to his own judgment. This indifference often ex--
tended to the point where the incumbent took it upon himself to lay
the cess directly. Usually he encountered opposition only when the
amount demanded was substantial.

The vestry also, however, proved something of a forum for expression of grievances and for exposing divisions of opinion in
the community. Construction of a new church, for instance, was often
attended by considerable furor when it came time to assign seats. In
this, an index of social standing, the clergy made enemies by intervening and often a more remote artiber, the bishop, was asked to settle
the dispute. In Clones, County Monaghan, a seating dispute resulted
in half the congregation vowing never again to enter the church. Even
the location of the church itself caused difficulty. Prestige, not
convenience, was often the determining factor. The vestry meeting
on Easter Monday afforded aggrieved parties an opportunity to vent
their frustrations, and violence was not unknown.[4] Protestants of
middle class origin used the vestry to upstage their gentry coparish-

ioners. Social climbing was never more in evidence than during the
Napoleonic Wars, when vestries were called upon to provide bounties
for enlistees, and to staff reserve units in their own parishes.
So intense was the competition for honorable places in the yeomanry
that the cess was frequently disrupted, and the Church went without
supplies while laymen measured the intentions and tested the stamina
of the competition.

Because clergymen were responsible to Dublin Castle for filling
the ranks of the militia, they were eager to see the problem resolved
satisfactorily and applied themselves to see that a solution was
found. Some Ulster parishes published an expression of their gratitude in 1808. They thanked their clergy for "the disinterested and
generous exertions made in reconciling the various interests of so
great a number of people, which, however small, are not therefore
contended for with less violence."[5] On other occasions, it appears,
the clergy were less successful as keepers of the peace in the vestries.

These disruptions were vexatious, but the Church continued to
champion the vestry as a living expression of the establishment concept. It pointed to the considerable work in welfare, law and
order, and local cooperation which would not be accomplished otherwise. But as in the case of so much of the Church of Ireland's
work, the vestry also incorporated a supreme weakness which growing
Catholic agitation after 1815 quickly underscored. Like tithes, the
vestry cess was laid upon the land; like tithes, it was in fact
paid by Catholic tenants. Catholics objected not so much to the

burden of the cess, which was generally small, but to its application. They were understandably reluctant to see the cess allocated
to the purchase of bread and wine for a denomination they thought
heretical, to clerks, sextons and applotters whose selection they
could not help determine, or to the beneficed clergy, whose pattern
of almsgiving they believed favored Protestants.

The casual disbursement of funds was first challenged in 1816,
when some parishes refused to pay the cess laid down by the clergy
and their Churchwardens without vestry approval.[6] After 1823, as
part of a general increase in political consciousness, Catholics
began attending vestry meetings and attempted to pressure those
voting to follow their wishes. By virtue of such pressure Catholics
sometimes secured grants for their own churches, a practice directly
opposed to the essence of the erastian system, or obtained appointment of Catholic schoolmasters.[7]

Catholic intervention coincided with a growing conviction that
as organs of local government vestries were ill-equipped to provide
essential services. Parliament discovered upon investigation that
many parishes were inefficiently and expensively managed. Funds were
appropriated to the repair and expansion of churches, when these
should have been financed by vigorous collection of first fruits.
Large sums went to organists, who were often kinfolk of vestry officials. In the cathedral parish of St. Canice in Kilkenny there were
only four Protestants, not even enough to fill the offices. The
utility of many appropriations for the parochial church was hotly
questioned: prayerbooks for all parishioners in morocco bindings;

a salary for a bell ringer in a church without a bell; heavy
allotments for altar wine; compensation to a former clerk after
being fired for dereliction of duty.[8]

It was almost inevitable, therefore, that the issue should
eventually surface in Parliament. Sir John Newport launched one
line of attack in 1823 when he renewed demands for more rigorous
collection of first fruits, an assessment which neither new legislation nor threats by public officials and ecclesiastics against
the clergy seem to have had much effect. Newport predicted that
revolution would follow inevitably if the Church of Ireland's
privileges were not dismantled. He was censured by the House of
Commons for his inflammatory remarks.[9]

In 1824 Newport introduced a motion condemning Church rates.
This motion was defeated by only sixteen votes. Goulburn, heed-
ing the storm signals, pledged to extend the powers of the Lord
Lieutenant over the Church. An amendment to previous legislation
on Church rates was thereupon approved.[10] In 1825 Newport opened
another attack by introducing a bill to reform the vestry system
itself. He reviewed the returns authorized by Parliament the previous year, and presented a series of instances which supported his
contention that the vestry rate was controlled neither in its collection nor in its disbursement. The first deficiency was due in large
measure to the exclusion of Catholics, which dated from the reign
of George I. This permitted the small Protestant community in rural
Ireland to levy rates without opposition. The second deficiency represented a flagrant disregard of the restraints imposed by law and

propriety. Newport's examples prompted mirth and displeasure in the House: an increase in the sexton's salary from ₤10 to ₤20 per annum "because the practice of ringing funeral bells was discontinued;" appropriations to maintain public property when the Corporation failed to allocate sufficient funds; several allocations at Castle Comber, Kilkenny, to a carpenter and a schoolmaster by the parish clerk, all three being the same person; a ₤36 bill for altar wine, with no record of any services having been performed in the parish. Newport did not advocate abolishing the vestry, but he wanted Catholics admitted on equal terms. So incontrovertible were Newport's instances of malfeasance, ignorance, and carelessness that Goulburn in reply "felt no disposition to oppose the bill."[11]

As approved by the House of Commons the bill stated that residents denied the right to participate in vestry sessions but who paid the assessed taxes might appeal to quarter sessions for an injunction against the cess. In the House of Lords the appeal provisions were dropped. This left matters much as they had been before Newport introduced his reforms. In February 1826, therefore, Newport moved for introduction of another vestry bill, and Goulburn agreed to support it. The "Ultras" protested that the bill "would degrade the Church Establishment and weaken its claims to the respect and affectionate gratitude of the people." They justified this position by pointing out that flexibility in the rules allowed the Established clergy to make grants to Catholic and Presbyterian communities. This promoted local amity. A long and desultory debate followed. Goulburn brought it to a close by pledging to "ascertain what the law was, and to collect and consolidate the whole of the acts of this subject into one, and in that one to introduce clauses for the removal of many of the grievances complained of."[12]

Goulburn redeemed this pledge in April 1827. By this time liberals had changed their position. To Goulburn's surprise they now suggested that Parliament should expand rather than reduce the operation of the vestry system. They hoped that incidents of "good fellowship and Christian feeling," when vestry funds had been used to support Presbyterian and Catholic projects, could be made legal and indeed compulsory. Even Newport retreated from his earlier sweeping condemnation of the vestry system. He rose to support the new proposal. In one of his less impressive parliamentary performances, Goulburn predicted that such a system would lead to the destruction of the Established Church even more surely than would ending the vestry system. He objected to any system which would enable the majority of the vestry "to lay a compulsory tax on a parish, opposed to the views of the minority of the vestry, and perhaps to that of the whole body of parishioners."

This was, of course, the central objection of Newport and his friends to the system already in existence. Heretofore the Tories had not complained of a vestry system which saw a minority bind the unfranchised majority, providing that the minority was Protestant. The idea of giving Catholics control was repugnant. Robert Inglis, one of the most articulate and dedicated "Ultras," took the high road. He dismissed the existing irregularities as so slight as to warrant no legislative attention. He condemned the new proposal because it denied Protestants an opportunity to practice spontaneous Christian charity. At length Peel rescued Goulburn from his plight. He dismissed Spring Rice's plan as impractical and Inglis' observations as fatuous. The vestries, Peel noted, "were to be considered as so many little Parliaments in their several parishes; but their powers ought to be as clearly defined as possible." It was a serious enough objection to Newport's views that he wanted the Established Church to be undermined. It was not less serious that Ireland might end up with a full-fledged system of local government without the machinery to control excesses stemming from it.[13]

The plan to make the vestry popular and powerful was thereupon defeated. Goulburn supplied a bill which eventually passed both houses. By virtue of this measure Catholics were admitted to vestry sessions for deliberation of all matters except church repair and setting church rates; these were reserved for the "exclusive vestry" of Protestant landholders. All those contributing to church rates could vote for cess for "general parochial purposes" and for Church-wardens, whose powers were now severely curbed and stated explicitly. Appeals against assessments would be made to justices a quarter or general sessions, not through church courts.

In Catholic eyes, the new law was inadequate.[14] In Parliament the issue was once more joined the following year. Newport opened proceedings by producing evidence to support his contention that since the Act of Union "no less than half a million" had been raised through vestry rates, and principally from Roman Catholics, for the support of the Church of Ireland. As O'Connell was to note later, the vestry reform Act of 1827 had in fact strengthened rather than weakened the power of the Protestant minority to use the vestry system to the prejudice of Catholics. Powers had been more clearly delineated, but the parameters had not necessarily been reduced. For example, whereas previously the vestry might repair churches, now they were empowered to levy rates for a new one. Whereas earlier bishops could use only ecclesiastical devices to force vestries to levy rates for church repairs when vestries refused to do so directly, now they might apply civil sanctions as well. Civil sanctions, needless to say, were much more effective. Most important, the "exclusive vestry" was not restricted in the amounts it might demand for Church repairs, and in the wake of the 1827 Act rates had risen substantially in some parts of Ireland.[15]

At the end of these discussions a motion to terminate the vestry system was redrafted and brought in as a bill by Newport, Spring Rice, and their friends.[16] In the House of Lords Baron Clifden noted in support of the bill that "every man acquainted with Ireland knows he could not ride the distance of three miles, without seeing a church in ruins. Now, however, a fancy had been taken to build churches. But it was very unreasonable that the Catholics should be compelled to pay for what . . . the Protestants had allowed to go to ruin."[17] The 1827 legislation was not amended, however.[18] In 1830 Stanley proposed some minor changes, most of which O'Connell pronounced "meaningless."[19]

Parliament's intransigence again prompted popular measure in Ireland to change the cess. The legislation of 1826, it was soon realized, was largely ignored by Protestants; they continued to appropriate funds for a variety of church-related purposes now outlawed. Catholic pressure to disband the system increased. The Established Church was reluctant to part with this source of income and preferred therefore to appease Catholics with larger grants to the poor and to their chapels. By 1831 it was clear, however, that the vestry system was disintegrating. Catholics turned meetings into tumults, hissed speakers from the galleries, and took the cess to court on whatever technical defects sharp lawyers could uncover.[20] Growing tithe agitation destroyed the vestry as a forum for arranging composition agreements. Arguments over furnishing Protestant churches led to near-violence. Catholics proceeded to vote down every proposed appropriation. This left churches without candles, organists and altar supplies, and vestry officials without salaries. At length the only appropriation supported by all parties was coffins for paupers. Protestants tore pages from cess books to hide extravagant assessments of previous years, and Catholics forced stampeded "exclusive vestries" into early adjournment.[21]

By the spring vestry, 1833, many parishes had suspended the cess altogether; in others, the inevitability of the collapse of the system prompted enterprising Protestants in exclusive vestries to lay heavy taxes for church repairs; they assumed that the government would forward the necessary funds instead of risking the riotous reaction of Catholics during collection. Finally even the Church conceded that the vestry system must be substantially reformed. Magee declared his readiness to surrender in a pamphlet published in 1832, and Stanley obtained similar expressions from Robert Blomfield, the Bishop of London.[22]

The last phase of the vestry debate in Parliament opened in March 1830, when O'Connell and others submitted petitions complaining about vestry rates in particular and the Established Church in general.[23] O'Connell sharpened the debate in April when he moved for changes in the 1827 Vestry Act so as to admit Catholics to the "exclusive" or "select" vestry . He impugned the motives as well as the provisions of the 1827 measure. Charging that the Act gave universal dissatisfaction and that indeed it "inflicted additional grievances" he demanded that the exclusive vestry be abolished entirely.[24] Goulburn defended the 1827 Act as the most which could be conceded without destroying the Establishment itself. "Ultras" accused O'Connell of advocating disestablishment under the guise of the vestry question. Peel claimed that the Irish Church should be sustained by Ireland, and that taxes on the land, such as those levied by the vestries, were appropriate. O'Connell concluded with a savage attack on the Church of Ireland. He accused it of "levying distress, and . . . pocketing the fees of that distress," for taxing "the poorest of nations" to maintain an alien ecclesiastical system. The motion was decisively negatived, 177 to 47, but many observers sensed that rural violence in Ireland would soon necessitate new measures.

Indeed, the tide soon turned against the ancient vestry system. Only three years elapsed before the Irish Church Temporalities Act of 1833 ended the use of the vestry cess for maintenance of the Established Church. It did not, however, destroy every aspect of the local

erastian arrangement. The beneficed clergy continued to preside over
the vestry, it was still held in the Anglican church, and Protestant
landlords continued to use the vestry to exercise their local influence. The vestry, therefore, continued to be the scene of annual
confrontations between Protestants and Catholics. In the spring of
1834 vestry participants in St. Michan's parish, Dublin, voted to
censure the presiding clergyman for his "bigoted conduct." Vestry
officials, now charged with responsibilities for paupers and local
ordinances, were almost universally denied their salaries in a demonstration of Catholic power.[25] Appropriations for the village school
were routinely voted down. In April 1836, after a siege of notices
about tumultuous vestry meetings the Dublin Evening Mail observed that
it could "not burden our columns or offend the public taste" by in-
serting any more of these stories. It regretted the damage done to
the churches during these meetings, when they were rendered "worse
than bear gardens."[26] By 1838 the chaos was complete and by 1839 most
could report "that no business of public interest was transacted.[27]
The vestry system, and the official place of the Established clergy in
local politics, had been destroyed by religious tensions, political
activism, and popular clamor.

The destruction of the vestry system in Ireland had far-reaching
consequences. As an expression of the role of the Established Church
in national life the vestry was far more important than episcopal
influence in high councils of government, for it embodied that joint
Church-state responsibility for social control so central to any functioning erastian system. In Ireland destruction of the vestry was par-

ticularly painful, because few other local institutions were able to fill the gap in local government, especially concerning social welfare services. In the brief interval between vestry reform in 1826 and resumption of agitation in 1831 much was done to coordinate local efforts in containing disease, enforcing quarantines, cleaning public streets, sustaining the poor, supplying coffins, and supporting orphans.[28] The imposition of a poor law in 1834, with its brutalizing workhouses, its impersonal regulations, and its distant supervision, was not an attractive substitute. For the Church of Ireland the loss of the forum for exercising influence far beyond its membership limitations was incalculable. The clergy retreated to their own flocks, severing or weakening ties with the Catholic and Presbyterian communities. Their wider aspirations, often supported by a liberal education and cosmopolitan outlook were perforce channeled into the narrower topics of evangelicalism and theological controversy.[29]

The immediate cause of the collapse of the vestry system was the tithe problem, already noted, and Catholic emancipation. The latter issue was born in the penal codes of the late seventeenth and early eighteenth centuries, nurtured by Ireland's brief period of legislative independence under Henry Grattan, sharpened still further by Pitt's abortive promises to Catholics in 1800, and sustained by growing sentiment in the united Parliament after 1800. King George III's scruples set off a sustained campaign of petitioning to Parliament which almost produced a favorable vote in Parliament in 1812 and 1813. Indeed, at this time the prospects of early passage of Catholic emancipation seemed good. Perceval reconciled himself to eventual surrender on the issue as early as 1810, and Stuart was convinced that the growing weakness of the Perceval ministry in 1812 would prompt this concession to Catholics .[30] The issue lost momentum there- after. English Catholics eventually declared their willingness to accept a veto on episcopal appointments in return for the emancipa- tion measure. George IV's visit to Dublin in 1821 recalled pledges he made in 1807 to promote Cathlics' grievances, and the appointment of the Marquess Wellesley as viceroy seemed to suggest the government might be prepared to move forward.

This optimism proved premature, and in 1821 the Establishment seemed as secure as ever. In 1823, however, O'Connell's Catholic association was founded, and in the autumn of the same year, John Doyle, Catholic Bishop of Kildare, declared his support for O'Connell's program. Archbishop Curtis, the Catholic primate, apologized to Wellington for Doyle's indiscretion, but the hierarchy rallied to Doyle's defense. The Catholic clergy was mobilized to collect the Catholic Association's rent. In 1825 Goulburn suppressed the associa- tion. In return the government promised emancipation, buttressed by state payment of the Catholic clergy and a higher franchise. This passed the Commons, but failed in the Lords, and O'Connell fashioned a new movement which conformed to the technicalities of the law. When Wellington displaced the Canningites, O'Connell opted for bold action, stood for Parliament at the Clare election, and won. The prospect of successful candidates being unable to enter Parliament threatened to undermine the entire system, and maneuvers began in earnest towards a resolution of the controversy.[31]

The Church of Ireland was not slow to respond to the crisis, but its plan of action remained somewhat confused. Every flutter of parliamentary activity brought pamphlets and petitions from clerical and lay Protestants in opposition to the system. Two arguments played a leading role. One was the conviction, widely held, that emancipation was for Catholics merely a stepping-stone to seizure and full power. One observer put the Protestant cause in clear focus in 1807:

> There is a peculiarity in the situation of Ireland, which
> in discussions of this kind should never be forgotten, and
> one which throws very considerable light upon the subject.
> It is a matter of unquestionable notoriety that the Catholics
> of Ireland look upon themselves as original and legal pro-
> prietors of the island; the rightful and inherent possessors
> of the soil; that the Protestants have forcibly intruded
> upon the country; and have transferred the property and
> influence from the Catholics to a Protestant Supremacy.
> Would not this simple aspect of the case, be sufficient to
> set aside volumes of argument in favor of Catholic Emanci-
> pation? Does it not clearly suggest to every thinking
> mind, that while such is the ruling premise of the Catholics,
> it is incompatible with the safety of the state, to admit
> them to the equal advantage of the constitution, as the
> Protestants are disposed of.[32]

Emancipation, then, however just in theory, was dangerous in practice. It was argued by others, however, that it was not supported by theory either. Emancipation would violate the essence of the union of the Churches in 1800, for it would single out the Irish portion of the Establishment for special danger, and certain destruction. It would endanger its temporalities by encouraging tithe resistance. It would not ease religious tensions, nor satiate Catholic demands.[33]

Aside from some heavy pamphlet barrages, however, the role of the Church of Ireland in opposing emancipation was curiously muted.

In part, as has been seen, this reflected a disinclination of the beneficed clergy to become deeply involved in agitation. Even the appearance of the Brunswick lodges and resurrection of the Orange movement did not immediately overcome this reserve.[34] In part it represented a feeling of the futility of forwarding petitions against emancipation to the Canningites, whose liberalism was firmly based, or to conservatives, whose firm support could always be anticipated. The restoration of a bona-fide Tory ministry under Wellington in 1828 was interpreted by the Church, therefore, as at least a temporary respite from the dangerous schemes of the Canningites and relief from the feeling of inevitable success which by 1828 was permeating the emancipation movement.[35]

Wellington's decision to introduce a bill for emancipation came as a distinct surprise to everyone and as a thunderclap to the Irish Church. Perspective shows quite clearly that Wellington had been contemplating the possibility of conceding Catholic emancipation for some time.[36] For Beresford and his clergy, however, the realization came late, and no frenzied campaign of opposition could alter Wellington's convictions. The Established clergy were now urged to participate actively in the Brunswick Clubs, but these organizations lacked both the great potential power of mass membership and the inspired leadership of an O'Connell. Beresford came forth with a highly impractical scheme of guarantees. He asked that Catholics be required to renounce papal infallibility and the power of priests to grant unconditional absolution. He wanted them to accept a separate hierarchy from that of England and whatever canons for control of the clergy the government

might see fit to formulate.[37]   John Jebb asked Peel, whose own conversion was no less startling to Churchmen than that of Wellington,
what motivated the conversion.   Peel replied, somewhat tactlessly,
"what would become of the temporalities of the Irish Church during
a civil war embittered by furious religious bigotry?"[38]   Beresford
then led two-thirds of the bench in signing a petition against emancipation, "a measure which we conceive would endanger the security of
the Established Church in Ireland." Wellington refused to affix his
signature, and emancipation passed.[39]

The significance of Catholic emancipation in the larger context
of British politics can hardly be overestimated. It showed the
power of mass movements, the strength of reformist ideals, the impossibility of governing Ireland without accommodating Catholic
wishes, and the power of the priests over the Catholic laity. All
of these had been impressed upon the Established Church's leaders
during the tithe resistance, if somewhat less dramatically. More
disturbing for the Church was the way in which emancipation was formulated and enacted into law. Well might Beresford complain to
Wellington that his counsel was being ignored, that measures were
being conceived which affected the Irish Establishement and about
which he was left in complete ignorance until the last minute, and
that the Irish Church counted for nothing in the government of the
realm.[40]   He was also well advised to suspect that further concessions
to Catholic sensitivites, even apart from tithes and Church reform,
could be expected in the future. Within a decade English prime ministers would look with indifference on Catholic bishops' use of cer-

ain ecclesiastical titles, though it violated the law, and later on

eel's concessions to Maynooth in L845.[41] From the vantage point of

he English Church these things were gratuitously provocative; for

he Church of Ireland they were confirmation of a diminishing stake

n the nation.[42]

This diminishing stake in national life was nowhere more appar-

nt than in the metamorphosis of those informal bonds which had cement-

d the Protestant ascendancy in the eighteenth century. By 1820 that

lmost indistinguishable set of interests of the penal code period,

ay and clerical, state and Church, had decayed. The Church lost its

verwhelmingly aristocratic mold. Leading families gradually ceased

o allocate their offspring between civil and ecclesiastical estab-

ishments. Informal communication declined. The state became more

eluctant to give the Church first priority in its policy and neglect-

d to demand from it much responsibility in the task of controlling

reland. Each constituent of the old ascendancy viewed the other with

reater detachment, and, eventually with the laity gradually ceased

o treat bishops with respect and deference. The bishops in turn

ecame evasive, defensive and embittered. The Irish bench vacillated

etween accusing Parliament and the incumbent ministry of conscious

eglect, insidious curiosity, and insensitive, heavy handed interven-

ion into the Church's affairs.

The Establishment's difficulties with Parliament after 1800 had

any antecedents. The Irish Parliament waxed anti-clerical on several

eparate occasions and the Church was saved only by the intervention

f the crown. After 1800 Parliament was intially much more accommodating, but Stuart's relations with Dublin Castle were anything but cordial.[43] The bench got along surprisingly well with the Fox-Grenville Whigs, and Bedford prided himself on the intimacy he was able to encourage with Stuart and others. After 1807 parliamentary mettle, ministerial mismanagement, and the Church's stubbornness on such relatively minor items as franking privileges produced many instances of embarrassment. Patrick Duigenen, self-appointed champion of the Church interest in the Commons, consistently managed to alienate his audience and aggravate problems. From 1812 to 1816, as a result, Stuart strongly advised against all parliamentary initiatives on behalf of the Church, whatever their value and defensibility.[44] In 1816 Alexander Knox noted that the state was pursuing a double standard towards the Irish Church: it upheld the union when it wanted to press Englishmen into Irish sees and benefices, and ignored the union when proposing reforms.[45] Robert Peel did much to mitigate the sharpest edges of this criticism by his delicately worded advice and generous compliments. His successor as Irish chief secretary, Henry Goulburn, was less adept in this respect. The liberal-minded Lord Lieutenant, Marquess Wellesley, delighted in "roasting bishops" at dinner and displayed an animosity for John Jebb, Bishop of Limerick, which almost caused an open breach with the Church.[46]

Goulburn was unable to diffuse the Wellesley-Jebb dispute, but he worked hard to meet the rising wave of parliamentary and popular criticism of the Church which came in the 1820s. The Irish secretary could not silence Newport, Hume, Burdett and Cobbett, but he did blunt their thrusts. Church leaders alternated between periods of militancy

and silent, almost passive, agony.[47] In Ireland bishops were quick
to complain of assaults on their dignity. Magee in Dublin was
chagrined "to have the heads of the Established Church, immediately
under the eye of the government of the country, held up to public
contempt and execration, by a set of popish priests."[48] By the end
of the decade Parliament had confirmed Catholic emancipation,
Wellington had neglected to include the Irish Church in his confi-
dences, and the Whigs were preparing for Church reform.

During the 1830s even the Whig appointed Whately was distressed
at the government's failure to communicate with the Irish bishops.
The Tory restoration in 1841 brought little of that intimacy which
Peel and Blomfield enjoyed in reference to the English Church.[49]
Irish bishops were perhaps happy enough to be left alone, and Beresford, fighting his rear-guard action to save what he could, kept
his letters to Dublin and London on a strictly formal basis. In
seventy years the process of alienation had become almost complete.
So far from the heady days of Archbishop Agar's pervasive influence
was it that the Irish Church refused even to meet with Gladstone in
constructive fashion as the disestablishment bill moved towards enactment.

Collapse of the vestry system, passage of Catholic Emancipation
legislation, and a growing estrangement of Church leaders from the
ministry of the day were bound to bring into question the utility and
necessity of the Establishment itself. The concept of establishment,
formulated rather haphazardly under Henry VIII, raised to general
approval under Elizabeth, and stamped with a convincing justification

by Hooker, had achieved in early nineteenth century-England a level
of acceptance which neither prospects of radical reform or signs of
institutional deficiency seemed to disturb. In Ireland the philoso-
phical exercises were equally convincing, but the reality was not.
The essential weakness of the Irish system was noted by Francis Plowden at the very beginning of the nineteenth century. The Church-state
relationship, he observed, had taken not the form of an alliance but
a dependence of the former on the latter. Rather than a system incorporating two independent jurisdictions, spiritual and temporal,
with an exchange of assistance emanating from these autonomous foundations, in Ireland there had developed a Church which was peculiarly
the product of state policy, ringed by foes and beset by internal
problems which it could not rectify .[50] But less delicately, the Irish
Church "in its unpurged and unreformed state, was very little else than
a mere political engine for supporting and fostering British interests
and English principles in this country; . . . It was indeed the only
bond that bound the political interests of the two nations together."[51]
It was, in the eyes of a noted political economist of the day, an experiment "never. . . attempted in any other country since the beginning of the world."[52]

Before 1800 the problem of defending the Irish Establishment,
while not always easy, was relatively uncomplicated. If one were to
assume that some Church must be established then it remained only to
choose among the three religious bodies of substance in the nation.
The Presbyterians claimed to be true heir to the Reformation. Their
fundamentalist tendencies and geographical imbalance, however, sug-

gested to most observers that Presbyterianism was incapable of
fulfilling the responsibilities of a state Church. Roman Catholicism
was limited by its overseas allegiance, its almost universal poverty,
its prostrate condition after the century's application of the penal
code, and its understandable difficulties in presenting its case
forcefully and articulately. After 1800 Catholicism came into contention, as it demonstrated loyalty to the state, a firm control over
its membership, a higher level of scholarship, and a tendency towards
steady growth at the expense of its competitors.[53] The Establishment
was forced to alter its defense. Against those who argued that the
majority religion should be established the Church replied that in
the entire United Kingdom the Anglican Church was in the majority,
and that in Ireland itself religion bore a special civilizing burden, which only the Anglican Church could fulfill.[54] It also pointed
out, with more effect, that Catholicism showed no interest in being
established, that it preferred to direct its principal loyalties
elsewhere. It pointed to its stake in Ireland's economic and social
life as evidence of its role in social control. The Church charged
low rents and thereby enhanced Ireland's prosperity. Disestablishment
would undermine all property rights in the nation and would destroy
an important contributor to the nation's stability.[55] Finally, the
Church produced evidence that it was, in the wake of internal adjustments made after 1800, moving towards majority status.[56]

The assault on the idea of establishment did not get under way
in earnest until after 1820, and in 1825 Catholic witnesses before
parliamentary committees on Ireland made a convincing case for their

contention that they neither opposed the present Establishment, nor
wanted the privilege for themselves. As John Doyle noted, the disadvantages of the state connection, as it had worked out in Ireland,
were so much greater than the privileges, that no Christian denomination anxious for its future prosperity would want the empty honor.[57]
The question, indeed, was raised by some Protestants themselves whose
own allegiance to the idea of establishment was not always above suspicion. In 1829 Ireland witnessed an extended battle in pamphlet form
between the Earl of Mountcashel, acting as devil's advocate, and several
of the Church's most prominent apologists, including Thomas Elrington
and Henry Newland.[58] The dispute, which seems to have been followed
attentively by much of the reading public, culminated in a determined
effort by the Church to explain, excuse, or justify those anomalies
which had not yet succumbed to the reforming impulse. This was not a
particularly convincing exercise, and it led some leading ecclesiastics
to indulge in unmistakable twistings of logic.[59] All this effort was
misdirected, however. After 1830 arguments relating to the concept of
establishment moved from proving which denomination should have the
honor, to a debate on whether to sustain the idea at all. In this contest, disestablishment began to take on ominous tones, and marked the
start of nearly forty years' deliberation on an alternative inconceiv-
able to members of the Church before 1800.

The disestablishment issue after 1830 was debated largely within
the framework of Benthamite assumptions about institutional efficiency,
and in this sense, Parliament's intervention in Church administration
in 1833 probably prolonged the Establishment by a decade or two. As

we have seen both radicals and conservatives wanted Church reform. Radicals wanted to transform the Church into a society promoting useful knowledge and "amiable morals". Conservatives wanted to resurrect its prerogatives and power, through it to inculcate in the Irish people strong doses of loyalty, morality, and Protestant theology. Radicals wanted little from the Church but its property, and this more than anything else conservatives were unwilling to concede.

In radicals' eyes the agency for transforming the Church of Ireland into a useful public body was government by commission. The first serious venture into this form of ecclesiastical administration in 1830 combined the inevitable inertia of bureaucracy with the calculated obstructionism of vested interests. The Commissions of 1830 and 1832 were staffed largely by ecclesiastics. They contrived to supply Parliament appropriate information too late for currently popular reform proposals. Bishops found ignoring requests for information emanating from these commissions even easier than those from parliamentary committees.[60] In the 1830s, therefore, the Tories were the winners. They were able to appropriate the Benthamite penchant for efficiency, not to remove revenues from the Church, but to make the Church itself more efficient. The effect was "to convert what had been a great system of patronage and private property into a responsible semi-public corporation."[61] Whether this "semi-public corporation" could achieve its goals was the next question; and most parties seemed willing to give it a chance to perform.

For thirty five years the Ecclesiastical Commission busied itself with Benthamite reforms. Zealous Churchmen infused a new level of pastoral effectiveness into clerical activity. Catholicism mourned the decline and death of O'Connell and then reeled under the impact of the famine. The prospect of disestablishment seemed real, but remote. In 1844 Henry Ward, member for Sheffield and an active partisan in opposing Peel's plan to increase the public support for Maynooth, tested political sympathy for disestablishment by offering a motion to examine Church temporalities. The motion was defeated 274 to 179. The tally suggested that while disestablishment was favorably thought of by a large minority of the House of Commons, effecting it was far from inevitable. Ward's motion, however, created its own internal whirlwind. His suggestion that Maynooth be funded out of the resources of the Established Church disoriented the "Voluntaries." Some of this group supported Ward in the hope of destroying the prevailing erastian system. Others opposed Ward because they feared more the prospect of a Catholic establishment.[62] Five years later, with Maynooth forgotten, a motion for disestablishment by Bernal Osborne was defeated by only 67 votes. The matter was not pressed, however. In Ireland Catholicism devoted its time and resources to a reconstruction of the Church after the famine. At length it emerged fiscally stronger and institutionally highly cohesive. In Britain the revival of Catholicism, its membership fed by an influx of Irish workers and its leadership drawn heavily from the Oxford Movement, touched Protestant nerves and indirectly protected the Irish Established Church. In Parliament the Independent Irish Party alluded to disestablishment but concentrated on land questions.[63]

The census of 1861 (the first to determine denominational allegiances) produced in public opinion a dramatic shift from indifference

to alarm. Within the Irish Church itself a complacency nourished by
isolated demonstrations of evangelical success and a generation of
political peace was abruptly shattered. The census revealed that the
Established Church commanded the allegiance of less than 12 per cent
of the population. Its losses in rural Ireland had been catastrophic.
Even its most celebrated evangelical experiments, such as Achill
Island, had made little impact upon denominational statistics. A
chorus of demands for disestablishment was heard in all quarters.
Cardinal Cullen, emerging as Ireland's architect of a militant counter-
Reformation Catholicism, committed his Church to disestablishment. In
political circles a sympathy for disestablishment was articulated in
the founding of the National Association of Ireland, committed to systematic exploitation of support within and without Parliament.[64] Public opinion expressed its displeasure at the disclosure of a dwindling
membership in large parts of Ireland, where episcopal lands continued
to sustain a wealthy coterie of aristocratic families and a superabundant ecclesiastical structure. Upon the death of Archbishop Beresford
in 1862 many expressed shock and dismay at the size of his private fortune.[65]

There were murmurings within the Church itself. In 1862 Archbishop Whately confided to Nassau Senior that the state was supposed to
tax people to do things the people could not do for themselves. By
this criterion Catholics' taxes were misdirected as far as sustaining
the Church of Ireland was concerned.[66] Maziere Brady, in influential
Church of Ireland clergyman, declared that "in proportion as the Church
Established seeks more earnestly to live as a Church, so will her posi-

tion as an Establishment become less tolerable."[67] While not subscribed to by a majority of Irish clergymen many members of the Church of Ireland concluded that the existing system sacrificed the welfare of the ecclesiastical polity to the interests of Irish landlords. Political developments once again convulsed by Fenian agitation and a powerful Catholic interest, suggested that the dangerous repercussions stemming from disestablishment might well be faced now.

As disestablishment gained public attention after 1864 old arguments in favor and in opposition were revived, and some new ones were advanced. The transformation wrought in Irish politics by nationalism and Catholicism gave added weight to the contention that the Establishment was alien, and that disestablishment was inevitably a part of any settlement of the Irish question as a whole. To the first the Church responded by noting how few Englishmen now held positions, great or small, in its structure, and how prominent was the influence of Rome in its adversary. In answer to the latter the Church predicted, and it turned out accurately, that disestablishment would resolve fewer problems than many supposed. Richard Chenevis Trench, Archbishop of Dublin after 1866, maintained that what the Irish craved was land. They would assault the Protestant interest until a desperate point was reached when England was forced to subdue Ireland to save the garrisoned Protestants. Thought of in terms of the events of 1894, this is not without its claims to wisdom. By undermining property rights, by weakening Protestantism, by driving those loyal to the Crown into rebellion and by removing from the countryside a valuable gentry interest, Trench believed disestablishment would only hasten the day of apocalypse.[68]

While Trench raised storm flags, however, his colleagues made
desperate efforts to avoid disestablishment. In doing so they proposed
changes within the Church more revolutionary than reformist. In 1864
the Irish bench of bishops advocated immediate abolition of 17 of 30
Irish cathedrals and chapters and suppression of 19 of 32 deanships
upon vacancy. They offered the ecclesiastical commission sweeping
powers to equalize clerical incomes and to revamp parochial jurisdictions. Submitted to Palmerston in 1864, the plan was ignored and soon
forgotten. In 1867, however, the Conservatives under Earl Russell
moved a Royal Commission to investigate the property and revenues of
the Church, and its conclusions, made public even as Gladstone deploy-
ed his forces for full disestablishment, were rejected by the Irish
bishops. Even with the Church the will to resist disestablishment had
ebbed. The long battle for ecclesiastical reform within an erastian
framework was over. The Church looked forward to independence, and
that most vexatious question of early nineteenth century Irish politics
and religion was laid to rest by Parliament's declared will.

Chapter X: Conclusion

The Church of Ireland which drew near to disestablishment after
mid-century was in some respects stronger and in other respects weaker
than it was at the beginning of the nineteenth century. Its clergy were
now reformed, better educated, more devout, more popular and better
employed. Its temporalities, still large but no obstruction to pastoral

efficiency, no longer occasioned tithe resistance and other violence.
Patronage remained, but was executed with due regard for the needs and
sensitivites of the Church.   Its beneficed clergy now reflected the
overwhelming preponderance of Irishmen, and its curates were sustained
in dignified fashion.   But it was also weaker.   The intimacy of the
state connection had vanished.   The prospect of conversion of the nation
had been dimmed.   The exercise of civic responsibilities on both the
national and local level had been curbed.   Its membership was still
heavily oriented towards the English connection and must be expected
to suffer any diminution of British influence or control.

The adventure of the Irish Church between 1800 and 1869 was not
simply an ecclesiastical one;   indeed, we must ask what its decline
as a social and political factor meant for Ireland.   It signified,
above all, that Ireland was not likely to be transformed into a nation
bound to Britain by a common culture and cemented by shared religious
and political values.   The continued minority position of the Establishment committed Britain to an experiment in religious and political
pluralism which, if ultimately unsuccessful, prompted a deeper examination of the efficacy of a state Church.   In Parliament the Church issue
encouraged wider legislative experiments in effecting administrative
reform, and prompted a secularization of local government to a degree
perhaps not yet fully appreciated.

The Church issue was also instructive as a study in institutional
behavior and development.   If it entered the nineteenth century as one
of the most unusual and ill-equipped ecclesiastical systems of its
time, this only reflected the burden of its own, and the nation's,his-

torical experience. If the Church was deficient in its conception
and program, no less so was the state to which it was formally allied
and in fact all too often subservient. As John Stuart Mill right-
fully observed, the most persistent tragedy of the British presence
in Ireland was the utterly unshakeable conviction of the government
of the day that Ireland was amenable to the same type of control as
proved effective in Britáin, and to the same combinations of inducements and admonitions. The Church of Ireland was a manifestation of
this attitude written large. Thus two developments destroyed the
Establishment's role as traditionally conceived by architects of
British policy. The first was a growing feeling within the Church
that it must be something more than a convenient mechanism for staff-
ing rural Ireland with a conscientious gentry and for providing a
Protestant presence. The second was a conviction outside the Church
that it must be something less than a system of privileges, property,
and wide prerogatives. The first measured the Church's effectiveness
as a religious institution, the second its worth as a mechanism of
social control. In 1800 the Church of Ireland scored poorly in both
fields.

It is easy to cite the aggravations with which the Church of
Ireland was associated in Irish life in the early nineteenth century.
It must also be remembered, however, that its severance from secular
responsibilities in the 1830s, its reformed temporalities, and finally
its complete disestablishment in 1869 did not make Ireland an easier
forum for the exercise of British control. Though Ireland was intensely
concerned with religious problems, its problems were not essentially

religious but economic. Agitation against the Established Church was not, in the final analysis, only an expression of religious feeling, although both Catholics and Protestants often concluded as much. The essential problem was land, a crucial commodity in a country short of natural resources and burdened with a superabundant population. Tithe reform, by partially reducing the tenants' burden of tilling the land, was a temporary palliative, but the survival of the rackrent system meant that the difficulty was not permanently resolved. The Church and its temporalities served for a long time to obscure from tenants, and, more tragically, from most landlords, a pervasive cancer of the rent system. Perhaps tithes did their greatest disservice to Ireland not in exciting the peasant to tithe resistance, but in deflecting attention from shortsighted landlord policies until Ireland confronted and was forced to endure the great famine, a national disaster of unparalleled proportions in nineteenth century Europe.

The Church of Ireland was, of course, more than an economic phenomenon. This became increasingly apparent during the process of internal renewal and revitalization. The Church was also more vulnerable to criticism than the landlords' system. As a religious institution it was judged by higher standards than were landlords, and as the Roman Catholic Church reasserted its power in Ireland this condemnation became more severe. Criticism, however beneficial ultimately, is never comfortable, and the oppobrium which accompanied the process of reform left scars on the Church which were slow to heal. But if perspective may be used to advantage, it is not likely that a modern observer of

the condition of the Church of Ireland in 1800 and again on the eve
of disestablishment would choose the former over the latter. Nor is
it likely that the religious configuration of modern Ireland would
have been changed to the Church's advantage by a continuation of
the erastian system which existed in 1800, in 1835, or perhaps even
in 1869.

FOOTNOTES

Chapter I: The Erastian Heritage 1535-1800

[1]This statement must be modified to acknowledge the appearance of Donald H. Akenson's The Church of Ireland: Ecclesiastical Reform and Revolution 1800-1885 (New Haven: Yale University Press, 1971). This fine work concerns itself with administrative reform.

[2]Robert Dudley Edwards, Church and State in Tudor Ireland: A History of the Penal Laws against Irish Catholics 1534-1603 (Dublin: Talbot Press, 1935, pp. 16, 25, 159.

[3]Calendar of Carew MSS (Howth), p. 485, quoted in A. Cooper, annotator, Whole Works of Sir James Ware, I, 537, noted in Edwards, Church and State, p. 143.

[4]Edwards, Church and State, pp. xxxix, xli-xlii.

[5]Ibid., p. 72.

[6]Dublin, Public Record Office, Calendar of State Papers of Ireland, I, 265 (Shirley, no. 75), noted in Edwards, Church and State, p. 195.

[7]C.S.P., III, (No. 463), 70; W. M. Brady, ed., State Papers Concerning the Irish Church in the Time of Queen Elizabeth, no. 86, cited in Edwards, Church and State, p. 267.

[8]Quoted in The Works of Dr. John Bramhall (Oxford, 1842), I, lxxx-lxxxii, noted in C.V. Jourdan, "The Rule of Charles I," in Walter Allison Phillips, ed., History of the Church of Ireland from the Earliest Times to the Present Day (3 vols.; London: Oxford University Press, 1933), III, 12-13.

[9]Bagwell, Ireland, I, 68.

[10]Lord Strafford, Letters, I, 187-89, noted in Jourdan, "Rule of Charles I," pp. 18-19.

[11]Rawdon Papers, p. 127, noted in R.H. Murray, "The Church of the Revolution," in Phillips, ed., History of the Church of Ireland, III, 119.

[12]Ireland, C.S.P. (1894-95), p. 82, cited in Murray, "Church of the Revolution," p. 169.

[13]J.C. Beckett, "The Government and the Church of Ireland under William III and Anne," Irish Historical Studies, II (March, 1941), p. 302.

[14]William Petty, Political Survey of Ireland (2nd ed., London, 1719), pp. 16-17.

[15]Michael MacDonagh, The Viceroy's Post-Bag: Correspondence hitherto Unpublished of the Earl of Hardwicke, First Lord Lieutenant of Ireland after the Union (London: John Murray, 1904), p. 99.

[16]"Primate" will refer only to the Archbishop of Armagh, the senior ecclesiastical official of the Church of Ireland. The Archbishop of Armagh was styled "Primate of All Ireland," the Archbishop of Dublin was styled "Primate of Ireland." In practice the latter was never referred to as primate.

[17]Sermon of January 20, 1760, quoted in Norman Ravitch, "The Social Origins of French and English Bishops in the Eighteenth Century," Historical Journal, VIII, 3 (1965), pp. 310-11.

[18]Ravitch, "Social Origins," pp. 318-19.

[19]Norman Ravitch, Sword and Mitre: Government and Episcopate in France and England in the Age of Aristocracy (The Hague, 1966), pp. 145-47.

[20]Ravitch, "Social Origins," pp. 322-323.

[21]Thomas B. Lundeen, "The Bench of Bishops: A Study of the Secular Activities of the Bishops of the Church of England and Ireland 1801-1871," (Ph.D. Dissertation: State University of Iowa, 1963), pp. 35-36.

[22]J.L. McCracken, "The Conflict between the Irish Administration and Parliament, 1753-6," Irish Historical Studies, III (1942), passim.

[23]William King, Archbishop of Dublin, to Dr. Charlott, April 1, 1715, noted in Charles S. King, A Great Archbishop of Dublin: William King, D.D., 1650-1729 (London: Longmans and Co., 1906), p. 220.

[24]W.D. Killen, Ecclesiastical History of Ireland (London: Macmillan and Co., 1875), II, 244; King to William Wake, Archbishop of Canterbury, July, 1722, cited in Richard Mant, History of the Church of Ireland from the Reformation to the Revolution (London, 1840), p. 380.

[25]Descendents of Cromwell's soldiers were now Catholics in areas

where no Protestant clergy resided: Hugh Boulter, Letters . . . to
Several Ministers of State in England, and some Others, Containing
an Account of the Most Interesting Transactions which have Passed in
Ireland from 1724 to 1738 (2 vols.; Dublin, 1770); I, II.

[26]Jonathan Swift, Dean of Christ Church, Dublin, "Considerations
upon Two Bills, etc." in The Prose Works of Jonathan Swift, Vol. XII,
Irish Tracts, 1728-1733 (Oxford: Shakespeare Head Press, 1955), pp.
191-92, quoted in Ravitch, Sword and Mitre, p. 135.

[27]Ibid., 110-22; other instances of this bias occur in Boulter,
Letters, pp. 11 (Jan. 19, 1824), 19 (April 29, 1725), 19 (May 1, 1725),
26 (June 3, 1725), 33-34 (Sept. 11, 1725), 85 (Dec. 3, 1725), 107 (Feb.
9, 1726), 115 (Feb. 18, 1726), 138 (June 10, 1727), 156 (August 26,
1727), 220 (Jan. 16, 1728), 220 (June 12, 1729), 272 (Dec. 14, 1729).
A rare instance in which Boulter suggested the appointment of an Irishman came when the temper of the Irish House of Commons was at a high
pitch; see Boulter, Letters, II, 23 (Aug. 7, 1730).

[28]Jonathan Swift to Thomas Pelham-Holles, 1st Duke of Newcastle,
July 3, 1725, cited in Mant, History of the Church, pp. 426-28.

[29]King to Joseph Gibson, Dec. 1, 1714, cited in Mant, History of
the Church, pp. 288-289.

[30]W. Killen, Ecclesiastical History, p. 332; King to Lord Carteret,
Lord Lieutenant, March 18, 1827, noted in Mant, History of the Church,
p. 460.

[31]Boulter, Letters, I, 165, 182-83.

[32]King to Charlott, April 20, 1715, cited in Mant, History of the
Church, p. 293; King to Edward Synge, Archbishop of Tuam, cited in King,
A Great Archbishop, p. 221.

[33]King to Edward Maule, June 9, 1722, cited in Mant, History of the
Church, p. 353; Boulter to Wake, Feb. 13, 1727, cited in Boulter, Letters,
I, 169-71; II, 182-83.

[34]King to Peter Brown, Bishop of Cork, Dec. 12, 1724, cited in Mant,
History of the Church, p. 426.

[35]W. Killen, Ecclesiastical History, II, 261; Boulter, Letters, II,
184-85; King to Gibson, Dec. 1, 1714; Swift to Newcastle, July 3, 1725,
cited in Mant, History of the Church, pp. 288-289, 426.

[36]J.C. Beckett, Protestant Dissent in Ireland 1687-1780 (London:
Faber and Faber, 1947), pp. 58-59.

[37]King to Wake, Nov. 10, 1719, cited in Mant, History of the Church,

p. 337, and in Killen, Ecclesiastical History, II, 29. Five years
earlier, King had noted that the Jacobite faction of the Established
Church had encouraged dissent to believe that accession of the
Hanoverians would facilitate a substitution of Dissent for the Church
of Ireland as the Establishment: King to Charlott, April 20, 1715,
cited in Mant, History of the Church, pp. 296-97.

[38]W. E. H. Lecky, Ireland in the Eighteenth Century, (5 vols.;
London: Longmans and Co., 1892), II, 200.

[39]Boulter, Letters, p. 182.

[40]Edwards, Church and State, p. 81; Boulter, Letters, II, 27.

[41]James A. Froude, The English in Ireland in the Eighteenth Century
(London; Longmans, Green and Co., 1886), II, 491-93.

[42]Anon., The Pedlar's Letter to the Bishops and Clergy of Ireland
(Dublin, 1760), noted in Lecky, Ireland, II, 20; Anon. Serious and
Seasonable Observations on . . . the Subject of Tithes, by a Curate.
(Dublin, 1787), pp. 70-71.

[43]Mant, History of the Church, p. 688; Killen, Ecclesiastical
History, II, 304; W. Brett, The Judgment of Truth, or Common Sense
and Good Nature, in behalf of Irish Roman Catholics (Dublin, 1770),
passim.

[44]Froude, The English in Ireland, II, 44-45, 211-212; Lecky, Ireland (London; Cabinet ed., 116-17), II, 15, 19-20; Killen, Ecclesiastical History, p. 332; Froude, The English in Ireland, II, 497.

[45]Constantia Maxwell, Country and Town in Ireland under the Georges
(Dundalk; W. Tempest, 1949), p. 351; Brett, Judgment of Truth, pp. 64-
65, 89-71; Beckett, Dissent, p. 99; Froude, The English in Ireland, II,
490-91.

[46]This type of criticism did not die in 1735, as shown in Amyas
Griffith, Observations on the Bishop of Cloyne's Pamphlet, in which
the Doctrine of Tithes is Candidly Considered (Dublin, 1787), pp. 24-
25. Although tithes were reduced in 1735, rising land values gradually
restored the Church's finances, and by 1785 it was again generally
agreed that the Church of Ireland was over-endowed; W. Killen, Ecclesiastical History, p. 313.

[47]Robert Fowler, Archbishop of Dublin, to Lord George Germain,
Feb. 5, 1780, Stopford-Sackville MSS, I, 267-68, noted in Beckett,
Dissent, p. 103.

[48]Lecky, Ireland, II, 34-35; Froude, The English in Ireland, II,
493-94; Anon., Farmer to Theophilus (Dublin, n. d.), pp. 34, 16.

[49] Henry Grattan to the Irish House of Commons, Jan. 17, 1788, in Collectanea Politica, I, 161-64.

[50] R.E. Burns, "Parsons, Priests, and People: the Rise of Irish Anticlericalism 1785-1789," Church History, xxxi (1962); Constantia Maxwell, Dublin under the Georges (London: G. S. Harrop and Co., 1940), p. 351.

Chapter II: Politics, Patronage and Preferment

[1] See Akenson, Church of Ireland, passim.

[2] The relative desirability of Irish dioceses during the eighteenth century has been analyzed by Donald Akenson in Church. By the early nineteenth century some changes had occurred, and the ten most sought-after sees might be listed in this descending order of importance: Armagh, Dublin, Derry, Cashel, Clogher, Tuam, Meath, Raphoe, Kildare, Waterford.

[3] Ravitch, "Social Origins," p. 317.

[4] Swift, "On the Bill for the Clergy's Residing on their Livings," in The Prose Works, XII, 181, quoted in Ravitch, "Social Origins," pp. 142-43.

[5] Lundeen, "Bench of Bishops," p. 73.

[6] Akenson, Church, pp. 12-23.

[7] Daniel A. Beaufort, Memoir of a Map of Ireland (London: W. Fadden and James Edwards, 1792), pp. 64-65.

[8] These returns are incomplete, inconsistent, and inaccurate. Tuam, Kildare and Cloyne are not represented on the list. In Ossory, Ferns, and Cork and Ross the totals were compiled on the basis of the number of parishes, not benefices. In a dozen cases the totals do not match. Later more accurate statistics were compiled, but by that time many of the distinctive conditions surrounding rights of presentation had been modified and they do not suggest the full complexity of the problem as it existed at the beginning of the century.

[9] William Stuart, Archbishop of Armagh, to Charles Brodrick, Archbishop of Cashel, Jan. 27, 1803, National Library of Ireland, Brodrick MSS, 8869/1.

[10] MacDonagh, G. C. Bolton, The Passing of the Irish Act of Union (London: Oxford University Press, 1966); Kevin B. Nolan, The Politics of Repeal (Toronto: University of Toronto Press, 1965).

[11]The Fifth Article of the Act of Union declared "that the Churches of England and Ireland, as now by law established, be united into one Protestant Episcopal Church, to be called, the United Church of England and Ireland; and that the doctrine, worship, discipline and government of the said United Church shall be, and shall remain in force forever, as the same are now by law established for the Church of England; and that the continuance and preservation of the said United Church, as the Established Church of England and Ireland, shall be deemed and taken to be an essential and fundamental part of the Union; and that in like manner the doctrine, worship, discipline and government of the Church of Scotland shall remain and be preserved as the same are now established by law, and by the Acts of the Union of the two kingdoms of England and Scotland." Statutes at Large, XLII, Part II, pp. 648-79.

[12]Robert Stewart, Marquess of Londonderry, Memoir and Correspondence of Viscount Castlereagh (12 vols.; London, 1848-53), III, 229-30.

[13]Henry Grattan, Memoir (5 vols.; London, 1834), IV, 390; Charles Cornwallis, Marquess Cornwallis, (3 vols.; London: J. Murray, 1859), II, 160-209.

[14]MacDonagh, Post-Bag, pp. 94-95, 207; Charles Agar to Hardwicke, October 26, 1801, February 23, 1805, Hardwicke MSS, 35731/131, 35756/235; Agar to the Irish Chief Secretary, August 6, 1805, Dublin, State Paper Office, Official Papers, Series II, Vol. I, Carton 528, No. 199/58.

[15]Lundeen, "Bench of Bishops," p. 50.

[16]Ibid.; II, 71; Bolton, Act of Union, p. 177.

[17]Stewart, Castlereagh, II, 31; III, 26, 309; Thomas O'Beirne, Bishop of Meath, to Hardwicke, June 27, 1801, quoted in MacDonagh, Past-Bag, pp. 73-74.

[18]Cornwallis, Correspondence, III, 170.

[19]Macartney to Thomas Pelham, First Lord Pelham, Home Secreatry, August 7, 1801, noted in MacDonagh, Post-Bag, p. 23.

[20]John Fitzgibbon, Earl of Clare, to William Eden, Baron Auckland, January 14, 1800, June 17, 1800, in McDowell, "Some Fitzgibbon Letters from the Sneyd Muniments in the John Rylands Library," John Rylands Library, Manchester, Bulletin, XXXIV (1952), p. 311.

[21]Ibid.

[22]Cornwallis to Henry Cavendish Bentinck, Earl of Portland, March 11, 1800, in Cornwallis, Correspondence, III, 209-210.

[23]Cornwallis had favored Agar, whose expectations, as has been seen, were disappointed.

[24]Elizabeth Johnston, Great Britain and Ireland, 1760-1800; A Study in Political Administration (Edinburgh; Oliver and Boyd, 1963), p. 70.

[25]Auckland to John Beresford, August 4, 1800, in William Beresford, Correspondence of the Right Hon. John Beresford Illustrative of the Last Thirty Years of the Irish Parliament (2 vols.; London: Woodfall and Kinder, 1854), I, 248-49.

[26]Cornwallis to Portland, quoted in MacDonagh, Post-Bag, p. 97.

[27]Cornwallis to the Bishop of Litchfield and Coventry, January 24, 1800; Cornwallis to Portland, March 24, 1800, in Cornwallis, Correspondence, III, 169, 217-18.

[28]Arthur Aspinall, ed., Later Correspondence of George III (Cambridge: Cambridge University Press, 1962 ff.), III, 378. Dr. John Randolph, Bishop of Oxford, became Bishop of London in 1809. Dr. Charles Manners Sutton, Bishop of Norwich, became Archbishop of Canterbury in 1805 and died in 1828.

[29]Countess of Bute to the King, Aug. 18, 1792, William Pitt to the King, Aug. 21, 1792, in Arthur Aspinall, ed., Later Correspondence, I, 608, 780, 580, 581; Lord Bute to Portland, Jan. 19, 1793, Welbeck MSS.

[30]The King to the Archbishop of Canterbury, Dec. 18, 1794, Jan. 4, 1800, A. Aspinall, ed., Later Correspondence, III, 306, 310.

[31]The King to Lady Charlotte Finch, July 13, 1800, A. Aspinall, ed., Later Correspondence, III, no. 2191.

[32]Stuart to the King, July 18, 1800, A. Aspinall, ed., Later Correspondence, III, 377-78.

[33]The King to Pitt, July 19, 1800, Aspinall, ed., Later Correspondence, III, 379.

[34]Cornwallis, Correspondence, III, 160, 218.

[35]Cornwallis to the Bishop of Lichfield and Coventry, Dec. 22, 1800, Kent Record Office MSS, in Aspinall, Later Correspondence, III, 436.

[36]MacDonagh, Post-Bag, p. 98.

[37]Charles Warburton, Bishop of Limerick, to Col. McMahon, December 10, 1813, Arthur Aspinall, ed., George IV, I, 343.

[38]The King to Lord Loughborough, Lord Chancellor, June 28, 1801; Moore, Archbishop of Canterbury, to the King, Jan. 29, 1801; the King to the primate, Jan. 29, 1801; the King to Moore, Jan. 29, 1801; Moore to the King, Feb. 2, 1801, in Aspinall, ed., Later Correspondence, III 474, 477-79, 481.

[39]Brodrick's elevation to Cashel was not due primarily to union engagements; his name was not on the patronage list entrusted to Hardwicke, though his family was both powerful and friendly to the government. The Home Secretary's recommendation of Brodrick must have helped: he noted that Brodrick knew the Irish language, in itself a significant comment on Brodrick's serious views towards his ecclesiastical responsibilities; Pelham to the King, Oct. 26, 1801, Aspinall, ed., Later Correspondence, No. 2546.

[40]Lord Hobart to Auckland, May, 1801, in Robert John Eden, Third Baron Auckland, ed., The Journals and Correspondence of William, Lord Auckland (4 vols.; London: R. Bentley, 1861-62), IV, 109-10.

[41]Stuart to Henry Addington, Viscount Sidmouth, Prime Minister, Nov. 27, 1801, Hardwicke MSS, 35771/152, Hardwicke to Addington, Dec. 22, 1801, Hardwicke MSS, 35771/154.

[42]Hardwicke to Stuart, Dec. 22, 1801, quoted in MacDonagh, Post-Bag, pp. 100-101, 101-104; Charles Abbot, Chief Secretary, to Stuart, Dec. 23, 1801, Hardwicke MSS, 35771/155-57.

[43]Stuart to Abbot, Dec. 27, 1801, Hardwicke MSS, 35771/157-160.

[44]Hardwicke to Addington, Abbot to Stuart, Dec. 28, 1801, Hardwicke MSS, 35771/160, 163.

[45]Stuart to Addington, Jan. 14, 1802, as quoted in Aspinall, ed., Later Correspondence, IV, 12-13.

[46]Hardwicke to Addington, December 28, 1801; Hardwicke to Stuart, December 29, 1801, MacDonagh, Post-Bag, pp. 107-109.

[47]Stuart to Hardwicke, December 31, 1801, MacDonagh, Post-Bag, p. 112.

[48]Hardwicke to Addington, December 29, 1801, Hardwicke MSS, 35771/166; Charles Lindsay, Secretary to Hardwicke, to Hardwicke, January 5, 1802, quoted in MacDonagh, Post-Bag, p. 112.

[49]Addington to Hardwicke, January 2, 1802, MacDonagh, Post-Bag, p. 11.

[50]Addington to Stuart, January 7, 1802, Stuart to Addington, January 14, 1802, MacDonagh, Post-Bag, pp. 113-14.

[51]Stuart to Addington, January 14, 1802, MacDonagh, _Post-Bag_, p. 116.

[52]Addington to Hardwicke, January 28, 1802, MacDonagh, _Post-Bag_, p. 117.

[53]The King to Addington, Feb. 16, 1802, quoted in Aspinall, ed., _Later Correspondence_, IV, 12-13.

[54]Abbot to Stuart, Dec. 23, 1801, quoted in MacDonagh, _Post-Bag_, pp. 101-104; Stuart to Abbot, Dec. 27, 1801, Dec. 31, 1801, Hardwicke MSS, 35771/157, 161-62.

[55]Stuart's decision to surrender the presidency of the charities as a gesture of his unhappiness was perhaps suggested to the King by Addington as a facesaving compromise.

[56]Lindsay to Hardwicke, Jan. 5, 1802, quoted in MacDonagh, _Post-Bag_, p. 112; Addington to Stuart, Jan. 11, 1802, Stuart to Addington, Jan. 14, 1802, Addington to Stuart, Jan. 23, 1802, Hardwicke MSS, 35771/174, 181, 182.

[57]Redesdale to Addington, Feb. 29, 1802, Sidmouth MSS, quoted in Aspinall, ed., _Later Correspondence_, IV, 12-13.

[58]Pelham to Hardwicke, July 21, 1802, MacDonagh, _Post-Bag_, p. 121.

[59]Hardwicke to Macartney, Aug. 1801, Macartney to Pelham, Aug. 7, 1801, quoted in MacDonagh, _Post-Bag_, pp. 23-24; Euseby Cleaver, Bishop of Ferns, to Hardwicke, May 9, 1802, June 9, 1802, Joseph Stock, Bishop of Killala and Achonry, to Lindsay, July 2, 1802, Hardwicke MSS 35734/210, 343, 35735/92.

[60]Hardwicke to Addington, Aug. 8, 1803, Marquess of Ely to Addington, Sept. 30, 1803, Hardwicke MSS, 35772/221, 35744/255.

[61]Hardwicke to Charles Yorke, Home Secretary, August 13, 1803, MacDonagh, _Post-Bag_, pp. 123-24; Hardwicke to Abbot, August 10, 1803, Hardwicke MSS, 35772/225.

[62]Lindsay to Hardwicke, Dec. 18, 1803, Hardwicke MSS, 35744/230; Lindsay to Marsden, Dec. 20, 1803, Dublin, S. P. O., Official Papers, Second Series, Carton 525, No. 260/5. He confessed to Marsden that he had devoted more time to seeing his friends than to parliamentary business, and, in a postscript, added, "Make me Raphoe if you can." Marsden and Hardwicke did.

[63]MacDonagh, _Post-Bag_, p. 122.

[64]Addington to Hardwicke, December 20, 1803, MacDonagh, _Post-Bag_, p. 123.

[65] Hardwicke to Charles Yorke, May 3, 1804, Hardwicke MSS, 35706/34.

[66] Hardwicke to Hawkesbury, May 24, 1804, Hardwicke MSS, 35709/37, 38, 39.

[67] Marquis of Waterford to Hardwicke, December 23, 1803, Hardwicke to Waterford, December 27, 1803, Hardwicke to Addington, December 28, 1803, MacDonagh, Post-Bag, pp. 126-29.

[68] Hardwicke to William Banks Jenkinson, Viscount Hawkesbury, May 26, 1804, Hardwicke MSS, 35709/43, 44.

[69] Ely to Hardwicke, May 11, 1804, Addington to Hardwicke, May 1804, "Substance of Lord Hardwicke's conversation with Lord Robert Tottenham, May 25, 1804," quoted in MacDonagh, Post-Bag, pp. 234-35, 137-39; Butson to Evan Nepean, Irish Chief Secretary, June 30, 1804, Hardwicke MSS, 35750/252.

[70] Hardwicke to John Beresford, Dec. 27, 1803, Hardwicke to Addington, Dec. 29, 1803, Hardwicke MSS, 35745/12, 34; Addington to Hardwicke, Jan., 1804, Beresford to Addington, Jan., 1804, Hardwicke to Addington, Jan., 1804, quoted in MacDonagh, Post-Bag, pp. 129-130; Lindsay to Hardwicke, Dec. 18, 1803, Hardwicke MSS, 35744/230.

[71] Ely to Hardwicke, May 11, 1804, Hardwicke MSS, in MacDonagh, Post-Bag, p. 133.

[72] Addington to Hardwicke, May 14, 1804, Hardwicke MSS, in MacDonagh, Post-Bag, p. 134.

[73] Hardwicke to Hawkesbury, May 24, 1804, Hardwicke MSS, in MacDonagh, Post-Bag, pp. 139-142.

[74] Hawkesbury to Hardwicke, June 18, 1804, Hardwicke MSS, Loftus to William Pitt, June 13, 1804, Hardwicke MSS, MacDonagh, Post-Bag, pp. 143-44.

[75] Waterford to Beresford, November 12, 1804, MacDonagh, Post-Bag, p. 213.

[76] Stuart to Hardwicke, September 28, 1804, Hardwicke MSS, MacDonagh, Post-Bag, p. 147.

[77] Hawkesbury to Hardwicke, May 20, 1804, quoted in MacDonagh, Post-Bag, pp. 136-37.

[78] Hardwicke to Lady Londonderry, Nov. 7, 1804, Hardwicke MSS, 35753/182, in David C. Douglas, general editor, English Historical Documents (New York: Oxford University Press, 1955-69), English Historical Documents, 1783-1832 (Arthur Aspinall and E.A. Smith,

eds., London; Eyre and Spottiswoode, 1959), p. 264.

[79]Hawkesbury to Hardwicke, December 1804, Hardwicke MSS, in Mac-Donagh, Post-Bag, p. 217.

[80]Hawkesbury to Hardwicke, May 20, 1804, quoted in MacDonagh, Post-Bag, pp. 136-37.

[81]Hardwicke to Cleaver, June 6, 1804, Hardwicke to Butson, March 27, 1804, Stock to Hardwicke, Jan. 11, 1806, C. Mongan Warburton, Dean of Ardagh, to Hardwicke, Oct. 26, 1801, Cleaver to Hardwicke, July 14, 1807, Stock to Hardwicke, Dec. 14, 1805, Hardwicke MSS, 35750/17, 35777/87, 35764/221, 35731/115, 35764/10.

[82]Hardwicke to Napean, June 9, 1804, quoted in MacDonagh, Post-Bag, p. 142.

[83]Cleaver to Hardwicke, May 9, 1802, Hardwicke to Cleaver, June 6, 1804, Hardwicke to Butson, March 27, 1804, Hardwicke MSS, 35734/210, 343, 35750/17, 35777/87.

[84]Stuart to Hardwicke, Sept. 28, 1804, Beresford to Hardwicke, June 26, 1804, Hardwicke to Beresford, July 10, 1804, Hardwicke MSS, 35752/264, 35750/207, 361.

[85]See: Richmond to Charles Lennox, Duke of Richmond and Lennox, to A. Wellesley, Irish Chief Secretary, July 1, 1807, in A.R. Wellesley, Duke of Wellington, Despatches, Correspondence and Memoranda of Arthur Duke of Wellington (8 vols.; London: John Murray, 1867-1880), Ireland, pp. 103-4.

[86]Union list of ecclesiastical engagements, Dec. 26, 1804, quoted in MacDonagh, Post-Bag, pp. 43-46.
    Archbishop of Cashel - To succeed to Dublin.
        (Translated accordingly, vice Fowler, deceased).
    Mr. Alexander - The Bench
        (Done. Appointed Bishop of Clonfert by the removal of Bishop
        Beresford to Kilmore, Kilmore to Cashel, and Cashel to Dublin.)
    Bishop of Killala - Strong assurances given to Lord Abercorn of
        his being translated, which Lord Cornwallis intended to do after
        he found an opportunity of removing the Bishop of Kilmore to a
        better See.
        (Translated to Londonderry, vice the Earl of Bristol, deceased.)
    Rev. Mr. French - The Bench of Bishops.
        (promoted to Waterford, vice Marlay, deceased.)
    Dean Warburton - Promised to recommend him strongly to Lord Hard-
        wicke on account of his general good character, and of his
        services during the Rebellion and the Union contest. Lord
        Cornwallis intended to have him promoted to the Bench after the
        Union Engagements had been filled. (The King has declared he

will never make him a Bishop. He was a Roman Catholic ori-
ginally; his name, Mongan, and his father an Irish harper.
He himself was a missionary, and acquired, by plausible
manners, to the amount of £2,000 a year and upwards of Church
preferment.)
Rev. Mr. Cleland - Tutor to Lord Castlereagh. Promised the
Rectorship of Armagh.
  (Promoted to the Precentorship of Armagh, vice Alexander.)
Rev. Richard Straubenzie Wolfe, Lord Kilwarden's nephew -
Better preferment. (He was promoted to the Prebend of Ticolme
and Rectory of Templepeter, in the Diocese of Leighlin and
Ferns; also to the vicarage of Dunlackney and Agha, in the same
diocese, vice Alexander, promoted. The above mentioned Prebend,
etc., vacated by the unfortunate assassination of Mr. Wolfe,
have been given to a son of Dr. Kearney, the Provost, to whom
I was desirous of an opportunity of showing a personal attention, the College being at present inclined to support his
Majesty's Government, and at all times an important body.
Rev. Mr. Besset - Promised a living of £500 or £600 a year, and
to resign his present preferment of £300 a year. Through him
managed Cope, M.P. for Armagh.
  (Not done, because the primate refused to present a person
  recommended by Government to his living.)
Rev. John Hill, brother to Sir. G. Hill - Promised preferment
and to be recommended to Lord Hardwicke for early promotion.
  (Promoted to the Prebend of Clonmethan, vice Lord Strange-
  ford, deceased.)
Rev. Mr. Paul, Lord O'Neill's tutor - His lordship has had a
promise that Paul should be promoted.
  (This was done accordingly by the Rectory and Vicarage of
  Knockbride, vice Thomas Smyth, deceased.)
Rev. John Molesworth Staples - Promised Lord Clifden to give him
a living.
  (Done by giving him a living in Co. Kildare.)
Rev. John Rowley - Promised his father, Mr. Clotionthy Rowley,
that he should be promoted.
  (Not yet done.)
Rev. Mr. Clemlow - Lord Cornwallis promised his uncle, Mr. Mathew,
that he would recommend him strongly for a preferment. (This
private wish was connected with a publick transaction.) His
uncle was an old acquaintance of Lord Cornwallis, but being one
of Lord Downshire's members, he was obliged to take away his
place. As some return, and to show that there was nothing
personal in it, he put down his nephew in the manner above
stated.
  (Mr. Clemlow was accordingly promoted to the Rectory of
  Westena, alias Vastina, in the diocese of Meath.)
The Rev. Dean Graves - was promised preferment both by Lord
Cornwallis and Lord Camden.
  (Promotion to the Deanery of Connor, vice Dobbs, deceased.)

Rev. Gilbert Holmes – a letter from Lord Cornwallis, 5th August, 1801, stated that Mr. Holmes has been forgot (sic).

(Promoted to the Deanery of Ardfect, vice Graves, promoted.) Exclusive of the above list of Positive Engagements in the Church, there are some applications which Lord Cornwallis would have been glad to have complied with, if proper opportunities had offered, and which are entered in a separate book of applications under similar circumstances.

Rev. Mr. Usher – A friend of Lord Belvedere.

(A supplementary engagement given in by Mr. Cook, and satisfied by the Deanery of Asnamurthis, in the Diocese of Meath, vice Himan, deceased.)

N.B. – Besides those, I have presented the Rev. Ponsonby G. Gouldsbury to the Rectory of Raddinstown, vacated by Dr. French, at the particular request of Mr. Smyth, member of the Co. Westmeath, as well as his colleague Mr. Rochfort. Rev. Mr. Lee, brother to the member for the county of Waterford, to the Deanery Kilmacduagh. Also Rev. Mr. Hunt, nephew of Mr. Hunt, an old Surveyor-General and very inefficient, thereby saving the expense of placing him on Income Incidents."

[87] Warburton to Duke of Buckingham, Jan. 12, 1798, Great Britain, Historical Manuscripts Commission, Report on the Manuscripts of J. B. Fortescue, Preserved at Dropmore (10 vols.; London: HMSO, 1892ff); Lundeen, "Bench of Bishops."

[88] Power le Poer French to Hardwicke, Nov. 4, 1805, Beresford to Hardwicke, July 18, 1804, Hardwicke MSS, 35763/108, 35751/56; also see MacDonagh, Post-Bag, pp. 73-74.

[89] A. Wellesley to Richmond, June 30, 1807, Wellington, Ireland, pp. 101ff.

[90] Hardwicke to the Countess of Londonderry, November 7, 1807, Hardwicke MSS, 35753/182.

[91] Charles Chester to Lindsay, Feb. 17, 1802, quoted in MacDonagh, Post-Bag, pp. 13-14.

[92] Hardwicke to Abbot, Aug. 9, 1803, Hardwicke MSS, 35772/224.

[93] Hardwicke to Nepean, June 9, 1804, noted in MacDonagh, Post-Bag, pp. 142-43; Wellesley to Stuart, Wellesley to Warburton, Bishop of Limerick Dec. 25, 1807, in Wellington, Ireland, pp. 78-79, 251-52.

[94] Stuart to Hardwicke, Sept. 28, 1804, Hardwicke MSS, 35742/264.

[95] Grenville to Windham, June 5, 1806, Bedford to Grenville, July 13, 1806, July 14, 1806, printed in Fortescue MSS, 179, 231, 234-35, 238.

[96] A. Wellesley to Richmond, June 28, National Library of Ireland, Richmond MSS, 58/7.

[97] A. Wellesley to William Wellesley-Pole, March 17, 1808, Ireland, p. 367.

[98] Warburton to McMahon, December 10, 1813, Aspinall, George IV, I, 343.

[99] A. Wellesley to Richmond, June 28, 1807, June 29, 1807, Wellington, Ireland, pp. 97, 98; A. Wellesley to Richmond, July 21, 1807, Richmond MSS, 58/34.

[100] Liverpool to Richmond, July 14, 1809, Dundas to Richmond, July 17, 1809, Egremont to Richmond, July 19, 1809, Richmond to Egremont, July 31, 1809, Richmond MSS, 71/1385, 59/171, 71/1367, 69/1245, 1254.

[101] Richmond to Liverpool, July 31, 1809, Richmond MS 71/1368.

[102] Liverpool to Richmond, July 26, 1807, Aug. 4, 1809, Aug. 31, 1809, Richmond MSS, 65/779, 71/1381, 1383.

[103] A. Wellesley to Richmond, June 22, 1807, June 26, 1807, June 28, 1807, June 29, 1807, July 22, 1807, July 24, 1807, Wellington, Ireland, pp. 93, 97, 98, 123, 127, 128.

[104] A. Wellesley to Richmond, Richmond MSS, 58/12; Wellesley to O'Beirne, May 27, 1807; Wellesley to Agar, June 9, 1807, Wellington, Ireland, pp. 67, 78.

[105] Ely to Spencer Percival, January 7, 1810, Prime Minister, Richmond MSS, 888.

[106] Denis Gray, Spencer Percival; The Evangelical Prime Minister 1762-1812 (Manchester; University Press, 1963), p. 22.

[107] Percival, memorandum, n.d. (1810), Richmond MSS, 66/888, Liverpool to Richmond, Sept. 7, 1808, May 25, 1809, Richmond MSS, 72/1628, 71/1388. This suggestion, which clearly originated in George III's mind, embarrassed politicians, because no English bishop wanted an Irish see (in 1800 only two bishops showed any interest in the Irish primacy!) and because no politician, burdened by an immense backlog of promises to Englishmen, favored granting an English bishopric to an Irishman: see A. Wellesley to Richmond, July 22, 1807, Richmond MSS 58/35.

[108] Richmond to Richard Ryder, Home Secretary, and Percival, Jan. 1, 1810, Richmond MSS, 62/504.

[109]Stock to A. Wellesley, June 27, 1807, Dublin, State Paper Office, Official Papers, Second Series, I (1790-1810), 537/231-35.

[110]Richmond to Ryder, Jan. 11, 1810, Richmond MSS, 62/495, 66/888.

[111]Wellesley-Pole, Irish Chief Secretary, to Richmond, March 26, 1810, Richmond MSS, 73/1699.

[112]Ibid., March 21, 1810, Richmond MSS, 73/1703.

[113]Richmond to Percival, Sept. 16, 1810, Richmond MSS, 61/360.

[114]Richmond, memorandum, Sept. 16, 1810, Richmond MSS, 61/360.

[115]Richmond to Percival, Sept. 16, 1810, Percival to Richmond, Oct. 12, 1810, Oct. 29, 1810, Richmond MSS, 61/360, 66/880; Wellesley-Pole to Richmond, Nov. 17, 1810, Richmond MSS, 73/1663.

[116]A. Wellesley to Richmond, July 21, 1807, July 22, 1807, quoted in Wellington, Despatches, Ireland, pp. 122-23; Warburton to Stuart, April 2, 1810, Stuart to Richmond, April 2, 1810, Brodrick to Stuart, April 3, 1810, Richmond MSS, 63/600.

[117]W. Wellesley-Pole to Stuart, April 10, 1810, Richmond MSS, 63/599.

[118]Richmond to Stuart, April 21, 1810, Richmond MSS, 63/898.

[119]Richmond to Wellesley-Pole, March 24, 1810, Richmond MSS, 64/643.

[120]Wellesley-Pole to Richmond, March 26, 1810, Richmond MSS, 73/1699.

[121]Richmond to Wellesley-Pole, March 30, 1810, Richmond MSS, 64/638.

[122]Ibid., March 31, 1810, Richmond MSS, 64/637; Percival to Ryder, April 1, 1810, Richmond MSS, 66/875.

[123]Bishop of Limerick to Stuart, April 2, 1810, Stuart to Richmond, April 2, 1810, Brodrick to Stuart, April 3, 1810, Richmond MSS, 63/601, 66/900, 63/600.

[124]Bishop of Limerick to Stuart, April 2, 1810, Richmond MSS, 601.

[125]Broderick to Stuart, April 3, 1810, Richmond MSS, 600.

[126]Stuart to Wellesley-Pole, April 8 [?], 1810, Richmond MSS, 1699a.

[127] Wellesley-Pole to Richmond, April 3, 1810, Richmond MSS, 73/1695; Stuart to Richmond, n. d. (c. April 6, 1810), Richmond MSS, 63/602; Wellesley-Pole to Richmond, April 10, 1810, Richmond MSS, 73/1691.

[128] Richmond to Wellesley-Pole, April 16, 1810, Richmond MSS, 64/632.

[129] Richmond to Stuart, April 21, 1810, Richmond MSS, 66/898.

[130] Stuart to Richmond, April 18 [?], 1810, Richmond MSS, 901.

[131] Wellesley-Pole to Richmond, March 21, 1811, April 11, 1811, May 17, 1811, Richmond MSS, 65/755, 719, 767.

[132] Richmond, memorandum, December 9, 1811, Richmond MSS, 565a.

[133] Ryder to Richmond, December 17, 1811, Richmond MSS, 63/567.

[134] Liverpool to Richmond, September 25, 1812, Richmond MSS, 74/892.

[135] Robert Peel, Irish Chief Secretary, to Richmond, June 8, 1813, Richmond MSS, 1467.

[136] Richmond to Peel, June 10, 1813, Richmond MSS, 71/1408.

[137] Richmond to Peel, June 20, 1813, Richmond MSS, 71/1404.

[138] Richmond to the Bishop of Cork, April 19, 1813, Richmond to Peel, April 24, 1813, Liverpool to Richmond, May 1, 1813, Richmond MSS 74/1836, 71/1436, 68/1102.

[139] Richmond to Peel, May 5, 1813, Richmond MSS, 68/1157.

[140] Peel to Richmond, April 28, 1813, Richmond MSS, 69/1180.

[141] Peel to Richmond, May 11, 1813, Richmond MSS, 1163.

[142] Liverpool to Richmond, May 1, 1813, Richmond MSS, 1102.

[143] Peel, memorandum, June 8, 1813, Peel MSS, 40283/102; O'Beirne to Peel, Oct. 20, 1812, Richmond MSS; Peel, memorandum, March 17, 1814, O'Beirne to Peel, Peel to John Wilson Croker, 1818, Peel MSS, 40235/169, 40280/135, 40281/98, 40284/127, 40295/90, 40294/152.

[144] John Leslie to Peel, Oct. 24, 1817, Peel MSS, 40181/130-31.

[145] Ibid.

[146]Talbot to Peel, May 6, 1818, British Museum, Peel MSS, 40194/250.

[147]Charles Chetwynd, Earl Talbot to William Gregory, September 10, 1819, December 13, 1819, printed in Augusta Isabella Gregory, Mr. Gregory's Letter-Box, 1813-1830 (London: Smith, Elder and Co., 1898), pp. 130-32.

[148]Liverpool to Richard Colley Wellesley, Marquess Wellesley, Lord Lieutenant, June 7, 1822, Wellesley MSS, 37299/187-90.

[149]Richard St. Lawrence to Peel, Feb. 27, April, 1822, Peel MSS, 40345/94.

[150]Liverpool to Wellesley, June 7, 1822, Wellesley MSS, 37299/187-90.

[151]Henry Goulburn, Irish Chief Secretary, to Wellesley, May 16, 1822, Wellesley MSS, 37299/122-24; Liverpool to Wellesley, June 7, 1822, Wellesley MSS, 37299/187-90.

[152]Goulburn to Wellesley, May 16, 1822, Wellesley MSS, 37299/122-24.

[153]Peel to Lloyd, May 15, 1822, Lloyd to Peel, May 16, 1822, quoted in Charles Stuart Parker, Sir Robert Peel . . . from his Private Correspondence (3 vols.; London: Murray, 1899), I, 324-25; Peel to Nathaniel Alexander, Bishop of Down and Connor, June 19, 1822, Peel MSS, 40347/90.

[154]Peel to Liverpool, Nov. 2, 1822, Kingston-on-Thames, Surrey Record Office, Goulburn MSS, II/14; Percy Jocelyn was deprived one year after the King had intervened personally, at the behest of Lord Roden, to translate Jocelyn to Clogher. Jocelyn was apprehended on a charge of homosexuality in the summer of 1822, and his arrest presented the government and the Church with a serious embarrassment. Liverpool wished to deflect attention from Jocelyn by accepting his resignation; Goulburn, Peel, and reform-minded Churchmen resisted (Goulburn to Peel, Peel to Goulburn, Aug. 17, 1822, Sept. 2, 1822, Peel MSS, 40328/112, 116-117). The trial took place in September and October, 1822 (Peel to Goulburn, Goulburn to Peel, Sept. 10, 1822, Oct. 24, 1822, Peel MSS, 40328/131, 160-161) and was given great, if discreet, coverage by the Irish press (see, for example, the Dublin Evening Post, July 25, Aug. 1, 31, Sept. 10, 14, 17, 21, Oct. 5, 24, Nov. 5, 7, 12). Jocelyn was sent abroad, sustained by a monthly allowance from his family. A year later he returned Ireland briefly, agitating Peel and Goulburn, who dared not expose him by ordering his arrest. Eventually he was induced to return to the Continent. (see Goulburn to Peel, Dec. 3, 1823, Peel to Goulburn, Dec. 7, 1823, Goulburn to Peel, Dec. 12, 1823, Dec. 15, 1823, Dec. 19, 1823, Dec. 26, 1823, Peel to Goulburn, Dec. 31, 1823, Goulburn to

Peel, Jan. 2, 1824, Peel MSS, 40329/237-38, 249-50, 251, 353-55, 257, 261, 263, 40330/1).

[155]William Bennett, Bishop of Cloyne, to Thomas Brooke Clarke, Aug. 6, 1820, Aug. 27, 1820, Northern Ireland Public Record Office MSS, D1108/13/74. Peel's role in this case clearly reflects his attitude toward the Church of Ireland. At first he opposed allowing Jocelyn to resign; this would be interpreted as leniency (Peel to Goulburn, Sept. 2, 1822, Goulburn MSS, II/14. When the trial was held, Peel urged vigorous prosecution (Peel to Goulburn, Nov. 11, 1822, Goulburn MSS, II/14. Jocelyn apparently escaped and Peel, now reversed himself, declaring that the publicity of a nationwide search would, for the Church, outweigh gains derived from application of the full force of the law. (Peel to Goulburn, Dec. 23, 1823, Goulburn MSS, II/14.) "Such a wretch as he is, is deserving of no consideration, but the blow, which would reach him, would inflict a dreadful wound on the Church." Also see Lord Liverpool, Prime Minister, to Peel, Nov. 2, 1822, Goulburn MSS, II/14.

[156]Liverpool to Wellesley, Aug. 7, 1822, Wellesley MSS, 37299/ 324-25.

[157]Goulburn to Peel, Oct. 18, 1822, Peel MSS, 40328/150-57; Edward Brynn, "A Church of Ireland Diocese in the Age of Catholic Emancipation," Historical Magazine of the Protestant Episcopal Church, XL (June, 1971), 185-196.

[158]Warburton to Peel, May 7, 1822, July 20, 1822; Peel to Warburton, Aug. 1, 1822, Peel MSS, 40347/43, 40348/33, 180-81, 185.

[159]Alexander to Peel, Dec. 24, 1822, Robert Fowler, Bishop of Ossory, to Peel, Nov. 4, 1822, St. Lawrence to Peel, Feb. 10, 1823, March 8, 1823, Thomas Elrington, Bishop of Ferns and Leighlin, to Peel, April 15, 1823, Peel MSS, 40353/213, 40352/218, 40354/298, 40355/48, 283; Goulburn to Wellesley, May 11, 1824, Wellesley MSS, 37302/261-62.

[160]Liverpool to Wellesley, Aug. 19, 1826, British Museum, Liverpool MSS, 37304/1778.

[161]Goulburn to Peel, Aug. 12, 1826, Peel MSS, 40332/84-87.

[162]Wellesley to Goulburn, Oct. 15, 1826, Goulburn MSS II/21.

[163]Goulburn to Peel, Aug. 15, 1826, Peel MSS, 40332/94.

[164]Ibid., Oct. 1, 1826, Oct. 16, 1826, Peel MSS, 40332/133-138, 146.

[165] Wellesley to Richmond, July 5, 1807, Wellington, Ireland, p. 107.

[166] Goulburn to Peel, Aug. 15, 1826, Peel MSS, 40332/94; Charles Arbuthnot to Henry, Earl Bathurst, Sept. 1, 1826, Great Britain, Historical Manuscripts Commission, Report on the Manuscripts of Henry Seymore, Third Earl Bathurst, Preserved at Cirencester Park. (Francis Lawrence Berkeley, ed.; London: HMSO, 1923), p. 614.

[167] See: Liverpool to Wellesley, Aug. 19, 1826; Wellington to Wellesley, Aug. 20, 1826, Aug. 21, 1826; Wellington to Liverpool, Aug. 30, 1826, Sept. 1, 1826, Liverpool to Wellington, Aug. 31, 1826, Wellesley MSS, 37304/181-206.

[168] Charles Arbuthnot to Bathurst, September 1, 1826, Bathurst MSS, p. 614.

[169] Liverpool to Wellesley, Aug. 19, 1826, British Museum, Liverpool MSS, 37304/1778.

[170] Arthur Wellesley, Duke of Wellington to Wellesley, Aug. 20, 1826, Liverpool MSS, 37304/181-85.

[171] Peel to Goulburn, Sept. 7, 1827, Goulburn MSS, II/16.

[172] Goulburn to Wellesley, April 5, 1827, Wellesley MSS, 37305/75-79.

[173] Goulburn to Peel, Oct. 28, 1826, Peel MSS, 40332/166-69.

[174] Peel to Goulburn, Nov. 1, 1826, Peel MSS, 40332/178.

[175] Goulburn to Peel, Dec. 2, 1828, encl., John George Beresford, Archbishop of Armagh, to Goulburn, Nov. 29, 1828, and Richard Laurence to Beresford, Nov. 15, 1828, Peel MSS, 40333/66-71.

[176] 3 Hansard's Parliamentary Debates, IV (1831), 1409-10; VI (1831), 1193-94, 1305-7.

[177] Peel to Earl Haddington, Lord Lieutenant, Jan. 4, 1835, cited in Parker, Peel, II, 285-86.

[178] Lord Elliot to Peel, July 15, 1842, cited in Parker, Peel, III, 38.

[179] Peel, memorandum, Nov. 13, 1844, cited in Parker, Peel, III, 120-21.

[180] Richard Whately, Archbishop of Dublin, to Wellesley, May 10, 1834, Wellesley MSS, 37307/39.

[181]John A. Russell, Thoughts on the State of the Established Church and on the Means by which its Efficiency may be Promoted (Dublin, 1835), p. 26.

[182]G. I. T. Machin, "The Maynooth Grant, the Dissenters and Disestablishment, 1845-1847," English Historical Review, LXXXII (Jan., 1967), 68; Gilbert A. Cahill, "The Protestant Association and the anti-Maynooth Agitation of 1845," Catholic Historical Review, XLIII (October, 1957), 284 ff.

Chapter III: The Movement for Internal Reform 1800-1830

[1]Stock to Hardwicke, Oct. 31, 1805, Knox to Hardwicke, Oct. 26, 1802, Knox to William Wickham, Irish Chief Secretary, Aug. 19, 1803, Lindsay to Hardwicke, Oct. 13, 1805, Butson to Hardwicke, Sept. 10, 1805, March, 1806, Hardwicke MSS, 35763/78, 35736/258, 35741/284, 35762/237, 42, 35766/344.

[2]Lindsay to Hardwicke, Oct. 13, 1805, Hardwicke MSS, 35762/237.

[3]Butson to Hardwicke, March, 1806, Hardwicke MSS, 35763/344.

[4]Stock to Long, Oct. 31, 1805, Hardwicke MSS, 35763/78.

[5]Knox to Hardwicke, Oct. 26, 1802, Hardwicke MSS, 35736/258; Robert Jones to Clarke, April 5, 1800, Johnson to Clarke, Feb. 22, 1801, Belfast, Northern Ireland Public Record Office MSS, D1108/B/16, 24.

[6]For a discussion of the following points in greater detail see Akenson, Church, Chapter I.

[7]In the late eighteenth century Irish deaneries ranged in value from ₤20 (Ross and Clonfert) to ₤1700 (Down). Derry and Raphoe were worth ₤1600, St. Patrick's and Clogher ₤800. Seventeen of thirty-two deaneries were worth between ₤100 and ₤300 per annum. See Mant, Church of Ireland, II, 659-70.

[8]Akenson, Church, pp. 6, 10.

[9]Vavasour to Brodrick, March 24, 1814, Brodrick to Vavasour, March 27, 1814, Vavasour to Brodrick, March 29, 1814, Patrick Duigenan to Brodrick, Jan. 5, Aug. 9, Sept. 3, 1815, Brodrick MSS, 8861/7.

[10]Arthur Young, A Tour of Ireland with General Observations on the

Present State of that Kingdom (2 vols.; Dublin, 1780) II, 81-82.

11Stewart, Castlereagh, II, 70-71.

12House of Commons, Report of His Majesty's Commissioners of Ecclesiastical Inquiry: Ireland, 1831 Vol. IX (1831), pp. 74 ff.

13Ibid.

14Ibid.

15Ibid.

16Warburton to Marquess of Buckingham, Jan. 12, 1798, Fortescue MSS, IV, 55-56.

17Alexander to Wickham, Aug. 19, 1803, Hardwicke MSS, 35741/284; Brodrick to William Bennett, Bishop of Cloyne, n. d. [probably February 1802], Brodrick MSS, 8888.

18John Russell, Duke of Bedford to William Grenville, April 14, 1806, Fortescue MSS, VIII.

19Meath to Abbot, March 21, 1804, in Charles Abbot, Baron Colchester, Diary and Correspondence (3 vols; London: J. Murray, 1861), I, 492-93; J. Petroic to Robert Ponsonby Tottenham Loftus, Bishop of Killaloe and Kilfenora, Aug. 4, 1810; Loftus to Petroic, Aug. 29, 1810, Lovett to Brodrick, April 24, 1804, Brodrick MSS, 8821, 8874/2.

20Thomas Brainard, Bishop of Limerick, to Brodrick, Aug. 3, 1802, Brodrick to R. Stopford, Bishop of Cork, Nov. 5, 1802, Stuart to Brodrick, May, 1805, Brodrick MSS, 5561/4, 8888, 8869/3. Knox to Stuart, May 1805, Brodrick MSS, 35759/214-222; Brodrick to Rev. Chitwood, May 3, 1804, Brodrick to Patrick Duigenan, July 16, 1804, Brodrick MSS, 8888.

21Lindsay, "memorial," n. d. Brodrick MSS, 8888.

22Bennett to Brodrick, Oct. 2, 1819, Brodrick MSS, 8892.

23Warburton, Bishop of Limerick, to Stuart, April 2, 1810, Richmond MSS, 63/601; Stuart to Brodrick, March 24, 1808, Brodrick MSS, 8869.

24Stuart to Brodrick, Feb. 3, 1808, Brodrick MSS, 8869.

25 1 Hansard, XXXV (1805), 51; Stuart to Brodrick, Feb. 8, 1805, Brodrick MSS, 8869/3.

[26]"Private Instructions," 1802, noted in Colchester, _Diary and Correspondence_, I, 301-302.

[27]Brodrick to Hardwicke, Aug. 10, 1801, John Porter, Bishop of CLogher, to Wickham, Aug. 19, 1803, Knox to Hardwicke, Dec. 13, 1804, Hardwicke to Butson, July 29, 1805, Butson to Hardwicke, Sept. 10, 1805, Hardwicke MSS, 35703/32, 35741/272, 35754/119, 35761/103, 35762/42; Hardwicke to Stuart, Nov. 8, 1802, Hardwicke MSS, 37776/54.

[28]Bedford to Grenville, May 2, 1806, _Fortescue MSS_, 128-30.

[29]Stuart to Elliott, APril 8, 1806, Bedford to Grenville, April 14, 1806, _Fortescue MSS_, VIII, 90-93, 98.

[30]Bedford to Grenville, April 14, 1806, May 2, 1806, Stuart to Bedford, n. d. (May, 1806), _Fortescue MSS_, VIII (1912), pp. 97, 128-29, 130-31.

[31]O'Beirne to Wellesley, May 16, 1808, quoted in Wellington, _Ireland_, p. 438; Stuart to Richmond, April 2, 1810, Richmond MSS, 63/900, 901.

[32]Wellesley to O'Beirne, May 27, 1807, Wellington, p. 62; Stuart to Richmond, April 18, 1810, Richmond MSS, 63/901.

[33]Wellesley to O'Beirne, Nov. 19, 25, Dec. 16, 1807, in Wellington, _Ireland_, pp. 191-94, 226-27; Stuart to Brodrick, March 24, 1808, Brodrick MSS, 8869/5; Wellesley to Robert Fowler, Archdeacon of Dublin, April 21, 1807, in Wellington, _Ireland_, p. 9.

[34]Mant, _History_, II, 434.

[35](Edward Stopford), "Statement of First Fruits Fund, 1823-4," Armagh Public Library, Beresford Papers, I.

[36]Akenson, _Church_, p. 126.

[37]O'Beirne to Brodrick, Feb. 23, 1803, Brodrick MSS, 8873. Young in 1780 estimated the wealth of the major dignities of the Church at the following:

Archbishops:		Deaneries
8,000	Armagh	150
5,000	Dublin	1,000
4,000	Cashel	300
4,000	Tuam	500

Bishoprics:

3,400	Meath (Clonmaienoise)	50
7,000	Derry	1,600
2,600	Raphoe	1,600
4,000	Clogher	800
2,000	Dromore	400
2,600	Kilmore	600
---	Down	1,700
2,300	Connor	200
2,600	Kildare	120
2,000	Ossory	600
---	Ferns	200
2,200	Leighlin	200
3,500	Limerick	600
---	Ardfert & Aghadoe	60
2,500	Waterford	400
---	Lismore	300
2,700	Cork	400
---	Ross	20
2,500	Cloyne	220
2,300	Killaloe	140
---	Kilfenora	210
3,700	Elphin	250
2,400	Clonfert	120
---	Kilmacduagh	120
2,900	Killala	100
---	Achonry	---

cf. Mant, History of the Church, pp. 659-60.

[38] Young, Tour, II, 81-82. By 1800 these figures had risen considerably.

[39] Charles Tottenham to Castlereagh, quoted in Stewart, Castlereagh, III, 323.

[40] O'Beirne to Abbot, Jan. 11, March 8, 1802, in Colchester, Diary and Correspondence, I, 345, 404-405.

[41] Stuart to Brodrick, Aug. 21, 1804, March 31, 1806, Brodrick MSS, 8869/3, 4.

[42] Ibid., Aug. 21, 1804, July 9, Dec. 11, 1809, Brodrick MSS, 8869/3, 5.

[43] Hardwicke to the Bishop of Killaloe, Oct. 23, 1802, Hardwicke MSS, 35776/68-70.

[44]Stuart to Brodrick, Feb. 7, 1802, NLI MSS 8869/8; Great Britain, Parliamentary Papers, Vol. CXXXV (Accounts, Vol. XVI), 1823, "Accounts Relating to the Church Establishment of Ireland," p. 34.

[45]Stuart to Brodrick, March 15, 1803, III Brodrick MSS, 8869/71.

[46]Great Britain, Parliament, Sessional Papers, Vol. I (1802-1803), pp. 371-87: "Bill to Enable the Commissioners of First Fruits in Ireland to Lend Certain Sums of Money (Interest Free) to Incumbents of Benefices there, for the Purpose of Enabling Them to Erect Glebe Houses and Offices Convenient for their Residence; and to make Provision for the Repayment of all Loans to be Made by the Said Commissioners"; Bill as Amended, Sessional Papers, Vol. I (1802-1803), pp. 529-37; Wickham to the Bishop of Killaloe, June 18, 1803, Dublin, S. P. O., Series II, Vol. I, Carton 522, No. 144.

[47]Ibid.

[48]Stuart to Brodrick, June 19, 26, 1803, Brodrick MSS, 8869/2; Hardwicke appears to have encouraged him in this separate initiative; Knox to Hardwicke, Dec. 13, 1804, Hardwicke MSS, 35754/119; Stuart to Brodrick, March 12, 1804, Brodrick MSS, 8869/2.

[49]Stuart to Brodrick, Feb. 18, 1804, Brodrick MSS, 8869/2.

[50]Knox to Hardwicke, Oct. 25, 1802, Hardwicke MSS, 35734/158; Stuart to Brodrick, April 8, 1803, Brodrick MSS, 8869/3.

[51]Brodrick to Irish Chief Secretary [?], June, 1805, S. P. O. Official Papers, Series 2, Vol. I, 529/208/7.

[52]Stuart to Brodrick, March 21, 1805, Brodrick MSS, 8869/3.

[53]Great Britain, Parliamentary Papers, "House of Commons, Orders for Ecclesiastical Returns," June 5, 1805, State Paper Office: Official Papers, Series 2 (Vol. I 1790-1810), 530/219/1.

[54]Stuart to Brodrick, Oct. 29, 1805, Brodrick MSS, 8869/3.

[55]O'Beirne to Castlereagh, May 10, 1800, Londonderry, Castlereagh, III, 253-56; O'Beirne to Brodrick, May 24, 1803, Stuart to Brodrick, Oct. 4, 1805, Brodrick MSS, 8873.

[56]1 Hansard, VI (1806), 154.

[57]Stuart to Brodrick, March 2, 1806, Brodrick MSS, 8869/4; Great Britain, Parliament, Sessional Papers, "A Bill for Enforcing the Residence of Spiritual Persons on their Benefices in Ireland," (1806), pp. 13-20, 1 Hansard, VI (1805), 172.

[58]1 Hansard, VI (1806), 428; Duigenan to Brodrick, March 12, May 10, 1806, Stuart to Brodrick, March 17, 1806, Brodrick MSS, 8861, 8869; Elliot to Grenville, Grenville to Elliot, April 6, 1806, Fortescue MSS, VIII (1912), 82, 94.

[59]1 Hansard, VI (1806), 186, 451.

[60]Ibid., 423, 428-31, 500, 559.

[61]Ibid., VII (1806), 117-23; Stuart to Brodrick, March 24, 1806, NLI, Brodrick MSS, 8869.

[62]Enclosure in Elliot to Grenville, April 6, 1806, Fortescue MSS, VIII (1912), 82; also see Stuart to Brodrick, April 24, 1806, Brodrick MSS, 8869/4; Grenville to Elliot, April 16, 1806, Fortescue MSS (Dropmore), VIII (1912), 100.

[63]See returns for Derry, Clogher and Down, submitted 7 January, 8 January, and 28 April, 1806, in Ireland, S. P. O. Official Papers (Second Series), I (1790-1810), Carton 529/208/2, 3, 6.

[64]Elliot to Grenville, April 6, 1806, Fortescue MSS, VIII (1912), 82; Stuart to Brodrick, April, 1806, Brodrick MSS, 8869/4. As the chief executive officer of the Established Church the sovereign had the right to conduct his own visitation, subject, of course, to the recommendation of the incumbent ministry.

[65]Grenville to Bedford, April 18, 1806, Fortescue MSS, VIII (1912), 105; Stuart to Brodrick, April 24, 1806, Brodrick MSS, 8869/4.

[66]Stuart to Bedford, April 27, 1806, Fortescue MSS, VIII (1912), 130-31; also see Stuart to Brodrick, April 29, 1806, Brodrick MSS, 8869/4.

[67]Bedford to Grenville, May 2, 1806, Fortescue MSS, VIII (1912), 128-29.

[68]Grenville to Bedford, May 6, 1806, Fortescue MSS, VIII (1912), 135; Stuart to Brodrick, May 12, 1806, Brodrick MSS, 8869/4.

[69]Bedford to Grenville, June 5, 1806, Fortescue MSS, VIII (1912), 176-77.

[70]Stuart to Brodrick, Aug. 4, 1806, Brodrick MSS, 8869/4. Bedford to Grenville, Fortescue MSS, VIII (1912), 128-29: Great Britain, Parliament, Sessional Papers, 1807, "State of the Irish Church, 1807," p. 16.

[71]Stuart to Brodrick, Nov. 28, 1806, Brodrick MSS, 8869/4.

[72]Great Britain, "State of the Irish Church, 1807," pp. 5ff. "An Account of the Number of Parishes in Ireland and of the Benefices or Unions of Parishes into which the same have been Distributed and Reduced. Also an Account of the Number of Churches and Glebe Houses that were Existing in Ireland in 1791, etc.", Ireland, S. P. O. Official Papers, 2nd Series, Vol. I (1790-1810), April 20, 1807, 531/231/1, 3.

[73]A. Wellesley to Stuart, June 9, 1807, quoted in Wellington, Ireland, pp. 78-79.

[74]1 Hansard, IX (April 20, 1807), 497-99.

[75]Ibid., 2, 1024.

[76]A. Wellesley, memorandum, summer [?], 1807, Peel MSS, 40221/1; A. Wellesley to Percival, Oct. 27, 1807, A. Wellesley to O'Beirne, Nov. 19, 1807, in Wellington, Ireland, pp. 150-51, 191-92.

[77]Percival to A. Wellesley, Nov. 3, 1807, A. Wellesley to Percival, Dec. 24, 1807, in Wellington, Ireland, pp. 173-74, 241.

[78]1 Hansard, IX (1807), 497-99.

[79]Ibid., 837-38, 906-7; A. Wellesley to Richmond, Oct. 27, 1807, Wellington, Ireland, pp. 150-51.

[80]Wellesley to Stuart, Jan. 6, 1808, in Wellington, Ireland, p. 288; Stuart to Brodrick, Feb. 3, 1808, Brodrick MSS, 8869/5; "Returns, . . ." Dublin, S. P. O., Official Papers, Second Series, Vol. I, Carton 535/252/2.

[81]A. Wellesley to Hawkesbury, February 11, 1808, Wellington, Ireland, p. 334.

[82]Stuart to Brodrick, March 24, 1808, Brodrick MSS, 8869/5; Newport in 1 Hansard, XI (1808), 67; Lord Auckland to Grenville, May 3, 1808, Fortescue MSS IX (1916), 199.

[83]Wellesley to O'Beirne, May 25, 1808, enclosing letter, Percival to A. Wellesley, n. d., in Wellington, Ireland, pp. 432-33.

[84]A. Wellesley, in 1 Hansard, XI (1808), 67-8.

[85]Ibid., pp. 719-20. See "Abstract of Legislation for Building Church Houses and Churches and Purchasing Glebes in Ireland," Wellington, Ireland, pp. 434-37.

[86]48 George III, c. 66.

87/Christopher Butson to A. Wellesley, Nov. 2, 1808, Ireland, S. P. O. Official Papers, 535/212/8.

88 1 Hansard, XI (1808), 277-82.

89 Ibid., pp. 282-85.

90 O'Beirne to A. Wellesley, May 16, 1808, in Wellington, Ireland, p. 438.

91 Wellesley perceived a need for 642 Glebe houses, of which 346 also required glebes, and estimated the total cost at ₤463,000 of which ₤276,800 would be devoted to the purchase of 346, 20 acre glebes, and ₤187,000 to the construction of glebe houses. To this would be added ₤230,000 for the construction of 230 new churches at ₤1,000 each. The cost of glebes would be amortized through rents. Glebe houses would be financed by sequestering the revenues of every living exceeding ₤200 until ₤187,000 was raised (plus the cost of supporting a curate in each sequestered benefice). If sequestration opposed, each benefice over ₤200 would be taxed at a multiple of the cost of glebe house construction to provide ₤187,000, plus interest, to the state. The only permanent burden on the state would be ₤230,000 for churches, to be amortised at an annual cost of ₤17,500: A. Wellesley, May, 1808, in Wellington, Ireland, pp; 435-37.

92 A. Wellesley to O'Beirne, Feb. 27, 1809, Wellington, Ireland, p. 592. For example, see the interesting communication of Bishop Butson of Clonfert respecting the reaction of his clergy to a parliamentary request in June, 1809 for a list of all livings receiving an income of less than ₤150. Many bishops ignored the request entirely, others requested additional time, complaining of their own residence in England and the refusal of their clergy to supply the requested information. Butson, no signal reformer himself, dispatched a circular letter to his recalcitrant clergy in October, 1809, noting that he had twice requested information, and that even the second had been "received with a very reprehensible disrespect . . . I am unwilling to recall to your recollection your oath of canonical obedience. But you be pleased to repair personally to my court at Clonfert upon the 13th (of November) and there advance such plea, as you may be able, in excuse for your contumacy, . . ." Butson complained even this did not work. Clonfert to Charles Sexton, Dec. 22, 1809, S. P. O. Official Papers, 2nd Series, 539/294/2.

93 Great Britain, Parliamentary Papers, "Accounts Relating to the Church Establishment," pp. 3-4; Edward Stopford to Beresford, Feb. 22, 1830; Edward Stopford, "Statement of First Fruits Fund, 1823-4", cited in Akenson, Church, p. 117; A. Wellesley to Richmond, May 12, 1808, A. Wellesley to Duigenan, May 25, 1808, A. Wellesley to Richmond,

June 6, 1808, Stuart to Brodrick, April 10, 1806, Henry Grattan
to James [Grattan], June 4, 1811, National Library of Ireland, MSS,
2111.

[94] Brodrick, memorandum, n. d. [probably 1809], Brodrick MSS,
8893/2.

[95] Stuart to Brodrick, June 10, 18, 28, 1810, Brodrick MSS, 8869/6.

[96] Liverpool to Peel, Nov. 7, 1812, Peel MSS, 40181/27.

[97] Stuart to Brodrick, March 1, 1812, April 14, 1814, Feb. 20,
1816, Brodrick MSS, 8896/6.

[98] Ibid., July 5, 1819, Feb. 7, 1822, Brodrick MSS, 8869/8; n. s.
Hansard, XI (1824), 890-98.

[99] "Abstract of Receipt and Expenditure from the 1st of May, 1801
to the 5th of January, 1815;" "Statement of Progress. . . in Improving
the Condition of the Established Church in Ireland . . . by . . . the
Board of First Fruits . . . 1801 to 1818," Dublin, S. P. O., Second
Series, 558/425/2.

[100] Great Britain, Parliamentary Papers, "Accounts Relating to the
Church Establishment," pp. 4, 33.

[101] Stopford to Beresford, Feb. 27, 1830, Armagh Public Library,
Beresford MSS.

[102] Akenson, Church, p. 121.

[103] Based on Great Britain, Parliamentary Papers, Vol. LXXVIII
(Reports, vol. V) "Papers Relating to the Established Church in Ire-
land " "Third Report of His Majesty's Commissioners on Ecclesiastical
Revenue in Ireland," "Fourth Report of His Majesty's Commissioners on
Ecclesiastical Revenue and Patronage in Ireland," cited in Akenson,
Church, pp. 128-29.

[104] 5 George IV, c. 91.

[105] Based on Akenson, Church, Table 32, pp. 128-29.

[106] Stopford to Beresford, July 6, 1828, Armagh Public Library,
Beresford Papers, I, Great Britain, Parliamentary Papers, Vol. CCLXXIX
(Accounts and Papers, Vol. XIX), "An Account of the Number of Facilities
or Dispensations which in the Last Ten Years Have Been Granted in Ireland," (1830), p. 1.

Chapter IV: The Irish Tithe Question 1800-1830

[1]Angus Macintyre, The Liberator; Daniel O'Connell and the Irish Party 1830-1847 (London: Hamilton, 1965), p. 169, quoting Anon., State of Ireland Considered, with an Enquiry into the History and Operation of Tithes (Dublin, 1810), p. 52, note 1.

[2]Beaufort, Memoir, p. 137.

[3]Akenson, Church, p. 95.

[4]Great Britain, "Third Report of His Majesty's Commissioners on Ecclesiastical Revenue and Patronage," and the fourth report on the same.

[5]Boulter to the Bishop of London, March 13, 1728, Boulter, Works, I, 232-33.

[6]40 George III, c. 23.

[7]The event was described in 1828 as "that enormous and unparalleled act of injustice committed by the gentry of Ireland, . . . which gave the great landholder an exemption from the tithe, on the mere condition of depopulating his estate, and substituting cattle in the place of human creatures." John Finlay, A Treatise on the Laws of Tithes in Ireland (1828), p. 477.

[8]Robert B. McDowell, Irish Public Opinion 1750-1800 (London: Faber and Faber, 1952), pp. 119-20.

[9]Lecky, Ireland in the Eighteenth Century, II, 34-35; Killen, Ecclesiastical History, II, 287.

[10]McDowell, Irish Public Opinion, pp. 119-20.

[11]Irish Debates, VII, 57-59; Froude, The English in Ireland, II, 497.

[12]Pitt to Rutland, November 7, 1786, printed in Charles Manners, Duke of Rutland, ed., Correspondence between the Right Honorable William Pitt and Charles, Duke of Rutland, Lord Lieutenant of Ireland, 1781-1787 (London: A. Spottiswoode, 1842), p. 159.

[13]Mant, History, II, 712-13.

[14]Orde to John Hely Hutchison, April 9, 1787, Hutchison to George Rose, June 19, 1788, Great Britain, Historical Manuscripts Commission, The Manuscripts of the Duke of Beaufort, the Earl of Donoughmore and Others, I, 310, 322-23.

[15] Parliamentary Register, VIII, 191-237 (February 14, 1788), IX, 442-64 (May 8, 1789)?

[16] Lecky, Ireland in the Eighteenth Century, II, 460-61. One hundred fourteen commissions and 60 Select Committees investigated Irish problems between 1810 and 1833; many were intimately concerned with the tithe problem.

[17] McDowell, Public Opinion, p. 121.

[18] Francis Plowden, The History of Ireland from its Invasion under Henry II to its Union in January, 1801 (3 vols.; London, 1805-1806), Vol. II, Part I, p. 389.

[19] 2 Hansard IX(1823), 374.

[20] Hervey to Pelham, January 16, 1798, in Bentley Gilbert, ed., English Historical Documents, (Oxford University Press, 1962ff.), p. 121.

[21] Cornwallis to Portland, March 26, 1800, in Cornwallis, Correspondence, III, 220-221.

[22] Bedford to Grenville, Jan. 14, 1807, Feb. 26, 1807, Fortescue MSS, IX, 9-14, 59-61.

[23] Buckingham to Grenville, Sept. 17, 1800, Fortescue MSS, VI, 319-20.

[24] Grenville to Bedford, March 11, 1807, Fortescue MSS, IX, 68-72.

[25] Bedford to Grenville, January 14, 1807, Fortescue MSS, IX, 9-12.

[26] Bedford to Grenville, Jan. 14, 1807, Bedford to Spencer, March 14, 1807, Grenville to Bedford, March 11, 1807, in Fortescue MSS, IX, 9-14, 82-97, VI, 68-72.

[27] William Blackstone, Commentaries on the Laws of England (4 Vols.; Oxford: Clarendon Press, 1765-69), II, 24.

[28] Samuel Percy Lea, Present State of the Established Church, or Ecclesiastical Registry of Ireland, (Dublin, 1814), pp. 105-22, in Dublin, Royal Irish Academy, Haliday Collection of Bound Pamphlets, 1051/8. See: Richard Bivin, The Ecclesiastical Law (9th ed., 1842).

[29] National Library of Ireland MSS, "Rates of Tithe Valuation, Clogher (1822)"; "Biblicus," History of Tithes (London: 1831), p. 35,

in Haliday, 1520/3; British Museum, Wellesley MSS, 38103/77; William Shaw Mason, A Statistical Account or Parochial Survey of Ireland Drawn up from the Communications of the Clergy (3 Vol.; Dublin, 1814), III, 440.

[30] House of Commons, "Report of the Committee . . . on Disturbances in Ireland," 1832 (677) XVI, Question 7295-97, 6668-71.

[31] John Wilson Croker, Sketch of the State of Ireland Past and Present (Dublin, 1808), pp. 31-32, in Haliday, 938/4; (Thomas Elrington), Letter from an Irish Dignitary to an English Clergyman on Tithes (London, 1807), p. 11, in Haliday, 907/5; McDowell, Irish Public Opinion, p. 120; Richard Woodward, Bishop of Cloyne, The Present State of the Church of Ireland (Dublin, 1787), p. 6; (Richard Whately), Evidence of the Archbishop of Dublin on Tithes (London, 1832), p. 11, in Haliday, 1553/1; (Thomas Elrington), Letter to William W. Pole, Irish Chief Secretary, on the Proposal for a Commutation of Tithes in Ireland (Dublin, 1810), p. 12, in Haliday, 979/9; Patrick Sarsfield O'Hegarty, A History of Ireland under the Union 1801-1822 (London: Methuen and Co., 1952), p. 84.

[32] Boulter to Bishop of London, March 13, 1728, in Boulter, Works, I, 234-35; William Rowe Lyall, The Nature and True Value of Church Property Examined (London, 1831); McDowell, Public Opinion, p. 120; S. N. (Thomas Elrington), Inquiry whether Disturbances in Ireland have Originated in Tithes (Dublin, 1822), pp. 12, 14, 20-21, in Haliday, 1256/2.

[33] Adam Smith, An Inquiry into the Nature and Causes of the Wealth of Nations (1828), III, 386-87.

[34] Anon., Letter to Sir [H.] Parnell in Reply to "Arguments and Plan for Commutation of Tithes in Ireland." By a Beneficed Clergyman (London, 1813), p. 29, in Haliday, 1044/8; Patrick Duigenan, A Fair Representation of the Present Political State of Ireland (Dublin, 1800), p. 58, in Haliday, 795/1; Anon., Letter to an M.P. on the State of Ireland. By an Irish Magistrate (Dublin, 1825), p. 88, in Haliday, 1346/4; S. N. [Elrington], Inquiry, p. 16.

[35] Duigenan, A Fair Representation, p. 55; S. N. [Elrington], Letter from an Irish Dignitary, p. 10; Anon., Serious and Seasonable Observations on . . . the Subject of Tithes, by a Curate, p. 23.

[36] Anon., Observations Occasioned by the Letter of J.K.L. [James Doyle], (Dublin, 1823), pp. 43-44, in Haliday, 1260/1; "Mediensis," Tithes no Tax (Dublin, 1823), pp. 30-31, in Haliday, 1289/5; Lyall, Nature and True Value, pp. 17-18.

[37]Anon., Short Papers on the Irish Church Question, no. 3 ("A Few Words on the Origin of Church Property in Ireland"), (Dublin, 1869), p. 4; Anon., Facts Respecting the Irish Church (Dublin, 1869), pp. 2-3.

[38]Olive J. Brose, Church and Parliament; the Reshaping of the Church of England 1828-1860 (Stanford: Stanford University Press, 1959), pp. 118-119.

[39]Croker, Sketch, pp. 49-50; S. N. [Elrington], Letter from an Irish Dignitary, p. 7.

[40]Ibid., pp. 5-6; Whately, Evidence, p. 52.

[41]Killen, Ecclesiastical History, II, 458; Richard [Laurence, Archbishop of] Cashel, Charge at the Visitation of Munster (Dublin, 1823), p. 25, in Haliday, 1263/3; Rev. Whitty of Glanheen to Brodrick, May 8, 1816, Brodrick MSS, 8861; Anon., Serious and Seasonable Observations, p. 54; S. N. [Elrington], Letter from an Irish Dignitary, p. 21; Anon., Letter to Parnell, p. 30; S. N. [Elrington], Letter to William W. Pole, p. 44.

[42]Ibid., pp. 19, 25; Dominick Trant, Considerations of the Present Disturbances in the Province of Munster (Dublin, 1787), p. 11; Duigenan, A Fair Representation, p. 59.

[43]Anon., Advice to the Protestant Clergy of Ireland by a Layman of the Church of England (Dublin, 1777), p. 22; Trant, Considerations on the Present Disturbances, p. 13; Charles Grant, Substance of the Speech . . . Delivered in the House of Commons 22 April 1822 (London, 1822), p. 25, in Haliday, 1248/1; Anon., Letter to Parnell, p. 26; S. N. [Elrington], Letter to William W. Pole, pp. 15-16; Anon., Sketch of an Amendment to Mr. Goulburn's Bills for the Composition of Tithes in Ireland (London, 1823), p. 14, in Haliday, 1258/1.

[44]Speech, Jan. 17, 1788, quoted in Collectanea Politica, II, 161-64.

[45]The Evidence Taken before the Select Committees of the Houses of Lords and Commons Appointed in the Sessions of 1824 and 1825 to Inquire into the State of Ireland (London; John Murray, 1825), pp. 79-80, 83; Anon., Reflections on the State of Ireland in the Nineteenth Century (London, 1822), pp. 223-25, in Haliday, 1247/3; Anon., Letters to the Archbishop of Armagh and . . . the Duke of Devonshire with Observations of the Tithe System (London, 1822), pp. 40-41, in Haliday, 1247/3; Report of the Committee for the Relief of the Distressed Districts of Ireland. Appointed . . . May 7, 1822 (London, 1823), p. 87, in Haliday, 1283.

[46]Croker, Sketch, pp. 43, 47-48; Anon., Letters to the Archbishop of Armagh, p. 30; Anon., Appeal to the King on the State of Ireland (London, 1822), p. 27, in Haliday, 1249/1.

[47]Anon., Short Statement on the Bishops Court in Ireland and Conduct of the Proctors in that Country (London, 1824), pp. 1-16, in Haliday, 1301/5.

[48]Henry Upton, Strictures on a Pamphlet Signed "Theophilus" . . . Respecting Tithes (Dublin, 1787), p. 7.

[49]Anon., Appeal to the King, p. 28; Anon., Short Statement on the Bishops Court, p. 10, S. N. [Elrington], Inquiry whether Disturbances, p. 48; Thomas Spring Rice, Considerations on the Present State of Ireland, etc. (London, 1822), p. 160, in Haliday, 1255/9.

[50]MacIntyre, Liberator, p. 172.

[51]Full and Authentic Report of all the Debates that Have Taken Place on the Irish Tithe Question in the Last Session of Parliament (Dublin, 1833), p. 6, in Haliday, 1577/1.

[52]Strictures . . . on . . . Theophilus, p. 32.

[53]J. Caldwell, Debates on the Affairs of Ireland in 1763 and 1764, pp. 656-59, noted in Lecky, Ireland in the Eighteenth Century, II, 19-20.

[54]Thomas Nowlan, Enquiry into the History of Tithe with a Plan for Modification (Dublin, 1808), pp. 50-51; in Haliday, 944/5; H. Woodward, Letter to Rt. Hon. E. G. Stanley on Tithes (Dublin, 1832), passim, in Haliday, 1553/3; Anon., An Essay on the Tithe System Showing its Foundation on the Laws of the Land (Dublin, n. d.), pp. 28, 29, 46, 47; Anon., Commutation of Tithe, by a Greable Charge upon Land. By a Beneficed Clergyman of the Established Church (London, 1816), p. 22, in Haliday, 1093/6; (William Parnell), Inquiry into Causes of Irish Discontent. By an Irish Country Gentleman (London, 1804), p. 10, in Haliday, 868/2; Earl Blessington, Observations Addressed to Marquis Wellesley (London, 1822), p. 36; Spring Rice, Considerations, p. 28; Grant, Substance, p. 24; Anon., Strictures . . . on . . . Theophilus, p. 37; Arthur Young, A Tour of Ireland with General Observations on the Present State of that Kingdom (3 vols., Dublin, 1780), II, 81.

[55]Nowlan, Enquiry into the History of Tithe, p. 54.

[56]Kilkenny Journal, March 12, 1831, p. 2, col. 4; April 6, 1831, p. 3, col. 1; May 16, 1833, p. 3, col. 3; G. Dymond, The Church and the Clergy, Showing that Religious Establishments Derive no Countenance

from the Nature of Christianity (London, 1832), pp. 50-51.

[57]Killen, Ecclesiastical History, II, 334; Plowden, History, Vol. II, Part II, appendix, pp. 141-65; George Ensor, Observations on the Present State of Ireland (Dublin, 1814), p. 36, in Haliday, 1064/2.

[58]Ensor, Observations, pp. 38-39; also see Anon., Letter to the Grand Jury of Armagh on Tithes. By a Killeavy Weaver (Dublin, 1808), p. 12, in Haliday, 944/2.

[59]Anon., Letter to the Grand Jury, pp. 14-15; Anon., Thought on the Protestant Ascendency in Ireland (London, 1805), p. 87, in Haliday, 874/3; Kilkenny Journal, Nov. 20, 1830, p. 3, cols. 4-5.

[60]Duigenan, Address to the Nobility, p. 101; Anon., Serious and Seasonable Observations, pp. 44-45.

[61]Anon., Serious and Seasonable Observations, pp. 44-45; Letters on Tithes in the "Dublin Journal" (Dublin, 1808), p. 29, in Haliday, 944/3; Mason, Survey, III, 439; J.C. Curwen, Observations . . . on the State of Ireland Principally Directed to its Agriculture and Rural Population (2 vols.: London, 1812), 384; S. N. [Elrington], Letter from an Irish Dignitary, p. 23.

[62][John Wiggins], South of Ireland: Hints to Irish Landlords on the Best Means of Obtaining their Rents (Dublin, 1824), p. 27, in Haliday, 1305/9; Anon., Report of the Committee for . . . Distressed Districts, p. 87; J.K.L. [Doyle], Vindication of Irish Catholics' Principles (Dublin, 1823), p. 30, in Haliday, 1260/1; Rev. Sir H. B. Dudley, Short Address to the Primate of all Ireland Recommending Modification of the Tithes of that Country (London, 1822), pp. 20-21, in Haliday, 1256/7; Grattan in the Irish House of Commons, 1788, noted in Mant, History of the Church of Ireland, pp. 713-14; William Carleton, The Tithe Proctor (London: Sims and M'Intyre, 1849), p. 389; Nowlan, Enquiry into the History of Tithe, pp. 51-52, Curwen, Observations, II, 80-81; Anon., Strictures on Theophilus, p. 34; Anon., Report of the Committee for . . . Distressed Districts, p. 82.

[63]Wiggins, South of Ireland, pp. 24-26.

[64]Froude offers a convenient if facile summary: "In his origin the tithe proctor was a parish officer, appointed and paid by the people, at a time when they were on a less painful footing with the Protestant clergyman . . . [Later] the tithe proctor, like his neighbors, became more grasping and avaricious . . . His trade was dangerous, and therefore he required to be more highly paid . . . He fleeced the flock and he fleeced their shepherd . . . [Since tithe proctors operated best where there were no rectors, vicars, schoolmasters, etc., he was] often

the officer of revenue besides, and would arrange his demands for
his own advantage, overcharging the tithes and pocketing the surplus,
and compensating the tithe-payer by undercharging his taxes . . ."
See Froude, Ireland in the Eighteenth Century, II, 493-94.

[65]Boulter to Wake, Archbishop of Canterbury, Feb. 27, 1727, in
Boulter, Works, pp. 172-73.

[66]Anon., Real Grievances of the Irish Peasantry. By a Clergyman
of the Established Church (London, 1825), pp. 10, 99-100, in Haliday,
1322/6; Killen, Ecclesiastical History, II, 80.

[67]Wellesley to Lord Clarina, Oct. 22, 1807, in Wellington, Ireland, pp. 144-46; Anon., Letter to Parnell, p. 20; Richard Bourke,
Bishop of Waterford and Lismore, to Peel, Nov. 9, 1815, Peel MSS,
40249/21; S. N. [Elrington], Letter from an Irish Dignitary, pp. 18-
19.

[68]Rev. William Phelan to the select committee of the House of
Commons, May 5, 1825, in Evidence, p. 38.

[69]Boulter to Bishop of London, March 13, 1728, in Boulter, Works,
I, 232-33; Boulter to Robert Walpole, Prime Minister, Aug. 9, 1737,
noted in Mant, Church of Ireland, pp. 556-57.

[70]Mant, Church of Ireland, pp. 711-12; M. de Lactoynaye, Rambles
through Ireland (2 vols.; Cork, 1798), I, 95; John Reade, Observations
on Tithes, Rents, etc. with Peculiar Reference to Ireland (Dublin, 1811),
pp. 45, 52-53, in Haliday, 996/4; Curwen, Observations, II, 189-90;
George G. Perry, History of the Church of England (3 vols.; London:
Saunders, Otley and Co., 1861-64), II, 542-43; Froude, The English in
Ireland, II, 524-27; S. N. [Elrington], Letter to William W. Pole,
p. 11.

[71]Reade, Observations on Tithes, pp. 85-86; J. K. L. [Doyle],
Letters on the State of Ireland (Dublin, 1825), p. 30, in Haliday,
1339/4; Anon., Dr. Doyle and Tithes (Dublin, 1881), p. 17, in Haliday,
1520/4; Killen, Ecclesiastical History, II, 328; Ballyshannon Herald,
Sept. 19, 1834, p. 3, col. 4; Sept. 26, 1834, p. 2, col. 5.

[72]B. Browne, Letter on the State of Ireland (London, 1822), pp.
10-11, in Haliday, 1248/1.

[73]Evidence before the Select Committee, June 4, 1825, March 22,
1825, in Evidence, pp. 40, 432.

[74]William Lamb, Viscount Melbourne, Home Secretary, to the Marquess Anglesey, Lord Lieutenant, Dec. 16, 1830, in Belfast, Northern

Ireland, Public Record Office, Anglesey MSS, 619/VI/3; J. A. Murphy, "The Support of the Catholic Clergy in Ireland, 1750-1850," His- torical Studies: Papers Read before the Sixth Annual Conference of Irish Historians, V, 116.

[75]Dudley, Address to the Primate, p. 7; Anon., Considerations on Commutation of Tithes, etc. By a Lay Protestant (Dublin, 1817), p. 21, in Haliday, 1114/8; William Sturch, Grievances of Ireland: Their Causes and their Remedies (London, 1826), p. 50, in Haliday, 1354/11.

[76]Anon., Dialogue between a Bishop and a Judge on Tithes (Dublin, 1831), pp. 11-12, in Haliday, 1520/5; Anon., Dr. Doyle and Tithes, p. 4; Dymond, The Church and the Clergy, p. 51.

[77]William Parker, Plan for Improvement of the State of the Irish Poor (Cork, 1816), p. 10, in Haliday, 1093/2; Anon., Dialogue, pp. 20-21; J. K. L. [Doyle], Letters, p. 353; Anon., Letter to an M. P., pp. 89-90; Anon., The Justice and Expediency of Continuing the Pro- testant Church Ascendency in Ireland Briefly Examined (London, 1835), pp. 1-2.

[78]George Cornewall Lewis, On Local Disturbances in Ireland and the Irish Church Question (London: B. Fellowes, 1836), appendix no. 1, pt. A; A. Atkinson, Ireland in the Nineteenth Century (London, 1833), pp. 171-72.

[79]Nowlan, Enquiry into the History of the Tithe, p. 60; Sturch, Grievances of Ireland, pp. 50-51.

[80]Croker, Sketch, passim; John Edwards, Interests of Ireland: A new Method with Confident Hope to Attach the Lower Classes to the Laws and Constitution (Dublin, 1814), p. 116, in Haliday, 1064/1; Anon., Letter to Parnell, p. 30; Jerome, Counte de Salis, Considerations on the Propriety of . . . Commutation of Tithes for Ireland (Armagh, 1813), p. 7, in Haliday, 1044/7; Reade, Observations on Tithes, pp. 57-58.

[81]Anon., Advice, p. 51; S. N. [Elrington], Letter to William W. Pole, p. 46; Croker, Sketches, pp. 6-7, 13; Anon., Strictures on . . . Theophilus, p. 45.

[82]Curwen, Observations, I, 385; Reade, Observations on Tithes, pp. 84-85.

[83][Whately], Evidence . . . on Tithes, pp. 25, 30-31, 41-42.

[84]V. Lavrovsky, "Tithe Commutation as a Factor in the Gradual Decrease of Ownership by the English Peasantry," Economic History

Review, XVI, 139; W. R. War, "The Tithe Question in England in the Early Nineteenth Century," _Journal of Ecclesiastical History_, XVI (1965), p. 67.

[85]A. Wellesley to Liverpool, October 22, 1807, Wellington, _Ireland_, pp. 142-43.

[86]A. Wellesley to Clarina, October 22, 1807, Wellington, _Ireland_, pp. 144-45.

[87]A. Wellesley to Ponsonby, October 26, 1807, Wellington, _Ireland_, p. 149.

[88]A. Wellesley to O'Beirne, November 2, 1807, Wellington, _Ireland_, pp. 160-61.

[89]A. Wellesley to Percival, November 6, 1807, Wellington, _Ireland_, pp. 162-63.

[90]Liverpool was still Hawkesbury; the title change was soon to come and is anticipated in the text. A. Wellesley to Hawkesbury, Oct. 22, 1807; A. Wellesley to Lord Clarina, Oct. 22, 1807; A. Wellesley to C. W. Ponsonby, Lord Chief Baron, Oct. 24, 1807; Ponsonby to A. Wellesley, Oct. 26, 1807; A. Wellesley to O'Beirne, Nov. 2, 1807; Percival to A. Wellesley, Nov. 3, 1807, A. Wellesley to Percival, Nov. 6, 1807; A. Wellesley to O'Beirne, Nov. 19, 1807, Nov. 25, 1807, Wellington, _Ireland_, pp. 142-43, 144-47, 148-49, 160-61, 162-65, 167-75, 191-92, 193-94.

[91]Bedford to Grenville, Jan. 14, 1807, _Fortescue MSS_, IX (1916), 9-12.

[92]Wellesley to Spencer Percival, with marginal notes by Percival and Hawkesbury, Nov. 6, 1807, in Wellington, _Ireland_, pp. 183-64.

[93]A. Wellesley to Hawkesbury, Dec. 14, 1807, in Wellington, _Ireland_, p. 225.

[94]1 _Hansard_, XI (1808), 79.

[95]_Ibid._, XIV (1809), 625-48.

[96]_Ibid._, XVI (1810), 658-89, XX (1811), 588.

[97]Infrequent clashes continued : _Clare Journal and Ennis Advertiser_, Nov. 17, 1808, p. 1, col. 4; correspondence concerning prosecutions for non-payment of tithes in 1809, Brodrick MSS, 8821/2; Jebb to Brodrick, May 3, May 14, 1814, Brodrick MSS, 8886/5; Ensor, _Observations_, p. 43.

[98] Richmond, memorandum, n. d., Richmond MSS, 60/275.

[99] Some average rates in 1817-21: wheat (5/2 to 8, with the average about 6/6), barley (4/6 to 6/11); oats (3/5 to 5/9); hay (2/11 to 4/0), flax (5/9 to 7/7); potatoes (5/9 to 6/9); Belfast, Northern Ireland Public Record Office, D/175.

[100] Duigenan to Brodrick, Aug. 29, 1815, Elrington to Brodrick, May 20, 1816, Brodrick MSS, 8861/7, 9; Warburton to Peel, Nov. 13, 1815, Peel MSS, 40249/68.

[101] Jebb to Brodrick, Nov. 13, 1815, Brodrick MOS, 8866/4.

[102] Robert Disney to Brodrick, Jan. 23, 1816, May 7, 1816, Brodrick MSS, 8861/8.

[103] Stuart to Brodrick, May 5, 1816, Elrington to Brodrick, May 1, 1816, Brodrick MSS, 8861/8.

[104] 2 Hansard, II (July 5, 1820), 221-23.

[105] The drive for possession of the land which identified tithe resistance and Irish nationalism is discussed in John Edwin Pomfert, The Struggle for Land in Ireland 1800-1823 (Princeton: University Press, 1930).

[106] Goulburn to Wellesley, Feb. 13, 1822, Wellesley MSS, 37298/200.

[107] Ibid., July 9, 1822, Wellesley MSS, 37299/278.

[108] Ibid., Feb. 22, 1822, Wellesley MSS, 37298/205-206.

[109] Liverpool to Stuart, Feb. 24, 1822, Liverpool MSS, 37300/291-97.

[110] Goulburn to Wellesley, Feb. 22, 1822, Feb. 26, 1822, Wellesley MSS, 37298/206-207, 209.

[111] Ibid., March 5, 1822, March 14, 1822, Wellesley MSS, 37298/207-208.

[112] Ibid., March 14, 1822, Wellesley MSS, 37298/207-208.

[113] Ibid., March 23, 1822, Wellesley MSS, 37298/209.

[114] Ibid., March 29, 1822, Wellesley MSS, 37298/210; Wellesley to Goulburn, February 23, 1822, Goulburn MSS, II/22.

[115] 2 Hansard, VII (May 15, 1822), 597-604; VII (June 19, 1822), 1147-98.

[116] Wellesley to Goulburn, July 5, 1822, Goulburn MSS, II/22.

[117] 2 Hansard, VII (June 13, 1822), 1037.

[118] 2 Hansard, VII (1822), 1029-37; "Draft of a Tithe Bill with Marginal Comments," c. April 15, 1822; Elrington to Peel, April 22, 1822, Peel MSS, 4032/50-61.

[119] Extract of a Letter from Lt. Col. Shawe to the Marquess Wellesley," Feb. 26, 1822, Wellesley MOS, 37298/269-71. This letter contains Shawe's interview with Wellington and Maryborough.

[120] O'Beirne, "memorandum," n. d. [1822], Wellesley MSS, 37298/289-90; Bishop of Raphoe to Wellesley, March 9, 1822, Wellesley MSS, 37298/295-27.

[121] Beresford to Liverpool, March 22, 1822, Wellesley MSS, 37298/346-48.

[122] Dublin, Patriot, March 19, 1822, p. 3, col. 4.

[123] Goulburn to Wellesley, June 15, 1822, Wellesley MSS, 37299/213-14; 2 Hansard, VII (1822), 1147-98.

[124] Copies of Diocesan returns on tithes are to be found in Wellesley's personal papers, as are several voluminous drafts of his own observations: see Wellesley MSS, 37298/381-83; 37299/2-30, 84-87, 253-58.

[125] Wellesley to Peel, Nov. 21, 1822, Wellesley MSS, 37300/69.

[126] Goulburn to Peel, Oct. 16, 1822, Peel MSS, 40328/147-49.

[127] Liverpool to Wellesley, Dec. 9, 1822, Liverpool MSS, 37300/88-96.

[128] Wellesley, "memorandum," n. d. (Dec., 1822), Wellesley MSS, 37300/92-98; Goulburn to Peel, Dec. 11, 1822, Peel MSS, 40328/288-91.

[129] Wellesley to Liverpool, Nov. 18, 1822, Wellesley MSS, 37300/24-25.

[130] Goulburn to Peel, Oct., 1824, Peel MSS, 40330/140-44; J. C. Erck,

Account of the Ecclesiastical Establishment in Ireland (Dublin, 1830), p. 41, in Haliday, 1474/4; Bedford to Liverpool, Feb. 15, 1823, Wellesley MSS, 37300/298-304.

[131] Goulburn to Wellesley, Feb. 20, 1823, Wellesley MSS, 37300/250-57.

[132] Liverpool to Beresford, Feb. 24, 1823, Wellesley MSS, 37300/291-96.

[133] "Memorial," March 7, 1823, Wellesley MSS, 37300/325-26.

[134] Anon., Reflections on the State of Ireland, p. 228.

[135] Goulburn to Peel, March 31, 1823, Peel MSS, 40329/56.

[136] Ibid., Jan. 21, 1823, Peel MSS, 40329/29-32.

[137] Goulburn to Wellesley, June 1, 1822, Wellesley to Goulburn, June 5, 1822, Goulburn MSS, II/21.

[138] 2 Hansard, VII (1822), 1039-40.

[139] Palmerston to Peel, March 27, 1823, Goulburn MSS, II/14; 2 Hansard, IX (1823), 370.

[140] Journal of the House of Commons, LXXVIII, 96, 149, 252, 254, 414.

[141] 2 Hansard, VIII (March 6, 1823), 494-501.

[142] Goulburn told Wellesley he had been tempted to say to the irate Archbishop, "in vastitate omnium Tuam professionem sacrosanctum futuram ipse putus?": Goulburn to Wellesley, March 8, 1823, Wellesley MSS, 37300/331-32.

[143] Goulburn to Wellesley, June 7, 1823, Wellesley MSS, 37301/118-19.

[144] 2 Hansard, VIII (April 21, 1823), 1132-34.

[145] Ibid., IX (May 30, 1823), 602-9.

[146] Ibid., IX (June 6, 1823), 802-810.

[147] Ibid., IX (July 8, 1823), 1452-56.

[148] Ibid., IX (July 9, 1823), 1490-93.

[149] Goulburn, "Compendium and Summary of Tithe Act as Sent to all

Clergy," Aug., 1823, Peel MSS, 40329/124-26.

[150]Goulburn to Peel, Sept. 1, 1823, Peel MSS 40329/131-32.

[151]Ibid., October 17, 1823, Peel MSS, 40329/172-74.

[152]Ibid.

[153]Ibid., Sept. 16, 1823, Peel MSS, 40329/139-40.

[154]Enclosure, Goulburn to Peel, Jan. 31, 1824, Peel MSS, 40330/17-19.

[155]"Tithe Returns," Oct. 26, 1824, Peel MSS, 40330/140-44.

[156]Goulburn to Wellesley, Feb. 3, 1824, Wellesley MSS, 37302/69.

[157]Wellesley, memorandum on tithes, n. d., Wellesley MSS, 37302/1-40.

[158]2 Hansard, X (1824), 1385-93; XI (1824), 421-25, 501-9. See 4 George IV, c. 99. For further details on parliamentary negotiations leading to the shaping of these terms, see; Elrington to Peel, April 21, 1823, Peel MSS, 40355/341; William Magee, "Notes on the Tithe Bill of 1823," March, 1823, Wellesley MSS, 37300/331; also see Goulburn to Wellesley, Feb. 27, 1824, Wellesley MSS 37302/112; Goulburn to Peel, March 18, 1824, Peel MSS, 40330/24-25.

[159]2 Hansard, X (March 24, 1824), 1385-93; XI (April 2, 1824), 69-71.

[160]Goulburn to Peel, Oct. 25, 1824, Peel MSS, 403301/138-39.

[161]Ibid., Oct., 1824, Peel MSS, 40330/140-44; J. C. Erck, Account, p. 41, in Haliday, 1474/4; Wellesley, memoranda, Feb. (?), 1828, Wellesley MSS, 37305/302-313.

[162]The applotment books referred to include the following entries in the Public Record Office, Dublin: Aghabog (1832: ass 1); Ballibea (1829: Class 12); Agnamullon (1829: Class 3); Errigal (1826: Class 65); Clones (1833: Class 37); Drumsnatt (1827); Kilbaron (1833: Box 78); Clontibret (1830: Box 40); Currin (1827: Box 46); Ematris (1830: Box 64); Donagh (1823: Box 50); Tyholland (1832: Box 160); Muchnoe (1827: Box 132); Monaghan (1826: Box 129); Carrickmacross (1824: Box 125). Also see: Moyen Jellett to Totenham Loftus, Bishop of Clogher, Oct. 22, 1827, Loftus MSS, 8821/16.

[163]Stafford, County Record Office, D. 260/M/OI/1879.

[164]MacIntyre, Liberator, p. 171.

[165]Ibid.

[166]House of Commons, "Second Report of the Select Committee of the House of Commons on Tithes, 1831-32," 508, XXI, minutes of evidence, Questions 5671, 5675.

[167]Ibid., pp. 265-72, 305-41, 349-64.

[168]Patrick O'Donoghue, "Opposition to Tithe Payments in 1830-31," Studia Hibernica, VI (1966), 69.

[169]L'Donoghue, "Opposition," passim; O'Donoghue, "Causes of Opposition to Tithes, 1830-38," Studia Hibernica, V (1965), 7-28; Geoffrey Locker Lampson, A Consideration of the State of Ireland in the Nineteenth Century (London: Archibald Constable and Co., 1907), pp. 148-79.

Chapter V: The Established Church and Irish Education

[1]28 Henry VIII, c. 15; 7 William III, c. 4; 8 George I, c. 12.

[2]12 Elizabeth I, c. 1.

[3]This is discussed in greater detail in Donald H. Akenson, The Irish Education Experiment: The National System of Education in the Nineteenth Century (London: Routledge and Kegan Paul, 1970), pp. 31-32.

[4]Ibid., pp. 73-75.

[5]Stuart to Brodrick, March 7, 1802, Brodrick MSS, 8869/1; O'Beirne to Abbot, Jan. 11, 1802, in Colchester, Diary and Correspondence, I, 343.

[6]Anon., Observations on the Present State of Charter Schools in Ireland (Dublin, 1806), pp. 17-18, in Haliday, 891/1; Stuart to Brodrick, Feb. 8, 1805, Brodrick MSS, 8869/3.

[7]Grenville to Bedford, May 6, 1806, Bedford to Grenville, June 15, 1806, Earl Spencer to Grenville, June 18, 1806, Fortescue MSS (Dropmore), VIII (1912), 135, 177, 194; R. B. McDowell, The Irish Administration 1801-1914 (London: Routledge and Kegan Paul, 1964), p. 234.

[8]A. Wellesley, "Memorandum on Education in Ireland," December

1807, in Wellington, Despatches, pp. 242-43.

[9]A. Wellesley to Stuart, Nov. 30, 1807, Wellesley to O'Beirne, Jan. 2, 1808, in Wellington, Ireland, pp. 200-201, 270.

[10]A. Wellesley to Percival, Oct. 27, 1807, and Rev. Stearne Tighe to A. Wellesley, Nov. 15, 1807, in Ireland, pp. 150-51, 186-88.

[11]D. Carolan Rushe, History of Monaghan for Two Hundred Years (Dundalk: The Dundalk Press, 1921), p. 183.

[12]Akenson, The Irish Education Experiment, p. 78.

[13]Great Britain, Parliament, House of Commons, First Report of the Commissioners of Irish Education Inquiry, 1825 (400), xii, pp. 31-37; R. Barry O'Brien, Fifty Years of Concessions to Ireland 1831-1881, 2 vols.; (London, 1885), I, 77-82, cited in Akenson, Irish Education Experiment, p. 82.

[14]Henry Newland, An Apology for the Established Church in Ireland . . . Addressed to the Earl of Mountcashel (Dublin, 1829), pp. 205, 207, 209; Thomas O'Beirne, Charge to the Clergy of Meath (Dublin, 1816), pp. 30-31, in Haliday, 1100/1; Anon., Practical Observations upon the Views and Tendency of the First Report of the Commissioners of Irish Education Inquiry (London, 1826), passim, in Haliday, 1364/1.

[15]Anon., Practical Observations, p. 10.

[16]Robert Steven, Remarks on the Present State of Ireland (London, 1822), p. 35, in Haliday, 1234/5; Anon., Inquiry into the Abuses of the Charter Schools (London, 1819), p. 50, in Haliday, 1161/2.

[17]Second Annual Report of the Baptist Society, for Promoting the Gospel in Ireland (London, 1816), passim; The First Report of the Commissioners of Irish Education Inquiry, pp. 82-84.

[18]First Report of the Irish Society for Promoting the Education of the Native Irish (Dublin, 1819), p. 28, in Haliday, 1172/1; Ibid. (Fourth Report), passim, in Haliday, 1250/1; First Report of the Commissioners of Irish Education Inquiry, pp. 82-84.

[19]Anon., Practical Observations, p. 10; Irish Society for Promoting the Education of the Native Irish, Twelfth Report, passim, in Haliday, 1250/5.

[20]Akenson, Irish Education Experiment, p. 88; Killen, Ecclesiastical History, II, 392.

[21] House of Commons, Report from the Select Committee on Foundation Schools and Education in Ireland, 1837-38 (701), vii, p. 11; George L. Smyth, Ireland: Historical and Educational (London, 1844, III, 232, quoted in Akenson, Irish Education Experiment, pp. 86-87.

[22] First Report of the Commissioners on Education in Ireland, pp. 37-58; Lord Cloncurry, Letter . . . to the Most Noble the Marquis of Downshire on the Conduct of the Kildare Street Education Society (Dublin, 1825), passim, in Haliday, 1364/1; Rev. E. F. Gregory, Observation on Opposition to Promotion of the Education of the Irish Poor (Dublin, 1822), p. 26; Society for Promoting the Education of the Poor in Ireland; Tenth Report (Dublin, 1822), passim.

[23] This is repeatedly confirmed in Mason, Parochial Survey.

[24] House of Commons, Fourteenth Report from the Commissioners of the Board of Education in Ireland: View of the Chief Foundations, with Some General Remarks, and Result of Deliberations, 1812-13 (21), vi, pp. 275-76, 331-32.

[25] Peel to Foster, March 25, 1813, Parker, Peel, I, 89.

[26] 1 Hansard, XXV (1813), 258, 264-65, 267-68.

[27] Brodrick to Stuart, n. d. [probably c. March 1, 1814] Brodrick MSS, 8888.

[28] Stuart to Brodrick March 12, 21, 1814, Brodrick MSS, 8869/7.

[29] Jebb to Brodrick, March 12, 1814, Brodrick MSS 8866/2.

[30] O'Beirne to Brodrick, March 13, 17, 1814, Brodrick MSS, 8873; also see Thomas St. Lawrence, Bishop of Cork, to Brodrick, March 10, 21, April 1, 1814, Brodrick MSS, 8891/7.

[31] Elrington to James Verschoyle, Bishop of Killala and Achonry, March 11, 1814; Verschoyle to Elrington, March 14, 15, 1814, Peel MSS, 40235/160, 166.

[32] McDowell, Irish Administration, p. 236; Akenson, Irish Educational Experiment, p. 79.

[33] Jebb, memorandum, July 5, 1814, Brodrick MSS, 8866/2.

[34] First Report of the Commissioners of Education, pp. 4-5.

[35] Ibid., pp. 58-60.

[36] Anon., Inquiry into the Abuses of the Charter Schools, passim, Anon., Observations on the State of the Established Church in Ireland (Dublin, 1822), passim, in Haliday, 1252/4.

[37] Anon., Essay on the Present State of Schools in Ireland (Dublin, 1806), p. 2, in Haliday, 891/13.

[38] See a discussion of these problems in: Rev. Poadar MacDoinnleibhe, "Schools in County Fermanagh 1824-1826," Clogher Record, V (1963, 96-120; Very Rev. Lorcan O'Meardin, "Schools in County Monaghan, 1824-26" Clogher Record, V (1963), 63-95; Pilib B. O'Mordha, "Notes on Education in Curren Parish [Drumully]," Clogher Record, V (1964), 251-262.

[39] Stuart to Brodrick, March 2, 1821, Brodrick MSS, 8869/8.

[40] Goulburn to Wellesley, June 10, 1825, Wellesley to Goulburn, June 14, 1825, Goulburn MSS, II/21.

[41] Akenson, Irish Education Experiment, pp. 94-95.

[42] Beresford to T. Franklin Lewis, Jan. 31, 1826, Aug. 28, 1826, reproduced in The Ninth Report of the Commissioners of Irish Education Inquiry, 1826-27 (516), xiii, pp. 6-7, 14-17.

[43] Akenson, Irish Education Experiment, p. 103.

[44] Circular letter by Robert Paunceforte, Secretary of the Commission of Education Inquiry, Jan. 26, 1825, Brodrick MSS, 8821/15.

[45] "Report of the Select Committee of the House of Commons to Examine Reports on Irish Education," The Christian Examiner and Church of Ireland Magazine, VIII (July 1828), p. 45.

[46] Wellesley to Goulburn, Sept. 14, 1825, Goulburn MSS, II/21.

[47] Fourteenth Report of the Society Promoting the Education of the Poor of Ireland [Kildare Place] (Dublin, 1826), p. 3, in Haliday, 1364/1.

[48] Society for the Education of the Irish Poor [Kildare Place]: Sixteenth Report (Dublin, 1827), passim, in Haliday, 1409/12.

[49] Goulburn-Wellington correspondence, Sept. 14, 1825, Goulburn MSS, II/21.

[50] Beresford to Goulburn, March 9, 1830, N.I.P.R.O. D664/A/132.

[51] Stanley to Grey, March 1831, National Library of Ireland MSS, noted in Akenson, Irish Education Experiment, p. 110.

[52] 3 Hansard, VIII (1831), 184-85; IX (1831-32), 893-95; X (1832), 851-70, 1176; XI (1832), 241-42, 1076, 1181-83; XII (1832), 323-27, 496-99, 537-42, 633-36, 980-82; XIII (1832), 1-6, 328-30, 278-79, 342-48, 548-54, 657; XIV (1832), 87-95.

[53] Solloway, Prelates, pp. 162-64.

[54] Arnold, Bishops and Deans, I, 172.

[55] Desmond Bowen, Souperism: Myth or Reality? (Dublin, 1970), p. 43.

[56] The credibility of this allegation is undermined in Akenson, Irish Education Experiment, p. 128.

[57] McDowell, Irish Public Opinion, p. 80.

[58] 3 Hansard, XVII (1835), 1230.

[59] Ibid., XIX (1835), 461-79, 482-84; XXV, (1836), 1013-21.

[60] McDowell, Irish Public Opinion, p. 81.

[61] 3 Hansard, X (1832), 870-73; XI (1832), 92, 320-23, 648-49.

[62] Ibid., xxxii (1836), 274-308.

[63] "Parliamentary Evidence on National Education in Ireland," Christian Examiner and Church of Ireland Magazine, 3 ser., III (Jan. 1838), 52, quoted in Akenson, Irish Education Experiment, p. 190.

[64] Rushe, Monaghan, pp. 247-50.

[65] These figures are produced in Akenson, Irish Education Experiment, pp. 198, drawn from Reports One through Ten of the Church Education Society; also see Ballyshannon Herald, May 31, 1839, p. 1.

[66] 3 Hansard, XVI (1833), 791.

[67] Richard Whately, Reply . . . to the Address of the Clergy of the Diocese of Dublin and Glendalough on the Government Plan for National Education in Ireland (London, 1832), pp. 8-10, noted in Akenson, Irish Education Experiment, p. 191; also see 3 Hansard, XXVI (1837), 1142-46.

[68] Whately to Spring Rice, Dec. 15, 1838, Monteagle MSS, 13, 370/11.

[69] Akenson, *Irish Education Experiment*, pp. 194-95.

[70] Nowlan, *Politics of Repeal*, pp. 28-30.

[71] Beresford to William Howley, Archbishop of Canterbury, April 12, 1845, N. I. P. R. O. MSS, D64/A/501.

[72] Beresford to Peel, May 31, 1845, Peel to Beresford, June 9, 1845, reproduced in *Report from the Select Committee of the House of Lords Appointed to Inquire into the Practical Working of the System of National Education in Ireland*, 1854 (525), XV, part II, pp. 1604-1605, 1607-13.

[73] James Godkin, *Education in Ireland: Its History, Institutions, System, Statistics and Progress form the Earliest Times to the Present* (London, 1862), pp. 103-104.

[74] Akenson, *Irish Education Experiment*, pp. 292-93; Anon., *Declaration in Favour of United Secular Education in Ireland by Members of the United Church of England and Ireland* (Dublin, 1866), pp. 5-6.

[75] Beresford to William Howley, Archbishop of Canterbury, April 12, 1845, N. I. P. R. O. MSS, D664/A/501.

Chapter VI: The Irish Church and Parliament in the Age of Church Reform,

1822-1833

[1] Olive J. Brose, *Church and Parliament: the Reshaping of the Church of England 1828-1860* (Stanford: Stanford University Press, 1959), pp. 1, 14-17.

[2] Gilbert A. Cahill, "Irish Catholicism and English Toryism," *Review of Politics*, XIX (1957), pp. 65-66.

[3] Mary Condon, "The Irish Church and the Reform Ministries," *Journal of British Studies*, I (May, 1964).

[4] One instance is Miss Condon's assertion that the Irish Church Temporalities Act of 1833 received "the consent of the primates." ("The Irish Church," p. 125). This is much too simple a reading of the attitude of Beresford and Howley.

[5] See Edward Brynn, "Irish Tithes in British Politics," *Historical Magazine of the Protestant Episcopal Church*, XXXIX (September, 1970), pp. 295-306, and "Some Repercussions," *passim*.

[6] G. I. T. Machin, "The Catholic Emancipation Crisis of 1825" English Historical Review, LXXVIII, (July, 1963), 458-82; Cahill, "Irish Catholicism," p. 67.

[7] William Magee to A. Wellesley, March 9, 1822, Wellesley MSS, 37298/295; Beresford to Liverpool, March 23, 1822, Beresford MSS, II/283-84.

[8] A. Wellesley, memorandum, n. d. (1822), A. Wellesley to Lord Clarina, Oct. 22, 1822, Peel MSS, 40221/1.

[9] A. Wellesley to Goulburn, Feb. 3, 1823, Goulburn MSS, II/22; Beresford to Wellesley, Feb. 14, 1823, Beresford MSS, 38.

[10] 1 Hansard, XXXIX (1819), 1454-58.

[11] John Mitford, Baron Redesdale, to Charles Abbot, Baron Colchester, Dec. 30, 1822, Magee to Abbot, July 20, 1823, in Colchester, Diary, III, 262, 268.

[12] 2 Hansard, VIII (1823), 367-416; Goulburn to Wellesley, March 5, 1823, Wellesley MSS, 37300/316-17.

[13] 2 Hansard, XI (1824), 532-88; XIII (1825), 1149-66.

[14] 2 Hansard, VIII (April 10, 1823), 802-812; XI (May 25, 1824), 890-99.

[15] 2 Hansard, XI (1824), 603-8, 775-76, 1432-34.

[16] William Dawson to Goulburn, Feb. 16, 1824, S. P. O.: Official Papers, Second Series, Carton 588E, No. 586/2; 2 Hansard, X (1824), 183-87.

[17] 2 Hansard, XI (1824), 918-19.

[18] Ibid., XII (1825), 1341-47.

[19] 2 Hansard, XIII (June 14, 1825), 1149-66.

[20] Ibid., XIV, (1826), 1205-8, 1253-54.

[21] Ibid., XIX, (1829), 131-35.

[22] Ibid., XIX, (1829), 906-13.

[23] James A. Reynolds, The Catholic Emancipation Crissis in Ireland 1823-1829 (New Haven: Yale University Press, 1954), p. 151; Beresford

to Howley, Feb. 10, 1829, Beresford MSS, 56.

[24]Beresford to Goulburn, Feb. 11, 1829, Beresford MSS, 54; Colchester, _Diary_, III, 605-6. Those bishops opposing Beresford were: Christopher Butson, Bishop of Clonfert and Kilmacduagh; William Bissett, Bishop of Raphoe; Richard Lawrence, Archbishop of Cashel and Bishop of Emly; Richard Ponsonby, Bishop of Killaloe; and, less directly, James Verschoyle, Bishop of Killala and Achonry and Robert Fowler, Bishop of Ossory. See Northern Ireland Public Record Office, D664/A/37-39.

[25]Rev. R. J. McGhee to Peel, Jan. 5, 1832, Peel MSS, 40402/171; James Graham to Edward Littleton, Oct. 8, 1832, National Library of Ireland, (microfilm) Graham MSS.

[26]Beresford to Edward Stanley, Irish Chief Secreatry, Beresford MSS, 19.

[27]Sidmouth to Talbot, April 23, 1819, S. P. O.: Official Papers, Second Series, II, 577/521/3; "Order of the House of Commons of 11 Feb., 1823 for an Account of All Unions and Divisions of Parishes from 1818," S. P. O.; Official Papers, Second Series, II, 587/549/2.

[28]Goulburn to Beresford, Dec. 16, 1829, N.I.P.R.O. D664/A/123.

[29]J. E. Jackson to Beresford, April 10, 1830, Stopford to Beresford, April 13, 1830, Representative Church Body Library, Beresford MSS, 5.

[30]2 _Hansard_, XXII, 1273-74, 1279, 1291.

[31]2 _Hansard_, XIII (May 18, 1830), 840-41.

[32]_Ibid._, 847.

[33]Stopford to Beresford, April 27, 1830, R.C.B.L., Beresford MSS, 6; Goulburn to Beresford, March 5, 1830, N.I.P.R.O. MSS, D664/A/31; Francis Leveson Gower, Irish Chief Secretary, to Beresford, March 6, 1830, Dublin, P.R.O.I., 737/55; 2 _Hansard_, XXII (1830), 1265.

[34]Goulburn to Beresford, March 5, 1830, N.I.P.R.O., MSS, D664/A/31.

[35]Beresford to Howley, Feb. 1, 1830, Beresford MSS, 59; Leveson Gower to Singleton, March 6, 1830, P.R.O.I., 737/58.

[36]Goulburn to Beresford, March 5, 1831, Beresford to Goulburn, Aug. 11, 1830, Goulburn to Beresford, Aug. 17, 1830, N.I.P.R.O., D/664/A.131, D/664/A/207-8; Leveson Gower to Beresford, March 6, 1830, Leveson Gower to Singleton, March 6, 1830, March 16, 1830, April 5, 1830,

P.R.O., IA/41/133; Great Britain, Parliamentary Papers, Vol. XCIII
(Reports, Vol. IX), Report of His Majesty's Commissioners of Ecclesiastical Inquiry, Ireland, 1831, pp. 1-2.

[37] Some idea of the conventional case of the Commission is seen
in Armagh Public Library, Beresford MSS, 4.

[38] Great Britain, Parliamentary Papers, (House of Commons), 1830,
Vol. VII, House of Commons Report on the Poor, p. 48.

[39] Stanley to Blomfield, Nov. 19, 1830, Beresford MSS, 37.

[40] Stopford to Beresford, May 17, 1830, Armagh Public Library,
Beresford MSS, V 5; Great Britain, Parliamentary Papers, Vols. DXXIII
(1834), CCXLVI (1836), D (1837) (Reports, Vols. XXIII, XXV, XXI),
Second, . . . Third . . . , and Fourth Reports of His Majesty's
Commissioners on Ecclesiastical Revenue and Patronage in Ireland.

[41] Great Britain, Parliamentary Papers, (Reports, Vol. XXXIII),
First Report of the Commissioners of Public Instruction, Ireland,
1835, pp. 9-45.

[42] Ibid., Vol. CCCLXXXVIII (Reports, Vol. XLVII), Parochial Bene-
fices, Ireland, 1835; Vol. XXXV (Reports, XXVII), Clerical Residence,
1833; Vol. DCCXXI (Reports, Vol. XXVII), Curates, Ireland, 1833;
Vol. LXXXI (Reports, Vol. XLVII), Clerical Residence, Ireland, 1835;
Vol. CD (Reports, Vol. XXVII), The Number of Churches in Each
Benefice or Union in Ireland, 1833; Vol. CCCXC-XCDXCI (Accounts and
Papers, Vol. XXVII), An Account of All Benefices in Ireland in which
Divine Service . . . Has Not Celebrated within . . . Three Years,
1833; Vol. CDXII (Reports, VI), Report from the Select Committee
. . . [on] Ecclesiastical Courts in Ireland. See Akenson, Church,
p. 165.

[43] A. Wellesley, memorandum, February 1833, Wellesley MSS, 37306/
49-59.

[44] Report of Sir John Harvey to Sir William Gregory, Dec. 23, 1830,
Dublin, S.P.O. Outrage Papers H. 120; Harvey to Sir John Harding, Oct.
21, 1830, Outrage Papers H. 119, noted in Patrick O'Donoghue, "Opposition", p. 69.

[45] Report of the Committee of the House of Commons on Disturbances
in Ireland, 1832, (677) XVI, questions 7295-7297, 6668-6671, cited in
O'Donoghue, "Opposition to Tithes," p. 9.

[46] Harvey to Gregory, Dec. 23, 1830, S.P.O. (Ireland), Outrage
Papers H. 120; House of Commons, Second Report of the Select Committee

of the House of Commons on Tithes, 1831-32 (508) XXI, 245, questions 2793, 3319, 3501, 3884, cited in O'Donoghue, "Opposition," p. 11, fts. 23, 26.

[47]Browne to Harvey, Dec. 14, 1830, Harvey to Stanley, Jan. 3, 1831, S.P.O. (Ireland), Outrage Papers H. 144.4; House of Lords, First Report from the Select Committee of the House of Lords ot Enquire into the Collection and Payment of Tithes in Ireland, 1831-32 (271) XXII, 1, pp. 39-40.

[48]Ibid.; See the testimony of Maj. George Brown, Inspector of Police, Kilkenny, in House of Lords, Minutes of Evidence [regarding] Collection of Tithes, 1831-32 (305), 179. Richard Wilson Greene, law advisor to the Irish government, declared: "The truth is that the legislature must be applied to, for the executive cannot take upon itself the assertion of the right of tithe, any more than of the right to rents, or the recovery of private debts." Ibid., appendix A, no. 31, quoted in Condon, "The Irish Church," p. 123.

[49]Harvey to Sir W. Gossett, letters of March and April, 1831, S.P.O. (Ireland), H. 18, 32, 35, 37, cited in O'Donoghue, "Opposition," p. 75, fts. 20-24.

[50]James Doyle, Letter to Thomas Spring Rice on the Establishment of a Legal Provision for the Irish Poor and on the Nature and Destination of Church Property (Dublin 1831). Bishop Doyle was alleged to have started the tithe war, and in fact did little to abate it. He declared that resistance should continue until the tithe was appropriated to its original purpose: one portion for the support of the clergy; another portion for public instruction; another for the building and repair of churches; a fourth portion for support of the poor. See J. K. L. [James Doyle], Letters on the State of Ireland (Dublin, 1825), pp. 32-33, 311-40; House of Lords, Minutes of Evidence (1831-32) 305, pp. 336, 343, 350-53; O'Donoghue, "Opposition," p. 76.

[51]Freeman's Journal (Dublin), June 21, 23, 28, 29, 30, 1831, July 29, 1831; Kilkenny Journal, June 22, 1831; Dublin Evening Post, June 21, 23, 24, 28, 30, 1831, July 28, 1831; Dublin Evening Mail, June 20, 22, 24, 27, 29, 1831; Harvey to Gossett, June 21, 1831, August 10, 12, 1831; 3 Hansard, I (1830), 1202-3, 1350, 1355; II (1830-31), 604, 11/6. See O'Donoghue, "Opposition," p. 77 and fts.

[52]House of Commons, First Report of the Commission for Ecclesiastical Inquiry, Ireland, 1833 (762) XXI, p. 201; Third Report, 1833 (762), XXI, p. 617; Fourth Report, 1833 (762), XXI, p. 673; 3 Hansard, II (1830-31), 29, 116, 350, 465-66, 727, 1001; Freeman's Journal, August 2, 8, 15, 20, 1831; Dublin Evening Post, July 12, 21, 23, 1831, August 27, 1831; Kilkenny Journal, August 6, 1831; Wexford Independent, August 2, 1832. See O'Donoghue, "Opposition," p. 78.

[53]3 Hansard, AI (1831), 906-10.

[54]Ibid., IV (1831), 239, 1092, 1169-70.

[55]Ibid., IV (1831), 1100.

[56]Ibid., VI (1831), 90-95, 871; VII (1831), 858-59; VIII (1831), 134-42.

[57]Ibid., IX (1831), 131; IV (1831), 1093-94.

[58]Wilbur Devereux Jones, Lord Derby and Victorian Conservatism (Oxford: University Press, 1956), pp. 26-27.

[59]Stanley to Blomfield, November 19, 1830, Beresford MSS, 37.

[60]William Lamb, Viscount Melbourne, Memoirs (ed. W. M. Torrens), (2 vols.; London: Macmillan and Co., 1872), I, 228.

[61]3 Hansard, XXIV (1834), 33.

[62]Ibid., IV (1831), 949.

[63]Jones, Derby, pp. 29-30.

[64]3 Hansard, X (1831), 136-55; Stanley to Beresford, Oct. 5, 1832, Stanley to Blomfield, Nov. 19, 1830, Beresford MSS, 20-37.

[65]A critical factor in 1831 was the position of the Whig Lord Lieutenant, the Marquess of Anglesey, whose recommendations on the tithe question were substantially more radical than those of Stanley. Stanley's admission to the cabinet in 1831 directly challenged Anglesey's position; a confrontation was made inevitable by ministerial discussion of the Irish church reform bill the following year.

[66]House of Commons, First . . . and Second Report[s] . . . on Collection of Tithes, 1831-1832, (508), XXI, 245, questions 3480, 3481, 2747, noted in O'Donoghue, "Opposition," p. 98.

[67]O'Donoghue, "Causes of the Opposition," pp. 13-15; House of Lords, Minutes of Evidence . . . [on] tithes, (1831-32), CCV, 272; House of Commons, Report on the State of Ireland, (1831-32), XVI, 431.

[68]O'Donoghue, "Opposition," pp. 93-96.

[69]Beresford to Howley, Dec. 9, 1831, Beresford MSS, 60.

[70]Ibid.

[71] Beresford in the House of Lords, 3 Hansard, XII (1832), 745-50.

[72] Stanley to Anglesey, Dec. 3, 1831, N.I.P.R.O., Anglesey MSS, T1068/36/132-33; Littleton, diary, Dec. 12, 1831, Stafford, County Record Office, Hatherton MSS, D/260/M/F/5, 26/7, f. 258.

[73] Anglesey's plan deserves more detailed consideration, for many portions of it were eventually realized under pressure from the radicals during the 1830s. The plan was prepared by Valentine Blake, a Catholic lawyer and a friend of the Lord Lieutenant and Dr. Francis Sadleir, later provost of Trinity College, Dublin. The plan was based on a projection of total revenues to be derived by compulsory tithe composition and rearrangement of the Church's administrative structure. The commission appointed to supervise these projects would also purchase existing leases on bishops' lands and let them out at competitive rents. After reimbursing the clergy the anticipated surplus could be used to eliminate the Church cess and to subsidise the Catholic clergy. Any further funds could be used for non-Church purposes. There were many controversial features, not the least of which was the prospect of paying the Catholic clergy. Even Bishops Doyle and O'Connell opposed it; O'Connell ahd been unwary enough to assent to it and in consequence had almost forfeited the leadership of the Catholic association. Peel also opposed it, for different reasons. Anglesey's program, then, while a worthy and far-sighted exercise, was doomed to failure, and he was miffed when the cabinet put it aside. See "Paper on Tithes and Church and Bishops' Lands, for the Consideration of the Cabinet," Jan. 18, 1832, Anglesey MSS T1068/36; Anglesey to Stanley, June 4, 1832, Anglesey to William Lamb, Viscount Melbourne, July 3, 1832, Anglesey MSS T1068/18, 35, f. 136; Anglesey to Brougham, Aug. 21, 1832, Brougham MSS, all noted in Abraham D. Kriegal, The Irish Policy of Lord Grey's Government," English Historical Review, LXXXVI (1971), the reading of which provided invaluable assistance for an understanding of Whig attitudes towards the Irish Church. Also see; Reynolds, The Catholic Emancipation Crisis, pp. 40-41; Peel to Gregory, March 21, 1825, quoted in Parker, Peel, 1, 369-70; and memorandum Aug. 11, 1828, Parker, Peel, 11, 58-60.

[74] Earl Grey, Prime Minister, to Anglesey, Feb. 5, 1832, Anglesey MSS, T1068/30/176.

[75] Stanley to Grey, Nov. 29, 1831, Durham, University of Durham, Grey MSS; Littleton, diary, Dec. 12, 1831, Hatherton MSS, D/260/M/F/5, 26/7, ff. 256-57.

[76] 3 Hansard, IX (1831), 259-78.

[77] Ibid., pp. 781-87.

[78] Ibid., X (1832), 2-7, 735-37.

[79] "Committee on Tithes: Stanley's Observations," circulated Jan. 5, 1832. H. O. 100/241/39-42.

[80] House of Commons, Report(s) . . . on the Collection of Tithes, 1831-32 (508), XXI (Reports from Committees, XVII), 245, p. xiii; Stanley to Grey, n. d. [late 1831], Grey MSS, noted in Kriegal, "The Whig Government," pp. 105-6. The Commons wanted the state to be the proprietor and collect a tax in lieu of tithes and the cess; the Lords wanted a general permanent composition collected by landlords as part of the rent: House of Lords, Second Report . . . on the Collection of Tithes, (1831-32), 303-5; House of Commons, Second Report on Tithes, (1831-32), XXI, 245, pp. iv, vii, viii, x.

[81] Lord Holland, Chancellor of the Duchy of Lancaster, to Anglesey, March 1, 1832, Anglesey MSS, T/1068/34/293-4.

[82] 3 Hansard, X (1812), 1281-82, 1305.

[83] Ibid., 1374; XI (1832), 134-202, 970-1012, 1042-76, 1113-56, 1234-44.

[84] Ibid., XII (1832), 572-91.

[85] Ibid., XI (1832), 1402; Great Britain, Parliamentary Papers, Vol. CCCXLVI (Bills, Vol. IV), "A Bill to Facilitate the Recovery of Tithes," 1831-32.

[86] 3 Hansard, XII (1832), 1363-66.

[87] 3 William IV, e. 41.

[88] Akenson, Church, p. 156.

[89] Anglesey to Grey, Feb. 10, 1832, Anglesey MSS, T1068/8/225.

[90] Anglesey to Stanley, March 21, 1832, June 4, 1832, Anglesey to Melbourne, July 3, 1832, Anglesey MSS, T/1068/18/35/136; Anglesey to Brougham, Aug. 21, 1892, Brougham MSS; Anglesey to Melbourne, Sept. 9, 1832, Anglesey MSS, T/1068/35/105; Anglesey to Graham, Oct. 6, 1832, quoted in C.S. Parker, Life and Letters of Sir James Graham, Second Baronet of Netherby 1792-1861 (2 vols., London: John Murray, 1907), I, 174; Anglesey to Holland, Oct. 21, 1832, cited in the Marquess of Anglesey, One Leg: The Life and Letters of Henry William Paget, First Marquess of Anglesey (London: Reprint Society, 1963), p. 264.

[91] 3 Hansard, X (1832), 1286-87, 1299-1302, 1331-74, XL (1832), 134-54.

[92] Ibid., XI (1832), 186, 191.

[93] Ibid., p. 1234.

[94] Ibid., X (1832), 1061-63; XIII (1832, 278, 761-62, 1161.

[95] Grey to Lord John Russell, paymaster-general, Oct. 25, 1832, cited in Spencer Walpole, The Life of Lord John Russell (2 vols.; London: Longmans, Green and Co., 1891), I, 190-91.

[96] 3 Hansard, XIV (1832), 95-112.

[97] Jones, Lord Derby, pp. 28-29.

[98] Stanley to Peel, April 22, 1832, Peel MSS, 40403.

[99] 3 Hansard, XI (1832), 1386.

[100] Ibid., XIII (1832), 1161.

[101] Ibid., XIV (1832), 228.

[102] Ibid., pp. 424, 719.

[103] Ibid., 242, 374-77.

[104] Great Britain, Parliamentary Papers, Vol. DXCIX (Bills, Vol. IV), A Bill to . . . Provide for the Establishing of Tithes in Ireland, 1831-32.

[105] Condon, "The Irish Church," p. 125.

[106] Stopford to Beresford, December 1834, Beresford MSS, 77.

[107] 3 Hansard, XX (1832), 579-83; Jones, Lord Derby, p. 28.

[108] Ibid., XVIII (1833), 1075-77.

[109] John Morley, The Life of William Ewart Gladstone (3 vols.; New York: Macmillan and Co., 1909), I, 133; Jones, Lord Derby, p. 28; Stanley to Goulburn, Aug. 2, 1832, Goulburn MSS, II/23.

[110] The Church question has, of course, received attention in recent scholarship, but not the role of the Church itself.

[111] Brose, Church and Parliament, pp. 43-46.

[112] Stanley to Grey, June 11, 1832, Sept. 24, 1832, Grey MSS.

[113]Lord Althorp, Chancellor of the Exchequer, to Graham, First Lord of the Admiralty, Sept. 25, 1832, Graham MSS; Stanley to Grey, August 4, 1832, Grey MSS.

[114]G. F. A. Best, "The Whigs and the Church Establishment in the Age of Grey and Holland," History, XLV (1960), 105.

[115]3 Hansard, I (1830), 574-75.

[116]Ibid., III (1831), 486; IV (1831), 768-69; Jones, Lord Derby, p. 27.

[117]3 Hansard, IV (1831), 1305-8.

[118]Ibid., VI (1831), 330-31.

[119]Ibid., 768-71, 1222.

[120]Ibid., 1305-7, 20-26.

[121]Ibid., IV (1831), 1409-10.

[122]Ibid., VI (1831), 1193-94.

[123]Owen Chadwick, The Victorian Church (2 Vols.; Oxford: University Press, 1966), I, 53.

[124]Wellesley, memorandum, Aug., 1833, Wellesley MSS, 37306/49-59.

[125]Enclosure in letter, Stanley to Peel, April 22, 1832, Peel MSS, 40611/164.

[126]"Stanley's Plan of Church Reform," Sept. 10, 1832, Grey MSS, cited in Kriegal, "The Whig Government," pp. 132-33.

[127]Stanley to Beresford, Oct. 30, 1832, Beresford MSS, 21.

[128]"Stanley's Plan of Church Reform," Grey MSS.

[129]Stanley eventually proposed reduction of bishoprics to ten: Dromore to Down and Connor; Clogher to Armagh; Raphoe to Derry; Elphin to Ardagh and Kilmore; Clonfert to Killaloe, Killala to Tuam; Kildare to Dublin; Cork to Cloyne; Waterford to Cashel and Emly; Ossory to Ferns; the province of Tuam to Armagh, and Cashel to Dublin, with Tuam and Cashel becoming bishoprics. This consolidation would realize a saving of Ŀ60,000.

[130]The sliding scale of taxation of clerical benefices in lieu of

first fruits was eventually established at the following levels:
₤200 or less equals nothing; ₤200-₤500 at 5%; ₤500-₤800 at 7%; ₤800-
₤1200 at 10%; ₤1200 and over at 15%. Deans and chapters would be
liable to the same rate. Since bishops' expenses were higher, they
would be taxed at the following rates: ₤4000 and less 5%; ₤6000 and
less at 7%; ₤10,000 and less at 10%; over ₤10,000 at 15%. This, with
abolition of church rates, would bring in ₤70,000 per annum. Certain
sees' revenues would be reduced. Chapters without duties would either
be abolished or have duties attached. Where no duty had been performed during the past three years commissioners might suspend appointment
of a minister. This was the program gradually decided upon by the
Grey ministry late in 1832 and even more gradually disclosed to Beresford.

[131]"Stanley's Plan for Church Reform," Grey MSS.

[132]Condon, "The Irish Church," p. 126.

[133]The theory that the graduated tax on benefices represented a
concession to Benthamite ideals is discussed in Condon, "The Irish
Church," p. 126, ft. 29.

[134]House of Commons, Second Report on Tithes, (1831-32), xxl (245),
xi.

[135]3 Hansard, XV (1833), 561-67.

[136]"Stanley's Response to Durham's Observations," Nov. 8, 1832,
Grey MSS, cited in Kriegal, "The Whig Government," p. 135.

[137]Elie Halevy, The Triumph of Reform (London: Ernest Benn, 1950),
pp. 142-43.

[138]Denis Le Marchant, Memoir of Viscount Althorp, Third Earl Spencer
(London: Richard Bentley and Son, 1876), p. 472.

[139]King William IV to Grey, Dec. 22, 1831, quoted in Henry, Earl
Grey, ed., Correspondence of William IV and Earl Grey from November
1830 to June 1832 (2 vols; London: John Murray, 1867), II, 54-55.

[140]Lord Durham, Lord Privy Seal, to Edward Ellice, Oct. 28, 1832,
National Library of Scotland, Ellice MSS, E/29/71, cited in Kriegal,
"The Whig Government," p. 136.

[141]Grey to Anglesey, Sept. 12, 1832, Anglesey MSS, T1068/30/229;
Grey to Brougham, Sept. 21, 1833, cited in John Cam Hobhouse, Lord
Brougham, Life and Times of Lord Brougham (3 vols.; London: William
Blackwood and Sons, 1871), III, 208-9; Grey to Russell, Oct. 25, 1832,
cited in Walpole, Russell, I, 190-91.

[142] Grey to Anglesey, June 11, 1832, Anglesey MSS, T1068/30/207.

[143] Ibid., Oct. 25, 1832, Anglesey MSS, T1068/30/239.

[144] Melbourne to Anglesey, April 4, 1831, June 30, 1832, cited in Lloyd C. Sanders, ed., Lord Melbourne's Papers (London: Longmans, Green and Co., 1889), pp. 180-81, 185-87.

[145] Melbourne to Anglesey, Sept. 12, 1832, Anglesey to Holland, Jan. 11, 1832, Melbourne to Anglesey, Dec. 20, 1830, Anglesey MSS, T1068/31/118, T1068/7/80, T1068/31/18-19; Littleton, diary, Aug. 10, 1833, Hatherton MSS, D/260/M/F/5/26/9, f. 37.

[146] Melbourne to Brougham, Sept. 20, 1832, Brougham MSS, cited in Kriegal, "The Whig Government," p. 138.

[147] Graham to Stanley, November 3, 1832, Graham, I, 173; Duke of Richmond, Postmaster General, to Graham, Nov. 11, 1832, Graham MSS.

[148] Anglesey to Holland, Oct. 21, 1832, cited in Marquess of Anglesey, One Leg, p. 264; Anglesey to Graham, Oct. 6, 1832, quoted in Parker, Graham, I, 174.

[149] Althorp to Grey, Aug. 6, 1832, Althorp MSS, cited in Kriegal, "The Whig Government," p. 140.

[150] Best, "The Whigs and the Church Establishment," p. 105.

[151] Christopher Darby to Charles Beresford, Sept. 13, 1832, enclosed in a letter, Charles Beresford to Lord John George Beresford, n. d., Beresford MSS, 8.

[152] Ibid.

[153] Beresford to Stanley, Sept. 22, 1832, Beresford MSS, 17.

[154] Ibid.

[155] Ibid.

[156] Grey to Stanley, Sept. 27, 1832, Grey MSS.

[157] Stanley to Beresford, Sept. 30, 1832, Beresford MSS, 18.

[158] Ibid.

[159] Beresford to Stanley, Oct. 4, 1832, Beresford MSS, 19.

[160]For contemporary reaction to Beresford's acquiescence, see: Lady Dorchester, ed., Recollections of a Long Life by Lord Brougham [John Cam Hobhouse] (6 vols.; London: John Murray, 1910), IV, 284; Henry Reeve, ed., The Grenville Memoirs (8 vols.; London: Longmans and Co., 1888), II, 330; 3 Hansard, XV (1833), 610; XVII (1833), 37, 980, 984. For modern concurrence in these reactions see: Condon, "The Irish CHurch," p. 125; Kriegal, "The Whig Government," p. 131.

[161]Durham to Ellice, Oct. 28, 1832, Ellice MSS, E/19/71-72, cited in Kriegal, "The Whig Government," p. 140.

[162]Russell to Grey, Oct. 20, 1832, quoted in Walpole, Lord John Russell, I, 188-89; 3 Hansard, XIV (1832), 377.

[163]Althorp to Grey, Oct. 20, 1832, Althorp MSS, cited in Kriegal, "The Whig Government," p. 141.

[164]Ibid.

[165]Russell to Grey, Oct. 25, 1832, British Museum, Holland House MSS; Grey to Russell, Oct. 25, 1832 and Holland to Russell, quoted in Walpole, Lord John Russell, I, 189-92; Grey to Althorp, Oct. 21, 1832, Le Marchant, Althorp, p. 446.

[166]Althorp to Grey, November 3, 1832, Althorp MSS, Althorp to Russell, Oct. 24, 1832, Duke University Library, Russell MSS, cited in Kriegal, "The Whig Government," p. 142.

[167]Anglesey to Holland, Oct. 21, 1832, Anglesey MSS, T1068/7/120.

[168]Grey to Althorp, Oct. 21, 1832, Althorp MSS, cited in Kriegal, "The Whig Government," p. 143.

[169]Holland to Russell, Oct. 26, 1832, Duke University Library, Russell MSS; Grey to Russell, Oct. 25, 1832, British Museum, Russell MSS, 38080/58-59; Grey to Althorp, Oct. 21, 1832, Le Marchant, Althorp, p. 446. Russell was comforted by his discovery that Althorp shared his views and still found it possible to remain in the government.

[170]Grey to Anglesey, Oct. 24, 1832, Holland to Anglesey, Oct. 24, 25, 1832, Anglesey to Holland, Oct. 27, 1832, Anglesey MSS, T1068/30/ 233-39, T1068/34/334-35, 340, T1068/7/124.

[171]Grey to Anglesey, Oct. 25, 1832, Anglesey MSS, T1068/30/239. Grey's increasing conservatism, however, should not obscure his basic unhappiness with the Irish Church. He contrasted, for instance, Irish bishops' light parliamentary duties and his own brother's burdens as

Bishop of Hereford: Grey to Brougham, Sept. 21, 1833, quoted in
Brougham, Lord Brougham, III, 208-9.

[172]The standard historical view that Durham was prepared to surrender on the Irish Church issue has been overturned by Miss Condon,
"The Irish Church," p. 127.

[173]Durham to Ellice, Oct. 28, 1832, Ellice MSS, E/29/71, cited in
Kriegal, "The Whig Government," p. 149.

[174]Ibid.

[175]Ellice to Grey, Nov. 5, 1832, Ellice MSS, E/18/95, cited in
Kriegal, "The Whig Government," p. 149; Richmond to Graham, Oct. 6,
1832, Graham MSS; Grey to Anglesey, March 5, 1831, Anglesey MSS,
T1068/30/79.

[176]Stanley to Beresford, Oct. 30, 1832, Beresford MSS, 14.

[177]Beresford to Stanley, Nov. 1, 1832, Beresford MSS, 22.

[178]Stanley to Beresford, Nov. 1, 1832, Beresford MSS, 23.

[179]Beresford to Howley, Richard Mant, Bishop of Down and Connor,
and John Brinkley, Bishop of Cloyne, Nov. 10, 1832, Beresford MSS, 65.

[180]Ibid.

[181]Mant and Brinkley to Beresford, Nov. 5, 1832, Beresford MSS, 66.

[182]Howley to Beresford, Nov. 17, 1832, Beresford MSS, 67.

[183]Graham to Stanley, Nov. 3, 1832, Graham MSS.

[184]Althorp to Grey, Nov. 3, 1832, Althorp MSS, cited in Kriegal,
"The Whig Government," p. 150. The ministry's difficulties are clearly
outlined by Professor Kriegal, pp. 150-155.

[185]Grey to Stanley, Nov. 3, 1832, Grey MSS.

[186]Stanley to Graham, Nov. 8, 1832, Graham MSS. Stanley in Dublin
negotiated with the ministry at a distance and at considerable inconvenience while Beresford at Armagh demanded their negotiations also
by conducted by post.

[187]"Observations on Stanley's Plan for Reform of the Irish Church,"

Nov. 8, 1832, Durham MSS, cited in Kriegal, "The Whig Government,"
pp. 151-52.

[188] "Stanley's Response to Durham's Observations," Nov. 18, 1832,
Grey MSS; "Lord Durham's Reply to Stanley's Remarks on Durham's
Observations of Stanley's Bill," Durham MSS. See Kriegal, "The Whig
Government," pp. 151-53, for a fuller elaboration of the Durham-Stan-
ley-Grey contest.

[189] Stanley to Graham, Nov. 21, 1832, Stanley to Grey, Nov. 29,
1832, Graham MSS.

[190] Althorp to Grey, Dec. 2, 1832, Althorp MSS, Graham to Stanley,
Nov. 18, 1832, Graham MSS; Grey to Stanley, Dec. 2, 1832, Grey MSS;
Stanley to Grey, Dec. 5, 1832; all cited in Kriegal, "The Whig Govern-
ment," pp. 152-53.

[191] Brougham to Grey, Dec. 5, 1832, Brougham, Lord Brougham, III,
245.

[192] Grey to Brougham, Dec. 4, 1832, Brougham to Grey, Dec. 9, 1832,
Brougham, Lord Brougham, III, 240-41, 248.

[193] Howley to Beresford, Dec. 22, 1832, Beresford MSS, 67.

[194] Beresford to Howley, Jan. 5, 1833, Beresford MSS, 69.

[195] Blomfield to Beresford, Jan. 1, 1833, Beresford to Blomfield,
Jan. 24, 1833, Beresford MSS, 2.

[196] Beresford to Stanley, Jan. 12, 1833, Beresford MSS, 25.

[197] Ibid., Jan. 24, 1833, Beresford MSS, 27.

[198] Stanley to Beresford, Jan. 28, 1833, Beresford MSS, 28.

[199] Ibid., Jan. 16, 1833, Beresford MSS, 26.

[200] Beresford to Stanley, Feb. 2, 1833, Beresford MSS, 29.

[201] Stanley to Beresford, Feb. 9, 1833, Beresford MSS, 30.

[202] Beresford to Stanley, Feb. 14, 1833, Beresford MSS, 31.

[203] Stanley to Beresford, Feb. 20, 1833, Beresford MSS, 32.

Chapter VII: The Irish Church and Parliament in the Age of Church

Reform   1833-1838

[1]3 Hansard, XV (1833), 576.

[2]Elrington to Newport, February 16, 1833, National Library of Ireland, Newport MSS, 796/26.

[3]Broughton, Lord Broughton, IV, 284; Littleton, Diary, Feb. 12, 1833, Hatherton MSS, D/260/M/F/5/26/8, ff. 153-55.

[4]Elrington to Beresford, Feb. 13, 1833, Beresford MSS, 72.

[5]Goulburn to Beresford, Feb. 13, 1833, Beresford MSS, 70.

[6]3 Hansard, XV (1833), 578-85.

[7]Elrington to Beresford, Feb. 13, 1833, Beresford MSS, 72.

[8]Howley to Beresford, Feb. 14, 1833, Beresford MSS, 8.

[9]Duke of Cumberland to Beresford, Feb. 1833, Capt. J. Jones to Beresford, Feb. 16, 1833, Beresford MSS, 136, 138, 84.

[10]Stanley to Beresford, Feb. 22, 1833, Beresford MSS, 35.

[11]Elrington to Beresford, Feb. 19, 1833, Beresford MSS, 85.

[12]Beresford to Howley, March 16, 1833, Beresford MSS, 90.

[13]Beresford to Elrington, Feb. 16, 1833, Beresford MSS, 83.

[14]Beresford to Goulburn, March 20, 1833, Beresford MSS, 86.

[15]Howley to Beresford, March 23, 1833, Beresford MSS, 92.

[16]Goulburn to Beresford, Feb. 13, 1833, Beresford to Goulburn, Feb. 16, 1833, Beresford MSS, 70, 71.

[17]Beresford to Laurence, March 21, 1833, Beresford MSS, 91.

[18]3 Hansard, XIX (1833), 550-51, 749-50.

[19]George Kitson Clark, Peel and the Conservative Party, (2nd ed., Hamden, Conn.: Archon Books, 1964), pp. 98-101, 114-21, 129-36, 151-95; P. J. Welch, "Bloomfield and Peel: A Study in Cooperation between

Church and State 1841-1846," Journal of Ecclesiastical History, XII
(April 1961), 71-84; Norman Gash, Mr. Secretary Peel (Cambridge, Mass:
Harvard University Press, 1961), passim; Norman Gash, Reaction and
Reconstruction in English Politics, 1832-1852 (Oxford: Clarendon Press,
1965), chapters III ("Church and Dissent: the Conflict"), and IV ("Church
and Dissent: the Compromise"), pp. 60-118: Edward Brynn, "Some Reper-
cussions of the Act of Union on the Church of Ireland, 1801-1820,"
Church History, XL (September 1971), pp. 281-96.

[20]See: Robert Shipkey, "Problems of Irish Patronage under the Chief
Secretaryship of Robert Peel, 1812-1818," Historical Journal, X (1967),
4-56; and Edward Brynn, "Irish Tithes in British Politics," passim.

[21]Duke of Cumberland to Peel, March 11, 1833, Howley to Peel,
March 21, 1833, Talbot to Peel, July 14, 1833, quoted in Parker, Peel,
II, 216-17.

[22]3 Hansard, XV (1833), 600-606.

[23]Peel to Goulburn, April 26, 1833, Parker, Peel, II, 218-20.

[24]3 Hansard, XV (1833), 561-76.

[25]Althorp's figures, while forecasting a surplus, in fact under-
estimated Church revenues: bishops' net revenues he estimated at
Ƚ130,000, of which Ƚ100,000 came from land; the proper totals were
Ƚ151,000 and Ƚ128,000 respectively. He estimated clerical tithes at
Ƚ580,000 to Ƚ600,000; they exceeded the latter figure by Ƚ10,000.
The gross revenues of deans and chapters were not Ƚ23,600, as he
thought, but with sums due to canons and prebends added, totalled
more than Ƚ152,600. See: 3 Hansard, XV (1833), 561-76, and Condon,
"The Irish Church," p. 128, footnote 40.

[26]3 Hansard, XV (1833), 608.

[27]Goulburn to Beresford, Feb. 13, 1833, Beresford MSS, 70.

[28]3 Hansard, XV (1833), 623-25.

[29]Ibid., XVII (1833), 1005-1007.

[30]Ibid., XVI (1833), 1399-1406; XVII (1833), 33-44.

[31]Ibid., XVII (1833), 1002-1003, 1005-1007.

[32]Ibid. Althorp showed that the combined revenues of Irish bishops
and clergy exceeded Ƚ730,000, more than enough for Church purposes.

Liberals thought his prediction vindicated when, after the death of three Irish bishops a year later, Littleton, the incumbent Irish Chief Secretary, could produce a surplus of Ł25,000.

[33] Ibid., pp. 44-49.

[34] Ibid., pp. 1003.

[35] Ibid., pp. 121, 138-39, 1127.

[36] Ibid., XV (1833), 973-74, 1150-53, 1191-99.

[37] Brougham, Lord Brougham, III, 188-89; the King's scolding was so oblique that contemporaries and some modern writers thought it referred not to the Church at all but to an adverse vote on Portuguese affairs: Greville, Memoirs, II, 390-93; III, 10, 14; Sir Herbert Taylor to Brougham, June 16, 1833, Grey to Brougham, June 19, 1833, Brougham, Lord Brougham, III, 190-201.

[38] Peel to Goulburn, May 25, 1833, Goulburn MSS, II/18; also in Parker, Peel, II, 221.

[39] 3 Hansard, XVII (1833), 1146-48.

[40] For a vociferous defense of the Church see Fraser's Magazine, VII (March 1833), 347-48, and Ibid. (April 1833), 476-81. Great stress was placed on the coronation oath, which bound ministers of the crown as much as the King himself, on infringement of property rights and other prerogatives,on reform of bishops' lands, which would destroy a profitable tenantry, and on the necessity for an independent clergy in Ireland, already endangered by tithe agitation and mortally endangered by the bill. The author noted that provision for suspension of service in benefices without churches, some of which benefices were late creations from oversized unions, would condemn to extinction the work of the Church in areas which would not have been affected if no reform had been attempted. The first attempt to circumvent reduction of bishops appeared in a formula whereby incumbents would appoint coadjutors. This would assure that no Protestant child went without confirmation and no clergyman went without easy access to episcopal consultation. Finally, there was the "treatened breach of the treaty of the union," placing part of the Church under its own head, the board of commissioners, a "complex pope replacing the headship of the crown."

[41] Peel to Goulburn, June 18, 1833, Goulburn MSS, 11/18, also quoted in Parker, Peel II, 222.

[42] Peel to Goulburn, June 21, 1833, Goulburn MSS, 11/18; also see

Clark, Peel, pp. 118-20; Littleton to Anglesey, June 23, 1833, Anglesey MSS, T1068/30/222-23.

[43] 3 Hansard, XVIII (1833), 1076-77.

[44] Ibid.

[45] Ibid., pp. 1150-52.

[46] Ibid., pp. 1152-62.

[47] Ibid., XIX (1833), 257-303.

[48] Peel to Goulburn, June 21, 1833, Goulburn MSS, 11/18; Clarke, Peel, pp. 118-20.

[49] 3 Hansard, XIX (1833), 257-303. The vote was 274 to 94. Goulburn had advised Peel to oppose it, believing Peel's support would prove embarrassing to the Lords should they decide to reject it: Goulburn to Peel, Peel MSS, 40333/158.

[50] David Large, "The House of Lords and Ireland in the Age of Peel, 1832-1850," Irish Historical Studies, IX (September 1955), 367-70.

[51] Grey to Anglesey, June 24, 1833, Anglesey MSS, T1068/30/306-307; 3 Hansard, XVIII (1833), 1073-74.

[52] Cumberland to Peel, March 31, 1833, Peel MSS, 40403/192.

[53] Wellington to Peel, July 23, 1833, quoted in Parker, Peel, II, 218.

[54] 3 Hansard, XIX (1833), 550.

[55] Ibid., pp. 550, 934-39.

[56] Ibid., p. 934.

[57] Van Mildert to Thorp, June 25, 1833, in Edward Hughes, "The Bishops and Reform, 1831-1833; Some Fresh Correspondence," English Historical Review, XVI (July 1941), 488.

[58] 3 Hansard, XIX (1833), 945.

[59] Brougham, Lord Brougham, III, 292. For Whigs' fears for the safety of the bill in the House of Lords see Taylor to Brougham, July 14, July 23, July 24, 1833, quoted in Brougham, Lord Brougham, III, 201-

205; Althorp to Lord Spencer, July 12, 1833, quoted in Le Marchant, Althorp, pp. 473-74; Greville, Memoirs, II, 390; Henry Lytton Bulwer, The Life of Henry John Temple, Viscount Palmerston (Philadelphia: J. B. Lippincott and Co., 1871), II, 161-65.

[60]Guy Le Strange, ed., Correspondence of Princess Lieven and Earl Grey (3 vols.; London: Richard Bentley and Son, 1890), II, 452.

[61]3 Hansard, XIX (1833), 303, 550; Althorp to Spencer, July 12, 1833, quoted in Le Marchant, Althorp, p. 473.

[62]Anglesey to King William, July 14, 1833, Anglesey MSS, T1068/7/ 184-89; Taylor to Brougham, July 14, July 23, 1833, quoted in Brougham, Lord Brougham, III, 296, 299.

[63]Greville, Memoirs, II, 394.

[64]Lieven to Grey, June 22, 1833, Correspondence, II, 450; Earl Eldon to Lady J. Bankes, July 16, 1833, quoted in Horace Twiss, The Public and Private Life of Lord Chancellor Eldon, with Selections from his Correspondence (2 vols.; London: John Murray, 1846), II, 317.

[65]3 Hansard, XIX (1833), 551-52; Large, "House of Lords," pp. 377-78.

[66]Clark, Peel, pp. 133-34; Wellington to Peel, July 23, 1833, Peel MSS, 40309/264-65.

[67]3 Hansard, XIX (1833), 1220, 1229.

[68]Earl Rosslyn to Mrs. Arbuthnot, July 24, 1833, quoted in Arthur Aspinall, ed., The Correspondence of Charles Arbuthnot (London: Royal Historical Society, 1941), pp. 172-73.

[69]Littleton, diary, July 25, 1833, Hatherton MSS, D/260/M/F/26/9, f. 25.

[70]3 Hansard, XX (1833), 1-4.

[71]Ibid., p. 118.

[72]Ibid., p. 287.

[73]Akenson, Church, pp. 172-78.

[74]See: W. Palmer, A Narrative of Events Connected with the Publication of the 'Tracts for the Times' (Oxford, 1843).

[75] Gash, _Reaction_, p. 81; Brose, _Church and Parliament_, p. 102.

[76] Peel to J. W. Croker, Sept. 28, 1833, quoted in Parker, _Peel_, II, 224.

[77] Lord Duncannon to Brougham, Sept. 12, Sept. 21, 1832, Brougham MSS, cited in Kriegal, "The Whig Government," p. 221.

[78] 3 _Hansard_, XVIII (1833), 659-61.

[79] Melbourne to Anglesey, May 9, June 3, 1833, Anglesey MSS, T1068/31/116, 176.

[80] Littleton to Anglesey, July 2, 1833, Hatherton MSS, D/260/M/01/2, f. 28.

[81] Littleton diary May 18, 1833, Hatherton MSS, D/260/M/F/26/8, f. 235.

[82] _Ibid._, July 11, 1833, Hatherton MSS, D/260/M/F/26/9, ff. 8-9.

[83] Littleton to Melbourne, Sept. 30, 1833, Hatherton MSS, D/260/M/01/2, f. 178.

[84] Littleton to Anglesey, June 11, 1833, Anglesey MSS, T1068/36/115.

[85] Littleton, diary, July 7, 1833, Hatherton MSS, D/260/M/F/26/9; f. 1.

[86] _Ibid._, July 7, July 8, 1833, Hatherton MSS, D/260/M/F/26/9, f. 3.

[87] Beresford to Grey, Aug. 14, 1833, Beresford MSS, 75.

[88] Littleton, diary, July 20, July 21, 1833, Hatherton MSS, D/260/M/F/26/9, ff. 12-17.

[89] 3 _Hansard_, XVIII (1833), 1953-57.

[90] _Ibid._, XX (1833), 341-45. Littleton produced the following information to support the million pound loan:

Tithes outstanding for 1830	0
Amount of tithe compensation claimed under the relief bill of 1832	Ŀ104,285
Amount collected	12,100
Amount outstanding for 1831	92,185

Amount due bishops, corporations and other bodies which had not availed themselves of relief during the previous session	20,000
Amount of tithes outstanding	112,185
Amount of tithes for 1832 not collected	300,000
Amount of tithes due for current year	600,000
Total amount of Church's tithes outstanding as of end of 1833	1,012,185
Amount of lay tithes outstanding	222,578
Total amount of tithes outstanding	1,234,763
Reduction for expense of collection by state (15%)	241,242
Balance to be loaned to tithe owners	993,521

[91] Ibid., pp. 351-54, 782-83, 820-21.

[92] Littleton to Anglesey, July 22, Aug. 20, 1833, Hatherton MSS, D/260/M/O1/2, ff. 79-80, 129; Grey to Beresford, Aug. 15, 1833, Beresford to Grey, Aug. 21, 1833, Beresford to Melbourne, Aug. 28, 1833, Beresford MSS, 93, 95, 103.

[93] Littleton, diary, Aug. 26, 1833, Hatherton MSS, D/260/M/F/26/9, ff. 49-50.

[94] Melbourne to Wellesley, Lord Lieutenant, Oct. 19, 1833, in Littleton, diary, Hatherton MSS, D/260/M/F/26/8, f. 231.

[95] Wellington to Croker, Sept. 30, 1833, John Wilson Croker, The Croker Papers: The Correspondence and Diaries of the Late Right Honourable John Wilson Croker, ed. Louis I. Jennings (3 vols.; London: John Murray, 1884), II, 217-18; the letter deserves quoting:

> The Irish Church bill, together with the measures above which [relate] to tithes, must destroy the Church of England in Ireland. We must not consider the Church of England, whether in England or in Ireland, as a religious establishment only. It promotes and encourages learning among its ministers, as well as piety, morality, good manners, and civilisation. The clergy are composed of the best educated gentry of the country. They owe much of their influence, particularly among the higher classes to that education and manners. But deprive the Church of its dignities, its honors and emoluments, pay the clergyman no more than is necessary for his bare subsistence, and enable him to raise his family in the cheapest and worst way in which a family can be reared, and we shall have deprived the Church of those ornaments which have given it strength and efficiency

as well as credit.

[96] Wellesley to Grey, Jan. 11, 1834, N. L. I., Wellesley Letter Book, 1834.

[97] Littleton to Melbourne, Sept. 21, 1833, Hatherton MSS, D/260/M/01/2, f. 165; Grey to Althorp, Sept. 29, 1833, Althorp to Grey, Oct. 3, 1833, Althorp MSS, cited in Kriegal, "The Whig Government," p. 240.

[98] Wellesley to Melbourne, Dec. 12, 1833, Wellesley Letter Book, 1834.

[99] Littleton to Newport, Dec. 31, 1833, N. L. I., Newport MSS, 796/4.

[100] Littleton to Wellesley, May 12, 1834, Wellesley MSS, 37307/68.

[101] Russell to Grey, Oct. 2, 1833, Grey MSS; Duncannon to Littleton, Nov. 6, 1833, Wellesley MSS, 37306/162-64.

[102] Littleton to Wellesley, Sept. 9, 1833, Littleton to Melbourne, Nov. 16, 1833, Hatherton MSS, D.260.M.01.2, ff. 159-60, 251-52; Grey to Wellesley, Nov. 22, 1833, Melbourne to Littleton, Nov. 22, 1833, Wellesley MSS, 37306/191, 202.

[103] Duncannon to Wellesley, Dec. 13, 1833, Wellesley MSS, 37306/246.

[104] Althorp to Littleton, Jan. 5, 1834, Wellesley MSS, 37306/308; Littleton to Wellesley, Jan. 31, 1834, Hatherton MSS, D/260/M/01/2, ff. 394-95.

[105] 3 Hansard, XXI (1834), 106.

[106] Ibid., p. 579. Applications by counties; Antrim, 3; Fermanagh, 4; Leitrim, 6; Londonderry, 11; Tyrone, 14; Monaghan, 17; Armagh, 19; Cavan, 23; Down, 30; Sligo, 37; Donegal, 44; Queens, 52; Dublin, 54; Mayo, 61; Meath, 63; Kings, 64; Roscommon, 67; Kerry, 70; Galway, 94; Waterford, 98; Kildare, 101; Limerick, 114; Clare, 144; Kilkenny, 160; Wesford, 198; Tipperary, 248; Cork, 303. All but one of the counties with low incidence are in the north.

[107] Condon, "The Irish Church," p. 131.

[108] 3 Hansard, XXI (1834), 572-91.

[109] Ibid., pp. 591-98.

[110] Ibid., pp. 572-91.

[111] 3 Hansard, XXI (1834), 628.

[112] See Chapter IV; also see Thomas S. Townshend, Facts and Circumstances Relating to the Condition of the Irish Clergy (Dublin, 1832), pp. 48-49; Graham to Stanley, July 3, 1834, quoted in Parker, Graham, I, 206-207; Stanley to Lord Ripon, Lord Privy Seal, British Museum, Ripon MSS, 40863/122-27.

[113] Beresford to Grey, Aug. 14, Aug. 21, 1833, Beresford MSS, 75, 95.

[114] Littleton to Wellesley, March 3, 1834, Hatherton MSS, D/260/M/01/2, f. 461.

[115] Ibid., May 2, 1834, Wellesley MSS, 37307/2-3.

[116] Ibid., ff. 4-5.

[117] Ibid., May 3, 1834, Wellesley MSS, 37307/9.

[118] 3 Hansard, XXIII (1834), 459.

[119] Ibid., 646-48, 651-52.

[120] Ibid., pp. 659-62.

[121] Ibid., p. 666.

[122] Memorandum from Stanley to Graham, entitled "Note handed to me in the House of Commons during Debate on Irish Church bill in May 1834," Graham MSS. Russell was alleged to have stated that "if there ever were a just ground of complaint on the part of any people against any grievance, it was the complaint of the people of Ireland against the present appropriation of tithes. . . ." Hansard supports this version. Stanley claimed he heard "if ever a nation had a right to complain of any grievance, it is the people of Ireland against the Church of Ireland." The meanings are quite different. See: 3 Hansard, XXIII (1834), 664-66; Greville, Memoirs, III, 100-101; Parker, Graham, I, 186-87; John, Earl Russell, Recollections and Suggestions 1813-1873 (London: Longmans, Green and Co., 1875), pp. 118-21; Jones, Lord Derby, pp. 45-46.

[123] Russell's motives have afforded historians cause to ponder their material. David Southgate in his Passing of the Whigs, 1832-1866 (London: Macmillan and Co., 1962), thought the statement unnecessary (p. 50). Kriegal regarded it a "blunder" perhaps due to Russell's frustration ("The Whig Government," p. 262). Other believe Russell wanted to secure the leadership of the party by ousting Stanley from the

government. Russell defended himself by declaring that Stanley had pledged the government to non-appropriation (Russell, Recollections, p. 120).

[124] Jones, Lord Derby, pp. 43-70; Best, "Whigs and the Church Establishment, pp. 115-16.

[125] 3 Hansard, XXIII (1834), 1396; Littleton to Welles ley, May 7, 1834, Wellesley, MSS, 37307/27.

[126] Russell, Recollections, p. 122; Littleton to Wellesley, May 28, 1834, Hatherton, MSS, D/260/M/01/3, f. 204. A commission of ecclesiastical inquiry was already in existence, being, as we have seen, one of the first initiatives of the Whig ministry in 1831. This commission was instructed to examine the practibility of dissolving unions of parishes in hopes of abolishing sinecures, attaching incumbents to benefices which provided their support, and increasing pastoral effectiveness. It was not instructed to determine the number of Protestants in each parish or the effectiveness of the clergy. See the testimony of J. G. Erck, Secretary to the Commissioners, in House of Lords, Minutes of Evidence (re) Collection of Tithes, 1831-32, CCV, 160, 165-67.

[127] Parker, Graham, II, 189; Greville, Memoirs, III, 38-39; 3 Hansard, XXIV (1834), 36.

[128] Peel to Goulburn, May 25, 1834, quoted in Parker, Peel, I, 243-44.

[129] King William to Peel, April 4, 1835, "A Statement of His Majesty's General Proceedings," Jan. 14, 1835, Peel MSS, 40303/143-52, 40302/203.

[130] Greville, Memoirs, III, 41; Broughton, Recollections, LV, 343, 34; Grey to Brougham, Nov. 5, 1833, Brougham, Lord Brougham, III, 316-17.

[131] 3 Hansard, XXIV (1834), 254-276.

[132] Thomas Spring Rice, Secretary for War and the Colonies, to Bourke, June 26, 1834, N. L. I., Monteagle MSS; Graham to Richmond, June 10, 1834, Graham MSS.

[133] Peel to Goulburn, May 25, 1834, Goulburn MSS, 11/18; also in Parker, Peel, II, 243.

[134] Peel to Arbuthnot, May 27, 1834, quoted in Parker, Peel, II, 247.

[135]Lambert to Durham, June 10, 1834, Durham MSS, cited in Kriegal, "The Whig Government," p. 272; Littleton to Wellesley, June 11, 1834, Hatherton MSS, D/260/M/01/3, f. 248.

[136]3 Hansard, XXIV (1834), 978-1000, 1209.

[137]Ibid., pp. 732-33, 1137-38.

[138]See Kriegal, "The Whig Government," pp. 277-79, and fts. 16-25.

[139]Henry Reeve, ed., Memoir and Correspondence relating to Political Occurrences in June and July 1834 by Edward John Littleton (London: Longmans, Green and Co., 1872); Brougham, Lord Brougham, III, 263-70; Sir Herbert Maxwell, ed., The Creevey Papers: A Selection from the Correspondence and Diaries of the late Thomas Creevey, M.P. (London: J. Murray, 1904), II, 255-56, 258.

[140]The King to Melbourne, July 9, 1834, Peel MSS, 192-94.

[141]Ibid., July 15, 1834, Peel MSS, 40303/205-209.

[142]Sir Robert Peel, Memoirs of the Right Honourable Sir Robert Peel (2 vols.; London: John Murray, 1858), II, 9.

[143]3 Hansard, XXIV (1834), 1285.

[144]Ibid., XXV (1834), 713-19.

[145]Ibid., pp. 992-93.

[146]Ibid., XXIV (1834), 731.

[147]Ibid., pp. 1190-93.

[148]Ibid., XXV (1834), 894.

[149]Ibid., XXIV (1834), 1146-47.

[150]Wellington to Sidmouth, April 1833, in George Pellew, ed., Life and Correspondence of the Right Hon. Henry Addington, First Viscount Sidmouth (3 vols.; London, 1847), III, 436ff; Greville, Memoirs, III, 73, cited in Clark, Peel, p. 181.

[151]3 Hansard, XXV (1834), 1196-99.

[152]Ibid., pp. 1167-71.

[153]Ibid., pp. 1171-72.

[154] Ibid., pp. 1190-93.

[155] Ibid., pp. 1193-96; Stanley to Ripon, July 25, 1834, Ripon MSS, 40863/122-27.

[156] 3 Hansard, XXV (1834), 1134-35; Littleton to Wellesley, Aug. 2, 1834, Hatherton MSS, D/260/M/01/3, ff. 381-82.

[157] Littleton to Gossett, Aug. 14, 1834, Hatherton MSS, D/260/M/01/3, f. 408; Greville, Memoirs, III, 68.

[158] Stanley to Goderich, July 25, 1834, Ripon MSS, 40863/122.

[159] Ibid.

[160] Peel to Goulburn, Sept. 3, Sept. 25, 1834, Goulburn MSS, 11/18.

[161] Beresford to Howley, Sept. 1, 1834, Beresford MSS, 105.

[162] Ibid., Aug. 29, 1834, Beresford MSS, 105.

[163] Beresford to Wellington, Nov. 11, 1834, Beresford MSS, 99.

[164] Beresford to the Duke of Northumberland, Nov. 13, 1834, Beresford MSS, 114.

[165] Wellington to Peel, July 5, 1834, Peel MSS, 40309/368.

[166] The King, private memorandum, Nov. 14, 1834, Peel MSS, 40303/230-31; Stanley to Ripon, Nov. 20, 1834, Ripon MSS, 40863/130-32; Baron E. von Stockmar, Memoirs of Baron Stockmar (2 vols.; London, 1872), I, 329; Duncannon to Littleton, Oct. 2, 1834, "Plans for Draft of Bill," (Nov. 1834), Wellesley MSS, 37307/181/82, 185-86.

[167] Rollo Russell, ed., Early Correspondence of Lord John Russell (2 vols.; London: T. Fisher Unwin, 1913), II, 46-47.

[168] W.S. Crawford, Observations on the Irish Tithe Bill (Dundalk, 1835), pp. 7-8; Henry D. Inglis, Ireland in 1834 (London, 1834), II, 208-10.

[169] Spring Rice to the Duke of Northampton, June 26, 1834, Monteagle MSS, 550/8-9; Russell to Spring Rice, Jan. 23, 1835, Spring Rice to Russell, Jan. 23, 1835, Spring Rice to Russell, Jan. 29, 1835, Russell, Correspondence, II, 74-75, 79-81.

[170] Herbert Taylor to Peel, March 4, 1835, Peel MSS, 40303/54-55.

[171] Greville, Memoirs, III, 148; the King to Melbourne, Nov. 14, 1834, memorandum, Nov. 14, 1834, Peel MSS, 40403/227-28, 229-30.

[172] Peel's declaration regarding the Irish Church:

> I cannot give my consent to the alienating of Church proper-
> ty, in any part of the United Kingdom, from strictly eccles-
> iastical purposes. But I repeat now the opinions that I
> have already expressed in Parliament in regard to the Church
> Establishment in Ireland - that, if by an improved distri-
> bution of the revenues of the Church, its just influence can
> be extended, and the true interests of the Established re-
> ligion promoted, all other considerations should be made
> subordinate to the advancement of objects of such paramount
> importance.

Quoted in Peel, Memoirs, II, 65.

[173] Stanley to Peel, Dec. 11, 1834, Peel MSS, 40405/61, and quoted in Peel, Memoirs, II, 36-42; Stanley to Ripon, Nov. 27, 1834, Ripon MSS, 40863/133.

[174] Peel to Stanley, Dec. 12, 1834, Peel MSS, 40405/120.

[175] Russell to Spring Rice, Jan. 23, 1835, Spring Rice to Russell, Jan. 29, 1835, quoted in Russell, Correspondence, II, 75-76, 78-80.

[176] Peel to Beresford, Feb. 14, 1835, Peel MSS, 40419/9.

[177] 3 Hansard, XXVI (1835), 66.

[178] Ibid., XXVII (1835), 13-22.

[179] Ibid., pp. 33-39.

[180] Ibid., pp. 13-23.

[181] Lord Haddington, Lord Lieutenant, to Goulburn, Feb. 14, 1835, Goulburn MSS, 11/24.

[182] Stopford, "Observations on the Tithe Bills," Aug. 1, 1833, Beresford MSS, 134.

[183] Haddington to Goulburn, Feb. 14, 1835, Goulburn MSS, 11/24.

[184] Stopford to Beresford, Jan. 30, 1835, Beresford MSS, 121; Peel to Beresford, Feb. 14, 1835, Peel MSS, 40414/9.

[185] Peel to Beresford, Feb. 14, 1835, Peel MSS, 40414/9.

[186] 3 Hansard, XXVI (1835), 23.

[187] Ibid., pp. 46, 55-56.

[188] Spencer to Russell, Jan. 28, 1835, quoted in Russell, Correspondence, III, 76-77.

[189] Melbourne to Grey, Feb. 11, 1835, Saunders, ed., Lord Melbourne's Papers, p. 253.

[190] Duncannon to Grey, Feb. 5, 1835, Grey MSS.

[191] Russell to Grey, March 13, 1835, Grey MSS, William Lamb, Viscount Melbourne, Memoir, ed. W. M. Torrens (2 vols.; London: Macmillan and Co., 1872), II, 106.

[192] Graham to Lord Howick, March 13, 1835, Graham MSS.

[193] Greville, Memoirs, III, 180.

[194] Parker, Peel, II, 292-303.

[195] Graham to the King, March 29, 1835, quoted in Parker, Peel, II, 292-303.

[196] Peel, memorandum, n. d., quoted in Parker, Peel, II, 301; also see Clark, Peel, p. 251, ft. 1.

[197] Graham estimated the revenues of the Church at ₤791,721, including tithe composition (₤534,433), episcopal revenues exclusive of tithes (₤141,896), deans and chapters and economy estates (₤5,399), minor canons and vicars choral (₤5,183), dignitaries, prebends and canons (₤6,560), glebe lands (₤68,250), and holdings of the perpetuity purchase fund (₤30,000): 3 Hansard, XXVII (1835), 361-74.

[198] Ibid.

[199] Parker, Graham, II, 223; Southgate, Passing of the Whigs, p. 50.

[200] Grey to Melbourne, Feb. 1, 1835, Russell to Melbourne, Feb. 11, 1835, quoted in Saunders, ed., Lord Melbourne's Papers, pp. 239, 252; Clark, Peel, p. 165.

[201] Hansard, XXVII (1835), 419-22.

[202] Ibid., pp. 422-25.

[203]Three weeks' debate consumed 440 pages in Hansard: 3 Hansard, XXVII (1835), 861-64.

[204]Ibid., pp. 980-84.

[205]Greville, Memoirs, III, 241, 243.

[206]3 Hansard, XXVII (1835), 957.

[207]Ibid., XIX (1835), 287-89.

[208]Peel declared that the Church's revenues were greatly overrated and its membership underestimated. Ward's resolution was "decidedly hostile to the Establishment;" the commissioners' income stood at Ł29,127, and expenses at Ł69,412 (Ł34,412 for operational expenses previously defrayed by the Church cess, and Ł24,000 for annual repairs to deteriorating churches). Even when tithe resistance ceases, Church revenues would not exceed expenses until a debt of Ł412,382 had been accumulated; at best this could not be amortized until 1873. The present bill would aggravate this deficiency by reducing tithe revenues, by making future reductions easy, by pegging rates to lowered grain prices. Peel added that if one estimated the Church's income at Ł377,779 (Ł288,163 in tithe revenue, Ł76,778 from glebes, and Ł12,838 from ministers' money), funds would not cover expenses as outlined in the Church Temporalities Act. Benefices with more than 50 Protestants totalled 1,121, giving each an average tithe revenue of Ł256. If incumbents in benefices of 50 to 500 Protestants were paid Ł200 per annum, those in benefices of 500 to 1,000 Ł300, and those in benefices of more than 1,000 members Ł400, the cost would exceed tithe revenue by Ł5,500 per year (Ł293,500 to Ł288,000). Glebe revenues, he concluded, must also cover defects in estimates of Irish revenues: 3 Hansard, XXIX (1835), 790-822.

[209]Mant to Mrs. Mant, July 10, 1835, Mant, Memoir, pp. 324-25.

[210]Ibid., July 17, 1835, Mant, Memoir, p. 327.

[211]Ibid., July 15, 1835, Mant, Memoir, p. 327.

[212]3 Hansard, XXX (1835), 716-17.

[213]Greville, Memoirs, III, 272; Broughton, Recollections, IV, 40.

[214]Edward Littleton to Robert Wilmot Horton, June 30, 1835, Derby, County Record Office, Catton MSS, "Letters from Lord Hatherton".

[215]Clark, Peel, p. 309.

[216]3 Hansard, XXIX (1835), 1067.

[217]Greville, Memoirs, III, 358.

[218]3 Hansard, XXX (1835), 119-22.

[219]Stanley to Ripon, Oct. 13, 1835, Ripon MSS, 40863/153.

[220]Robert Peel, A Correct Report of the Speech Delivered . . . on Inauguration into the Office of Lord Rector of the University of Glasgow and at the Public Dinner at Glasgow (7th ed., London: John Murray, 1837).

[221]Lord Wharncliffe to Peel, c. May 12, 1837, Peel MSS, 40423/209-38.

[222]Ibid.

[223]3 Hansard, XXXIII (1836), 22.

[224]Great Britain, Parliamentary Papers, Vol. CCXVIII (Bills, Vol. I), A Bill for the Better Regulation of Ecclesiastical Revenues and the Promotion of Religious and Moral Instruction in Ireland," 1836; 6 and 7 William IV, c. 99.

[225]Great Britain, Parliamentary Papers, Vol. CCLXXXVIII (Bills, Vol. I), A Bill for the Better Regulation of Ecclesiastical Revenues, 1837.

[226]Beresford, Draft of a speech on the tithe bill, July 1836, Beresford MSS, 135; 3 Hansard, XXV (1836), 1170-71, 1251-52.

[227]Mant, Memoir, pp. 362-63, 385-86.

[228]3 Hansard, XXXIV (1836), 22.

[229]Whately to Melbourne, Oct. 16, 1835, Saunders, ed., Lord Melbourne's Papers, p. 299.

[230]3 Hansard, XXXVIII (1837), 1375.

[231]Southgate, Passing of the Whigs, p. 63.

[232]Greville, Memoirs, III, 270.

[233]Wharncliffe to Peel, May 13, 1837, Peel MSS, 40423/227-29.

[234]Mulgrave to Russell, April 8, 1837, Russell MSS, P. R. O. 30/22/2E.

[235]Ibid., December 16, 1836, Russell MSS, P. R. O., 30/22/2D.

[236]Graham to Dean Jackson, Jan. 23, 1839, Graham MSS.

[237]U. Henriques, Religious Toleration in England 1787-1833 (London: Routledge and Kegan Paul, 1961), pp. 140-41. Carless Davis has noted that "one unexpected result of the Reform Act of 1832 was that the electorate showed itself even more violently interested than the old in questions which appeared to involve religious principles; and the Tories reaped the chief advantage of this circumstance." H. W. Carless Davis, The Age of Grey and Peel (Oxford: Clarendon Press, 1929), p. 161.

[238]Gladstone noted that "it appears not too much to assume that our Imperial legislature has been qualified to take and has taken in point of fact a sounder view of religious truth than the majority of the people of Ireland in their destitute and uninstructed state." W. E. Gladstone, The State and its Relations with the Church (London: John Murrary, 1839), p. 80.

[239]Such as in the Edinburgh Review, XXXVIII (1823) and XLIV (1826), as noted in Gash, Reaction, p. 60, ft. 1. He also produced the following quote from the Weekly Police Gazette, a radical rag of varying influence: "The clergy, as a body, are, in despite of their gowns, and bands, and oaths, a swarm of detected, blasted infidels. The living is their God. Toryism is their creed, knowledge is their aversion and libertinism is their practice."

[240]Gash, Reaction, p. 74.

[241]See The Times, Jan. 30, Feb. 5, 14, 23, Dec. 17, 31, 1835; Feb. 11, 20, May 7, July 2, 4, Aug. 20, 23, Sept. 5, 10, 28, 1836 for the "no popery" crusade of the Conservative clubs; also see Proceedings of the Protestant Association, Tenth Annual Report, May 1846, for the role of "no popery" among labor groups threatened with an Irish influx.

[242]Peel to Goulburn, Jan. 3, 1836, Peel to Wellington, Feb. 10, 1836, in Parker, Peel, II, 318, 322, 494-96.

[243]Elie Halevy, The Age of Peel and Cobden (New York, 1948), pp. 174-75.

[244]Greville, Memoirs, III, 354.

[245]Melbourne to Lansdowne, Dec. 26, 1836, in Torrens, Melbourne, II, 214-15.

[246]Stopford, "Sundry papers relating to the Irish Church bill," n. d. Beresford MSS, 128. The Earl of Ripon noted that continued tithe resistance had raised the debts incurred by the Ecclesiastical Commis-

sioners to ₺229,000. Meanwhile, nothing had been done towards building new churches and glebe houses, or the improvement of smaller
livings. Melbourne then admitted the Irish Church Temporalities Act
had in fact something of a "speculative character . . . and that the
amount of money to be supplied from the probable resource was found
to be greatly below the amount that the framers of the measure supposed." 3 Hansard, XLII (1838), 437-45, 447-48.

[247] Stopford, "On Residence," n. d., Beresford MSS, 128.

[248] Whately to Wellesley, Jan. 30, 1835, Wellesley MSS, 37307/349-
56.

[249] Peel to Wellington, March 28, 1837, in Parker, Peel, II, 344-47.

[250] O'Connell to Warburton, Dec. 29, 1836, quoted in Walpole,
Russell, I, 273.

[251] Taylor to Russell, Jan. 2, 1837, in Walpole, Russell, I, 274.

[252] Lord John Russell, Letter to the Electors of Stroud on the Principles of the Reform Act (2nd ed., London, 1839), pp. 30-31.

[253] Akenson, Church, p. 191.

[254] Charles Greville, A Journal of the Reign of Queen Victoria from
1837 to 1852 (3 vols., London: Longmans, Green and Co., 1885), I, 92.

[255] Ibid., p. 93.

[256] Frederick Shaw to Beresford, Mar. 17, 1838, N. I. P. R. O. MSS,
D664/A/351.

[257] Beresford to Goulburn, April 6, 1838, N. I. P. R. O. MSS, D664/
A/359.

[258] Stopford to Beresford, April 20, 1838, N. I. P. R. O. MSS,
D664/A/361.

[259] Ibid., I, 100.

[260] 3 Hansard, XLIII (1838), 1202.

[261] 1 and 2 Victoria, c. 109. See MacIntyre, Liberator, p. 190;
Daniel Kinahan, A Digest of the Act of Abolition of Tithes (1838),
V-XXXIII; Great Britain, Parliamentary Papers, Vol. CCCV (Accounts
and Papers, Vol. XLIII), Return of Tithe Arrears, 1844, p. 2.

[262] Parker, _Peel_, III, 65.

[263] _A Bill Entitled An Act to Alter and Amend Several Acts Relating to the Temporalities of the Church of Ireland_, H. L., 1847 (193) iii.

[264] Gladstone to Manning, April 26, 1845, March 8, 1846, April 5, 1846, Gladstone MSS, 44247/264-67, 289-92, 298-305; in Machin, "Maynooth" p. 63.

[265] Gash, _Reaction_, p. 94.

[266] Olive Brose, _Church and Parliament_, pp. 118-119.

[267] Cahill, "Protestant Association", pp. 276-77.

[268] This is discussed in greater detail in Chapter IX.

[269] Gash, _Reconstruction and Reaction_, pp. 72-75.

[270] Croker to Peel, April 20, 1845, Peel MSS, 40565/7-8.

[271] Ellice to Russell, March 31, 1845. Russell Papers, P. R. O., 30/2240.

Chapter VIII. The Life of the Church 1800-1869

[1] Wellesley to the Bishop of Cork, Dec. 27, 1808, Wellington, _Despatches: Ireland_, p. 514; Liverpool to Richmond, May 11, 1809, Richmond MSS, 71/1389; Liverpool to Peel, Oct. 24, 1813, Peel MSS, 40181/51-53.

[2] Rev. George Miller to Edward Johnson, May 10, 1822, Dublin, S. P. O., Official Papers, Second Series, Carton 577, No. 525/4; Aspinal, ed., _George IV_, I, 343, footnote.

[3] O'Beirne to Brodrick, May 24, 1803, Brodrick MSS, 8873; Curwen, _Observations_, II, 178-79.

[4] A. Wellesley to Knox, Jan. 9, 1809, Jan. 14, 1809, Wellington, _Ireland_, pp. 525-537.

[5] Anna L. Evans, _The Disestablishment of the Church of Ireland_ (Lancaster, Pa., 1929), p. 98.

[6] _Cobbett's Political Register_ (August 3, 1822).

[7] Annual Register, 1822, appendix, p. 425; Dublin, P. R. O. MSS, U2293, Jocelyn to Beresford, Aug. 13, 1822; Beresford to Goulburn, Aug. 21, 1822, Beresford to Goulburn, Sept. 28, 1822, Wellesley to Goulburn, Aug. 3, 1822, Goulburn to Wellesley, Sept. 20, 1822, Goulburn MSS/21.

[8] Francis Bamford and Arthur Wellesley, Seventh Duke of Wellington, eds., The Journal of Mrs. Arbuthnot, (2 vols.; London: Macmillan, 1950), I, 183.

[9] Lundeen, "Bench of Bishops," p. 12.

[10] Evans, Disestablishment, p. 98.

[11] Desmond Bowen, The Protestant Crusade in Ireland, 1800-70 (Dublin: Gill and Macmillan, 1978), passim.

[12] Fitzgibbon to Eden, January 14, 1800, in McDowell, "Some Fitzgibbon Letters," p. 311.

[13] Solloway, Prelates, pp. 49-50.

[14] Bowen, Souperism, p. 75.

[15] W. J. Fitzpatrick, Memoirs of Richard Whately (2 vols.; London, 1864), I, 146.

[16] Leveson Gower to Peel, Nov. 2, 1829, Dublin, P. R. O., M737/179; Fitzpatrick, Whately, I, 151-52; John Redcliff to Sir William Gossell and Stanley, Aug. 10, 1831, S. P. O., Official Papers, Second Series, Vol. II (1810-1831), Carton 588E/586/21.

[17] Fitzpatrick, Whately, I, 90-96.

[18] E. L. Woodward, The Age of Reform 1815-1870 (Oxford: Clarendon Press, 1938), p. 488.

[19] Brougham in 1863 claimed an "indistinct recollection of urging Grey to appoint Whately." Fitzpatrick, Whately, I, 85-86.

[20] Grey to Bathurst, Aug. 21, 1831, Bathurst to Grey, Aug. 22, 1831, Howick Papers, noted in Chadwick, Victorian Church, I, 53.

[21] Fitzpatrick, Whately, I, 250-51, 290-315.

[22] Whately to Wellesley, Jan. 28, 1834, Wellesley MSS, 37306/348.

[23] Chadwick, Victorian Church, I, 54.

[24] Brose, Church and Parliament, pp. 35-36; 3 Hansard, X (1832), 873.

[25] Dr. Wills, Lives of Illustrious and Distinguished Irishmen, VI, 387, quoted in Fitzpatrick, Whately, I, 132.

[26] Stuart to Brodrick, March 20, 1813, Brodrick MSS, 8869/7.

[27] Charles Lindsay to Wellesley, Dec. 28, 1827, Wellesley MSS, 37305/211.

[28] Anon. to Brodrick, April 23, 1815, Hannah More to Brodrick, Nov. 4, 1815, Brodrick MSS, 8861/7.

[29] Lundeen, "Bench of Bishops," p. 23.

[30] Warburton to McMahon, June 14, 1813, in Aspinall, ed., George IV, I, 257.

[31] Ibid., July 20, 1813, in Aspinall, ed., George IV, I, 267-68.

[32] Gregory, Letter-Box, p. 131.

[33] Bowen, Souperism, p. 72.

[34] Stuart to Brodrick, Feb. 7, 1822, Brodrick MSS, 8869/8.

[35] Jebb to Brodrick, Nov. 29, 1817, copy, Brodrick to Jebb, Nov. 13, 1817, Jebb to Brodrick, Jan. 18, 20, 1819, Stuart to Brodrick, Feb. 7, 1822, Brodrick MSS, 8866/5, 6, 8869/8.

[36] Leslie Stephen and Sidney Lee, eds., Dictionary of National Biography (Oxford: Oxford University Press, 1885-1900), X, 696-97.

[37] Bennett to Brodrick, Oct. 2, 1819, Brodrick MSS, 8892.

[38] Stuart to Brodrick, July 5, 1819, Brodrick MSS, 8869/8.

[39] William Magee, Evidence . . . on the State of Ireland, pp. 14-15; Newland, Apology, p. 165.

[40] R. B. McDowell, The Church of Ireland, 1869-1969 (Boston: Routledge and Kegan Paul, 1975), p. 10.

[41] DNB, VIII, 532.

[42] R. S. Gregg, Memorials of the Life of John Gregg (Dublin, 1879), pp. 67, 121, 209-10, in McDowell, Church, pp. 10-11.

[43] George Madden to Thomas Lockwood, Aug. 10, 1811, Brodrick MSS, 8861/5.

[44] O'Beirne to Brodrick, June 27, 1803, Brodrick MSS, 8873.

[45] Whately's proposal for a seminary was couched in terms which inevitably inspired fears of an institution in which the clergy would be exposed to the intellectual discipline and dogmatic method then associated with Maynooth.

[46] Croker, Sketch, p. 39; Ensor, Observations, p. 34.

[47] H. Blake, Letters from the Irish Highlands of Cunnemarra (London, 1825), pp. 147-49.

[48] Lovett to Brodrick, April 19, 1800, Brodrick MSS, 8874/4.

[49] Stuart to Brodrick, April 24, 1812, Brodrick MSS, 8869/6.

[50] National Library of Ireland, Loftus MSS, 8821; Ballyshannon Herald, June 6, 1834, p. 4.

[51] James Brandon to A. Laberlauch, May 23, 1816, N. I. P. R. O. MSS, D1108/B/60.

[52] Ballyshannon Herald, Aug. 26, 1831, p. 2.

[53] William Porteus to Loftus, October 17, 1826, Loftus MSS, 8821/15.

[54] William Owens to Thomas Brooke Clarke, absentee encumbent of Innismacsaint, Dec. 1799, Jan., March, April, 1800. N. I. P. R. P. MSS, D-1108/B/13; Thomas Irwin to Clarke, May 25, 1816, Robert Richardson to Clarke, June 24, 1820, Irwin to Clarke, July 26, 1821, James Kidney to Clarke, June 15, 1822, N. I. P. R. O. MSS, D1108/B/57, 68, 70, 71, 82; memorial from Thomas Gutbridge and Arthur Trotter, Churchwardens of Rossory, Nov. 20, 1832, Loftus MSS, 8821/18.

[55] Blake, Letters from Highlands, pp. 148-49.

[56] Thomas O'Beirne, Charge to the Clergy of Meath (Dublin, 1800), p. 13, in Haliday, 801/9.

[57] O'Beirne to Brodrick, March 31, 1803, Brodrick MSS, 8873; O'Beirne, Charge to the Clergy (1804), p. 10; O'Beirne to Brodrick, Sept. 4, 1813, March 9, 1818, Brodrick MSS, 8873.

[58] Stuart to Brodrick, May 18, 1805, Hardwicke MSS, 35759/96; Brandon to Clarke, Nov. 8, 1814, J. I. P. R. O. MSS, D1108/B/49; William Magee, Charge to the Clergy of Dublin (Dublin, 1822), pp. 32-33, in Haliday, 1225/1.

[59] Henry Lloyd to Loftus, Sept. 19, 1810, Loftus MSS, 8821/3.

[60] Stuart to William Elliot, April 8, 1806, Fortescue MSS, VIII (1912), 90.

[61] Bennett to Brodrick, Oct. 2, 1819, Brodrick MSS, 8892.

[62] Lovett to Brodrick, July 12, 1804, Jan. 15, 1805, Brodrick MSS, 8869.

[63] Brodrick to unknown correspondent, May 3, 1810, Richard Wynne to Brodrick, Sept. 10, 1814, Brodrick MSS, 8888, 8861/7.

[64] Stuart to Richmond, April 18, 1810, Richmond MSS, 63/901.

[65] Duigenan to Brodrick, Dec. 10, 1811, January 4, 1812, Wynne to Brodrick, Jan. 25, 1812, Brodrick to Forster, Feb. 13, 1812, Symes to Brodrick, June 4, 1812, Brodrick MSS, 8861/5, 6.

[66] O'Beirne to Brodrick, March 31, 1805, Brodrick MSS, 8873; Loftus to Henry Boyd, Oct. 7, 1810, Loftus MSS, 8821/3; Loftus to James Cochrane, Aug. 21, 1812, P. R. O. MSS, M2287; Loftus to Clarke, Nov. 8, 1824, N. I. P. R. O. MSS, D/108/B/88; "Clogher Visitation Book, 1824," N. L. I. MSS, 2757.

[67] Richard Warburton to Brodrick, April 6, 1814, Brodrick MSS, 8861/7.

[68] Lord Sanford to Loftus, Jan. 16, 1809; Loftus to Sanford, Jan. 26, 1809, Loftus MSS, 8821/2.

[69] Loftus to unnamed correspondent, March 17, 1810, Loftus MSS, 8821/3.

[70] A. Wellesley to Richmond, June 30, 1807, in Wellington, Civil Correspondence: Ireland, pp. 101-102; N. R. Parkenham to Henry Goulburn, Aug. 9, 1822, Dublin, S. P. O., Carton 664.

[71] Lovett to Brodrick, Oct. 8, 1803, Feb. 19, 1806, Brodrick MSS, 8874/1, 2; J. W. Rogers to Loftus, Jan. 19, 1809, Loftus MSS, 8821/2; William Owens to Clarke, June 1801, N. I. P. R. O. MSS, D1108/B/28; Richard Graves to Brodrick, Sept. 13, 1819, Brodrick to Graves, Sept.

20, 1819, Thomas Gough to Brodrick, Oct. 5, 1819, Brodrick MSS, 8861/10.

[72]W. H. Pratt to Loftus, Oct. 8, 1828, Loftus MSS, 8821/16.

[73]Brandon to Clarke, Sept. 20, 1812, April 7, 1813, N. I. P. R. O. MSS, D1108/B/49; William Miller to Loftus, Aug. 30, 1813, Loftus MSS, 8821.

[74]Killen, Ecclesiastical History, II, 353; John Healy, History of the Diocese of Meath, 2 vols.; (Dublin: Association for the Propagation of Christian Knowledge, 1908), II, 353; Mant. History, II, 738-39.

[75]Thomas O'Beirne, Charge to the Clergy of Meath (Dublin, 1820), pp. 4-5, in Haliday, 1177/9.

[76]Dublin Evening Mail, quoted in Fitzpatrick, Whately, I, 130.

[77]Thomas Newenham, A Statistical and Historical Inquiry into the Progress and Magnitude of the Population of Ireland (London, 1805), p. 307.

[78]Mason, Survey, III, 14 ff.

[79]Anon., Essay on the Comparative Number of Protestants and Roman Catholics in the United Kingdom (Dublin, 1812), p. 14, in Haliday, 1003/8; Newland, Apology, pp. 190-195.

[80]Ballyshannon Herald May 31, 1839, p. 1.

[81]Dublin, P. R. O. "Official Papers," Carton 522; Ecclesiastical Group 144, Item 1 (June 18, 1803); House of Commons, "Returns of the Clergy, 1824" James O'Connor, History of Ireland 1798-1924 (2 vols.; New York; E. Arnold and Co., 1926), p. 223. On the eve of disestablishment the Irish Church Commission reported the distribution of members among benefices as follows: over 5,000 members in 4 benefices, 2,000 to 5,000 in 63, 1,000 to 2,000 in 115, 750 to 1,000 in 100, 500 to 750 in 122, 200 to 500 in 336, 100 to 200 in 254, 40 to 100 in 287, 30 to 40 in 59, 20 to 30 in 48, under 20 in 92. House of Commons, Report of Her Majesty's Commissioners on the Revenue and Condition of the Established Church in Ireland, 1867-68, XXIV, Appendix, p. 249. See P. M. H. Bell, Disestablishment in Ireland and Wales (London: SPCK, 1969), pp. 32-33 for further discussion.

[82]McDowell, Church of Ireland, pp. 12-13.

[83]House of Commons, First Report of the Commissioners on Ecclesi-

astical Revenue and Patronage, Ireland, 1833, (742), XXI; Evans,
Disestablishment, p. 99.

[84] Edward Stopford, "Returns of the Clergy, 1824", Beresford's Correspondence, XI, 154; Mason, Survey, III, 460; 3 Hansard, XXIX (1835),
885-86; Brose, Church and Parliament, p. 113.

[85] Stopford, memorandum, 1838, Beresford's Correspondence, XI, 152;
Bell, Disestablishment, pp. 31-32.

[86] Anon., Thoughts on the Protestant Ascendancy, pp. 90-93.

[87] Ibid., p. 90.

[88] New Irish Magazine and Monthly National Advocate, I (September
1822), p. 86, in Haliday, 1245/1.

[89] Ensor, Observations, pp. 30-31.

[90] Anon., The Improved Antidote, Supposed to be More Active in Ex-
pelling Poison, than a Late Invention by the Rev. Sir Harcourt Lees,
in which Catholics are Vindicated form his Abuse (Dublin, 1820), p.
17, in Haliday, LL81/1.

[91] Newenham, Inquiry, p. 318.

[92] Anon., Reflections on the State of Ireland, pp. 197-98.

[93] New Irish Magazine, p. 86; Irish Protestant and Faithful Examiner,
(Nov.-Dec. 1822), 109-110, in Haliday, 1245/1.

[94] O'Beirne, Charge, (1816), pp. 13-14.

[95] Thomas O'Beirne, Charge to the Clergy of Meath (Dublin, 1822),
pp. 8-9, in Haliday, 1230/5; Charge, (1822), p. 9.

[96] A. O'Callaghan, Observations on the State of Religious Feeling
in Ireland (London, 1827), pp. 130-31; 1 Hansard XXXIX (1819), 1455-
58; n. s. Hansard, XII (1825), 1341, 1346; XIII (1829), 1149-57, 1159-
60.

[97] Kilkenny Journal, March 26, 1831, p. 3; Ballyshannon Herald, June
19, 1835, p. 3; Report of the Committee for the Relief of the Distressed
Districts, pp. 45, 47; M. Seymour, Speech . . . on the Conduct towards
Protestant Tenants of the Irish Aristocracy (Dublin, 1829), passim. in
Haliday, 1444/7; Magee, Evidence . . . on the State of Ireland, pp. 1-4.

[98] Anon., Observations on the State of the Established Church, pp. 49-82; Ballyshannon Herald, Aug. 21, 1840, p. 3.

[99] Ballyshannon Herald, Sept. 26, 1834, p. 4; W. H. C., Letter to Earl Mount Cashel on the Distribution of Church Revenues (Dublin, 1829), p. 5, in Haliday, 1446/12.

[100] William Mayne to William Lennard, Nov. 2, 1811, N. I. P. R. O. MSS, 01232.

[101] Beech to Loftus, July 10, 1809, Rev. L'Estrange to Loftus, July 8, 1809, Rev. Hamilton to Loftus, July 13, 1809, Loftus MSS, 8821/21; John Palliser to Brodrick, Jan. 18, 1804, Brodrick MSS, 8861/4; George Miller to Loftus, Jan. 25, 1825, Loftus MSS, 8821/14; House of Commons, Papers Relative to Building a Church in the Parish of Devenish, printed March 15, 1824.

[102] There is an interesting collection of letters illustrating these points in the Loftus MSS during the years 1810 and 1813. The confrontation resulted from the construction of a new church in Roscrea, and the subsequent assignment of seats provided an opportunity for an eruption of long-repressed community antagonisms.

[103] Statistical information is reproduced in Brynn, "Church of Ireland Diocese," passim.

[104] Richard Lawrence, Charge at the Visitation of Munster (Dublin, 1833), p. 32, in Haliday, 1263/3.

[105] Determined by comparing the frequency of names on the Clogher lists in the following sources: Charles Coote, Statistical Survey of the County of Monaghan (Dublin, 1801), pp. 223-31; Rushe, History, pp. 155-59, 167-68, 185-90; "Clontibret Applotment Book," Aug. 30, 1830, P. R. O. MSS, Box 40; and from private correspondence, especially the Loftus MSS.

[106] McDowell, Church of Ireland, pp. 13-14.

[107] Anon., Thoughts and Suggestions on the Education of the Peasantry of Ireland (London, 1820), p. 29, in Haliday, 1179/7.

[108] William Magee, Charge of the Clergy of Raphoe (Dublin, 1822), pp. 17-18, in Haliday 1230/2; House of Lords, "Minutes of Evidence," 1824, p. 235.

[109] Anon., Letter to the Hon. J. Abercrombie, M.P., on the New Irish Tithe Bill (Dublin, 1824), pp. 65-66; Ballyshannon Herald, March 6,

1840, p. 2; William Magee, Charge to the Clergy at Raphoe (Dublin, 1822), pp. 17-18, 20, in Haliday, 1230/2.

[110] Anon., Thoughts and Suggestions on the Education of the Peasantry of Ireland (London, 1820), p. 27, in Haliday, 1179/7; Anon., Letters to the . . . Archbishop of Armagh and . . . the Duke of Devonshire, p. 38; James Doyle, Letters on the State of Ireland (Dublin, 1825), p. 73, in Haliday, 1339/4.

[111] Ballyshannon Herald, March 6, 1840, p. 2.

[112] Anon., Three Months in Ireland by an English Protestant (London, 1827), p. 42, in Haliday, 1380/7.

[113] Killen, Ecclesiastical History, II, 421.

[114] Maxwell, Dublin under the Georges, p. 339.

[115] Ballyshannon Herald, Dec. 2, 1831, p. 2, Sept. 25, 1835, p. 3, Sept. 21, 1838, p. 3, Sept. 14, 1838, p. 3: these are instances drawn from all over Ireland. Also see John Jebb to Brodrick, Dec. 26, 1821, Brodrick MSS, 8866/8.

[116] Digest of Evidence Taken before Select Committees of the Two Houses of Parliament, Appointed to Inquire into the State of Ireland 1824-25 (London, 1826), pp. 128-29, 140, 143-44, in Haliday, 1235/1; George White, Digest of Evidence on the First Report of the Committee on the State of Ireland (Dublin, 1825), p. 9, in Haliday, 1336/1; Dublin, S. P. O., Catholic Association Papers, Feb. 27, 1824, noted in Reynolds, Catholic Emancipation, p. 32; evidence of Michael Collins. House of Commons, Select Committee . . . on the State of Ireland, p. 68; evidence of John Dunn, Ibid., p. 7; New Irish Magazine, I (Sept. 1822), 233.

[117] Murphy, "Support of the Catholic Clergy," p. 106.

[118] House of Commons, Select Committee (1825), p. 37; Ballyshannon Herald, May 23, 1834, p. 2.

[119] W. R. LeFanu, Seventy Years of Irish Life (London: Macmillan, 1894), p. 45; Grant, Substance of a Speech, p. 66; House of Commons, Select Committee . . . on the State of Ireland," p. 33.

[120] Report of the Committee for the Relief of the Distressed Districts of Ireland, p. 148.

[121] Curwen, Observations, I, 235-36.

122 Anon., One Year's Administration of Lord Lieutenant Wellesley in Ireland (London, 1823), passim, in Haliday, 1282/1; Anon., Recent Occurrences in Ireland in a Letter to a Friend in England (London, 1823), pp. 182-83, in Haliday, 1282/3; Magee, Charge (1822), passim; New Irish Magazine, I (Sept. 1822), 235.

123 Irish Protestant, I (Nov.-Dec. 1822), 112.

124 Anon., One Year's Administration, p. 81; Anon., Recent Occurrences, passim; Thomas Elrington, Charge to the Clergy of Leighlin and Ferns (Dublin, 1827), passim, in Haliday, 1389/7-11.

125 Magee to Wellesley, Sept. 17, 1823, Wellesley MSS, 37301/283-85.

126 Goulburn to Peel, Sept. 23, 1823, Peel MSS, 40329/141-43.

127 Magee to Goulburn, Sept. 27, 1823, Peel MSS, 40329/157-58.

128 Goulburn to Peel, Oct. 8, 1823, Oct. 22, 1823, Dec. 26, 1823, Peel MSS, 50329/156-57, 183, 259-61.

129 Goulburn to Wellesley, Feb. 6, 1824, Wellesley MSS, 37302/91-92.

130 Peel to Wellesley, Feb. 7, 1824, Goulburn to Wellesley, Feb. 9, 1824, Wellesley MSS, 373021/76, 97-98.

131 Wellesley to Peel, Feb. 17, 1824, Wellesley MSS, 37302/101.

132 Goulburn to Wellesley, Feb. 27, 1824, Wellesley MSS, 37302/107-109, and Wellesley, memoranda, n. d., Wellesley MSS, 37302/145, 147-49.

133 Goulburn to Wellesley, March 3, 1824, Plunkett to Wellesley, March 4, 1824, Wellesley to Plunkett, March 7, 1824, Peel to Wellesley, March 7, 1824, Goulburn to Wellesley, March 9, 1824, March 16, 1824, Peel to Wellesley, March 16, 1824, Wellesley MSS, 37302/155-57, 163-67, 177-78, 179-85, 189-90, 219-22, 224-26; "Copy of the Amended Act with Lord Wellesley's Remarks in the Margin," March 17, 1824, Wellesley MSS, 37302/227-30; 2 Hansard, X (1824), 1453-65; XI (1824), 39-41, 48-49, 174-78.

134 2 Hansard, XIII (1825), 1011-25; Peel to Northumberland, July 11, 1829, Peel MSS, 40327/32; Beresford to Leveson Gower, Aug. 3, 1829, Dublin S. P. O., Official Papers, Second Series, Carton 588N, No. 680/6.

135 In one parish alone there were several acts of violence against

the clergy or their property between 1830 and 1840: <u>Ballyshannon Her-</u><u>ald</u>, Jan. 6, 1832, p. 2, June 12, 1835, p. 2, Aug. 21, 1835, p. 2, Aug. 1, 1838, p. 3, July 31, 1840, p. 2.

[136]<u>Dublin Weekly Register</u>, July 23, 1823.

[137]Magee to Goulburn, Sept. 27, 1823, Peel MSS, 40329/157.

[138]Report of William Knox, Bishop of Derry, Sept. 17, 1805, in Dublin, P. R. O., S. C. P., Carton 409, No. 1063/4; Christopher Butson, Bishop of Clonfert, 1822, P. R. O., S. C. P., Carton 668.

[139]Curwen, <u>Observations</u>, I, 237; <u>Report of the Committee for the</u> <u>Relief of the Distressed Districts</u>, p. 64; Elrington, 1823, in Dublin, P. R. O., S. C. P. Carton 941, No. 5340.

[140]Sirr, <u>Trench</u>, pp. 55, 57, 100; Sirr, <u>Trench</u>, Aug. 4, 1813, Dublin, P. R. O., S. C. P. Carton 415, No. 1538/19, <u>Trench</u>, March 24, 1820, Dublin, P. R. O., S. C. P. Carton 427, No. <u>2172/39</u>.

[141]Curwin, <u>Observations</u>, II, 167-232.

[142]Blake, <u>Letters form the Irish Highlands</u>, p. 149.

[143]O'Beirne, <u>Charge</u> (1800), pp. 17-18.

[144]Rev. Peter Dunn, <u>A Sermon Preached before his Excellency, Philip,</u> <u>Earl of Hardwicke, Lord Lieutenant, President, and Members of the Asso-</u><u>ciation for Discountenancing Vice . . . 19 November 1801</u> (Dublin, 1815), p. 30, in Haliday, 1084/1; Whately, <u>Evidence of Tithes</u>, p. 81; Magee, <u>Charge</u> (1822), p. 17; Anon., <u>Observations on the State of the Established</u> <u>Church</u>, pp. 28-29; Anon., <u>Letter to the Right Hon. Charles Grant from</u> <u>an Irish Layman of the Established Church on the Subject of a Charge</u> <u>Lately Published and . . . Delivered . . . by the Lord Bishop of Killa-</u><u>loe and Kilfenora</u> (Dublin, 1820), p. 22, in Haliday, 1177/8.

[145]Mant, <u>Charge to the Clergy of the Diocese of Killaloe</u> (Dublin, 1820), p. 35, in Haliday 1177/7.

[146]Kendall, <u>Letters to a Friend on the State of Ireland, the Roman</u> <u>Catholic Question, and the Merits of Constitutional Religious Distinc-</u><u>tions</u> (2 vols.; London, 1826), I, 254.

[147]Beresford to Goulburn, October 14, 1824, Goulburn to Beresford, October 21, 1824, Goulburn to Peel, October 28, 1824, Peel MSS, 40330/153.

[148]Grant, Substance of a Speech, p. 25; Magee, Charge (1822), p. 17; Thomas O'Beirne, Charge to the Clergy of Meath (Dublin, 1800), p. 36, in Haliday, 80.1/9; E. A. Kendall, Letters to a Friend, I, 254; Anon., Observations on the State of the Established Church in Ireland (Dublin, 1822), pp. 49, 82, in Haliday, 1232/4; Mant, Charge to the Clergy of Killaloe (Dublin, 1820), p. 22, in Haliday, 1177/7; Kenneth Connel, The Population of Ireland 1750-1845 (Oxford: University Press, 1950), p. 166; Blake, Letters, pp. 144-45; Peter Dunn, A Sermon preached before . . . the Association Incorporated for Discountenancing Vice, 19 Nov. 1801 (Dublin, 1815), p. 30, in Haliday, 1084/1. John Jebb expressed the clergy's role in society better than anyone else:

"The character of the parochial clergy is, in many important respects, different from that of their English brethren; and nowhere more remarkably, than this, that a larger proportion are gentlemen; but indeed without large pecuniary resources, for they are usually younger brothers with slender patrimonies, but in habits, manners, and education, assuredly not inferior to any members of the respectable families, from which they spring. This peculiarity enables them to fill a place, to discharge a function, comparatively unknown in England. I mean that of enlightening, of civilizing, and (if the expression may be used) of moralizing the country gentry; with us in very many districts, from the predominance of absentee proprietors, the parochial rector, though not overburdened with wealth, is the first gentleman of his neighborhood and where his comparative rank and consequence may not be so great, education and enlargement of mind enable him, with the best effect, to give the tone to society. In England, where the country gentleman for the most part, have been somewhat refined and have a mind more or less cultivated by good literature, this influence of the clergy is by no means equally needful, and indeed were it needful, such influence could be little exercised, from the small incomes, the imperfect education and the humble birth of a great majority of the beneficed clergy.

"This influential character of our parochial clergy, as acting upon the upper orders of society, is an invaluable property of our Irish Church. Assuredly it is with the higher classes, that any solid permanent, and unsophisticated improvement can be particularly expected to commence. It is among those classes, that we would look for the few evidences of Christian excellence, which are perhaps, to Providence, history, and [undecipherable] the grace and ornament of the Church.

"But it is not only, or chiefly among the higher classes, that the beneficial influence of our clergy is exerted. It would argue a gross ignorance of human nature to maintain, that a civilized and cultivated clergyman is disqualified by his habits and attainments to speak with feeling to the humblest peasant. The fact in Ireland is directly the reverse; his rank in society, conciliates the respect of the populace, above all others . . . . His seniority and condescension engage the affections of a people, more sensible to the names, the matter of rank. Is it hazardous to say that those who are acquainted with the interior of the Irish Church will be most ready to bear witness that the most zealous and efficient of our parish ministers are drawn from the more elevated ranks of life? But, as I have already hinted, the best clergy, though frequently comfortable, are seldom rich. Further to impoverish their pockets would be materially to abridge their usefulness. Their usefulness is perhaps not sufficiently appreciated. The clergy are far above the inclination to praise themselves; their best services are often performed in the most remote and least frequented districts. If the poor were asked, who are your most liberal benefactors?, they would most assuredly answer . . . the clergy of the Established Church. This is not included as a merit, but stated as a fact . . . . We have many non-resident landlords, and those who do reside are frequently absent; and for long intervals. This I do not complain. Their duty often requires it. Convenience often justifies it. But the clergyman is permanently on the spot. His avocations make him familiar with the district, and he cannot see the distress without attempting to relieve it . . . ." Memorial, John Jebb to unknown correspondent Jan. 5, 1814, Brodrick MSS, 8866/2.

[149] Ensor, Observations, p. 34; Gamble, View of Society, p. 123; Blake, Letters from the Highlands, p. 146.

[150] H. Rowder to Loftus, Dec. 1, 1823, Loftus MSS, 8821/3, O'Beirne to Brodrick, n. d., Brodrick MSS, 8873.

[151] Anon., Letter to an M.P., pp. 94-95; Rev. F. Thacheray, Defence of the Clergy of the Church of England (London, 182?) pp. 30-31, in Haliday, 1256/8; Anon., Observations on the State of the Established Church, p. 33; Richard Mant, Charge at Down and Connor (Dublin, 1824), p. 48, in Haliday, 1302/2; Ballyshannon Herald, July 6, 1832, p. 2.

[152] Clarles Warburton to the Marquess of Buckingham, Jan. 12, 1798, Fortescue MSS, LXIX (1905), 55-56; Lovett to Brodrick, April 16, 1800, Oct. 1, 1803, Brodrick MSS, 8874/1.

[153] Anon., Probable Consequences of Catholic Emancipation. By a Member of the Established Church (Dublin, 1819), pp. 51-52, in Haliday, 1155/5.

[154] J. K. L., Letters on the State of Ireland, p. 275.

[155] Clare Journal and Ennis Advertiser, Oct. 13, 1808, p. 4, Nov. 28, 1808, p. 1, April 17, 1809, p. 2; Kilkenny Journal, April 26, 1815; Ballyshannon Herald, Dec. 21, 1832, p. 1, March 1, 1833, p. 4, April 17, 1835, p. 2, Aug. 5, 1838, p. 3, Aug. 17, 1838, p. 4.

[156] Bowen, Souperism, passim.

[157] Evidence of clerical effectiveness: Parker, Plan for Improvement, p. 11, Report of the Committee for the Relief of the Distressed Districts, p. 47; Anon., Observations on the State of the Established Church, p. 46; Charges of clerical ineffectiveness; John Jebb, Charge to the Clergy of Limerick (Dublin, 1823), p. 41, in Haliday, 1263/2; Parker, Plan for Improvement, p. 12; Anon., Authentic Report of a Discussion Between Three, Roman Catholic Clergymen and Three Protestant Clergymen (Dublin, 1824), passim. in Haliday, 1294/3; description of clerical philanthropy: F. Page, Observations on the State of the Indigent Poor of Ireland (London, 1830), pp. 51-52, in Haliday 1491/9; Kilkenny Moderator, March 13, 1833, p. 2, March 1, 1834, p. 3; Ballyshannon Herald, Sept. 12, 1834, p. 3; Dublin Evening Post, Dec. 2, 1834, p. 1; Kilkenny Moderator, March 14, 1835, p. 2; Ballyshannon Herald, June 19, 1840, p. 2.

[158] Parker, Plan for Improvement, pp. 114-16; Page, Observations, pp. 32-33; Kilkenny Moderator, Oct. 11, 1834, p. 4.

[159] Kilkenny Journal Oct. 6, 1813, p. 3; Ballyshannon Herald, Dec. 2, 1831, p. 1; Killen, Ecclesiastical History, p. 466.

[160] Society for the Relief of Protestants: First Annual Report (Dublin, 1838), passim, in Haliday, 1712/8; School for Sons of the Irish Clergy: Report (Dublin, 1839), passim, in Haliday, 1743/6.

[161] Reports, Aug. 24, 1807, July 6, 1810, July, 1815, Dublin P. R. O., State of the Country Papers, first series, Vol. 410, No. 1120/59; Vol. 411, No. 1276/6; Vol. 418, No. 1171/61-63; Reports, 1814, July 1815, 1819, P. R. O., S. C. P. Vol. 417, No. 1565/64 ff., Vol. 418, No. 1711/61-63; Vol. 426, No. 2084; Reports, May, June, October, 1824, P. R. O., S. C. P., Vol. 445, No. 2623/1-4; Report, March 1820, 1828, Dublin, P. R. O., S. C. P., Vol. 427, No. 2172/39, Nos. 2882/31-68, 71, 73, 2885/10; "Return of the Clergy to the Bishop of Clogher, 1834-35," N. L. I. MSS, 2744.

[162] Irish Protestant, passim.

[163] Machin, "No-Popery," passim. Goulburn to Peel, Oct. 28, 1824,

Peel MSS, 40330/153.

[164]Statistical information is reproduced in Brynn, "Church of Ireland," passim.

[165]Newland, Apology, p. 136. Of the total repaired and constructed, about 25% were restorations of existing structures, a process often as expensive as laying a new foundation.

[166]O'Beirne, Charge to Meath, p. 10.

[167]N. L. I. MSS, 1620/14.

[168]Diocese of Ferns Visitation Book, Diocese of Leighlin Visitation Book, N. L. I. MSS, 2743.

[169]Triennial Visitation for 1826, Dublin, P. R. O. MSS, M2514.

[170]O'Beirne, Charge (1816), p. 4.

[171]Letters from Castleblayney: Lord Blayney and Others on the Non-Residence of the Beneficed Clergy in Ireland (Dublin, 1822), preface, pp. 1-15, in Haliday, 1232/3.

[172]V. H. Forster, A History of Killeevan Parish, Diocese of Clogher (Monaghan: Monaghan Press, 1958), pp. 16-17.

[173]3 Hansard, XXVII (1835), 917-18.

[174]Henry D. Inglis, Ireland in 1834: A Journey Throughout Ireland (2 vol.; London, 1834), II, 166.

[175]Croker, Sketch, p. 39.

[176]W. H. C., Letter to Earl Mount Cashel, pp. 10-11; Jane Whately, Life and Correspondence of Richard Whately, D. D., Late Archbishop of Dublin (Dublin, 1866), p. 81.

[177]Whately to the Provost of Trinity College, March 3, 1834, Wellesley MSS, 37306/282-87.

[178]Beresford to Wellesley, April 22, 1834, Wellesley MSS, 37306/425.

[179]Whately to Wellesley, May 10, 1834, Wellesley MSS, 37307/39-41; "Memorial" from nineteen fellows of Trinity College, May 16, 1834, Wellesley MSS, 37307/50-51.

[180]Whately to the Provost, May 16, 1834, Littleton to Wellesley, May 17, 1834, Wellesley MSS, 37307/52-62, 69.

[181]Anonymous correspondent to Creevey, Oct. 5, 1828, Creevey, Creevey Papers, III, 175-76.

[182]Inglis, Ireland, II, 166; Anon., Letters to the Archbishop of Armagh, p. 38; Kilkenny Journal, Dec. 25, 1830, p. 4, col. 4.

[183]Memorial to Charles, Marquis Cornwallis, from Charles Graham, Gideon Ousley, Methodist Preachers, Oct. 23, 1800, Dublin, P. R. O. "Official Papers: Ecclesiastical Papers, 1790-1831," Carton 513, Group 74, No. 9.

[184]Kirwan, Discourse, p. 31, in Bowen, Souperism, pp. 30-32.

[185]Samuel Madden, Memoir of the Life of the Late Rev. Peter Roe (Dublin, 1842), p. 321.

[186]A. O'Callaghan, Thoughts on the Tendency of Bible Societies, as Affecting the Established Church . . . (Dublin, 1816), pp. 46, 49. See Rev. B. O'Donohue, A Congratulatory Letter to the Rev. A. O'Callaghan, on His Masterly Discipline of the Bible Society (Dublin, 1816), passim, in Haliday 1089/1.

[187]A. O'Callaghan, Bible Society Against Church and State (Dublin, 1817), passim, in Haliday, 1109/3; Rev. William Phelan, The Bible, not the Bible Society, Being an Attempt to Point Out that Mode of Disseminating the Scriptures (Dublin, 1817), p. 71, in Haliday, 1109/1.

[188]Thomas O'Beirne, Charge to the Clergy of Meath (Dublin, 1818), pp. 14, 18, in Haliday, 1137/1.

[189]Charles Lovett to Evelyn John Shirley, May 15, 1822, N. L. I., Shirley MSS, 11/32.

[190]O'Callaghan, Observations, p. 55.

[191]Bowen, Souperism, p. 105.

[192]Anon., The Improved Antidote, passim: Rushe, Monaghan, pp. 190-94; DNB, XI, 836.

[193]Ballyshannon Herald, Sept. 19, 1834, p. 2, June 26, 1840, p. 1.

[194]Bell, Disestablishment, p. 34.

[195] Ballyshannon Herald, Jan. 2, 1835, p. 1, June 19, 1835, p. 3.

[196] William Fitzgerald, Thoughts on the Present Circumstances of the Church of Ireland (London, 1860), pp. 18-30, quoted in Bell, Disestablishment, pp. 34-35.

[197] First Report of the Irish Protestant Association (Dublin, 1836), passim, in Haliday, 1677/6; Society for the Relief of Protestants, passim.

[198] Rev. John A. Russell, Thoughts on the State of the Established Church and of the Means by Which its Efficiency may be Promoted (Dublin, 1835), p. 17; C. Forster, ed., Thirty Years Correspondence between John Jebb and Knox, (2 vols., London, 1834), II, 238-39; Walter-Bishop Mant, Memoirs . . . of Richard Mant (Dublin, McGlashan and Gill, 1857), pp. 362-63.

[199] R. J. McGhee, Episcopal Duty etc., Considered as to Ireland (Dublin, 1835) p. 50; H. S. M. Mason, Reasons for Employment of the Irish Lingua in Scripture Instruction to the Peasantry (Dublin, 1835), passim, in Haliday, 1622/10; Whately, Whately, pp. 60, 73.

[200] Thomas W. Freeman, Pre-Famine Ireland (Oxford: University Press, 1957), p. 146, quoting in part: Achill Mission and the State of Protestantism in Ireland: A Statement Delivered by the Rev. Nagle at a Meeting of the Protestant Association 1838 (London, 1839), p. 8.

[201] Miller, Church of Ireland, 1844, p. 124.

[202] Brose, Church and Parliament, pp. 124-25. Whately clarified this in writing to the Bishop of Landaff in 1832; he wanted "only a regular legislative government of the Church - call it convocation, synod, assembly or what you will. The bishops are governors of the Church only in the same sense as justices of the peace are of the state: the King is supreme in all cases, ecclesiastical as well as civil [but] his single power [are not laws. He] has no business to legislate for the Church; no one else has any right to do so." Whately to Bishop of Landaff, Sept. 9, 1832, Fitzpatrick, Whately, I, 197.

[203] Convocation (Ireland) . . . Copies of Letters from His Grace the Archbishop of Dublin to Her Majesty's Secretary of State for the Home Department . . ., 562, H. C. 1864, XLIV; W. Fitzgerald, The Revival of Synods (London, 1861), pp. 9-12.

[204] McDowell, Church of Ireland, p. 31.

[205] Bell, Disestablishment, pp. 36-37.

[206] Parker, Plan for Improvement, p. 67.

[207] W. Maziere Brady, Essays on the English State Church in Ireland (London, 1865), p. 154, cited in Bell, Disestablishment, p. 65.

Chapter IX. The Road to Disestablishment 1822-1869

[1] Thomas Nowlan, Enquiry into the History of Tithe, p. 10; William Whittaker to Rev. Thomas Brooke Clarke, 10 Oct., 1823, N. I. P. R. O. MSS, D1108/B/73.

[2] Edward Stopford, Present Situation of the Church (Dublin, 1833), p. 10.

[3] Clare Journal and Ennis Advertiser, May 5, 1808, p. 4, col. 4; Clontibret Vestry Book, II/96 (April 14, 1800, March 30, 1807, April 30, 1807, June 7, 1813); Representative Church Body Library MSS, J14, pp. 196, 229-30, 231, 250.

[4] Robert Tottenham Loftus to Dean Roper, Dec. 11, 1824, N. L. I. MSS, 8821/4; petition to Bishop of Clogher, n. d. [winter, 1824], N. L. I. MSS, 8821/14; Benson to Loftus, n. d. [winter 1814], Roper to Loftus, Feb. 17, 1825, Harris to Loftus, May 9, 1825, Irvine to Loftus, May 14, 1825, Harris to Loftus, March 2, 27, 1826, N. L. I. MSS, 8821/14, 15.

[5] See Clontibret Vestry Book II/96 (Aug. 3, 16, 1803, Oct. 3, 1803, Jan. 7, 1804, Feb. 21, 1804, March 2, 6, 1804, April 7, 1806, Aug. 31, 1809, April 14, 1811), pp. 211-13, 215, 227-28, 237, 241, R. C. B. L. MSS, J14.

[6] See, for example, Thomas Irwin to Clarke, May 25, 1815, N. I. P. R. O. MSS, D1108/B/57, pt. 2.

[7] William Magee, Evidence . . . on the State of Ireland (Dublin, 1825), p. 10, in Haliday, 1330/9; James Anderson to Loftus, May 21, 1825, N. L. I. MSS, 8821/12; Robert Magee, Archbishop of Dublin, May 13, 1825, House of Lords, "Minutes of Evidence," 1825, p. 488.

[8] N. S. Hansard, XII (1825), 617-21.

[9] 2 Hansard, VIII (April 21, 1823), 1132-34.

[10] Ibid., X (February 26, 1824), 496-97.

[11] 2 Hansard, VIII (1823), 802-12, XI (1824), 890-99; Goulburn to Peel, Dec. 27, 1825, Peel MSS, 40331/277; 2 Hansard, XV (1826), 47-62; XVII (1827), 208-23; XXIV (1830), 70-83, 838-59.

[12] Ibid., XIV, 439.

[13] Ibid., XV (1826), 544-48.

[14] 7 George IV, c. 72.

[15] 2 Hansard (April 27, 1830), 83-88.

[16] N. S. Hansard, XVII (1827), 208-223.

[17] Ibid., XVII (1827), 324-25.

[18] Ibid., XVIII (1828), 1223-37.

[19] 3 Hansard, I (1831), 486; IV (1831), 572.

[20] Kilkenny Journal, Sept. 15, 1830, p. 3, Nov. 20, 1830, p. 3, April 6, 1831, p. 3.

[21] Kilkenny Journal, April 6, 1831, p. 3, May 2, 1832, p. 1; Ballyshannon Herald, April 12, 1833, p. 3.

[22] Whately, Evidence . . . on Tithes, p. 10; Stanley to Blomfield, Nov. 19, 1830, Beresford MSS, 37.

[23] 2 Hansard, XXIII (March 16, 1830), 390-91.

[24] Ibid., XXIV (April 27, 1830), 83-103.

[25] Ballyshannon Herald, May 2, 1834, p. 3; April 15, 1835, p. 3; April 24, 1835, p. 3.

[26] Ibid., April 24, 1835, p. 3, April 8, 1836, p. 2.

[27] Ibid., April 7, 1837, p. 1, taken from the Dublin Evening Mail; Derry Journal, quoted in Ballyshannon Herald, p. 2; Ibid., May 3, 1839, p. 3.

[28] See, for example, Ballyshannon Herald, Nov. 18, 1831, p. 2, Nov. 21, 1831, p. 1, Nov. 25, 1831, p. 2. For diverse observations on the Irish Poor Law as a replacement for the vestry system, see: Rev. Richard Ryan, Letter to Rt. Hon. E. G. Stanley in Answer to Dr. Doyle's Letter (Dublin, 1831), p. 8, in Haliday, 1522/7; Stephen L.

Gwynn, The History of Ireland (London: Macmillan and Co., 1923), p. 441; Whately, Richard Whately, p. 136; Ballyshannon Herald, June 26, 1840, p. 3, July 17, 1840, p. 3, July 24, 1840, p. 3.

[29]English vestries were reformed in 1831 in an attempt to reduce their oligarchical tendencies and to make them "operative little parliaments:" 3 Hansard, VII (1831), 879-91; VIII (1831), 486-90, 690; X (1832), 1107.

[30]Percival MSS, draft of cabinet memorandum, undated [e. 1810], noted in Gray, Percival, p. 22; Stuart to Brodrick, May 10, 1812, Brodrick MSS, 8869/6.

[31]Reynolds, Catholic Emancipation, pp. 11-28.

[32]Anon., Letter to Lord Castlereagh on the Present Political State of Ireland (London, 1807), p. 10, in Haliday, 903/4.

[33]1 Hansard (1812), 744-48; J. Leslie Foster's testimony, in House of Lords, "Minutes of Evidence," 1825, p. 71; Rev. William Phelan's testimony, in House of Commons, "Select Committee, Minutes of Evidence," 1825, p. 38.

[34]G. I. T. Machin, "The Catholic Emancipation Crisis of 1825," English Historical Review LXXVIII (1963), p. 469; Ibid., "The No-Popery Movement in Britain in 1828-1829," Historical Journal, VI (1963). George Fisher, Strictures on the Antidote, L'Abeja, and Cursory View of Sir Harcourt Lees, Bart. (Dublin, 1820), p. 16 in Haliday, 1181/1; Richard Lawrence, Charge to Munster (Dublin, 1826), p. 2, in Haliday, 1374/7.

[35]Jebb to Inglis, Nov. 19, 1824, Peel Papers, 40370/23-24; Reynolds, Catholic Emancipation, p. 28.

[36]G. I. T. Machin, "The Duke of Wellington and Catholic Emancipation," Journal of Ecclesiastical History, XIV (Oct., 1963), 190-208.

[37]Wellington, Despatches, II, 596-607.

[38]Howley to Beresford, Feb. 6, 1829, Beresford MSS, 57; Jebb to Peel, Feb. 11, 1829, Peel to Jebb, Feb. 11, 1829, Peel MSS, 40398/233.

[39]The petition is included in Colchester, Diary and Correspondence, III, 605-606; Beresford to Wellington, Wellington to Beresford, April 1, 1829, N. I. P. R. O. MSS, D664/A/50, 51.

[40] Clyde J. Lewis, "The Disintegration of the Tory-Anglican Alliance in the Struggle for Catholic Emancipation," Church History, XXIX (March, 1960), p. 40.

[41] 3 Hansard, XL (1838), 898-905; XLVII (1839), 1235-36.

[42] Cash, Reaction, p. 95; Carless-Davis, Age of Grey and Peel, p. 160.

[43] Stuart to Brodrick, March 15, 1805, Brodrick MSS, 8869/3.

[44] 1 Hansard, XXII (1812), 486; Duigenan to Peel, Nov. 17, 1812, Peel MSS, 40223/72; Wellesley to O'Beirne, Feb. 27, 1809, in Wellington, Ireland, p. 592; this stubbornness on franking privileges constitutes one of the most interesting minor indications of Irish bishops' slow adjustment to changed circumstances: see Brodrick to Alexander, Feb. 15, 1822, Elrington to Peel, April 29, 1826, Peel MSS, 40386/202; Stuart to Brodrick, March 29, 1812, March 3, 1813, March 21, 1814, Brodrick MSS, 8869/6, 7.

[45] Alexander Knox, memorandum, June 4, 1816, N. L. I. MSS, 13, 385; O'Beirne, "Charge" (1816), p. 10.

[46] Anon., Letter to the Right Hon. Charles Grant on the Determination he has Announced of Withholding the Usual Parliamentary Aid from the Association in Capel Street and his Hostile Designs Against the Incorporated Society (Dublin, 1820), passim, in Haliday, 117911. Wellesley to Goulburn, Oct. 9, 1826, Goulburn MSS, II/18.

[47] See 1 Hansard, XXXIX (1819), 455, 1458; Jebb to Brodrick, Feb. 9, 1821, Brodrick MSS, 8893/3; n. s. Hansard, XI (1824), 1165; Ibid., XII (1825), 1341-45; Ibid., XIII (1825), 1149-66; XIV (1826), 1253-54; XXI (1829), 906-13.

[48] Magee to Peel, Sept. 27, 1823, Peel MSS, 40329/157.

[49] Hansard, XL (1838), 353-57; Welch, "Blomfield," p. 84.

[50] Plowden, The History of Ireland from its Union, pp. 140, 337.

[51] Carleton, The Tithe Proctor, p. 413.

[52] Nassau Senior, A Letter to Lord Lowick on Legal Provision for the Irish Poor, in Journals, Conversations and Essays Relating to Ireland (London, 1868), p. XII.

[53] Anon., Thoughts on the Protestant Ascendency, p. 87; John Gamble,

558

Views of Society and Manners in the North of Ireland (London, 1819), p. 219; Anon., Reflections on the State of Ireland, pp. 187-88.

[54]Anon., Letter from an Irish Dignitary, p. 24; Duigenan, A Fair Representation, pp. 47, 48, 54.

[55]Ryan, Letter to Stanley, pp. 24-25; Dublin Evening Mail, Jan. 16, 1835, p. 3; Anon., Letter to an M.P., p. 106.

[56]Anon., Letter to an M.P., p. 102; 1 Hansard, XXXIX (1819), 1556-57; Lord Redesdale to Abbot, Nov. 18, 1824, in Colchester, Diaries and Correspondence, III, 349.

[57]House of Commons, Report of the Select Committee, 1825, pp. 394-95, 431, 537; Alexis De Torqueville, Journeys to England and Ireland, (ed. by J. P. Meyer, London: Faber and Faber, 1958), p. 12, Murphy, "Support of the Catholic Clergy," p. 118.

[58]Anon., Correspondence between the Bishop of Ferns and Earl Mount Cashel on the Church Establishment (Dublin, 1830), in Haliday, 1492/3; Anon., A Review of the Correspondence between the Earl of Mount Cashel and the Bishop of Ferns (Dublin, 1830).

[59]Newland, Apology, pp. 110-11; Anon., Detail of Facts Relating to Ireland (Dublin, 1822), p. 125, in Haliday, 1247/2; J. B. McCrea, Principle of the Church Reform Bill (Dublin, 1833), pp. 34-5, in Haliday, 1557-2; Anon., Dr. Doyle and Tithes, p. 15; Anon., Remarks on a Letter from Lord Cloncurry to the Duke of Leinster (Dublin, 1822), p. 11, in Haliday, 1234/1; Anon., Letter to an M.P., p. 99; William Magee, Charge at the Visitation, St. Patrick's Cathedral Dublin (Dublin, 1826), p. 37, in Haliday, 1374/5.

[60]Wellesley's memorandum of August, 1833 noted the impact of these Ecclesiastical Commissions in thwarting reforms. Conservative politicians managed to have the powers of the commissions cast in vague terms, and the bishops, who inevitably dominated the membership lists, interpreted their responsibilities in the most limited terms possible: Wellesley MSS, 37306/49-59.

[61]Brose, Church and Parlimaent, pp. 118-21.

[62]Machin, "Maynooth," p. 68.

[63]Parker, Peel, III, 65; Bell, Disestablishment, p. 40.

[64] Roman Catholic	4,505,265	77.6
Established Church	693,357	11.9
Presbyterian	523,291	9.0
Methodist	45,399	2.5

See: E. R. Norman, The Catholic Church and Ireland in the Age of Rebellion, 1859-73 (London: Routledge and Kegan Paul, 1965), Chapter 4: Birth of the National Association.

[65] Evans, Disestablishment, p. 98; Godkin, Ireland and Her Churches, p. 435.

[66] Whately in conversation with Senior, Nov. 16, 1862, in Senior, Journals, II, 277.

[67] Maziere Brady, Essays on the English State Church in Ireland, p. 154, in Bell, Disestablishment, p. 65.

[68] See Bell, Disestablishment, Chapter I, for a thorough analysis of these arguments as they were presented in the final years of the Establishment.

BIBLIOGRAPHY

I. Primary Source Materials

The Church of Ireland featured prominently in parliamentary de-
bates and in investigations undertaken on Parliament's behalf between
1800 and 1838. Manuscript material prominently featured in this study
is housed in the British Museum (Hardwicke, Peel, Wellesley, Liverpool,
Russell, and Ripon MSS), the National Library of Ireland (Brodrick,
Richmond, Monteagle, Gratton, Church of Ireland, Loftus, and Newport
MSS), Republic of Ireland Public Record Office MSS, Northern Ireland
Public Record Office (Thomas Brooke Clarke, and Anglesey MSS), Trinity
College, Dublin (Beresford, Stock, and Whately MSS), the Representa-
tive Church Body Library (Leslie, and Beresford MSS), Armagh Public
Library (Beresford MSS), University of Durham (Grey MSS), Surrey Record
Office Kingston-on-Thames, (Goulburn MSS), Staffordshire County Record
Office, Stafford (Hatherton MSS), Derby County Record Office, Derby
County (Catton MSS), State Paper Office, Dublin, and the Public Record
Office, London.

In several instances important manuscript material has been
printed:

Aspinall, Arthur, and E. Anthony Smith, eds. English Historical Documents, 1783-1832. London: Eyre and Spottiswoode, 1959.

Aspinall, Arthur, ed. Correspondence of Charles Arbuthnot. London:
Royal Historical Society, 1941.

_____. Later Correspondence of George III. Cambridge: Cambridge
University Press, 1962 ff.

Auckland, Robert John Eden, Third Baron, ed. Journals and Correspondence of William, Lord Auckland. 4 vols. London: R. Bentley,
1861-62.

Bamford, Francis, and Arthur Wellesley, Seventh Duke of Wellington,
eds. Journal of Mrs. Arbuthnot. 2 vols. London: Macmillan,
1950.

Beresford, William. Correspondence of the Right Hon. John Beresford
Illustrative of the Last Thirty Years of the Irish Parliament.
2 vols. London: Woodfall and Kinder, 1854.

Boulter, Hugh. Letters . . . to Several Ministers of State in England.
2 vols. Dublin, 1770.

Colchester, Charles Abbot, First Baron. Diary and Correspondence. 3 vols. London: J. Murray, 1861.

Douglas, David C., ed. English Historical Documents. New York: Oxford University Press, 1955-69.

Great Britain. Historical Manuscripts Commission. Report on the Manuscripts of Henry Seymore, Third Earl Bathurst, Preserved at Cirencester Park. Francis Lawrence Berkeley, ed. London: HMSO, 1923.

_____. Report on the Manuscripts of J.B. Fortescue, Preserved at Dropmore. 10 vols. London: HMSO, 1892 ff.

Gregory, Augusta Isabella, ed. Mr. Gregory's Letter-Box, 1813-1830. London: Smith, Elder and Co., 1898.

Greville, Charles. A Journal of the Reign of Queen Victoria from 1837 to 1852. 3 vols. London: Longmans, Green and Co., 1885.

Grey, Henry, Earl, ed. Correspondence of William IV and Earl Grey from November 1830 to June 1832. 2 vols. London: John Murray, 1867.

Jennings, Louis I., ed. The Croker Papers. 3 vols. London: John Murray, 1884.

Le Strange, Guy, ed. Correspondence of Princess Lieven and Earl Grey. 3 vols. London; Richard Bentley and Son, 1890.

McDowell, Robert B., ed. "Some Fitzgibbon Letters from the Sneyd Muniments in the John Rylands Library." John Rylands Library, Manchester, Bulletin, XXXIV (1952).

Maxwell, Herbert, ed. The Creevey Papers. London: J. Murrary, 1904.

Melbourne, William Lamb, Viscount. Memoirs. W.M. Torrens, ed. 2 vols. London: Macmillan and Co., 1872.

Reeve, Henry, ed. Greville Memoirs. 8 vols. London: Longmans and Co., 1888.

_____. Memoir and Correspondence Relating to Political Occurrences in June and July 1834, by Edward John Littleton. London: Longmans, Green and Co., 1872.

Russell, Rollo, ed. Early Correspondence of Lord John Russell. 2 vols. London: T. Fisher Unwin, 1913.

Rutland, Charles Manners, ed. Seventh Duke. Correspondence between the Right Honourable William Pitt and Charles, Duke of Rutland,

Lord Lieutenant of Ireland, 1781-1787. London: A. Spottiswoode, 1842.

Sanders, Lloyd C., ed. Lord Melbourne's Papers. London: Longmans, Green and Co., 1889.

Wellington, A.R. Wellesley, Second Duke. Despatches, Correspondence, and Memoranda of Arthur Duke of Wellington. 8 vols. London: John Murray, 1867-1880.

II. Contemporary Secondary Sources

The Halliday Collection of contemporary pamphlet literature housed in the Royal Irish Academy, Dublin, is invaluable. Personal correspondence and memoranda available in print include:

Brougham, John Cam Hobhouse, Viscount. Life and Time of Lord Brougham. 3 vols. London: William Blackwood and Sons, 1871.

_____. Recollections of a Long Life. 6 vols. London: John Murray, 1910.

Bulwer, Henry Lytton. The Life of Henry John Temple, Viscount Palmerston. Philadelphia: J.B. Lippincott and Co., 1871.

Cornwallis, Charles Cornwallis, Marquess. Correspondence. 3 vols. London: J. Murray, 1859.

Fitzpatrick, W.J. Memoirs of Richard Whately. 2 vols. London, 1864.

Gash, Norman. Mr. Secretary Peel. Cambridge, Mass.: Harvard University Press, 1961.

Grattan, Henry. Memoirs. 5 vols. London, 1839.

King, Charles S. A Great Archbishop of Dublin: William King, D.D., 1850-1729. London: Longmans and Co., 1906.

Le Fanu, W.R. Seventy Years of Irish Life. London: Macmillan, 1894.

Le Marchant, Denis. Memoir of Viscount Althorp, Third Earl Spencer. London: Richard Bentley and Son, 1876.

Londonderry, Robert Stewart, Marquess. Memoir and Correspondence of Viscount Castlereagh. 12 vols. London, 1848-53.

Madden, Samuel. Memoir of the Life of the Late Rev. Peter Roe. Dublin, 1842.

Mant, Walter-Bishop. Memoirs . . . of Richard Mant. Dublin: McGlashan and Gill, 1857.

Melbourne, William Lamb, Viscount. Memoir. W.M. Torrens, ed. 2 vols. London: Macmillan and Co., 1872.

Morley, John. The Life of William Ewart Gladstone. 3 vols. New York: Macmillan and Co., 1909.

Paget, Henry William, First Marquess of Anglesey. One Leg. London: Reprint Society, 1963.

Parker, Charles Stuart. Life and Letters of Sir James Graham, Second Baronet of Netherby, 1797-1861. 2 vols. London: John Murray, 1907.

_____. Sir Robert Peel . . . from his Private Correspondence. 3 vols. London: Murray, 1899.

Peel, Robert. Memoirs. 2 vols. London: John Murray, 1858.

Pellew, George, ed. Life and Correspondence of the Right Hon. Henry Addington, First Viscount Sidmouth. 3 vols. London, 1847.

Russell, John Russell, Earl. Recollections and Suggestions, 1813-1873. London: Longmans, Green and Co., 1875.

Stephen, Leslie and Sidney Lee, eds. Dictionary of National Biography. Oxford: Oxford University Press, 1885-1900.

Stockmar, E. von, Baron. Memoirs. 2 vols. London, 1872.

Twiss, Horace. The Public and Private Life of Lord Chancellor Eldon, with Selections from His Correspondence. 2 vols. London: John Murray, 1846.

Walpole, Spencer. The Life of Lord John Russell. 2 vols. London: Longmans, Green and Co., 1891.

Whately, Jane. Life and Correspondence of Richard Whately, D.D., Late Archbishop of Dublin. Dublin, 1866.

Several contemporary analyses of the Church of Ireland offer important information:

Erck, J.C. Account of the Ecclesiastical Establishment in Ireland. Dublin, 1830.

Godkin, James. Education in Ireland. London, 1862.

Mant, Richard. History of the Church of Ireland from the Reformation to the Revolution. London, 1840.

Perry, George G. History of the Church of England. 3 vols. London: Saunders, Otley and Co., 1861-1864.

Senior, Nassau. Journals, Conversations and Essays Relating to Ireland. London, 1868.

III. Modern Secondary Sources

A. Books

Akenson, Donald H. The Church of Ireland: Ecclesiastical Reform and Revolution. New Haven: Yale University Press, 1971.

_____. The Irish Education Experiment: The National System of Education in the Nineteenth Century. London: Routledge and Kegan Paul, 1970.

Beckett, J.C. Protestant Dissent in Ireland, 1687-1780. London: Faber and Faber, 1947.

Bell, P.M.H. Disestablishment in Ireland and Wales. London: SPCK, 1969.

Bolton, G.C. The Passing of the Irish Act of Union. London: Oxford University Press, 1966.

Bowen, Desmond. Protestant Crusade in Ireland, 1800-70. Dublin: Gill and Macmillan, 1978.

_____. Souperism: Myth or Reality. Dublin, 1970.

Brose, Olive J. Church and Parliament: the Reshaping of the Church of England, 1828-1860. Stanford; Stanford University Press, 1959.

Carless Davis, H.W. The Age of Grey and Peel. Oxford: Clarendon Press, 1929.

Chadwick, Owen. The Victorian Church. 2 vols. Oxford: Oxford University Press, 1966.

Edwards, Robert Dudley. Church and State in Tudor Ireland: A History of the Penal Laws against Irish Catholics, 1534-1603. Dublin: Talbot Press, 1935.

Evans, Anna L. The Disestablishment of the Church of Ireland. Lancaster, Pa: University of Pennsylvania, 1929.

Forster, V.H. A History of Killeevan Parish, Diocese of Clogher.

Monaghan: Monaghan Press, 1958.

Freeman, Thomas W. Pre-Famine Ireland. Oxford; Oxford University Press, 1957.

Froude, James A. The English in Ireland in the Eighteenth Century. 2 vols. London: Longmans, Green and Co., 1886.

Gash, Norman. Reaction and Reconstruction in English Politics, 1832-1852. Oxford: Clarendon Press, 1965.

Gray, Denis. Spencer Perceval: The Evangelical Prime Minister 1762-1812. Manchester: Manchester University Press, 1963.

Gwynn, Stephen L. History of Ireland. London: Macmillan and Co., 1923.

Halevy, Elie. The Age of Peel and Cobden. New York, 1948.

_____. The Triumph of Reform. London; Ernest Benn, 1950.

Healy, John. History of the Diocese of Meath. 2 vols. Dublin: APCK, 1908.

Henriques, U. Religious Toleration in England, 1787-1833. London: Routledge and Kegan Paul, 1961.

Johnston, Edith. Great Britain and Ireland, 1760-1800: A Study in Political Administration. Edinburgh: Oliver and Boyd, 1963.

Jones, Wilbur Devereux. Lord Derby and Victorian Conservatism. Oxford: Oxford University Press, 1956.

Killen, W.D. Ecclesiastical History of Ireland. London: Macmillan and Co., 1875.

Kitson Clark, George. Peel and the Conservative Party. 2nd ed. Hamden, Conn.: Archon Books, 1964.

Lecky, W.E.H. Ireland in the Eighteenth Century. 5 vols. London: Longmans and Co., 1892.

Locker Lampson, Geoffrey. A Consideration of the State of Ireland in the Nineteenth Century. London: Archibald Constable and Co., 1907.

MacDonagh, Michael. The Viceroy's Post-Bag: Correspondence Hitherto Unpublished of the Earl of Hardwicke, First Lord Lieutenant of Ireland after the Union. London: John Murray, 1904.

McDowell, R.B. The Church of Ireland, 1869-1969. Boston: Routledge and Kegan Paul, 1975.

_____. The Irish Administration 1801-1914. London: Routledge and
    Kegan Paul, 1964.

_____. Irish Public Opinion, 1750-1800. London: Faber and Faber,
    1952.

Macintyre, Angus. The Liberator; Daniel O'Connell and the Irish Party,
    1830-1847. London: Hamilton, 1965.

Maxwell, Constantia. Country and Town in Ireland under the Georges.
    Dundalk, Ireland: W. Tempest, 1949.

_____. Dublin under the Georges. London: G.S. Harrop and Co.,
    1940.

Nolan, Kevin B. The Politics of Repeal. Toronto: University of
    Toronto Press, 1965.

Norman, E.R. The Catholic Church and Ireland in the Age of Rebellion,
    1859-73. London: Routledge and Kegan Paul, 1965.

O'Brien, R. Barry. Fifty Years of Concessions to Ireland, 1831-1881.
    2 vols. London, 1885.

O'Hagarty, Sarsfield. A History of Ireland under the Union 1801-1822.
    London: Methuen and Co., 1952.

Phillips, Walter Allison, ed. History of the Church of Ireland from
    the Earliest Times to the Present Day. 3 vols. London: Oxford
    University Press, 1933.

Pomfret, John Edwin. The Struggle for Land in Ireland, 1800-1823.
    Princeton: Princeton University Press, 1930.

Ravitch, Norman. Sword and Mitre: Government and Episcopate in France
    and England in the Age of Aristocracy. The Hague, 1966.

Reynolds, James A. The Catholic Emancipation Crisis in Ireland, 1823-
    1829. New Haven: Yale University Press, 1954.

Rushe, D. Carolan. History of Monaghan for Two Hundred Years. Dundalk:
    Dundalk Press, 1921.

Southgate, David. The Passing of the Whigs, 1832-1866. London: Mac-
    millan and Co., 1962.

B. Articles

Beckett, J.C. "The Government and the Church of Ireland under William

II and Anne." Irish Historical Studies, II (March 1941).

Best, G.F.A. "The Whigs and the Church Establishment in the Age of Grey and Holland." History, XLV (1960).

Brose, Olive J. "The Irish Precedent for English Church Reform: the Church Temporalities Act of 1833." Journal of Ecclesiastical History, VII (October 1956).

Brynn, Edward. "A Church of Ireland Diocese in the Age of Catholic Emancipation." Historical Magazine of the Protestant Episcopal Church, XL (June 1971).

_____. "The Church of Ireland in the Age of Catholic Emancipation, 1800-1841." Rocky Mountain Social Science Journal, (1971).

_____. "Irish Tithes in British Politics." Historical Magazine of the Protestant Episcopal Church, XXXIX (September 1970).

_____. "Robert Peel and the Church of Ireland." Journal of Religious History, (1974).

_____. "Some Repercussions of the Act of Union on the Church of Ireland, 1801-1820." Church History, XL (September 1971).

Burns, R.E. "Parson, Priests, and People; the Rise of Irish Anti-clericalism, 1785-1789." Church History, XXXI (1962).

Cahill, Gilbert A. "Irish Catholicism and English Toryism." Review of Politics, XIX (1957).

_____. "The Protestant Association and the Anti-Maynooth Agitation of 1845." Catholic Historical Review, LXIII (October 1957).

Condon, Mary. "The Irish Church and the Reform Ministries." Journal of British Studies, I (1964).

Hughes, Edward. "The Bishops and Reform, 1831-1833: Some Fresh Correspondence." English Historical Review, XVI (July 1941).

Kriegal, Abraham D. "The Irish Policy of Lord Grey's Government." English Historical Review, LXXXVI(1971).

Large, David. "The House of Lords and Ireland in the Age of Peel, 1832-1850." Irish Historical Studies, IX (September 1955).

Lavorovsky, V. "Tithe Commutation as a Factor in the Gradual Decrease of Ownership by the English Peasantry." Economic History Review, XVI.

Lewis, Clyde J. "The Disintegration of the Tory-Anglican Alliance in the Struggle for Catholic Emancipation." Church History, XXIX (1960).

Machin, G.I.T. "The Catholic Emancipation Crisis of 1825." English Historical Review, LXXVIII (1963).

_____. "The Duke of Wellington and Catholic Emancipation." Journal of Ecclesiastical History, XIV (1963).

_____. "The Maynooth Grant, the Dissenters and Disestablishment, 1845-1847." English Historical Review, LXXXII (January 1967).

_____. "The No-Popery Movement in Britain in 1828-1829." Historical Journal, VI (1963).

McCracken, J.L. "The Conflict Between the Irish Administration and Parliament, 1753-6." Irish Historical Studies, III (1942).

McDougall, Donald J. "George III, Pitt, and the Irish Catholics, 1801-1805." Catholic Historical Review, XXXI (October 1945).

Murphy, J.A. "The Support of the Catholic Clergy in Ireland, 1750-1850." Historical Studies: Papers Read before the Sixth Annual Conference of Irish Historians, V.

O'Donoghue, Patrick. "Causes of Opposition to Tithes, 1830-38." Studia Hibernica, V. (1965).

_____. "Opposition to Tithe Payments in 1830-31. Studia Hibernica, VI (1966).

O'Mordha, Pilib B. "Notes on Education in Curren Parish." Clogher Record, V (1964).

O'Meardin, Lorcan. "Schools in County Monaghan, 1824-26." Clogher Record, V (1963).

Ravitch, Norman. "The Social Origins of French and English Bishops in the Eighteenth Century." Historical Journal, VIII (1965).

Shipkey, Robert. "Problems of Irish Patronage under the Chief Secretaryship of Robert Peel, 1812-1818." Historical Journal, X (1967).

War, W.R. "The Tithe Question in England in the Early Ninettenth Century." Journal of Ecclesiastical History, XVI (1965).

Welch, P.J. "Bloomfield and Peel. A Study in Cooperation between Church and State, 1841-1846." Journal of Ecclesiastical History, XII (April 1961).

C. Dissertations

Acheson, Alan R. "The Evangelicals in the Church of Ireland, 1784-1859." Ph.D. Dissertation: Queen's University, Belfast, 1967.

Lundeen, Thomas B. "The Bench of Bishops: A Study of the Secular Activities of the Bishops of the Church of England and Ireland, 1801-1871." Ph.D. dissertation, State University of Iowa, 1963.

Colchester, Charles Abbot, First Baron. Diary and Correspondence.
3 vols. London: J. Murray, 1861.

Douglas, David C., ed. English Historical Documents. New York; Oxford
University Press, 1955-69.

Great Britain. Historical Manuscripts Commission. Report on the Manuscripts of Henry Seymore, Third Earl Bathurst, Preserved at Cirencester Park. Francis Lawrence Berkeley, ed. London: HMSO, 1923.

_____. Report on the Manuscripts of J.B. Fortescue, Preserved at
Dropmore. 10 vols. London: HMSO, 1892 ff.

Gregory, Augusta Isabella, ed. Mr. Gregory's Letter-Box, 1813-1830.
London: Smith, Elder and Co., 1898.

Greville, Charles. A Journal of the Reign of Queen Victoria from 1837
to 1852. 3 vols. London: Longmans, Green and Co., 1885.

Grey, Henry, Earl, ed. Correspondence of William IV and Earl Grey
from November 1830 to June 1832. 2 vols. London: John Murray,
1867.

Jennings, Louis I., ed. The Croker Papers. 3 vols. London: John
Murray, 1884.

Le Strange, Guy, ed. Correspondence of Princess Lieven and Earl Grey.
3 vols. London; Richard Bentley and Son, 1890.

McDowell, Robert B., ed. "Some Fitzgibbon Letters from the Sneyd
Muniments in the John Rylands Library." John Rylands Library,
Manchester, Bulletin, XXXIV (1952).

Maxwell, Herbert, ed. The Creevey Papers. London: J. Murrary, 1904.

Melbourne, William Lamb, Viscount. Memoirs. W.M. Torrens, ed. 2
vols. London: Macmillan and Co., 1872.

Reeve, Henry, ed. Greville Memoirs. 8 vols. London: Longmans and
Co., 1888.

_____. Memoir and Correspondence Relating to Political Occurrences
in June and July 1834, by Edward John Littleton. London: Longmans,
Green and Co., 1872.

Russell, Rollo, ed. Early Correspondence of Lord John Russell. 2 vols.
London: T. Fisher Unwin, 1913.

Rutland, Charles Manners, ed. Seventh Duke. Correspondence between
the Right Honourable William Pitt and Charles, Duke of Rutland,

Lord Lieutenant of Ireland, 1781-1787. London: A. Spottiswoode, 1842.

Sanders, Lloyd C., ed. Lord Melbourne's Papers. London: Longmans, Green and Co., 1889.

Wellington, A.R. Wellesley, Second Duke. Despatches, Correspondence, and Memoranda of Arthur Duke of Wellington. 8 vols. London: John Murray, 1867-1880.

II. Contemporary Secondary Sources

The Halliday Collection of contemporary pamphlet literature housed in the Royal Irish Academy, Dublin, is invaluable. Personal correspondence and memoranda available in print include:

Brougham, John Cam Hobhouse, Viscount. Life and Time of Lord Brougham. 3 vols. London: William Blackwood and Sons, 1871.

_____. Recollections of a Long Life. 6 vols. London: John Murray, 1910.

Bulwer, Henry Lytton. The Life of Henry John Temple, Viscount Palmerston. Philadelphia: J.B. Lippincott and Co., 1871.

Cornwallis, Charles Cornwallis, Marquess. Correspondence. 3 vols. London: J. Murray, 1859.

Fitzpatrick, W.J. Memoirs of Richard Whately. 2 vols. London, 1864.

Gash, Norman. Mr. Secretary Peel. Cambridge, Mass.: Harvard University Press, 1961.

Grattan, Henry. Memoirs. 5 vols. London, 1839.

King, Charles S. A Great Archbishop of Dublin: William King, D.D., 1850-1729. London: Longmans and Co., 1906.

Le Fanu, W.R. Seventy Years of Irish Life. London: Macmillan, 1894.

Le Marchant, Denis. Memoir of Viscount Althorp, Third Earl Spencer. London: Richard Bentley and Son, 1876.

Londonderry, Robert Stewart, Marquess. Memoir and Correspondence of Viscount Castlereagh. 12 vols. London, 1848-53.

Madden, Samuel. Memoir of the Life of the Late Rev. Peter Roe. Dublin, 1842.

Mant, Walter-Bishop. Memoirs . . . of Richard Mant. Dublin: McGlashan and Gill, 1857.

Melbourne, William Lamb, Viscount. Memoir. W.M. Torrens, ed. 2 vols. London: Macmillan and Co., 1872.

Morley, John. The Life of William Ewart Gladstone. 3 vols. New York: Macmillan and Co., 1909.

Paget, Henry William, First Marquess of Anglesey. One Leg. London: Reprint Society, 1963.

Parker, Charles Stuart. Life and Letters of Sir James Graham, Second Baronet of Netherby, 1797-1861. 2 vols. London: John Murray, 1907.

_____. Sir Robert Peel . . . from his Private Correspondence. 3 vols. London: Murray, 1899.

Peel, Robert. Memoirs. 2 vols. London: John Murray, 1858.

Pellew, George, ed. Life and Correspondence of the Right Hon. Henry Addington, First Viscount Sidmouth. 3 vols. London, 1847.

Russell, John Russell, Earl. Recollections and Suggestions, 1813-1873. London: Longmans, Green and Co., 1875.

Stephen, Leslie and Sidney Lee, eds. Dictionary of National Biography. Oxford: Oxford University Press, 1885-1900.

Stockmar, E. von, Baron. Memoirs. 2 vols. London, 1872.

Twiss, Horace. The Public and Private Life of Lord Chancellor Eldon, with Selections from His Correspondence. 2 vols. London: John Murray, 1846.

Walpole, Spencer. The Life of Lord John Russell. 2 vols. London: Longmans, Green and Co., 1891.

Whately, Jane. Life and Correspondence of Richard Whately, D.D., Late Archbishop of Dublin. Dublin, 1866.

Several contemporary analyses of the Church of Ireland offer important information:

Erck, J.C. Account of the Ecclesiastical Establishment in Ireland. Dublin, 1830.

Godkin, James. Education in Ireland. London, 1862.

Mant, Richard. History of the Church of Ireland from the Reformation to the Revolution. London, 1840.

Perry, George G. History of the Church of England. 3 vols. London:
Saunders, Otley and Co., 1861-1864.

Senior, Nassau. Journals, Conversations and Essays Relating to Ireland. London, 1868.

III. Modern Secondary Sources

A. Books

Akenson, Donald H. The Church of Ireland: Ecclesiastical Reform and
Revolution. New Haven: Yale University Press, 1971.

_____. The Irish Education Experiment: The National System of Edu-
cation in the Nineteenth Century. London: Routledge and Kegan
Paul, 1970.

Beckett, J.C. Protestant Dissent in Ireland, 1687-1780. London:
Faber and Faber, 1947.

Bell, P.M.H. Disestablishment in Ireland and Wales. London: SPCK,
1969.

Bolton, G.C. The Passing of the Irish Act of Union. London: Oxford
University Press, 1966.

Bowen, Desmond. Protestant Crusade in Ireland, 1800-70. Dublin:
Gill and Macmillan, 1978.

_____. Souperism: Myth or Reality. Dublin, 1970.

Brose, Olive J. Church and Parliament: the Reshaping of the Church of
England, 1828-1860. Stanford; Stanford University Press, 1959.

Carless Davis, H.W. The Age of Grey and Peel. Oxford: Clarendon Press,
1929.

Chadwick, Owen. The Victorian Church. 2 vols. Oxford: Oxford University Press, 1966.

Edwards, Robert Dudley. Church and State in Tudor Ireland: A History
of the Penal Laws against Irish Catholics, 1534-1603. Dublin:
Talbot Press, 1935.

Evans, Anna L. The Disestablishment of the Church of Ireland. Lancaster, Pa: University of Pennsylvania, 1929.

Forster, V.H. A History of Killeevan Parish, Diocese of Clogher.

Monaghan: Monaghan Press, 1958.

Freeman, Thomas W. Pre-Famine Ireland. Oxford; Oxford University Press, 1957.

Froude, James A. The English in Ireland in the Eighteenth Century. 2 vols. London: Longmans, Green and Co., 1886.

Gash, Norman. Reaction and Reconstruction in English Politics, 1832-1852. Oxford: Clarendon Press, 1965.

Gray, Denis. Spencer Perceval: The Evangelical Prime Minister 1762-1812. Manchester: Manchester University Press, 1963.

Gwynn, Stephen L. History of Ireland. London: Macmillan and Co., 1923.

Halevy, Elie. The Age of Peel and Cobden. New York, 1948.

_____. The Triumph of Reform. London; Ernest Benn, 1950.

Healy, John. History of the Diocese of Meath. 2 vols. Dublin: APCK, 1908.

Henriques, U. Religious Toleration in England, 1787-1833. London: Routledge and Kegan Paul, 1961.

Johnston, Edith. Great Britain and Ireland, 1760-1800: A Study in Political Administration. Edinburgh: Oliver and Boyd, 1963.

Jones, Wilbur Devereux. Lord Derby and Victorian Conservatism. Oxford: Oxford University Press, 1956.

Killen, W.D. Ecclesiastical History of Ireland. London: Macmillan and Co., 1875.

Kitson Clark, George. Peel and the Conservative Party. 2nd ed. Hamden, Conn.: Archon Books, 1964.

Lecky, W.E.H. Ireland in the Eighteenth Century. 5 vols. London: Longmans and Co., 1892.

Locker Lampson, Geoffrey. A Consideration of the State of Ireland in the Nineteenth Century. London: Archibald Constable and Co., 1907.

MacDonagh, Michael. The Viceroy's Post-Bag: Correspondence Hitherto Unpublished of the Earl of Hardwicke, First Lord Lieutenant of Ireland after the Union. London: John Murray, 1904.

McDowell, R.B. The Church of Ireland, 1869-1969. Boston: Routledge and Kegan Paul, 1975.

_____. The Irish Administration 1801-1914. London: Routledge and Kegan Paul, 1964.

_____. Irish Public Opinion, 1750-1800. London: Faber and Faber, 1952.

Macintyre, Angus. The Liberator; Daniel O'Connell and the Irish Party, 1830-1847. London: Hamilton, 1965.

Maxwell, Constantia. Country and Town in Ireland under the Georges. Dundalk, Ireland: W. Tempest, 1949.

_____. Dublin under the Georges. London: G.S. Harrop and Co., 1940.

Nolan, Kevin B. The Politics of Repeal. Toronto: University of Toronto Press, 1965.

Norman, E.R. The Catholic Church and Ireland in the Age of Rebellion, 1859-73. London: Routledge and Kegan Paul, 1965.

O'Brien, R. Barry. Fifty Years of Concessions to Ireland, 1831-1881. 2 vols. London, 1885.

O'Hagarty, Sarsfield. A History of Ireland under the Union 1801-1822. London: Methuen and Co., 1952.

Phillips, Walter Allison, ed. History of the Church of Ireland from the Earliest Times to the Present Day. 3 vols. London: Oxford University Press, 1933.

Pomfret, John Edwin. The Struggle for Land in Ireland, 1800-1823. Princeton: Princeton University Press, 1930.

Ravitch, Norman. Sword and Mitre: Government and Episcopate in France and England in the Age of Aristocracy. The Hague, 1966.

Reynolds, James A. The Catholic Emancipation Crisis in Ireland, 1823-1829. New Haven: Yale University Press, 1954.

Rushe, D. Carolan. History of Monaghan for Two Hundred Years. Dundalk: Dundalk Press, 1921.

Southgate, David. The Passing of the Whigs, 1832-1866. London: Macmillan and Co., 1962.

B. Articles

Beckett, J.C. "The Government and the Church of Ireland under William

II and Anne." Irish Historical Studies, II (March 1941).

Best, G.F.A. "The Whigs and the Church Establishment in the Age of Grey and Holland." History, XLV (1960).

Brose, Olive J. "The Irish Precedent for English Church Reform: the Church Temporalities Act of 1833." Journal of Ecclesiastical History, VII (October 1956).

Brynn, Edward. "A Church of Ireland Diocese in the Age of Catholic Emancipation." Historical Magazine of the Protestant Episcopal Church, XL (June 1971).

_____. "The Church of Ireland in the Age of Catholic Emancipation, 1800-1841." Rocky Mountain Social Science Journal, (1971).

_____. "Irish Tithes in British Politics." Historical Magazine of the Protestant Episcopal Church, XXXIX (September 1970).

_____. "Robert Peel and the Church of Ireland." Journal of Religious History, (1974).

_____. "Some Repercussions of the Act of Union on the Church of Ireland, 1801-1820." Church History, XL (September 1971).

Burns, R.E. "Parson, Priests, and People; the Rise of Irish Anti-clericalism, 1785-1789." Church History, XXXI (1962).

Cahill, Gilbert A. "Irish Catholicism and English Toryism." Review of Politics, XIX (1957).

_____. "The Protestant Association and the Anti-Maynooth Agitation of 1845." Catholic Historical Review, LXIII (October 1957).

Condon, Mary. "The Irish Church and the Reform Ministries." Journal of British Studies, I (1964).

Hughes, Edward. "The Bishops and Reform, 1831-1833: Some Fresh Correspondence." English Historical Review, XVI (July 1941).

Kriegal, Abraham D. "The Irish Policy of Lord Grey's Government." English Historical Review, LXXXVI(1971).

Large, David. "The House of Lords and Ireland in the Age of Peel, 1832-1850." Irish Historical Studies, IX (September 1955).

Lavorovsky, V. "Tithe Commutation as a Factor in the Gradual Decrease of Ownership by the English Peasantry." Economic History Review, XVI.

Lewis, Clyde J. "The Disintegration of the Tory-Anglican Alliance in the Struggle for Catholic Emancipation." Church History, XXIX (1960).

Machin, G.I.T. "The Catholic Emancipation Crisis of 1825." English Historical Review, LXXVIII (1963).

_____. "The Duke of Wellington and Catholic Emancipation." Journal of Ecclesiastical History, XIV (1963).

_____. "The Maynooth Grant, the Dissenters and Disestablishment, 1845-1847." English Historical Review, LXXXII (January 1967).

_____. "The No-Popery Movement in Britain in 1828-1829." Historical Journal, VI (1963).

McCracken, J.L. "The Conflict Between the Irish Administration and Parliament, 1753-6." Irish Historical Studies, III (1942).

McDougall, Donald J. "George III, Pitt, and the Irish Catholics, 1801-1805." Catholic Historical Review, XXXI (October 1945).

Murphy, J.A. "The Support of the Catholic Clergy in Ireland, 1750-1850." Historical Studies: Papers Read before the Sixth Annual Conference of Irish Historians, V.

O'Donoghue, Patrick. "Causes of Opposition to Tithes, 1830-38." Studia Hibernica, V. (1965).

_____. "Opposition to Tithe Payments in 1830-31. Studia Hibernica, VI (1966).

O'Mordha, Pilib B. "Notes on Education in Curren Parish." Clogher Record, V (1964).

O'Meardin, Lorcan. "Schools in County Monaghan, 1824-26." Clogher Record, V (1963).

Ravitch, Norman. "The Social Origins of French and English Bishops in the Eighteenth Century." Historical Journal, VIII (1965).

Shipkey, Robert. "Problems of Irish Patronage under the Chief Secretaryship of Robert Peel, 1812-1818." Historical Journal, X (1967).

War, W.R. "The Tithe Question in England in the Early Ninettenth Century." Journal of Ecclesiastical History, XVI (1965).

Welch, P.J. "Bloomfield and Peel. A Study in Cooperation between Church and State, 1841-1846." Journal of Ecclesiastical History, XII (April 1961).

C. Dissertations

Acheson, Alan R. "The Evangelicals in the Church of Ireland, 1784-1859." Ph.D. Dissertation: Queen's University, Belfast, 1967.

Lundeen, Thomas B. "The Bench of Bishops: A Study of the Secular Activities of the Bishops of the Church of England and Ireland, 1801-1871." Ph.D. dissertation, State University of Iowa, 1963.

INDEX

Biographical Note: entries are listed by rank and identified, where applicable, by highest office held between 1800 and 1869.

Irish and English convene in London (1835), p. 317.
Jonathan Swift on, p. 12.
patronage powers of, p. 34.
recruitment of in eighteenth century, p. 14.
recruitment from chaplains to Lord Lieutenant, p. 33.
translation of, pp. 32, 61.

Blackstone, William, definition of tithes, p. 145.

Board of First Fruits, pp. 61, 107, 109.
    Act to strengthen, p. 130.
    deficiencies of, p. 127.
    reduction in government support for, p. 131.

Boulter, William (Archbishop of Armagh), p. 17.
    on landlords' opposition to tithes, p. 159.
    on tithes, p. 158.

Brodrick, Charles (Archbishop of Cashel) pp. 35, 44, 45, 70, 78, 346, 422.
    on clerical support for schools, p. 206.
    on non-residence, p. 103.
    President of Board of First Fruits, p. 113.
    role in Board of First Fruits after 1809, p. 130.

Brougham and Vaux, John Cam Hobhouse (Baron), pp. 259, 261.

Brunswick Clubs, p. 398.

Buckingham and Chandos, p. 143.

Busby, Charles, p. 62.

Butson, Charles (Bishop of Waterford), p. 52.
    on glebe house construction, p. 127.
    on disorder in diocese, p. 91.

Canning, George, p. 228.

Cashel, Archdiocese of, p. 17.
    Synod of, p. 136.

Castlereagh, Robert Stewart (Viscount), pp. 55, 57, 112, 142, 143.

Cathedral chapter, description of, p. 93.
    offices, p. 31.

Catholic Association, p. 398.